Christ
Our
Mediator

Christ
Our
Mediator

Thomas Goodwin

Sovereign Grace Publishers, Inc.
P.O. Box 4998
Lafayette, IN 47903

*Printed In the United States of America
By Lightning Source, Inc.*

CONTENTS

The original title of this treatise was, *A Discourse of Christ the Mediator*, first printed in London in **1692**, 13 years after the death of this great servant of God. We have taken it from Volume V of the Nichol's Series of Great Divines, reproducing it by photolithography.

Thomas Goodwin will no doubt be found in the first rank of Christian writers when God passes out His rewards at the coming Judgment. Not only was he one of the pillars on which the golden age of theology was hung in the seventeenth century, but a close investigation would find that nearly everyone worth his salt in succeeding centuries were in some large measure dependent on the thought of Thomas Goodwin. Notable among these are Jonathan Edwards, John Gill, George Whitefield, and John Wesley (that's right! John Wesley fed heartily on Goodwin's writings.)

Goodwin, of course, along with John Owen and Jeremy Burroughs, founded the Congregational Church. And it was Goodwin who wrote the first draft of the Savoy Confession of Faith (which was unanimously adopted with hardly a change). But the genius of the man would not and could not be circumscribed by denominational lines. In any period when God sends reformation and revival into His churches, one can quickly find that Goodwin has burst in upon hungry, tender souls with a feast of spiritual delights which can be found in no other author from the advent of time.

Of all the sublime subjects tackled by and opened by Goodwin, this subject of the mediatorship of Christ is at the very top. This is a famous book, and justly so. However learned the reader, however near he may have drawn to God, he is certain to find in these pages fountains of living water which he never before dreamed to be a part of the legacy left us by our Savior God. Let no man fail to read each page! When there is gold lying so near to the surface, can one quarrel about the need for labor? He who digs here will thrill as he uncovers each new nugget of truth!

OF CHRIST THE MEDIATOR.

BOOK I.

God the Father's eternal counsel and transactions with Christ, to undertake the work of redemption for man, considered as fallen.

CHAPTER I.

*The exposition of the words of the text.—What is the great design of the gospel.
—The excellency of the knowledge of it.—The highest attainment is to see
the gospel in its original, those eternal transactions between God the Father
and God the Son for the salvation of man.*

*And all things are of God, who hath reconciled us to himself by Jesus Christ,
and hath given to us the ministry of reconciliation; to wit, that God was in
Christ, reconciling the world unto himself, not imputing their trespasses unto
them; and hath committed to us the word of reconciliation.—2 Cor. V.
18, 19.*

These words do summarily tell us what is the argument of that great mystery of the gospel, as it concerneth sinners, viz., reconciliation. Therefore he styles it the 'ministry of reconciliation:' that is the title he gives the doctrine of it; and withal further explains this, 'To wit,' says he, 'that God was in Christ, reconciling the world;' and so the foot of the angels' evangelical song, wherein they sung forth the main end of Christ's nativity, was reconciliation: Luke ii. 14, 'Glory to God in the highest, and on earth peace, good will towards men.' This reconciliation consists of two parts, peace and good will.

The full scope of the words you may conceive, as I have cast them into this frame; and withal, what also is the sum of all the discourse upon them.

First, The word *reconcile* imports the whole of mankind to have been once created in an estate of amity and friendship with God. For to reconcile, is to make friends again, and argues former friendship. And this sets and limits the subject of these eternal transactions between God the Father and the Son, to have been man considered as fallen.

And *secondly,* the whole lump of man being fallen off from God into a deep rebellion, and become of the devil's side and faction, God, who is infinite in love and rich in mercy, bearing everlasting and secret good will to some of these now become rebels, in all ages hath maintained certain lieger ambassadors in the world, to treat with this rebellious rout, and to conclude a peace betwixt them and him : 2 Cor. v. 20, ' Now then we are ambassadors for Christ, as though God did beseech you by us : we pray you in Christ's stead, be ye reconciled to God ; ' and hath furnished them (as all other ambassadors use to be) with a large and gracious commission, the title of which is, ' The ministry of reconciliation ; ' ' And hath given to us the ministry of reconciliation,' ver. 18. The sum of which commission hath these two principal parts.

1. On the part of him, to publish and proclaim his royal and gracious intentions towards them. For when two are at variance, there can be no hope of peace and reconciliation, unless the party wronged and injured shew an inclination (at least) to listen to an agreement. Now as to that, he hath empowered and commanded them with all confidence and credence to declare ;

First, That whereas they might conceive him most unjustly to be averse to the very motion of it, that yet he, for his part, is not only contented and inclined to listen to an agreement, but is and hath been ever so fully willing and desirous of it, that he hath made it as it were his chief business, and as that which he hath plotted to bring about ; and that he for his part hath been reconciling the world to himself by Christ. ' God was in Christ reconciling,' yea, and from everlasting hath been. And though all things else are of him, as ver. 18 he prefaceth unto this, yet this mainly above all other things. Take the whole of them, ' All things are of God, who hath reconciled us.' He hath been (as it were) *totus in illo*, wholly bent upon this of all things else. And whereas it might yet be thought, that he being so just, and having declared himself so jealous a God, sensible of the least injury, so tender of his glory, and jealous of the least violation or wrong done thereto, that he therefore would require and propound to have full satisfaction from them first, as the condition of his and their accord and agreement ; which that they, or any other creature for them, either were able or willing to perform, was utterly out of all hope. Therefore,

Secondly, He bids his ambassadors declare, that as to that point men need not trouble themselves, nor take care about it ; for he himself hath further been so zealously affected in this business, that he himself hath made full provision, and took order for that aforehand, and done it to their hand ; ' He hath been in Christ, reconciling the world ; ' that is, in him and by him, as a mediator, and umpire, and surety between them and him, this great matter hath been taken up and accorded. For he and Jesus Christ his only Son have from all eternity laid their counsels together (as I may so speak with reverence), to end this great difference ; and they both contrived and agreed, that Christ should undertake to satisfy his Father, for all the wrong was done to him, all which he should take upon himself, as if he were guilty of it ; ' he was made sin,' 2 Cor. v. 21, that is, a surety and a satisfaction for it. And God the Father, upon it, is so fully satisfied, as he is ready not only not to impute their sins to them, ver. 19, but to impute all Christ's righteousness to them, and to receive them into favour more fully than ever they were. ' He was made sin, that they might be made the righteousness of God in him.'

2. The second part of our commission is what concerns men, the parties to be reconciled ; and God hath given us, his ambassadors, full power and

authority to deal with men about it, and to strike up the compact and perfect this agreement into a full and final issue and end, with charge to tell this message indefinitely to all and every man in the world; and that founded upon this ground, that reconciliation is to be obtained from God for some in the world: and thereupon to exhort all and every one that hears it to be reconciled. And men accordingly are to seek it as thus revealed to them by us; and these exhortations are to be entertained by them, as if God had exhorted and persuaded them thereunto. So ver. 20, ' Now then we are ambassadors for Christ, as though God did beseech you by us: we pray you in Christ's stead, be ye reconciled to God.'

And this, my brethren, is the gospel, which is the best news that ever ear heard, or tongue was employed to utter, which took up God's thoughts from all eternity, and lay hid in his breast, and which none knew but his Son and Spirit; a news so blessed and worthy of all acceptation, which as soon as it brake out, heaven and earth rang with joy again: the angels could not hold, but, as ambitious to be the first relaters of it, posted down to earth to bring the news of it: Luke ii. 13, 14, ' And suddenly there was with the angel a multitude of the heavenly host praising God, and saying, Glory to God in the highest, and on earth peace, good will towards men.'

And this being committed unto us to be the dispensers of it, this makes our very feet beautiful in the eyes of broken-hearted sinners: Rom. x. 15, ' And how shall they preach, except they be sent? as it is written, How beautiful are the feet of them that preach the gospel of peace, and bring glad tidings of good things!' This makes our calling envied (if possible it were envy should befall those blessed spirits), envied of the angels themselves, to whom God hath not betrusted this glorious embassy, the most honourable employment that ever creature dealt in: Heb. ii., ' The law was given by angels,' ver. 2; ' but God hath not put into subjection to the angels the world to come, whereof we speak' (speaking of the gospel, ver. 5), for which Paul brings in that long and famous thanksgiving, 1 Tim. i. 11, 12, ' According to the glorious gospel of the blessed God, which was committed to my trust. And I thank Jesus Christ our Lord, who hath enabled me, for that he counted me faithful, putting me into the ministry.' He accounted that the greatest mercy which Jesus Christ (next his own salvation) had shewn him, and wherein he made him a pattern of his super-excelling grace, that he committed the gospel to his trust, which of all other doctrines tend the most to the good of men: 1 Tim. i. 15, ' This is a faithful saying, and worthy of all acceptation, that Christ Jesus came into the world to save sinners; of whom I am chief.' Tit. iii. 7, 8, ' That, being justified by his grace, we should be made heirs according to the hope of eternal life. This is a faithful saying, and these things I will that thou affirm constantly, that they which have believed in God might be careful to maintain good works. These things are good and profitable unto men.' What things? See ver. 4, even this doctrine of salvation; ' and these things,' saith he, ' I would that thou affirm constantly,' ver. 8. For this is the power of God unto salvation; as Rom. i. 16, ' For I am not ashamed of the gospel of Christ: for it is the power of God unto salvation, to every one that believeth, to the Jew first, and also to the Greek,' i. e., it is the most powerful and prevailing means to subdue the rebellious hearts of men, and overcome them; and whereas the preaching of the law makes men often sturdy, this proclamation of pardon and reconciliation brings men in as voluntaries, and that by troops; Luke xvi. 16, ' The law and the prophets were until John: since that time the kingdom of God is preached,' (that is, the gospel), ' and every man presseth into it.' Intimating that before, when the law was most preached, and the gospel but sparingly (and but as a parenthesis, as it were), there were few brought in ; but the gospel brought them in by heaps and multitudes (for so the opposition there stands), with which men were so taken and affected, that glad was he that could get in with pressure and crowding.

And therefore we likewise freely profess to you, that these things we would affirm constantly (were men fitted, broken, and humbled), and preach in a manner nothing else, for it is the sum and upshot of our ministry, as the title is given it in the text, ' the ministry of reconciliation.' And we would desire to know nothing among you but Christ ; as Paul speaks to the Corinthians, 1 Cor. ii. 2, ' For I determined not to know any thing among you, save Jesus Christ, and him crucified :' and this chiefly, Christ as crucified to reconcile you, crucified before your eyes in the 'gospel. Gal. iii. 5, ' He therefore that ministereth to you the Spirit, and worketh miracles among you, doeth he it by the works of the law, or by the hearing of faith ?' And as for you, your work, τὸ ἔργον, is to believe ; ' This is the work of ₁God' (says Christ, John vi. 29), ' to believe iu him whom God hath sent.' So our τὸ ἔργον, our work, is to preach him to you whom God hath sent, that you may believe in him ; and therefore we account it our misery that we are fain to spend the most of our time in making ourselves work, as in preaching the law we do ; and are fain to come with the great hammer of the law, and break all your bones in pieces, that we may then, as it is in Isa. lxi. 1, ' preach the gospel, and bind up the broken-hearted.' It is tiresome to us that we must take men by the throats, and arrest them by the law (as we do), in the name of the great God, and haul them to prison, and there shut them up ' under the law,' as the apostle's phrase is, Gal. iii. 23, that then we may bring them Christ's bail, and by preaching the gospel, proclaim ' liberty to the captives, and the opening of the prison to them that are bound ;' as the allusion is, Isa. lxi. 1, ' The Spirit of the Lord God is upon me ; because the Lord hath anointed me to preach good tidings uuto the meek : he hath sent me to bind up the broken-hearted, to proclaim liberty to the captives, and the opening of the prison to them that are bound.'

And we do withal protest before God and men this day, that when we come to preach it, we yet tremble to do it more than any doctrine else ; for we are afraid that men should lie still in their sins : those that are drunkards should be drunkards still, and unclean still, and lest those who withhold the truth in unrighteousness (their consciences telling them that they live and lie in known sins), lest they should go on to do so still after the delivery of it ; which if they shall do, they had better have been in hell than in the assembly of saints to hear the gospel. We tremble therefore at it, as knowing that men cannot hear it and disobey it, but under an extraordinary curse, oftentimes a final one, and such a one as Christ cursed the fig-tree with when he said, ' Never fruit grow on thee more.'

But to come unto that which is my main and principal intendment, and scope of this text, and which is the first and original part of the gospel, viz., the everlasting transaction which the Father had with his Son, in calling him to the work of redemption of us men, considered as sinners. Other pieces of the gospel, as those on Christ's part, his fitness for the work, his ability and performance, in being made sin and a curse, do in their due place follow upon other texts. But attend at present unto the fountain and original of them all, unto that which sets all the wheels going from eternity; the story of which, were it but for the antiquity thereof, is well worth the hearing, being withal the greatest intercourse and treaty, about the greatest affair, between persons of the highest sovereignty and majesty, that ever was transacted either in heaven or earth, or ever will be. And accordingly, the highest form or rank of Christians, termed ' fathers,' have for their attainments this mark and character set upon them, ' to know him that was from the beginning,' as the highest pitch of all: 1 John ii. 14, ' I have written unto you, fathers, because ye have known him that is from the beginning. I have written unto you, young men, because ye are strong, and the word of God abideth in you, and ye have overcome the wicked one.' The apostle speaks with some allusion to what is the glory of old men, and so suitably of old men in Christ. They use to boast of knowing things that are of antiquity and of elder years, as having fallen under their observation, as it is the property of young men to boast of their strength and vigour: Prov. xx. 29, ' The glory of young men is their strength, and the beauty of old men is the grey head,' i. e., their wisdom; which lies in their grey heads, and which ariseth from their having the prospect of former times. John, therefore, correspondently commends strong men, grown up in Christianity, for their strength, as the peculiar excellency of that age in Christ. ' You are strong' (says he), ' and have overcome the wicked one.' But he commends fathers in Christ for their knowledge in things most ancient; and because the story of him that was from the beginning is the ancientest of all other that ever was, it is therefore made their excellency to know it, and is commended to their study; and the knowledge of the eternal transactions of God the Father for man's salvation is the highest of their attainments.

CHAPTER II.

Some observations premised.—That it is to the Father the reconciliation is made, and to him the affair is chiefly attributed.

Ere I come to the particulars of these transactions between God the Father and the Son for our salvation, I will premise some general observations out of the text, which shall make way for what follows.

The great business of reconciliation (as I said) is both the subject of the gospel and of this text, which tells us of those two great persons by whom this great business was transacted, and brought to such a pass, as men may come to be reconciled, and friends with God again; and what they are, that is, God the Father, the party wronged and injured, and Christ the means of reconciliation, the umpire and mediator between both: ' God was in Christ reconciling the world.'

By God is therefore meant a distinct person from Christ; for in the former words it is said, that ' he hath reconciled all things to himself by Christ.' And that person is the Father, as other scriptures tell us.

Obs. 1. That the Father is the person to whom reconciliation is made. Not but that it is made to the rest also. But,

First, Because he being the first person, the suit against us runs in his name especially, though it be the quarrel of all the rest of the persons, and the injury done against all the rest. Thus in colleges, and such common societies, their suits against others are commenced in some one's name, as the master's or the like, whose name is used for the whole; and so this common quarrel and suit of trespass, which the whole Trinity hath against us, is commenced in God the Father's name for all the rest; and therefore Christ is said to be an ' advocate with the Father,' 1 John ii. 1, as the party betrusted to take the atonement, and make an end of the quarrel in the name of all the rest. And,

Secondly, Because as creation is attributed to the Father especially, so the covenant of works, the law, the covenant we were created under, being a covenant made especially with the Father in the name of the rest, therefore sin, which was the transgression of that covenant, is said to be, as it were, especially against him; for in the dispensation of that covenant he ruled immediately. And as the sins against the second covenant are said to be in a more especial manner against Christ and the Holy Ghost, so those against the first, which occasioned the performance of reconciliation, are said to be against the Father. Because therefore the transgressions of the first testament, as they are called, Heb. ix. 15, are especially said to be committed against him, therefore he takes upon him as the person especially aggrieved, and so the reconciliation is said to be made to him.

Thirdly, And further, because the other two persons have other distinct offices in the work of reconciliation. The Son he is to transact the part of a mediator, as the person by whom reconciliation is to be performed; and the Holy Ghost, he is to make report of that peace and atonement made, and shed abroad the love of both. Rom. v. 5, ' And hope maketh not ashamed; because the love of God is shed abroad in our hearts by the Holy Ghost, which is given unto us.' He speaks of God's love in reconciling us : ver. 8, 9, 10, ' But God commendeth his love towards us, in that, while we were yet sinners, Christ died for us. Much more then, being now justified by his blood, we shall be saved from wrath through him. For if, when we were enemies, we were reconciled to God by the death of his Son : much more, being reconciled, we shall be saved by his life.' Therefore, the Father he bears (if any such part) the part of him that receives into favour, and to whom we are to be reconciled.

To illustrate this, we are in the same sense and respect said to be reconciled to the Father, in which we are taught especially to pray to the Father, ' Our Father,' &c. For the Son and the Spirit do bear other parts in our prayers : the Son, he is the master of requests, the intercessor, in whose name therefore our prayers are to be made. The Holy Ghost, he is the inditer of our prayers, and helper of our infirmities; Rom. viii. 26, 27, ' Likewise the Spirit also helpeth our infirmities : for we know not what we should pray for as we ought; but the Spirit itself maketh intercession for us with groanings which cannot be uttered. And he that searcheth the hearts knoweth what is the mind of the Spirit, because he maketh intercession for the saints according to the will of God.' Therefore the Father, he is expressed as the party we pray unto; and thus it is in like manner in the business of reconciliation. It is the Father to whom it is and was to be made, and therefore by him to be first promoted and set on work.

Obs. 2. Observe in the second place, that as he is made the special person to whom the reconciliation is made, so the whole business is in an especial manner attributed to him.

Though it be done and performed wholly by Christ as the mediator, yet the Father is he who sets all on work, and is said to reconcile by Christ to himself. It is not only that Christ hath been about reconciling us to him, but that he hath been a-reconciling us to himself, and that in Christ, as having the first, and chief, and main hand in the work, as well as being the person to whom reconciliation is made.

God the Father was not as other parties injured, that use to carry themselves as mere passives in an agreement when it is to be wrought; who, though they are at length brought to it, yet they will not seem to condescend to have any hand in it, or to be the first movers or the seekers of it. But God the Father carried himself otherwise in the reconciling of us; he is active in it, he moves it and sets it on foot, and useth his interest in his Son for the effecting of it. In general he is said especially to do two things.

First, He it is that draws the platform of all the works that the other two persons do put their hand to effect. Christ says, that he himself doth nothing but what he sees the Father first do; John v. 19, ' Then answered Jesus, and said unto them, Verily, verily, I say unto you, The Son can do nothing of himself, but what he seeth the Father do: for what things soever he doeth, these also doeth the Son likewise.' So that he, the Father, is the great plotter and contriver, that draws the draught; for it is added, he shews all to the Son: ver. 20, ' For the Father loveth the Son, and sheweth him all things that himself doeth: and he will shew him greater works than these, that ye may marvel.' As David the father drew, and gave Solomon the son, the pattern of the temple which he was to build, so God gave Christ the platform of reconciliation, of the temple his church, when he would have it built. The platform is especially attributed to him, the effecting of it to the Son; and therefore Christ calls them the works which the Father hath given him to finish: John v. 36, ' But I have greater witness than that of John: for the works which the Father hath given me to finish, the same works that I do, bear witness of me, that the Father hath sent me.'

And, *secondly*, he not only draws the platform of them, how he would have them done, but the first purpose and resolution to have them done, that is attributed to him also. Therefore Christ resolves all into his Father's will; ' Even so, Father: it seemed good in thy sight,' Mat. xi. 26. And so this mystery and draft of reconciliation is called the ' mystery of his will;' Eph. i. 9, ' Having made known unto us the mystery of his will, according to his good pleasure, which he hath purposed in himself.' The *mystery*, because he draws the plat; and *of his will*, because he resolves thus and thus to have it done; who is said, ver. 11, ' to work all things according to the counsel of his will.' His counsel draws the draught, and his will resolves thus to have it done; and all this is there especially attributed to the Father.

Obs. 3. That he is not only made to have the first hand in it, but a universal hand in it also. ' All things are of God, who hath reconciled us to himself.' And all things in the business of salvation and reconciliation are from him; that, as it is said of Christ in the matter of creation, that ' all things were made by him; and without him nothing was made,' &c., John i. 3, so Christ says, that he ' can do nothing, but what the Father first doeth,' John v. 19.

So as we find, that all in the matter of reconciliation is attributed both to Christ, and also to God the Father, which makes it indeed a great mystery, that all should be attributed to both; so that we are beholden to both for all.

Christ is said to be ' all in all' unto us, Col. iii. 11; and yet all that he s to us, he is to us of the Father. 1 Cor. i. 30, ' But of him are ye in

Christ Jesus, who of God is made unto us wisdom, and righteousness, and sanctification, and redemption.'

As, *first*, all blessings and benefits we have by Christ are of the Father, as the first donor and giver, though by Christ; as Paul blesseth him for blessing us with all spiritual blessings in Christ: Eph. i. 3, 'Blessed be the God and Father of our Lord Jesus Christ, who hath blessed us with all spiritual blessings in heavenly places in Christ.' Christ is indeed wisdom and righteousness, which contains all that our needs require. But who made him all these? He is not any of these, not the least of these, but as the Father hath made him unto us wisdom, &c. 1 Cor. 1. 30, 'Who is made to us of God,' &c. So as all is to be attributed as much to him as to Christ.

Yea, all we have, and all we are in Christ, is said to be of him; 'Of him ye are in Christ Jesus,' in the same place. We are indeed in Christ, but yet of God in Christ. He gives all the being we have in Christ, all our subsistence in him, to which those blessings belong, that we are first in Christ, and then have all blessings in him. He attributes all this to be of the Father.

Now how all this is to be attributed to both, St Paul hath elsewhere taught us, using this very distinction, 1 Cor. viii. 6, 'The Father, of whom are all things, and we in him; and one Lord Jesus Christ,' as mediator, 'by whom are all things, and we by him.' *By* and *of* puts the distinction, which we have observed.

Yea, and *thirdly*, Jesus Christ as mediator, is all and wholly of him the Father, and by his appointment. Whatsoever he is or hath as mediator, is ordained to him by the Father. Therefore Christ is said to be his king: Ps. ii. 6, 'Yet have I set my King upon my holy hill of Zion.' And Christ is called his servant too: Isa. xlii. 1, 'Behold my servant, whom I uphold; mine elect, in whom my soul delighteth: I have put my Spirit upon him; he shall bring forth judgment to the Gentiles.' And it is said also, that God the Father appointed him a priest: Heb. iii. 1, 2, 'Wherefore, holy brethren, partakers of the heavenly calling, consider the Apostle and High Priest of our profession, Christ Jesus: who was faithful to him that appointed him, as also Moses was faithful in all his house.' And it was God the Father who raised him up as a prophet: Deut. xviii. 15, 'The Lord thy God will raise up unto thee a prophet from the midst of thee, of thy brethren, like unto me; unto him ye shall hearken.' And therefore, too, Christ is styled an heir of his appointment: Heb. i. 2, 'Hath in these last days spoken unto us by his Son, whom he hath appointed heir of all things, by whom also he made the worlds.'

Yea, *fourthly*, whatever Christ did for us, in doing or suffering, it was what his Father appointed him. All that he was to do, Luke ii. 49, and all he was to suffer, Acts ii. 23, it was his Father's cup, and he mingled it.

Yea, *fifthly*, all the glory he hath as mediator, the Father is said to give him, John xvii. 22. And though it be no robbery for him to be equal with God, yet that great name he hath, God is said to have given him. Philip. ii. 6–11, 'Who, being in the form of God, thought it not robbery to be equal with God; but made himself of no reputation, and took upon him the form of a servant, and was made in the likeness of men: and being found in fashion as a man, he humbled himself, and became obedient unto death, even the death of the cross. Wherefore God also hath highly exalted him, and given him a name which is above every name: that at the name of Jesus every knee should bow, of things in heaven, and things in earth, and things under the earth: and that every tongue should confess that Jesus Christ is Lord, to the glory of God the Father.'

And the reason of all this is that which is given there, even ' the glory of the Father.' The end of Christ's great name, and all that honour we are to attribute to him is, ' to the glory of God the Father,' ver. 11. Though Christ hath a name above every name, which we are to magnify and adore, yet all this his name is to the glory of the Father, who hath the revenue of all. And therefore when the Lord Jesus Christ gives up his dispensatory kingdom to his Father, as mediator, God shall be ' all in all :' 1 Cor. xv. 28, ' And when all things shall be subdued unto him, then shall the Son also himself be subdued unto him that put all things under him, that God may be all in all.' Why? Because all was originally from him, therefore all shall end in him, and he shall be all in all.

CHAPTER III.

What as to our salvation was done by God the Father from all eternity.—The meaning of that phrase, ' God was reconciling us in Christ.'—That God took up a strong resolution and purpose to reconcile some of the fallen sons of men to himself.—His motives were not any thing in us, but purely his love, and his delight in mercy.—His love in thus designing salvation to us magnified by several considerations.

These things being premised, we come now to shew what God the Father hath done towards this business of reconciliation, how far he hath advanced it and set it forwards.

Now the main of his work was transacted secretly from everlasting, as we have it here also expressed to us, 1 Cor. v. 19, ' God was in Christ.' He had said in the former verse, He hath actually reconciled us, believers, by Jesus Christ; but yet lest they should think that this was a business begun of late to be done by him, then when Christ died, and they were converted, he further says, that he hath made it his main business from all eternity, ' God was in Christ reconciling the world.'

And to this purpose the alteration of the phrase is observable, that speaking of actual reconciliation, as performed by Christ, and applied to them who were now believers, he saith, ' He hath reconciled us by Jesus Christ,' διὰ Ἰησοῦ Χριστοῦ; but, speaking of this transaction from everlasting, he says ἐν Χριστῷ, ' God was *in* Christ reconciling the world.'

And it is the observation of a great divine,* though not upon this text, yet putting the difference between these two phrases, of what God is said to do *in Christ* and *by Christ*, as in many places they are used; that when God is said to reconcile in Christ, or the like, it implies and notes out those immanent acts of God in Christ; the preparation of all mercies and benefits we have by Christ, from him, and laying them up in him really for us in Christ, as in our head, in whom God looked upon us when we had no subsistence but *in him;* when God and he were alone plotting of all, framing of all that was after to be done by Christ for us, and applied unto us. But the particle *by whom* imports the actual performance of all this by Christ, and application of it to us, Eph. i. 3, 4, ' Blessed be the God and Father of our Lord Jesus Christ, who hath blessed us with all spiritual blessings in heavenly places in Christ:' ver. 4, ' According as he

* Zanchy.

hath chosen us in him before the foundation of the world, that we should be holy and without blame before him in love.' We are said to be blessed with all spiritual blessings *in* Christ, so that God was then a-justifying us in him, a-reconciling us in him.

And further to enlarge this notion, we may observe these three phrases severally used—*in* Christ, *for* Christ, and *through* Christ.

1. *In* Christ, as here and elsewhere.

2. *For* Christ, as to you it is given to suffer for Christ: Philip. i. 29, ' For unto you it is given in the behalf of Christ, not only to believe on him, but also to suffer for his sake.'

3. *Through* Christ, as I am able to do all things through Christ: Philip. iv. 13, 'I can do all things through Christ which strengtheneth me.'

1. When he says *in* Christ, he speaks of Christ as of a common head, whom God looked at as such, when he endowed us with all blessings in him, by way of a covenant with him for us.

2. *For* Christ notes out Christ as the meritorious cause, for whose sake we obtain those blessings, for he was to purchase them.

3. And the third notes out Christ as the efficient cause, that dispenseth that grace, as a king, to us.

Let us therefore first begin with what God the Father hath done, who was the chiefest in that secret transaction between him and Christ from everlasting, which is the groundwork of all in the gospel, which is therefore said to have lain hid in God: Eph. iii. 9, ' And to make all men see what is the fellowship of the mystery, which from the beginning of the world hath been hid in God, who created all things by Jesus Christ.'

And we will begin at that which was the spring and first moving cause of all in him, and that is, his will and good pleasure.

First, He took up a strong purpose and resolution to reconcile some of the sons of men to him, though they would or should turn rebels against him; and this purpose began from him, and in him first. Hence the gathering together of all in one, that is, the uniting and knitting his church to himself in one head, who were scattered from him. The gaining and winning them in again is said to be the mystery of his will, and attributed to his good pleasure, whereof he gives no reason, but a purpose taken up in himself, even according to his good pleasure which he hath purposed in himself: Eph. i. 9, 10, ' Having made known unto us the mystery of his will, according to his good pleasure, which he hath purposed in himself:' ver. 10, ' That, in the dispensation of the fulness of times, he might gather together in one all things in Christ, both which are in heaven, and which are on earth, even in him.' Which he hath purposed in himself, that is, whereof there is no other motive nor first mover or occasioner, but himself, and this is there attributed chiefly to the Father.

To say no more; this he resolved upon, and would have effected, and this with infinite delight in the project of it, so as he should be gladder to see this business effected and brought about, than any that ever he should set his hand unto; his heart was more in it than in all things else. ' All things are of God,' but this above all.

And it was a great matter that he should pitch so peremptorily and resolutely on this course rather than any other, for he might have took up other purposes enough suitable and advantageous to his ends, but this pleased him above all other, Col. i. 19, 20, ' For it pleased the Father, that in him should all fulness dwell,' ver. 20; ' And (having made peace through the blood of his cross) by him to reconcile all things unto himself; by him,

I say, whether they be things in earth, or things in heaven.' For these enemies he could have destroyed, and have been glorified in their just destruction. He was able enough to bear the loss of souls. What is it to him that the nations perish ? He should not have weakened himself a whit by cutting off all the rebels, as kings do, whose glory consists in the multitude of their subjects. Neither had he any need of friends ; he was happy enough afore they were, and could be as happy still without them. And if he would have friends, had he not the angels ? that were constant friends to him, to delight in. One would think he should have prized their friendship more for the faithfulness of it ; and if he had a mind to others, he could have created new ones. But out of these very stones he would have a new generation raised up, a seed of well-willers, or a generation of children to Abraham. And yet as God offered to Moses, he might have done in this our case, Num. xiv. 12, 'I will smite them with the pestilence, and disinherit them, and will make of thee a greater nation, and mightier than they.' God might have made the offer of all greatness and glory to Christ, and as for us, might have destroyed us one and all, and have packed us all to hell for rebels. He had prisons enough to have held us, which kings often want in a general rebellion ; yea, and he would have been glorified in that our just destruction also. There was therefore no necessity put him upon this resolution, but his good pleasure, which was in himself, which made him say within himself of the sons of men, as in allusion to what is in Jer. viii. 4, 'Shall they fall, and not arise ? shall he turn away, and not return ?' His mind lingered after them, and he is glorified more in the services than the sufferings of men ; and he had angels enough already, thousand thousands, and ten thousand times ten thousands, and he would have some men that should see his glory, bless him, and be blessed of him. He loves variety ; to have two witnesses at least, he creates two worlds, heaven and earth, in them two several sorts of reasonable creatures as inhabitants ; upon them he would shew two several ways of salvation, and all to shew his manifold wisdom: Eph. iii. 8–10, ' Unto me, who am less than the least of all saints, is this grace given, that I should preach among the Gentiles the unsearchable riches of Christ ;' ver. 9, 'And to make all men see what is the fellowship of the mystery, which from the beginning of the world hath been hid in God, who created all things by Jesus Christ:' ver. 10, 'To the intent that now to the principalities and powers in heavenly places might be known by the church the manifold wisdom of God.' And if you would further know, What should be the reason of this strange affection in our God, why ? The Scripture gives it.

Our God being love, even love itself, 1 John iv. 16, 'And we have known and believed the love God hath to us. God is love ; and he that dwelleth in love dwelleth in God, and God in him.' Our God loving, where he sets his love, with an infinite love as himself is, which love of all things else in him he loves to shew the utmost of, and of all works, works of love have the most delight in them, therefore mercy is called his delight, his darling: Micah vii. 18, 'Who is a God like unto thee, that pardoneth iniquity, and passeth by the transgression of the remnant of his heritage ? He retaineth not his anger for ever, because he delighteth in mercy.' Our God being thus love, and mercy his delight, he would gladly shew how well he could love creatures, he was most glad of the greatest opportunity to shew it ; therefore he resolves upon this course, to reconcile enemies, whatsoever it should cost. And the more they should cost him, the gladder should they* be. The making of a thousand new friends could not have expressed so much love as the reconciling one enemy. To love and delight in friends, who had never wronged him, was too narrow, shallow, and slight a way. He had heights, depths, breadth of love: Eph. iii. 18, 'May be able to comprehend with all saints what is the breadth, and length, and depth, and height.' Which heights and depth of love he would make known, and which nothing but the depths of our misery could have drawn out.

And that this is the reason, see Rom. v. 8, 10, 'But God commendeth his love towards us, in that, while we were yet sinners, Christ died for us.' Ver. 10, 'For if, when we were enemies, we were reconciled to God by the death of his Son, much more, being reconciled, we shall be saved by his life.' God commends his love towards us, that whilst we were yet enemies, he gave his Son for us, not to be born only, but to die. Both our being sinners, and his giving his Son, commends or sets out his love; and that he might commend it, he pitcheth on this course. And that this love should be pitched upon men, not the angels that fell, it yet further commends his love. There were but two sorts of sinners whose sins could be taken away; and of the twain, who would not have thought but the fallen angels should have been propounded first, and have passed more easily? They were fairer and better creatures than we; and if he regarded service, one of them was able to do him more than a thousand of us. When he had bought us, he must be at a great deal of more trouble to preserve and tend us, than we were able ever to requite in service and attendance upon him. He must allow us much of our time to sleep, and eat, and to be idle in; to refresh our bodies, and tend us as you would tend a child; rock us asleep every night, and make our beds in sickness; Ps. xli. 3, 'The Lord will strengthen him upon the bed of languishing: thou wilt make all his bed in his sickness;' and feed us himself in due season. Whereas the angels, they could stand in his presence day and night, and not be weary. And, besides, the nature of the angels had been a fitter match a great deal for his Son. They are spirits, and so in a nearer assimilation to him. Who ever thought he should close to match so low as with us? All this makes for us still the more love, for it was the more free. And the more unlikely it is that he could love such as we, the more his love is commended. The less we could do for him or for ourselves, the more it would appear he did for us. He is honoured more in our dependence than our service. He hath regard to the lowness of his spouse and handmaids, and lets the mighty go, principalities and powers; he loves still to prefer the younger, and make the elder serve them, Rom. ix. The angels are ministering spirits for their good. Among men he culls out still the poor, the foolish, not many wise or noble; and he makes as unlikely a choice amongst his creatures.

CHAPTER IV.

That God, in pursuance of his gracious design to save sinners, exercised his wisdom to contrive the fittest means of accomplishing it.—Though God might have pardoned sin without satisfaction, yet he would not; and the reasons of it.

As God's purpose was thus strongly bent upon the salvation of men, so his wisdom and counsel were exercised about the means whereby it might

* Qu. 'he'?—ED

be effected; and it is a business that requires the depths of his wisdom. We silly men set upon many projects, which at first view delight and affect us; and we are hot upon them, which yet upon consultation we find not feasible, and so leave them, meeting with such difficulties in them as we know not how to compass them; though when the heart is fully set upon any business, it will set wit and invention a-work to find out all means that wit can reach to.

Now, as God's strong purpose and delights were in this great work, so also his depths of wisdom were in it also. Therefore God's will is said to have counsel joined with it, to work all by counsel, Eph i. 11. He works all by counsel, to effect and bring to pass what his will hath pitched upon, and the stronger his will is in a thing, the deeper are his counsels about it; and this business, as he resolves to have it carried, will prove such as will draw out his depths of wisdom.

And therefore as you have seen his will thus strongly pitched upon it, as his highest and deepest project, to manifest the dearest affection in him to the utmost, so you shall now see his wisdom soar as high (indeed infinitely) out of our sight, thoughts, and imaginations, to find out a correspondent means, not only to effect it, but in effecting it to shew both love and wisdom, and give full satisfaction to his justice, which was infinitely beyond the reach of any created understanding to have found out.

There was one way indeed which was more obvious, and that was, to pardon the rebels, and make no more ado of it; for he might if he had pleased have ran a way and course of mere mercy, not tempered with justice at all. He might have pardoned without satisfaction. I will not now dispute it; only this I will say for the confirmation of it, to punish sin being an act of his will, as well as other works of his *ad extra*, may therefore be suspended as he himself pleaseth. To hate sin is his nature; and that sin deserves death is also the natural and inseparable property, consequent, and demerit of it; but the expression of this hatred, and of what sin deserves by actual punishment, is an act of his will, and so might be suspended.

But besides that this way would not manifest such depths of love, though thus to have pardoned one man had shewn more love than was shewn to all the angels who never sinned; it also was not adequate and answerable to all those his glorious ends, and purposes, and other resolutions in this plot, which he will be constant unto, and make to meet in it (and it is the proper use of wisdom to make all ends meet); and God will not break one rule or purpose he takes up; and he hath other projects afoot besides. For,

First, He meant to give a law, whereof he will not have the least *iota* to perish or be in vain; Mat. v. 18, 'For verily I say unto you, Till heaven and earth pass, one jot or one tittle shall in nowise pass from the law, till all be fulfilled.' Which law might both discover what was sin, and what a heinous thing it was, and shew by a threatening the punishment which it naturally doth deserve, and what the sinner might expect in justice from him; this was necessary, for where there is no law there is no sin; Rom. v. 13, 'Sin is not imputed where there is no law.' And otherwise there should have been no sinner actually capable of punishment.

Secondly, Giving this law he takes upon him to be a judge, and the judge of all the world; for in the very making of the law he declares himself to be so.

Thirdly, If so, then he is engaged upon many strong motives to shew his justice against sin in that punishment he threatened ; though still in that he is judge of all the world, and maker of the law, he could if he pleased forbear to execute those threatenings (seeing a note of irrevocation was not added to them) ; for he that made the law may repeal that part of it, yet most strong motives these are to execute them.

For is he not the judge of all the world ? And is it not a righteous thing with God to render vengeance ? 2 Thess. i. 5, 6, ' Which is a manifest token of the righteous judgment of God, that ye may be counted worthy of the kingdom of God, for which ye also suffer :' ver. 6, ' Seeing it is a righteous thing with God to recompense tribulation to them that trouble you.' 'And shall not the Judge of all the world do right?' Gen. xviii. And is he not therefore to set a copy to all judges else, being judge of all the world ? *Primum in quolibet genere, est mensura reliquorum.* And is not he an abomination to him, that justifies the unrighteous and condemns the innocent ? Prov. xvii. 15. These may not dispense with the laws, because they are but his justices ; and though he might dispense, being the supreme judge, yet if all the world be his circuit, and he means to condemn the angels by the law, and shew his justice on them, how will he clearly overcome when he judgeth them ? as it is in Rom. iii. 4. Stop their mouths, as it is at the 19th verse, if he shews not his justice against those sins he pardons. And though he might say to them, Pay what you owe ; what is that to you ? yet even the men he pardons, and pardons to that end to shew his mercy, would esteem sin less, and pardon less, if it were procured and obtained lightly ; and should sin, which is the greatest inordinacy, and would not be brought in compass in his government, which doth order all things, be left to its extravagant course, and passed unregarded, and escaped as free as holiness ?

And again, are not all his attributes his nature, his justice as well as mercy ? his hatred of sin, as well as the love of his creature ? And is not that nature of his pure act, and therefore active, and therefore provokes all his will to manifest these his attributes upon all occasions ? Doth not justice boil within him against sin, as well as his bowels of mercy yearn towards the sinner ? Is not the plot of reconciliation his masterpiece, wherein he means to bring all his attributes upon the stage ? And should his justice, and this expressed by a law, keep in and sit down contented, without shewing itself ? No ; and therefore he resolves to be just, and have his justice and law satisfied, as well as to justify the sinner ; Rom. iii. 26, ' To declare, I say, at this time his righteousness : that he might be just, and the justifier of him that believeth in Jesus.' And as to run a course of mere rigorous justice pleased him not, so likewise nor to stretch the pure absolute prerogative of mercy. Wherefore some of the fathers have, after the manner of men, brought in mercy and justice here pleading ; the project of mercy was his delight, as mercy is, Micah vii. 18. And he had resolved above all to shew it. But then justice also is his sceptre, whereby he is to rule, and govern, and judge the world. Wherefore his wisdom, as a middle attribute, steps in, and interposeth as a means of mediation between them both, and undertakes to compound the business, and to accommodate all, so as both shall have their desire and aims, their full demonstration and accomplishment.

CHAPTER V.

To the effecting of all the designs, both of justice and mercy, it was necessary that a full and complete satisfaction should be made, which we being unable to pay, divine wisdom thought of another person to undertake and to do it for us.—That God's justice is contented with this commutation of the person, since hereby that attribute is more glorified, and all the ends of the law answered, than if we [the offenders had in our own persons suffered the due punishment of sin.

This accomplishment of all the designs, both of justice and mercy, must be by satisfaction, by full and adequate ransom, ἀντίλυτρον; 1 Tim. ii. 6, 'Who gave himself a ransom for all, to be testified in due time;' which is *redditio æquivalentis pro æquivalenti*, which the sinner of himself would never have been able to perform. There is no thinking of it; Rom. v. 6–8, 'For when we were yet without strength, in due time Christ died for the ungodly.' Ver. 7, 'For scarcely for a righteous man will one die: yet peradventure for a good man some would even dare to die.' Ver. 8, 'But God commendeth his love towards us, in that, while we were yet sinners, Christ died for us.' We are said to be without strength, and it is there brought in, as the great demonstration of Christ's love in dying for us, when we were yet without strength. And if nothing we are, much less anything we have or can offer; the blood of bulls and goats is not able; it is not possible to take away sin by it: Heb. x. 4, 'For it is not possible that the blood of bulls and of goats should take away sins.' Add to them all the creatures that are the appurtenances of man, which man hath to give, as gold, silver, precious stones, not the whole world of them would do. For nothing less noble than man can be a sufficient surety for man's life, which sin deprives us of. All such things are not worth a soul, which is to be lost for sin, said he that paid for one; Mat. xvi. 26, 'For what is a man profited, if he shall gain the whole world, and lose his own soul? or what shall a man give in exchange for his soul?' And as it is in Micah vi. 7, 'Will the Lord be pleased with rivers of oil? nay, with thy firstborn of thy body for the sin of thy soul?' There is no proportion; God would never have turned away so fair a chapman, if his justice could afford so cheap a commutation. And as not rivers of oil, so nor rivers of tears, which (as all other actions that come from us) are defiled, and become but as puddle-water.

His wisdom therefore thought of a commutation, so as that that satisfaction should be performed by a surety in our stead, who might be a mediator and umpire, and who might take our sins upon himself, and upon whom God might lay the iniquity of us all, Isa. liii. 6, and exact the punishment, as Junius reads it; that might become a surety: Heb. vii. 21, 22, 'For those priests were made without an oath; but this with an oath, by him that said unto him, The Lord sware, and will not repent, Thou art a priest for ever after the order of Melchisedec;' ver. 22, 'By so much was Jesus made a surety of a better testament;' that might make satisfaction, being made sin : 2 Cor. v. 21, 'For he hath made him to be sin for us, who knew no sin ; that we might be made the righteousness of God in him.' That being 'made of a woman, might be under the law,' Gal. iv. 4. 'But when the fulness of time was come, God sent forth his Son, made of a woman, made under the law,' and who so might give and expose himself as a ransom and ἀντίλυτρον, a sufficient adequate satisfaction.

And his justice will be content to admit of such a commutation, and that such a satisfaction should be performed by a surety in our stead. For when all parties are satisfied, and no wrong is done to any, justice may well be satisfied. For if the parties undertaking it be willing, *volenti non fit injuria*, and the great undertaker having power over that thing which he offers to lay down for satisfaction, being lord of it, no other one is wronged.

Neither is the party to be satisfied wronged, if he that undertakes it be of ability fully to satisfy and to fufil what he desires, and if, being the law-giver, he be willing to assent to this act of his, and to accept it. For, being Lord of his own law, he may dispense with the letter of it, if so be those holy ends, which his counsel had in making it, be accomplished and attained; and if the reason of the law and lawgiver be satisfied, then is the law. Now the ends and grounds of giving God's law were to declare and shew forth his justice, and hatred against sin wherever he found it. Now his justice and hatred of sin is as fully manifested when punishment is executed upon a party assuming our sins on himself, and undertaking to be a surety, as if the sinner himself were punished; if not more, in that *he* doth but un-dertake it for another, and yet is not spared. As God is said to hear our prayers, and fulfil his promise, when he answers to the ground of our prayers, though not in the thing; so are the cries of sin, or* justice against the sinner, answered, and God's threatenings fulfilled, when another is punished, because all the ends of the lawgiver are fully accomplished. It is true, the tenor and letter of the law is dispensed with, but not the debt; that is as fully exacted as ever. It is but a dispensation of the party obliged, not of the obligation itself, or of the debt, or of the reason why the debt is exacted. It is not wholly *secundum legem*, nor yet *contra*, οὐδὲ κατὰ νόμον οὐδὲ κατὰ νόμου, ἀλλὰ ὑπερ νόμον καὶ ὑπερ νόμου,† it is a saying no less solid than elegant, and therefore the more elegant, because it was anciently used in another case. And although the law doth not mention or name a surety, and the malefactor's single bond be only mentioned therein, and the threatening directed against him, and his name is only in the project, be-cause the law in itself supposeth as yet none else guilty, and can challenge none else, yet if some other, that is lord of his own action, subject himself to the law willingly, which will of his is a law to him, and the lawgiver himself, that is lord of the law, accepts this, as seeing the same ends shall be satisfied for which he made the law; in this case the law takes hold of the surety or undertaker, and he may let the malefactor go free.

And now that his wisdom hath found a course and way of mediation between his justice and his mercy, yet who is there in heaven and earth should be a fit mediator, both able and willing to undertake it, and faithful to perform it?

CHAPTER VI.

The great difficulty was, to find out a person of strength equal to so high an undertaking.—Neither angels nor men could have found out or presented a fit person.—God manifest in the flesh, for redemption of man, was a mystery above all the thoughts of angels or men, and was worthy only of God's wisdom to find out.

The difficulty is still behind, a mystery so great as would have nonplussed heaven and earth, angels and men, *Nodus Deo vindice dignus.* So as if

* Qu. 'for'?—ED.
† That is, ' Neither against the law nor according to the law; but above the law and for the sake of the law.'—ED.

God had referred it to a consultation of men and angels, and empannelled all intelligible natures upon this grand jury for to save men, and offered but thus fairly; though none of you can do it, yet find you but out the way and person, and I will set my power to the effecting of it; they would have returned in a verdict and bill of *Ignoramus*. After millions of years' consultation, their thoughts would not have presumed to have waded into this depth, so far as to think that justice might dispense in the least measure with so holy a law, and admit a commutation.

But impossible it was they should have thought of the person that should give full satisfaction to his justice, it passed all created powers to perform it (as I shall shew when I shall shew Christ's ability to this work), and as it passed their power to effect it, so their skill and reach. We who could never have found out a remedy for a cut finger, had not God prescribed and appointed one, could much less for this, it being a case of such difficulty. The devils they could not imagine any way, no more for us than for themselves, and therefore tempted man, thinking him when he had sinned sure enough, and hell gates so strongly locked, that no art could find or make a key to open them, or power to break them open. Adam, poor man, he trembled, and knew not which way to turn him, and thought God would have flown upon him presently. The good angels, they know it but by the church: Eph. iii. 10, 'To the intent that now unto the principalities and powers in heavenly places, might be known by the church the manifold wisdom of God.' In this strait God himself aforehand set his depths of wisdom a-work to find out one, in and by whom all things might be accommodated, and out of those infinite depths found out and invented a way and means of effecting our reconciliation, even in the incarnation and death of his own Son. Before the wound given, he provided a plaster; and to allude to Abraham's speech, provided a sacrifice unknown to us, and a sufficient remedy to salve all again, which otherwise had been past finding out.

For the assumption of our nature into one person with the Son of God, was a thing thought credible when revealed, because possible, yet hardly so conceived, even by Mary, when it was told her by the angel: Luke i. 34, 'How can this thing be?' says she. There is nothing in all the works of nature to make a correspondent example for it; yea, nature denies such a composition, to confound heaven and earth. All other religions abhor it. It was the great stumbling-block of the Jews, as they object it to him : John x. 33, 'The Jews answered him, saying, For a good work we stone thee not; but for blasphemy, and because that thou, being a man, makest thyself God.'

But suppose that mystery had been made known, as some say it was, to the angels, that Christ in our nature should be a head, a mediator of union, the stomaching of which, say some, was their fall; yet to have imagined him a mediator of reconciliation, and that he should satisfy God for us, and be made sin and a curse, they would have trembled to have thought it, if God had not first said it. Nay, when Christ told his apostles what he was to suffer, their thoughts seemed to abhor it; 'Master, spare thyself,' says Peter: Mat. xvi. 21, 22, 'From that time forth began Jesus to shew unto his disciples, how that he must go unto Jerusalem, and suffer many things of the elders, and chief priests, and scribes, and be killed, and be raised again the third day;' ver. 22, 'Then Peter took him, and began to rebuke him, saying, Be it far from thee, Lord: this shall not be unto thee.'

This invention therefore God's wisdom alone is to have the glory of, and

therefore it is called, 'the hidden wisdom of God, as in a mystery:' 1 Cor.
ii. 7, 'But we speak the wisdom of God in a mystery, even the hidden
wisdom, which God ordained before the world unto our glory.' The chief
piece of which mystery is God manifest in the flesh: 1 Tim. iii. 16, 'And,
without controversy, great is the mystery of godliness; God was manifest
in the flesh, justified in the Spirit, seen of angels, preached unto the Gentiles,
believed on in the world, received up into glory;' which, had God not revealed, none could ever have reached, for it 'lay hid in God:' Eph. iii. 9,
'And to make all men see what is the fellowship of the mystery, which from
the beginning of the world hath been hid in God, who created all things
by Jesus Christ.'

And which when revealed is, without controversy, so great a mystery,
1 Tim. iii. 16, that the very revelation of it is the greatest argument that
can be brought to prove the truth of our religion; for all men that understand it, must and will with amazement acknowledge and confess, that so
great a plot could not have been hatched in the womb of any created understanding. As sin was our invention, Eccl. vii. 29, so Christ alone was God's;
and therefore Christ is called, 'The Wisdom of God,' which is not spoken of
him essentially as second person, but *manifestativè* as mediator, because in
him his wisdom to the utmost is made manifest.

CHAPTER VII.

When God's wisdom had found out a fit person, yet since this must be his only
Son, here was a greater difficulty for him to overcome; how to give him for
us.—The depths of God's love here, as of his wisdom before, seen in not
sparing his own Son, but exposing him to all the rigours of justice, which
would not make the least abatements.—It was of free choice that he made
thus of his Son to be a Redeemer, to which he was not obliged or necessitated.
—He appointed his Son to death for us, and laid his injunction and charge
on him to perform this his will.

Now the person is found out, and the way clear how it should be done,
which difficulty his wisdom hath expedited; yet the finding out the person
hath brought a greater with it; for if none but he that was his Son could
do it, and though a Son, yet if he become a surety, justice will not have
him spared. 'He that spared not his own Son, but delivered him up for
us all, how shall he not with him also freely give us all things?' Justice
would abate nothing; 'Without blood there is no remission,' and not the
best blood of his body would serve, but of his soul too. He must bear our
sins: Isa. liii. 5, 'But he was wounded for our transgressions, he was
bruised for our iniquities: the chastisement of our peace was upon him;
and with his stripes we are healed.' He must pay God in the same coin
we should, and therefore must 'make his soul an offering for sin:' Isa. liii.
10, 11, 'Yet it pleased the Lord to bruise him; he hath put him to grief:
when thou shalt make his soul an offering for sin, he shall see his seed, he
shall prolong his days, and the pleasure of the Lord shall prosper in his
hand. He shall see of the travail of his soul, and shall be satisfied: by his
knowledge shall my righteous servant justify many; for he shall bear their
iniquities.' And if he be made sin, he must be made a curse; and which
is more than all this, God himself must be the executioner, and his own
Son the person who suffers, and no creature could strike stroke hard enough

to make it satisfactory. Many a tender mother hath not the heart to see her child whipped, much less to whip it herself, although she knows it to be for its own profit and good, when it is in fault; but God here in this case must put his Son to grief, Isa. liii. 10.

To find out the way to accomplish it, and the person by whom, drew out but the depths of his wisdom; but now, if the business go forward, it will draw out the depths of his love. It cost him but his thoughts afore, now it must cost him his Son, the Son of his love. If it were to sacrifice worlds for us, he could have easily created millions, and destroyed them again for us; as he gave nations for their sakes, Isa. xliii. 4. But what? To sacrifice his only Son, here was the difficulty.

And if this be the only way (God might have said), bury the invention of it in eternal silence; let it never be made mention of or come to light, that ever there were such a thing; let it here die, rather than Christ die; and therefore though his heart was much set upon this project, yet this might likely have dashed all, that nothing should serve but the death of his Son; his will might be more set upon this business of reconciling us, than ever on any, but yet not upon such terms as these. He might be glad to see it done, yet not to cost so dear.

Behold therefore and wonder, and stand aghast! He takes this way to choose, and chooseth Christ to this work; and thus to choose him was God the Father's work, and indeed a work of wonder. Isa. xlii. 1, 'Behold my servant, whom I uphold; my elect, in whom my soul delights.' And so Mat. xii. 18, 'Behold my servant whom I have chosen, in whom my soul is well pleased.' That ever these two should be put together in one sentence,—Scil., 'In whom my soul delights,' with this, 'Behold my servant whom I have chosen,' to such a harsh and difficult a business; yet that was the very reason of this choice, therefore he chooseth him, and therefore it is mentioned with it; for the more he loved him, the more love he should shew in giving him for us.

And observe it. It is made an act of choice in him, full and free. He had other ways; at least, he was no way necessitated unto this. He might have destroyed us, and lost nothing by us. He might have pardoned us, and shewn more love therein than unto millions of new created friends. Yea, suppose a creature could have satisfied, yet he takes this way to choose; it suits with the utmost extent of all his ends. If the sacrifices of bulls and goats could (as they could not), have taken away sin, yet these 'thou wouldst not,' says Christ, Heb. x. 8, 'but a body hast thou fitted me. He takes away the first' (says the apostle, Heb. x. 9), 'that he may establish the second.' That is, he layeth aside all other means (if other could be supposed), and chooseth this, and however resolves to take this course ex abundanti; and as in making his promises it is said, Heb. vi. 17, 'God being willing more abundantly to shew to the heirs of salvation the immutability of his counsel, confirms them by an oath,' which puts an end to all controversies; ver. 16, 'And because he can swear by no greater, he sware by himself.' So say I in this: What if God, ex abundanti, if upon supposition other means could have done it; yet out of his abundance of love to us, whom he thinks he can never love enough, nor to shew his love, do too much for; what if he means to give his Son because he cannot give a greater, and so at once to give the greatest instance of his love and justice: of his love, in that he is not only content to commute the punishment, but lay it on his Son; of his justice, in that he will not only punish sin in us, but even in him. He will not spare his own Son, Rom. viii. 32, and so he will make sure work indeed, and put an end to all suppositions, fears, yea, possibility of miscarriage ; a way whereby to accommodate all things so fully, as all conveniences requisite to this work should concur, yea, abound indeed in Christ's alone mediation. The demonstration of which doth depend upon the second part of the story, when we hear what Christ did do to the effecting of it.

So as it is, and may be a great question, whether God hath shewn more love in pitching on this way, when by other means he might have saved us if he would ; or if no other means could be had, and God was confined to this, yet that God would do so much rather than we should not be saved ? We could have had pardon without Christ, yet to have not pardon only, but Christ also, this is infinitely more. The pardon of sin is a greater gift than millions of worlds ; but to have pardon through Christ, and Christ with the pardon, though but of one sin, is more than the pardon of worlds of sins.

And, further, consider what he chose Christ unto ; ' He appointed him to death,' as the apostle says of himself in another case. Therefore Peter, 1 Pet, i. 18, 19, speaking of our redemption by his blood ; ' which (says he) was verily foreordained before the foundation of the world.' So as he chose him not as a head only, but as a lamb to be slain : Rev. xiii. 8, ' And all that dwell on the earth shall worship him, whose names are not written in the book of life of the Lamb slain from the foundation of the world.'

I have elsewhere * shewed how he was appointed to be an heir ; but there is some dignity in that, and yet it was a humiliation in him to take that by appointment which was his own by natural inheritance ; but to be appointed to death so long afore, and to such a death, and there was not a circumstance in it but his Father appointed it, that it should be thus shameful, thus painful, &c., this was love indeed ; Acts ii. 23, ' Him being delivered by the determinate counsel of God, ye have crucified and slain.' All was done by the determinate counsel of God. He not only secretly determined it, but which is more, called him to it, moved him in it himself to undertake to do all this ; for calling and election of us are two distinct things ; and so in the designing of Christ to this office, they are to be considered apart.

Now the Father was not only the contriver and designer, but had the heart (such was his love to us) to be himself the first propounder also of it to him, and withal to tell him he was to be the executioner, or he should not be satisfied by him for sin. And who should break this to Christ, and persuade him, or bring him off to be willing to it ? No creature had interest enough in him, to be sure. None of us did ever speak to him to die, nor no creature mentioned it for us ; for none durst so much as to think it. Who did then ? His Father owns it as his own work ; Isa. xlii. 6, ' I have called thee in righteousness ;' and it was necessary he should. Both because,

First, Christ was not to begin to offer it of himself. That conceit of Bernard's, bringing Christ in offering himself for poor man (as he doeth), saying, ' Take me, sacrifice me for them,' hath no ground, for he doeth nothing but what his Father propounds ; John v. 19, 20, ' Then answered Jesus, and said unto them, Verily, verily, I say unto you, the Son can do nothing of himself ; but what he seeth the Father do : for what things soever

* In the ' Discourse of the Knowledge of God the Father, and his Son Jesus Christ.' In 2d volume of his Works.—[Vol. IV. of this edition.—Ed.]

he doeth, these also doeth the Son likewise. For the Father loveth the Son, and sheweth him all things that himself doeth : and he will shew him greater works than these, that ye may marvel.' He is the second person, and all motions are to begin and come from the Father, who is the first person. And as to this particular, Christ speaks in this wise, John viii. 42, ' I came from God, neither came I of myself, but my Father sent me.'

Secondly, It being an office, and an office of priesthood, he was to be appointed to it. Heb. v. 4, 5, ' No man takes this honour to himself, but he that was called of God, as was Aaron. So also Christ' (though he had all excellencies and abilities in him) ' glorified not himself to be made an high priest for us.'

God therefore called him to it; and this as making it his own business, as he was pleased to account it, and as such commended it to Christ, and therefore Christ calls it his ' Father's business:' Luke ii. 49, ' And he said unto them, How is it that ye sought me ? Wist ye not that I must be about my Father's business ? '

And now will you see how and in what manner it was he called him, and be amazed at it, to see how earnest he is in it. See his own words (as the Holy Ghost, the great secretary of heaven, who alone was by at that great council, hath recorded it), Heb. v. 5, 6, ' So also Christ glorified not himself to be made an high priest; but he that said unto him, Thou art my Son, to-day have I begotten thee. As he saith also in another place, Thou art a priest for ever, after the order of Melchisedec ;' where we find the very words he spake to him recorded, ' He that said to him, Thou art my Son, this day have I begotten thee, says in another place,' which records another passage then spoken, ' Thou art a priest for ever, after the order of Melchisedec.' The Holy Ghost brings in both these, and joins them together, and brings that which was in the first as the argument or motive which God used to him to persuade him, when he moved him to it. He that said, ' Thou art my Son,' says, ' Thou art a priest ' also, to shew the ground of authority which he urgeth in it. He that was his Father, and so had power to appoint his Son his calling (as other parents have), appointed him as his begotten Son thus to be a priest. And therefore he tells him, in the first speech, that he is his Son, and he begat him ; and therewithal wooes him, that as he was his Son, and he his Father, and puts him in mind of all that mutual love which was between them upon so high a relation ; and so much the higher, by how much the thing communicated was greater, in that he was God by his begetting him ; that therefore and thereupon he would take on him this so hard and harsh an undertaking. He calls him indeed, and speaks (as if he meant not to be denied) in the highest language of a father, and useth his whole interest in that, mentions the deepest obligation, and he notes out the time ; it was on his birthday, ' *This day* have I begotten thee.' As parents often dedicate their children, when first born, to such and such a calling, as Hannah did Samuel to the priesthood, so doth God his Son. Yea, he is yet more earnest, he laid his express command on him, John x. 18, though the other mentions the most commanding argument and relation of all other, viz., as he was his Son. All obedience as due on Christ's side, and authority on his Father's, are spoken in such a word. Yea, and yet to shew more vehemency and earnestness, he adds an oath to it, Heb. vii. 21, ' He swore he should be a priest,' and when he hath done, records it. ' It is written of me,' and that ἐν κεφαλίδι τοῦ βιβλίου, in the first page, or beginning of the book of his decrees ; yea, and puts his seal to it, ' Him hath the Father sealed,' John vi. 27. By all which he precludes him from a refusal, to prevent all supposition of denial.

God the Father, you see, hath done all that lies in him, and yet no more than was necessarily required to this work, as was in part said before, and may be further observed out of the 10th verse of the 10th chapter of the Hebrews, wherein he says, ' We are sanctified through his will, through the offering of the body of Christ ;' having reference to that his will of calling him, before expressed in that 5th chapter, without which Christ's offering had not been satisfactory, or of force to sanctify us.

CHAPTER VIII.

Christ's acceptance of the terms which God the Father propounded to him for man's redemption.—That his willingness in the undertaking proceeded not only from the love he had for us, but from that which he did bear unto his Father, and his desire to obey him, and to perform his will.—That the elect, redeemed by Christ, were first God the Father's, and by him given in trust and charge to Christ to save them.

Now the next thing to be considered is, how this motion takes with Christ's heart, which his Father makes, and what he says to it, how he answers it again, and how willingly. And this is as necessary as the former; for besides that it could not be forced on him; for, John v. 26, ' the Father hath given him to have life in himself, and so to have power over his life.' John x. 18, ' I have power over my life, and none can take it from me.' Besides that, if it came not of him freely, it had not been satisfactory ; for *satisfactio est redditio voluntaria*, it must be a voluntary payment; and as our disobedience was free, so must his satisfaction be. Though he had at last yielded, yet if he sticks at it we are undone, if he makes but an objection. And is it not infinite love he should not, being he was the party to undergo so much debasement? How did the eldest son's stomach rise, when but the fat calf was killed for the prodigal? But the eldest, only begotten Son of God, must sacrifice himself for enemies (not the sacrificing of worlds would serve, whereof he could have created enough), and yet not a thought did arise contrary to his Father's will. So his own words, in answer to the former call of his Father, do shew, ' Lo, I come to do thy will, O God,' Heb. x. 7. The psalmist, from whence the words are borrowed, hath it, ' I delight to do thy will,' Ps. xl. 8. ' Lo, I come ' (says Christ); I am as ready, as forward, O God, as thou to have me ; not willing only, but glad ; I delight to do thy will. As the sun rejoiceth to run his race, so the Sun of righteousness to run his, for he was ' anointed with the oil of gladness above his fellows,' Ps. xlv. 7. He was as glad to do this work as ever he was to eat his meat : John iv. 34, ' Jesus saith unto them, My meat is to do the will of him that sent me, and to finish his work.' ' With desire' (saith he) ' have I desired it:' Luke xxii. 15, ' And he said unto them, With desire I have desired to eat this passover with you before I suffer.' He longed as much, and was as much pained, as ever woman with child longed to be delivered, till this work was accomplished. Luke xii. 50, ' But I have a baptism to be baptized with, and how am I straitened till it be accomplished.'

It was well for us that his Father struck thus strongly in. For, take the business in itself, you know how unwelcome it must needs be to Christ: 'Father, if it be possible' (says he), 'let it pass;' yet because it was his Father's will, he submits, 'Not my will, but thine be done,' Mat. xxvi. 39. As it was his Father's will, he had no reluctancy, neither would simply all our cries or mediation have ever moved him, no more than straws can move a mountain; but that it was his Father's will, it was enough.   For besides that reason for it, John x. 30, 'I and my Father are one' (saith he), and so have one will and agree in one, there is another thing in it most prevalent, seeing that his Father entreats him thus to do it.   The Father resolves to hear him in all things; and should not he then hearken to his Father, especially when his request is made upon his birthday ('This day have I begotten thee'), when all requests are rendered more easy and facile to be granted; as Herod on his would give to the half of his kingdom? What, and as he was his Father and he his Son,—'Thou art my Son,'— this overcame him.   John x. 17, 18, Though he had life in his own hand, yet (says he) I lay it down, because my Father loves me.   Surely his Father being so earnest in it, he would not deny him, especially when he added a command to it.   This is the reason he likewise gives, John x. 18, 19, 'I have power to lay down my life, and this command I have received of my Father.' It had stuck with him from the first, and he remembered it still.   His Father had power (as other fathers have, to dispose of the calling of their sons) to dispose of him; and though he was so great a Son, equal to so great a Father, yet, being a Son, he is not exempted from obedience.   Philip. ii. 8, 'And being found in fashion as a man, he humbled himself, and became obedient unto death, even the death of the cross.' Heb. v. 7, 8, 'Who in the days of his flesh, when he had offered up prayers and supplications, with strong crying and tears, unto him that was able to save him from death, and was heard in that he feared: though he were a Son, yet learned he obedience by the things which he suffered.   And when his Father shall add an oath to it also (that is an end of all controversies between man and man, Heb. vi. 16, much more between the Father and Son), and last of all sets his seal to it, it must stand good, for his seal stands sure, 2 Tim. ii. 19, there is no breaking of it; and therefore all these made Christ fully willing.

And this is therefore to be in a more especial manner taken notice of; that we may consider for whose sake principally Christ did die, and undertake it, and thus see whom so much we are beholden to.   Though Christ did it out of love to us, yet chiefly for his Father's entreaty and command, and out of love to him.   So Christ says, John xiv. 31, 'That the world may know that I love the Father, and that as he gave commandment, so I do.'   He spake this when he was to go to suffer, for, saith he, 'Arise, let us go hence.'

In the sixth place, as his Father recommended the business to him, so also he gave especial recommendation of the persons for whom he would have all this done; for he gave those of the sons of men unto Christ whom he would have reconciled, and this with a charge to bring them to salvation.

Hence Christ, when he was to offer up himself, he commits and commends them at his death again to his Father and to his love, upon this great ground and motive, that he himself gave them first to him; alleging that he himself came to have a share in them, by his gift and commendation: John xvii. 6, 'Thine they were, and thou gavest them me.'   A strange gift it was, which he must yet pay for, and must cost more than they were worth, and yet he takes them as a gift and favour from his Father; which also when he had bought, he likewise begged at his Father's hands, in John xvii. 20, 21, 24.

And observe that they were first his Father's; first thine, and then mine by thy gift; and this was not a late or new acquired propriety of God's in them, but an ancient one, which Christ puts him in mind of, 'Thine they were.' So that as the Father gave him his work he was to do, ver. 4, so he gave to him the persons for whom he should do it; ver. 6, so as both things and persons, 'all things whatsoever thou hast given me, are of thee,' ver. 7. As he doeth nothing of himself, but what he sees the Father do; so as mediator (and though mediator) he saves not a man but whom his Father did give him, nor puts a name in more than were in his Father's bill. John vi. 37, 38, 'I came not to do mine own will, but the will of him that sent me.' And this is spoken in relation, not to the business only he was to do, but of the persons also that were to be reconciled; for it follows, ver. 39, 'This is his will, that of all which he hath given me I should lose none.' And they are not said to be then given to Christ only when they are called and begin to believe, but before, even from everlasting (of which transaction we now speak); for, John vi. 37, 'All the Father giveth me shall come to me;' therefore they are not then said first to be given when they came, but before.

And hence, by reason of his Father's giving of them to him, he calls them his sheep, and that before they are called, which as yet were not of the fold, but which were yet to bring in; John x. 16, 'And other sheep I have, which are not of this fold: them also I must bring, and they shall hear my voice; and there shall be one fold, and one shepherd.' Yea, and he calls himself such a shepherd, whose own the sheep are; John xvi. 2, 3, 4, 'They shall put you out of the synagogues: yea, the time cometh, that whosoever killeth you will think that he doeth God service. And these things will they do unto you, because they have not known the Father, nor me. But these things have I told you, that, when the time shall come, ye may remember that I told you of them. And these things I said not unto you at the beginning, because I was with you.' Ver. 11, 12, 'Of judgment, because the prince of this world is judged. I have yet many things to say unto you, but ye cannot bear them now.' He was owner of them (as all shepherds are not), and delighteth to use a phrase of propriety. His own sheep they are. How his own, but by gift from his Father, and by special love and care of his own? And their names he knows. John x. 14, 'I am the good Shepherd, and know my sheep, and am known of mine.' As God by name is said to know who are his; and therefore their names are said to be written in the Lamb's book as well as in his Father's: Rev. xiii. 18, 'Here is wisdom. Let him that hath understanding count the number of the beast: for it is the number of a man; and his number is six hundred threescore and six;' yea, they are written in his heart. And as the high priest had the names of all the tribes written on his breastplate, so had Christ the names of all his written in his heart, by a pen of adamant, by the will of his Father, written with ever-living and everlasting love; so as the letters can never be worn out.

And as he gave them to be his, so also with a special charge to bring them to salvation, to lose not one of his tale and number. John vi. 38, 39, 'This is my Father's will, who sent me,' says Christ, 'for which I came down from heaven, that of all that he hath given me, I should lose nothing.' As Laban required his tale of Jacob, so doth God of Christ. When he sent him he gave him that charge, 'This is the will of him that sent me.'

I come with this errand, charge, and message, which therefore Christ had still in his eye, yea, and looks at it as a duty enjoined him; 'Them I must bring,' says he, John x. 16, which hath relation to that command laid on him.

And as Judah became a surety to Jacob his father for his younger brother Benjamin, to bring him safe to him out of Egypt—Gen. xliii. 9, 'I will be a surety for him, and if I bring him not unto thee, and set him not before thee, let me bear the blame for ever '—so did Christ for his younger brethren, whom God, through him as their captain and chief leader, would bring to glory: Heb. ii. 10, 11, 'For it became him, for whom are all things, and by whom are all things, in bringing many sons unto glory, to make the Captain of their salvation perfect through sufferings. For both he that sanctifieth and they who are sanctified are all of one : for which cause he is not ashamed to call them brethren.' Who therefore had the charge of conducting them, and to that end he took flesh, and in regard to it gives an account to his Father of them; 'Behold I and the children which God hath given me.' And you may observe how careful he was in this his account, and how punctual in it: John xvii. 12, 'Those thou gavest me I have kept, and none of them is lost, but the son of perdition.' He is exact in his account, as appears in that he gives a reason for him that was lost, that he was a ' son of perdition,' and so excuseth it; and to this end God also gave him, as he was mediator, power over all flesh, that he might be enabled to give eternal life to those God gave him : John xvii. 3, ' And this is life eternal, that they might know thee the only true God, and Jesus Christ whom thou hast sent.'

CHAPTER IX.

That upon Christ's accepting this agreement, God the Father, to reward him, engages to bestow all the blessings which he should purchase to those redeemed by him.—That all these blessings of grace and eternal life were promised to us in Christ from all eternity.

Christ thus willingly undertaking to die, and to fulfil his Father's will, his Father, to gratify him, enters into a covenant with him, and binds himself to him to bestow the worth and value of all his obedience in all spiritual blessings (both of grace and glory, which that his death should purchase), to those whom he had given him, and that he and his children should have it out in everlasting revenues of grace and glory. As Christ undertook to God, so God undertakes to Christ again, to justify, adopt and forgive, sanctify and glorify those he gives him. All the blessings his love intended, Christ was to purchase them; and all the blessings Christ's death did purchase, he promiseth Christ to bestow on those whom he purchased them for, so as his labour should not be in vain.

This you may observe out of many places ; as, in general, Isa. liii. 10-12, ' Yet it pleased the Lord to bruise him ; he hath put him to grief: when thou shalt make his soul an offering for sin, he shall see his seed, he shall prolong his days, and the pleasure of the Lord shall prosper in his hand. He shall see of the travail of his soul, and shall be satisfied; by his knowledge shall my righteous servant justify many ; for he shall bear their iniquities. Therefore will I divide him a portion with the great, and he shall divide the spoil with the strong ; because he hath poured out his soul unto death : and he was numbered with the transgressors ; and he bare the sins of many, and made intercession for the transgressors ;' where God makes a promise unto Christ that he should see his seed, and see the travail of his soul, and should be satisfied ; for my righteous servant shall justify many, and thus because he underwent so much sorrow and grief so willingly, as it is in the former part of the chapter, and the joy of this was it that made him undergo it so willingly : Heb. xii. 2, ' Looking unto Jesus, the author and finisher of our faith ; who for the joy that was set before him, endured the cross, despising the shame, and is set down at the right hand of the throne of God.' And that his joy was this, that he should prolong his days, and though he died in the travail, yet should see the travail of his soul ; as though a woman be in great pains, yet her joy is, that a man-child is brought forth into the world. And so it was with Christ ; his joy is, that many children should be brought to glory, and by this he should be satisfied, namely, that many should be justified by him, as it follows there (for nothing else will satisfy Christ), ' and that he should divide the spoil with the strong ; because he poured out his soul to death,' ver. 12. That is, he triumphed over hell and death, and by the conquest spoiled principalities and powers, and obtained heaven and everlasting righteous-ness, by which himself is not of himself made the richer. God therefore allows him to divide it and give it away to others. And God considered also how that in this work he was his servant, ' My righteous servant,' says he, ' shall justify many.' He was his servant, and did his business in it, and should he have no wages nor rewards ? Yes he should ; and the only reward he seeks for, is the salvation and justification of his elect, and of those whom God hath given him. And therefore we find this very cove-nant bargain-wise struck up, and by way of a most elegant dialogue expressed to us, Isa. xlix., which chapter is, as I may call it, the draught of the covenant, or deed of gift, betwixt Christ and his Father for us ; wherein Christ first begins and shews his commission, as the ground of the treaty between them ; intimating unto his Father that he had called him to this great work : ver. 1, ' Listen, O isles, unto me ; and hearken, ye people, from far ; The Lord hath called me from the womb ; from the bowels of my mother hath he made mention of my name.' And fitted him for it : ver. 2, ' And he hath made my mouth like a sharp sword ; in the shadow of his hand hath he hid me, and made me a polished shaft ; in his quiver hath he hid me.' He therefore expects what fruit and reward he should have of all his sufferings.

His Father offers (as it were) low at first, and mentioneth but Israel only as his portion ; ' Thou art my servant, O Israel, in whom I will be glorified,' ver. 3. Then he, as thinking them too small an inheritance, too small a purchase for that great price, foreseeing the hardness of their hearts, and how few of them would come in, not worth his coming into the world for, so that if the gleanings of them were all, he says, ' He should labour in vain, and spend his strength for nought,' ver. 4. Though, how-ever, he satisfies himself with this, ' My work is with thee, O Lord,' &c. ; namely, that his main end of undertaking it was for his Father's sake, and in obedience unto him.

God therefore answers him again, and enlargeth and stretcheth his cove-nant further with him : says he, ' It is a light thing that thou shouldest be my servant, to raise up the tribes of Israel,' &c. ' I will give thee for a light to the Gentiles, that thou mayest be my salvation to the ends of the earth,' ver. 6. And, ver. 8, ' I will give thee for a covenant to the people,'

&c. God, you see, makes this covenant with him, to save both Jews and Gentiles, as the reward of his death.

And this compact you have also expressed, Ps. ii. 7, 8, where, after he had called him to this office (which then he calls the decree, ' I will declare the decree : Thou art my Son ; this day have I begotten thee'), he subjoins this covenant made upon it. ' Ask of me, and I shall give thee the heathen for thine inheritance, and the uttermost parts of the earth for thy possession.' And this was shadowed out by that famous covenant made with David for his seed, for an eternal kingdom : Ps. lxxxix. 4, 5, ' Thy seed will I establish for ever, and build up thy throne to all generations. Selah. And the heavens shall praise thy wonders, O Lord : thy faithfulness also in the congregation of the saints.' And ver. 28, 29, ' My mercy will I keep for him for evermore, and my covenant shall stand fast with him. His seed also will I make to endure for ever, and his throne as the days of heaven.' Which covenant was made with David, as a type of Christ, and is to be meant as spoken of Christ ; and that covenant too made by God with him for his spiritual seed. That covenant is called ' the sure mercies of David,' and is applied to Christ as that spiritual David ; Acts xiii. 34–37, ' And as concerning that he raised him up from the dead, now no more to return to corruption, he said on this wise, I will give you the sure mercies of David. Wherefore he saith also in another psalm, Thou shalt not suffer thine Holy One to see corruption. For David, after he had served his own generation by the will of God, fell on sleep, and was laid unto his fathers, and saw corruption : but he, whom God raised again, saw no corruption :' who therefore is called David, as here and elsewhere ; and that oath God made to David, shewed the everlasting oath and covenant made to Christ for his seed : Ps. cxxxii. 10, 14, ' For thy servant David's sake, turn not away the face of thine anointed. The Lord hath sworn in truth unto David ; he will not turn from it ; of the fruit of thy body will I set upon thy throne.'

And hence further to confirm this, we find, Titus i. 2, that ' eternal life is promised afore the world began ;' which is to be understood in relation to this covenant. A promise then was made ; that is, an expression of an engagement, which is more than a purpose, for a promise is an expression of a purpose ; and to whom can this be understood to be made so long afore but to our head Christ ? And we were then looked at by God only as in him ; to whom therefore for us he promised to give eternal life as the fruit of his death. This very covenant, therefore, that God struck with Christ for us, this was the promise meant ; which was, that as he should die, so he would as certainly bestow the fruit and revenue of his death in glory on those he gave to him.

So as though God had never expressed any promise to us, yet having made it to Christ for us, he would have performed it ; therefore he adds, God that cannot lie hath made this promise ; and further says, that as before all worlds he made this promise and covenant with Christ, so in due time he hath further manifested this his word by preaching, &c. All the promises that now are revealed are but the manifestation of that grand promise ; but copies, as it were, of that which was made to Christ, in whose breast the original of our records are kept, and the application of those promises to us is but the writing out the counterpane* of what was done in heaven. As all promises are made in him, so all promises were first made to him, and to us as one with him. Therefore, says the apostle, ' Not to seeds, as of many, but to seed, as of one, which is Christ,' Gal.

* That is, ' counterpart.'—Ed.

iii. 16, who in our name, and for us, took a deed of gift from God the Father, for all blessing we are to enjoy, before the world was. And therefore also, 2 Tim. i. 9, ' Who hath saved us, and called us with an holy calling, not according to our works, but according to his own purpose and grace, which was given us in Christ Jesus, before the world began.' There is grace spoken of as given us in Christ ere the world began, which place explains the former ; for as the former says it was promised, so this, that grace was given us, and as then promised to Christ for us, so then also given us in Christ, God looking on us as one with Christ. Which promise is made upon that his promise to his Father, to give himself for us. The sum of all is : his Father promiseth to him to give all spiritual blessings in him, and then makes a deed of gift to him for our good and use ; even as goods may be given to and by a feoffee in trust for one that is yet not born. And so our life is said to be ' hid with Christ in God ;' and so it was from everlasting there laid up by God with Christ.

And hence also we find that all blessings which God in time bestows are said to be given in Christ, ere they are actually to us. So Eph. i. 3, ' God hath blessed us with all spiritual blessings in Christ.' So his purpose of saving us is said to be purposed in Jesus Christ : Eph. iii. 10, 11, ' To the intent that now unto the principalities and powers in heavenly places, might be known by the church the manifold wisdom of God, according to the eternal purpose which he purposed in Christ Jesus our Lord.' So to be reconciled in Christ here in the text. So, speaking of our redemption, he says, ' which is in Christ Jesus;' Rom. iii. 24, ' Being justified freely by his grace through the redemption that is in Jesus Christ.' So all grace is said to be given in Christ, 2 Tim. i. 9, before the world was.* So 2 Tim. i. 1, ' Paul, an apostle of Jesus Christ by the will of God, according to the promise of life which is in Christ Jesus.' The promise of life is said to be in Jesus Christ. Now the phrase notes out a transaction, an endowment of all these on us, not first immediately in ourselves, but in Christ for us, and on us in him.

Hence likewise in Scripture we read of promises, not only conditional, that he that believes and repents shall be saved, but also absolute; as that in Jeremiah, ' This is my covenant, to give them a new heart and a new spirit, and they shall walk in my commandments,' Jer. xxxi. 33, wherein he undertakes to fulfil the conditions themselves ; and that covenant must needs be made with Christ first, and mediately for us ; and he only knows for whom it is made, even for those his Father gave him.

CHAPTER X.

What is the reason that though we receive all these blessings by Christ, and on the account of his merits, yet they are said to be given to us of pure grace.

And upon this covenant made with Christ, and compact between God and him for us, comes it, that all things we have by Christ, though purchased by him, are yet said to be by grace, as well as by Christ's merits, because they are bestowed by a compact with Christ, by virtue of which compact his merits are accepted for us ; so that though Christ laid down a price worth all the grace and glory we shall have, yet that it should be accepted for us, and all'that grace bestowed on us, comes from this com-

* *Vide* Athan. Ora. iii. cont. Arianos.

pact and covenant made by God with Christ to accept it for us. And the acceptation of it for us depends as much on that covenant made with Christ as on his merits. Therefore, Heb. x. 10, our sanctification and salvation is ascribed as much to God's will and covenant with Christ (of which he spake, ver. 7) as to Christ's offering himself; for he says, 'By which will we are sanctified, through the offering of the body of Christ.' And therefore, as it is said that Christ died, so also it is God that justifies; Rom. viii. 33, 'Who shall lay anything to the charge of God's elect? It is God that justifieth;' justifies freely by his grace; Rom. iii. 24, 'Being justified freely by his grace, through the redemption that is in Jesus Christ.' Though Christ hath laid down a sufficient price, and equal to the guilt of our sins, yet that God justifies us for it is an act of grace. Why? Because the acceptation of it for us was out of covenant ; and therefore our divines say against the Jesuits, that his merits are merits *ex compacto*, and not which absolutely could oblige God to us. Though they be equal to our demerits by sin, yet it is only that relation that they had to this covenant made with Christ which gave acceptation to them for us.

And the reason is, because to satisfy for another, especially in corporal punishments, requires the compact and willingness of the party to be satisfied, to accept it for him that should else undergo it. Let the satisfaction be never so equivalent to the wrong, yet without a covenant of the party to be satisfied it may be refused. Therefore umpires use to bind the parties in bond to stand to their word ; *Quando aliud offertur quam est in obligatione, satisfactio est recusabilis*, say the schoolmen. So Ahab offered Naboth as good a vineyard as his own, yet he might refuse it, as he did. This covenant therefore which God made with Christ, to bestow all the merits of his obedience on us, which he called him unto, is the main foundation of all our happiness. As it obliged and engaged God firmly to us in Christ, so it makes all that Christ purchased to be of grace. Though he paid an equivalent price to what we should have done, and much more, yet it is accepted for us out of a covenant of grace. And therefore in Rom. v. 17, though the apostle shews and proves that there is more merit in Christ's obedience to justify than in Adam's sin to condemn, yet the imputing of it to us he calls 'abundance of grace, and the gift of righteousness.' Though it was an abounding righteousness, yet there was an abounding of grace to accept it for us, and it is derived by way of gift.

And the ground of all is because of this covenant made by God with Christ for us, upon which the acceptation of all depends.

CHAPTER XI.

That upon the conclusion of this agreement or covenant of redemption, there was the greatest joy in heaven ; the divine persons exulting in the delightful thoughts, that so many wretched, lost creatures should be effectually saved.

And now our reconciliation being brought to this blessed issue by God the Father and his Son, their greatest delights have been taken up with it ever since, so as never in like manner with anything else. There was never such joy in heaven as upon this happy conclusion and agreement. The whole Trinity rejoiced in it (which is the last thing, and the *coronis* of this discourse), they not only never repented of what they had resolved upon ; 'he swore, and would not repent,' Heb. vii. 21 ; but further, their chiefest delights were taken up with this more than in all their works *ad extra*. God's heart was never taken so much with anything he was able to effect; so as the thoughts of this business, ever since it was resolved on, became matter of greatest delight unto them.

This you may see, Prov. viii. 30, 31, ' Then I was by him, as one brought up with him : and I was daily his delight, rejoicing always before him; rejoicing in the habitable part of his earth; and my delights were with the sons of men.' Where you have that curious question in part resolved, what God did before the world was made ? How that eternity was run out, and what the thoughts and delights of the great God most ran on ? You have it resolved by one that knew his mind, and was of his council, the ' mighty Councillor,' as being the Wisdom of his Father, as he is there styled that was before God made the world, Prov. viii. 22, 23, ' The Lord possessed me in the beginning of his way, before his works of old. I was set up from everlasting, from the beginning, or ever the earth was.' ' Then was I' (says he, ver 30) ' all the while by him,' that came out of his bosom, John i. 18, and who therefore compares himself in this Prov. viii. to a child brought up with the parent : ' so was I' (says he) ' brought up with him.' And what did they together ? Two things.

1. They delighted one with and in another, the Father that he was able to beget such a Son like him, and of equal substance with himself : ' I was daily his delight,' and he mine, ' rejoicing always before him.' And this was and would have been delight enough to them, though no creature had ever been made.

2. But, secondly, next to that, what did they delight in most ? It follows, ' rejoicing in the habitable parts of his earth; and my delight was with the sons of men.' And observe it, that next to those internal, essential, and personal delights each in other, the greatest and dearest unto those two divine persons were their delights in ' the sons of men ;' of all God's works *ad extra*, in these they most took pleasure.

Now, what is it concerning them should afford God and Christ such thoughts so long aforehand, but this plot concerning them of reconciling them again ? For to look and foresee them all at one clap turned rebels against him, and view them mustering together in troops against him, this could minister none but sad and disconsolate thoughts, and it pained him at the heart to think of it : Gen. vi. 5, 6, ' And God saw that the wickedness of man was great in the earth, and that every imagination of the thoughts of his heart was only evil continually. And it repented the Lord that he had made man on the earth, and it grieved him at his heart.' What was it delighted him then ? Men delight only in their friends, not enemies. Was it in them then, as they were at first created in a state of friendship, that God was pleased ? No. Then there were but a couple to delight in; but this delight is said to be ' in the sons of men,' all the earth over, ' in the habitable parts of the earth,' which implies he had some in all parts inhabited who were the desire and delight of his eyes. And besides, that first friendship was not worth the thinking of, it lasted so little while, and ended in so great and general a breach. These delights then were most in this, to think that he should win to him and gain the love of these accursed rebels whom he himself loved so dearly, and that he should shew that his love, by an unheard of way, that should amaze angels and men, to take away their sins, and reconcile them to himself again by the incarnation and death of his Son ; and tie them to him by an everlasting knot, which their sins should not untie again, nor separate from that his love. This took up his delights (in the plural); he delighted to think of it again and again; his double delights (as some paraphrase it) were in this, insomuch as he glads himself with the continual thoughts of it again and again. Which may appear by another scripture added unto this, which tells us how his thoughts did run upon this so dear a design to him (speaking after the manner of men), above all else, and that they were taken up with it; as it useth to be with us, when we are deeply affected with anything. So Ps. xl. 5, 'Many,' says he, 'are the wonderful works that thou hast done, and thy thoughts to us-ward cannot be reckoned.' His mind hath ran on them from everlasting, that his thoughts cannot be numbered. There are many works of wonder which he hath done for us, which hath exercised these his thoughts towards us, but above all in this we have been speaking of; therefore he passeth by all other works, and mentions this very transaction, and calling of, and covenant with, his Son, which we have all this while been speaking of, as that wherein these his thoughts have been most spent and exercised with delight. So ver. 6–8, 'Sacrifice and offering thou didst not desire; mine ears hast thou opened: burnt-offering and sin-offering hast thou not required. Then said I, Lo, I come: in the volume of the book it is written of me, I delight to do thy will, O my God: yea, thy law is within my heart.'

And by all this you see that our salvation was in sure hands, even afore the world was; for God and Christ had engaged themselves by covenant each to other for us, the one to die, the other to accept it for us.

And though Christ was yet to come and die, yea, and though there were not one word of promise written that was made to us expressing God's mind, yet this everlasting obligation made all sure that it should be done.

So as had I no other news to tell you, and could not secretly assure you of these passages from everlasting, they might be enough to persuade and over-persuade you to come in for mercy and grace with him; but much more when it shall be further told you, what Christ hath done to the accomplishment of all this, and what fulness was in him for it, which makes up the second part of this glorious story.

BOOK II.

The sole and peculiar fitness of Christ's person for the work of redemption.

For verily he took not on him the nature of angels ; but he took on him the seed of Abraham.—Wherefore in all things it behoved him to be made like unto his brethren, that he might be a merciful and faithful high priest in things pertaining to God, to make reconciliation for the sins of the people.— HEB. ii. 16, 17.

CHAPTER I.

The fitness of Christ's person for the work of a mediator, hath a great influence to make it successful and prosperous.

IN the first chapter, the apostle shewed that our mediator was God, and the Son of God. In this second, he shews that he is man also, and a man made of the same lump with other men, and flesh and blood as well as we. And he knits up all with this, that thus it behoved him to be, that he might be a priest to reconcile us to the Father. That therefore which these two chapters drive at, is to shew the personal fitness, in all relations and respects, that was in Christ for the work of mediation between God and us. A point therefore to be insisted on, because it is the drift of these two whole chapters, and is indeed the foundation of all that follows, concerning his offices and works ; which therefore he mentions not here only, but had intimated it before, in ver. 10. To which we may add that in Heb. vii. 26, ' For such an high priest became us, who is holy, harmless, undefiled, separate from sinners, and made higher than the heavens.' So that his singular fitness for this work is a thing that the Scriptures would have us to take special notice of, and which God aimed at in choosing him unto it, for,

First, In general, to give a reason or two of it. Fitness in the person that goes about a matter of reconciliation, is more behoveful and available to further it, than all the means and satisfaction besides that can be made. For reconciliation is a matter of friendship, and therefore it is to be wrought in a friendly way, and a word from a fit person will ofttimes more prevail to effect it, than a great ransom from, and much entreaty by another. ' How forcible are right words !' as Job says—fit words, rightly placed and ordered, but especially when from a fit person ; the person adds grace and acceptation to them.

Secondly, In reconciling us, God likewise had a special regard to this. He aimed not only to have satisfaction made to his justice, and so to be sure to have an equivalent ransom, but that he might be fully pleased. He would have it carried on in the most pleasing and suitable way that might be, that so his mind might receive full content in it, and that his love might rest in it with delight, and that his wisdom also might infinitely please itself in the sweet harmony, the consent, and the fit accommodations of all things in it; to see all aptly meet and accord for the making of his covenant, as it might be sure, so ordered in all things (as the phrase is, 2 Sam. xxiii. 5). But above all, that this confluence of fitness should be especially in the person that was to perform it; one that should be most pleasing to himself and most fit for the business, even so fit, as none fitter.   Thus the apostle, in the text, giving-the reason why God made him the ' Captain of our salvation,' and appointed him to suffer : ' It became him,' says he, 'for whom and by whom are all things, in bringing many sons to glory, to make the Captain of their salvation perfect through sufferings;' that is, seeing this work of redemption was the grand plot and master-piece of him who is both the efficient and end of all things, and that the bringing of many sons to glory was of his works and ends the master-piece, it became him therefore to take such a course to do it as was worthy of him, and as might most of all and best of all suit with all his ends, and with that work which contains all his other works eminently in it.   And therefore it was meet for him to make choice of the fittest person that could be found in heaven or earth to be his captain, and to make him, in saving us, as perfect as was possible, as full and complete a Saviour in his person and in his works as could be.   And that nothing might be wanting in him which might be thought fit for him who was our Saviour to perform, he was to suffer the utmost of sufferings, rather than he should not be a full, perfect, and complete Saviour; ' God made him perfect through sufferings;' for (as Christ tells his disciples, Luke xxiv. 4) ' it behoved him thus to suffer.'   And it was his speech to John, Mat. iii. 15, ' Thus it becomes us to fulfil all righteousness.'   And surely that God, who did all things else in a due proportion, in weight and measure, and this, in his works of an inferior kind and mould, the works of creation (wherein we yet see he hath artificially suited one thing to another), will much more in this transcendent work of redemption cause the greatest harmony to meet in the plot and contrival of it.

And so I come to the point delivered, namely,

That there is a fulness of fitness in the person of Christ for this great work of reconciliation between us and God.

First, I say, ' In the person of Christ.'   For although in the works of his mediation there may a great correspondent fitness be observed, and a harmonious proportion, both in relation to the benefits they are to procure for us, and between themselves (as was before observed), yet we must now in this head bind ourselves only to the fitness in his person ; and therein also carefully sever such considerations as tend to discover his fulness of abilities for this work, many of which are apt to fall under this head. Which notwithstanding we will keep as immixed as we can from these, which argue his fitness, and reserve those other for a second head.

Secondly, There is not only ' a fitness,' but a ' fulness of fitness ;' so that suppose others besides him had been able, yet none so fit, or in whom there is an universal concurrency both of fitnesses and abilities.   And therefore he is designed out for this work with an emphasis: Col. i. 20, ' And (having made peace through the blood of his cross) by him to reconcile all things unto himself; by him, I say, whether they be things in earth, or things in heaven.'   ' By him, by him, I say ;' and so ' in him' is with the like emphasis repeated, as denoting him to be eminently fit above all others, in Eph. i. 10, ' that, in the dispensation of the fulness of times, he might gather together in one all things in Christ, both which are in heaven, and which are on earth, even in him.'

This premised, we will proceed by degrees, and we shall find, that there was nothing in his person but what fitted him for this work.

Consider what he was before he took our nature ; what this *he* was, mentioned in the 16th ver., ' *He* took,' &c.   For he was a person of himself ere he took our nature.   And this refers to the first chapter, where the apostle shews that he was God, and the Son of God : Heb. i. 3, 5, ' Who, being the brightness of his glory, and the express image of his person, and upholding all things by the word of his power, when he had by himself purged our sins, sat down on the right hand of the Majesty on high ;' ver. 5, ' For unto which of the angels said he at any time, Thou art my Son, this day have I begotten thee ?   And again, I will be to him a Father, and he shall be to me a Son ?'   And thus it behoved him to be, that was our priest.

It behoved him to be God.   It was not fit that any mere creature should have the honour to be the mediator and reconciler.   Could we suppose that a creature had been able to have performed it, yet it had been no way fit.   The honour of this place and office was too transcendent for any mere creature ; and nothing is more unseemly and uncomely than an office of dignity and honour misplaced, as Solomon tells us.   And this crown of honour would not have fitted and sat well on any creature's head.   An honour I call this office, and that the most transcendent ; for to be a priest, was to be taken out, and separated from, and above other men, to draw nigh to God for them ; Heb. v. 1, ' For every high priest, taken from among men, is ordained for men in things pertaining to God, that he may offer both gifts and sacrifices for sins.'   And therefore it is such ' an honour ' (says he at the 4th ver.) ' as no man takes to himself, but he that is called of God, as was Aaron.'   And yet, what was the high priesthood of Aaron in comparison with this ?   A mere shadow ; not so much as an image of it, as is said of the types of the law : Heb. x. 1, ' For the law having a shadow of good things to come, and not the very image of the things, can never with those sacrifices, which they offered year by year continually, make the comers thereunto perfect.'   It was but as the office of a king-at-arms in comparison of a real king indeed.   And therefore this priesthood, to offer real satisfaction, is accounted such a glory, as Christ himself (though full of all infinite perfections, and in whom the fulness of the Godhead dwells) took not upon him till he was called ; as chap. v. ver. 5, ' So also Christ glorified not himself to be made an high priest ; but he that said unto him, Thou art my Son, this day have I begotten thee.'   The phrase used is, that ' he glorified not himself to be made an high priest,' &c.   It is not an honourable office only this, by which phrase Aaron's is expressed to us, but it is glorious.   He being to be not an ' high priest' only, but to be ' a great high priest:' chap. iv. 14, ' Seeing then that we have a great high priest, that is passed into the heavens, Jesus the Son of God, let us hold fast our profession.'   Yea, it is so glorious as is fit for none but the King of glory, who is the only wise God.   Which therefore, as it is so glorious, as Christ, till called unto it, takes it not on him, so it is so transcendent a glory, as God will not bestow it on, or call any to it, but him who is God.   ' My glory' (says God) ' I will not give unto another,' Isa. xlii. 8.   And this office he accounts part of it.   Read the words going before (and which occasioned that speech), and you shall find that they are spoken of the bestowing this office upon Christ, and the glorifying him by calling him to it : ver. 6, 7, ' I the Lord have called thee, and will give thee for a covenant,' &c.   And then follows, ' My glory will I not give unto another.' As God will not give his praise and worship to graven images (as in the words following), so nor this glory to any creature, not to any other but to one who is God equal with himself. And consider but that one main end and consequent of his mediation there expressed, that he was to be made a covenant for the people; that is, the founder and striker up, and mediator of a new covenant for us (as he is called, Heb. ix. 15)— yea, a surety, not only of a new covenant, when an old one is made void, but of a ' better covenant' (as he is called, Heb. vii. 22), ' established upon better promises' (as it is Heb. viii. 6)—a better covenant than the angels stand under, who yet are the most glorious of all the creatures. And therefore ' he hath obtained' (says the text there) ' a more excellent ministry, by how much he is the mediator of a better covenant :' not brought into a better covenant, or made under a better covenant (which is our happiness), but the maker of that better covenant itself, yea, so as to be made that covenant; and it will be evident that it was not fit for any mere creature to undertake so great an office.

CHAPTER II.

That it was necessary for our mediator to be God.—He could not otherwise have been present at the making of the eternal covenant of redemption.— None but God could have the power to bestow such great blessings as are those of the covenant.—None but God could be the object of our trust, faith, and hope, and obedience.—None but God could be sufficiently able to succour us at all times.

That Christ the Son of God was the only fit person to be the mediator, will appear plainly to us upon these considerations :

I. If you consider that it was fit that he who thus made a covenant for us should be present at the making of it, and at the first striking of the bargain, and should be privy to the plot, and know the bottom of God's counsel in it, and the depth of all his secrets, and should know for whom and what he was to purchase, and upon what conditions ; now then this plot and covenant, having been as ancient as eternity, even an everlasting covenant, and it being requisite that God should have our mediator by him from eternity, with whom he might strike it for us, and also that he should know all God's secrets, and be admitted into all his counsels from eternity, therefore no creature could be capable of this. ' For who of them hath been his counsellor ?' And who knows his depths of election, which are past finding out ? as Rom. xi. 33, 34, ' O the depths of the riches both of the wisdom and knowledge of God ! how unsearchable are his judgments, and his ways past finding out !' ver. 34, ' For who hath known the mind of the Lord ? or who hath been his counsellor ?' God may say to all the creatures as he said to Job, Where were you when the plot of redemption was laid, and the platform thereof drawn, and the book of life penned, and the names of my redeemed ones put in ? None but he whose name is ' Wonderful, Counsellor, The mighty God, and everlasting Father,' as Isa. ix. 6, was capable of all this ; which names of his are put into that promise of him as mediator, because it was requisite that our mediator should be all this. And now he being the mighty God, he might be of counsel with God from eternity, he was present at the first pricking down our names, and foreknew all God's choice. He stood at God's elbow and consulted with him whose names to put in ('Then I was by him,' says he, Prov. viii. 30), and so became their everlasting Father, begetting them in the womb of eternal election.

II. If we consider the conditions of the covenant, no mere creature was fit to undertake them ; neither those on God's part, nor those on ours.

1. Not those on God's part. Was it fit that a mere creature should be God's executor, and have power to leave such legacies, as the promises of heaven, pardon of sin, &c., are ? Without whom, and without whose blood, all those promises had been of no force, but had been nothing worth ; as Heb. ix. 15–18, 'And for this cause he is the mediator of the new testament, that by means of death, for the redemption of the transgressions that were under the first testament, they which are called might receive the promise of eternal inheritance.' Ver. 16, 'For where a testament is, there must also of necessity be the death of the testator.' Ver. 17, 'For a testament is of force after men are dead : otherwise it is of no strength at all whilst the testator liveth.' Ver. 18, 'Whereupon neither the first testament was dedicated without blood.' Was it fit that a mere creature's hand and seal should be required to God's own will and testament, or else it could not be of force ? Certainly it was too much. And therefore the apostle, ver. 14, having shewed how Christ ' by the eternal Spirit offered up himself' (that is, by his Godhead, &c.), he adds, ver. 15, 'For this cause he is the mediator of the new testament.' Hence it was that he became the founder of it, that he was ' the eternal Spirit,' God immortal, else he had not been capable of being mediator of such a testament ; a testament also, whereby he not only was to undertake to make satisfaction, and to make good*all God's legacies, but to make good in us the conditions on our part, by writing the law in the heart. For that is the new covenant, as Heb, viii. 10, 11, ' For this is the covenant that I will make with the house of Israel, after those days, saith the Lord ; I will put my laws into their mind, and write them in their hearts ; and I will be to them a God, and they shall be to me a people :' ver. 11, ' And they shall not teach every man his neighbour, and every man his brother, saying, Know the Lord : for all shall know me, from the least to the greatest.' And if the mediator had not engaged to do this, God would not have dealt with him, for he will make sure work in the covenant, since it was to be a covenant ordered in all things, and sure ; 2 Sam. xxiii. 5, ' Although my house be not so with God ; yet he hath made with me an everlasting covenant, ordered in all things, and sure : for this is all my salvation, and all my desire, although he make it not to grow.' And what creature could do this ? Or was it fit that God should put so much trust in any creature, who ' finds folly in his angels, and puts no confidence in his saints ? ' God would not vouchsafe to treat or trade with any mere creature, upon so high and deep engagements, nor enter into partnership with them, to share alike, as in that covenant thus made God and the mediator of it were to do.

2. The part which we bear in the covenant, and our actings in it, rendered it unmeet that any but the Son of God should have the administration of it committed to him. For,

First, If we consider what is the business and acts of our faith, it will be evident that it was fit and requisite that our mediator should be such a one as we might rely upon, and trust in. Now was it fit that any mere creature should be made and set forth to us as the object of our faith ? And yet it is that faith which is the most suitable condition for the covenant of grace ; as Rom. iv. 16, ' It is therefore of faith, that it might be by grace ; and sure to all the seed.' And that faith must pitch upon our mediator as upon a corner-stone laid by God, as a sure foundation (as Paul and Peter speak), so as he that believeth might not come to be ashamed : 1 Pet. ii. 6, ' Wherefore also it is contained in the scripture, Behold, I lay in Sion a chief corner stone, elect, precious: and he that believeth on him shall not be confounded.' Would it then have been, or could any arm of flesh have thus secured us, or under-propped our hearts? Or was it fit that any creature should be propounded to us, as the object of our faith as justifying, and so be ' set forth as a propitiation through faith in his blood,' and mediation; and so we to be justified by faith in him (as the apostle's expressions are in Rom. iii.)? No, this is an honour not fit to be put upon any creature ; no, not on all the angels and saints. Take, not Peter only (on whom the papists say the church is built), but the whole church and family of God in heaven and earth, and we say indeed, that ' we believe the catholic church,' but not ' in the catholic church;' we believe only in God, and in Jesus Christ. Any creature had been too weak a foundation to build the faith of the church upon ; they could not have borne the weight of it. And therefore, 1 Tim. iii. 16, when the apostle had said, ' God manifested in the flesh,' he adds, ' believed on in the world,' for if he who was manifest in the flesh had not been God, he could not have been the object of faith. And, indeed, it was fit for us that we should have one whom we might fully trust, and whose sufficiency might answer all our fears. For if a creature had been our mediator, we would have been afraid of a miscarriage in the business, as there was such a cause of fear whilst the concern was in the hands of our father and head, Adam ; and we should still have feared that the devil might overcome us and him again ; and though he had held out many years, yet we would have been afraid that one day he might fail and have perished. Besides, we should continually have feared, that the guilt of our sins weuld revive again in our consciences, for conscience being subject to God only, no mere creature therefore could still it, or purge it ; but it is the eternal Spirit alone that can do it, as the apostle shews, Heb. ix. 14, ' How much more shall the blood of Christ, who through the eternal Spirit offered himself without spot to God, purge your conscience from dead works to serve the living God?' And it is God alone that can subdue iniquities : Micah vii. 18, 19, ' Who is a God like unto thee, that pardoneth iniquity, and passeth by the transgression of the remnant of his heritage ? He retaineth not his anger for ever, because he delighteth in mercy.' Ver. 19, ' He will turn again, he will have compassion upon us ; he will subdue our iniquities ; and thou wilt cast all their sins into the depths of the sea.' Therefore, to take away all fears, it was fit that our reconciler should be God. And therefore, Isa. xxxv. (throughout which the coming of Christ is foretold) ver. 3, ' Strengthen you' (says the prophet) ' the feeble hands,' &c., . . . ' say unto them that are of a fearful heart, Be strong, fear not : behold, your God will come with vengeance,' namely, to destroy the enemies of your salvation ; he says it again, ' God will come with a recompence ;' and then again he speaks it, ' he will come and save you ;' and he goes on to shew his kingdom, ver. 5, 6, 7, ' Then the eyes of the blind shall be opened, and the ears of the deaf shall be unstopped.' Ver. 6, ' Then shall the lame man leap as an hart, and the tongue of the dumb sing : for in the wilderness shall waters break out, and streams in the desert.' Ver. 7, ' And the parched ground shall become a pool, and the thirsty land springs of water : in the habitation of dragons, where each lay, shall be grass, with reeds and rushes.' Any other saviour would have needed salvation himself, except him who is salvation itself, and so Christ is called : Luke ii. 28–30, ' Then took he him up in his arms, and blessed God, and said,' ver. 29, ' Lord, now lettest thou thy servant depart in peace, according to thy word : ' ver. 30, ' For mine eyes have seen thy salvation.'

The second condition is obedience, even that we should wholly give up ourselves to his service for ever, which also comes in in our indentures, and is mentioned in the covenant on our parts, and which, out of thankfulness, we could not but perform, as a due to him that should be our mediator. For he that should have reconciled us must have bought us, and so delivered us from death and hell ; and if so, we must then by all right and equity have been his servants for ever.   Now surely, God would not have us so obliged to any mere creature, as wholly to serve and obey it ; and therefore it was fit that none but God himself should save and buy us out ; 1 Cor. vii. 23, ' Ye are bought with a price : be not the servants of men.' To prevent which inconvenience, God himself would redeem us, that we might serve none but him : ' Him only shalt thou serve,' for it is his due. The apostle also judgeth it an equal thing that men should live to him who died for them, to redeem them from death.   Thus, 2 Cor. v. 14, 15, ' We thus judge,' saith he, ' that in that he died for all, they who live should not henceforth live unto themselves, but unto him who died for them.'   It was therefore no way fit that any mere creature should be employed in this work.   It was fit that none should do so much for us, but only he who made us ; for to justify us, and to restore us out of this miserable, lost condition, was more than at first to create us.   For our misery was worse than a not-being ; and should it ever be said that a creature had done as much for us as God did at the first ?

Thirdly, Besides all this, would we not have had such a Saviour (to choose) as might know our hearts, and be able to succour us ? on whom we might rest securely, that he knows God's mind, and searcheth the deep things of him, and who is his counsellor ?   And therefore, when he speaks to us kindly, we may be sure God means us good, and in whose face we may read God's mind.   Would we not have such a Saviour as might have an unlimited power over all flesh to defend us, so that nothing shall be able to withstand our salvation ?   As John xvii. 2, ' As thou hast given him power over all flesh, that he should give eternal life to as many as thou hast given him.'   Now such an one must be God, who can save not only the body, but the soul too.   All the creatures, as they can destroy the body only, so they can save the body only ; and of the two it is more easy to destroy than to save.   When the people of Israel were to be led into Canaan, and so to be carried through the wilderness, and through many enemies and difficulties, they hearing (Exod. xxxiii. 2) that an angel should go before them, and drive out the Canaanites (ver. 3), and that God would not himself immediately go up with them, it is said, that ' all the people mourned because of this ; ' yea, and Moses also (at the 12th verse) was fearful of a mere angel's conduct, his heart was not secured thereby, as it would have been if God himself would have been pleased to go with them. And therefore he says to God, ' Thou hast not let me know whom thou wilt send with me.'   And yet God had told him that an angel should.   But Moses seemed not to understand God, but would have had another answer. Thus, when we are fearful and cannot trust to the conduct or undertaking of one employed for us, we use to say, to a friend that puts it off and sends another, You leave me, and send I know not whom with me ; that is, one that I am not secure of, one in whose sufficiency I cannot rest for the per-

formance. And this therefore (ver. 4) is called ' evil tidings.' In Exod.
xxiii. 20, before this, there was an angel promised to go before them, namely,
Christ the angel of the covenant, who indeed was God (for, ver. 21, he says,
' My name is in him '), and then the people's hearts were quieted. So
that some think that this other angel in the 23d* chapter was but some
mere created angel, whom when they heard to be substituted in God's stead
to be their leader, then they mourned ; and then Moses also complained.
However, if it were the same angel, yet they understood it and conceived of
it to be a creature, and not the Son of God. By which you see that the
people desired that no creature, no, not an angel, should be their leader
(though one angel could destroy a host of men in a night), but they would
have God himself or none. And so if we had been to have chosen a
' captain of our salvation,' a head and governor ' to bring us unto glory,'
as the apostle speaks, Heb. ii. 10, and withal had known that there was
speech in heaven of, and so a possibility, of having the Son of God for this
our captain, how would we have said as he did of Goliath's sword, ' There
is none like to this saviour !' Or as they of Joseph, ' Can we find such
another one as this ?' And on the contrary, if God had instead of him
sent but an angel to redeem us, how would we have mourned, as the people
there did, and as John did, Rev. v. 4 ; and have said as Moses, ' We
know not whom thou wilt send with us ' ? We will therefore conclude
with that which God speaks, Isa. xliii. 11, ' I am the Lord, and besides me
there is no Saviour.'

CHAPTER III.

Of the three persons in the Godhead, the Son is the fittest to be mediator.—
What are the reasons of it.

We have seen it was meet our redeemer should be God, and the Godhead itself cannot become a redeemer but as subsisting in a person, one of
three. Now which of the three so fit as is the Son ? The oath and
decree of God makes the Son to be appointed to this office. And the
reasons of the fitness and meetness of this second person are :
First, If we consider the relations of the three persons among themselves,
he is of all the fittest to undertake this work.
1. It was meet the ἰδιώματα, or the proper titles by which the persons of
the Trinity are distinguished, should be kept and preserved distinct, and no
way confounded. He that was to be mediator it was meet he should be the
Son of man, the son of a woman as his mother, as I shall shew anon; and
this title and appellation will fitliest become him that is a Son (though of
God) already ; and it was not fit there should be two sons, or two persons
in the Trinity to bear the relation or title of sons. For instance, that
the Father should in any respect be said to be a Son, or to have a mother,
or call David or Abraham father, was most improper; so as this would not
become him. And so in like manner it was as unfit for the Holy Ghost,
who himself was to have the hand in his conception, to be called a Son ;
but that the Son of God should is not improper, for he is a Son already.
2. It was meet that the Son of God should be this mediator, that the due
order that is between these three persons be also kept. The Father is the
first, the Son the second, the Holy Ghost the third ; and he that is to be

* Qu. ' 33d '?—ED.

mediator must be called to it, and sent by another person, therefore the Father is not to be mediator; for both the Son and the Holy Ghost being from the Father in subsisting, are not to send the Father, who is the first. And as the order of their subsisting, so of their working; and therefore the Holy Ghost, he likewise being the third person, cannot so fitly be mediator; for though he might be sent from the Father and the Son, as he proceeds from both, yet his work and task is to work from the Son, and to take off his work wrought first, as the Son is to take from the Father: John v. 19, 20, 'Then answered Jesus and said unto them, Verily, verily, I say unto you, The Son can do nothing of himself, but what he seeth the Father do : for what things soever he doth, these also doth the Son likewise. For the Father loveth the Son, and sheweth him all things that himself doth : and he will shew him greater works than these, that ye may marvel.' And as in order of subsisting, the person of the Spirit proceeds from him, so in order of working, his work is from the Son's work; 'He shall take of mine,' says Christ, 'and shew it to you;' John xvi. 13–15, 'Howbeit when he, the Spirit of truth, is come, he will guide you into all truth : for he shall not speak of himself: but whatsoever he shall hear, that shall he speak : and he will shew you things to come. He shall glorify me : for he shall receive of mine, and shall shew it unto you. All things that the Father hath are mine: therefore said I, that he shall take of mine, and shall shew it unto you.' And therefore he that is to be mediator to redeem must be the Son, who may send the Holy Ghost to apply his work, who, being the last person, is to appear last in the world, and take the last work, which redemption is not, but the application of it. And therefore,

3. The Father is the person to whom the redemption is to be paid in the name of the persons; to whom the reconciliation is made by the redeemer; and the Holy Ghost is he that most fitly should apply that redemption unto us the redeemed. Therefore the redemption itself fitly falls to the Son's share.

And *secondly*, As thus to preserve the due decorum among the persons, so also in respect of the work itself, it was most proper to him.

1. He being the middle person of the three, bears the best resemblance of the work, to be a mediator, to come between for us, to the other two. Herein the work and the person suit. He was from the Father, and the Holy Ghost from him, and it is he in whom, as it were, the other two are united, and are one, and so he is not* able to lay hands on both. As the nature of man is a middle nature between the whole creation, earthly and heavenly ; and as for one and the same person to be both God and man was a middle rank between God and us men ; so is the Son of God a middle person between the persons themselves.

2. It best suited all the particular benefits of redemption, and the ends thereof. Many divines, for the demonstration of this, allege that the second person being that Word by whom all things were made, as Heb. i. 2 and John i. 3, that therefore it was fit for him to restore all ; and it is certain that in those places his working all things is alleged on purpose to shew it was meet he should be the restorer of them. It becomes him who hath such an interest in the first building, that he should found them anew and repair them. It is alleged also that he was the life of man in innocency: John i. 4, 'In him was life, and the life was the light of men ;' and therefore he was fittest to restore that new life. Eph. ii. 1, 'And you hath he quickened, who were dead in trespasses and sins.' Ver. 5, 'Even when we

* Qu. 'he is' ?—ED.

were dead in sins, hath quickened us together with Christ (by grace ye are saved).' Also that he being the image of God, therefore to restore it in man when it was lost, the best way was to set forth the original image, and to bring our decayed image to this to be conformed. But I allege not these to this purpose, as not being certain whether these things are spoken of him, considered simply as second person, or as foreseen and decreed to be God-man (as I have elsewhere * shewn), which design, besides the work of redemption, served to all these ends and purposes. But I shall mention one, which is the main end of his being mediator, and for the bestowing which redemption maketh way; that is, adoption, and making us sons, which is made one of the greatest benefits of all other, Eph. i. 5. Now it is certain that to convey this to us, of all persons the Son was the fittest; Gal. iv. 4, 5, ' God sent forth his Son, made under the law, to redeem them that were under the law, that we might receive the adoption of sons.' Where there is a double antithesis or opposition : (1.) Christ a Son, to make us sons ; (2.) Christ made under the law, to redeem us that were under the law. We were slaves under the law ; who then was so fit to redeem us as the King's Son ? We were servants ; who then so fit to convey sonship as the eldest Son ? And to sinners convey sonship he could not, till they were redeemed, as that place shews. God was to be a Father to us, and in whom or for whose sake so fitly as for his Son's, through our union and marriage with him ? Heaven and the glory of it is called adoption : Rom. viii. 23, ' And not only they, but ourselves also, which have the first-fruits of the Spirit, even we ourselves groan within ourselves, waiting for the adoption, to wit, the redemption of our body ;' and to bestow this on us by a right of inheritance, for whom was it so proper as for God's own Son, the heir of all things ? This is manifest further by these scriptures : John xx. 17, ' I go to my Father and to your Father;' and ' In my Father's house are many mansions,' John xiv. 2. As if he should have said, I am his eldest Son, I can bid you welcome thither. And so in Rom. viii. 17, ' Ye are heirs and co-heirs with Christ;' and in many the like places.

Some divines say that no person else could have been mediator, because sonship was to be derived to us ; for nothing, say they, is communicated by grace to us but is first in the Godhead, or in some person in the Godhead, who is made ours, and so it is derived through fellowship with him. Thus we are made wise because God is wise, holy because God is holy, and we made partakers of the divine nature, which is the image of what is in God. Now therefore, in like manner, if we be sons, it must be through a sonship found in one of the persons, and our communication with that person, and so we are made sons because he is. I will not say it could not have been otherwise ; sure I am it was fittest and comeliest it should be so.

And also that we should be accepted graciously, and beloved of God, which of ourselves, without a mediator, we could not be ; who so fit as the Son to make us thus accepted, who is the first beloved, the Son of his love, as he is called, Col. i. 13, ' Who hath delivered us from the power of darkness, and hath translated us into the kingdom of his dear Son.' But the Holy Ghost proceeds from both *per modum amoris*, and so is rather the reflection of love of both, wherewith God loves his Son and himself also.

Then the Son was fittest to be the mediator in respect of all those offices that belong to the performance of this great work.

* In the ' Discourse of the Knowledge of God the Father, and his Son Jesus Christ.' In 2d Vol. of his Works.—[In Vol. IV. of this Series.—ED.]

As *First*, If we regard the office of high priest, who so fit as the Son, the eldest Son, to be so ? it being the birthright of the eldest in the family, by the law of nature, to be the priest. Therefore, Heb. v., to prove that he was a priest, the apostle presently cites that saying out of the second Psalm, ' Thou art my Son, this day have I begotten thee,' as being all one with that other which follows, quoted out of Ps. cx., ' Thou art a priest for ever.' And especially when the work of our salvation and his mediation was to be transacted by intercession ; none so fit to be an advocate with the Father (as John speaks) as Jesus the Son. 1 John ii. 1, ' My little children, these things write I unto you, that ye sin not. And if any man sin, we have an advocate with the Father, Jesus Christ the righteous.'

Secondly, If we consider the office of being a prophet, none so fit for this as the Word and Wisdom of the Father ; therefore, Heb. i. 1, it is said that in the last days God hath spoken by his Son. Who so fit to break up God's counsels as the mighty Counsellor, and next in counsel to himself ? ' None hath seen God at any time ;' but it follows, ' The only begotten Son, who is in the bosom of the Father, he hath declared him,' John i. 18.

And so, *thirdly*, for the kingly office, none so fit as the heir, as sons use to be ; none so fit to have all judgment and the kingdom committed to him as God's Son.

And last of all, if we consider the inauguration into these offices and work of mediation, it was by an anointing, as all those offices of old were. He was to be the Messiah, and God's Anointed ; now the Father (as was meet) was to be the Anointer : so Acts iv. 27, ' For of a truth, against thy holy child Jesus, whom thou hast anointed, both Herod and Pontius Pilate, with the Gentiles, and the people of Israel, were gathered together ;' and the Holy Ghost was to be the oil with which he was to be anointed above his fellows ; as it is expressly, Acts x. 38, ' How God anointed Jesus of Nazareth with the Holy Ghost, and with power : who went about doing good, and healing all that were oppressed of the devil ; for God was with him.' So as in this respect none but the Son was capable of these offices, and to be Messiah or the Anointed one ; and so accordingly he was consecrated a priest for ever.

CHAPTER IV.

That it was necessary our mediator should be man.—The reasons why the angelical nature would not have been proper for this work ; and therefore why Christ assumed not that, but the nature of man.

That which next is to be demonstrated is, that if Christ be a mediator, he must be something else than mere God or second person ; as the text saith, ' He took to himself the seed of Abraham.'

For, *first*, if he be a reconciler he must become a priest, and offer up something by way of satisfaction to God ; so Heb. viii. 3, ' Every high priest is ordained to offer gifts and sacrifices : wherefore of necessity he must have somewhat to offer ;' and that which he offers must needs yet be greater than all things but God. For nothing else would be a sacrifice great enough to expiate sin ; and therefore that which he offers must some way be himself, for otherwise there could nothing be greater than all things, and yet withal something else than God. And therefore still it is said, ' he offered himself.' But if he be God only, he cannot be sacrificed nor offered up.

And again, *secondly*, if he be God only, he should reconcile us to his own self; but he that is a reconciler must be some way made diverse from him unto whom the reconciliation is made, for he is to be a surety to him; and therefore Christ being made man, he, as 'οιχονομιχῶς, or ministerially considered, is diverse from himself as φυσιχῶς considered, viz., as he is the Son of God, and so is fit to become a party between us, and to reconcile us to himself.

And, *thirdly*, if he be a reconciler and mediator, he must become some way subject to God, and less than God *ratione officii;* as he says, ' My Father is greater than I,' John xiv. 28, for he must subject and submit himself, and be obedient, and be content to be arrested by the law. He must become an intercessor and entreater, and so become subject, as Christ did, who, when he was equal with God, humbled himself: Phil. ii. 6–8, ' Who, being in the form of God, thought it not robbery to be equal with God: but made himself of no reputation, and took upon him the form of a servant, and was made in the likeness of men: and being found in fashion as a man, he humbled himself, and became obedient unto death, even the death of the cross.'

Now, then, if he must take up some creature or other, it must be a rational creature; and therefore there being but two sorts of creatures reasonable, angels and men, they are both mentioned in the text as those that only were capable and fit for this assumption. The disputes of some schoolmen, that the Son of God might have assumed any creature, though unreasonable, into one person with himself, are in a manner blasphemous. And, to be sure, if such an assumption had been possible, yet unfit.

First; for his person, for which we see the reasons of the schoolmen, for there was reason that he that is taken up to this glory should be capable of knowing and loving God.

And secondly; and above all, for this work, for he must be holy: Heb. vii. 26, ' For such an high priest became us, who is holy, harmless, undefiled, separate from sinners, and made higher than the heavens.' Such a high priest became us as was holy, he should not fulfil the law else. He must love God, for love is the fulfilling of the law. He must have an understanding and a will. He must be full both of grace and truth: of truth in his understanding part, of grace in his will. And he was to become obedient to God for us, and to have a holy will; for the will of the Godhead could not have become subject.

Now, then, seeing there are but two rational natures, angels and men, that can stand for this place, it is to be considered which of these two is the fitter.

Now, consider this fitness as it relates to the person of the Son of God simply so considered; and so the nature of angels was `a fairer match for him by far. But an angel, though a more fit match for him who is a Spirit, and they spirits, and so there is a nearer assimilation, and which he would have assumed and united to himself (for his soul, when separate, was still united to him); yet it was not so fit for this business to reconcile us, therefore he says, Heb. ii. 16, at no hand he took their nature. He supposeth it possible, he would not else have instanced in it, but he by no means supposeth it as fit; for ' it behoved him to be made like unto his brethren.'

First, It was not so fit for us that he should assume the angelical nature, it was not so fit,

1. That we, being the persons to be reconciled, should be beholden

to a stranger, but to a kinsman of our own nature. It was a law in Israel that their prince should not be a stranger; and it was meet to take place in this, that one should not be a mediator who is a stranger.

2. That the relations that were to be between us and him might be founded upon the greatest nearness, and so more natural and kindly, it was meet that the mediator should be of the same nature with us.

(1.) He that reconciled us was to be head to us; and it was fit the head and the body should be, as near as could be, of the same nature, homogeneal, not diverse, else there would be a monstrosity in it.

(2.) We were to be made sons in him, and he to be our brother, and therefore to be of the same nature, Cant. viii. 1.

(3.) He was to be a husband to us, and man and wife must be of the same nature, that she may be bone of his bone and flesh of his flesh.

3. That he might more naturally love us more, and we him, it was fit that he should take our nature. Likeness is the cause of love. Brethren that are like each other, love more than the other of the brethren use to do; therefore God made man in his image at first, that so he might be the nearer object of his love. But if he will take up our nature also to himself, how will this raise his love yet higher! His end in reconciling was to make us like himself, and therefore he made himself like to us, and we being to partake of a divine nature from him, he partakes of a human nature with us; and therefore he was made in the likeness of man. Kings, whom they love, they use to apparel like themselves; their favourites were so of old. As men are to love men better than angels, because made of one blood, and God did it on purpose; so Christ seeing his own nature in us, and that we are given him, cannot but love us the better; he cannot be averse to his own flesh and blood.

Secondly, An angel's nature would not have been so fit for the business or work itself; for,

1. Seeing that justice permitted a commutation, it was but comely that yet justice might be satisfied in all other points as near as possibly might be. It was but fitting that satisfaction should be made in the sameness of nature at least, seeing it could not be by the same individual persons. This reason seems to be rendered, Rom. viii. 3, 'For what the law could not do, in that it was weak through the flesh, God sending his own Son, in the likeness of sinful flesh, and for sin condemned sin in the flesh.' He took the likeness of sinful flesh, to condemn sin in the flesh. Also this was meet, that the very same nature that was contaminated and defiled might be cleansed and purified, that they who are sanctified, and he that sanctifieth, might be of one nature: Heb. ii. 11, 'For both he that sanctifieth, and they who are sanctified, are all of one: for which cause he is not ashamed to call them brethren.'

And, 2. Seeing that we fell by the sin of a man, God (that in his wisdom and justice loves like proportion to be made up, himself making all things in due order and measure) ordained that we should be redeemed by a man. This reason is intimated 1 Cor. xv. 21, 'Since by man came death, by man also the resurrection of the dead;' and so by the like parallel reason, seeing by man came sin, by man came redemption; the like proportion the apostle also holds forth, Rom. v. 15–18, 'But not as the offence, so also is the free gift. For if through the offence of one many be dead; much more the grace of God, and the gift by grace, which is by one man, Jesus Christ, hath abounded unto many. And not as it was by one that sinned, so is the gift: for the judgment was by one to condemnation, but the free gift is of many offences unto justification.   For if by one man's offence death reigned by one ; much more they which receive abundance of grace, and of the gift of righteousness, shall reign in life by one, Jesus Christ.   Therefore, as by the offence of one judgment came upon all men to condemnation ; even so by the righteousness of one the free gift came upon all men unto justification of life.'

Thirdly, If we consider the obedience which the mediator was to perform for us, it was not fit he should be an angel.   For,

1. He was to fulfil the whole law, and every iota of it, and that in a double respect.

(1.) For our righteousness.

(2.) For our example.

Now in either of these respects an angel was not so fit ; for the angels were not capable of fulfilling so many parts of the law as a human nature is.   An angel could not perform the ceremonial, as to be circumcised, &c.; nor half the moral, as to be subject to parents, to be temperate, sober, to sanctify the Sabbath, &c.   But it became him that was our mediator (as far as possibly might be) to fulfil all (that is, every part of) righteousness.

2. He was to fulfil all this righteousness by way of example.   Socinus he would make it all the intent of Christ's coming into this world (but blasphemously); yet this was requisite, that Christ should set us the greatest example of holiness.   1 Peter ii. 21, ' He left us an example that we should follow his steps: who, when he was reviled, reviled not again, nor was guile found in his mouth.'   He was to be a visible example; now so an angel's obedience could not have been.   He was to be a perfect example and copy —Follow me as I follow Christ, says Paul, 1 Cor. xi 1—now so an angel could not have been.   All duties of obedience that are performed in the body, as we are men, they are not capable of; the second table is cut off to them ; their obedience is only spiritual, and the duties of the first table.

As thus an angel's nature only could not have fulfilled that law we were to have fulfilled, so much less could it have suffered what was requisite. They could have endured God's wrath indeed, but not that other curse which went out in the letter against us; they could not die, not return to dust, and bodily death was threatened, ' To dust thou shalt return.'   They had no body and soul to be separated by death, and therefore could not be a sacrifice for sin, for without blood there is no remission: Heb. ix. 22, ' And almost all things are by the law purged with blood ; and without shedding of blood is no remission ;' for without blood it had not been extensive, a full redemption.   Now the angels have no blood to lay down nor shed.

Lastly, It was not so fit that we should be reconciled by angels, but by one in our own nature, that so the devils might be the more confounded. Now seeing the devil had out of malice ruined man's nature, God would have man's nature to destroy the works of the devil, as 1 John iii. 8, ' He that committeth sin, is of the devil ; for the devil sinneth from the beginning.   For this purpose the Son of God was manifested, that he might destroy the works of the devil.'   And God, to the devil's confusion, would have him led captive by one who is man.   So Heb. ii. 14, ' He took the nature of man, that he might by death destroy him that had the power of death.' It is a reason given of his assuming it.   If this great act had been done by an angel, the devil might have said he had met with his match, and so was foiled ; but to have it done by a weak man, one that was once a babe, a suckling, this was a mighty confusion of him.   And thus it is noticed in the 8th psalm, which is applied to Christ, ' Out of the mouths of sucklings thou hast ordained strength, that thou mightest still the enemy and avenger,' Ps. viii. 2. And this very confusion and revenge upon Satan, who was the cause of man's fall, was aimed at by God at first; therefore is the first promise and preaching of the gospel to Adam brought in rather in sentencing him than in speaking to Adam, that the seed of the woman should break the serpent's head, it being in God's aim as much to confound him as to save poor man.

CHAPTER V.

That it was fit that our mediator should be both God and man in one person, that so he might partake of the nature of both parties, and be a middle person between them, and fill up the distance, and bring them near to one another. —That he might be in a better capacity to communicate unto us his benefits, and that he might be capable of performing what our redemption required.

We see then how much it behoved Christ to be man as well as God, and indeed both, for a mediator is a mediator between two, Gal. iii. 20; and those two between whom a mediator must go, were God and man; and therefore it is said that there is but one mediator between God and man, the man Christ Jesus, 1 Tim. ii. 5. And this was most fit; for,

First, Hereby he participates of both natures, and so his person doth bear a resemblance of the work in general. Mediation was the business, and who so fit as a middle person? Therefore, first, he became *medius,* a middle person, and then a mediator; first *medius,* then *medians*—a middle person in regard of participation of both natures, and then a mediator in regard of reconciliation and reconciling both natures. And a middle person, not in order only, as men are between angels and beasts, and as a middle rank of men are between those above them and under them, but of participation, as having the natures of both. A middle person not in place only, as Moses when he stood between God and the people, Exod. v. 5, but in person. A *medium,* not only between God and us, but one with God and us, and symbolising with both. Therefore our divines say, that *mediatio operativa* is founded, and hath influence from his *mediatio substantialis,* that his works of mediation, whereby he mediates for us, ariseth from his person, that they arise from both natures, so as both natures have an influence into all his works, and they are the works of both, so that he might be *totus mediator,* a whole, entire mediator, in his person and in his works.

And, *secondly;* Hereby he is of equal distance and difference from both; as he is God he differs from us, as he is man he differs from God. Yea, and as he is mediator he takes on him a differing person as it were from himself, and what he is essentially, as being only the Son of God; for he became lesser than himself in his office, and emptied himself, and so is a fit mediator between us and himself also as he is the Son of God, *Differt Filius incarnatus, οἰκονομικῶς, à seipso φυσικῶς.* The Son incarnate differs ministerially from what himself is naturally. As we say in philosophy, *Una et eadem res à seipsa diversa est, modo et ratione.* One and the same thing is differenced from itself by a different *modus,* or manner of existing.

Thirdly; Hereby he is indifferent also between both, so as not to take part with the one more than with the other, ready to distribute to both with unequal hands their due, and be faithful to both: Heb. ii. 17, ' That he might be a merciful and faithful high priest in things pertaining to God, to make reconciliation for the people.' Lo here are the matters both of God and man referred to him, for the cause of both was to be committed to him, Τὰ πρὸς Θεόν, and τὰ πρὸς ἡμᾶς, therefore he partakes of both, and is distant from both, as a middle thing participates of both extremes, and toucheth both.

Fourthly; He was to make peace between both, and take away hostility, therefore he takes pledges both out of earth and out of heaven. He takes the chief nature on earth and the chief in heaven, thereby to still the enmity, and to part us who were fighting each against other, we against God, and God against us. Now having our nature and God's, he had two hands able enough to part us, he could take hold of God's strength, and hold his hands, as it is Isa. xxvii. 5, and so make peace ; and having our nature, he had a hand to take hold of our hands also.

Fifthly; He is hereby able to draw near to both, and bring both together, and so make us one; for is not he fit to do this, that is both God and man ? He joins our nature first with God in his own person, and makes both one there, that so God and man becoming one in person, he might the easilier make God and man one in covenant. God and man were at division, and when he would make *utrumque unum,* he becomes *et unum ex utroque.* He by this means is in a friendly way able to treat with both, and hath a hand to shake with both. He is become ' the man God's fellow,' Zech. xiii. 7. If he had been God's fellow, and not the man God's fellow, he might have drawn near to God, and yet we have been never the nearer ; and yet if not more than man, and so God's fellow (which no mere man could be) he could not have approached to God ; as Jer. xxx. 21, ' And their nobles shall be of themselves, and their governor shall proceed from the midst of them ; and I will cause him to draw near, and he shall approach unto me : for who is this that engaged his heart to approach unto me ? saith the Lord.' Who but he could have engaged his heart, or assumed the boldness to have drawn near unto God ? And yet withal he being the man God's fellow, we may draw nigh to him, and come to God by him, as the phrase is in the epistle to the Hebrews ; for why, he comes out of the midst of us, as in the same Jer. xxx. 21. Thus Heb. iv. 15, 16, ' For we have not an high priest which cannot be touched with the feeling of our infirmities ; but was in all points tempted like as we are, yet without sin. Let us therefore come boldy unto the throne of grace, that we may obtain mercy, and find grace to help in time of need.' And Heb. x. 21, 22, ' And having an high priest over the house of God ; let us draw near with a true heart, in full assuranĉe of faith, having our hearts sprinkled from an evil conscience, and our bodies washed with pure water.'

Sixthly; He could hereby communicate the benefit of all he did for us unto us, which without it had not been done, *Participavit de nostro, ut communicaret suum :* He partakes of ours, that he may communicate to us his. We are to participate the divine nature, 2 Pet. i. 4, and therefore he takes part of ours. If we were to have righteousness from him, it was fit our own nature should be the fountain: John xvii. 19, ' For their sakes I sanctify myself that they may be sanctified ;' *I,* that is, my deity, sanctifies *myself,* that is, my human nature, which he calls himself, because it was one in person with himself. It was fit that that nature that sinned should be sanctified to ' condemn sin in the flesh,' Rom. viii. 3. And hence it is the benefit of his righteousness is not extended to angels, because he that sanctifies and them that are sanctified are of one, Heb. ii. 11, which he and angels are not ; and therefore his merits reach not in a proper and direct way unto them.   The intense worth indeed of his benefits ariseth from his abilities and sufficiency personal, but the extension from his so proper fitness that he was a man, and therefore reacheth only to men.

Seventhly; That which he was to do for us required he should be both God and man.   For consider but the principal parts of the work that he was to do, and it was fit that he should be both, that what did not become the one nature the other might do.

1. He was to keep and fulfil the law, and be subject to it, and to merit by keeping it.   Now if he had not been man he could not have been subject to the law; therefore he was made of a woman, and made under the law; first, therefore, made of a woman, that so he might be under the law: Gal. iv. 4, ' But when the fulness of the time was come, God sent forth his Son, made of a woman, made under the law.'   And if he had not been God, he could not have merited for us by that his keeping the law, for he had done but what was required and what was a due, and so it could have reached but to himself; for all creatures, when they have done all they can, are but unprofitable servants; and he that merits must do it by his own strength, for otherwise ' what hast thou that thou hast not received ? '

2. He that is our mediator must die and overcome death, for he was to rescue us from death, and destroy him that had the power of it.   Now if he had not been man, he could not have died; therefore he took such a body as we have that he might die; he could not have tasted of death else : Heb. ii. 9, ' But we see Jesus, who was made a little lower than the angels for the suffering of death, crowned with glory and honour; that he by the grace of God should taste death for every man.'   Ver. 14, ' Forasmuch then as the children are partakers of flesh and blood, he also himself likewise took part of the same ; that through death he might destroy him that had the power of death, that is, the devil.'   And if he had not been God he could not have raised himself: Rom. i. 4, ' And declared to be the Son of God with power, according to the spirit of holiness, by the resurrection from the dead :' therefore, John x. 18, ' I lay down my life,' saith he, ' and take it up again.'

(1.) He had not had a life to lay down if he had not been man, for the Godhead could not die.

(2.) If he had not been God he could not have merited by laying it down.   It must be his own, not in the dominion of another; now the lives of creatures are not their own, and therefore their laying of them down cannot merit.

(3.) He must have it in his own power ; if another could take it away he could not have merited, for it must be a voluntary laying it down, and there is no mere man but another may take away his life from him if God prevent not; but Christ, having his life wholly in his own power, resigned it, therefore that centurion said he was God, Mat. xxvii. 54.

(4.) He could not else take it up again.   None ought to die but man ; none could give up his life, and reassume it, but God : he had the passive power to die, as man, the active power, to die of himself, as God.

(5.) And so for enduring the wrath of God ; if he had not been man he had not had a soul to be heavy to the death ; and if he had not been God it had died through heaviness, if the Godhead had not upheld him that upholds all things.

(6.) Also he was to be a judge : and that he could not be unless he had been God ; and also an advocate : and that he could not be, unless he had been man.

CHAPTER VI.

How the two natures, the divine and human, which are so different, are united into one person, Christ God-man.—That the Son of God did not assume a human person, but the nature.—The reasons why a human person could not have been assumed.—It was our whole nature which the Son of God took, both soul and body.—The reasons which made this necessary.

And now that we have the reasons that he was to be both, you will ask how can this be that he should be both ? The text resolves it, and says, ' He took to himself,' Heb. ii. 16. The meaning is, he did take man's nature into one person with himself. He not only took on him, but to him, ἐπιλαμβάνεται, *assumpsit ad. Assumpsit non hominem personam, sed hominem in personam* ; he took not the person of a man, but man to be one person with himself. ' He took the seed of Abraham ' to himself, that is, to subsist in himself, not of itself, and to have his subsistence communicated to it ; this nature being as an appendix, as a part of him subsisting in him, but communicating the subsistence of that divine person to the human nature that they are personally one, as truly as soul and body joined become one man ; and therefore the phrase is, that this second person was ' made flesh:' John i. 14, ' And the Word was made flesh, and dwelt among us (and we beheld his glory, the glory as of the only begotten of the Father), full of grace and truth.' Though God dwells in the saints in heaven, and fills them with his fulness as a cause efficient of all their glory and their chiefest good, yet they are not so united as that God can be said to be made the saints; but Christ may be said to be made man, and to be as essentially man as he is God ; made, not as the water was made wine, and ceasing to be water, but both natures remaining distinct, are made one person, so as both became one Lord and one Christ ; there is one Lord, 1 Cor. viii. 6, ' But to us there is but one God, the Father, of whom are all things, and we in him : and one Lord Jesus Christ, by whom are all things, and we by him ;' God and man personally one. So 2 Cor. v. 14, ' For the love of Christ constraineth us ; because we thus judge, that if one died for all, then were all dead.' One is said to have died for all, that is, but one person, though there were two natures, God and man, yet but one person of both. That as in the Trinity there are three persons in one nature and Godhead, so here are two natures, one in person and subsistence (the manner of which union hath no similitude in nature to express it by), so as in the concrete the man Christ may be called God, and the Son of God (so Luke i. 35, ' That which shall be born of thee, shall be called the Son of God'), though the manhood cannot be called the Godhead. And then this second person is said to dwell in that nature : Col. ii. 9, ' The fulness of the Godhead ' is said to ' dwell in him bodily ;' and so notes out a permanent union, not God to dwell in him only by his graces, but the Godhead is said to dwell in him, and the fulness of the Godhead to fill that human nature, as fire fills the iron that is in it*—and not to dwell in him as in the saints by grace, and as being their portion, uniting himself to them as an object they love, as God is said to be all in all in the saints in heaven, and as the Spirit dwells in us, sanctifying, &c., and as the same Spirit dwells in Christ, —substantially dwelling in him, σωματικῶς ; that is, not only in a body, noting out the subject in which, but the manner, personally, bodily. Now the Grecians put σῶμα to express a person, σώματα πολλὰ τρέφειν. And so

* Qu. ' that it is in ' ?—ED.

Thucydides, σώμασι πολεμεῖν. As the Hebrews put soul for person : Exod.
i. 5, the souls came out of the loins of Jacob ; the Grecians use the word
body, so that *bodily* is *personally*.

God communicates his presence to all creatures, his grace to the saints ;
but the Son of God communicates his personality, his subsistence, to the
man Christ Jesus—this is the highest communication, for his nature is
communicable to none but the three persons—so as our nature and Christ's
person is one ; not in office only, as two consuls or bailiffs in a town, that
have a joint commission ; not as man and wife only, who are in a relation
one flesh ; not spiritually only, as Christ and we his members are one spirit,
as the head and members are one ; but they are personally one. So as
when we see a man, we say, there is such a man, such a person ; so when
you shall see Christ at the latter day, you may say as John doth, 1 John
v. 20, ' This is the true God, and eternal life.'

God is the *principium* of subsistence to all, but in Christ he is the *terminus subsistendi*, yet not so as if the personal property were communicated
that is incommunicable, as to be begotten of God, and to subsist of itself,
but that the second person becomes a foundation of subsistence to the
human nature of Christ, as an oak is to the ivy.

Now to shew the grounds why this was fit (which is the proper scope of
this discourse) why this union was requisite, and fitted him for the work of
mediation. Had he not been thus God and man, he could not have been
mediator. For,

1. It being necessary he should be God and man, and remain perfectly
God and perfectly man, and the Son of God, and the same person that he
was, therefore they could no way else be united to do us good ; for they
could not the one be changed into the other, for God was immutable ; and
it was impossible that the nature of man should become the nature of God,
since the essence of the Godhead is incommunicable. And if they had been
so united as that a third person out of both had been made, as when the
elements are made one in a man's body, as the soul and body make one
man, besides the impossibility of it, it had not served this turn. For he
that redeems us must be God and man, therefore there is no way but that
the personality of the second person be communicated to the human, both
natures remaining united in one person ; it cannot be more nor less. If the
personality of the Son of God had been communicated only by power and
grace, &c., then his actions had been of God as the author or efficient, but
not actions of the person of the Son of God, as his personal actions, which
should have received a worth from him.

And, 2. This will fit us well ; for now all that Christ as God doth, the
man Christ shall be said to do for us, that so it may be ours ; and all that
Christ man doth, Christ God shall be said to do, that it may have an infinite merit in it. For as there is a communication of the personality of
Christ to the manhood, so of acceptance of all the human nature doth : 1
Pet. iii. 18, ' For Christ also hath once suffered for sins, the just for the
unjust, that he might bring us to God, being put to death in the flesh, but
quickened by the Spirit.' And therefore the blood shed shall be called the
blood of God, as well as the man is called the Son of God : so Acts xx. 28,
' Take heed therefore unto yourselves, and to all the flock, over the which the
Holy Ghost hath made you overseers, to feed the church of God, which he
hath purchased with his own blood.' And so the Lord of glory is said to
be crucified : 1 Cor. ii. 8, ' Which none of the princes of this world knew :
for had they known it, they would not have crucified the Lord of glory.'

And as the person is one, so the redemption, and all that both did, became one work of mediation, and one is said to die for all, Christ as one, God and man ; so as, when he offered up the human nature as a sacrifice, he may be said to offer up himself, for it is himself, and he poured out his own soul : Heb. ix. 14, ' How much more shall the blood of Christ, who, through the eternal Spirit, offered himself without spot to God, purge your con· science from dead works, to serve the living God?' Isa. liii. 12, 'Therefore will I divide him a portion with the great, and he shall divide the spoil with the strong ; because he hath poured out his soul unto death : and he was numbered with the transgressors ; and he bare the sin of many, and made intercession for the transgressors.'

Now then, if this manhood be assumed into one person with the Son of God, then it could not remain a person of itself; and so the text also intimates, calling him ' the seed,' Heb. ii. 16, as not a person, but a human nature ; so as though he took our nature, and an individual particular nature, yet that nature was not a person. Therein indeed his human nature differs from ours ; but that difference is not in any part of the substance' of our natures, but only in a complement of being, or rather a modification of being, a difference in the manner of subsisting : it is no more.

(1.) The nature is the same for being and substance.

(2.) It is an individual nature.

But (3.) it is not a person of itself apart for subsistence, for that is properly called a person that subsists in itself; though we all have our being in God, and exist by him as in a cause thereof, yet we do not subsist as one with him as a person ; that is, we are persons apart and alone of ourselves, and God and we are two persons, but our nature in Christ is one with God, and in God.

The reasons of this are two.

1. It was not indeed possible that a person (as the second person was) should assume another person, subsisting of itself, into personal union with him : it had been a contradiction, and therefore it is impossible. For that two persons, remaining two, should become one, is a contradiction ; even as to say of an accident (the nature of which is to subsist in a substance), that it subsists in itself, is a contradiction. Now to be a person of itself is to subsist of itself alone ; this is the condition of its subsisting as it is a person ; and therefore here in the 16th verse of this Heb. ii., when he speaks but by way of supposition of the second person's assuming the nature of angels, he doth not say, he took not on himself ' an angel,' but ' not of angels,' that is, the nature of angels ; for to have assumed the person of an angel had been a contradiction, and so such a phrase of speech was not fit to have been used so much as in a supposition.

2. As it was not possible that the second person of the Godhead should take the person of a man into union with himself, so it was not fit (the demonstration of which is that which I in this discourse did aim at) for the work of mediation. For although it was necessary for that work that he should be an individual particular man as we are, particularly existing— for else he could not merit, nor act, nor suffer, for all merits and actions are of individuals—yet if he had subsisted of himself, and been a person of himself as man, all that merit and actions of obedience would have been but for himself. If he had been a person of himself apart, so his merits would have been for himself apart ; and he subsisting in his own bottom, and in himself as a person, must have stood by his own obedience, and so all his obedience would have been but enough for himself, and have been

shut up in himself, and confined to himself. But he having an individual nature of man as we all have, without a propriety of subsistence, all his obedience may be common for all others, and as many as he shall please to communicate it unto may have a share in it. It may be a common salvation, as it is called Jude 3, 'Beloved, when I gave all diligence to write unto you of the common salvation, it was needful for me to write unto you, and exhort you, that ye should earnestly contend for the faith which was once delivered unto the saints.' For our nature in him, as it is human, is not circumscribed or enclosed with a proper subsistence of its own, but lies like a field unenclosed, not hedged in with personality, as all our natures are.

And to this purpose observe the phrases whereby the Scripture expresseth this nature assumed by the Son of God, which are such as do imply, that that which was assumed was only a human nature, and not a person. As when it is said, ' He took the seed of Abraham,' Heb. ii. 16, not a person, but ' the seed,' our nature. *Semen est intimum substantiæ*, the quintessence of nature, but notes not out a person. So the Word is said to be made flesh ; that word flesh noteth out but one nature assumed, not a person ; and therefore the apostle speaking of Christ, he makes him the person, and his flesh or human nature but as an appendix : Rom. ix. 5, ' Whose are the fathers, and of whom as concerning the flesh Christ came, who is over all, God blessed for ever. Amen.' And so in Luke i. 35, ' And the angel answered and said unto her, The Holy Ghost shall come upon thee, and the power of the Highest shall overshadow thee : therefore also that holy thing which shall be born of thee shall be called the Son of God.' The angel there speaks of Christ's human nature, which was to be born of Mary, not as of a person but as of a thing, in the neuter gender : ' That holy thing which shall be born of thee shall be called the Son of God.' And besides, he, the man Christ, could not have been called the Son of God if he had been a person apart of himself, for one person is not predicated of another ; the husband cannot be called the wife, though most nearly united, for they are two persons. And therefore likewise Christ himself, when he was to take our nature, speaking of that which was to be assumed, saith, Heb. x. 5, ' A body hast thou fitted me ;' *me* notes out the person, the other is but a body assumed ; so he calls it, because himself as God was the person ; this was not a person but the nature of man, therefore he calls it a body, and so Col. i. 22, ' in the body of his flesh through death, to present you holy and unblameable, and unreprovable in his sight :' it is ἐν τῷ σώματι τῆς σάρκος, in that body of his flesh.

But though he subsisted not as an entire person, yet it was fit and necessary that he should be a whole and perfect man entire, so as though he took not a person on him, yet he took our whole nature for substance, every way as perfect as ours, in all the parts of it, both of soul and body : ' He was made like us in all things,' says the apostle, Heb. ii. 17. There was nothing wanting essential to either, or for the perfection of either part of our nature, for he will be like us in all things, in all members of our bodies, and faculties of our souls. It is called flesh indeed, and a body, but yet lest only a body should seem to be meant, he elsewhere is called ' a man,' ' the man Christ Jesus,' as having all belonging to a man ; and he is called ' that man' in Acts xvii. 31 : ' Because he hath appointed a day, in the which he will judge the world in righteousness, by that man whom he hath ordained ; whereof he hath given assurance unto all men, in that he hath raised him from the dead.' He had a perfect body as ours, and a soul, and both united, and so was a whole man.

1. For the body, Col. i. 22, it is called ' the body of his flesh.' They thought he had been a spirit, but in opposition to their conceit, ' It is I,' says he, Mat. xiv. 27 ; ' and feel,' says he ; ' hath a spirit flesh, and blood, and bones ?' Luke xxiv. 39. And this was fit, that the similitude of our union might be the nearer, and that we might be truly called ' members of his body,' as being ' of his flesh and of his bones :' as Eph. v. 30, ' For we are members of his body, of his flesh, and of his bones.' Also because he was to reconcile us ' in the body of his flesh through death,' Col. i. 22, by bearing our sins upon his body on the tree : 1 Peter ii. 24, ' Who his own self bare our sins in his own body on the tree, that we, being dead to sin, should live unto righteousness : by whose stripes ye were healed.' If he had not had the body of a man, he could not have been fastened to the tree, nor endured our sorrows, the pains of death. And again, as all our members are weapons of unrighteousness, therefore he was to take them all, to sanctify all to God, and make them weapons of righteousness.

And that body did not want a soul, for his ' soul was heavy unto death,' Mat. xxvi. 38. And it was meet it should be so, for first the chief suit and threatening for sin was against the soul : ' The soul that sins shall die,' Ezek. xviii. 20 ; therefore he must ' pour out his soul to death,' Isa. liii. 12, and it is the redemption of the soul that is precious : Ps. xlix. 8, ' For the redemption of their soul is precious, and it ceaseth for ever ;' that is the chief thing to be redeemed, and that is so precious, as nothing but a soul could be a fit price. He was made like us therefore, that he might succour us in all respects : Heb. iv. 15, ' For we have not an high priest which cannot be touched with the feeling of our infirmities ; but was in all points tempted like as we are, yet without sin ;' Heb. ii. 17, 18, ' Wherefore in all things it behoved him to be made like unto his brethren, that he might be a merciful and faithful high priest in things pertaining to God, to make reconciliation for the sins of the people. For in that he himself hath suffered, being tempted, he is able to succour them that are tempted.' And now our greatest temptations are in our souls, and therefore he had a soul to be tempted in all things, sin only excepted ; and so he knows how to pity our souls, and the distress of them, and he joys to be a ' shepherd of our souls :' 1 Peter ii. 25, ' For ye were as sheep going astray ; but are now returned unto the Shepherd and Bishop of your souls.'

And then, 2, both body and soul must be united, else the body could not die ; for bodily death is the separation of soul and body, and that was threatened against us, and therefore to be executed on our mediator ; and therefore when he died, it is said, ' He gave up the ghost,' Mat. xxvii. 50.

And he must be a whole, perfect man, for this reason too, because he was to be a priest and a sacrifice both, and the priests in the law were to be perfect men in all parts of their bodies. If they had any blemish, they were not to be priests. And so the sacrifices were to be whole burntofferings, therefore a whole man was to be offered up by the Son of God.

And he being to redeem the whole man, it was fit he should take the whole human nature. All that was lost was to be saved by him : Luke xix. 10, ' He came to seek and to save that which was lost.' There was not that thing in man that was lost (as all was), but he saved it, and therefore took the whole of man into union with himself.

CHAPTER VII.

That it was not only fit that Christ should be man, but such a man as to be like us in the matter and substance of his body—And to be like us in his production and birth, to be born of a woman, as we are.—What are the reasons of this—What is the reason why Christ, though born of a woman, is yet without sin.—Why he is man, and of the Jewish nation.

Now seeing he was thus to be a man, let us consider what manner or kind of man every way qualified was fittest in this business, and we shall find that such a man did God every way make him ; for he must have a human nature fitted for him on purpose : Heb. x. 5, ' Wherefore when he cometh into the world, he saith, Sacrifice and offering thou wouldest not, but a body hast thou prepared me.' ' A body hast thou fitted me,' so some read it, *adaptasti*, fitted him with a body for the purpose. And indeed if for all other works God chooseth out fit instruments, then surely for this great work of all works else ; and accordingly divines call his human nature *instrumentum Deitatis*, the instrument of the Godhead. It is not every kind of body will fit him for this purpose of reconciling. Some schoolmen have thought that not any other human nature but that which was assumed could have been assumed; sure I am a greater fitness could not have been in any, and all to make up this his personal fitness for a mediator full, that in him all fulness might be found to dwell.

Now concerning what qualifications are to be in him for this work, we have this general rule given us here in Heb. ii. 17, ' That it became him in all things to be made like to us who were his brethren ; ' so as the liker he should be to us, the fitter mediator he should be for us, and that for the very reasons before mentioned, that because justice admitted of a commutation, it would yet come every way as nigh to have a full and proportionable satisfaction as could be. As satisfaction must be made in a nature of the same kind, by man, not an angel, so in such a nature a man as should be as near akin to us, and like us, as the matter would possibly permit, so as the business of reconciliation be not hindered nor evacuated by it; for then he should have lost his end.

First, Whereas he might have been a man of the same nature with us, consisting both of body and soul, and yet have been created immediately, as Adam was, out of nothing, yea, or out of matter in heaven (as some do dream), as his body itself is now heavenly and spiritual, and therefore called ' the heavenly man,' 1 Cor. xv. 48, 49 : yet that he may be like to us, he will take human nature of the same lump with ours, and out of which ours is taken. So here in Heb. ii. 14, ' He took part of the same ; ' the same flesh and blood that we have ; and again, ver. 11, ' Both he that sanctifieth and they who are sanctified are all of one:' he says, not only that both are one for nature and kind, but all are ' of one,' that is, one lump and mass, that so he might be a little the more akin to us, our countryman, being made of the same earth we are of. If he had been made of heavenly matter he had been countryman to the angels rather, for heaven is their country ; yea, he had been utterly a stranger to us, though of the same nature ; as a man dropped from heaven would be, as some conceive Melchisedec his type to have been. And the reason there given is proper and pertinent, for he was to sanctify us ; and he that sanctifies and they that are sanctified it is meet they should be ' of one.' The ground of this reason is taken from that of the Levitical law, by which the first-fruits sanctified the whole lump or mass which those fruits were taken out of; and they by this sanctified the rest, because they were of the same lump or mass, as it is expressed, Rom. xi. 16, 'For if the first-fruit be holy, the lump is also holy: and if the root be holy, so are the branches.' They were not only of the same species of creature that the rest were of, but growing out of the same earth that the rest of the fruits did. Now Christ, as he is called 'the *fruit* of the womb,' Luke i. 42, so the 'first-fruits,': 1 Cor. xv. 20, 'But now is Christ risen from the dead, and become the first-fruits of them that slept;' which, though spoken of the resurrection only, yet holds in all, even to his very nature. He is in all things wherein he is like us the first-fruits, and therefore is to be made like us in all, that he might be the first-fruits. And he was to sanctify others of mankind; and this he had not so fitly and correspondently, according to the law of nature, done, had not both they and he been all of one. And besides God meant not to create anew any of mankind, and therefore he made woman of man rather than of nothing, intending to make out of Adam all which he meant to make, even Christ and all. But then,

Secondly, He might have been made of the same lump, if made of some man, in that manner as Eve was out of Adam, made of a rib, or some such part of mankind. But he resolves to come nearer yet, and to be made as like in all things as may be, and therefore he will be made of the same kind of matter that we all are made of, even of seed, which is the quintessence, the elixir of man's nature, *intimum substantiæ;* and therefore the first title and appellation he was known by unto the sons of men was ' the seed of the woman:' Gen. iii. 15, 'And I will put enmity between thee and the woman, and between thy seed and her seed; it shall bruise thy head, and thou shalt bruise his heel.' So Acts xvii. 26. God hath made mankind all of one blood, that so they might love one another; and he will have this man that is to be our redeemer to be of the same blood, that is, of seed, which is the blood of man concocted to an height, and therefore he is not only called a man, but the ' Son of man,' Mat. xvii. 12. Eve, though made out of man, was not *filia hominis*, a daughter of man; nor Adam, though a man, yet not a son of man; no. In the genealogy, Luke iii. 38, Adam is called the son of God; but Christ is to be the Son of man as well as man, and that by being made of seed, which all men are made of; and so in Heb. ii. 16, ' He took not the nature of angels, but the *seed* of Abraham.' And the reason is given in the next verse here, that he might call us brethren, and not be ashamed of us. A brother is more than of the same nature, it notes one made out of the same blood. And God would have the same blood run in his veins that runs in ours. And this fitted him the more to be a redeemer, and to have right to do it by the Levitical law also, for it was proper to a brother to redeem, and a stranger could not: Levit. xxv. 25, ' If thy brother be waxen poor, and hath sold away some of his possession, and if any of his kin come to redeem it, then shall he redeem that which his brother sold.' So that the church comes to have her wish: Cant. viii. 1, ' Oh that thou wert as my brother,' &c. For so Christ is. Yea,

Thirdly, He will come yet nearer, even in the manner of his production, or being made a man, as like as may be to that of ours, as near as possibly might be, so as not to take infection. He will be made of seed, even by a conception, and lie in the womb, and grow up there, from a tear, a drop, by degrees, as man doth, and be born, and be a suckling as we, as Ps.

viii. 2 speaks of him, and therefore he is called the fruits of the womb : Luke i. 42, 'And she spake out with a loud voice, and said, Blessed art thou among women, and blessed is the fruit of thy womb.' And more expressly, Luke i. 31, ' Thou shalt conceive in thy womb, and bring forth a son,' speaking to Mary. You see Christ is like to us in being produced both by the same way, and to lie in the same place, that secret and dark chamber that all mankind lies in. Conception is the groundseil (as I may call it) of our nature, which sin had infected, and it was rotten and corrupted, and from it the leprosy was spread over all the walls of this building : ' In sin my mother conceived me,' says David, Ps. li. 5, and Christ coming to repair and restore us from the very foundation, sanctifies that very way of production, conception, and consecrates the curious room and privy chamber that all mankind lies in. Man is said by the psalmist to be curiously wrought ' in the lower parts of the earth,' Ps. cxxxix. 15 ; and Christ descends even thither, that so he may ascend the higher. He takes his flight thus low, in that he ascended, he descended first into these lower parts of the earth, which surely is part of the apostle's meaning, in comparing it with that psalm : Eph. iv. 9, 10, ' Now that he ascended, what is it but that he also descended first into the lower parts of the earth ?' ver. 10, ' He that descended is the same also that ascended up far above all heavens, that he might fill all things.' And that we may be where he is, as he prays, John xvii. 24, he will condescend for a while to be where we were, enclosed in the womb. And that we may come to his place, his mansion-house in heaven, his Father's house, he will first come down to our place, our mother's house, for such is the womb. And therefore he is still called ' the seed of the woman,' and ' made of a woman ;' Gal. iv. 4, 5, ' But when the fulness of time was come, God sent forth his Son, made of a woman, made under the law ;' ver. 5, ' To redeem them that were under the law, that we might receive the adoption of sons ;' to the end that he might be fitted to redeem us. This reason is expressly added there, ' that he might redeem us that were under the law.' And this woman was yet a virgin, as you shall see by and by, ' A virgin shall conceive :' Isa. vii. 14, ' Therefore the Lord himself shall give you a sign ; Behold, a virgin shall conceive, and bear a son, and shall call his name Immanuel.' One reason of it, besides that which I shall anon give, might be, that God would take a new course in the rearing up this human nature, differing from what was taken afore. If he had made him out of man, or the rib of a man, so he had made the woman before ; if out of nothing, so he had made the first man before. But to make him of a woman, and the seed of the woman, by conception, without man, this was a new thing in the earth, as the prophet speaks, Isa. xliii. 19. And God herein kept some further correspondency also with man's sinning, that (as was observed before) as by a man came death, so by man should come the resurrection ; God observed a proportion in it. So here, a woman afore destroyed us, and was ' first in the transgression ;' nevertheless, both she and we shall be saved by her child-bearing, or that child-bearing (as some interpret that place, 1 Tim. ii. 15). And Adam laid all the blame on the woman (reflecting withal on God) : Gen. iii. 12, ' And the man said, The woman whom thou gavest to be with me, she gave me of the tree, and I did eat.' And therefore God presently, to meet with him, says, ' The seed of the woman,' not the man, shall break the serpent's head ; as if he had said, Thou hast laid the fault on me for giving thee a woman, because she hath been the occasion of thy fall ; but I will be even with thee (but it is in mercy, as God's revenges on his children are). Thou shalt have cause to thank me more for this woman, than thou now hast done; for 'the seed of the woman shall break the serpent's head;' and so doth God reprove him, and for his unthankfulness puts the honour upon the woman.

Obj. Yea, but now in the *fourth* place, you will say, this kindred is too nigh, he had better have married our nature further off, and at a greater distance; for thus he is in danger to be made sinful. Doth not the psalmist say, 'In sin my mother conceived me,' Ps. li. 5. Doth not the apostle say, 'And such an high priest became us as was separated from sinners'? Heb. vii. 26. Why, then, the work of our redemption will be spoiled by this way of conception of Christ, and he be unfitted for the work.

But for answer, though there is a *concipiet*, yet not a *genitus est*; though there is a conception, yet not a generation. It is conception upon generation defiles. Man begets in his image, but Christ was not begotten, but conceived only. He comes so near, you see, that it is but the cutting of a hair keeps him from being infected; and so though he will have the same substance, yet separate from sinners, as there the separation means *quantum ad culpam*, as to sin; *non naturam*, as to nature. And therefore though he will be conceived in the same place we are, and be of the same substance with us, yet not after the same way; and it is not the substance that defiles, or the place, but the way of framing our natures. We are framed by generation of man and woman, he but by conception only of a woman, but made by the Holy Ghost; so in our Creed, 'conceived by the Holy Ghost;' so in Luke i. 25, 'The Holy Ghost shall overshadow thee;' and Mat. i. 20, 'That which is conceived in her is of the Holy Ghost.' Not σπερματικῶς, but δημιουργικῶς, as the builder framing and forming his body. Therefore it is not said he was *begotten* of a woman, but *made* of a woman, *non genitus, sed factus*, and therefore he is called 'The man from heaven,' though the matter of his body was from earth, 1 Cor. xv. 47, 48. And to this purpose it is observable, that Heb. x. 5 is with difference spoken of Christ's human nature and ours, 'A body hast thou prepared me;' that is, God did it, and not man by generation, which is the ordinary way of producing men, and the only way of conveying sin. The parents, they are therefore said to beget a man, not because they afford matter and stuff, but because there goes a forming power, *vis plastica*, as philosophers call it, that doth prepare the matter, form it, and, to use the word which is here, doth καταρτίζει, articulate it for the soul, which is the utmost they do, and for which they are said to beget, and wherein the very *formalis ratio* of generation lies. Accurately therefore to distinguish this production of the human nature of Christ from the ordinary, though he useth the same word, that signifies the manner of making our bodies by way of articulation, yet he expresseth it as done by another hand, 'Thou hast prepared it,' the Holy Ghost performing that which the *vis plastica*, or forming power, in all other generations useth to do. Luke i. 35, 'And the angel answered and said unto her, The Holy Ghost shall come upon thee, and the power of the highest shall overshadow thee: therefore also that holy thing which shall be born of thee, shall be called the Son of God.' That though the matter is the same, and this formed by articulation, as ours is, yet it is done by the power of the Most High, and therefore exempted from sin; therefore he adds, 'That holy one that shall be born of thee shall be called the Son of God.' For because generation by men is the only way of conveying sin, and the *formalis ratio* of generation lies in that *vis plastica*, whereby a parent forms the birth (as philosophy teacheth), therefore his body, though made of the same matter, seed, that ours is, and that seed articulated into the same shape ours is, yet because by another hand, ' the power of the Most High,' therefore he is a holy one separate from sinners, his body being a tabernacle which ' God pitched, not man,' Heb. viii. 2.　Not of this building, not built as man's is, not by the same hands, as Heb. ix. 11, ' But Christ being come an high priest of good things to come, by a greater and more perfect tabernacle, not made with hands, that is to say, not of this building.'　Man reared it not, nor jointed it, nor framed it, but ' A body hast *thou* (O God) prepared.'　And therefore this body was of a virgin without a father, that as Melchisedec is said, Heb. vii. 3, to be without father and mother, so Christ as man was without father, and as God without a mother, who is therefore the stone cut out of the same quarry with us, but ' without hands,' Dan. ii. 45, that is, the help of nature, or by a man.　And it was necesssary; for,

1. Otherwise his human nature had been a person (the inconvenience of which you heard afore) for *terminus generationis est persona*.　What is produced by generation is a person.　And,

2. He had otherwise had two fathers, which nature abhors, that one person should have two fathers.

And in preparing this nature of Christ, the Holy Ghost sanctified that matter, and purified it, as goldsmiths do gold from the dross.　And his business being to part sin and our flesh, it was fit he should take such flesh as, though once sinful, yet now sin was parted from it.　It is generation defiles, for that which is born of the flesh is flesh, John iii. 6, and that as from a man, by whom sin is conveyed ; but it follows in the same place, that which is born of the Spirit is spirit.　Now, of Christ it is said that which is conceived in thee is of the Holy Ghost : Mat. i. 20, ' But while he thought on these things, behold, the angel of the Lord appeared unto him in a dream, saying, Joseph, thou son of David, fear not to take unto thee Mary thy wife : for that which is conceived in her is of the Holy Ghost.'　It is not the matter nor the place we are conceived in defiles, but the being begotten by a man in the ordinary way of nature, upon which the law of nature seizeth, by which a man is to beget in his own likeness. And therefore the difference of the phrase used here in Heb. ii. 11, of Christ and us ; and that in Rom. v. 12, speaking of our coming from Adam, is observable.　Here, in Heb. ii. 11, Christ and we are said to be ' of one,' that is, of one lump ; but the phrase that is used, Rom. v. 12, when the apostle speaks of the propagation of original sin, runs thus, ' By one man sin entered,' because all came by and of that one man.　And therefore though Christ be made a Son of Adam, Luke iii. 38, as made of that substance and matter derived from him, yet not in regard of the same way of conveying that matter, by fleshly generation of a man, which is the natural channel of conveying his image and original sin.　And yet,

Fifthly, To make up this disproportion, he will in all other respects be yet the more like to us ; and seeing he must not take sinful flesh, yet he will take the likeness of sinful flesh, as Rom. viii. 3, ' For what the law could not do, in that it was weak through the flesh, God sending his own Son, in the likeness of sinful flesh, and for sin condemned sin in the flesh.' He partakes of flesh and blood, Heb. ii. 17 ; and by flesh and blood are meant infirmities of all sorts, he excepts sin only, a body passible ; he might have had a body exempted from all sufferings or misery, but he would not.　And this assumption of frail flesh was the first part of satisfaction for sin, and the condemning sin in our flesh is attributed to it,

Rom. viii. 3. He took not indeed personal infirmities, as sickness, but what were common to man's nature; he did bear *dolores nostros*, our griefs, not of John or Peter, not such evils as came from the particular sins of men, but such as flowed from the common sin of man; nor such as do spring from sin, as not despair, though fear; and those he took was to shew his love, and as they were part of the curse, that he might be able to pity us, and that he might suffer and die and feel the pains of death, in all which he was left to infirmity; as you have it, 2 Cor. xiii. 4, 'For though he was crucified through weakness, yet he liveth by the power of God: for we also are weak in him, but we shall live with him by the power of God toward you.' And so in this text, he was 'partaker of flesh and blood,' that is, of the infirmities of man's nature, as well as of the nature; that through death he might destroy him that had the power of death, that is, the devil. If he had not taken this frail flesh, he could not have died.

Hitherto you have heard every way what manner of man he was, and such as in all respects was fittest for him to be, in all things. But there are two things yet to be added, and both such as will make him yet fitter. I add them that you may every way see a fulness in it. Therefore,

Sixthly, Man's nature, you know, was diversified into two sexes, male and female. Now, which of the two was the fittest for him to assume? And this is a distinct consideration from all the former. Of the two, a male was fittest; and such was he. It is not so directly in the text, and yet all that is spoken of him runs in the masculine gender, *him* and *he;* and so this is included: Mat. i. 21, 'Thou shalt bring forth a *son*,' and, ver. 25, 'she brought forth her first-born son;' and so Luke ii. 22. For he was to be our high priest, and consecrated to God as holy, and so thereby to sanctify his brethren, as Heb. ii. 11 hath it; and so was the first male child by the law, which is on purpose noted, Luke ii. 23, 'Every male that openeth the womb shall be called holy to the Lord.' And again, all his other offices required it. He was to be a prophet, and to teach God's will first, Heb. ii. 2, 3, and for ever to be in the great congregation; and a woman is not to teach in the church. He was to be a king, and to rule his church; and a woman is not to usurp authority over the man. He was to be a husband, and his church a spouse; and only a male could fitly bear that relation. And besides all this, there was this further harmony in it, that as by the male, the man, not the woman, sin is said to enter into the world, Rom. v. 19; so by the man we should be restored. And thus indeed both sexes came to share in this honour—the male, in that Christ himself is a man; the female, in that she yet was the instrument of bringing him forth into the world. He is of the woman's seed, but of man's sex, that so both male and female might be all one in Christ Jesus.

There is now but one thing left, and that is, seeing God hath appointed several bounds to man's habitation, though all are made of one blood, of what country or kindred of men was it fittest for our Redeemer to be of? God pitched it on what of all was fittest, that he should be 'of the seed of Abraham.' This Heb. ii. 16 you see also hath it; and so I could not but take notice of it. As he took the nature of man, not of angels, so he took the seed of Abraham more eminently than of any other nation; although he had by some of his progenitors Gentiles' blood in him, yet he was of Abraham in a lineal descent: Rom. ix. 4, 5, 'Who are Israelites, to whom pertaineth the adoption, and the glory, and the covenants, and the giving of the law, and the service of God, and the promises;' ver. 5, 'Whose are

the fathers, and of whom as concerning the flesh Christ came, who is over
all, God blessed for ever. Amen.' I will not mention any other reason
of this, but what is proper to set out his fitness the more for this work.
It was well for us that he took Abraham's seed, for so in him all nations
were blessed, as was the promise, Abraham being father of all the faithful.
But especially he was thereby engaged to keep the whole law for us; for
Abraham's seed were all to be circumcised, and he that was circumcised
was a debtor to the whole law: Gal. v. 3, 'For I testify again to every
man that is circumcised, that he is a debtor to do the whole law.' And
so the law will take hold of him, and so hereby he was made under the
law; and this was one reason why he was a male child also, for they only
were circumcised. Thus you see Christ hereby engaged to keep the law
for us, yea, to satisfy for sin; for the ceremonial law was a bond against us,
which he must cancel and destroy.

CHAPTER VIII.

*The Uses.—Since God hath thus fitted us with a Mediator, we may be assured
that he will fit us with all other things.—Let us choose Christ to be our only
Saviour, and trust in none but him.—Is he God?—Let us not then fear or
doubt.—Hath he taken our nature?—Let us admire his love in this, and
consider our own privilege.—Let us endeavour to fit our natures all that we
can for fellowship with him.*

We will now come to uses of all this. And surely the doctrine of Christ
will afford many; for his person is the most useful of any in heaven and
earth. I deferred the uses until the last, that so you might view the frame
of the doctrinal part, as set together without separation.

I. The first uses shall be from this, That God chose him to be mediator,
because of his fitness above all other.

1. Hence learn and be assured, that that love which thus fitted thee
with a Saviour, will much more fit thee with all other things which thou
hast need of. Thou shalt have the fittest condition, the fittest calling, the
fittest yoke-fellow, the fittest estate, 'food convenient,' as Agar speaks:
God will fit thee in everything. Thus he sought out a 'meet help' for
Adam, Gen. ii. 20. The fulness of fitness in Christ to be a saviour is a
pawn for fitting and suiting thee with all things else; for he that gave
Christ gives all besides: Rom. viii. 82, 'He that spared not his own Son,
but delivered him up for us all, how shall he not with him also freely give
us all things?' And believe that as all things do meet in Christ, and
nothing is wanting that may make him a fit and meet saviour for thee, so
all things shall conspire, all things shall suit and kiss each other; sins,
afflictions, mercies, yea, all God's dealings shall work together for thy good.
Be quiet therefore, and trust him in all; 'lean not,' as Solomon says, 'to
thine own wisdom,' Prov. iii. 5. Thou knowest not what is fittest for
thee, as the sons of Zebedee did not when they asked for a place that was
not fit for them. The physician knows what is fit for his patient better
than he himself does; and so does God. He takes measure of thy spirit,
and knows the composition of it; and so orders his prescripts accordingly.
We cannot judge what is fit for us, God only can. If thou hadst seen
Christ in the flesh, poor and despised (as he was whilst on earth), thy
carnal heart would have judged him as unlikely and as unfit a man to be

the saviour of the world as the Jews did; Isa. lii. 14, 'His countenance was so marred.' Thou wouldst never have thought that a carpenter's son should build God a church; that a man unlearned should be the prophet of God's people. The Jews refused him as an unfit stone to be laid in their building, whom God had yet hewn out on purpose, as being only fit to be made 'the head stone of the corner,' as a stone elect and precious: Isa. xxviii. 16, 'Therefore thus saith the Lord God, Behold, I lay in Zion for a foundation a stone, a tried stone, a precious corner-stone, a sure foundation: he that believeth shall not make haste;' 1 Pet. ii. 6, 7. And as much mistaken are men in judging of their own condition.

2. Is Christ every way so fit a saviour? Then choose him, and rest in him alone. It is necessary that a saviour you should have; for otherwise you perish; and it is as necessary that you should have Jesus Christ, or else you must have none: for there is, there can be, no other. But yet, suppose you should have your choice of many, nay, suppose there were as many saviours as men to be saved (as many as the papists would make), yet he so transcends, that if ye all knew him, you would all make choice of him, and refuse all others. As 'who is a god like to our God?' so, who is a saviour like to our Saviour? Isa. xliii. 11, 'There is none besides him.' What do you therefore mean, to stand demurring and deliberating whether you should take him or no for your Lord and King, as the most men do? Do you look for any more such Christs, or can you have a better, a fitter saviour? Let this encourage you also to be willingly subject to him. What greater motive can there be to this, than that of all princes he is the fittest to be thy king (and none fit to be king of saints but he), and of all husbands he is the fittest to rule over thee? It grieves no man, nor do any think much to be subject to such a governor as all men with one consent acknowledge to be most fit for them: 'The people rejoice,' says Solomon, 'when the righteous are in authority,' Prov. xxix. 2. Now that the Lord Christ is King, 'let the earth rejoice, and the multitudes of the isles be glad,' Ps. xcvii. 1.

II. The second sort of uses may be taken from this, that our saviour is God.

1. Is he who is thy saviour God? Then fear not to commit thyself to him. 'Thy God is thy saviour.' If 'God will justify' (though there were no mediator), 'who should lay anything to thy charge?' Rom. viii. 33. Surely none would open their mouths against you; 'The Lord that chooseth Jerusalem rebuke thee,' said the angel unto Satan, Zech. iii. 2; but if God will also be thy mediator, and die for thee, then much more art thou safe: 'Who shall condemn?' as the apostle says, 'It is Christ that died.' Do you know and consider who he is that died for you? It is even 'Christ that died,' Rom. viii. 34; who in the beginning of the next chapter, he tells them, is 'God over all, blessed for ever.' 'In his days Judah shall be saved,' Jer. xxiii. 6. It shall be so, says the prophet, 'for his name is Jehovah our righteousness.' 'Say to the feeble of heart, Fear not: for your God will save you,' Isa. xxxv. 4. When princes will themselves in person go into the field, how doth it encourage their subjects and soldiers? Now Jesus Christ, who is God, came down into the field himself: 'Who is this that comes from Bozrah?' Isa. lxiii. 1. 'It is I,' says Christ, 'that am mighty to save.' 'The heathens thought that if their gods should but come down, they were sure of the victory. Now God came down, and was found amongst us as a man, and is become a 'Captain of salvation,' Heb. ii. 10; therefore let fear have no entertainment with you.

Only in the second place,

2. If he be God; although this may raise your hearts not to fear discouragements (I speak to you whose hearts are set to be saved), yet it may withal strike the greatest and most awful dread upon your spirit, and provoke you to fear this your saviour, and not to deal presumptuously with him, nor to slight him, and play fast and loose with him, thinking you may have salvation at any time. No ; he is God ; and 'God will not be mocked,' Gal. vi. 7. You must carry yourselves towards him as towards God himself. Because Christ came to be a saviour, and hath a nature so full of meekness, therefore men think to deal with him as they please. But, as God elsewhere says, Ps. xlvi. 10, ' Be still, and know that he is God.' Therefore, when God sent him before the Israelites, Exod. xxiii. 21, he bade them ' beware of him, and provoke him not ; for,' says he, ' he will not pardon your transgressions ' (that is, he will not pardon you upon any other than gospel terms and limits) : ' for my name is in him :' that is, he is God as well as I, and therefore will not suffer you to lie in such sins as cannot stand with the rules in his word, and yet pardon you. Think not to deal so with him. He will save you upon no other terms than I myself would by him. And therefore the apostle, when he had shewn how Christ was God as well as man, in the first and second chapters to the Hebrews, to the end that ' he might be a faithful high priest to God,' as well as ' a merciful high priest to men ' (ver. 17 of the second chapter), that is, such a saviour as was not so made up all of mercy to men, but that withal he is as faithful to God. From this therefore the apostle in the third chapter makes this use, and bids them ' consider what an high priest they have ' (ver. 1), who was and will be ' faithful to God that appointed him,' ver. 2. And he bids them to consider this, to this end, not to neglect the present opportunity of salvation, and think to put Christ off for the present, and come in to him when they please, in that he is so merciful a saviour. But (says he, ver. 7) consider, that as ' the Holy Ghost says, To-day, if ye will hear his voice, harden not your hearts ;' so take heed how there be in you an evil heart, to depart from him, he being ' the living God,' ver. 12. Remember how he dealt with the Israelites in the wilderness (his Father's name being in him), and how he sware against them, and said, ' They should not enter into his rest.' Read the whole chapter, and you will find this use made of it, as by the apostle elsewhere it is. So, 1 Cor. x. 4, 5, 6, I would have you, brethren, says he, ver. 1, to consider that our fathers had Christ for their captain, as we have (ver. 4), and they had him offered unto them in the ordinances ; but they tempting him, ' with many of them God was not well pleased ;' that is, Christ was not well pleased (for, ver. 9, they are said to have tempted Christ), and he, being God, ' destroyed them in the wilderness.' For in that he was God, he would not be so dealt withal by them. These things therefore are examples unto us (as he there concludes that discourse), that we may know and consider what a saviour we have to deal withal : who, as he is man (and therefore you might expect all mercy from him), so he is God also, and will be faithful unto God to save men, but this upon his Father's own conditions. And if we seek not salvation according to his own rules, he will take part with his Father against us, for his Father's name is in him. And yet,

3. Withal we may fetch this ground of encouragement against the guilt of great sins for time to come, that he is God, therefore able to pardon us. Were he mere man, though he had our nature, yet he would not endure us. So much mercy as serves to pardon us, never entered into the heart of any

mere creature : ' I am God, not man, therefore you sons of Jacob are not consumed.' But the human nature of Christ being united to the Son of God, his will in pardoning doth accompany the divine will, and goes along with it ; and as in all acts else, so in forgiving, it is able to hold pace with him.

III. A third sort of uses are taken from this, that he who is God hath took our nature, our whole frail nature, unto himself, in that humbled way mentioned.

1. Admire we the love of God towards us, which (if ever it was shewn in anything) is shewn in this ; and therefore this is made the great act of love, his ' emptying himself,' and ' becoming nothing,' as it were, that he being equal with God, ' took upon him the form of a servant.' Solomon made a wonder of it, that he whom ' the heavens of heavens cannot contain,' should vouchsafe to dwell in ' temples made with hands,' 1 Kings viii. 27. But this is nothing to his being personally united to the human nature, and to dwell bodily and personally in it, and so to be made one with the house in which he dwells, and which he himself built, that is, he to be made a creature, who made all creatures. It is to be admired that God would ever have it said that a creature was God, and that God is become a creature ; yet so it is said, John i. 18, ' The Word was made flesh.' For him to be made a creature is more than for us to become nothing, or for an angel to become a worm. It is therefore made a mystery, a great mystery, that all stand aghast at, as well angels as men (and this ὁμολογουμένως, even with one consent), that ' God should be manifest in the flesh :' 1 Tim. iii. 16, ' And, without controversy, great is the mystery of godliness : God was manifest in the flesh, justified in the Spirit, seen of angels, preached unto the Gentiles, believed on in the world, received up into glory.' And if he be made a creature, let him be made the best of creatures, an angel, there being such nobleness in them above what is in us. Their perfections are the measure of ours, and our perfection is expressed but by being like to them. Our estate in heaven is to be ὡς ἄγγελοι, ' as the angels.' Likewise the chiefest wisdom in any man is but as an angel's (as it is said of David). They for their substance are spirits, and therefore in a nearer degree of assimilation unto God, they are the fitter matches for him who is a spirit. Again, if he will assume anything of ours, let it be our souls only, for our bodies are ' vile bodies,' Philip. iii. 21. But such was his love to us, that he will take both, because he means to redeem both, and to make our bodies glorious like his own body. And how doth the apostle in this, Heb. ii. 16, set forth his love in this, that οὐ δήπου, ' at no hand he took upon him the nature of angels,' though he could have done it easily, and with more personal honour, but he would ' in no wise' entertain a thought of it. Such was his love to us, that he refused that match, his heart being fixed on us. He lets ' principalities and powers' go, and ' hath respect to the lowness of his handmaid,' Luke i. 48, the mean estate of our nature. But yet, if he take our nature, let him take it at its best, whilst in a state of innocency ; let him marry it in its prime, and (as the high priest was to do) when it is a virgin uncorrupted, unpolluted with sin or misery, or rather, let him take it such as it is now in heaven, all glorious. But he will, out of his love to us, take our nature on him when it is at the worst, and then make it glorious, and us like him. When we are traitors, and out of favour, he will marry flesh and blood out of our stock and kindred, so to bring us into favour again. Was it not unparalleled love in Jonathan then to love David, when he was in disgrace with his father ? Much more would it have

been for him, out of his love to David, as then to have married one of his children. How exceeding much more then is the love of Christ towards us?

2. For all which, as we should admire his love, so withal we should consider our privilege by having our nature so advanced. What a pawn and pledge of love is it to us, to have one of these bodies of ours made more glorious than all the angels? To whom charge is given, when he ' comes into the world,' to ' worship and adore him,' Heb. i. 6. Who is to have them, and all things else put under his feet, and is to be their Lord and judge, and they all but to be his guard. What a prerogative is it that our nature should be in him made higher in court than any queen can be in the court of any king; and thus it is, seeing he is one in person with God, not in conjugal relations only, and the rest of his brethren are advanced to be his queen, and the angels to be but his and her guard and servants. And as this is the privilege of our nature, so some of the. ancients have thought, that the revealing of God's purpose in it unto the angels before their fall was the occasion of the same, and that their casting out of heaven was a punishment of their proud stomaching of the honour done unto our nature, that it should be advanced so far above them (as the apostle speaks, Eph. i. 21). And it should teach us not to dishonour and defile this nature (which God hath so honoured) with intemperancy, uncleanness, or any base or noisome lusts. It also may encourage us to come with boldness to the court of heaven and throne of grace, for that our nature is chief in favour there. Heb. iv. 14, ' Seeing we have so great an high priest passed into the heavens, let us hold fast our profession.' And seeing he was man, ' touched with our infirmities, let us therefore come boldly unto the throne of grace, that we may find grace and mercy in time of need.' When one of a kindred is advanced and made a favourite at court, how will every one of his alliance (though never so far off) challenge kindred of him, and seek favour by him, and hope to be advanced too? And Christ is ' not ashamed' of us, his poor kindred; but being allied to us by his nature, he deigns to call us brethren, and is grieved that we come no oftener to him, with petitions of favour to be put up by him. And he not only called us brethren, when himself was with us in a poor estate here below, and lived in our houses amongst us, but likewise when he was risen again, and thereby entered into possession of his kingdom. Even then the first message that he sent, and the first words that he spake, were those in John xx. 17, ' Go to my brethren, and say unto them, I ascend unto my Father, and your Father,' &c. You see his preferment alters him not; after his resurrection he calls them brethren. We should therefore improve this our affinity and kindred with him; he took it on him for that very purpose. And,

3. In that he took upon himself such a human nature as should be every way fit for the business of mediation that he was to perform for us, let us endeavour to fit ourselves all that we can, for communion and fellowship with him. The reason why we live here absent from him so long, though contracted to him already, is, to be fitted for his bed in heaven, and for everlasting embraces. Even as Esther was a long while preparing for Ahasuerus his bed, so are we here in preparing for glory; as it is, Rom. ix. 23, ' And that he might make known the riches of his glory on the vessels of his mercy, which he had afore prepared unto glory.' The bride dresseth herself here in this life; Rev. xix. 7, ' Let us be glad and rejoice, and give honour unto him: for the marriage of the Lamb is come, and his wife hath made herself ready,' and prepares to meet her Lord, with whom she must live for ever. And look, as he took our nature, let us take his; labour we

to be changed into his image, being made partakers of the divine nature. As he took our whole nature, to save the whole of it, so let us consecrate the whole to him, and ' be sanctified throughout in body, soul, and spirit ;' as 1 Thess. v. 23, ' Cleanse we ourselves from all pollution of flesh and spirit,' soul and body, 2 Cor. vii. 1. And as he came as near in likeness to our nature (as was shewn) as possibly he could, in conception, in birth, and in everything, yet so as he might avoid sin, so should we come as near to him as is possible. Be we ' like him in all things.' In his power and prerogative indeed we cannot ; they are as incommunicable to us, as our sin was to him ; but in graces and in holiness we may, in meekness and humility we may. And as he took up our infirmities, so take we up his cross ; be we willing to be ' made conformable to him in sufferings' for him. And as his human nature subsists wholly in the second person, losing its own proper personal subsistence to be one with him, and to become a fit instrument together with him of our salvation ; so be we content to lose ourselves and our own personal proprieties, to subsist only in him and to him, and to be for ever serviceable unto his glory.

BOOK III.

The fulness of abilities which are in Christ to accomplish the work of our redemption, which are impossible to be found in any other person.

*For it is not possible that the blood of bulls and of goats should take away sins. Wherefore, when he cometh into the world, he saith, Sacrifice and offering thou wouldest not, but a body hast thou prepared me: in burnt-offerings and sacrifices for sin thou hast had no pleasure: then said I, Lo, I come (in the volume of the book it is written of me) to do thy will, O God. Above, when he said, Sacrifice, and offering, and burnt-offerings, and offering for sin thou wouldest not, neither hadst pleasure therein; which are offered by the law; then said he, Lo, I come to do thy will, O God. He taketh away the first, that he may establish the second. By the which will we are sanctified, through the offering of the body of Jesus Christ once for all.—*HEB. X. 4-10.

CHAPTER I.

The all-sufficient abilities to accomplish our redemption, demonstrated from God the Father's calling him to it, which he would never have done had not he known him able.—From God's engaging also to furnish him with abilities.—From Christ's undertaking it, which he did upon the knowledge which he had of himself, as equal to the great performance.—From the greatness and excellency of his person, who, being God-man, is able to do anything.—The reasons which induced God to fix on this way of salvation, to be by the blood of his Son.—An answer to that objection, how God is said to pardon us freely by his grace, when yet he requires full satisfaction to be made.

HAVING at large laid open that sole peculiar fitness which is in Christ for the work of reconciliation, we will now come to discover likewise that all-sufficient fulness of abilities in him for the accomplishment of this great work, in all particulars required to it. Which, *first*, in the general, your faith may be helped in the persuasion of by these demonstrations.

Demonstration 1. Because God the Father did call him to this great work. And had not Christ been fully able to bring you to heaven, without all possibility of miscarriage, God would never have pitched upon him. Man may sometimes choose one for a place of office and honour, who yet is not sufficient to discharge it, because they are mistaken in men's abilities; but God could not be mistaken, but must needs know, that Jesus Christ was able to go through without miscarrying, and therefore he pitched upon him. In Ps. lxxxix. 19, ' Then thou spakest in vision to the Holy One, and saidst, I have laid help upon one that is mighty; I have exalted one chosen out of the people.' That whole psalm is a prophecy of Christ, under the type of David, and hath in it much of the gospel, which is called ' the sure mercies of David.' The state of the people of Israel when David came to the crown (if you take the psalm of the type David) was a shattered state; Israel was a racked people, all was distracted, tottering, and broken ; Saul their king, and Jonathan his son, slain ; themselves overcome and routed by the Philistines; their religion, state, and all were desperate and staggering; but God chose David, an able governor, to restore all, and so ' laid help on one that was mighty.' In Ps. lxxv., David speaking of his coming to the government and kingdom, ' when I shall receive the congregation,' ver. 2, adds, ver. 3, ' The earth' (namely, the land of Judea), ' and all the inhabitants thereof, are out of course : I bear up the pillars of it.' Now, he therein was a type of Christ (who often in the prophets is called David); for when we were without strength, being captived by Satan, forlorn and undone, and no creature able to help us, then did God ' lay help on one that was mighty ;' that is, he laid the task of saving us upon Christ, who was able to do it. Thus also, Heb. vii. 16, ' He was made a priest, not after the law of a carnal commandment, but after the power of an endless life ;' that is, he was armed with power to execute the office of priesthood for ever, and to overcome all difficulties ; and therefore he is said to have been made after the power of an endless life, and not after the law of a carnal commandment, as other priests were. And, ver. 18, the apostle says their office was weak, and not able to bring things to perfection. Those priests were not able to satisfy God, nor to carry on the work ; but Christ had the power of an endless life, because Christ had power to lay down his life and take it up again, to survive the encounter of his Father's wrath, and then to live for ever, and intercede for us, and so to go through-stitch with the work, and without once fainting, much less succumbing or sinking under it, or failing in bringing it to its full perfection.

Demonst. 2. In that God called him, he undertook to make him able ; for besides that God knew Christ to be able, and therefore called him, it may be further said, that in calling him he undertook to make him able. Men, if they find one not able for an office to which he is called, cannot give him abilities ; but God, when he gives a call, gives likewise abilities. Thus of Christ it is said, Isa. xlii. 1, 4, 6, ' Behold my servant, whom I uphold ; mine elect, in whom my soul delighteth : I have put my Spirit upon him : he shall bring forth judgment to the Gentiles. He shall not fail nor be discouraged, till he have set judgment in the earth : and the isles shall wait for his law. I the Lord have called thee in righteousness, and will hold thine hand, and will keep thee, and give thee for a covenant of the people, for a light of the Gentiles.' ' Behold my servant, whom I uphold,' saith he; ' mine elect, whom I have called in righteousness.' That is, I have both called him to this office, and that in righteousness. I have not forced it on him, nor put him upon this hard task unwillingly. (1.) He is *my elect;* I chose him of all that ever were or shall be. (2.) I have *called* him in righteousness ; that is, he being not unwilling to undertake it, but consenting to it. And (3.) I *promised* faithfully to stand by him, and not to leave him in it. And (4.) He being *my servant* in it, therefore certainly I will uphold him through it, as it is, ver. 6. God promiseth that he will ' hold his hand,' that he sink not (even as Christ held up Peter by the hand from sinking), and will keep him so as (ver. 4), ' he shall not fail or fall short' to accomplish the work of mediation, in the least tittle ; nor shall he be discouraged, or (as it is in the original) broken (and yet he was to undergo that, which would have broken the backs of men and angels, and have pushed them all to hell), but he shall be backed with all the power that God hath, even that *he* hath who made the heavens (as it follows, ver. 5), which he mentions as engaging all that power in it.

Demonst. 3. Christ was willing to undertake it, and therefore surely he knew himself able to go through with it, for otherwise he would never have undertaken it. A wise man will not undertake an enterprise which he is not able to manage and go through with; and Christ much less, he being the Wisdom of his Father. He will not do as a foolish builder that sets upon a work which he is not able to finish. What wise man will enter into bond for another, for more than himself is worth, and so run a hazard of lying in prison all the days of his life? Surely no wise man will do this; and much less would Christ undertake to be our surety, if he had thought himself insufficient to pay; therefore certainly he knew that he was able to perfect and consummate the great work of our reconciliation before he took it upon him.

Demonst. 4. In that he is God as well as man, therefore he must needs be able for any undertaking, be it never so hazardous. If it had been possible for his Father to have forsaken him (as he complained that for a time he did), and afford him no succour, no support, but leave him to himself, nay, do his utmost against him, and make known against him the power of his wrath (as indeed he did), yet he is able alone to uphold himself, for that the ' fulness of the Godhead dwells bodily in him,' Col. ii. 9, and therefore there was an impossibility of miscarriage, as you have it, Acts ii. 24, ' It was not possible that he should have been held under the pangs of death.' If anything would have held him, it would have been death and hell; for then his power was put to it to raise himself; but it was impossible that he should be held by them, because he was God. It is one of his great names, Isa. ix. 7, that he is the mighty God: therefore he is mighty and able to save himself and others.

Now the particulars of all that salvation whereunto this all-sufficiency of his is required, are many; as (not to name all) to make your peace, pardon your sins, bring you into favour, send his Spirit into your hearts, to change them, and dwell there for ever, to subdue your enemies, defend and keep you blameless unto the great day, and then to raise you up, and glorify you for ever.

But the foundation of all these lies in that all-sufficiency that was found in Christ to satisfy for sin and to justify sinners; for by that satisfaction sin was removed, which before did separate between God and us, and was a hindrance of all blessings from descending upon us; for there cannot be so much as peace whilst sin remains; and by Christ's satisfaction sin being removed, then likewise all the blessings wherein salvation consists, and which God's free favour intended to bestow, were also purchased by him. And however that the application of all be performed by degrees, yet the purchase of all was laid in that one satisfaction of his, ere he offered to set a foot out of the grave. And therefore, Heb. x., he is said, ' by that one offering' (which was the great and last payment), ' to have for ever perfected those that are sanctified;' that is, to have done all that which was to be done for that blessed estate of perfection which he was to bring them unto. The all-sufficiency of which satisfaction is that particular subject that we are now to handle, the opening of which we reduce to these two heads:

I. More generally; That in Christ, and him alone, there was an all-sufficiency or fulness of abilities to be found, to satisfy for sin, and to justify sinners.

II. More particularly; That all the several particular parts of, and what is requisite to complete the justification of a sinner, are fully found in Christ's satisfaction: so that there is in it a fulness and perfection of parts also.

I. For the first of these, viz., That in Christ, and in him alone, there is an all-sufficiency to satisfy for sin, and to justify sinners, I will (as a ground for it) take for my text Heb. x. 4–10, ' For it is not possible that the blood of bulls and of goats should take away sins. Wherefore when he cometh into the world, he saith, Sacrifice and offering thou wouldest not, but a body hast thou prepared me: in burnt-offerings and sacrifices for sin thou hast had no pleasure. Then said I, Lo, I come (in the volume of the book it is written of me) to do thy will, O God. Above, when he said, Sacrifice, and offering, and burnt-offerings, and offering for sin thou wouldest not, neither hadst pleasure therein (which are offered by the law); then said he, Lo, I come to do thy will, O God. He taketh away the first, that he may establish the second. By the which will we are sanctified, through the offering of the body of Jesus Christ once for all.'

For the opening of this point out of these words we will proceed by degrees, first premising such observations as shall make way for the clearing of it.

Obs. 1. You see that the project that he mentioneth is the taking away of sins; and nothing had been more easy for God to have done. He might have taken away the sins by taking away the sinners, and so have made short work of it, taking them both out of the way at one stroke, by which course he might have caused sin to cease, as Ezekiel speaks, Ezek. xxiii. 48. But this is not his meaning; for his purpose is, so to take away sins as the sinners might stand still; that is, that they might stand in judgment, and be justified in his sight. There are some even among sinners whom he bears a secret good-will unto, and hath done so from everlasting; but their sins have separated between him and them, and he would fain separate their sins as far off from them, that so he might draw near to them, and communicate himself fully and freely unto them. And because sin is a burden which they can neither stand under nor throw off themselves :—' a wounded spirit who can bear?'—and further, they can never give thanks enough for his benefits received, much less satisfy for sins; therefore he resolves to have them took off, as the word ἀφαιρεῖν seems to signify.

But then again, for to take away sins only is but half the design. The 4th verse indeed mentions no more, because the ' blood of bulls' could not do so much; yet that same ' will of God,' mentioned in the 7th verse, had a further aim, not only to take away sins, that he might not hate us, but further to give us such a righteousness as for which he might have more cause to love us than ever, and loving to delight in us. His will meant not only peace or pardon to us, but grace and favour. It was as they sang, Luke ii. 14, ' Goodwill towards men,' as well as ' peace on earth.' His will is to have us adopted and graciously accepted, as well as pardoned: Eph. i. 5, 6, ' Having predestinated us unto the adoption of children by Jesus Christ to himself, according to the good pleasure of his will, to the praise of the glory of his grace, wherein he hath made us accepted in the beloved.'

But then again, thus to have taken sins off from them might have been done by a sole, free act of pardon passed from him, and he needed not to

have made any more ado about it.   I dare not say the contrary, as some
are bold to do ; for this reason sways with me, namely, to punish sin being
but an act of his will (as all his other works *ad extra* are), and not of his
nature; for what is the reason else that he sometimes suspends the punishing of wicked men, out of the riches of his forbearance ?   It is because to
punish them is but an act of his will.   If it were an act of his nature, then
whosoever sinned should die for it immediately ; but it being an act of his
will, he may suspend it, as he oftentimes doth.   And if for a while he thus
forbears, why might he not have done so for ever, and so wholly pardon ?
Surely there is no reason to the contrary.   To hate sin indeed is an act of
his nature, but to express his hatred by punishing is an act of his will, and
therefore might be wholly suspended.   And that which yet further confirms
me in it is, that Christ, when he prayed that ' the cup might pass from
him,' Mark xiv. 36, useth this argument, ' All things are possible to thee.'
The thing he entreated for was, that the cup might be taken away; and he
intimates this as the ground of his prayer, that it was possible to God,
that notwithstanding he was resolved to have the world saved, yet to have
that end of his brought about another way, though in view there is none
that we know of but this.   Now there was a truth in this, else Christ
would not have used it as an argument to this purpose.   The impossibility
lay only in God's will to have it done by Christ's satisfaction, and no
way else ; which therefore Christ submitted unto—' not my will, but thine
be done'—only nature in him, to shew its averseness to that cup as simply
in itself considered, sought a diversion.   And to shew that there was
another way, he useth this as the greatest argument, thereby the more
to set forth his and his Father's love, that he yet underwent this most
difficult one.

Obs. 2. Therefore, secondly, observe in the general, that for to take away
sins God takes means into consideration.   Why else do bulls and goats
come into consideration here ?   He means not to use his sole prerogative
in it, but to do it fairly; and though by a bare act of his will he might
have done it, yet his will working by counsel, Eph. i. 11, he thought it not
so fit to do it.   The apostle therefore speaks of blood here, and in Heb.
ix. 22, 23, he also says, that ' without blood there is no remission.'   He
will have blood for satisfaction ; and, ver. 23, the apostle makes it a
necessity that there should be sacrifices, yea, better sacrifices than the
blood of bulls and goats.   It was necessary (says he), not absolutely, but
in regard of God's resolution to satisfy justice.   And therefore the heathens
offered sacrifices to pacify their incensed gods ; this thought being innate
in every man's nature, that God must be satisfied, the reasons of which
(namely, why God required satisfaction) I shewed in that first part of the
story of the gospel* (in God's eternal transaction with Jesus Christ), only I
will now but use the ground of it which lies in the text itself.

1. Consider that the project is to take away sins (as hath been shewed);
and then for to make way for the manifestation of this it was necessary to
give a law, which might both discover what sin was, and how heinous ;
and also shew by a threatening annexed, that punishment which it naturally
deserves, and what the sinner might in justice expect from God.   This was
necessary; for otherwise, ' where there is no law there is no transgression;'
at leastwise ' sin is not imputed where there is no law,' Rom. v. 13, and
then there would have been no sins actually capable of mercy, or none to
pardon.   Now then, upon God's giving this law, he *ipso facto* takes upon
* Qu. ' Glory of the Gospel' ?   In Vol. IV. of this series of his works.—ED.

him to be a judge, and the judge of all the world; for in the very making of the law he declares himself to be so. So then he is engaged, upon many strong motives, to shew his justice against sin, in punishing it according as he had threatened (as I then shewed).

2. Consider that if he hath satisfaction it must be perfect and full ; for why else is the blood of bulls and goats here rejected, and that with an impossibility ;—' It is not possible that they should take away sins '—but because his end was to have perfect satisfaction? It is true he might have accepted of that for an acceptilation (as they call it), which should not so fully have answered his justice ; for if he might have pardoned without any satisfaction at all, then certainly he might have accepted of so much or so little. If he might wholly pardon he might then abate, and take but something. And the reason of it is the same with the former ; for it being an act of his will, he might (as Christ said) ' do what he would with his own;' he might forgive all or require all; forgive part or require but part. Though full satisfaction be not given, yet the laws of men use to give some damages, though never so little, unto the party wronged ; though not for satisfaction, yet for an acknowledgment of the injury. But God will have satisfaction to the full, or none at all. He stands upon it, and therefore it is that the apostle saith, that the blood of bulls and goats cannot possibly take away sin. If God had only required an acknowledgment of that satisfaction which a sinner was to make him, he might then have accepted of the blood of bulls and goats to satisfy his justice. But on the contrary, in Rom. iii. 26, he declares himself to have ' set forth Christ as a propitiation, that he might be just, and a justifier of him that believes in Jesus.' And if he speaks of justice in it, surely an imperfect satisfaction is not worthy to have that name put upon it. In like manner the Scripture speaks of a price paid to redeem us, which argues it to be special justice; the word *redemption* itself (which is so frequently used) doth likewise argue it ; and it differs from buying but in this, that it implies a buying anew that which was one's own before, but yet by a price; so that this justice of God came to set a price that it would have ; and if justice sets a price it will have a full one. We use to say, What I give I give, but what I sell I sell. When men indeed are frightened for lack of money, they will sell their goods at any under rate ; but God was no way necessitated ; he could have improved his glory another way, and in the mean time have lost nothing by us. Therefore if God will sell, and his justice sets the price, he then will have his full price ; he will make a wise bargain, and not see our ransom undervalued. That phrase in 1 Cor. vi. 20, ' Bought with a price,' may seem to be a tautology, and as if one should say, ' He speaks with his mouth;' for if they be bought, they must needs be bought with a price. But there is an emphasis in the phrase ; the word *price* is added to note that he hath bought them indeed, and over-bought them, and that he hath paid for them, and that a full price. Therefore, 1 Tim. ii. 6, it is called ἀντίλυτρον, that is, a ransom every way answerable and adequate. And besides these reasons intimated, add these :

(1.) All God's works are perfect in their kind, Deut. xxxii. 4. God loves not to do things by halves ; if therefore he goes about to shew his justice, he will do it perfectly or not at all.

(2.) If God should have required something that was not fully satisfactory, then the sinner relieved would have been apt to have thought and spoken of it as if it had been fully such, and would have been ready to have upbraided God therewith, as being not so much beholden unto him for cutting off part of the payment due. We see how conceited proud nature is of its own performances ; and notwithstanding that God, to convince it of its own inabilities, has set forth his Son as making so transcendent a satisfaction, yet it would needs esteem that little which it is required to do, merely as an acknowledgment of thankfulness, to be in lieu of satisfaction, and accordingly it stands upon it ; and we have much ado to break ourselves of this conceit. How much more then would we have done this if God had required no other ?

(3.) As to prevent the false conceits of our hearts, so also [for the full quiet and security of our spirits, God did ordain that there should be a full satisfaction made, that so we might have perfect peace in our spirits, as it is Isa. xxvi. 3, ' Thou wilt keep him in perfect peace, whose mind is stayed on thee ; because he trusteth in thee ;' and trust perfectly upon it, as 1 Peter i. 21. If it had been an imperfect satisfaction, the soul of man would still have been solicitous and doubting, it would still have been prying and questioning whether God would have accepted it or no, fearing it had not been full enough. Wherefore, as to take away our unthankfulness, so to prevent our infidelity, it was to be a perfect satisfaction, even such as his justice shall require no more at our hands.

Quest. But a question may here arise. How can God be said to pardon freely by his grace, when yet his justice requires a full satisfaction ?

Ans. The answer is, that both may well stand together. And therefore we have both joined together : Rom. iii. 24, 25, ' Being justified freely by his grace, through the redemption that is in Christ.' And clearly to solve this doubt, consider,

1. That it is of grace that this satisfaction is transmitted, and translated from us unto another ; which satisfaction, when it should come from another for us, God was no way bound to accept of; and yet he doth accept it freely. To illustrate which, there is this difference between satisfaction for damage in goods, and for injuries in point of honour (which is the thing wherein God accounts himself mainly wronged), that satisfaction for goods (which we call restitution) may be performed for the debtor by another person, and stand as good and valid as if himself had done it. But if it be to be made in point of honour, or that the punishment be to reach the life of the party wronging, then to commute or transmit it, it was a matter of free grace and pardon.

2. It was free grace unto us, however, because we were wholly spared. All is freely remitted to us, although he ' spared not his own Son,' as it is said, Rom. viii. 32, and especially in that this was done to this end, that he might spare us. A type of this were those two goats in the old law, whereof the one was sacrificed, and the other let go free, and was called the scape-goat. And although mercy would not have been so much shewn in accepting what was a defective and imperfect satisfaction from ourselves, as if mercy had wholly and alone supplied and made up all, yet it was shewn as much in accepting what another performed for us (though that satisfaction was never so perfect) as if it had wholly forgiven it.

3. If furthermore we consider, that it was his Son from whom this satisfaction was exacted, one so dear to him, and one who of himself was free from all such obligations, and put upon it by God, the more to shew his grace, this makes it to be mere grace ; and indeed the more grace, by how much the satisfaction was greater. And therefore God is said ' to commend his love in this, that Christ died for us,' Rom. v. 8. And Eph. i. 7, we are said ' by him to have redemption through his blood, even the forgiveness

of sins, according to the riches of his grace.' Had Christ been one nearer to us than to him, or had he been wholly a stranger to God, it might then have been esteemed to have less of grace in it ; but in that he spared not his own Son, that he might spare us, this makes grace the more to abound in it, though the satisfaction be never so perfect.

CHAPTER II.

That in Christ alone there was sufficient ability to take away sin.—The weakness and insufficiency of any creature for this work demonstrated.—That it is for the greater honour of Christ to effect that, which none could do besides him.—The insufficiency of any creature proved by an enumeration of particulars.—That the blood of all sacrifices could not have such an efficacy.—That we were unable to satisfy God by anything which we could suffer, or do.—That all the saints are as unable to help us in this case.—That it is beyond the power of angels themselves.

These observations having been sent before to make way, we come now to the main point at the first propounded, viz., That in Christ, and in him alone, there is an all-sufficiency of abilities to take away sins ; and that seeing God stood upon a full and perfect satisfaction, he alone was able to effect it. Which proposition we will branch out into two, and those both of them founded upon the text.

I. That it was not possible for any of the creatures to have made satisfaction, and to have taken sins away.

II. That in Christ's offering up himself as a sacrifice, there was an all-sufficiency to do it.

I. The creatures could not satisfy God, nor take away sin. The handling and proving of this tends so much the more to set forth and advance Christ's all-sufficiency. As therefore, in shewing his fitness, we made it appear that his office was fit for no creature, but only for himself, so now in declaring his abilities for this office, we will shew that none besides him was able to perform it. And for proof of this, we need go no further than the apparent drift and scope of this text, and of this epistle, which as it is to shew the perfection of Christ's oblation once offered, so it was withal to shew the weakness of all other offerings, even of those appointed by God himself under the old law ; and to that end, comparing them all along with this sacrifice of his Son. In which comparison you may observe,

1. That a sufficient worth and value was the thing that God stood upon, (as hath been said). So Heb. ix. 23 : ' It was therefore necessary that the patterns of things in the heavens should be purified with these ; but the heavenly things themselves with better sacrifices than these.' The apostle speaks of the worth and betterness of sacrifices, ' better sacrifices than these.' So he speaks of a sacrifice that should perfect them for whom it was offered : Heb. x. 14, ' For by one offering he hath perfected for ever them that are sanctified.' And chap. vii. 26, 27, he mentioneth abilities to save, as being required in him who was our high priest : Heb. vii. 25–27, 'Wherefore he is able also to save them to the uttermost that come unto God by him, seeing he ever liveth to make intercession for them.' Ver. 26, ' For such an high priest became us, who is holy, harmless, undefiled, separate from sinners, and made higher than the heavens ;' ver. 27, ' Who needeth not

daily, as those high priests, to offer up sacrifice, first for his own sins, and then for the people's : for this he did once, when he offered up himself.'

2. You may observe, all other sacrifices were laid aside as weak, and wanting of this worth and value. So the apostle saith, ' The law made men high priests who had infirmities :' Heb. vii. 28, ' For the law maketh men high priests which have infirmity ; but the word of the oath, which was since the law, maketh the Son, who is consecrated for evermore.' There was an infirmity and a weakness that accompanied all the sacrificers and sacrifices. And for this weakness of theirs, there was a ' disannulling of that commandment,' for the ' weakness and unprofitableness' of it, ver. 18. And Heb. ix. 9, he tells us, ' They could not make him perfect who did the service,' and also that all those sacrifices, as they could not make the offerer himself that did the service perfect, much less could they make them perfect for whom they were offered : Heb. ix. 9, ' Which was a figure for the time then present, in which were offered both gifts and sacrifices, that could not make him that did the service perfect, as pertaining to the conscience :' Heb. x. 1, ' For the law having a shadow of good things to come, and not the very image of the things, can never with those sacrifices, which they offered year by year continually, make the comers thereunto perfect.' All which argues, that God would have such a satisfaction as should make men perfect, that is, should be fully able to satisfy his justice, and their consciences. And therefore also here in the text God is brought in, consulting about, or considering and weighing all other sacrifices ; and when he had found them all too light, the text says, he laid them all aside, and pitched upon, and established this of Christ. And therefore you see this proffer of Christ, ' Lo, I come,' comes in after God's refusal of all others as ineffectual ; ' then said I, Lo, I come :' Heb. x. 5–7 ' Wherefore, when he cometh into the world, he saith, Sacrifice and offering thou wouldest not, but a body hast thou prepared me :' ver. 6, ' In burnt-offerings and sacrifices for sin thou hast had no pleasure :' ver. 7, ' Then said I, Lo, I come (in the volume of the book it is written of me) to do thy will, O God.' Thus Gal. iii. 21, ' If there had been a law that could have given life, righteousness had been by the law.' The apostle speaks as if God would have taken that, or any other course, if it could have been sufficient. And Gal. ii. 21, ' Do I frustrate the grace of God ?' says he, ' If righteousness be by the law, then Christ died in vain.' What he says of the law may be said of all means else, if any other could be supposed. The same reason that is there given against the law (namely, that the grace in Christ's dying and justifying us, would be frustrated) holdeth as well, to exclude the supposed possibility of any other means to make us righteous. For by that reason it appears, that God's aim and end in Christ's dying was to advance the glory of his grace, which consists in having the monarchy and sole prerogative in saving sinners attributed unto it ; the height of whose honour and eminency is this, that it alone reigns, and hath nor could have any competitor therein. And therefore if there could be supposed to be any other means, Christ's death would then lose something of its peculiar glory ; which if it should, he would account himself to have died in vain ; for the glory of his aim had been defaced and frustrated, and his end in his account as good as lost. As it is the excellency of God, that he is God alone, and there is none besides him, so of Christ, that he alone is our saviour, and that there is none besides him. But take this as still spoken in opposition to all creatures only ; for otherwise that former supposition, that God could have pardoned us by a mere act of grace without Christ's satisfaction, doth

not detract from this glory of Christ's death, which is not to take away from free grace, and to be accounted in comparison of it, the principal and only saviour. Christ is content that the free grace of his Father should share with him in it, and himself to be in this work God's servant. But this competition of Christ is with all other means by creatures; the excluding the possibility of which to perform our redemption, makes Christ sole heir to this kingdom and monarchy of grace, which is destructive of the dominion of sin, and so endears his death to us : ' He hath a priesthood that passeth not away,' Heb. vii. 24, as the high priest did by reason of death. But he dies not; and his office is such, as if he should lay it down, there is not any creature in heaven or earth that could take 'it up. The fullest trial and manifestation of this is made in a case of less difficulty (which evidently reacheth this of satisfaction), in the fifth chapter of, the Revelation, where, as a prologue to that ensuing prophecy (which begins chap. vi.), there is a solemn proclamation made by a strong angel, who ' spake with a loud voice,' ver. 2 (as that which might come to the hearing of all creatures) : and the matter of this proclamation was this challenge, ' Who is worthy to open the book' (namely of the Revelation, which was sealed in the hand of God, that sat upon the throne, ver. 1), ' and to loose the seals thereof?   And there was none' (so it is in the original, that is, no reasonable creatnre ; we read ' no man,' but that is too much limited), man or angel, ' in heaven, or in earth, or under the earth, that was able to open the book, or so much as to look thereon.'   And John was at this discouraged, and ' wept much,' ver. 4, as thinking, here must be an end of all, and that he should have no further vision. But God did premise this on purpose to shew the difficulty of the work, and to spoil all creatures of the glory of it, and the more to set off and make illustrious the sole power and worth that was in Jesus Christ for this work ; even as men in their fictions use to do, when they would greaten some one man, whose story they write.   For after this nonplus and dejection, a stander-by comforts him, and bids him ' not weep : for lo, the Lion of the tribe of Judah hath obtained to open the book,' &c. And presently a lamb comes, approacheth the throne, and takes the book out of his right hand, ver. 6, 7.   And upon that all the chorus of twenty-four elders and four beasts (who are there the church representative of saints on earth), do fall down before the lamb, and set this crown of glory upon his head alone, with this new song and shout, ' Worthy art thou,' &c., and thou alone ; unto which the angels give a respond of praise, ver. 11, 12, and heaven, and earth, and all creatures, echo to it, ver. 13. Now how much more might all this solemnity have been used about satisfaction to be made for sin ? To approach the throne, and take the book, and open it, was far less than to have the heart to break through an army, and approach God in his fury and fulness of wrath for sin, and to sustain that wrath, and satisfy it by overcoming it.   And this is more than intimated in that very chapter ; for (ver. 9) the elders in their song do attribute this power of Christ to open the book, unto the merit of a far greater work done, even this of our redemption, and Christ's satisfaction for sin : ' Thou art worthy,' say they, ' to take the book, because thou wast killed, and hast redeemed us to God by thy blood.'   And how far off then will all creatures be found to be, and how short of worth and power to redeem a sinner by their blood, who were all not worthy so much as to look on that book, much less to open it, not worthy to reveal this redemption, much less to effect it ? Than which there cannot be a stronger proof for this my assertion. Thus much in general. Now secondly,

II. To demonstrate this by an induction and an enumeration of all particular means, which may be any way supposed able to help us.

1. First, Take the blood of bulls and goats, and add to them all the creatures which man is lord of, and which are his to give ; yet this whole world of creatures would not be a sufficient sacrifice for sin. In Micah vi. 7, there is one comes off with a good round price, 'Will the Lord be pleased with thousands of rams, or with thousands of rivers of oil ? or shall I give my first-born for my transgression ?' And nature is apt to be thinking of such sacrifices. But if justice could have afforded it so cheap, God would not have turned away so fair a chapman ; yet he there turns him away. One reason for which is there intimated, namely, that sin is the sin of the soul, but all these are but the appurtenances of, or at the highest, but fruits of the body : ' Shall I give the fruit of my body for the sin of my soul ?' The soul, which is lost and forfeited by sin, is (as Christ says) more worth than a whole world, Mat. xvi. 26. Yea, the life of the body is more worth in a man's own estimation than all that he possesseth ; ' All that a man hath will he give for his life,' Job ii. 4 ; but the ' redemption of the soul is ' yet much more ' precious,' as the psalmist speaks, Ps. xlix. 8. And as a king's ransom is more than another man's, so is the redemption of the soul, which in worth exceeds all creatures, more than of all other creatures besides. And yet further, the sin of the soul cannot be recompensed by the loss and sacrifice of the soul itself ; for by sin the glory of God suffers detriment, but by a soul's loss the good of a creature only is damaged. It is a rule current in cases of morality and justice, that the injury of a supreme order is not made good by things of an inferior rank unto it. What recompence will the forfeiture of a murderer's goods give to a man for his life, or for that of his friends ? What satisfaction can money give for a dishonour cast upon a man's good name, which Solomon says is ' better than riches' ? Prov. xxii. 1. So what is the fruit of a man's body (as it is in Micah vi. 7) to the sin of his soul ? Verily there is no proportion. Yea, it falls short in the estimation of a man's own conscience.

Unto this disproportion the apostle adds another, Heb. ix. 23, that the blessings to be purchased and obtained by this satisfaction are heavenly ; but all such sacrifices as these are but things earthly ; and therefore better sacrifices than these are required. All such external sacrifices are but enough (if enough) to sanctify the ' pattern of heavenly things ;' that is, the types of the law ; and this too, but only as they were ' shadows of things to come.' Wherefore ' it was necessary that the heavenly things themselves' (the substance) ' should be purified with better sacrifices than these.' Now grace is heavenly, and pardon of sin must come from heaven, even out of God's bosom ; and will God (think we) exchange heavenly commodities for earthly treasures ?

Again, the apostle adds a third disproportion unto these, Heb. ix. 14, all such sacrifices cannot reach to the conscience. We have consciences to be purged, and what are such outward things to purge a man's conscience ? As plasters outwardly applied cannot reach to benefit the heart or lungs ; so neither can these reach the conscience. They might sanctify the outward man (as he there speaks), to purge away a ceremonial outward uncleanness, but not the inward, Jer. ii. 22, ' Though thou wash thee with nitre, thy iniquity is open before me,' says the Lord. All these could not satisfy a man's conscience, much less God's justice. Therefore those that were exercised in sacrifices, their consciences were unquiet, as both the Jews' and heathens' were.

2. As for ourselves, there was no hope that ever we should satisfy God by aught that either we can do or suffer.

(1.) Not by suffering anything. And for this, take the highest instance. If there were any hope to satisfy by sufferings, it would be by the sufferings of men in hell, because they are the utmost and the most extreme punishment that are threatened as the reward of sin, and whereby God recovers all that may be had out of the creature. A man would think that after millions of years expired, the torments which men there suffer should satisfy for sin; but they do not. Those eternal flames in which their souls are scorched do nothing purify or diminish the stain of one sin: they may indeed destroy the sinner, but they can never take away the sin; for therefore it is that they shall for ever suffer. He must for ever remain to be punished, because for ever he remains a sinner. And it is also a certain and sure rule, that *nulla pœna nocentis est peccati deletiva;* no punishment of a person nocent is deletive of sin. The sin can never be taken away or blotted out by it.

(2.) Nor by doing; for,

First; We are not able by all our works to satisfy our own consciences, which still prick us in the midst of them; much less can we satisfy God, who is greater than our consciences. In Rom. v. 6, the apostle gives us all up for desperate and past recovery; 'When we were without strength,' says he, 'Christ died for us.' We had no strength left us wherewith to do anything; neither could all the strength that the law could put into us, by quickening and exciting our consciences to do good works, anything avail us. So, Rom. viii. 3, the apostle tells us, that 'what the law could not do, for that it was weak through the flesh,' that Christ came to do. If anything had been done by us, it must have been by the help of the law in our consciences, directing, inciting, and carrying us on to obedience. But, saith he, our corruption still weakeneth the power of the law, that it cannot do any good upon us, in us, or by us. As when nature is spent, physic is said to do no good through the weakness of the patient, so nor the law through the weakness of the flesh. And therefore it follows, there being no help in ourselves, 'God sent his Son in the similitude of sinful flesh, and condemned sin in the flesh.' Neither,

Secondly; Are we thus weak only, but also ungodly; and so are all our works. There is not only a weakness in all that the flesh can do, but also a wickedness or enmity; so that 'they who are in the flesh can never please God;' as Rom. viii. 8. Yea, it is impossible they should, for their works are all defiled; and though they were good, yet,

Thirdly; They could not bring our persons into favour. For sin, breaking the first covenant, by the tenor of which our works did keep our persons in favour; hence we have forfeited all honour to our persons for ever, and so unto all our works also, that look, as traitors when their persons are condemned, all their works are void in law, so are ours. So that if we could suppose ourselves to love God, yet *dilectio illa nos quidem faceret dilectores, sed non dilectos;* though thereby we might be called lovers of God, yet they could not make us beloved of him again.

Fourthly; As we have forfeited all favour to our persons for ever, so we have forfeited too the having any graces, or gifts of grace, whereby we might be supposed to come into favour. For sin hath put in a bar against us, this being the eternal demerit of it, that the former grace be never more bestowed upon any of that former interest; for it is wholly made void unto all ends and purposes. And therefore, ere ever new grace be bestowed, the guilt, and forfeiture, and desert of sin must be forgiven ; and how can we ever come to obtain that for ourselves ?

Fifthly ; If that demerit be cut off by free pardon, and grace be anew bestowed, then that grace becomes a new favour, for which alone we can never be thankful enough by the power of all the grace we receive. We run into a new debt, which we can never requite or satisfy for, much less by that can we pay our former debts. Therefore,

Lastly ; Grace received anew, though in and through Christ, it may indeed come to please God, as a token of our thankfulness (and so it doth), yet can it never so much as justify us. The graces of godly men made perfect in heaven shall (it may be) be as much and more than that of the angels. Now then, suppose it such in this life, yet all that grace would not justify us, because we once forfeited all of it, and the receiving of it now were a new mercy. The grace of them who are in heaven may indeed please God, but it cannot justify them, and therefore much less could it ever come to satisfy God for sin. And besides, *debitum peccati est infinitum,* the debt and guilt of sin is infinite, because against an infinite God. Graces would be but finite, because in us, and because ours, who are finite creatures, as our graces also are. So then, you see, ourselves could not make God any satisfaction.

3. If you go to all the saints, they are unable to help you ; Mat. xxv. 1, 2, 8, 9, ' Then shall the kingdom of heaven be likened unto ten virgins, which took their lamps, and went forth to meet the bridegroom :' ver. 2, ' And five of them were wise, and five were foolish :' ver. 8, ' And the foolish said unto the wise, Give us of your oil, for our lamps are gone out :' ver. 9,' ' But the wise answered, saying, Not so, lest there be not enough for us and you ; but go you rather to them that sell, and buy for yourselves.' The foolish virgins go to the wise, and say, ' Give us some of your oil,' that is, of your grace. They would have had some of the others' graces to help them, but the wise virgins answered, ' No, lest there be not enough for us and you ; but go you rather and buy of them that sell.' The saints then (you see) have grace little enough for themselves ; all the grace they in heaven have is little enough to save them, and all the grace they have is borrowed, and cannot justify themselves, much less therefore can it satisfy for another. The papists, who so much extol works, though they say, indeed, that good works do merit for the saints themselves, yet not that they can satisfy for another.

4. Go from them to the angels. If they were a grain lighter, they would be found too light, and their kingdom would depart from them, and themselves would be stripped of all their happiness. They need confirmation in their estates themselves ; it is well that they keep their own standing, and their heels from being tripped up. All they can do in obedience to the law, they owe it ; and how can one debt be paid with another ? God says of them, Job iv. 18, ' that he finds folly in them.' If God's curious eye inquire and search into them, they will be found defective of that holiness which he desires, though they be the works of his hands, and though they have such a holiness as is the perfection of their natures ; and (so far as such creatures can be), they be perfectly righteous. But yet if they be compared to that holiness wherewith God is delighted, and that which the curious eye of his purity would require, he finds a folly in them. And therefore they need not only a mediation of union to confirm them in grace, but further, for this end, that God may be pleased with them and their works ; he being so curious, that but for a mediator (whose holiness wholly

satisfies his exact eye), he would be pleased with no works of his own hands whatever, but would rend, and tear, and throw all away, as not yet worthy enough of him, even as curious artists do their best draughts, as not satisfied with them. Yea, if the angels were but one grain wanting, scruple not to say, they would be cast down, yea, fall down, and become devils. And therefore how can all that they can do be able to help you, seeing they have little enough for themselves?

So you see, upon a survey of all particulars, that no creature could make satisfaction to God for sin.

CHAPTER III.

That the most perfect creature, though having all the perfections of Christ's human nature, yet could not be our redeemer.—The utmost extent to which the power of any creature can reach, to save himself or others, which yet all fall short of that which was to be performed for our redemption.

Add to all these the utmost supposition that can be made, of the most transcendent perfection of grace that may possibly be bestowed upon any mere creature. Take the supposition which some of the schoolmen have made, that as God appointed Adam, a mere creature, to convey and derive grace to all his posterity, so if we with them suppose, *first*, some one mere creature as a head, appointed to satisfy for sin, and convey grace to sinners (as Christ doth); and, *secondly*, suppose this mere creature filled with as much grace habitual as Christ had, as much love, humility, &c., only that grace of union to a divine person set aside, which so transcendently elevates all in him above created perfections, and then such a supposition cannot be denied. *Thirdly*, Suppose a transcending degree of favour and glory appointed as the reward of that grace, more than is borne towards all other creatures; yet though this creature should lay down all that glory, quit itself of all that happiness, and subject itself to all those torments which Christ's soul underwent for us, to the end that our punishment might be cut off, and we brought unto favour, all this could no way deal with justice to satisfy for sinners, and restore them to favour. Which now we will endeavour to make good from those more near and intimate demonstrations, which hold forth in them the true grounds why no mere creature can satisfy for sin, upon no supposition, how high soever. By all which the superabundant grace and glory of Christ will the more appear, whose cause herein we plead, and who pleadeth ours in heaven.

And, *first*, to make the clearer entrance, and the better explication and stating of this point, let us consider and examine how far the graces of a mere creature, how great soever, have gone, or can go, to advantage and promote either the owner of them, or another, in the way of salvation; and so see the utmost extent of their abilities, and where they have and must fall short. Which will likewise afford us evident demonstrations how far short they come of satisfaction for sin, or justifying of a sinner.

I. Let us see what they can do for the owner and possessor of them.

1. They can and do justify the possessor of them, if he have never sinned. Thus the grace and works of the angels do justify them before God; which yet is much for God to accept of, for he 'seeth folly in his angels;' yet this privilege he vouchsafes to their own grace. And thus to be justified, is

no more than to be accounted righteous before God's tribunal, and so worthy
to live in his sight, and by means of it to enjoy their present condition
of happiness. And thus Adam's grace in innocency did justify him : God
by his law and ordination pronouncing him righteous by it (whilst he continued in it), as wanting nothing which his law required in him for happiness
and life. And though grace in Adam and in the angels did, by a natural
law and just ordination of God, justify them before him, so as, God looking on their works, did pronounce them righteous in his sight, according
to his law, yet this law or ordinance was founded upon no other obligation from God than the ordinances and laws of providence towards other
creatures, even such as the ordinances of day and night (as he speaks of
them); and so it was but such as when God saw all the creatures which
he had made keep the ordinances which he had set them in, he pronounced
that they were all good, namely, in their kind, Gen. i. 31, they continuing
(as the psalmist says, Ps. cxix. 91) according to their ordinances. So
whilst man continues in the ordinances which God hath set him in, he
pronounceth him good in his kind, that is, righteous ; righteousnsss being
his proper goodness, and such to him, as the proper goodness of all creatures are in their kind unto them. And as this righteousness was due to
him, and so created in him, not by merit, but as the native perfection
without which he could not be a man, so was this pronouncing of him
righteous (and to be in God's favour whilst he continued in that goodness)
not due of merit (for what can we do towards it ?), but only as a due approbation and suitable reward and consequence of his goodness, meet for God
to bestow, according to that special law of nature which God had created
him in. And so I understand that same *ex debito*, Rom. iv. 4, where the
apostle, speaking of the covenant of works (which was the covenant of
nature), he says, ' the reward was of debt, not of grace ; ' that is, there was
a reward that was a natural due to it (which is opposed to mere grace),
which notwithstanding is not of merit, nor could that deserve it at God's
hands ; only it was meet and due, in a natural way, that God should so reward it.

2. The grace of such a mere creature can preserve itself, and increase itself. Therefore Christ compares it unto mustard-seed, the least of all seeds,
which yet grows up to be a great tree ; and so the stock that Adam had he
might have kept, by the power that God had given him. As Adam might
have maintained his bodily life unto eternity by food, so his spiritual life
by keeping the law—' do this and live.' So that grace in a pure creature
before the fall might possibly have kept its station. Yet,

3. It could not, nor cannot absolutely confirm and establish such a creature in a state of justification, which is a further thing than simply to justify, as to give perseverance in grace is more than to give grace. Thus
the angels, though always they be justified by their own grace, yet no acts
of their own did, or could, procure a confirmation in that grace, or strength
and security that they should not, nor could not, fall. It is an incommunicable property of Jehovah not to change, and to have no ' shadow of turning,' James i. 17. It is therefore judged by all divines that this benefit
they have by Christ.

4. Much less can the grace of a mere creature (or ever could) merit a
higher condition ; to do which is more than to confirm the continuance of
the present condition. Adam could not earn a condition of a higher rank,
nor by all his works have bought any greater preferment than what he was
created in. To compass it was *ultra suam sphæram*, above his sphere; he

could never have done it. As, for instance, he could not have attained that state in heaven which the angels enjoy. What says Christ? 'When you have done all you can, say, You are unprofitable servants,' Luke xvii. 10. This he could no more do than other creatures by keeping those their ordinances can merit to be 'translated into the glorious liberty' which they wait for, and shall have at the latter day. The moon, though she keep all her motions set her by God never so regularly, yet she cannot thereby attain to the light of the sun as a new reward thereof. And thus no more can any pure creature of itself, by all its righteousness, obtain in justice a higher condition to itself. And therefore the angels, by all their own grace, have not to this day earned a better condition than they were created in. And yet all this falls short of satisfying for sin, as we shall see anon.

II. We have taken a view of all that which all the grace of a mere creature can do for the owner of it; let us now, secondly, see what it can do for another. And,

First, We may safely say, it can avail less for another than for the person himself. For what it doth for another it doth by virtue of what it first doth for itself. If it brings another into favour, it must needs be much more beloved itself.

Secondly, We grant that it might have been a means of conveying righteousness, through God's goodness and appointment of it, unto another. For so Adam's grace should have done to all his posterity. For as he falling we now inherit his sin, so if he had stood we by the same law should have had his righteousness conveyed unto us ; and so much indeed may the grace of a creature that never fell do for another. But then take in these cautions with it.

1. That other must be one who also never fell, it could not do thus for those that were once sinners, though it might convey righteousness to another that never sinned.

2. Though a creature that never sinned might have a stock of righteousness conveyed from another (as we should have had from Adam), yet that creature must still continue to be justified by its own righteousness, besides by what was conveyed from that other (even as well as the conveyer himself was by his own righteousness to have lived), and so might notwithstanding have fallen away. For Adam's righteousness, and the imputation of it, would not alone have been sufficient to justify us eternally ; but our justification must have been continued by our own righteousness. For as although we have Adam's sin conveyed to us, yet we are condemned for our own sins besides, and not only for his ; so Adam's righteousness being conveyed to us, we must afterwards have had, and must have continued to work, a righteousness of our own. He was only a means to give us a stock wherewith to begin, all which we might have spent, and it was likely we should.

So that, in the last place, to draw up all, by a comparison from the less to the greater, it will appear how far short the power of grace in mere creatures doth come of satisfying for another's sin. You see how little it can do for itself; and it must needs be able to do less for another than for itself, and less for a sinner than for either. It may justify itself, and the possessor of it may actually live by it, but not so another. For though that other may have righteousness conveyed to him at first, yet he must ever after live upon his own. The creatures' grace cannot confirm itself in a perpetual state of justification for time to come, much less merit a better condition. But to satisfy for sin is beyond all these; it is as much as to merit a better condition, and more.

(1.) It is as much, for satisfaction hath to do with justice as well as merit; for to merit is to do that which justice itself shall count truly worthy of such a reward. And so to satisfy is at least to offer that for a satisfaction, which justice itself offended cannot but think worthy to be accepted in recompence. The one undertakes to deserve of justice rewarding, the other to pacify and fully content justice offended. And,

(2.) It is more; and therefore the papists themselves, who say that a man's own grace may merit for himself, yet deny it to be able to satisfy for another's sin. And reason is for it; for,

First; In meriting a better condition, a man earns but of another's goods, and undertakes to do something worthy of a better reward; and there is in it but *comparatio rei ad rem.* But in satisfying for injuries, he undertakes to repair personal wrongs; which it is so much harder to repair, as men love their own persons more than their goods. A poor man may earn some of a nobleman's goods by a day's work; but can never satisfy him for a disgrace.

Secondly; To satisfy for sin is more than to do something worthy of a higher and better condition; because there is a greater distance between a sinner's estate, and justification to be attained, than is between the estate of one already justified, and a higher condition of favour; such as was between the estate of Adam and that of an angel. There was not such a gulf (as Christ says) or distance between Adam's earthly state and theirs, as is between an offender and the favour of God; which by his offence is wholly forfeited. He when innocent was much nearer the most glorious condition which any creature was capable of. Even as a good subject, though never so poor and mean, who yet never offended, is nearer the dignity of a duke, and more capable of it, than one who is a traitor, and so hath forfeited not only his honour, but his life and the privilege of a subject.

CHAPTER IV.

The inability of the creature to redeem us, demonstrated from the nature of the satisfaction.—First, That which the law required, a creature could not answer for us, neither in obeying the precept, nor suffering the penalty.

This premised, we will now more distinctly consider whereunto satisfaction must be made, wherein it must consist, and according to what it is to be proportioned.

There are two to be satisfied before ever a sinner can be justified, viz., God and the law. For as the evil of sin is expressed by its enmity unto both these (as Rom. viii. 7, where the flesh is said to be 'enmity against God and his law'), so answerably may the satisfaction that is to be made for it be measured out by both. I confess that both come to one; for satisfy the law, and you satisfy God, and so *e contra:* yet we may take the distinct consideration of each as a help in the search, and for the finding out wherein true satisfaction for sin is to consist.

First; For the law. No mere creature could satisfy that for us, or make compensation for sin, as it is the transgression of it.

1. In general; let us measure satisfaction by the worth of the law, and of every iota of it, which sin doth what in it lies to make void and of none

effect.   In Ps. cxix. 126, ' They have willingly,' says David, ' destroyed thy
law :' that is, what they did tended to destroy it; though yet it doth it
not : for not one iota of it shall pass.   Now seeing satisfaction is *redditio*
æquivalentis pro æquivalenti; that which is given in way of restitution must
be of an equivalent worth to that which is endamaged; what therefore can
any mere creature have to render to God, equivalent to this his law ?   For
is not the least tittle of the law worth heaven and earth, and so all in it,
even saints and all, because God's prerogative lies at stake in it ?   Is it
not the *regula*, the pattern, yea, the original copy of all the grace which the
saints have ?   For all grace is but the copy of the law.   And doth it not
command all that is in them ?   What have they then to be deprived of that
is worth it ?

2. Let us more particularly consider those special debts which the law
requires satisfaction in and for ; which, according to the two main parts of
the law, are answerably two.   As all laws, so this, hath,

First, A preceptive part, ' Do this and live ;' and this requires exact
obedience to every tittle of it.

Secondly, A penal part.   If we trespass in the least, it exacts a punishment ; and that is, eternal death.

Now therefore when we transgress in the least, we hence first grow into
a double debt, and become debtors to both parts of the law ; and the reason
hereof is, because all laws require both.   So the laws of men do ofttimes
require not only restitution and satisfaction to be made to the party wronged ;
but they enjoin a further punishment as a satisfaction to the law itself,
which was contemned and broken.   And therefore in many cases, though
no hurt be done, the trespasser failing of his purpose, yet the law takes
notice of the attempt, and punisheth him for it ; because therein the law
is contemned.   For in such trespasses against men there is a double wrong :
the one to the party injured, whose goods or honour is impaired ; and the
other to the law, which is scandalised by it.   And so he is not only to
satisfy for the personal damage, but also for the public offence, and the
vitiosity of the act in breaking order ; and so a double satisfaction is to be
made.   Thus also it is in debts : for there is both the principal, and the
forfeiture also.   So likewise in the Levitical law, when a man had wronged
his neighbour in goods, he was to do two things ; not only to make restitution due to the party wronged, and that double at least, as part of a punishment also, but he was to satisfy the law besides, and to offer sacrifice.   And
in case of debt, before instanced, until a man hath paid it, he is to lie in
prison, to satisfy the law.

(2.) We having sinned, do owe satisfaction to God in respect of his law ;
and that in a double relation and respect : first, on our parts ; secondly,
on God's part.

First, On our own.   As we are creatures, we owe him service ; and as
we are sinners, we owe punishment.

And Secondly, On God's part.   We owe satisfaction to him, both as he
is our lord, our creator, and owner, that hath right to us ; and also as he
is our lawgiver.

[1.] As he is our lord he hath a right to us, and as a creditor he gave
us ourselves and graces : and we are his goods, and so do owe him active
obedience.

[2.] As he is our lawgiver, so he hath the right of a judge, to whom for
our neglect we do therefore owe punishment.   For God hath over us both
jus crediti or *dominii*, and *jus rectoris;* he is lord of his law, and lord of

us; and we are his subjects, and also his servants; and there is in equity very good grounds for both debts. For we owe him subjection for his benefits bestowed, although there were no law : but then in regard of his ὑπεροχή, his transcendent excellency, he is our lawgiver and judge ; and so he might give us these laws, though it could be supposed that we had no such benefit from him.

Obj. And [3.] Whereas it may be said that the bearing the punishment due to the offence against the law, may seem to stand for that debt of obedience to the law ;—

Ans. The answer is, that it is clean otherwise; for we owe both punishment for sin past, and obedience also. And the reason is evident, namely, in that punishment for sin is but an appendix to the law, and not that which the law chiefly intends ; for it principally aims at obedience, and does therefore indeed threaten punishment to keep the creature to obedience ; and therefore to endure the punishment is no satisfaction to the law. As though a debtor should live in prison all his lifetime, yet he should be in debt still ; and therefore could not be said to satisfy the law, because the principal intent of the law is to recover a man's goods. So that we are for ever bound to God by a double debt, a *debitum pœnæ*, a debt of punishment, and a *debitum negligentiæ*, a debt of neglect ; both which are to be satisfied for.

Now for neither of both these debts can either we ourselves, or any creature for us, ever satisfy God.

(1.) Not we ourselves ; for we can never discharge the debt of active obedience, though God should exact no more ; for part of it is neglected already ; and you may as well call back time that is past, as satisfy for what is past, because we are bound to God for our whole time, even to eternity. If an apprentice were bound to his master for ever, and he run away at any time, he can never satisfy his master for his time lost. If he were bound indeed but for seven years, then he might afterwards serve out his time, though he ran away for a while.

(2.) Nor can any mere creature be ever able to give satisfaction in our stead, upon the same grounds. It is true indeed, that a mere creature might perform and undergo this and all other kind of obedience that the law requires, both active and passive ; but not so, as that both, or either of these obediences so performed by it, should be satisfactory to the law for us, or stand us in stead. We will prove this, of each severally, and of both jointly. And first of either of them singly.

[1.] The active obedience performed by any mere creature for us could not discharge or satisfy that debt of active obedience which we owe to God, so as we should have any benefit by it. Such a creature may indeed perform it, so as to profit himself (as Job speaks, Job xxxv. 8), but not so as to profit us and himself by way of satisfaction. The reasons of which are,

First, Because his whole self, and all he can do, is in all respects wholly and altogether subject to the law already for himself, and he can plead no privilege of exemption whereby he should be any way free from this total subjection to the law. And therefore the law commanding him, and all the relations and respects that are in him, all that he can do is little enough for himself to satisfy the law. This is the reason which the saints themselves give to put others off with (for I would not give you school reasons herein, but scripture reasons) : Mat. xxv. 8, 9, the wise virgins said to the foolish, when they came to them for oil, ' We have little enough for ourselves.' All the money which any creature can make, will but serve to satisfy what the law requires for himself, and he hath nothing over and above what the law can challenge, to benefit another. ' Do this, and live,' says the law to all that are ' under the law,' and altogether under it. And it is as much as they can do to live by the law themselves. They have little enough for themselves, and nothing over. And this reason holds as fully in the best creature that can be supposed to have never so much grace (set that of hypostatical union aside, which is Christ's sole prerogative), as it doth in that creature that hath never so little. For all the grace that any creature hath, be it of never so large a revenue, he holds by the same tenure, namely, the tenure of the law, that one of never so low a degree of grace doth hold his by. And the law doth as fully exact all he can do, as being his own debt, as it doth the other's. Even as a man that hath never so much land, if his tenure from the lord in chief be the same by the law with that of another man who possesseth but a cottage ; and the conditions of both are to pay the whole revenue (their own mere and bare subsistence set aside), the former is as much disenabled to pay another's rent as the latter, though he hath never so great revenues. In this case he that hath the least hath no lack ; for God accepts what a man hath, and he that hath never so much hath nothing over. There is an equality or proportion, as the apostle speaks in another case.

If we consider the ground of the law's thus requiring the whole, it will afford a further reason. The ground why the law requires this, lies in two things :

1. That whatever the creature hath, it hath received it from God : And,

2. So received it, and upon such terms as to give an account of it. So as after it is given, God still challengeth a right in it, as being wholly his. Hence all that a mere creature hath, or can have, it owes to God.

1. Because it hath it wholly from God ; and therefore God challengeth all again, and obligeth the creature as a debtor to him for the benefit received. And then withal there cannot any respect of propriety be found, which a mere creature can challenge, in what it hath received, as having a title to it, distinct from that which God claims to himself; but all is wholly and alone his. And therefore the creature can never lay out anything for another, which it can call its own stock, and say, This is mine to dispose of, and I have enough besides to account with God for myself another way ; for ' what hast thou,' says the apostle, ' which thou hast not received ?' 1 Cor. iv. 7.

And, 2dly, it receives all from God so as to give an account, as a mere steward unto him. So the apostle Peter speaks, ' A steward of the manifold grace of God,' 1 Peter iv. 10, and so accountable to him for all. Now it is as impossible for a mere creature to satisfy God for another's debt, or he is as unable to do it, as the steward can undertake to pay his master for his fellow-servant's debt, out of the money his master hath betrusted him with. For what can be in this case given is the master's own already, and in having all resumed, the master hath no more than what he should have ; this being a certain rule and principle in equity, that it is impossible to satisfy another man with what is wholly his own already. And upon this ground doth the Lord refuse sacrifices for sin, even because they are all his already ; ' All the beasts of the forest are mine :' Ps. l. 8–11, ' I will not reprove thee for thy sacrifices, or thy burnt-offerings, to have been continually before me ; ' ver. 9, ' I will take no bullock out of thy house, nor he-goats out of thy folds :' ver. 10, ' for every beast of the forest is mine, and the cattle upon a thousand hills.' Ver. 11, ' I know all the fowls of the mountains; and the wild beasts of the field are mine.' Therefore David, 1 Chron. xxix. 14, acknowledgeth it mercy enough that God would but accept of their offerings for themselves : ' What are we that we should offer thus freely even for ourselves ?' He considers both God's transcendent excellency in himself, and that total dependence which they had on him for all; as it follows, ' Of thine own have I given thee,' and how can that satisfy the debt ? Sin indeed is our own, which we owe for; but obedience, that is not our own, but comes from the grace of God, and from his enabling. Indeed, if God had given us grace, as friends give gifts each to other, to do what they please with them, without requiring any account of them, then we might have payed him with that which he hath given us. But he gives grace to us as he does talents unto servants. And therefore he requires answerable service and improvement of those talents, of which he takes account according to the number given; and if they be not well used, he takes them away. ' And when we have done whatever we can, we are unprofitable servants too,' Mat. xxv. 14 to 30. And it is impossible for one who is wholly a servant, to satisfy his master for the debt of another. *Inter servum et dominum nulla intercurrit justitia*, says Aristotle, speaking of mere servants as in those times, because such a servant is *pars domini*, part of his master's goods. And herein let the supposition made hold good, as, let the creature have never so much grace, so much the more is he disenabled to satisfy for another; for the more grace he hath received, the more service is required from him; ' Much is required from him to whom much is given,' Luke xii. 48. Yea, the obligation upon himself is the greater, and binds him to do so much the more; and therefore he can as little, yea less, spare anything for another, as he that hath less.

In the second place, for passive obedience, that cannot be satisfactory for another. For,

1. Even so much passive obedience as any creature can undergo, is in itself in strict terms of justice due unto God from the creature, though not as a punishment, yet as a trial of obedience, if he should be pleased to lay it upon the creature. How else could Paul wish himself ' accursed from Christ for his kinsmen and brethren' the Jews ? Rom. ix. 3; and this as a duty surely. For he did not supererogate therein, nor do more than God might require. It was no more than what was due unto him.

2dly. Both of these obediences must be jointly performed by him that undertakes to satisfy; and it is impossible for him so to perform both.

! (1.) Both must be performed jointly; for passive obedience alone would never pay both debts. To cast a man into prison pays not the creditor, and punishment is required by God as he is the judge of the world; it is *jus rectoris*, and we owe obedience to him besides, as he is a creditor. And though God be content with passive obedience from those in hell, because it is all he can get of them, yet he is not satisfied with it, and therefore they are for ever to abide there. It is true that he improves it to his glory, in that it shews the various ways of his manifestation of his attributes upon creatures; but yet, simply in itself it would not satisfy it. Furthermore, the threatening of punishment is (as was said) but the appendix of the law, not the primary intent of the lawgiver; and therefore God doth not simply delight in it, nor is he satisfied with it.

(2.) There is an impossibility that any creature should perform both of them jointly and together, which it must do if it satisfy. For from that creature, though never so excellent, an eternity both of active and passive obedience would be exacted; and he could not dispatch or end either, nor perform both together. If the obedience that is set him might be ended, or if both could be performed together, he might satisfy; but the law exacts both for ever of us. And therefore the psalmist makes the redemption of the soul too precious for any creature to meddle with, Ps. xlix. 8, giving this reason why a man 'cannot redeem his brother; so precious is the redemption of a soul, and it ceaseth for ever;' that is, it shall never be accomplished; so the phrase is taken elsewhere. The work is so precious, as it requireth eternity to do it in. So that that which the best of creatures should do, or suffer for us in any finite term of time, would not satisfy for what was due from us to eternity, but it doth require yet a further and infinite worth in the obedience to be added to supply that eternity, and it is an utter impossibility to perform both together for ever. Look, as it is impossible to 'serve two masters, but that a man must lean to the one, and neglect the other,' Mat. vi. 24, so it is impossible for the creature to carry along both these obediences together. For when he were obeying the whole law, how could he at the same suffer? And when he were suffering, how could he obey the whole law? All the graces then exercised would have been only patience, and all little enough to afford him that; there would have been no room for the exercise of other graces. And as God calls us not to do and suffer at the same time, for both cannot stand together, so neither could any creature do and suffer at the same time for us. If indeed he could first despatch the active part, and then encounter the torments due unto us, and despatch them also, then there might be hope; but this he cannot; and to perform both to eternity is impossible.

But yet by making as free and large concessions as are imaginable, further to shew the impossibility of it, suppose that passive obedience and suffering for us would stand for both debts; and suppose also, that if their lives went for ours, they then might satisfy as well as we can, seeing theirs are as good as ours; and therefore, if eternal death in us be a satisfaction to God's justice (which if it be not so, God then loseth by sin, and then he would not have let it come into the world), then it might be so in them for us, and we be freed, yet consider the inconveniences that will follow:

1. They must always be satisfying, and it could never be said, 'It is finished.' They must lie by it till they have paid the uttermost farthing, which they can never do, no more than we ourselves can; and so they could not take away sins from us, for we could not have an acquittance till the debt were paid, we could not be justified till our surety were acquitted. Therefore, 'if Christ had not risen,' says Paul, 'we had yet been in our sins,' 1 Cor. xv. 17. And therefore the psalmist says, of the redemption of the soul by any creature, Ps. xlix. 8, 'it ceaseth for ever,' that is, shall never be accomplished, but shall always be a-doing, and never ended, and so, we never be the better, nor the nearer having our bonds cancelled. And this is the reason why sacrifices were rejected, even because every year they were still forced to offer them: Heb. x. 1–4, 'For the law having a shadow of good things to come, and not the very image of the things, can never with those sacrifices, which they offered year by year continually, make the comers thereunto perfect: ver. 2, 'For then would they not have ceased to be offered? because that the worshippers once purged should have no more conscience of sins;' ver. 3, 'But in those sacrifices there is a remembrance again made of sins every year;' ver. 4, 'For it is not possible that the blood of bulls and of goats should take away sins.' And, ver. 11, it is said, that 'they stood daily offering the same sacrifices.'

2dly. Suppose yet further, that God, to whom eternity is but as one instant, should give us in our bond, when the other had entered in his, because though it be to eternity a-paying, yet to him it were as good as paid in hand presently. Suppose this, yet notwithstanding, one just man or angel could satisfy but for one of us. Life could go but for life, and 'a tooth for a tooth,' as the law runs ; and so he must sacrifice as many creatures as good as we are for ever, as he meant to save of us men. That one creature's obedience would not, as Adam's righteousness, have extended to many, for that was a favour, but this a debt. And we cannot pay many bonds with one sum which is due for one ; for every one is a distinct debt and obligation.

3dly. If we grant all this, yet what creature would have had so much love in it towards us as willingly to sacrifice itself for us ? Which it must fully do, or else it cannot be satisfaction ; for *satisfactio est redditio voluntaria*, says the school. The apostle, Rom. v. 7, says, that 'peradventure for a good man some would dare to die.' Mark it, he makes a *peradventure* of it, and it must be for ' a good man ;' that is, one profitable to him, as they expound it ; and seeing death is φοϐερῶν φοϐερώτατον, he must be very hardy and daring that would do it. But to encounter God's wrath, who dares do it ? Jer. xxx. 21, ' And their nobles shall be of themselves, and their governor shall proceed from the midst of them ; and I will cause him to draw near, and he shall approach unto me : for who is this that engaged his heart to approach unto me ? saith the Lord.' The prophet there making a promise of Christ to be a mediator, and one that should be able to draw nigh to God, he gives this reason, ' For who is there that engageth his heart to draw nigh to me ?' As if he had said, none else durst have stepped in, to encounter me for you ; especially, not for enemies both to God and themselves. There is need of a mediator to reconcile us and the angels, as that place in the Eph. i. 10 may seem to imply, where the apostle says, that ' God made known unto us the mystery of his will, that he might gather together in one all things in Christ, which are in heaven and earth :' making us, as friends to himself, so one to another ; and if so, then antecedently, they could not be the reconcilers. And further, the holier they were, the less must they needs love us ; and so not of themselves would they ever undertake such work for us.

4thly. Suppose yet further, that any had so much love, or would have been so hardy to venture, as with Paul to wish they may be accursed ; yet if they were in hell but half an hour, they would repent themselves, and wish themselves out again, and so it had been spoiled for ever being satisfaction, which must throughout be voluntary, as our disobedience was. And therefore God would not trust to their help in so weighty a business, wherein his own will was so engaged. It is said in Job iv. 18, ' Behold he puts no trust in his servants.' Which though he might in ordinary works of obedience, yet he will never rely on them for so great a matter. He finds folly even in the angels, they are mutable. He trusted one man once for all, only in matter of obedience to his law, which was easy and sweet to him ; but see how he failed and left all, and that upon no great or strong temptation. He therefore will never hazard the second Adam to be a mere creature in a matter of punishment, which that he may be willing to undergo, he must be fed with some delight or hopes of ease. No ; he will make sure work now.

5thly and lastly. Suppose any creature had been so full of excellency, as that the sufferings of it alone could have been satisfactory for all that God meant to save, and according to the supposition formerly made, that he having more grace than all mankind, and so, being made heir to more glory than all mankind besides, would have been content to lay all aside, and to have subjected himself for ever to undergo all our' punishments ; yet considering all this must have been done by him, in obedience unto God, and for his sake (for otherwise it could not have been accepted, in that satisfaction for another must be voluntary on both parts, both on his that undertakes it, and also by the consent and acceptation of him that is wronged), if the case had thus stood, then this inconvenience would have followed, that a creature should have been obedient unto God, yea, and performed the highest obedience unto God, whom yet God never should have had an opportunity to reward, because he was to be in hell for ever.   And God will never be so behind-hand with any creature that shall do him service, much more so great a service as this would be.

CHAPTER V.

That no creatures could make that satisfaction which an injured God required.—
They cannot compensate the wrong done to him by sin, nor repair the loss
of his honour.

We have seen what satisfaction the law requires, and how far the creature would fall short of that.   Let us, secondly, now see what satisfaction God requires.   And although *re ipsa*, in the thing itself, it comes all to one to satisfy God and to satisfy his law, and both these heads be really coincident, yet our understandings may take a distinct consideration from each, which will serve the better to clear this point.

Now to make way for the demonstrations I intend, let us define in general what satisfaction is, and wherein it is to be made.

Satisfaction in general is, when so much clear emolument ariseth to the party wronged, as was impaired by the trespass committed.   Now all such damages to be repaired do usually consist either in goods or honour ; and satisfaction for goods is usually called restitution, but satisfaction for honour is it which is more properly called satisfaction.

Now we may consider a wrong done to God both these ways, and an answerable satisfaction requisite.

First, For that of goods ; though it be a thing which God doth not much reckon, yet something is considerable about it ; and therefore the prodigal's wild course is expressed and aggravated by this, that he spent his father's ' goods and substance in riotous living,' Luke xv. 13.   Therefore also God compares himself to a householder, who commits goods and talents unto his servants, to be by them improved, Mat. xxv. 14, and who, when he reckons with them, doth count up their waste and expense thereof upon their lusts ; and therefore they are said to ' consume them upon their lusts,' James iv. 3, that is, so to engross them to themselves, and as it were consume them, that God gets nothing by the things which he hath made.   By reason of sin he hath no profit by those creatures which sinners have committed to them, and the world becomes loss unto him. And though God stands not much upon this (as neither will I stand long upon the handling of it), yet this much is soon demonstrated, that no creatures were ever able to make satisfaction for losses of this kind : they

are not able (as Esther said in another case) to make good, or ' countervail
the king's loss,' Est. vii. 4.

Now, to instance in some particulars :

1. Sin by a forfeiture had quite destroyed this world, if Christ had not
upheld it. And can all the graces in the creatures make another, or uphold this from falling ? Surely no.

2. It blotted grace out of the heart of man ; and can the power of all the
creatures make one dram of grace ? Yea, could we so much as have lighted
our candles, that were blown out, at their tapers ? Surely no.

3. By sinners the law was destroyed also : Ps. cxix. 126, ' They have
destroyed thy law.' Now, if you would set a price upon the law, one tittle
of it is more worth than heaven and earth.

4. Through sin was much service due unto God lost. For that we may
reckon amongst goods, as a master doth the service of an apprentice. Although all sinners should presently cease to offend God any more, yet still
God hath lost so much service from them for the time past. Now all mere
creatures being God's servants, and owing all their endeavours and services
unto him for themselves, no one of them therefore can do two men's work,
because they owe all they can do for themselves, and so they can never
repay that loss of service past. God did hire mankind into his vineyard
for all eternity ; and though we could suppose they had not committed any
positive sin, yet if God had but only lost so much service from them, and
the sin of that neglect had annihilated them (and it doth as good as anni-
hilate them to God, and therefore he accounts and calls them lost ; as the
' lost sheep,' the ' lost son,' &c.), and then, if God had come to have
entered into terms with any mere creature for these losses, and should have
said, Give me but the creatures you have spoiled, make me a new world,
for your sin hath spoiled this, and ' subjected it to vanity ;' had any of
them power to have done it ? Surely no. When God would confute Job's
contending with him, he doth but ask him, whether he could make the
least creature, yea, or being made, command it : ' Thou !' (says God)
' where wast thou when I laid the foundations of the earth ?' Job xxxviii. 4.
' Hast thou commanded the morning since thy days, or caused the day-
spring to know its place ?' ver. 12. ' Out of whose womb came the ice ?'
ver. 29.' ' Canst thou lift up thy voice to the clouds' (and bid them rain),
' that abundance of waters may cover thee ? Canst thou send lightnings
that may go, and say unto thee, Here we are ?' ver. 34, 35. And though
thou canst do none of all this, yet dost thou contend with me ? ' Let me
see' (says God) ' what thou canst do,' Job xl. 7, 8, 9. If thou couldst
make or command the least creature, then ' I will confess to thee that thine
own right hand can save thee,' ver. 14. Can all the angels in heaven (as
powerful as they are) make one hair of thy head ? Can they set ordinances
in heaven ? Job xxxviii. 33. The philosophers feigned them to be but the
movers of those wheels and orbs, not the founders of them. They cannot
set the clock, much less make it. And can they make grace, or can they
make the law whole again, which sin had broken ?

But the truth is, that herein God expected not, nor is he capable of any
satisfaction or restitution of goods, for ' none can be profitable to him,'
Job xxii. 2, 3. When that formalist thought to oblige God by sacrifices ;
' If I were hungry' (says God), ' would I tell it thee ?' Ps. l. 12. ' The
world is God's, and the fulness thereof,' says the apostle, 1 Cor. x. 26.
And again, ' Who hath given to him, and he shall be recompensed ?' Rom.
xi. 35. No ; it is glory only that the creature is capable to give him. So

it follows there in Ps. l. 15, ' Thou shalt glorify me.' God is not as a king, whose tribute lies as well in goods as in honour ; but all the tribute he expecteth or exacteth from the creature consists in honour, for that is the end of all his works. He made all things for his glory ; ' I formed it,' says he in the prophet, ' for my glory,' Isa. xliii. 7. ' Of whom, and to whom, are all things, to whom be glory for ever,' says the apostle, Rom. xi. 36. And herein also, though it be most true that the creature can contribute nothing to God's essential glory, yet to his manifestative glory it may, and doth ; at least the creature may take from it, as by sin it doth. And the reason is, because this kind of glory is revealed in and by creatures. Now it is in this that God expects satisfaction, and that this satisfaction in point of honour does much more infinitely transcend the power of any creature, is the thing which I am now to demonstrate.

Let us therefore in like manner come to the particulars wherein God's honour suffers by sin, and shew how irrecompensable the injury therein is by creatures.

1. If it were no more than to satisfy for that tribute of honour left behind-hand unpaid, for the neglect of that homage due to God, and which is to come in by our service of him, what a quarrel must it needs breed, not to be composed or taken up by any creature ! You know, kings that have homage due to them from other kings, their equals, though the tribute itself, or thing to be paid, be small, yet if it be neglected, what wars and stirs hath it bred, merely because it is a matter of honour neglected ! Hence also the neglect of paying a small acknowledgment (suppose a pepper-corn, or the like), or of doing some petty service yearly, do ofttimes forfeit great estates, because they are acknowledgments of honour to the lord of whom the tenants hold ; and so being omitted, they are neglects of an honour that is due. Now, the like slight being offered towards God, how great a wrong doth he account it ; if no more, yet because there is a neglect of his honour in it ! If indeed the terms of our service between God and us did stand upon free mutual conditions of bargain, as when freemen are hired, and work only for wages, who if they neglect a day's work, it is but calling in so much of their wages, and they are even again with him that hired them ; if it were thus between God and us, the matter were easier to be reconciled ; but it carries a dishonour with it, such as are those neglects of service to a great prince, which service is not due by any bargain for wages, but out of subjection, or as to a lord by way of knight-service, not out of love only and liberty, but out of respect and homage. God is desirous of nothing but honour from you, and all the honour the creatures can give him is too little for him ; it satisfies not, neither answers to his vast desires of being glorified, nor to the dues of his most glorious excellency. And therefore if any be behind-hand unpaid by any of his creatures, it is a loss by creatures irreparable, for they render no overplus to make it up, and he cannot but account it so much loss to him ; and should they now do what they can, still God would want of his due.

2. Satisfaction is to be made for honour debased also ; for sin casts a soil of disgrace and debasement upon the honour which God hath, and goes about to despoil and rob him of it. It is said, Rom. ii. 23, ' In breaking the law thou dishonourest God ;' there is a dishonour cast upon him by it, yea, it toucheth upon the height of his honour ; which will appear,

(1.) In that every law of his is backed with his prerogative, and is a note of his absolute sovereignty; James iv. 12, 'There is one lawgiver, who is able to save and to destroy;' that is, he is the supreme potentate of all the world, the absolute Lord paramount; and this is shewn and declared in giving his law, and is therefore answerably denied by the creature in every breach of every law, to which every sin is an affront.

Now, as amongst men, kingly authority being the summity, the supremacy, the transcendency of all honour, therefore the law hath so fenced it, that whatsoever is immediately directed against it, or is a denial of it, is rebellion, and *crimen læsæ majestatis;* and to disgrace a king's personal perfections is not so much, nay, to speak dishonourably of the personal imperfections of a king, dishonoureth him not so much as to oppose his kingly power and dignity; as to say that kings are not so learned or so valiant as many other men, this is not in account so high a dishonour to them, because it toucheth not upon their sovereignty and princely dignity, for they may notwithstanding be acknowledged and obeyed as kings. But whatever tends to impair and blemish that their prerogative and dignity, is held to be the height of dishonour, as kingly authority is the sublimity and top of honour. So now in breaking the least law of God, we do deny the sovereignty and kingly authority of God. To despise any of God's works, and slight them, is a dishonour to the Maker, as Solomon says; but to slight his law is more, because that his transcendent excellency and kingly authority is thus engaged in it. Some of the schoolmen fondly reason to diminish and lessen the heinousness of sin, saying that all the evil of sin lying simply in this, that it is the breach of God's law, therefore it is not properly an injury to God, no otherwise than as a thing contrary to his will; as when a master commands a servant to do a thing, and he doth the contrary, and so, though indeed he displeaseth his master thereby (as doing a thing contrary to his command), yet, say they, it is no injury. But they do not consider that not only God's will is engaged in his law, but also his supreme authority, the law being made by his prerogative, and by the same prerogative backed and commanded. Kings indeed, in their laws, do not lay all the weight of their authority upon every law, but God doth. And therefore every sin is not only a transgression of his will, but a debasement of the sovereignty of his will. Hence in the promulgation of God's laws there runs this preface, 'I am the Lord thy God;' therefore do this, Exod. xx. 1. So that his sovereignty is slighted in every sin, and in it thère is a contempt of his crown and dignity.

Sin is not only a dishonour to him simply as he is a supreme lawgiver, but unto all his other personal glorious perfections. Every contempt of the authority of a prince reflects not upon his personal virtues, but sin reflects upon all God's excellencies; as upon his goodness, &c., for men seek that happiness and goodness in the creature which is to be had in God alone, and so profess him not to be the chiefest good. There is no attribute upon which a disgrace is not cast by the sins of men; yea, and therefore they tend to make him no God: Titus i. 16, 'In their works they deny God.' Traitors may aim to unking a prince, and to that end rebel against him, and yet their treason not reach unto his life. But God's sovereignty, and perfection, and glory are himself, and his life, the least detraction from which is to destroy the whole; for *quicquid est in Deo Deus est,* whatever is in God is God himself. It is true indeed that in the event those hurt not God, no more than snow-balls thrown against the sun can hurt it. God dwells in light which darkness cannot approach or touch. Sin hurts him no more than grace benefits him. But yet injuries and dishonours are not measured in morality by the event only, but by what is the *terminus*, the thing they tend to; which is to un-God the great God, and despoil him of all his titles. To resolve to kill a king is accounted treason, as well as to do it, and so punished for such; therefore Solomon did put Adonijah to death. Even as he who hates his brother is counted a murderer, 1 John iii. 15, so he who hates God is a murderer of God. Now, every sinner is said to hate God, Rom. i. 30, *peccatum est Deicidium.* It is true that physically sin is but *privatio boni finiti*, of that good which we might have in God, not *boni infiniti*, or *Dei*, not the privation of God as in himself, but as he is to be participated by us. Yet as the astronomers call the interposition of the moon between the earth and the sun the eclipse of the sun, though the sun doth really lose no light by it, but only the earth; yet because it makes the face of the world below to be as if there were no sun, it is therefore commonly called the eclipse of the sun, and not of the earth; so may it be said of sin. It is in the guilt of it a privation of God, and of his glory, and of his law; because, though indeed and in truth we only are the losers, yet it makes to us as if there were no God, as if God had no being; and so it may be said to be the eclipse of his being, viz., to us. Therefore men are said to 'live without God in the world,' Eph. ii. 12, and without the law, 1 Tim. i. 9; and to be 'deprived of the glory of God,' as being not manifested in them nor by them, Rom. iii. 23. Now, if it be so that the sinfulness of sin thus lies in so great a dishonour to so great a God, what satisfaction can then be made for the demerit of it by all the creatures? For in this respect it transcends in evil, and outweighs all the goodness that is either in the persons or graces of all the creatures. Indeed it is true, if we take sin physically, as it is a privation of the contrary habit of grace and of our good only, that then it hath no more evil in it than grace hath goodness; for as sin separates from God— 'Your iniquities have separated you from me,' Isa. lix. 2—so grace draws the soul nearer to God, and so makes a man as happy as sin makes him miserable: 'To draw near to thee is good,' says the psalmist, Ps. lxxiii. 28. But this is not that special evil in sin for which satisfaction is required, as neither is it the chief matter of our repentance for sin; for no man satisfies for an evil done to himself, neither is it sin's having so much evil in it against us that hinders a mere creature from satisfying; which notwithstanding was that that misled some of the ancient schoolmen, who upon that ground thought a pure creature might satisfy for sin; all their reasons running upon the evil of sin as a privation of grace, and of God to us only, and as he is our good; not considering that over and above it is an evil against God himself: Jer. ii. 19, 'It is an evil and a bitter thing to forsake God.' And sin is accordingly called 'enmity against God,' Rom. viii. 7, and 'a provoking the eyes of his glory,' Isa. iii. 8. It is likewise said to be against him: so says David, Ps. li. 4, 'Against thee, thee only have I sinned.' He looked not so much at the wrong to Bathsheba and Uriah, as at the dishonour done to God; and this is the eminent evil to be considered in sin; for as God is the chiefest good, so himself is the measure of all other good and evil. Now, then, the evil of sin lying thus in so great a dishonour unto God himself, no creature can make amends for it. For,

1. Dishonour, which reflects upon a person of worth, cannot be satisfied for but by a person equally worthy and honourable; for the satisfaction must be made by restoring of honour again, and that will depend upon the honour and worth of the party honouring. The restoring of honour is to

be measured by the same rule, and weighed at the same balance, that the honour of the person dishonoured is measure by. As, therefore, honour is in itself a personal thing, so the repairing of it again depends upon the personal worth of him that goes about to repair it. Were we and God equal, so as there were as much worth in us to honour him withal, as our dishonouring of him comes unto, then indeed, if we went about some way to restore again that honour that was impaired by us, we might perhaps satisfy for it. And yet the law is so tender of dishonour, that in case of defamation it is not enough for a person equally honourable to submit, and to say as much for a man as he hath said against him ; that is accounted* satisfaction ; but the law enjoins a penalty besides. But however, the restoring of honour being a thing personal, doth therefore depend upon the honour of that person who is to restore it; for *honor est in honorante,* honour is in him that honours ; the meaning of which saying may well be this, that honour depends upon the worth of the party honouring. Therefore we see that honour from a mean peasant is not esteemed or accounted of by one that is highly noble. And hence it is, that wrongs in point of honour offered by inferiors to superiors do oftentimes transcend satisfaction. It is not so in goods ; a poor man may satisfy a king in goods, in case he be able to restore, as well as another. And the demonstration of of this is, that the best way of satisfaction to be made by such inferiors being to submit themselves, and that submision being a due from them already, and no more than the distance of their ranks calls for, it therefore reacheth not to satisfaction. And thus it is in common esteem, and that founded upon what is in the things themselves, and not upon common opinion only. And therefore it is evident, that though the creatures should do that which might bring in as much glory to God as was lost, yet, because of the distance and disproportion that is between the persons, it would never satisfy. The aggravation of a dishonour ariseth not so much from the fact as from the disproportion between the persons ; for honour is not *inter res,* but *personas,* it concerns not things, but persons. To strike, or offer to strike at a magistrate (though we hurt him not), the heinousness of the fault lies not so much in the fact, as in the disproportion between the persons. Therefore though in the old law ' a tooth for a tooth' was satisfaction enough between private men, yet not so in case of hurting a magistrate, or striking a man's parent, which was death by that law, because of the dishonour done to them thereby. So upon the same ground, for a mad man to strike the king is death by our laws, not in respect of the fact or of his intention, but in regard of the transcendent honour of the person of a king, and the disproportion and inferiority that is in him that strikes him. Now the disproportion between God and us is so infinite, that it makes our sinning a dishonour *altioris ordinis,* of a higher kind than is recompensable by creatures.

And to enlarge this demonstration further. If no creature can make unto God a reparation of goods (as was shewn), then much less can it make satisfaction for his glory impaired. For goods are extrinsecal to a man's person, and therefore the loss of them a man less regards ; yea, the greater spirit a man is of the less he cares for goods; and indeed the wrong therein becometh less; even as to wrong a poor man in his goods is worse (because of his need) than to wrong a rich man ; but the greater any one is in spirit the more he regards honour, and that far above his goods. Men will lose their blood rather than suffer a hair of honour to perish ; which disposition, though it be often set wrong in men, yet it is a spark of God's image, and a

* Qu. ' is not accounted '?—ED.

resemblance of what is in him. God can bear the loss of creatures and worlds, and never be touched with it; but he will not lose one ray of honour. For glory is a personal thing: it is the lustre of his person which he carries and wears about him; and it is intrinsecal to him, which goods are not; and therefore God is willing to lose creatures, thereby to gain the more glory. So he casts away the most of men and angels for his own glory. ' My glory,' says God ' I will not give to another,' Isa. xlii. 8. But his goods he doth : ' He gave the earth and all the fulness thereof unto the sons of men,' Ps. cxv. 16. He gives worlds and kingdoms away even to the basest of men (says Daniel, Dan. iv. 17), but he will part with none of his glory, that is proper to himself, unto any of them. Of all the goods he possesseth, his children are the dearest unto him; he 'gives nations for them,' Isa. xli. 2, and once he gave his Son for them; they are ' the apple of his eye;' and he that toucheth them, toucheth the apple of his eye.' But his glory is dearer to him than all his children, for ' he formed them for his glory,' as the same prophet there also says, Isa. xliii. 7. How hard is it to pacify jealousy when a man's spouse is deflowered : ' It is the rage of a man, and he will not regard any ransom,' as Solomon says, Prov. vi. 34, 35. How hard then must it needs be to pacify God, who is said to be jealous of nothing but his honour ?

Again, 2. Though it be but the manifestation of God's glory, which hath a soil and a reflection cast upon it by sin, not his essential glory (which loseth nothing by sin, as it gains not, nor is increased by all the works that Christ or God himself hath done), yet not all that the creatures can do is worth the least beam of that his glory as it is to be manifested. For that is the end for which they were all made, and is therefore better than they. And besides, all they can do to the advancing of it they do owe it already ; and God stands not in need of them to manifest it; he could have let them remain in the womb of nothing, and have raised up others to glorify him.

3. In that sin strikes at God's being, what is there in the creatures that can make amends for it, they being but shadows of his being, and he the substance, whose name alone is *I am?* The over-shadowing, therefore, of the eclipse of his being is more than the destruction of ours.

Obj. Yea, but you will object, and say that the grace of a mere creature may seem to vie with all the evil that is in sin, and this in point of honour. For as sin is against God, so grace, though but in an impure creature, can say, ' I am for God;' and as sin sets up another god, so this grace glorifies God as God. Now God being the object of both, why should they not alike set a worth or a demerit upon what is done, and God accept of grace, which is for him, as much as condemn and punish sin, the aggravation of the sinfulness of which is, that it is against him ?

Ans. For answers unto this :

1. Though it be true that sin hurts him no more than grace benefits him (in that God is capable neither of benefit nor hurt); even as clouds take no more from the sun than candles add to it; and therefore in Job xxxv. 6, 7, it is said, ' What dost thou to him if thou beest righteous, or against him if thou sinnest ?' For nothing is opposed to God immediately, but only to him in his works. As no darkness can obscure the sun itself, though his beams it may intercept, so sin may dim the manifestative glory of the Father of lights. Yet as we measure not kindnesses or injuries by the event, but by what they are in the acts themselves (as treason is not punished according to the event, but according to the nature of the act plotted or purposed), so are we to do by sin.

And, 2. If we compare the ingredient qualifications considerable in the one, and in the other, as the one is an injury and the other an act of obedience, we shall find a great disproportion between them.   For,

(1.) If an injury is accounted more evil and blameworthy than all kindnesses praiseworthy and to be accepted, then when the injury is an undue act of us, unworthy of all the obligations between us and another whom we wrong, when it is causeless, and when the kindnesses we do are all due from us, herein lies the disproportion which makes the obliquity of the injury of sin the more transcendent.   All the obedience we perform is due from us to God : ' You do,' says Christ, ' what you ought to do,' Luke xvii. 10.   But in this (as Christ again says), ' we hate God without a cause,' John xv. 24, 25.   And ' what iniquity have you found in me,' says he, ' and for which of all my perfections or kindnesses to you, do you sin against me ?' John x. 32.   Now it is this inequality that lies between the one and the other, that makes the obliquity of the one to exceed the goodness of the other.   As for example : for a child to love his father, though it be good and commendable, yet in so doing he doth but his duty, and even what nature teacheth to do ; therefore this is not so praiseworthy, as to hate his father is odious, for he therein goes against his kind, there is an unnaturalness in it ; and, therefore, we see that one such act does more discommend one to men, than all former acts of dutiful and loving obedience do or can commend him.   The being due does diminish of the praise and commendation of what is good : ' If you love those that love you' (says Christ, Luke vi. 33, 34), ' what thanks have you ?'   No reward attends such a love, although it be good, because it is a due and suitable act ; but ' love your enemies,' says he, unto whom (in regard of any obligation to them) nothing is due, and ' then your reward shall be great ;' this is praiseworthy indeed.   I may turn this speech and say, that to obey God, and love him, and exalt him as God, though it be good, yet what is it but what is due from you, and that which all obligations tie you to ?   ' What does God require of thee, O man,' says Moses, ' but to love and fear him ?' Deut. x. 12.   He requires but what is reasonable and due.   Now to do all this is not thankworthy, for if you knew him, you could not choose but love him ; but to be rebellious to him, to be an enemy to one so good and so glorious, and one unto whom you are so much beholden, this is unsufferable.

(2.) As in regard of the undueness of the act, as from us to God, there is a greater obliquity in sin than goodness in grace, so in regard of God also.   Though the act of a creature obeying God doth intend glory to him, as much as a sinner doth intend dishonour to him, yet the sin is more, and that in regard of him who is the object of both.   For,

[1.] All the honour which we can give God is but his due already.   We do but attribute that to him which is his own already, and that independently without us.   What do we in being holy and obedient ?   We exalt him as God ; why, he is God already, whether we exalt him or no, yea, what we can do this way falls short of that which is his due in himself, for, Nehem. ix. 5, ' He is above all blessings and praises.'   But the very *formalis ratio* of sinning against him, is to set up another god, and so to attribute that to him which is not, or that which is below him, that is thereby to affix a new title of disgrace upon him, utterly unworthy of him.   As for the eye to call the light beautiful and glorious, and to admire it, what is it but only to speak that of it which it is already ?   But for the eye to call light darkness, this is *de novo* to coin and put a disparagement upon it, and sin is a new invention of our own, as Ecclesiastes speaks, Eccl. vii. 29, to dishonour

God. Thus unbelief makes God a liar; and what a wrong is that? It is not recompensable by all our acts of faith in believing that he is true; for to believe so, is but to declare what is his already; but the other is the invention of a falsehood obtruded upon him by men. For one to speak truth is but little or no commendation, for a man speaks but what is; but to tell a lie, is to invent a new thing that is false, and therefore how odious and shameful is it. Now, every sin is a lie concerning God, ' changing the truth of God into a lie,' Rom. i. 25. It declares that of God which is not. And to be the inventor of new gods, or of false things of God, what an evil is it? Again, to love God and honour him, is a thing due to his name— ' Give him the praise due to his name,' Ps. xxix. 2—and his excellency challengeth it. Now to love goodness, what is it! So to love God; but what an incongruity is it to hate goodness? For subjects to honour their king, whose title and prerogative is independent upon them, is not so much to him, as it is a dishonour for one man to disparage his title, and to go about the setting up of another king. Now God's glory is in and from himself; and therefore he hath reason to account it more dishonour to him, that one man should rebel, than honour to him, that all should obey him. When I honour him, his honour ariseth from himself, not me; as the glory of the sun shining in the water is not from the water, but from the sun. So when we reflect glory on God, that glory ariseth not out of what we do, but is in himself already. But the dishonour of him is wholly in us. We are the sole inventors of it, and there is no such thing extant, except in a sinner's heart.

[2.] Add to this, that all the grace wherewith we glorify God is not a man's own, but sin is wholly his own; so John viii. 44, when he sins, he sins ἐκ τοῦ ἰδίου, from his own; and so in Jude 16, their lusts are called their own; and, Eccl. vii. 29, they are said to be our inventions.

Again, [3.] If the compass and measure be taken of that dishonour which sin tends unto, there will be found a wider distance between the two terms of its reach, than there is of the honour that the creature can give to God, or than it doth extend itself unto. For the measure and compass of the dishonour is plainly this, to make the great God no God; these are the terms the least sin stretcheth itself unto, in the scope and tendency of the act, though not in the event, nor in the intention of the sinner. But when the creatures glorify God, though they should ' glorify him as God,' as far as the creatures can do it, yet if you take the measure of the utmost elevation of his glory by them, there still remains an infinite distance between the honour which they aim to give him, and what is in himself, so that it falls so far short, that it is infinite goodness in God to accept it.

As the conclusion therefore of this answer, and closure of this discourse, I will super-add these few demonstrations drawn from the effects, to shew clearly, and confirm this, that the least sin transcends in evil the worth of all created graces, which puts all out of question, and makes the whole demonstration undeniable; for satisfaction being *reductio ad æqualia*, a reducing of things to an equality, therefore if all their graces cannot make so much goodness as shall counterbalance the evil of sin, it is impossible they should ever satisfy. Now that they do not, appears by these demonstrations.

First, One sin, when it is committed by the best of creatures, prevails more with God to condemn him, than all his righteousness to justify him. If one of the angels did never so much, so great, so long service, yet if, after millions of years, he sinned in the least, all the forepast service would be forgotten. As a favourite that hath done much service at court, or in the wars; if, after all, he should be found guilty of one treason, that one act would put a blot upon all his former services, and render them nothing-worth. If a man doth not all things, yea (more than that) ' continues not in all things,' he is accursed, Gal. iii. 10. Now if sin were not more evil in God's judgment (whose judgment is righteous) than all obedience is good, then this could not be. It is not as the pharisees dreamed, that men should be justified, if their good works were more than their sins; as if their good works being weighed, and found exceeding the other in number, they should therefore carry it; no, a world of good works will be found too light for the least dram of sin.

Secondly, The demerit of sin is more than the merit of goodness can be, for that the evil that is in sin does truly deserve death; not only in relation to, or by virtue of, a penal law arbitrarily given, or out of a voluntary compact and agreement between God and the creature, but in its own nature. That threatening, 'Thou shalt die the death,' is not added *ex compacto* only, neither depends it merely upon an outward declaration of God's will, but further, sin is such an evil as, in the nature of the thing, deserves death, and that immutably. Therefore that δικαίωμα τοῦ Θεοῦ, that judgment of God written in all men's hearts, says that ' they who do such things are worthy of death,' Rom. i. 82; and so also Rom. vi. 23, ' The wages of sin is death.' But if you put all the grace in the world together, it cannot merit at God's hands his favour. God may out of his bounty oblige him-self by a promise to reward it, but it is not out of the worth of the thing. So it follows there, in that Rom. vi. 23, ' The gift of God is eternal life;' you see what an apparent difference the apostle puts between the one and the other. In like manner, Luke xvii. 10, it is said, ' When you have done all,' if you could suppose you had done all, yet ' you are unprofitable servants :' for God's right over us is founded upon his excellence; and accordingly, our obligation to serve God is not from his benefits only, but from a due unto his own excellencies. And therefore, although there were no reward for our service, yet service were due from us. So says Aristotle : If any man transcendently excel all others, that man is to be king over them, and they are bound to serve him. Yea, and therefore the privilege to justify a man is separable from our graces (as in men sanctified by the gospel), but so is not condemnation from sin. And therefore, although sin in the godly redounds not in the event to the persons, to condemn them, by reason of Christ's righteousness imputed, yet all that righteousness makes not but that sin in its own nature deserves death; and so they are to judge themselves for it, as worthy to be destroyed. But all the grace that is in them doth not only not justify them *ipso facto ;* but it hath wholly and for ever lost that privilege. Which argues that it is not seated in the nature of grace to justify, as to demerit death is seated in the nature of sin : for then, though the effect might be retained, yet that property would be inseparable from it.

And *Thirdly*, That the strength of sin was greater than that of grace, appears by this also, that it is able to expel grace out of the heart, as it did out of Adam's; but all the grace of all the creatures could not restore it.

Fourthly, It is counted more mercy to pardon one sinner, than goodness to reward and save all the angels. More riches are attributed even to God's mercy and patience towards wicked men, than to his simple goodness to-wards other creatures innocent, though never so holy.

CHAPTER VI.

That Christ hath made full reparation of all which was lost by sin.—The glory of the law, which sin had darkened, is by him perfectly recovered.—And God's image, which sin had defaced in man, is more fully restored in him.

We have seen the power of all the creatures set up, and at a loss as to this, the greatest and most difficult business that ever was set on foot, viz., the taking away of sins. Let us now come to lay open that fulness that is in Christ for this work ; before which all these difficulties that have been put, and all our sins likewise, will vanish and melt away, as clouds before the sun. A fulness it is that answers to every defect, and to every particular objection made. I will begin with that satisfaction that is to be given to God ; for in the wrong to him doth the principal knot and difficulty lie.

First, If God should stand upon satisfaction to be made, in point of goods (which yet, as I said, he doth not), Christ hath therein abundantly made amends. Which although he reckons not as any part of his satisfaction, which only consists in his obedient humbling of himself, yet it may be considered as part of the surplusage and redundancy of it. Let justice come and bring in her bill of damages, and see if Christ hath not abundantly given satisfaction for them : as,

1. Will the complaint be of the loss, spoil, and waste made of the world, and of all the creatures therein, and of the unjointing that frame, unto the danger of the destruction of it, which no creature is able to repair or to uphold ? Then let it withal be remembered that he that had undertook to satisfy God had his hand in making this old world, and 'without him it had not been made,' John i. 3. It is a consideration that both that evangelist, and the author to the Hebrews (Heb. i. 2), as likewise the apostle to the Colossians (Col. i. 16), do all suggest to this very purpose, thereby to shew Christ's ability to satisfy for sin. And if God would yet further desire new worlds to be made him for satisfaction, Christ could make enough. And it may be further pleaded, that this world (as we see) stands and continues still, notwithstanding all the sins committed in it, and that justice had destined it to present ruin the first day that man should sin. Now whose power is it that upholds it ? Is it not Christ's, whose very word is able to underprop it ? So Heb. i. 3, ' Upholding all things by the word of his power ;' who with one hand holdeth his Father's hands from destroying this world, and with the other upholds it from tottering. Yea, if it were no more but this, that he who made the world would vouchsafe to admit himself into it, and become a part of it ; and that he whom God did never make nor create, but from eternity begat, would be ' made flesh,' and become a creature and servant (which was an addition to God's goods, and worth all that he had made besides), this might make reparation for all such damages. And again, at whose expenses are all things here maintained ? Are they not at Christ's ? The Father did as it were deny to lay out any more power or patience in upholding the world, till he should be paid for it ; and did not Christ undertake this, and at his due time lay down a price that fully bought it ? who is therefore called the ' Lord that bought,' 2 Pet. ii. 1, as wicked men, so all the world. And that he who made the world, and is joint-heir with God, and hath as much right to it as he, should, to satisfy him, lay down his right, put himself out of all, and then take it up upon a new title, when it was his before, so buying what

himself made, and what was his own : that he should become poor, even not worth the ground he went on when he came into the world, and should suffer himself not to be owned (as John speaks), yea, to be cast out of the vineyard, as one that had nothing to do with it; will not all this make amends, will not this poverty rise to great riches ? The apostle Paul tells us so.   Wherefore this may well make satisfaction to God for goods lost.

2dly, If justice complain of the law defaced, and as it were abolished by sin ; if she plead that through it the righteous law is made void, and of none effect, and so bring it in, in this inventory of wasted goods, considered only as it is a copy of God's will, an expression of his holiness, an effect of his wisdom, and monument of the same, the least *iota* of which is so precious, as not all in heaven and earth can make amends for its loss :—should justice make this complaint, then let the reply be, that our Redeemer's head was in the making of that law; and that the hand of him who was the ' Mighty Counsellor,' did guide the pen that wrote it in Adam's heart at first ; and further, that himself is the substantial image of God, and the πρωτότυπον of the law.   And besides, when it was lost, and no copy on earth to be found, he it was that wrote it in the consciences of men fallen.   In which sense the apostle John says, that it is he who ' enlightens every man that comes into the world,' John i. 9.   And because that was but an imperfect copy, it was he that further delivered the law, of which David says it was perfect : Ps. xix. 7, ' The law of the Lord is perfect, converting the soul : the testimony of the Lord is sure, making wise the simple ;' and renewed it on Mount Sinai, Gal. iii. 19.   And in the fulness of time himself came, and vindicated it from all corrupt glosses in his preaching, fulfilled it in his life, and in fulfilling it, writ it out again with his own hands, and so set a more perfect copy than ever was extant in the hearts and lives of angels.   ' I came not to destroy the law,' says he, ' but to fulfil it.' Yea, and if all the copies of the law that are in the world were burnt, they might be all renewed in his story, insomuch that he is reckoned a new founder of it.   ' A new commandment' (says the apostle, 1 John ii. 8), ' write I unto you,' and so the apostle Paul speaks of ' fulfilling the law of Christ,' Gal. vi. 2.   ' Bear ye one another's burdens, and so fulfil the law of Christ.'   Yea, and suppose, that that covenant (which is the first story and copy of God's will and wisdom) had been utterly lost (like as some of Solomon's books were), yet he by his works of mediation makes a new story of another wisdom infinitely more glorious, viz., the gospel, whereof he is the sole founder, and of whom it is written as being the subject of it, the least line of which is worth all the law, so that the angels stand amazed at the ' treasures of wisdom' that are to be found therein, being deeper than ever were revealed in the law.   The law, *that* ' came by Moses, but grace and truth came by Jesus Christ,' John i. 17—a new volume of truths, which had not been true, if he by his blood had not made them so.

3dly, Though God's image be lost by sin, yet he is such an image of him, as the very sight and beholding of him renews it, and changeth men into the same image : 2 Cor. iii. 18, ' But we all, with open face beholding as in a glass the glory of the Lord, are changed into the same image from glory to glory, even as by the Spirit of the Lord.'   Yea, the image which he renews is a better image than that of Adam's, it is of a higher strain and key, and raised by higher motives.

4thly, As for loss of service, to repair it, ' He took on him the form of a servant,' Phil. ii. 7.   And such a servant he was, as was not to have been hired amongst all the creatures.   They all could not do the work that he did ; ' The government of the whole world is upon his shoulders,' Isa. ix. 6. He easeth his Father of it for the present, and when he hath brought him in infinite revenues of glory, he will at last ' deliver up the kingdom to him,' 1 Cor. xv. 24, with a greater surplusage than else would have been had out of that begun course of providence taken up at the creation. And if you will not reckon that as part of satisfaction, yet consider the service he did in the priest's office, wherein God acknowledged him his servant. He despatched more work in those thirty-three years wherein he lived, yea, in those three hours wherein he suffered, than ever was or will be done by all creatures to eternity. It was a good six-days work when the world was made ; and he had a principal hand in that, neither hath he been idle since ; ' I and my Father work hitherto,' says Christ, John v. 17. But that three hours' work upon the cross, was more than all the other. Eternity will not have more done in it, than virtually was done in those three hours ; so as that small space of time was τὸ νῦν æternitatis. As they say of eternity, that it is all time contracted into an instant, so was all time, past, and to come, into those few hours, and the merit of them. For he then made work for the Spirit, and indeed for all the three persons, unto eternity. He then did that which the Spirit is writing out in grace and glory for ever, yea, and all that ever was or will be done towards the saints, was then perfected : ' He perfected for ever them that are sanctified, by that one offering :' Heb. x. 12, 14, ' But this man, after he had offered one sacrifice for sins for ever, sat down on the right hand of God ;' ver. 14, ' For by one offering he hath perfected for ever them that are sanctified.'

CHAPTER VII.

That Christ hath repaired the loss of honour which God sustained by sin.— Satisfaction in point of honour being to be measured by the excellency, dignity, and reputation of the person satisfying.—Christ being God-man, in this respect makes the greatest which could be.

But the greatest evil of sin lies in the injury by it done unto the honour, and sovereign glory, and to the person of God himself, which is the thing that makes sin so heinous, that the difficulty of satisfying God herein is insuperable by all the creatures (as hath been shewed), unto which, notwithstanding, we shall see Christ is as much enabled, as we have seen him to be unto the former, to make amends for the damage which God sustained.

Honour (as was said) being a personal thing, and a due resulting out of personal perfections, answerably therefore satisfaction therein is fundamentally to rise out of, and to be measured by, the personal worth, dignity, excellency, and reputation of the person who undertakes to satisfy. Wherefore, as the foundation of this great demonstration, let us consider briefly the personal worth of Christ our surety, as from whence all his satisfaction receives its force and value, and so we will go on to shew what his person hath done to make amends therein ; and then by comparing (as we go along) both what he is, and what he hath done to satisfy, with what is in the dishonour done to God by sin (which is the thing to be satisfied for), you will see all the disproportions that have been mentioned and can be thought of, to make sin so above measure sinful, exceeded, and wholly overcome. Now as a ground-work to this, I will take but that one place ;—

Who, being in the form of God, thought it no robbery to be equal with God : but made himself of no reputation, and took upon him the form of a servant, and was made in the likeness of men: and being found in fashion as a man, *he humbled himself, and became obedient unto death, even the death of the cross.* —PHIL. ii. 6–8.

A place full and adequate to my scope, wherein (you see) the apostle argues the efficacy of Christ's merit, and the worth of it, from hence, that being equal with God, viz., in glory (as the opposite to *he humbled himself* shews), he should be humbled ; and that he should humble himself, and become obedient, &c., and all for the glory of God the Father. Every word is weighty, and speaks satisfaction ; and that he, so great a person, for greatness of glory equal with God ; for right to glory, one that thought it no robbery to challenge it ; for the kind of glory which was his due, it was not accidental, but, substantial, ' being in the form of God ;' that he should be emptied of all, and lay aside that honour, which was due unto him, yea, suffer all his glory to be debased, and his honour laid in the dust, and himself to be humbled to the greatest and basest of evils, death, and of all deaths the most shameful, ' the death of the cross,' and not humbled passively only, but that he should voluntarily ' humble himself, and become obedient,' and that the object of this subjection should be but actions only, not* himself, his person, so as all that he did or suffered reflected on himself, and his person was humbled in all ; and all this, to recover God's honour lost, it was ' to the glory of God the Father' (as the closure of all hath it) ; surely all this (as you will see) must needs make a full amends.

Now for the clearing of this point and demonstration, whence it is that this satisfaction ariseth, I will proceed by degrees, until a full satisfaction shall rise up to all your apprehensions, in a way of just reason, as there did unto God himself, by that one oblation of Christ himself for us.

And, *first*, let us consider the worth of the person, upon which the worth of the satisfaction doth depend. And to the manifesting of this, consider we first, that Christ had an essential glory, as he is God, which was the foundation and groundwork. This I need not insist upon, all knowing it, and taking it for granted, though divers interpreters judge it not to be that glory which the text doth directly and in the first place intend, yet to be ultimately supposed, as that which is the original ground of all that oriental transcendent glory, which as God-man he parted withal, for satisfaction to God. And though it be true that this glory of his, as he is merely God, cannot be debased or diminished, and so can never properly become the matter of satisfaction for sin, but it is another glory, which I shall speak of presently, is the matter of it ; yet this is it that was the cause and rise of that God-man's glory, and that doth give the original worth and value to all that Christ did or suffered. You shall still find that the Scripture puts the efficacy of his actions upon the worth of his person ; for, indeed, it is the dignity of the person that dignifies the work. God had respect first to Abel, then to his sacrifice, for the sake of Abel. Therefore, in a proportion, the more worth and esteem the person is of with God, the more worth the actions are. And therefore, as the worth of Christ's person was infinite, so must the worth of his actions be. His person raiseth his actions *in statum sibi similem*, unto a state suitable to himself, as a king doth his children to a state answerable to his own. And as the human nature, being personally united to the Godhead, is raised unto a transcendent privilege by virtue of that union, which no other creature hath, so the actions thereof do, by virtue of the Godhead, come to have *similem statum*, they are raised to a proportionable state also. And as the human nature is

* Qu. ' not actions only, but' ?—ED.

sanctified through that union with the divine, with a sanctification beyond that of habitual graces (as the schoolmen have rightly observed and descried), so the actions thereof are *deitate perfusæ*, they have a divinity in them. As the human nature of Christ, by reason of its union with the Godhead, hath more worth and dignity communicated to it than is or could be in all creatures—' in all things he had the pre-eminence,' Col. i. 18—and therefore when he comes into the world, it was said, ' Let all the angels worship him,' which honour no creature must have ; so his actions and graces are translated into as high a rank of dignity, above the graces and actions of creatures, and this by his person, even as his very human nature is exalted above the rank of all creatures. And this makes his blood to be precious blood indeed, in that it is the ' blood of God,' Acts xx. 28. The worth of this person being substantial, it doth *se totum transfundere*, it transfuseth, or rather casts its whole worth upon his actions, to the utmost of it. And as all the fulness of the Godhead is said to dwell in (Col. ii. 9), and to be personally communicated to, the manhood, making it as glorious as a creature can possibly by God be made, so the whole person doth cast a glorious brightness or lustre, and reflecteth upon the actions he doth in that nature all that personal worth that is communicable. And surely this will equal the proportion of evil that is in our sins ; for as the offence was against an infinitely glorious God, so the works done to take away the offence were wrought by one as infinite. And as the chiefest accent* of the offence lies in this, that it was against an infinite majesty, so the greatness of the satisfaction made lies in this, that it was performed by the mighty God ; which proportion could never have been filled up by any creature who was not God, satisfaction in point of honour depending upon the equal worth of the person honouring, and the person dishonoured. And though the human nature (which is in itself finite) be the *principium quo*, and the instrument by which and in which the second person doth all that he doth ; and therefore answerably the physical being of those actions is but finite *in genere entis*, yet all those articles being attributed to the person who is *principium quod*, the principle which doth, and unto which all is to be ascribed (for *actiones sunt suppositorum*, actions are attributed to the persons, because that is said only to subsist), therefore the moral estimation of them is from the worth of the person that performs them. And thus though the immediate principle, the human nature, be finite, yet the radical principle, the person, is infinite. And both natures being one in person, what the one is said to do or suffer, the other is said to do and suffer ; and therefore his blood is called ' the blood of God.' Yet this is not so to be understood (nor was it necessary unto satisfaction to God) as if the worth of the actions of this person should be as infinite as the person is, essentially and substantially ; for Christ's merits could not be infinite, as God's attributes are ; but it is enough to satisfaction, that they might be valued such in a moral estimation ; for thereby it holds an answerable proportion unto the evil of sin. For as the evil of sin is said to be infinite morally only, and in repute, and *objectivè*, as it is against an infinite person, and not essentially infinite, as the object of it is ; so answerably the satisfaction that it requires to be made for it, needs not to be essentially and physically infinite (for that were impossible), but it is enough if it be, as sin itself is, morally such, and in its value such, which then it will arise to be, when the person that performs it is infinite ; and so this will come to be subjectively infinite, as from an infinite person, as sin is objectively infinite, as against an infinite

* Qu. ' ascent '?—ED.

God. And such a person is the second person in the Trinity, and such therefore is his righteousness, it being the righteousness of him who is God.

But, *secondly*, although this essential glory of the Godhead gives the worth and value to all the actions that Christ did, yet in itself it was not capable of being debased, nor he of being emptied of it; nor could this therefore properly become the object matter which should be offered up to God for satisfaction. For as, in our sinning, God's essential glory is not nor cannot be injured by us, but it is wronged only in the shine and lustre of it, in the putting of itself forth before us creatures, or the manifestations of it (wherein though the essential glory of his Godhead is not obscured, but the manifestation of it only, yet the injury reflects upon that his essential glory, because that was it that was manifested), so in like manner is it in Christ's satisfaction. Christ's essential glory, as he is only God, could of itself alone never have satisfied for sin; for satisfaction in point of honour being to be effected by the lessening of glory in the satisfier, to give glory to him that is to have satisfaction, thence therefore the essential glory of the Godhead (which cannot be impaired of itself), if it remained unmanifested, it could never satisfy. But if this second person, putting himself forth to be manifested, will suffer himself to be obscured in that glory which is due to him when he comes to manifest himself, this indeed will come in to be fit matter for satisfaction.

For, *thirdly*, if the Godhead of Christ had gone about to manifest itself in works only, or such ways as are common to the other persons of the Trinity with himself, as by creating of worlds, making of laws, &c., he had not by those ways satisfied neither; because the other persons had had as joint an interest in all such kind of manifestations as himself had, and the obscurement of him in such manifestations had reflected equally upon the other two persons as upon himself. Wherefore over and above that his essential glory, he must have a manifestative glory, an outward, visible brightness of glory, and that also such as must become personal, and proper, and peculiar to him, so as to none of the other persons; that as it may be capable of being obscured, so also that obscurement of it may reflect upon his person, and upon it alone.

Therefore, *fourthly*, the Son of God, if he make satisfaction for sin, must necessarily be supposed first to take, or to have taken on him the nature of some reasonable creature, either of mankind or of the angels, into personal fellowship with himself; which would be both a peculiar way of manifesting himself and of his glory not common to the other two persons, and would also draw in all his personal excellencies into such an engagement, as that, both in the manifestation of himself in that nature assumed, his personal glory may be interested, and also, in the obscurement and clouding of himself in that manifestation, all these his excellencies may be said to be abased likewise, and so come to reflect upon the whole person himself, who is thus glorious, and upon all that is in him: and thus fitly come to make a full satisfaction.

Now, in the *fifth* place, let us consider what a manifestative glory is due to the Son of God, if he assume a creature into one person with himself. And herein consider we, that that nature or creature which he shall assume (be it man or angel) must by inheritance exist in the form of God, Phil. ii. 6; which ' form of God' I here take not to be put for the essence of God, as neither is ' the form of a servant,' in the following sentence, taken for the nature of man simply considered, but for that debased appearance in which he in our nature came into the world, not as a Lord, glorious, but covered with infirmities; and this expression seems to be all one with that, Rom. viii. 3, ' He came in the likeness of sinful flesh.' And so in like manner the ' form of God' here, is that God-like glory, and that manifestation of the Godhead, which was, and must needs be due to appear in the nature assumed; for *form* is put for an outward appearance and manifestation, in respect of which Christ, as God-man, is called ' the brightness of his Father's glory,' Heb. i. 2. Brightness (you know) is not the substance of light, but the appearance of it. And so also he is called ' the image of the invisible God,' Col. i. 15. The meaning of which is this, that whereas God's essential glory is invisible (for ' he dwells in light that no man can approach unto,' 1 Tim. vi. 16). Christ assuming our human nature, becomes the image of it, and so makes it visible to us, God having stamped all his glory upon his face, that we might see it in him: 2 Cor. iv. 6, ' For God, who commanded the light to shine out of darkness, hath shined in our hearts, to give the light of the knowledge of the glory of God, in the face of Jesus Christ.' So that if the Son of God will assume our nature, then it will follow that unto that nature there is due a God-like glory, so much transcending all creatures, that all might plainly see and say, certainly that nature is united to God; surely that man must needs be God as well as man: Hence,

1. He was to be endowed with privileges answerable to the dignity of the person assuming that nature; for if that nature becomes one in person with the Son of God, he becomes one in the privileges of the person also, and so that nature is to have a glory, ' as of the only begotten Son of God' (as the evangelist speaks, John i. 14), proper and peculiar to him. And so, besides that essential glory of his Godhead, there will necessarily be due to that person, in that nature assumed, a more manifestative glory shining forth, than could have arisen to God any other way; for God manifested in the flesh personally, must needs have (as his due) more manifestative glory, and so manifest more of the essential glory of the Godhead, than God manifested in all his other works, be they never so transcendent: even as there is more honour due unto a king, if he in person shew himself, than if his arms only be set up, or proclamation be made in his name. And in this respect Christ God-man may be said in a safe sense to be ' equal with God,' as here in the text, not in essence, but in a communication of privileges: that as God hath life in himself alone, and it is a royalty incommunicable to any mere creature, so this Son of man, when once united thus unto the Godhead, is also said to ' have life in himself,' John v. 26, this equality, or *ἰσότης*, not being to be understood of equality in proportion, but of likeness, and is all one with that which Zechariah speaks of his manhood, when he calls him ' the man God's fellow,' Zech. xiii. 7, one in joint commission with him. And thus Christ himself interprets it, John v., when the Jews, looking at him as a mere man, had objected it unto him as blasphemy that ' he made himself equal with God;' ver. 18 (it is the same word that is here used in the text), Christ answered them, ver. 19. And you find that his answer runs upon this, that even as he was Son of man (which was it that made them to stumble so at his former words), his privileges were such by the union with the second person, that he had a true kind of partnership with God the Father in his privileges, and such as did arise to a likeness, though not to an essential equality: so ver. 19. It is true (says he), ' The Son can do nothing of himself, but what he sees the Father do; and yet whatever things he doth, these also doth the Son likewise.' And so, he goes on to shew, that he could do like things to his

Father, and how he was to be honoured as his Father, ver. 23; and had life in himself, as his Father had, ver. 26; and had all judgment committed to him, &c. And that he might be understood to speak this of himself as God-man, he expressly adds, ' Because he is the Son of man,' ver. 27.

2. And hence, *secondly*, unto the Son of God thus dwelling in a human nature (when it shall be first assumed), all this honour and glory is due: it is proper to him; and therefore it is here said in the text, ' he thought it no robbery' for him to challenge it. Yet of all things God is tender of his glory; 'I will not give my glory to another,' Isa. xlii. 8. But Christ God-man dares challenge such a glory as we have been speaking of, as his due, and it is no robbery for him to do it, because it is his right. As, is worship to be performed unto God? So it is to be given to Christ as dwelling in a human nature: Ps. xlv. 11, ' He is thy Lord, worship thou him.' Yea, ' let all the angels worship him,' when he comes into the world, and so as considered with his manhood, Heb. i. 6: and ' Worthy art thou' (say the saints and angels, and all creatures) 'to receive honour and glory;' and so ' they fall down before him,' Rev. v. 12. And therefore this high character of him is put in, 1 Cor. ii. 8, that ' they crucified the Lord of glory.' He was Lord, and possessor of all the glory that God hath, for as his Father hath given him to have life, so glory in himself also, as in that John v. And here in the Philippians he is said to exist in this glory, Phil. ii. 6, not that his human nature had this glory actually put upon it at first (for he was born as we are, and took upon him the form of a servant); but because thus to exist in this glory was his due, from which he could not be put by; so as, if God would ordain him to subsist personally in a human nature, it was his due to have existed thus gloriously in the form of God, and not in the form of a servant, which is put in to shew how the form of a servant was merely arbitrary in him, in that another form was due to him, and in respect of that dueness is accounted as really existent, with an existency of right (for it should so have done), which is a real existency; even as one that is born a king, though he for some end take on him a mean condition, yet he being born a king does so exist, and it prejudiceth not his right all that while, for it is innate and bred with his existing. And therefore the Scripture speaks of Christ even as Son of man, as if as Son of man he had been in heaven, and had come down: not that actually he had been there, but because it was his right to have been there the first moment of the assumption of that nature. Thus John iii. 13, ' And no man hath ascended up to heaven, but he that came down from heaven, even the Son of man who is in heaven.' He (you see) says, that he is in heaven.

Thus much shall suffice to have shewn the foundation of satisfaction, from the qualifications and requisites in the person.

CHAPTER VIII.

What this excellent and glorious person did for satisfaction, brings more honour to God than ever sin had done dishonour.—The glory which redounds to God from this person's condescending to assume human nature, and that too in such a low condition, and meanest circumstances.

Now to come to the second head proposed, namely, to shew what it is in or of such a person that may become, or is the matter of this satisfaction offered up to God, for the debasement of his glory by sin. To clear this, I will first shew what it is that God reckons not upon for satisfaction in this person; what God cuts off from the account, because he would be sure to have full satisfaction *in specie*, in kind, which will also serve the more to set forth the fulness, the abundancy of Christ's satisfaction, when God accepts not of what might have been so accounted, but stands upon more; which Christ performs to him.

As, 1. The very condescending of the second person, who natively and essentially is so great, to assume man's nature, although in this form of God described, invested with all that manifestative glory spoken of, and this from and upon the first moment of his assuming it; if this act of assuming had been done and undertaken principally in order and with intention to satisfy God, by bringing in a new glory to him, greater than that which he lost by him, and this without the least humbling of himself; I ask, why might not this in just reason have been accounted satisfaction?

For (1.) he had thereby lessened himself to give glory to God. For in that assumption, and in that communication of himself to a creature, he takes on him such relations as do in some respects abate of the height of his native personal glory, as he is considered merely as second person; and in respect to this assumption, he is made less than what before he was. For now it may be said of him, as it was by himself, that ' his Father is greater than he,' John xiv. 28, whereas he might have kept himself in a full equality to him in all respects for ever, and to have had no such diminishing respect affixed to him.

And (2.) by this voluntary act alone he had brought in unto God a new and further revelation of the Godhead than ever was obscured by sin; and it is certain that he had never assumed man's nature, and thus lessened himself, but that so he might manifest the glory of the Godhead in such a manner as otherwise it never should have been. Therefore for him thus to lessen himself, to the end to manifest and exalt the glory of the Godhead the utmost way it could be, or more than otherwise it should have been, might not this make amends for the glory that sin would take from God? And the reason of this is, that satisfaction being a return of as much glory as was lost, and that by this means (if no other were added) more manifestative glory would come in unto God than either was or ever could have been debased or impaired by sin, why therefore might it not have been accounted satisfactory, if it had been ordered simply unto this end? And further also, even this would have served to fill up many of those disproportions found in the evil of sin. For as the evil of Adam's sin (which was the first sin) lay in this, that he who was a creature affected and aspired to be as God—He is become as one of us, said God, Gen. iii. 22— so Christ's obedience, in assuming our nature, would herein have answered it, that he that is God becomes a creature, and on the other side is become as one of us men; so to bring in a new honour unto God. So that, look how high our nature would have ascended, so low doth he descend; and as sin is a turning from God to the creature, so in this act the Creator descends from the height of his glory to become a creature, and join himself in a nearer union with us than wherein we in sinning affected to join ourselves to the Creator.

And then again, 2. All the works and actions which, in that nature thus assumed, in this height of glory that becomes due to it, he will set himself about to work, and to shew forth the glory of the Godhead of his Father, and of himself; even these also, by reason of that worth which his personal perfections do contribute unto them, might haply be estimated sufficient to give satisfaction in point of honour, though no further debasement be laid upon our nature in him. As suppose that he would have done nothing therein but work miracles, utter his treasures of wisdom, shew forth his holiness and power, &c.; yet these being from a person so infinitely glorious, have therefore an infinite worth in them all, even as all his actions, now he is in heaven, have ; for the person is infinite, and he it is that gives this acceptance and this lustre to them. And these would also have brought more glory to God than was lost, and so would have countervailed our sins. For all the actions that he doth, and all the glory that he hath now he is glorified, are all ' to the glory of God the Father ' (as this text hath it), and therefore if in all that he had ever done he had as directly glorified himself as now in heaven, yet all of those actions being further and besides, to the glory of God the Father, they might superabundantly have made amends for the dishonour that sin brought him.

But God reckons all this not as any part of that satisfaction which we are a-seeking after. He accepts not simply the assumption of our nature, though never so glorious, and he accepts it not, although it were a lessening of the second person. In the Scripture I find nothing for it, and what God reckons not satisfaction to him, we must not account such. Neither do I affirm it, having only pleaded what might be argued (and what haply God might have reckoned), thereby the more to advance that satisfaction which Christ hath performed in this human nature ; the like whereof I did when I discoursed the point of satisfaction for goods. It is indeed the foundation of satisfaction, and makes way to it, but is not a part of it. And so the actions of him now glorified in heaven, though they have so much worth in them, yet God reckons them not to be͵a part of satisfaction ; for that was all finished here in his humbled estate, ere ever he ascended.

And the reason of this, why this assumption of our nature in a glorious condition, or the actions thereof, are not mentioned in Scripture as any part of satisfaction may be ; both because the sole end of Christ's assuming our nature, *quoad substantiam mysterii*, for the substance of this mystery, was not (as I have elsewhere* shewed) the redemption of man; but there were other ends, which taken all together are as great as this, if not greater ; as, the manifestion of God to the utmost. God could not have been manifested to the utmost, but by lessening one of the persons of the Trinity by an hypostatical union ; as also because God would make the subject of all the parts of satisfaction to be Christ, God-man, and not the second person simply so considered, and therefore he must be supposed ordained to assume man's nature, ere he becomes a fit subject for satisfaction. But the act of assuming our nature is the act of the second person, merely so considered ; and so, though done in order to satisfaction, as being the foundation of it, yet is not a part of it. And thus all this glory spoken of being due to the person in this nature, and so to shine forth in this nature ; for him to lay it aside when he assumes this nature, and for him then to take the form of a servant, instead of this glorious form and manifestation of the Godhead ; this draws the manhood also into the merit of such a debasement, because a greater glory was due unto him ; and he might be truly said to exist in his glory whenever that nature was assumed, for so he ought to have done, and it might have been stood upon.

So then, the first ingredient into this satisfaction lies in the laying aside

* In the ' Discourse of God the Father, and his Son Jesus Christ,' Book iii., chap. 1, 2, 3, 4, in the second volume of his Works. [Vol. IV. of this Edition.—ED.]

the glory due to the second person when he should dwell in a human nature; and instead thereof, taking on him the form of a servant, and the likeness of men, or of 'sinful flesh,' as Rom. viii. 3, that is, frail flesh, subject to infirmities and miseries, as ours is here. And so the total sum of that satisfaction which God reckons of as such, is here also cast up first and last to have been, the taking the form of a servant, humbling himself, being emptied, or of no reputation, and becoming obedient in his life, and this to the death of the cross, as being the last part of this payment. And this (you will see) will in so great a person amount to and become the matter of a full and just satisfaction indeed, even to a flowing over. Which is the second thing in this head we inquire and seek for.

In the second place therefore, positively to lay down and define wherein Christ's satisfaction unto God for sin in point of honour lies; it is in brief this, viz., Christ's voluntary laying aside all the glory that was due to his person in his human nature assumed, and his submitting himself to the utmost debasement due to sinners, in pure obedience to his Father, thereby to restore and return glory unto God for the diminishing of it by sin. This God required, and this Christ performed, and this is satisfaction indeed, even to flowing over. God in his demanding satisfaction stood so much upon his glory, that,

1. He would not be contented with the mere lessening of this great person, in assuming our nature glorious; but he will have him take upon him (as this text hath it) the form of a servant, and be found as men here on earth, even clothed with the same frail condition of passible nature that sinful men are found in; nor,

2. Will he be contented with such actions from Christ in that nature debased, whereby Christ might seek and shew forth his own glory immediately and directly—'I seek not my own glory' (says Christ, John ix. 50), 'but the glory of him that sent me'—but he will have him perform such actions, and submit to such sufferings, as shall take away glory from him, and obscure and veil his glory due to him. He will have him take the form of a mere servant, and become wholly obedient, and not be for himself at all; who yet might think it no robbery to seek his own glory directly with God's. Nor,

3. Will God be satisfied to have this his glory a little veiled, and in some parts clouded; but he will have him robbed and spoiled of all manifestative glory whatsoever due unto him. He will have him emptied, or made of no reputation, as it is here; the Messiah shall have nothing left (as Daniel speaks, Dan. ix. 26), not a grain or mite of the riches of his glory which he could call his own, as God doth. Yea, if there be any debasement worse than other, he will have him obedient to it, even to death; and if any death be more shameful than other, he will have him submit to it, even the death of the cross. And,

4. God will have all this come from him willingly, heartily, and freely. He is not only thus to be humbled, but he must 'humble himself,' as the text also hath it; who indeed was so great that no other could do it, without his own free consent; and all this to the glory of God the Father.

And ere we go any further, do but think with yourselves that if a person, such as in the first head hath been described, who is equal with God in glory, will, to glorify God and exalt him, not only condescend to lessen himself, and that so much as to have it said, the second person is made a creature; but will further, at the command of his Father, lay aside even that glory which is still due to him when thus made man, yea, even empty himself wholly of all that glory personally due to him, and take on him the form of a servant instead thereof; and yet further, will actually become obedient in the performance of all such actions, not only which it was meet so great a person glorified in heaven should employ himself in, and shew his own, and his Father's glory jointly in, but such as men on earth shew their subjection in, both as mere creatures and as sinners; yea, and not only so, but will be obedient to the utmost of sufferings, even to death, and to the most shameful and ignominious death, the death of the cross; and will perform all this voluntarily, with an intention of mind and will, directing all to this sole end, so to make God alone glorious by and through his own utter debasement and obscurement, falling down thus low to exalt and set God up thus high, by his having so great a person, and in himself so glorious, thus obedient to him, and lowered for his glory's sake; I appeal even to the justice that is in all men's hearts, if it doth not both equalise the dishonour done to God by sin, and also bring in a greater overplus of glory than was taken from God by it, and so make a full amends.

CHAPTER IX.

The principal matter of Christ's satisfaction was not only in a diminishing of his glory, but despoiling him of it.—And that he did this willingly, he humbled himself.—And that his person was the subject of this debasement and humiliation.

But to speak yet more distinctly, the matter of his satisfaction lies in these three things principally, all which are in the text.

I. That it was not only a lessening of his glory, but a despoiling and emptying him of it, or a making him of no reputation.

II. That this was voluntary in him; *he humbled*, actively; it is not said *he was humbled*, passively.

III. That the subject of this humbling was *himself*, considered both as the subject-author of all this obedience, and also as the subject-matter involved in this obedience and debasement: ' he humbled himself.'.

I. It was an emptying himself of glory to glorify God; which, in the strictest way that justice can require, becometh properly and truly satisfaction in point of glory debased. To clear this, let us consider the difference between giving honour simply, and giving satisfaction for honour. We give mutual honour to one another without debasing ourselves, as inferiors to superiors, and superiors to inferiors, by mutual uncovering of the head each unto other. But if satisfaction in point of honour be strictly stood upon, then some acts of humbling are exacted from the party that is to satisfy, even a taking down of the glory of the one, to restore it to the other; examples whereof we often see, by the sentence of such courts as deal in point of honour and the restitution of it. Now to make use of this in the point in hand. A mere creature indeed cannot give the simple tribute of glory that is due unto God, but by humbling itself some way, either in obedience or worship; all the acts of which have a humbling of the creature in them. Thus the angels cover their faces, and cry, ' Holy, holy, holy,' &c., and the elders cast down themselves and their crowns, and cry, ' Worthy art thou to receive honour and glory.' And the reason is, because of the transcendent distance and disproportion between God and mere creatures; his glory being so high and sovereign, that they cannot shew forth the greatness of it, but by veiling their own glory before him. Thus the distance between kings and ordinary men, being in the institution of it so high and sovereign, the greatness of their majesty and glory cannot be held forth but by their subjects debasing of themselves, and falling down before them. And in this respect, the creature's debasement could never have satisfied for God's honour lost and impaired; because all its debasements are but suitable ways to give and shew forth that glory of God which is simply due from them although they had never sinned. But Christ, though he were lessened indeed (as became God-man), yet still, this man being one person with God, and so God as well as man, and so being by right of inheritance in joint commission with his Father, and set up in such a kind of equality, as hath been shewn, hence, as two kings in joint commission for the government of a kingdom, and by a like right, though they give glory each to other, yet not by debasement of their glory ; so nor was Christ to have done, as now in heaven he doth not, where, though he intercedes for us, yet *more regio*, as a king, ' sitting' (not kneeling, as on earth) ' at God's right hand ;' and *stilo regio*, in the language of a king—' Father, I will,' as John xvii. 24. It is not performed in a way of a humbling debasement, though in a way that argues a lessening of him. And thus he might have kept his state and majesty, as now in heaven he doth, and have given glory to God for ever, upon such terms, and by such ways, as should withal have held forth his own glory jointly and as directly as his Father's. Thus, at the latter day, when he comes to judge the world, he will come in his fullest glory, and ' every knee shall bow to him, to the glory of God the Father ;' this being his due, that he should be honoured together with his Father : ' That all should honour the Son ' (says Christ, speaking of that judgment committed to himself), ' even as they honour the Father,' John v. 22, 23. Thus indeed he might (as now he doth) have glorified God. But then all this in him would not have been satisfaction for the impairing and diminution of God's glory by sin. This is no way to be effected (no, not by Christ), but by a humbling, a lowering, a debasement, an emptying himself of glory, to restore it to his Father. For look, as in point of goods restitution is not made but by a parting with some of that man's goods that is to satisfy, to be added to his who is to be satisfied, so in point of honour, if satisfaction for dishonour (which is a taking away of honour, or reflecting disparagement on him who is dishonoured) be to be performed, there must in like manner be a taking away of, or a parting with, honour and glory in the satisfier, done for the injured person's sake, to give again unto the dishonoured, so as his glory shall be made up, or shewed forth by the other's debasement. For else it ariseth not to a proportion, which is the rule of justice in such cases. Therefore, nothing but a debasement can make a full amends for a debasement; but when so, then a proportion is observed; and honour can never be repaired but out of another's honour impaired, for it must be paid in its own coin; and in this case, you cannot repair a loss to the one, but you must impair it to the other. And this is the true reason why Christ, now he is glorified in heaven, though he be as full of action and employment as ever, and all to the glory of his Father, as much as those actions were which he performed here below ; yet all that now he doth in heaven hath not a meritoriousness in it, nor is it accounted of as being satisfactory for sin, as what he did here below was ; yet all those actions have an infinite worth in them, in respect of the person performing them, considered merely as an agent and efficient cause of them ;

and they are infinitely acceptable to God (as glorifying him) to other ends; but still, they arise not to answer the proportion that in justice satisfaction requires. For though they are the actions of Christ considered as an inferior, and one made less, and that in order to the glorifying of God, yet so as he still having a right to be glorified with God in all jointly, and as directly as God himself is to be glorified, and accordingly, all these actions, as immediately holding forth his own glory as his Father's; therefore, though God reckons and accounts of them as a glorifying of himself, yet not as a satisfaction to himself for his glory impaired, because Christ is not humbled in any of them, so as by a debasement in them to give glory unto God, but does now share with God in the tribute of glory that comes in, as being his due. But here on earth he abated of, and hid his glory; he was emptied of it, to the end that thereby what was lost to him might accrue unto God; which debasement does truly and properly become fit matter for satisfaction.

II. That which gives worth and acceptation to this debasement of his, to make it satisfactory, is, that himself, or his person (so great a person), is included in it: ' He humbled himself and became obedient; ' and so, this obedience of his, being in such a way of debasement, does draw and take into it all his fore-named personal perfections, to contribute an infinite dignity, worth, and satisfactoriness unto all he did or suffered; and this, from the consideration of *himself* as being included therein, and so in a double respect and relation giving a double gift unto his obedience, as I may so speak.

1. If his person be considered as the worker and efficient cause of all he did or suffered, and withal, as the root from whence it sprung, and as the subject author of all those graces and self-denials, this gives a worth to his obedience and sufferings.

2. As his person and all his excellencies are yet further involved as the *materiale*, the subject matter itself of this his obedience, as that which he offered up in all that he either did or suffered, so the honour of his person not only gives an influence of worth into his works of obedience, as he is the efficient of them, but further, in that his honour was reflected upon in them all, and he debased himself therein. And thus his person is doubly enwrapped in all he did; and therefore, in the text, it is said, 'He humbled himself and became obedient;' that is, in his actions of obedience himself was humbled and made subject. There is a reduplication, *he* and *himself*, noting that they came from his person, and that they again reflected upon his person, and were not only proceeding from *persona infinita*, in an infinite person, but are *circa personam infinitam*, concerned about him.

1. Now for the first; Consider him but as the subject author of them; and yet even so, all his graces and actions, in his person thus humbled, receive an infinite value and worth from him. Therefore the efficacy of his righteousness is put upon this, that it was the righteousness of God and our Saviour, that is, our Saviour who was God. So 2 Peter i. 1, ' Simon Peter, a servant and an apostle of Jesus Christ, to them that have obtained like precious faith with us, through the righteousness of God and our Saviour Jesus Christ.' And though this relation of his actions unto his person simply and alone considered in Christ as glorified, God accounts not satisfaction, yet they coming from Christ as humbled, he accepts of all his graces and actions, not only as having an infinite worth in them, but also as part of satisfaction. And to that end he considers this in them, that they are

all from a person so infinite, and in that respect they add a distinct worth to that satisfaction, which thus humbled he performs, from this other that follows ; which is,

2dly, That his person is further to be considered as the *materiale*, the matter of all his obedience, namely, in this respect, that his person was debased in all that obedience of his, so that it came to pass, that this his obedience was not only accepted because the offerer of it, the sacrificer, was a person of that worth, but also in that himself and his glory became the sacrifice and offering itself. He not only gave honour to God by his actions, and with his graces ; but did also therein give away his own honour, the honour of his person.   I will make this plain to you by a place of Scripture, namely, Heb. ix., where that that gives weight and efficacy to his blood to 'purge our consciences' (which all the sacrifices in the world could never have done, as the apostle says, verses 13, 14), is made to be this, that ' through the eternal Spirit he offered up himself,' as the 14th verse concludes. Whence observe, that he, viz., his person with his Godhead, was considered not only as the offerer (which those words import, ' through the eternal Spirit'), or as the author of that action of sacrificing, as the priests were of those sacrifices of the law (which is the first consideration mentioned in the former part of this distinction), but besides, himself was the thing offered, as those words shew, ' offered up himself.' So that that action had a double respect to his person, both as the subject author and as the matter, both as the sacrificer and as the sacrifice.   The priests, they offered indeed, but it was the gifts which people brought, so as therein the priest was one thing, and the sacrifice another ; but here Christ was both offerer and offering ; there the giver was one thing, and the gift another ; but here Christ was both the giver and gift : Eph. v. 2, ' Who hath loved us, and given himself for us, an offering and a sacrifice to God.'   And this is that which the Scripture mentions to have given a further infinite over-balancing weight of merit and satisfaction, and distinct from the former, unto all that Christ did, namely, that in all he still gave away himself.   They were not mere actions from him and in him, but such as included himself as given, and humbled in them.   This, as the places above mentioned, so that in Heb. i. 3 does plainly shew, ' having by himself purged our sins ;' mark it, not by actions merely from him, but by himself humbled in these actions and sufferings.   And therefore the same author to the Hebrews puts the main value upon himself considered as the person offered, and not only on himself considered as the offerer ; and indeed he distinctly mentions both.   For throughout the 7th chapter he shews that it was necessary he should be the priest, the offerer, that should sacrifice, and so appease God's wrath, shewing oppositely, the insufficiency of the Levitical priests, although their sacrifices had had no defect, and so concludes, that ' such an high priest became us,' &c., ver. 26 ; and yet because all the merit lay not in the bare person of the priest as an offerer, had not the sacrifice itself been answerable, therefore he further shews in the 9th and 10th chapters, the worth of that sacrifice also which by this our high priest was offered, which was no other than himself.   And this the apostle shews as considered apart by itself from the former consideration ; and therefore in like manner he oppositely shews the weakness and unworthiness that was in all the Levitical sacrifices and things offered, as he had formerly done of those offerers, chap. vii., still mentioning the worth of that one sacrifice of himself ; shewing that he was also the person offered, and that *that* was it which gave that super-eminent worth to his offering, to take sins away.   And it is plain that the apostle considers both these, for he argues the perfection of his satisfaction from both.

Now to clear this distinction by comparing an instance or two together; when Christ wrought a miracle, turning water into wine, this was an action from him merely as the author of it, and wherein he humbled not himself, which therefore made up no part of satisfaction. It was from him, but it reflected not thus upon, nor included his person thus in it. But when he was circumcised, and became obedient to his parents and to the law, all these actions, as they were from his person, so also they included in them the humiliation of himself, and had therefore the whole worth of the person who did or suffered them communicated unto them, as being included in them, and as reflecting upon the whole honour of his person in a way of debasement; for his glory is himself. Therefore in all his obedience, doing, and suffering, his glory being reflected upon, or debased, his person is said to be involved in the matter of it, as a king's honour is, when he doth an action that debaseth himself.

Or if you will yet more accurately consider how many ways himself or his person was included in this, then in a word to sum up all.

1. His obedience was from an infinite person as the cause thereof.

And, 2, performed likewise in himself as the immediate subject thereof; the difference between which two is evident; for the Holy Ghost, who is God, when he prays in us, and helpeth our infirmities, and makes intercession for us, though he be the efficient of the prayers made, yet these are not wrought in himself, but in us as the subject of them, and therefore are called our prayers. And hence these actions of his in us have not this great worth in them, though he be the author of them. But Christ's satisfaction and intercession were not only effected by him, but further, were performed in himself as the subject in whom the action doth reside, and to whom it appertains for ever.

3. It was not only performed by him, and in him, but himself was the matter of the obedience; 'he gave himself.' And so near an alliance of his obedience unto his person, must needs every way add an infinite worth unto it. Thus much for the second requisite to the matter of satisfaction.

III. Now, in the third place, add this other also, that all his obedience and humiliation was voluntary and arbitrary.

1. Voluntary, 'He humbled himself;' which I know is included in what hath been even now said in that second head fore-mentioned; yet something there is, that the distinct notion of it addeth to all the former, and it is a necessary requisite in satisfaction, which cannot be without it. Wherefore all that Christ did was voluntarily done by him; 'he humbled himself.' For submission and obedience forced, or to give honour to another out of constraint, can never satisfy, but rather prejudiceth it. And as honour sought for by the person himself who is to be honoured is not honour (as Solomon saith), so constrained submission in the person honouring another, redounds not to the honour of him who is to be honoured, and so not to satisfaction. And therefore among other defects in the satisfaction to arise from the punishment of men in hell, this is justly to be reckoned one, that all that submission and punishment of men and devils is not voluntary, but forced. But now, this of Christ's was voluntary; 'he became obedient.'

Yea, and 2, it was voluntary in a further consideration than can be attributed to the obedience of any creature, in that it was arbitrary in Christ as well as voluntary. He might have stood upon it by reason of his prerogative and equality with his Father, and was at liberty whether he would do that which he did, or not do it. And this the text intimates, when it premiseth unto this his obedience, that he was existing ' in the form of God,' and ' equal with God ;' that is, he might have stood upon his terms not to have subjected himself in any such way of humiliation ; yet ' he humbled himself, and became obedient.' The creature's obedience, though never so voluntary, cannot thus be said to be arbitrary ; ' A necessity lies upon me to preach' (says Paul), ' and woe is unto me if I do it not ;' and yet he preached willingly. It is a due from them, but not so from Christ. And this added unto it, makes it fully and properly satisfaction. And thus much for this second head, the matter of this satisfaction.

CHAPTER X.

The greatness and super-eminent worth of this satisfaction, as performed by such a person.—That hence the acts of his obedience exceed in goodness all the evil that is in sin, and that therefore they make full reparation, since they honour God more than ever sin had dishonoured him.

Now having thus seen the excellencies of the person who was to satisfy, Christ God-man, which excellencies have an influence into the worth and merit of this satisfaction made, and having also viewed the ingredients into the matter of this satisfaction for the dishonour done unto God, I will now come to rear upon these as foundations, demonstrations of the super-eminency that must needs be in the materials of such a satisfaction performed by such a person ; which makes the third and last head propounded. And whereas there were presented many insuperable mountains of difficulty, that lay in the way of all the creatures to satisfy for sin, which they could never pass over or remove ; and such vast gulfs of disproportions between God's dishonour and debasement by sin, and all the creatures' abilities to repair and restore it, by reason of the distance between God himself and them, such that nothing in or from them could ever make up or fill ; you shall now see all and every one of those mountains overtopped and levelled, and before this our mediator, Christ God-man, become a plain, all those chasms and chinks being filled up, and the way of satisfaction made so even and plain, that our faith may pass over it, and walk in it, assisted and supported even with reasons deduced from principles of justice and equity ; and so all the principles of understanding in us may come to see and receive full satisfaction in this satisfaction of his.

In making of this reddition, I shall not be able exactly to keep unto the same method I held in the beginning of this discourse, viz., to bring in the mention of every particular of this satisfaction, in the same order that I marshalled each of those particulars of the creatures' non-satisfaction, so as to set the one against the other in a parallel rank. For the disposing of such materials as do follow in the way of a natural consequence one from the other, must be suited unto the matter itself, not in an artificial, but according to the natural dependence wherein one thing may appear to arise from another. Hence, therefore, when I was to shew the creatures' inabilities, I so ranged and placed those things that should demonstrate, and in such an order, as might, by the consequence that one thing held upon another, best set forth the creatures' insufficiencies, which therefore was most suitable to that subject. And accordingly, now that I am to speak of the abilities that are in Christ, I must present the fulness of them in each

of those particulars so as will best suit with this subject, by setting forth
one particular after another, as they arise from or depend each on other :
arguing in an orderly way from what is to be considered in him that makes
this satisfaction, to make it by degrees rise up to its height and fulness ;
yet so as there shall be no particular ground of difficulty that made it
impossible for the creatures to satisfy, that shall be left out unsatisfied in
these demonstrations of the fulness of Christ's satisfaction, although not in
the same method that in the former part was observed.

The first and lowest consideration, from whence I shall begin to argue
this satisfaction of his, is that which was in the former head given, viz.,
that himself, or his person, is to be considered as the subject of all his graces
and obedience. And let us first see how much even this will contribute
towards the satisfactoriness of his obedience, and equalise the evil and dishonour by sin, and how far it will carry this on.

You may remember how, in the first part of this discourse, viz., the
demonstration of the creatures' inability to satisfy, I shewed both how far
short the graces of a mere creature, never so pure and innocent, do fall, as
not having any worth in them, more than to justify themselves, and that by
God's appointment too ; and likewise how much sin exceeded in evil the
goodness and worth of all mere creatures' graces, and that they did no way
so much honour God as sin dishonoured him. Now let us from this first
consideration, that so infinite a person is the subject of grace and obedience,
shew both,

1. How much their graces are exceeded ; and,
2. Also the evil of sin thereby.

1. These his humbling graces (as I call them), for such only are matter
of satisfaction, and his actions of obedience springing therefrom, infinitely
excel those of mere creatures, conceive them never so vast and large. That
which makes grace more excellent than any other creature, and so is the
true measure of the greater or lesser worth in grace or holiness, is that it
is the participation of the divine nature. Now take but an estimate in your
thoughts of the vast difference between the participation of the divine nature
in Christ, which makes his graces and obedience accepted, and that in mere
creatures. The participation of the divine nature in the grace of creatures,
is but by way of a mere shadow, likeness, or similitude, something resem-
bling ; and so the worth thereof is but such as you would have of the picture
of a king, that is somewhat like him. But the grace of union (as divines
call it, and that in way of distinction from Christ's own graces habitually
considered, as well as from those in mere creatures) which derives worth
into Christ's graces and obedience, is a kind of communication of the Godhead itself personally united, and so diffusing answerable worth and acceptation afore God into the actions of human nature thus united. The difference
herein is such, that whereas in mere creatures, standing afore God under a
covenant of works, and the covenant by mere right of creation is no other,
it is merely their graces and actions that make their persons accepted in
such a covenant, and they have no worth from the person at all whose
graces they are, but the person from them. Now, contrarily, the graces
and actions of Christ do not dignify the person so much, as the person them.
So that look in a proportion how much his person exceeds all the creatures,
so much in their capacity, and measure, and in a moral value, must his
graces and actions of obedience excel all theirs. It is true, that for kind
his grace and ours are and would be the same, for ' of his fulness we receive
grace for grace,' John i. 16. But look, as what a transcendent distance

there is between the worth and excellency that is put upon the body and the actions thereof in a man (by reason of that eternal soul that dwells in it, and is substantially united to it), and the actions of a beast, so that one and the same kind of earth is made capable of, and is to be a partner of eternal life, and of heavenly glory, by reason of the soul in a man, whereas that in a beast is ordained but to a life of sense.   Look in like manner how those actions are ennobled (comparatively to those of beasts), wherein the members of man's body are employed as weapons of righteousness, so that they are actions of eternal consequence, and acceptation with God.   Now an infinitely greater transcendent distance is there between the worth which the person of Christ doth communicate to the human nature, and the actions thereof, or of his person therein (it being thereunto substantially united), and the worth which the person of mere creatures, though supposed to be as full of habitual grace as Christ himself, can communicate to their actions. Though for metal they had been the same that Christ's were, yet wanting this royal stamp of the Deity upon them, they had not been coin that would have passed for payment and satisfaction.   His glory is substantial, and communicates its worth to the utmost to all and every action, so far as the act is capable, even as the whole king's image is stamped upon three-pence as well as sixpence; yet sixpence is of more value, because the matter is capable of more ; and so one action of Christ was capable of more worth than other, yet so as in them all there was an infinite moral dignity from the person.   And again, as all the Godhead in all his fulness is said to dwell in him and his person, so all the whole worth that the substantial excellency of the person can translate is in like manner stamped upon all his actions.   And though the human nature, which in itself is finite, be the *principium quo*, the instrument of all, by whom and in whom the second person doth all he doth, and therefore answerably the physical being of those actions is but finite, *in genere entis*, take them as created productions ; yet all Christ's actions being attributed to the person who is *principium quod* (for *actiones sunt suppositorum*, actions are attributed to and said to be of the persons that perform them, because that is said only to subsist), there-fore the moral estimation of them is infinite.   And though the immediate principle, the human nature, be finite, yet the radical principle, the person, is infinite, and they being one in person, what the one is said to do, the other is said to do also ; and therefore Christ's obedience is called ' the righteousness of God,' and the obedience of God.

2.   Yea, *secondly*, his graces do for this respect so far exceed any that are in creatures, that their goodness (as, Ps. xvi. 2, it is called) equals the utmost evil can be supposed in sin.   For as the offence is against an infinite glorious God, so the holy works are wrought by one as infinite.   And as the highest accent of the essence of sin lies over this head, that it was against an infinite majesty, so the greatness of the satisfaction herein lies, that it was performed by the mighty God.   Which proportion could never have been filled up by any creature who was not God ; satisfaction in point of honour depended upon the equal worth of the person honouring and disgraced.

Yet it is not so to be understood, nor was it necessary, that the worth of the actions should be as infinite as the person, essentially and substantially. For Christ's merits could not be infinite as God's attributes are, nor so loved by God as his attributes are, but that they are so in a moral estima-tion was enough.   For look, as though sin was infinite, yet not so essen-tially, so justice required not an obedience essentially and naturally infinite, but personally infinite, which Christ's is, it being the righteousness of him that is God.

The second thing propounded to be proved was, that his graces and actions of obedience did exceed in goodness the utmost evil that was in sin, which we saw no creature's graces did, or can be valued to do.

1. In the general, the evil of sin lies in this, that it is committed against the great God, and that God is the object of it: so as the utmost aggravation of the evil of sin is taken at the highest but from the worth of the object, God and his glory, against whom it is committed; but the worth of all his graces and actions being taken from the person, the subject, the efficient, from whom they do proceed, look how much more reason there is that the person, who is the author and subject of his actions, should convey more worth to his own actions than a person who is but an object of another's action can do to the action of that other, so much doth his graces, having a person that is God for the subject of them, exceed the evil of sin that is against God, the mere object thereof. For the subject conveys worth to his own actions, as the father conveys nobleness to his child; his child inherits it from him, and so an action doth worth from the person from whom it is natively derived; but that worth, and so that evil too, which it hath from the object is but extrinsecal and borrowed, and therefore the denomination of actions is taken rather from the subject than the object. As when a man understands an angel never so perfectly as the object of his understanding, it is called human knowledge, because man is the subject of it, and it is his knowledge; though the object it is conversant about be an angel, it is not called angelical knowledge. So by the same reason actions derive more proper worth and merit (for both worth and denomination arise from the same root) from the person from whom they come, and in whom they are, than from the person unto which they tend. And therefore though sin be done against God as the object, and so is heinous, yet because this satisfaction was made by God as the subject of it, therefore it is more meritorious than sin can be demeritorious. This satisfaction sucks more nobleness from the subject of it, which is the root it grows upon, than sin can take evil and blackness from the external shadow the Father of lights casts upon it by the sinner's eclipse of him. And the reason is, because all participation is founded upon union, mutual relation, and conjunction, and the more remote and further off the union and relation is, the less a thing participates from it. Now the relation and conjunction between the act and the object is but extrinsecal, it is an external conjunction that is between them, such as is between a man's eye and the sun, they remain strangers still; but the relation, conjunction, and kindred, that is between a person and his actions, is nearer, it is intrinsecal, such as is between the sun and the beams that flow from it, which is yet nearer when the person himself is included in the matter of the very action, as in this of Christ it is, whose person is intrinsecally included as the necessary part of the satisfaction itself. Now if this, that God is but the object of sin, doth cast such a heinousness upon the acts of it which come from us, if such a remote far off extrinsecal relation and conjunction brings forth so much demerit, and makes sin to abound in sinfulness, what will the satisfaction which comes from so great a person as Christ, God-man, and includes that person as a part of the satisfaction itself, how will this nearer union and relation between this person and his actions beget worth and dignity in them?

But then add to this further that other consideration mentioned, which will make a second head of this demonstration, that himself was not only the subject of his graces and actions of obedience, but that himself and his personal worth were included and involved therein as the matter also of the satisfaction (as I shewed at large); hereby it comes to pass that the evil of sin is again afresh exceeded to a flowing over. For as the relation between the act and the subject from whom, and in whom, is more near (as is said) than between the act and the object, so the subject matter, the *materiale* of the action *circa quam* hath a nearer affinity than the subject *in quo*, for it includes it, enwraps it into itself. And so did all Christ's obedience enwrap his glory in it and robbed him of it, and so he sacrificed it to God; and hereby God comes to have honour paid him double, over and over, not only honour returned him from a person as honourable and glorious as himself, which makes it infinite, and more than ever sin took from him, for *honor est in honorante*, actions of honour take value from the person; and as one king may render honour to another when as yet he keeps his state, so might Christ have honoured God, manifesting himself in a glorified condition. But God hath not this single but a double subsidy and tribute of honour; he will have Christ lay down his glory to glorify him, he will have the forfeiture, and not the principal debt only. And as Christ's obedience reduplicates upon his person, he humbled himself, so the honour due to God is reduplicated also, so that as the apostle says, there is superfluity in his satisfaction, 1 Tim. i. 14. For as if when he who was the Lord of so many worlds became poor for us, it must needs purchase infinite riches, as the apostle speaks, so if he who was equal in glory to God will debase himself at God's command, to glorify and give honour to him, and give up his own glory to add as it were to his Father's, what honour must needs redound to God thereby? John xvii. 3, 4, ' Father' (says he), ' give me the glory which I had ere the world was; I have glorified thee on earth;' as if he had said, I have laid aside the glory which I had afore the world was, all this while, and which was all this while my due, have left heaven and come to earth, and all to glorify thee on earth, ' Now glorify me,' &c. Christ reflects upon, and draws and includes all his glory to contribute and impute this double worth and satisfaction to his obedience.

And to make this demonstration the more full and satisfactory, let us more particularly consider what was that special damage and injury sin did unto God. It was (as I shewed) the obscuring of the glory of God, and reflecting dishonour to him. Now then let us but weigh together, as it were, in two scales, that exceeding weight of the glory of Christ, who was debased, with the glory of God the Father, which was obscured by sin, satisfaction being a reducing things to an equality, and a making of amends in what is lost or endamaged; and if it be in point of honour, it is requisite that as much and as great an honour be debased to make restitution, as was reflected upon or taken away. And here you may remember that satisfaction in point of honour doth depend upon the worth and reputation, of the person that satisfies for it; and what was the worth of Christ in his personal dignity I have spoken to, what is meet for the point in hand. And from thence it is evident that such worth of the party honouring, equally balances all the dishonour which sin had thrown upon God.

But, 2dly, as was also shewed, this satisfaction of Christ is not simply a giving honour to God, but a giving away his honour to make God's glory the more illustrious. Now, therefore, Christ made all his honour a sacrifice to God (I shewed how himself was the matter of the sacrifice), and therein indeed might especially be said to sacrifice himself, and to humble

himself, and it is the principal meaning of those expressions, for his glory
is himself. As a king, consider him as a king, and his glory is himself,
for his being a king is wholly matter of honour, and consists in nothing
else ; and therefore we use the word ' *His Majesty*,' for the king ; so God is
called ' the God of glory,' Acts vii. 2 ; and ' the Father of glory,' Eph. i. 17 ;
and Christ, ' the Lord of glory,' 1 Cor. ii. 8 ; and the Jews paraphrasti-
cally use to say, ' the glory of God,' to express God himself ; and we also
in ordinary speech, speaking of a man of worth doing anything dishonourable or unworthy of him, we say, ' he doth below himself,' for his honour
is himself ; and to any spirit that is noble, it is a nearer thing than wives,
children, goods, or whatever. Now all this in men is but a spark of that
image in God and Christ ; and in Scripture phrase it is said of God, that
' he made all things for himself,' that is, for his honour. And though
the honour that he hath by it is but a manifestative honour and extrinsecal, yet because himself is interested in it, and it is his, therefore it is
called himself, and he is as tender of it as of himself, ' My glory I will not
give to another,' Isa. xlii. 8.

Now, therefore, let us come to weighing, and put these two glories in the
scales, God's obscured by sin, and Christ's debased for sin.

A double glory God hath.

1. The one essential, the glory of the Godhead in itself.

2. A manifestated glory unto us. And the first is reflected upon by sin,
the other detracted from.

And Jesus Christ, the second person, God-man, hath answerably a
double glory, as was shewn, the one essential and equal to that of his
Father ; the other due to be manifested in and upon his assumption of our
nature. Now look, whatever can be said of the proportion of dishonour
done to either of these glories by sin as concerning God, the like may be
said of the debasement done to and performed by Christ, in respect of both
those his glories also.

And first compare we the reflection and shadow cast upon their essential
glory on either side, and at least the scales will be even. The essential
glory of God, although it cannot really be impaired by sin, yet it is reflected
on by sin, and so that that glory which is impaired (as his manifestative
is), being a peculiar belonging to his person, and indeed is himself (as was
said), hence all the essential greatness that is in God is taken in to aggravate the guilt of sin, and hence there is a denomination given to our acts
of sinning, as if they were destroying and dishonouring the Godhead ; as
Rom. i. 23, speaking of the sin of idolatry, ' They changed,' says he, ' the
glory of the incorruptible God into the image of a corruptible man, and
creeping things.' He speaks as if they had utterly destroyed the Godhead,
and turned him into a creature ; thus a denomination is given to sin, as
reflecting on the eternal Godhead and essence of it.

Now, then, to answer this evil in sin, and make all even, it must be
remembered what was afore said, that Christ that was debased was God,
and his glory essentially equal to his Father ; and that though that his
essential glory was not impaired, yet all the debasement of his person in
the human nature reflected as much upon that, as that of sin doth any way
upon God's. When he appeared in our flesh, I may say, he changed the
glory of the incorruptible God into the image, yea, the reality, of a crucified
man, a malefactor, the scum and dung of the earth, yea, a worm and no
man. And as sin hath a denomination, as if it did thus and thus to the
essential Deity itself, so hath Christ's sufferings a denomination of reflect-

ing on his Godhead in all its sufferings ; it is called 'the blood of God,' Acts xx. 28, and God may be said to have died, and to have been crucified; and so it is said, ' They killed the Prince of life,' Acts iii. 15, and ' crucified the Lord of glory,' 1 Cor. ii. 8. Now then all that substantial glory of his comes in (as was said) as the foundation, to give worth to all he did or suffered, as reflected upon hereby. For as no creature could have satisfied, because they have no radical internal worth to fill up this disproportion, theirs is but a borrowed and extrinsecal glory ; so if Christ had had no other, if indeed his glory had been but a borrowed glory, extrinsecal and but by representation, and but as called God, as kings are in name, not really and substantially (as the Arians and Socinians teach), then his being himself made ' of no reputation,' when his glory lay but in reputation, would have had no satisfaction in it. God, who had a substantial glory reflected on by sin, would never have regarded or accounted of receiving any honour from the humbling of such a one. What is it to have a king-at-arms, or one that doth but personate a king, crouch unto a king ? What glory is it to the sun to have the stars to pull in their glory, and be put out, and not to shine, whenas all their glory is borrowed from itself ? The creatures, although they may rob God of glory, and reflect dishonour upon God, and seem to eclipse him by sin, yet they can add no glory to him, as the moon, which receives light from the sun, may interpose between it and the earth, but she can noway add to the sun's brightness, or make it more illustrious, no, not although she disappears in the presence of him, and looks pale. And no more would all the debasements of the creature, though directed and intended to give glory unto God. But if there were another sun as glorious as this, and you should see it hide its brightness in this sun's presence, as if not worthy to shine together with it, that the sun might alone appear ; or if you should see a king as great in majesty as ours come and leave his kingdom and royalty, and debase himself to honour our king, what an honour adds this to the king, whenas it would not be so much for a subject to do this. (And this makes the pope's glory so extravagant and transcendent, that kings give their glory and power to him, and kiss his feet.) Now so did Christ lower his glory to God's, when he was equal in substantial glory to him. All the glory of the creatures is but accidental, put upon them as garments are, they shine *alienis radiis*, as stars with another's beams. Thus in kings, all their glory is accidental to their persons, therefore Christ says, the glory of the lilies exceeded that of Solomon, Mat. vi. 29, because it was native and inbred in comparison of his. But Christ's is glory substantial, residing in his person, as light in the body of the sun. Accidental glory, such as in kings, doth not give a worth to all their actions ; they sleep, eat, drink, &c., as other men, and these actions are no more royal in them than in other men ; they do not all they do as kings ; but where substantial glory dwells, it transfuseth a value into every thing that is done ; and therefore Christ's glory, being his essence (as he · is God), it diffuseth a royalty on all his actions, and so the least debasement of him to give glory to God, how infinite a value must it put upon it ! He having (as I shewed out of the text) an equal glory to his Father, and so his condescension makes at least the scales even.

But then there are even in this respect some considerations that make the reflection of dishonour on Christ's substantial glory, greater than that by sin on God's, and so to outweigh it.

1. Because the creatures' act is but a tendency, or at most an attempt to

eclipse this glory of God, and therein falls short in comparison; for it is but as if a mote should go about to eclipse the sun, when the sun shines round about it still. But these debasements of the Son of God, equal with God, are real, and they being arbitrary and done by himself, and from himself, are therefore greater and deeper than what the creature could any way effect, for he himself, that is God, debaseth himself.

2. Yea, and *secondly*, there is a personal glory proper to the second person as such, which was lessened and reflected on, besides his essential glory, as I may so distinguish it. For there is an essential glory common to all three persons, the glory of the Godhead, which is properly the object of sin ; and few or no sins are peculiarly against that proper personal glory of any of the persons apart. When we sin, we sin no more against the Father, than against the Son and Holy Ghost ; and even that'sin against the Holy Ghost is rather against the effects of the Holy Ghost than against his person distinctly considered of by the sinner. Now then, in this debasement of Christ, there was not only a reflection on his Godhead, as it is common to him with the other two persons, but that personal glory proper to him, as he was the second person, was in a further peculiar manner reflected on ; and this in every debasement of his. Yea, that personal glory was in some respect lessened. For besides that his Father was greater than he in a true sense, upon the assuming of man's nature, he was also made less than other men, and the *terminus* or subject of this lessening or diminution was truly the Son of God. For although it cannot be said that the Godhead suffered, yet of the second person it may now truly be said, he suffered as well in, as that he was made, flesh. Now the personal glory of the other persons is not debased or lessened by sin, because they do not personally manifest themselves ; but the second person did personally manifest himself, and present himself to men ; and his person was made the sole butt, mark, subject, *terminus* of all the dishonour done the Godhead in him. His person was singled out to bear it, and be the sole receptacle thereof ; so as he being thus debased, this dishonour reflected on his person and the glory thereof, besides what in common fell upon his essential glory, his Godhead, and so he came to have a further and more special debasement than the Godhead had by sin.

But then, in the *second* place, let us make the comparison between the obscuring the manifested glory of God detracted from by sin, and the dishonour done to Christ's manifested glory, which is the second thing, and you will find his losses in that manifestative glory that was due to him to exceed God's losses in the dishonour done to his. For as was said, the manifestative glory due to Christ at his appearing in the flesh personally, must needs be more than what the Godhead any other ways could have ever manifested in effects, be they never so transcendent. As more honour is due unto a king if he appears in person than if his arms only be set up, or proclamation be made in his name, or than unto his picture or coin, so by the like reason unto ' God manifested in the flesh' (as it is said of Christ, 1 Tim. iii. 16) a greater manifestation of glory is due than unto God, but manifest in his works, as Rom. i. 19, 20 ; and so more was to have shone in Christ, the express image of the invisible God (as Col. i. 15, and Heb. i. 3), than in God's works, which are but the footsteps of the invisible things of God ; or in his law, which is but the shadow of his glory : Heb. x. 1, ' For the law having a shadow of good things to come, and not the very image of the things, can never with those sacrifices which they offer year by year continually make the comers thereunto perfect.' Now that manifested glory of God's (of which alone properly and really sin is the obscurer and the detracter from) is but that which shineth in his law, which we sin against, or as he is manifested to us in his works; and this glory due to shine in Christ's person manifested in the human nature must needs infinitely transcend the glory of all those, yea, and in his person doth now shine more of the Godhead dwelling in him than in all his own works of redemption wrought by himself, which yet exceed those of creation wrought by God. And therefore, that he should empty himself of all that glory due to him the first hour he assumed our nature, he must needs lose more than God did or ever can come to lose by sinners, and so the satisfaction in that respect doth superabound. Yea, and this manifestative glory was as truly his due as his Father's glory was due to him, or ought to have been given the Father by us his creatures, either upon the manifestation of his glory in his works or holy law, in which the Godhead shined; for because such a glory was his right, therefore all that great name or dignity he hath above the angels he is said to have ' by inheritance,' Heb. i. 4.

CHAPTER XI.

That upon the whole it is evident that there is all in the satisfaction made by Christ which justice can require.—An enumeration of the several pleas which may be framed against the sinner, and how they are all answered by what our Redeemer hath performed.

Now these general grounds of satisfaction for sin being laid, if justice will yet contend, or Satan, or the sinner's conscience, dare to avouch or produce any of those particulars which were found in sin, so transcendently sinful as exceeded all the creature's satisfaction, I make proclamation here in open court, and do challenge heaven and earth, things visible and invisible, to bring in their bills and aggravations of a sinner's sinfulness; and they shall see a just, and full, and particular discharge unto highest satisfaction. And for a trial we will go over all those particular damages in honour which afore were mentioned, and require satisfaction for them, and you shall see that what Christ hath done, will in all things punctually and particularly make amends for them.

First, If we reckon honour due to God left behind unpaid, which all the creatures are never able to restore, because all they can do is due for themselves, and therefore they cannot afford an overplus of glory to repay what is lost, yet Christ is able to make amends. For he who was thus glorious to the highest degree (and it was his due by inheritance), he laid aside his honour, ' made himself of no reputation,' so the text says, yea, emptied himself of all, became vain, left himself disrobed and despoiled of all: ' I am a worm and no man,' says the psalmist, Ps. xxii. 6, of him ; he made himself nothing, became nothing, not in being or substance, but in account and reputation. It is said of Herod and his men, they did set him at nought, made nobody of him ; and when we saw him ' we esteemed him not,' says the prophet, speaking concerning the Jews' usage of him, Is. liii. 8. Yea, they called it blasphemy in him when he but meekly challenged his own, and told them for their good he was the Son of God. If God should reckon what manifestation of glory all those that have, or shall sin against him, had been able, or ought to have brought in to him, and which through their negligence and omission is now for ever lost, it will be found to hold no proportion unto what was to have been manifested in Christ God-man the first hour of his assumption. For when he had assumed our nature personally, there must needs be a greater brightness (as the author to the Hebrews styles it, Heb. i. 3), a more glorious gleam or issuing forth of splendour was to accompany and shine forth in that nature so united, than could possibly result to God out of all other ways of revealing himself whatever. Because they all are of a lower kind, and inferior unto this. This is a manifestation of the Godhead *altioris ordinis*, of a superior kind and order to all other. If himself personally appears, his glory must also appear as the glory of the only begotten Son of God. But he suffered all this utterly to be veiled and clouded, though sometime, perchance, as it were, a beam broke forth through a cranny, that, as John says, 'we saw his glory, as the only begotten Son of God,' John i. 14. Which yet was rather to make them believe what he was, than any way to glorify himself; but otherwise, he stole into the world as a prince disguised, and lived as an exile, debarred and kept from wearing the crown of glory, which should have been set upon his head the first hour. He stood out of his glory for three and thirty years, which was due to him as soon as he was conceived, therefore it comes in, 'Jesus was not yet glorified,' John vii. 39. What! not yet; not after thirty-three years' dwelling in flesh and debasement? Why, to stay for his crown one hour, in that one hour he should lose more than ever God could lose, in all that the creatures could afford him, in all those ways he had manifested himself to them by, unto eternity, or in any other way than by the assumption of a creature he could ever shew. And yet, I say, this glory was his due the first minute; for when he came into the world, when he first landed, it is proclaimed, 'Let all the angels of God worship him,' Heb. i. 6, and even as much was due then as he now wears in heaven, or as he put forth 'on the holy mount.' He hath not increased his personal glory by his own merits; *nil meruit sibi;* in that respect he deserved as great and high a name for personal glory as he hath now in heaven, for the great name he hath by inheritance, Heb. i. 4. I say, personal glory as much was his due the first day; for I confess there is a glory shines out of his works of mediation, and a glory of his offices, which is additional to his personal glory due unto his person. If a mere creature, that had done never so much service to God, had been content to have stood out of that glory, which, as a reward, God had promised unto him, this would not have satisfied for God's loss of honour by sin, as this of Christ doth; for, besides that the loss of the creature had not been equal to what God lost, as his was (as hath been shewn), even more than God could otherwise expect in his manifestation in his works; the glory due to that creature as a reward of its service being but by promise, out of favour, could never have come up to satisfaction. But the glory due to Christ was by inheritance descended to him, when once united to God, by natural right, so as though he was man, yet that man being one in person with the Son of God, is not to be reckoned the adopted Son of God, but the natural Son of God; and so his glory was answerable, not borrowed, but natural to him and by right; not as one who holds it by promise only, but as inheriting it. 'We saw his glory, as of the only begotten Son of God,' John i. 14; a glory that was proper to him, such as he who was the Son of God must necessarily have, and that by inheritance, as his right. Thus much for the first part of the bill—honour lost to God.

Well, but justice will plead yet further damage, not only of honour omitted and neglected to be given, but of honour robbed, stolen from God and given away to creatures, and so debased ; ' Changing the glory of the incorruptible God, into an image made like to corruptible man and fowls,' &c., Rom. i. 23. Now, behold, Christ did that which well may make amends, for he not only emptied himself, and stood out of honour, but humbled himself to the death of the cross ; which, besides the pain, had also the highest shame accompanying it, put upon his person in it ; therefore we find both joined, Heb. xii. 2—' He endured the cross, and despised the shame.' And now, bring in all the objections and aggravations of dishonour done to God, and see them all equalled and exceeded in his debasement.

First, Doth the evil of sin lie in a dishonour done by such base creatures as we are, to a God so glorious? And is it indeed the infinite disproportion between him and us makes the guilt thereof so heinous ? Why, if this person, so great as Christ was, and whose essential glory is equal with his Father, if he will subject himself to the lowest debasement that is possible, so as between that his glory, the glory of his person, and this his debasement, shall be as great a distance every way found as between the creatures and the glory they are able to give to God, or God to receive from them ; this must needs answer to, and fill up the disproportion. But there was a greater distance ; for he that is equal with God, takes ' upon him the form of a servant,' and will subject himself to God; and if that be not low enough, he subjects himself to the basest of creatures, yea, and will fall lower yet, to the basest condition of creatures, yea, as low as hell itself, and for substance endure the same anguish which the damned there do ; and shall not this make amends? If sin hath offended God's glory as far he can be offended, *quantum offendibilis est,* he subjects himself *quantum subjicibilis est,* as far as he can be subject. If sin exalts a creature above God, in lieu of it God will debase himself below all creatures, and of all conditions take the basest ; will not this his falling so low rise up in all apprehension to highest satisfaction ?

Again, *Secondly,* If you say God's prerogative and sovereignty is affronted by every sin ; Christ, though he can stand upon his prerogative as much as God, being equal with him, yet he lets it fall, lays it down, yea, stands and holds up his hand at a bar as a malefactor. Yea, it is that very prerogative of his, and his being a king, that was the greatest exception which they had against him, *gloria fit crimen,* his glory is turned into his shame; he is condemned to death for an usurper and an impostor, for saying he was the Messiah, and king of the Jews. It was written as the title on his cross, of what he suffered for ; and though he tells them that he was a king, and above a king, which was that good confession which Paul puts Timothy in mind of, which he made afore Pilate, yet Pilate thinks himself a better man than he : ' Have I not power to condemn thee ? ' And will not Christ, thus divesting himself of all his royalty, in like manner make amends ?

Thirdly, Is not only God's prerogative, which he backs his law with, contemned, but all his glorious perfections slighted and denied, as his wisdom, holiness, &c. ? So were all the excellencies in Christ debased.

1. His person was debased ; ' He said he was the Son of God ; let God save him if he will have him,' say they of him when he hung on the cross. Mat. xxvii. 43.

2. All his offices are blasphemed.

(1.) Prophetical ; ' Prophesy to us,' say they in a jeer when they buffeted him, Mat. xxvi. 68, ' and tell us who it was that smote thee.' He will one day tell him that did it, at the day of judgment !

(2.) Also, his kingly office ; Mat. xxvii. 42, 'If he be the king of Israel, let him come down,' said they, mocking him.

And*(3.) his priestly office also ; 'He saved others, himself he cannot save,' say they in despite, Mat. xxvii 42. They say this when he was doing that very thing they mocked him for, namely, saving others ; it was his business he hung upon the cross to finish.

As thus his person and offices, so all his attributes suffered contempt. Though he was the Wisdom of his Father, and discovered more than appears in all the works of creation and the law, yet how is he slighted as unlearned ! He knows not letters (say they, John vii. 15). And who are his followers ? None but the people that know not the law, John vii. 49. And how is Moses preferred before him ! John ix. 29, 'As for this fellow, we know not whence he is.' So how do they scoff at his omniscience, 'Tell us who it is that smote thee,' Mat. xxvi. 68. As if when they had blinded him, and covered his eyes, they thought they had hoodwinked his all-seeing eye also. He that is truth itself is counted a deceiver of the people ; yea, he that is holiness itself is reckoned amongst transgressors, Isa. liii. 12, yea, the greatest of sinners ; and this not by men only, but by God himself, by whom he was made sin that knew no sin, 2 Cor. v. 21, so that by imputation he was the greatest sinner that ever yet the world had, as Luther used to speak. He was made, as it were, a sink into which the guilt of all sin was drained : 'The iniquities of us all did meet in him,' Isa. liii. 6. His body on the tree was made the centre of all sins, as so many lines coming in upon him from the circumference of all ages. Yea, and he was not only to be accounted a sinner by others, but he was himself to do such actions whereby he *ipso facto* acknowledged himself such, as to fulfil the ceremonial law, to be circumcised, &c., which was our bond, whereby we acknowledged ourselves debtors to the law ; and he set his hand to it, as acknowledging the debt. And now methinks he that was holiness itself should least of all have brooked this dishonour. What ? Made *sin !* Why ? It is that which he only hates, which his pure eyes abhor to look upon, and yet he must quietly bear the name of it, and take upon him the guilt of it, as if it were his own ; a greater indignity than for the chastest woman to be called a whore. I will say no more but this ; he that was the great God was called devil, and content to put it up.

Lastly, The being and life of God makes sin most odious, as being that which sin, in the nature of the act, tends to take away from God : for (as was said) as he that hateth his brother is a murderer, 1 John iii. 15, so he that hateth God is a murderer of him (though it doth him no hurt) in the attempt or rather tendency of the act, though not in the attempt or intention of the sinner ; and therefore the life of all mere creatures will never make amends, no more than the life of a traitor ever can for murdering his prince ; only it is all the satisfaction that can be had. And so in hell God takes their lives for it, because it is all that can be gotten. But now come we to Christ ; he of whom it is said that he 'hath life in himself,' John v. 26, and is the 'living God,' is content really to be murdered and put to death. Murderers (says Peter to the Jews, Acts iii. 15), 'ye have killed the Prince of life ;' and Paul says, 'They crucified the Lord of glory.' And though it was but in the flesh that he was crucified, as Peter elsewhere distinguisheth, yet the life he laid down was the life of his person ; and as it is called the blood of God which was shed, so this was the life of God which was taken away ; therefore, John x. 17, 18, Christ there calls it his life ;—'I have power to lay down my life, and take it up again.' None could say so much but he who was God, but he who is the Lord of life; and it is more plainly expressed, 1 John iii. 16, 'Hereby we perceive the love of God, because he laid down his life for us.' It was the life of God, and that in so true and real a sense, as therein the utmost of his love appeared. Yea, further, he not only died, but death held him a while under it, as a conqueror of him, therefore, Rom. vi. 9, death is said to have once had dominion over him. Now this true and real laying down of his life must needs be more satisfactory unto God than the attempt, or rather tendency, that is in the act of sin to take God's life away can be reputed heinous.

You may remember, when we did set forth (in that first part of this discourse) sin's sinfulness, and the evil of it against God, wherein it was that it exceeded all the goodness of the creature (which yet was for God, as well as sin is said to be against God), we pitched it upon this, the undueness of the act of dishonour done to God by the creatures; whereas all the honour their graces bring in to him, is due from them towards him. Now therefore let us see if, even in this particular, the evil of sin be not exceeded by Christ's satisfaction also, that nothing may be omitted that may satisfy a sinner's reason about the all-sufficiency of this satisfaction. This undueness of the act of dishonour was the highest and utmost aggravation of man's sinfulness, and did cast the balance, and was found to weigh heavier than all the creatures' goodness. Now let us put Christ's debasement of himself into the balance with it, and we shall see it far over-balanced even by this, that all this debasement of his to glorify God was infinitely more undue; which naturally riseth thus to all men's apprehensions.

1. In that it was such a way of giving honour to God by him, as God himself could no way challenge as his due from the second person towards him; for he was equal with him. He did owe indeed (as all the persons do one to another, a mutual honour) an honour unto God, even as kings mutually honour one another; yet still but as equals use to do. And if as man, being made inferior to God, he owed subjection, yet still not in this way of debasing himself. He honoured his Father, and his Father the Son, from all eternity; for as they love one another, so they give honour one to another. But that God should have honour this way, by having his Son, a person his equal, become inferior to him, and obedient, and that so far as to death, and to profess that he did it freely at his command, this was in itself more than could be challenged, as due from him, by God, and therefore must needs be a full amends for any dishonour thrown on him by sin. It is as if the king of Spain should come out of his own kingdom, and admit himself into this of ours, and subject himself to our king and his laws, thereby to make our king seem greater; what an honour were it to him! More than all his subjects can do to him all sorts of ways in which they can be subject.

And 2. As Christ's debasement was thus undue, in respect that God could not exact it from him but by his own voluntary compact, so most of all undue it was, if we consider that which so often hath been inculcated, viz., the glory that himself could challenge as his due, and that by right of inheritance; and how great that was, and how due it was, hath been declared; and for him to be so debased, how infinitely undue was it in this respect also! Of sin's undueness it may be said, 'Hear, O heavens; and hearken, O earth;' that men should sin and rebel against the great God, so undue an act it is, and unworthy of the creature. But when we think or speak of this debasement of the Son of God, equal with God, to whom so much glory is due, O stand astonished at it, all you angels and men;

and with mere amazement fall and shrink into your first nothing, to think that ever it should be said, and be a truth, that the great God, the Lord of glory, should be crucified, the Lord of life killed. I appeal to you all, if this be not an act infinitely more unworthy, and as much out of course, more horrid to the thoughts of men and angels, than sin can be supposed to be. That a base creature should sin against God, it is a thing to be wondered at indeed as a strange indignity; but yet the creatures, if they know themselves, may well know, yea, and fear, that they being but creatures, they may do it too soon, as the best of them did; and it was a wonder rather that any stood. But that the Lord of glory should be thus debased and killed, no creature durst have thought it, if they had conceived it possible; but it is so abhorrent as it could never have entered into their thoughts, had not God done it; and it is marvellous in our eyes.

And *lastly*, That sin may have nothing left to boast of, and that we may omit nothing that may or hath been any way pleaded about sin's sinfulness, but see it out-pleaded, and cast, and exceeded by this satisfaction of Christ's, let us put into the balance likewise those evil effects mentioned also in that first part of this discourse, whereby the heinousness of sin was demonstrated to transcend the goodness of the creatures' graces in any effects of their goodness: you shall find the effects of Christ's righteousness to abound far above them.

For, first, his actions, by reason of the dignity of his person, do please God more than sin can displease him. For if our works, although full of sin, are yet, by reason of our union with Christ as our head, made so acceptable as to please God more than the sin in them doth displease him, how must his own works be accepted, wrought in himself, in our nature hypostatically united to him !

Secondly, And therefore if sin hath that inseparable evil (as was said) in the nature of it, that where it is found it condemns all, though the creature had been in former times never so righteous, nor never so long such, so hath Christ's righteousness that inseparable royalty to save and justify, though sins be never so great and many. So Rom. v. 17, he compares both the one and the other: 'If condemnation came by one man's disobedience, how much more shall, by an abundance of his righteousness, justification be unto life?' So as if he will impute this righteousness, and account it to the ugliest sinner in the world, then by virtue of the imputation he cannot but justify him, and pronounce him as worthy of eternal life as the greatest and the holiest angel in heaven. For this righteousness claims it by the merit of it, when once the sinner can call it his. And although one sin spoils and makes void all the good in any creature, though it hath been of never so long continuance, yet his righteousness, on the contrary, is sin-proof for time to come, and hath the worth of his person, who is the great God, to give power to it to prevail against all sins past, present, and to come; it is an 'everlasting righteousness,' Dan. ix. 24, such as which sinners can never spend or evacuate. And if sin take away the justifying power from grace, his righteousness takes away the condemning power from sin: 'There is no condemnation to them that are in Christ;' for it 'condemneth sin itself.' Rom. viii. 1, 3, 'There is therefore now no condemnation to them which are in Christ Jesus, who walk not after the flesh, but after the Spirit.' Ver. 3, 'For what the law could not do, in that it was weak through the flesh, God sending his own Son in the likeness of sinful flesh, and for sin condemned sin in the flesh.'

CHAPTER XII.

That all the pleas which the law can make against a sinner are by this satisfaction of Christ also fully answered.

And now we have shewn such abundant satisfaction given to God in point of his honour, the law methinks may well sit down and never so much as mention the debt that is its due. Yet if the law will needs bring in her bill also, there will be found satisfaction full enough for its claim also.

And first, in general, what is the law? The will, word, and command of the great God. Well, but Christ is the Word of his Father in a higher and more glorious sense; the original of this word and law. This is but the copy of what is substantial in him; he is therefore called ὁ λόγος, 'the Word,' John i. 1. Yea, and is not Christ the maker and the giver of that law? Gal. iii. 19. And if he that made the law will be 'made under the law,' as, Gal. iv. 4, he was, and enter into bond to the law, and give the law power over him, as a servant and an apprentice to it, make himself a debtor to it and fulfil it, will not this make amends? We might make very short work with the law's suit but by calling for her bond, which once she had to shew against those Christ died for. Therefore let the law shew and bring in that bond into open court. She returns answer, that she hath it not; we find then that it is 'taken out of the way,' Col. ii. 14. But how, and by whom? Not surreptitiously, and by stealth, or by force and violence, but openly in the face of the court of justice. And by whom? Christ blotting it out, nailing it to his cross, and 'triumphing openly,' says the 15th verse, and before the judge's face. The moral law, that was the creditor, and the bond which God appointed the Jews to give in, whereby to acknowledge the debt, was the ceremonial law; therefore says the apostle, 'he that is circumcised' (upon which the bond was entered into, and sealed) 'is a debtor to the whole law.' Now, in token that the debt is paid, we find the bond cancelled; and now she hath nothing to shew against believers so as to condemn us, and this is evidence sufficient. But yet if the law, or any legal conscience, would notwithstanding have further satisfaction, and put us to prove and shew how the particular debts due thereunto were paid and discharged, both that of service to be done, and fulfilling all the law, by active obedience, and then by passive obedience also, and know how the punishment and curse threatened was undergone, the particular discharge is yet upon record. Christ hath done both fully; and what he hath done and suffered hath that in it which the obedience and sufferings of no pure creature could have had, nor could have satisfied as his hath done. It is a point I shall speak of after, when I shall shew the fulness of parts that is in his obedience; yet I shall say a little now, and enough to stop the law's mouth, for this is but a ruder draught of what more particularly we will fill up.

First, He fulfilled the law in service and obedience performed unto it for the space of thirty-three years: John viii. 29, 'I do always the things that please him.' The text too says, 'he was a servant,' and obedient *usque ad mortem,* until death, Philip. ii. 8, and therefore all his life. He there mentions that obedience in lieu of service due by us; and although creatures could fulfil the law, yet they could not perform it for us, and for themselves too, because the law requires all they can do for themselves, and what they do is not their own ; but what Christ doeth shall stand for both. To go no further now than the text for clearing this ;—

First, Though as Christ was man, the law required obedience of him for himself, when once he is become a man, and had once assumed our nature, yet being before his assumption equal with God (which the text on purpose mentions to shew the worth of his obedience), and at his choice to have continued free for ever from all subjection ; that he should take upon him voluntarily this condition of a servant (as the phrase ' he became obedient' importeth, and he was *servus factus, non natus*, so Gal. iv. 4, ' made under the law'). This act of such a person, and thus free, doth make all the obedience he upon this performed, to stand both for himself and for others also; for the righteousness the manhood performed, his person had no need of. And then again the assumption of this nature was agreed on by covenant, and this by a more ancient law and decree made in heaven ere there were any creatures extant to give the moral law unto ; whereby it was agreed that the service he did in that nature should justify others ; so Isa. liii., ' My servant shall justify many ; ' though a servant, yet his service was not for himself, but others. And again, though as a man he is subject, yet that man is personally united to the Godhead, and so partakes of all his royalties, whereof one is to be Lord of the law, Mat. xii. 18 ;* and therefore his fulfilling the law is truly the obedience of God, the Lord thereof, as well as his blood is the blood of God. The creatures have no relation or privilege whereby they can plead exemption from the law, but so can he ; but all that the creatures have is necessarily and wholly subject, and therefore all which they can do is only for themselves. But his person is equal with God, and in that relation (which over-balanceth all other) is free and subject, not necessarily, but voluntarily, and that by a covenant made on purpose, the condition whereof was to assume the nature and the form of a servant in it, merely to justify others; and therefore will stand good for us against the law. Jehovah, that hath no need of acquisite righteousness, is our righteousness, Jer. xxiii. 6. And,

Secondly, Though creatures could not by their active obedience satisfy for another, because what they did was not their own, nay, it was but borrowed, yet he could say his soul was his own (as we use to speak) and that his life was his own, which no creature could say ; they cannot say their service is their own, and grace their own. And this propriety in what he had, did, or suffered, the Scripture often puts an emphasis upon, as that which conduceth to satisfaction, as when it is said he washed us with his own blood, Rev. i. 5. And ' I will lay down my life, and take it up again ; ' and, John xvi. 14, ' he shall receive of mine.' And though, as some of the schoolmen object, Christ's human nature and all his actions were *sub dominio Dei*, under the dominion of God, as creatures, and God had an interest in them, yet this human nature, and all that it could perform, was in another relation so peculiarly the second person's own, as it was not the other persons', namely, his own by personal union, which propriety was incommunicable to the other persons. Habitual grace, though it was the work of the Holy Ghost, Luke i. 35, yet due unto the human nature when united as its own ; and as the human nature was to be called not the adopted Son of God, but the natural, so the grace in that human nature might be called, now it is united to the Godhead, co-natural to him. And though the first grace of union was mere grace, yet that grace was

* Probably a misprint for Mark ii. 28.—ED.

vouchsafed to the human nature, not the divine, subsisting in the second person, who as such is the person who owneth all both graces and actions in the human, and is the proprietor of them; and he it was who was lessened by that assumption. Yea, and besides, when once that human nature is assumed, then all the dues and rights of that person, as to be full of grace, and Lord of glory, &c., was due and proper to him as the only begotten Son of God: John i. 14, 'And the Word was made flesh, and dwelt among us (and we beheld his glory, the glory as of the only begotten of the Father), full of grace and truth.' And grace was not given to him as a mere servant to give account of, but he entered upon it as a Lord; for if he be 'the Lord of glory,' as 1 Cor. ii. 8, then the Lord of grace too; and he is not as Moses, as a servant, but as a Son in his own house, Heb. iii. 5, 6; and so there are these great and just respects upon his obedience, that it was free, and his person not subject to that law which he fulfilled.

And whereas the creatures must have gone over their works again and again to eternity, done nothing but written the blurred copy of their obedience, copy after copy, in their lives, and so have made nothing perfect, there is in Christ a fulfilling of it but once by him, which will serve for that eternal debt of active obedience. And as by once offering of himself, Heb. x. 14, so by one righteousness and obedience, Rom. v. 18; that is, once gone over, he is able to justify us for ever. And therefore he tells his apostles, a little afore his death, that he had now but one thing to do, and that was to drink of the last cup; and how do I long, says he, till it be accomplished! And at his death he tells his Father, John xvii. 4, 'I have finished the work which thou gavest me to do.' And so he having despatched the active part, he had space enough left to undergo the passive, which, as I shewed in the first part of this discourse, no creature was capable of. Nay, further, he can do both at once: in obeying, suffer; and in suffering, obey; and each successively, so as God shall be no loser by the one or the other, and in the end can say of both, 'It is finished.' Thus much for the debt of active obedience.

Secondly, Now, if we come to passive obedience, we shall find that he was able so to undergo it, as shall put that worth into it, as it shall soon be finished, and be yet satisfactory.

First, Whereas no creature could have so much as borne the imputation of sin (which yet was necessary to satisfaction), for it would have withered and shrivelled up all their grace, because their grace is all but washy stuff, and but as a gilding by gold slightly overlaid; now Christ's grace is substantial, it was as gold itself, therefore it was sin-proof. He can be made sin, and yet his grace continue, as ours doth not, when Adam's sin is imputed. Grace maintains itself in him, not by a covenant of works, but by the personal union and the rights thereof, and so can bear the guilt of all our sins, and his grace never a whit the worse for it; his person is unpeccable, and so uncapable of hurt by the imputation of sin.

Secondly, The life and comforts thereof, which he lays down, and sacrificeth, is his own. His life is not due to God, as is the creatures', for it is given him 'to have life in himself,' John v. 26. 'And I have power over my life to take it up and lay it down,' says he. God, that hath power over life and death, hath not power over his: John x. 17, 18, 'Therefore doth my Father love me, because I lay down my life, that I might take it again.' Ver. 18, 'No man taketh it from me, but I lay it down of myself. I have power to lay it down, and I have power to take it again. This commandment have I received of my Father.' So as whatever he loseth in suffering for us shall be his own, he will not borrow anything to suffer with, but all he offers is his own, as it must be, if it be a mediating death. He was able to offer up himself, and so be his own sacrifice, altar, and priest; he borrowed nothing; and this all at once; and this no creature could do.

1. He being God, was able to be his own priest, and in dying offered up himself to God, and needed no other priest: so Heb. ix. 14, 'through his eternal Spirit he offered up himself.' Yea, and

2. He finds a sacrifice also, which was in a true respect his own, a respect wherein it was not God's, himself offering up his body, Heb. x. 10, and pouring forth his soul an offering for sin, Isa. liii. 10. And,

3. He is the altar himself: Heb. xiii. 10, 'We have an altar whereof they have no right to eat, which serve the tabernacle.' And so he offers all upon his own cost, and borrows nothing.

Thirdly, Now in the last place, let us take a brief survey of all those inseparable inconveniences (mentioned in the first part of this discourse) which we found to attend upon and clog the passive obedience of all mere creatures, if they should presume to undertake it, and you shall see them all to melt away, and come to nothing before his fulness. As,

First, The creatures would very hardly have so much as dared to die and undergo it for us: Rom. v. 7, 'For a good man peradventure one would dare die:' Jer. xxx. 21, 'Who hath engaged his heart,' says God, 'to draw nigh unto me?' No creature durst do it, but only, 'this one that shall come out of the midst of you' (as there); 'he shall draw near to me.' He durst encounter with his Father's wrath; he hath the hardiness to encounter with it, and to bear it and not be broken. The wrath of God it broke the backs of angels, but, Isa. xlii. 14, 'My servant,' says he, 'whom I uphold, shall not be broken.' Again,

Secondly, Will he be overcome with it, or always satisfying? No; whereas if any of the creatures had had the boldness to undertake it, yet they must have been always satisfying, and so we should never have come to have our bond out; but Christ will bear it, so as to come at last to say, 'It is finished,' as he did say at his death. He that was to be our mediator, was to rise again as a conqueror over death, to overcome hell, God's wrath, and not lie wrestling under them to eternity; for if he had lain by it, and had been kept in prison, so long the debt had not been paid. If ever therefore he will justify us by his death, he must overcome and rise again, else we should still be in our sins, as 1 Cor. xv. 17, 'And if Christ be not raised, your faith is vain; you are yet in your sins.' And this no creature could ever do, God's wrath would have held him tugging work to eternity, and they never have risen again from under it. He that overcomes that, must be as strong as God himself. Yea, and he must do this himself, by his own power too. It was not enough to be raised up, as Lazarus was, by the power of another; that will not serve to satisfy for a sinner. For that power that raised him, must first satisfy and overcome God's wrath, eluctate, and break open the prison doors. Now if another power than his own had done it, that party that helped him had been in part the mediator, and so not he. But Christ being God, he is able to do all this, and to do it by his own power. For,

1. Being God, he was backed with that power that was able to raise him up, and to loose the pains of death; yea, and it was impossible he should be held thereof, says Peter, Acts ii. 14. Those pains of death there mentioned were from the wrath of God, which would have stayed all the creatures

in the world for* ever rising; and the place implies that those pains would not have let him go till they were loosened and overcome; for if possible, they would have held him; but being he was God, it was not possible; but he takes hell-gates, like another Samson, and throws them off their hinges, carries them away, and swallows up death in victory.

2. He could raise himself up; 'Destroy this temple,' says he, John ii. 19, and 'I have power to raise it up,' I myself. The body could not raise itself, nor the soul have joined itself to that body; therefore if he had been but mere man, he could never have done it, but that Spirit, the eternal Godhead, could: 1 Peter iii. 18, 'He was put to death in the flesh,' that is, his human nature, 'but quickened in and by the Spirit,' that is, his Godhead united thereunto. And he will thus overcome, not by mere power, by force, but in a way of justice, so as justice itself shall willingly let him go free, as being itself first satisfied. Yea, he will overcome upon such terms that it shall be unjust to hold him any longer, unjust, and so impossible in that sense also; for he will in a few hours pay the whole debt, undergo the whole wrath due; that which the creatures' strength could endure but by drops (and therefore endures it ever), he will be able to bear at once, so as justice itself shall say, It is finished, and I am satisfied.

And further, when he hath despatched it, there will be time enough left, even an eternity of time, to reward him in, and to be glorified with the glory he had before the world was. This was another inconvenience attended the creatures' satisfaction, that it must always be a-satisfying, and so should never have been rewarded; which God would never put any creature to, for then he should require and accept the highest obedience from a creature whom he should never have time to reward for it. But Christ can so satisfy as there will be time enough to reward him in. Yea, and he needs but a little time to satisfy in, and then he will survive and live again to call for his reward: 'He shall prolong his days, and see his seed, and be satisfied,' Isa. liii. 11. And therefore in this text we read of 'a great name above every name,' which as a reward God gave him for his being obedient unto death, Phil. ii. 9. And,

3. Thirdly, Will his satisfaction serve but one sinner (as also I shewed would be the case if creatures had performed it; yea, God must have sacrificed as many innocent creatures as he meant to save sinners)? No; Christ's satisfaction will serve for worlds, Rom. v. 17, 18. He is able to bring in such abundance of righteousness as abounds to many.

4. And in the last place, to crown the conclusion of this discourse with an additional weight of glory, that is more than all that hath been spoken. What will there be but just enough in this his obedience to make satisfaction for sin, and procure peace for sinners? The creatures they could not have done so much. No! But his will not only satisfy and make peace, but also reconcile, make friends: Col. i. 20, 'And, having made peace through the blood of his cross, by him to reconcile all things unto himself; by him, I say, whether they be things in earth, or things in heaven.' His righteousness will not only pacify vengeance, but there is enough in it to bring us into favour with God. The worth and grace of his person is such, and he so beloved, as it makes us, though sinners, graciously accepted in his beloved, Eph. i. 6, brings us into a degree of favour infinitely greater than ever, and more lasting. He is the natural Son of God, the beloved in whom God's soul is well pleased; and his love being conveyed to us through him, it falls upon us with more strength and fervour than ever. And also

* That is, 'from.'—ED.

this offering up himself was so sweet a smelling sacrifice to God (as Eph.
v. 2), that although God expressed never so much anger against Christ as
when he hung upon the cross, yet he was never so well pleased by him as
then ; nay, he was more pleased than he had been displeased with all the
sins the creatures have or can commit. The damned spirits their punishment satisfies not ; vengeance can never suck out blood enough ; and yet
if what they did could satisfy, it would never rise so high as to please God,
never be of worth enough to bring them into favour again. But here when
first vengeance had sucked its full, and falls off satisfied, then the favour of
his person, the willingness of his obedience, purchaseth an overplus, a redundancy of merit, a surplusage of riches, ' unsearchable riches,' Eph. iii. 8,
not only able to pay our debts the first day (and that is the least part of the
benefit by it), but enough besides to purchase heaven itself as a portion for us,
the favour of God. Yea, as much there is of it as we can spend or take out
in glory to eternity. God had large thoughts of great and glorious blessings to be bestowed upon his people, and the righteousness of Christ is as
large in merit as God's heart in purposes, adequate thereto ; therefore the
apostle makes God's grace and Christ's righteousness of equal extent, so
that what God intended to be bestowed, his righteousness hath purchased :
Rom. v. 17–20, ' For if by one man's offence death reigned by one ; much more
they which receive abundance of grace, and of the gift of righteousness, shall
reign in life by one, Jesus Christ.' Ver. 18, ' Therefore as by the offence
of one judgment came upon all men to condemnation ; even so by the
righteousness of one the free gift came upon all men unto justification of
life.' Ver. 19, ' For as by one man's disobedience many were made
sinners, so by the obedience of one shall many be made righteous.' Ver.
20, ' Moreover the law entered, that the offence might abound. But where
sin abounded, grace did much more abound.' Yea, the merit of this his
obedience is so great, as it shall never be rewarded to the full ; the saints
shall not have to eternity the full worth of it out in glory.

BOOK IV.

Christ's willingness to the work of redemption from everlasting till
he accomplish it.

But in those sacrifices there is a remembrance again made of sins every year.
For it is not possible that the blood of bulls and of goats should take away
sins.   Wherefore when he cometh into the world, he saith, Sacrifice and
offering thou wouldest not, but a body hast thou prepared me: in burnt
offerings and sacrifices for sin thou hast had no pleasure; then said I, Lo,
I come (in the volume of the book it is written of me) to do thy will, O God.
Above when he said, Sacrifice and offering and burnt offerings and offering
for sin thou wouldest not, neither hadst pleasure therein (which are offered
by the law); then said he, Lo, I come to do thy will, O God.   He taketh
away the first, that he may establish the second.   By the which will we are
sanctified, through the offering of the body of Jesus Christ once for all.—
HEB. X. 8–10.

CHAPTER I.

That there are two things to be considered in the obedience which Christ per-
formed, the will and the deed.—That from all eternity he expressed his
willingness, in his consent to undertake the work.

As in all our obedience there are two principal ingredients to the true
and right constitution of it, the matter of the obedience itself, and the principle and fountain of it in us : whereof the one, the apostle calls the deed,
the other, the will—which latter God accepts in us, oftentimes without,
always more than, the deed or matter of obedience itself—even so in
Christ's obedience, which is the pattern and measure of ours, there are
these two eminent parts which complete it.

I. The obedience itself, and the worth and value of it, in that it is his,
so great a person's.

II. The willingness, the readiness to undertake, and the heartiness to
perform it.   The dignity of the person gave the value, the merit to the
obedience performed by him.   But the will, the zeal in his performance,
gains the acceptance, and hath besides a necessary influence into the worth
of it, and the virtue and efficacy of it to sanctify us.   All which you have
in the text.   The 'offering up the body of Jesus:' there is the matter.
The 'obedience of him to death:' there is the will by which he offered it
up: ' by which will.'   As calling not only for a distinct, but a more eminent consideration, and both necessarily concurring to our sanctification
and salvation; ' By which will we are sanctified.'   Now the story of his
willingness to redeem and save, or the will by which we are sanctified, is a
story of four parts.

1. Of his actual consent and undertaking the work, made and given to his Father from everlasting.

2. The continuance of that his will to stand to it from everlasting, unto the time of his incarnation and conception.

3. The renewal of this consent when he came into the world.

4. The stedfast continuance of that will all along in the performance, from the cradle to the cross.

And 1. As to his voluntary undertaking it 'afore the world was.' In the handling and discovery of those transactions of God the Father with him about the work of redemption, I have spoken something of Christ's willingness and consent, as it was there necessary; for else I could not have set forth the issue and conclusion of that treaty made by the persons shewing themselves; yet so as I reserved enough to make it a distinct head, when I should come to Christ's part. And so I here begin with it; for it was then, as was said, left by God the Father with him, and did wholly lie upon him.

It was necessary that Christ's consent should be then given, even from everlasting, and that as God made a promise to him for us, so that he should give consent again unto God. Yea; and indeed it was one reason why it was necessary he that was our mediator should be God, and existent from eternity, not only to the end he might be privy to the first design and contrivement of our salvation, and know the bottom and the first of God's mind and heart in it, and receive all the promises of God from God for us, but also in this respect, that his very consent should go to it from the first, even as soon as his Father should design it. And it was right meet it should be so; for the performance and all the working, operating part was to be his, and to lay* all upon his shoulders to execute, and it was a hard task, and therefore reason he should both know it with the first, seeing he was extant together with his Father, and should also from the first contrivement by his Father give his consent to it. It was fit that both his heart and head should be in with the first. And you have all in one Scripture, Isa. ix. 6, where, when Christ is promised, 'Unto us a child is born, unto us a son is given,' observe under what titles he is set forth unto us: 'Counsellor, the mighty God, the everlasting Father.' Where everlastingness, which is affixed to one, is yet common to those other two. The 'everlasting Counsellor,' as well as 'everlasting Father;' for he was both *Counsellor* and *Father*, in that he was the *mighty God*, and all alike from everlasting. For, being God, and with his Father as a Son from everlasting, he must needs be a *Counsellor* with him, and so privy unto all God meant to do, especially in that very business, for the performance of which he is there said to be given as a son, and born as a child, and the effecting of which is also said to be laid wholly on his shoulders. Certainly in this case, if God could hide nothing from Abraham he was to do, much less God from Christ, who was God with him from everlasting. And as he was for this cause to be privy to it for the cognisance of the matter, so to have given his actual consent likewise thereunto: for he was to be the father and founder of all that was to be done in it. And in that very respect, and in relation to that act of will then passed, whereby he became a father of that business for us, it is he is styled the 'everlasting Father,' and that from everlasting *à parte post*. For it is in respect of that everlastingness he is God, and so father from everlasting, as well as God from everlasting; a counsellor for us with God, a father of us, and our salvation. God's counsellor, because his wis-

* That is, 'lie.'—ED.

dom was jointly in that plot and the contrivement of it: and father both of us and this design, because of his will in it, and undertaking to effect it. In that his heart and will were in it as well as the Father's, he was therefore the father of it as well as God, and brought it to perfection.

I acknowledge the Scripture is more sparing in recording that hand and will that the Son of God had in it as from everlasting. And I have long apprehended this to be the reason of it; because his will is so necessarily and naturally resolved into his Father's will, they having but one will between them (as I have elsewhere alleged it upon this very argument), but chiefly because what was done as in the point of our salvation from everlasting, it is and was the proper honour of God the Father; and so the concurrence of the Son is swallowed up in the Father's contrivements about it; and the rather also, because the Son hath manifested his willingness so abundantly in the very performing it, which necessarily imported and required this everlasting consent of his, and argues it. Hence so little is explicitly said of it. But as the work of redemption performed in time is attributed to the Son, so these works from everlasting to the Father. And therefore all the speech is of what he then did; how he made promise to Christ, and blessed us in him with all spiritual blessings, and sware he should be priest upon the very day he begat him, in Heb. v., which refers both to his eternal generation and call to the office of priesthood, from the same everlasting, as well as to that in time.

Yet there are two things said elsewhere, that imply Christ's full consent given from everlasting, in answer unto that oath of God. For it is not barely said, as in that place, that he was 'made a priest' passively, as dedicated only by his Father to the priesthood, that might have been supposed to have been without his own actual consent given; like as parents, from the births of their children, have dedicated them to the ministry, or the like calling, [as Hannah did Samuel without his knowledge; and thus also Sampson was a Nazarite. But it was not so here, that his being made a priest then by his Father, is elsewhere interpreted by his being made a 'surety of a covenant.' So Heb. vii., by comparing the 21st and 22d verses together. In the 21st verse that oath is mentioned, 'The Lord sware and will not repent, Thou art a priest.' And this is interpreted by an inference from it, ver. 22, 'By so much was Jesus made surety of a better testament.' Now, this oath, though it was recorded and uttered by David, Ps. cx., after Moses' law supposed given, as the last verse of that chapter insinuates, yet we elsewhere find this covenant to be called an everlasting covenant, and the everlasting gospel, as Rev. xv., as that which had been made and lain hid in God from everlasting, à parte post, as the apostle, speaking of the gospel, plainly insinuates, Rom. xvi. 25, 26, 'The mystery kept secret since the world began; but now is made manifest, according to the commandment of the everlasting God,' which special attribute of eternity is there given God, to signify that though he had 'kept it secret since the world began,' and but now revealed it, yet he had framed and contrived it from everlasting and afore the world. And it is certain, that as all promises in the word are but the copies of God's promises made to Christ for us from everlasting, so these oaths and covenants recorded in the word are but the copy of that oath and covenant struck betwixt God and Christ from everlasting. These the extracts, those the original.

Now, then, if the intent of God's oath was to make a covenant of it, and not only a promise but a covenant, then Christ's consent is manifestly imported. If it had only been called a promise from God, that would not necessarily have implied Christ's consent, though it would have implied his existence or being then, as I have used to argue from that place, Titus i. 2, 'In hope of eternal life, which God that cannot lie promised before the world began.' But it being called further a covenant, it doth import two; for as a mediator is not of one but two, so a covenant is always the consent of two, and not of one only; it cannot be a covenant else. You use to say, to every bargain two words must go; the meaning is, the consent of two parties. So to every covenant; it had not been a complete covenant else. If God had sworn to it; yea, if Christ himself had been secretly willing, yet if by his consent expressed it had not been struck up, it had not been a covenant. A purpose also it might have been called, but not a covenant.

Yea, and let me further improve it. If Christ had not fully and perfectly consented, it had not been a perfect covenant. Yea, and if he had not at first propounding of it (which was from everlasting) come off to it, without taking any time to deliberate, it had not been an everlasting covenant; that is, from everlasting.

But (which is more) the second person did so fully engage himself, that God calls him not only his covenanter, but his covenant. It is in that place, Isa. xlix. 8, out of which I have elsewhere shewed how the covenant was struck dialogue-wise. You may see there how it was driven; and after he had shewn upon what considerations Christ came off to it, he thereupon in the 8th verse calls him his covenant.

And if it be objected that a covenant may be made without the consent of both parties, for God says, 'This is my covenant,' when he promiseth to give to us (who had not then consented) a 'new heart,' &c. Yet for answer, consider that this promise alleged was necessarily made first to Christ for us, and was driven covenant-wise with him; and in that respect it is that it becometh to be called a covenant; as thus it respects us, because indeed made with him for us first, and so made known unto us. The meaning is, that therefore it is that God promiseth on his part to give us a new heart, because Christ promised afore to him, for his part, to work redemption for us, otherwise it could not have been called a covenant till we had consented.

Then (2.) the word, 'He was made a surety,' doth argue it also, for that evidently imports an undertaking on Christ's part: and so as the oath was God's, so the suretyship was Christ's. And a surety, 'Εγγυος is a plighter of his troth, by 'striking hands,' as the phrase in the original, Prov. xxii. 26.

Now 2. for the second interval of the continuance of that his willingness from everlasting unto the time of his coming to perform it, that is as evident also out of Prov. viii. 30, which shews how his delights were in it all the while; and therefore his heart was more especially set upon it than all works else. But this I have also spoken unto elsewhere.

CHAPTER II.

That Christ renewed his consent as soon as he came into the world.—That his human nature from his first conception agreed to it.—That this is apparent from the scope and intent of the twenty-second Psalm.

*But in those sacrifices there is a remembrance again made of sins every year. For it is not possible that the blood of bulls and of goats should take away sins. Wherefore, when he cometh into the world, he saith, Sacrifice and offering thou wouldst not, but a body hast thou prepared me.—*Heb. X. 3-5.

The other two parts of his willingness come now to be handled.

I. His willingness and consent renewed, when he came into the world, to perform what he had undertaken and covenanted for from everlasting.

II. The constant and fixed posture of his will, and heartiness in the work all along, during his lifetime, and in his death, till he had finished it, John xiii. 1. I shall not need to pursue this any further than unto his death, for the rest of his work in heaven was pleasant work, and but as the reaping the joyful harvest of his seed sown in tears.

The first I call the will of dedication, or consecration of himself by a vow to this great work, then solemnly made and given when he came into the world; the latter, the will of execution or performance. The first is like the dedication of the temple, which was his type, and was a most glorious action, and fundamental to all that followed; and calls for an answerable regard and observation from us. The dedications of the outward temple, the type of his body, the tabernacle made without hands, were the most solemn actions recorded in the Old Testament. And the first dedication had to accompany it the greatest hecatombs and sacrifices that ever were afore or after, joined with a large, set, and powerful prayer, composed by Solomon, and upon record. The other by Zerubbabel had a yearly feast, called the 'feast of the dedication,' to celebrate the memorial of it. But 'a greater than Solomon is here,' and a more glorious dedication of that temple, which was the glory of that second, as Haggai had foretold, Hag. ii. 9. What sacrifices of prayers should we then offer up to God upon the news thereof?

I. For the first, Christ's willingness and renewed consent when he came into the world. These words hold forth eminently two things concerning it.

1. The time of Christ's dedicating himself.

2. The dedication itself.

1. The time you see is at the very instant of his coming into the world, to undergo this great work and service. 'When he comes into the world, he says,' &c. This must needs be observed (as it is) a great and mighty secret, that the very words that God the Son then used to God the Father, at the moment of his incarnation (when he was to take our nature, to become flesh, and appear in this world as a part thereof), should be recorded, which words were before known alone to the three persons; which yet the Holy Ghost, the great secretary of heaven, hath vouchsafed to reveal unto us; for the great concernment of them, as to our salvation, so to our knowledge thereof. The words were first uttered by David, prophetically of Christ, Ps. xl. 6, 7, and the apostle not only interprets them of Christ, but adds that which David mentioned not. David speaks not a word of the

time that the date of this speech should be at, viz., when he should come into the world. No; this is one of Paul's secrets, revealed to him by the Holy Ghost, and could have been known from no other hand. You have the like speech recorded of the Father's to Christ, when he came first to heaven, by the same David, though the time thereof is more clearly hinted there, in the words themselves, Ps. cx. 1, ' The Lord said to my Lord, Sit thou on my right hand, till I make thine enemies thy footstool.'

The great inquiry next will be, who this *I* was, in Heb. x. 7, that should then utter it? Whether the second person only, as now being to take up our nature, or withal, the human nature concurring with him in that consent.

1. That it was the speech of the second person, then existing, is evident. For it was spoken when the Holy Ghost was framing the body or human nature in the womb; ' A body hast thou fitted me: lo, I come.' For he is the person, the *me*, and the *I*, that took up that body into one person with himself. He was more concerned than that human nature, and gave more away by his incarnation and the sufferings that followed; and therefore his willingness was the more requisite and eminent, and to that end recorded for our comfort. Thus at the instant when the human nature was a-making, and so was not capable as yet to give consent, yet had the great and total sum of glory due to it upon its union with that person, given away for thirty-three years to come, by him that was indeed the person that assumes it. Then did the second person (that is the person to whom all actions are attributed) express his readiness and willingness, ' Lo, I come.' And to shew he did it the most deliberately, and *consultò*, as we say, it is prefaced how he had taken aforehand consideration of all ways else; and now that his Father had took a summary of all other means, that might be in pretence to redeem mankind, and how all would prove invalid, giving one instance for all the rest, as of which the experiment fully has been made, namely, sacrifices and burnt-offerings; and so by that one instance for all other, at once declaring that all creature sacrifices would be too light, and of no value: ' Sacrifices and burnt-offerings thou wouldst not.' And he speaks withal as one who had consulted his Father's decrees, ' the volume of that book' written in heaven, wherein all our names are written, Heb. xii. 23, and had there seen all the whole work set down, and every tittle of God's will he was to perform or suffer. And now when it was come to the very moment of time set down, the fulness of time, Christ the Son offers himself to perform every jot of it; and doth not so much as stay expecting his Father's answer in return, or that he should speak anew to him about it, or move him in it, but prevents him. He says, ' Lo, I come;' as carrying all this in his heart written there, and precisely remembering the time, the moment; for you see himself is only here to speak to his Father.

So then you have the speech which at that instant not only the angel spake to his mother on earth, Luke i. 28–38, but here also that which the Son spake in heaven. And it speaks all willingness, yea, heart and zeal not to fail a moment, ' Lo, I come to do thy will, O God.' And it is with an *Ecce*, ' Lo and behold' how ready I am to do it.

2. It is worth our next inquiry what consent, and when it was, that the human nature, that body which he assumed, actually did first give.

(1.) It was necessary that this human nature should likewise consent and be willing; for as it was a distinct nature from the divine, so it had a distinct will, and also it was concerned, being to be made the subject of all the sufferings, the sacrifice to be given away and offered up, as the 10th verse hath it. It is necessary that it consent too, when it is able to put forth an act of consent, and of a deliberate will. The fundamental consent was the divine person's, and the act of assuming our nature, and coming into the world, and writing his name among creatures, was solely and singly the act of the divine person. But yet there is to be an accessory consent of the human nature, now married into one person with the divine, concerning this.

(2.) The question will be about the time, whether at his first coming into the world this consent was actually given ; or, that the consent of the human nature was included, as of one under age, in the consent of the divine person, the Son of God.

For answer; how soon, and when first, the human nature gave his consent, is hard to say.

1. This may safely be affirmed, that as soon as, or when first he began to put forth any acts of reason, that then his will was guided to direct its aim and intentions to God as his Father, from himself as the mediator. And look, as in infants' hearts, if they had been born in innocency, there would have been sown the notion of God, whom they should first have known in and by whatever they knew else ; and the moral law being written in their hearts, they should have directed their actions to God and his glory, through a natural instinct and tendency of spirit ; the principal law written in their hearts then, and wherein holiness consists, being to direct all to God and his glory. Thus it was in Christ when an infant, and such holy principles guided him to that, which was that will of God as to him, and to be performed by him ; and which was to sway and direct all his actions and thoughts, that were to be the matter of our salvation and justification, which were to be exerted according to the capacity of reason, as it should grow up more and more. Hence therefore this law, from the very first of his acting intelligently, must move and predominantly carry all along with the motion of it, as the *primum mobile* doth all the rest of the spheres. And look, as it would have been necessary that the law of love to God, and aiming at his glory, should have acted all thoughts and imaginations rational in infants in innocency, or they had not acted holily, as parts and pieces of mankind ought to do, when they acted, so Christ, being not only a man that had the law of holiness in him, but also the Messiah or mediator by special office and calling, and accordingly had that special law of his office written in his heart, it was as necessary to the performance of that office, that all thoughts and acts of understanding, &c., should be directed to God by him from the first, as works and parts of mediation, as it was for him, as a man, to address them all unto God's glory, as parts of holiness or righteousness. For else he had not discharged his office and calling from the first, nor had those first dawnings and actings of his will, thoughts, and affections, been involved and included as parts and pieces of his mediation, as the other parts of his obedience afterwards were. But now what Christ did when a child, hath a meritoriousness in it, as well as what he did when he was a man grown ; and also what he suffered, his very circumcision is made influential into our sanctification, through the merits and virtue of it, as well as his after being baptized when thirty years old. And therefore for certain his actions, which proceeded from will and understanding from the first, had in their proportion the same meritorious influence.

The Twenty-second Psalm, which was peculiarly made for, and in the name of Christ, doth expressly and directly tells us not only that God took him out of the womb, and that he was cast upon God from the womb, ver. 9, 10, the latter of which may be passively understood of God's care of him ; but further, ' Thou didst make me hope when I was upon my mother's breasts,' ver. 9. ' And thou art my God from my mother's belly ;' or, as Ainsworth reads the words, ' The maker of me to trust at my mother's breasts.' Which words cannot be understood only in a passive sense, but do import acts of faith miraculously drawn forth from him to God as his God. As also those words, ' Thou art my God,' may well be taken to import how he had owned and relied upon him as his God from his mother's womb, shewing how that then he had owned him as his God, with an act of faith, as truly as in ver. 1, when he cried out, ' My God, my God,' &c., when on the cross.

But that I insist on is to observe to this purpose the coherence of his words all along afore, as also in this passage. Christ had pleaded ' their fathers trusted in thee, and were delivered,' ver. 4, 5 ; and ver. 8, he alleged how that that his faith upon God as his God, and as a Father to him, as his only begotten Son, and the Messiah and Saviour of the world, was the thing he was reproached and upbraided with now when on the cross : ver. 7 and 8, ' All they that see me laugh me to scorn : they shoot out the lip, they shake the head, saying, He trusted on the Lord that he would de-liver him : let him deliver him, seeing he delighted in him.' I say, this was the reproach cast on him in particular, viz., how that he had with con-fidence given out and taken upon him, as being the Son of God and Messiah, and for his trusting on God under that special relation to him, was the thing they jeered. Thus it is expressly, in the citing of that place by Matthew, Mat. xxvii. 43, ' He trusted in God ; let him deliver him now, if he will have him : for he said, I am the Son of God.' Now then, in the next verses of the psalm, he allegeth in answer to his reproach, ' Thou didst make me hope at my mother's breasts.' Which in its coherence is as if he had said, did the fathers trust thee with that faith, as men thine elect use to trust thee withal ? Why, lo, Lord, I began to trust thee sooner than ordinarily any of them do, or ever did, even at the breast when an infant ; and, Lord, thou hearest them mock me, that I trusted I was thy only begotten Son ; and now, Lord, this was the very thing thou causedst me to trust and have assurance of, when at my mother's breasts. Yea, and I did it then in that sense, and with that faith I now on the cross do call thee my God withal, as being that beloved Son of thine, my Father and my God, in whom thou delightest. And with this faith it hath been that I have owned thee as my God all along, even from the very womb.

Now then, if Christ had an actual faith then on God as his God, answer-able to his personal interest in and relation unto God as his God, and so in his proportion such as holy men have in their measure, and from their interest in God as adopted sons, suitably to their condition and estate when they come first to believe ; then that faith in him must needs in time rise up to faith and apprehension of him, as a Father to him, as the only begotten, the Messiah. For else his faith had fallen short of that object of it which was proper and peculiar to him and his state and condition. And if this be at all wondered at, that Christ's human nature should do it so soon, Christ himself tells it here as a wonderful work of God towards him in that human soul of his, in that he celebrates God as the maker of him to trust, or ' thou causedst me to trust then,' and thou that drewest me out of the womb, and didst miraculously form me there, didst draw my soul then to believe in thee as my Father.

Neither are these mine apprehensions alone upon this place, but the same I have found to be in one late learned commentator* on the words, who says, *Nos hunc versum de Christo interpretamur, in quo cum ab instanti conceptionis fuerunt omnes thesauri sapientiæ et scientiæ absconditi, potuit ab instanti conceptionis omnem suam curam et spem,. ut homo, in uno Deo figere et locare.* Christ having in him, from the instant of his conception, all the treasures of his wisdom and knowledge hidden in him, it might be so, that, from the instant of his conception, he as a man might fix and place all his care and hope in God alone. And to that end he quoteth also this place, Heb. x. 7, my text, ' When he came into the world, he says,' &c.

Now there are two speeches in the 40th Psalm more proper to apply to the soul of that human nature assumed.

1. ' My ear hast thou bored through,' is appliable more properly to the human nature than to the divine ; and so to be understood to be the voice of the human nature rather than of the divine.

Now, what is it to have an ear bored through ? It is to be made willing and obedient to do God's will, as a servant is to do his master's. You know how that one that was purely a servant, and for ever such, he had his ear bored, Exod. xxi. 6. This was typical. He that had his ear bored through gave his consent first, which is implied in those words, ' And if the servant shall plainly say, I love my master, my wife, and my children, I will not go out free.' If he would be free, he was to forsake his wife and children, which were a motive to many to live as a servant with them. The human nature now united might have stood upon it, not to enter into any service ; that is, as in respect of his own prerogative, being taken up into an equality with God. But, says Christ, I love my Father, and therefore I will serve him in the work of redemption : John xiv. 31, ' That the world may know that I love the Father, and as the Father gave me commandment, even so I do.' He also loved his wife, his spouse, his church, &c. He will have her live with him, he must serve for her company, and he loves his children particularly (as that speech imports, ' Lo, here am I, and the children thou hast given me'). This moved Christ to serve, as Jacob did Laban : Eph. v. 26, ' Husbands, love your wives, even as Christ loved the church, and gave himself for it.' He should not have her society else, as himself speaks : John xii. 23, 24, ' Except the Son of man die, he must abide alone,' or be in heaven alone, without his church's company. Neither is it the phrase only that complies with this sense, but you have another scripture doth manifestly apply this phrase to Christ, in this sense of willing obedience : Isa. l. 5, ' The Lord God hath opened mine ear, and I was not rebellious, neither turned away back.' Do you know his voice that speaks it, and about what ? It is your Saviour's. I will give you a comfortable token you shall know it by : ver. 4, ' The Lord God hath given me the tongue of the learned, that I should know how to speak a word in season to him that is weary. He wakeneth morning by morning, he wakeneth mine ear to hear as the learned.' You know who afterwards said of himself, ' Come to me, all ye that are weary, and I will ease you,' Mat. xi. 28, as you have it in the margin. And will you know what the work was for which God had opened his ear ? ' And I am not rebellious,' says he. It was the hardest piece of it, to which of all other, if to any, he should have been unwilling. It follows, ver. 6, ' I gave my back to the smiters, and my cheeks to them that plucked off the hair ; I hid not my face from shame and spitting.' Read Matthew the 26th and 27th chapters. But is that all, that he was not rebellious or refractory to it, his ear was

* *Muis* in Ps. xxii. 9.

bored, he drew not his back away? No: 'I give my back to the smiters,' &c. It was his own free act, as elsewhere it is said, Gal. ii. 20, 'He gave himself.' And whereas the servant in the type had but one ear bored through, of Christ the psalmist says in the plural, 'My ears' (so it is in the original) 'hast thou bored through,' to note an abundance, an overplus of willingness; as when we say, a man hears of a thing with both ears, it notes he hears of it, and hears of it again. Christ was all ear, to shew he was all obedience. His ear bored is put for the whole: as the apostle in,-terprets it, 'A body.'

2. There is another speech argues this consent to have been the human nature's also, when he says, speaking of his willingness, 'Thy law is in my bowels;' written there habitually from the womb, which cannot be meant of the divine nature. And yet even when he assumed this human nature, the law of God, and this special law of the mediatorship, was written there. That phrase shews (as I said at first) that it was by instinct, such as natu-rally it would have been in infants in innocency. Now, this is more than simply to have an ear bored, to give consent; it is to have his law made natural to him. And it is in the midst of the bowels, in the will, the affec-tions, that are the centre of the soul, and the middle of it. But the apostle speaks this of him when coming into the world. And these speeches being manifestly proper to the human soul and will, and being compared with these passages of the 22d Psalm, they all together do strongly argue that, in a miraculous way, the human soul of Christ did then give up itself to this whole work.

And so to conclude this, look as his mother consented to the angel's message before she conceived of him: Luke i. 31, says the angel, 'Thou shalt conceive, and shalt call his name Jesus.' And in the middle of his delivery of it, she had not as yet conceived him, for, ver. 35, he says still in the future, 'The Holy Ghost shall come on thee, and shall overshadow thee,' &c. And when the angel had done his message, ver. 38, 'Mary said, Behold the handmaid of the Lord' (I give myself up to him); 'be it unto me according to thy word.' And so thereupon she conceived of him; for, Luke ii. 21, it is said, 'his name was called Jesus, which was so named of the angel before he was conceived in the womb.' And therefore, till the angel had done his message, she conceived not of him, and so not till her own consent was given. And as God had hers that she might be freely the mother of him, so in like manner God, it would seem, had the consent of that reasonable soul of Jesus presently after his coming, and being made the Son of God. And so was fulfilled that which in the pro-phecy was foretold he should utter: Isa. xlix. 1, 'God hath called me from the womb,' as well as made mention of his name (Jesus) from his concep-tion; as it follows there, 'From the bowels of my mother he hath made mention of my name.' Which, though spoken of others (as of Cyrus), it imports but God's ordaining him from that time to that work; yet we may apply it to Christ, considering all that is said afore; as also that this is not passively spoken of him, as that of Cyrus and others, but is recorded as to be uttered by himself, 'The Lord hath called me from the womb,' &c. It may import more, even how Christ did then answer his call, and gave up himself to this work; but of this more anon.

And thus again, as his conception was at Nazareth, Luke i. 26, so he was every way Ναζαραῖος, a Nazarite, given up to God ,from the womb, given up by the second person that assumed that nature, given up by the human nature, the soul of it assumed, by a miraculous work of God, as was his conception itself, given up by his mother also, who assents to all that the angel said of him, to have such a child to be conceived in her: ' Be it according to thy word,' said she.   Lastly, a Nazarite by God's own dedication and separation of him then to it, in the message of the angel, which was sent by him.

CHAPTER III.

Shewing the mystery of that appellation given him, 'Jesus the Nazarite,' to have been, that he was thus dedicated from his very conception to this great work.

And he came and dwelt in a city called Nazareth, that it might be fulfilled which was spoken by the prophets, He shall be called a Nazarene.—MAT. II. 23.

There was no name more ordinarily and familiarly given to Christ, and that by all sorts of persons, than this, ' Jesus of Nazareth,' and ' Jesus the Nazarite.'   It was given him by the Jews, John xviii. 5, 7, Mat. xxvi. 71; by angels: (1.) the bad, Mark i. 24; (2.) the good, Mark xvi. 6.   Yea, this appellation obtained so among all, that it was put by Pilate, the Roman Governor, into the superscription upon the cross, in all three languages, ' Jesus the Nazarite,' John xix. 19; and was further used by his apostles, as glorying to own him under that title after his ascension; so Acts ii. 22, and chap. iii. 6, iv. 10.   Yea, and himself, after his ascension, doth from heaven decipher himself thereby: Acts xxii. 8, ' I am Jesus (ὁ Ναζωραῖος) the Nazarite.'

Now it so fell out, in the providence of God guiding the idiom or manner of speech in that language, that a Nazarene or Nazarite signified both an inhabitant of the city Nazareth, as also one that by profession and vow was peculiarly separated and dedicated to God.

The Jews, as they gave this name unto Jesus, intended no other thing thereby than that he was an inhabitant of and dweller in the city of Nazareth; as you say a Londoner, noting out an inhabitant of the city of London.   And so it is given to Christ, Ναζαρηνὸς, Luke iv. 34, compared with John i. 46, where it is τὸν ἀπὸ Ναζαρὲθ, that is, one of the inhabitants of Nazareth.

But Matthew tells us that God had a further design in guiding those Jews to this appellation, to hold forth a higher mystery, namely, that this was the great Nazarite, vowed and separated unto him, of whom all the votaries or Nazarites of the Old Testament were types.   And therefore he is termed by Matthew and others ὁ Ναζωραῖος, the great Nazarite, those having been his shadows, even as he is called the last Adam, 1 Cor. xv. 43; the true David, Acts xiii. 34.

The words of Matthew to this purpose are these, Mat. ii. 23, ' And he came and dwelt in a city called Nazareth,' which was the only occasion why the Jews termed him Jesus of Nazareth, or Nazarene; but it had this mystery further in it, ' That it might be fulfilled which was spoken by the prophets,' of him that was to be the Messiah, ' that he shall be called,' that is, be, ' a Nazarite.'

Now, under the Old Testament, the writers of which are generally called the prophets, all that were dedicated or consecrated unto God by vow of their parents from their birth, or that separated themselves unto God in a special vow of holiness and obedience above others of their brethren, these were termed Nazarites; as Joseph, Gen. xlix. 26, 'The blessings of thy father have prevailed above the blessings of my progenitors, and to the utmost bounds of the everlasting hills they shall be on the head of Joseph, and on the crown of the head of him that was separate from his brethren.' And Samson also, Judges xiii. 5, 'For, lo, thou shalt conceive and bear a son, and no razor shall come on his head; for the child shall be a Nazarite unto God from the womb.' And whoever he was that vowed his person to God, and not his goods only, was by the law called a Nazarite: Num. vi. 2, 'Speak unto the children of Israel, and say unto them, When either man or woman shall separate themselves to vow a vow of a Nazarite, to separate themselves to the Lord.' All which were acted as types and shadows of the dedication of himself, to be after this made by this great votary, who was the substance of them in this particular, as in all things else he was of all his other forerunning types, in what was attributed to them.

There may other royal qualifications and characters of Christ the Messiah fall into this, that he was called a Nazarite, as will in the current of this discourse appear; but this of his being vowed to God was the great and main thing intended thereby, as Joseph and Sampson and others were.

The main difficulty herein is, how the examples and the law of those Nazarites should be esteemed prophecies of him, as Matthew here says, 'That it might be fulfilled which was spoken by the prophets.'

It is a known and a taken-for-granted truth, that those names and things spoken of the eminent types of Christ, are by the evangelists and apostles given unto Christ, whom they prophetically signified, as more truly, and in a more transcendent manner, belonging to him than unto the persons themselves to whom they were first given unto; as eminently fulfilled in him, yea, and as more really intended of him than of them, as appears by many instances of the like kind.

Thus when Paul to the Hebrews would prove Christ to be the Son of God, in that peculiar manner as never man, yea, nor angel, ever was: Heb. i. 4, 5, 'Being made so much better than the angels, as he hath by inheritance obtained a more excellent name than they. For unto which of the angels said he at any time, Thou art my Son, this day have I begotten thee? And again, I will be to him a Father, and he shall be to me a Son?' He would here prove that Christ's name given him in the Old Testament, was 'the Son of God,' and so the Son as no angel. He cites a speech spoken of, and to Solomon, 'And again I will be to him a Father, and he shall be to me a Son.' Now where are these words to be found, or how come they to be meant of Christ? The words are only found, 2 Sam. vii. 14, 1 Chron. xxii. 10. No way can be devised but this, that what God speaketh of Solomon is more properly intended of Christ; *De Solomone vero*, more than *de Solomone mero*. David's Son was but a shadow. Yea, and which is stranger, he quotes it to prove that Christ the Messiah was the Son of God in such a transcendent manner as Solomon was not, even that he was the only begotten Son, whereof Solomon's sonship was but a shadow. This and many the like must be resolved into this general rule, that what is attributed to the type his shadow, must needs be in a more divine and super-eminent manner ascribed to him the substance. For if so excellent persons in their highest excellency were

but his types, then what are those excellencies in him, a person so divine ?
I might exemplify all this more clearly in the apostle's quoting, and that as
a proof too, what was said of the first Adam, that he was an earthly man,
a living soul, to fore-prophesy Christ's super-excelling dignity of his being
the Lord of heaven, a quickening Spirit, a second Adam : 1 Cor. xv. 44, 45,
' It is sown a natural body; it is raised a spiritual body. There is a natural body, and there is a spiritual body. And so it is written, The first
man Adam was made a living soul; the last Adam was made a quickening
Spirit.' And multitudes of other instances might be given ; as that in
Hosea xi. 1, ' Out of Egypt have I called my Son,' quoted by Matthew in
this chap. ii. ver. 15. Now then parallel this of Matthew, concerning
Christ his being a Nazarite, with that of his being a Son under the type of
Solomon, and a second Adam, &c., and you will readily say as Matthew
here, This name of Nazarite was commonly given him, that it might be
fulfilled which was spoken by the prophets, He shall be called a Nazarite.
So as, although there were no other scriptures in the prophets to foresignify
this thing, than these which were his types, yet that alone is sufficient to
call for Matthew's πληρωθῇ, 'that it might be fulfilled' ; yea, and the name
and thing more eminently fulfilled in him than it was in them ; and he a
more transcendent votary, made more holy and more sanctified than
they all.

CHAPTER IV.

*That Samson, and other Nazarites of the law, were types of Christ the great
Nazarite, who dedicated him to the holy work of redemption.—By what
rules and reasons we may judge that Christ was in this respect typified by
those Nazarites.*

Two things here are to be further inquired into.
I. By what it doth appear that Samson and Joseph, and those by the
law of vows that were Nazarites under the old law, were therein types of
our Jesus, termed the Nazarite.
II. How he, being a Nazarite, or a devoted person, from his very conception and education in his younger years, was fore-signified, and how
fitly and correspondently his being termed a Nazarite from the city Nazareth (which Matthew affirms) falls in herewith ; as also by what a wonderful providence it came to pass that this great and important title of the
Christ, Nazarite, should commonly and ordinarily be given him by the
Jews themselves, they intending it only to signify that he was an inhabitant of the city Nazareth, and but to vilify him ; but God intending it further to signify his dedication and consecration to the work of redemption
from his conception, and all along in his education, Nazareth being the
place of both.
I. To clear the first, viz., How Samson and other vowed Nazarites
appear to be types of Christ.
1. In general, even by the same rule that we know Adam and Solomon to have been types of him, and that what was said of them is to be
applied to him, who yet are nowhere in the Old Testament called his
types. And as we receive the testimony of Paul, that so applies it from
them, so we may here do this of Matthew by the same warrant ; though
we had no other special application of these types unto Christ in the Old
Testament.

The general rule which the apostles went by, and which the Jews themselves assented unto, and their teachers taught them, was, that whatever eminent and extraordinary excellency was found in any of their ancestors renowned in the Old Testament, or in the ceremonial law, that all such foresignified the Messiah to come, as the perfection and centre of them. This themselves acknowledge of David, who yet was not styled a saviour or deliverer, as Samson and Joseph are expressly termed, which was also the eminent character and work of our Jesus ; this I say they acknowledge of Melchisedec, David, Solomon, the high priest among the Jews, their kings, &c. Then if it be so, that special institution of the Nazarite must mean the like. And the reason is undeniable ; for what excellency was it that a Nazarite, a votary under the old law, took upon him the profession of ? Why a peculiar and more singular holiness, separation, consecration of their person unto God, in some special service which they were by vow or dedication obliged unto above their brethren, which they expressed by a peculiar strictness in abstaining from wine, and the like, which others did not. Thus Num. v. 2-5, ' Speak unto the children of Israel, and say unto them, When either man or woman shall separate themselves to vow a vow of a Nazarite, to separate themselves unto the Lord ; he shall separate himself .from wine and strong drink, and shall drink no vinegar of wine, or vinegar of strong drink, neither shall he drink any liquor of grapes, nor eat moist grapes, or dried. All the days of his separation shall he eat nothing that is made of the vine-tree, from the kernels unto the husk. All the days of the vow of his separation there shall no razor come upon his head ; until the days be fulfilled, in the which he separateth himself unto the Lord, he shall be holy, and shall let the locks of his hair grow.' He shall be holy, that is, peculiarly, singularly holy. Now then, if civil excellencies in public persons were types of him, as kings, &c., then sacred much more, and that of special holiness and consecration to God above any other.

Peculiar holiness, whether real or ceremonial, did make a Nazarite ; therefore, in Num. vi. 8, he is called ' holy to the Lord.' And a Nazarite is translated by the Septuagint ἅγιος, a holy man ; especially they were termed such, when these were joined with their being saviours and deliverers of the people of God. All such were eminently, and must be acknowledged, types of him that was to be the great saviour and deliverer whom the Jews expected.

2. Particularly, to give the reasons for it.

(1.) Joseph, both for his excelling in holiness above his brethren, as also his eminent advancement over them, was an apparent type of Christ.

[1.] For holiness. It might seem by the story he was devoted thereto from his younger years, when his brethren were vain and wicked, which is discovered in the story by this, that when he was seventeen years old, he, detesting their sinful ways, brought the report thereof unto his father, being a reprover of his brethren, for which his brethren hated him. That other, of his dignity, is more apparent. For these reasons he is twice called a Nazarite.

First; By Jacob, his father, in his prophecy, for so that his last speech concerning his son was, Gen. xlix. 26, ' The blessings of thy father have prevailed above the blessings of my progenitors, unto the utmost bounds of the everlasting hills ; they shall be on the head of Joseph, and on the crown of the head of him that was separate from his brethren.' In the original it is, ' That was a Nazarite among his brethren.'

Secondly; And then by Moses it is again repeated, as of mystical importance, Deut. xxxiii. 16. And in this last place, the Septuagint hath it δοξασθεὶς ἐπ' ἀδελφοῖς, 'He was glorious above his brethren.' And added unto this was (as you all know) Joseph, his being a saviour, and so acknowledged by Jacob. And he was so, upon record, in the bringing the first fruits, acknowledged by all his posterity : ' My father was a Syrian ready to perish,'* and who saved them ? Joseph. And the Gentile Egyptians, they also acknowledged it, Gen. xlii. 2, ' Thou hast saved our lives.' And he was one separated, singled out by God, and sent afore to save them. Joseph was beloved of his father, so Christ is the beloved ; Joseph was blessed above all, and his house in him, Gen xlix. 26, Deut. xxxiii. 16, so we are blessed in Christ. Eph. i. 3, ' Blessed be the God and Father of our Lord Jesus Christ, who hath blessed us with all spiritual blessings in heavenly places in Christ.' Joseph was carried into Egypt, so Christ too : Mat. ii. 15, ' Out of Egypt have I called my Son.' Joseph sold to the Gentiles, was a saviour to the Jews and Gentiles, so Christ too. Joseph was suddenly advanced out of prison, Christ in prison, Is. liii. 8, taken out of prison, and then ascended. Joseph in his advancement forgives, so Christ on the cross ; and when he came first to heaven, as a testimony thereof, he converted three thousand of the Jews that had crucified him. Joseph's brethren bow to him ; and of Christ it is said, ' All knees shall bow to him.'

And because that this title Nazarite was, in Joseph's example, used to design and note out one that excelled his brethren, and was a ruler over them, as Joseph was ; hence further, the word *Nezer* and *Nazer* was after used to express the oil and mitre that consecrated the priest, also the crown that was set upon their kings ; so as their kings, prophets, and priests were Nazarites all of them in the type. Thus the mitre on the high priest's head, in which holiness to the Lord was written, Ex. xxix. 6, is called *Nizri;* and chap. xxxix. 30, the oil that anointed his head, Lev. xxi. 12, is called 'the holy oil,' and the word for holy there is *Nezer.* And the diadem of the king is termed by the same name *Nezer,* 2 Sam. i. 10, Ps. lxxxix. 4, and Ps. cxxxii. 18, as being a sign of his separation from his brethren. So, then, this name seems to set the mitre and crown upon Christ's head. In plain words, they were all Nazarites, kings, priests, and prophets. Now, take in all these, and I am sure you must have prophets enough that came in to call him Nazarite, in recording the stories of these his types ; those that call him ' Holy, holy, holy,' as angels do, Isa. vi., or seeing his glory, as Dan. ix., call him ' most holy,' those who call him separated ; Heb. vii. 26, ' anointed,' as Joseph, ' with oil above his brethren,' Heb. i. 9 ; a person sanctified to his works, as he speaks of himself, when to die, John xvii. 19. What need I quote any more ? All these express his being a Nazarite.

(2.) Of Sampson, it is yet more expressly said, Judges xiii. 15, that he should be called ' a Nazarite to God from the womb.' And to what end was that separation of his from the womb made, and he marked out thereby? It follows, ' He shall begin to save or deliver Israel out of the hands of the Philistines their enemies.' And he killed these enemies, and delivered that people without weapons, by the jaw-bone of an ass, a contemptible instrument for such a slaughter ; and at last died out of an heroicness of spirit, by an extraordinary warrant, for it was effected by an extraordinary strength renewed upon him ; and so he was a greater con-

* Deut. xxvi. 5.—ED.

queror in his death than in all his life. You know how easy and natural it is to find all these in our Jesus. But how his being consecrated from the womb was a type of Christ (that is the main intended by me), I shall explain in the second head.

In the mean time, the result of these two types is to represent Christ as a Nazarite, eminently for these three things.

1. Excelling holiness and strictness of life, which was the law of Nazarites.

2. Dominion or rule over their brethren, as their kings and priests were, and Joseph, and Sampson, judge of Israel.

3. Being a saviour and deliverer from death and enemies. 'Sampson began to deliver,' &c., Judges xiii. 15.

Now, all these are found to have met in our Christ, as is the import of that ordinary appellation given him, 'Ιησοῦς Ναζαραῖος, Jesus of Nazareth, or the Nazarite, which are usually coupled together.

1. Jesus is the name of Saviour given him at his conception: Mat. i. 21, 'Thou shalt call his name Jesus: for he shall save his people from their sins.' And then Nazarite imports his being separated to that work, namely, to save, as in that speech of the angel he was declared to be, whilst his conception at Nazareth was effecting in the virgin's womb.

2. For holiness. The first time that we read of, wherein he was called Jesus the Nazarite, was by Satan, Mark. i. 24, and Luke iv. 34. And there, by the providence of God, this is added and confessed by that evil spirit, 'I know who thou art, the holy one of God, that eminent holy one, of whom all other eminent holy ones were types,' which was the import of the name Nazarite. Now, compare this with what is said of Samson, his type, Judges xiii. 5, 'He shall be a Nazarite unto God,' or 'of God;' and the Septuagint translates Nazarite sometimes ἅγιος, one holy; and so to be an holy one of God, and a Nazarite to God, is all one. But of Samson, his being his type in his conception, more hereafter.

3. His being king. Go to the cross, you find it written there, 'Jesus of Nazareth,' or, 'the Nazarite, King of the Jews.'

CHAPTER V.

How Christ was presignified as a Nazarite by these types.—The parallel between him and Samson.—How God having thus in the type foretold that Christ should be a Nazarite, so wisely ordered it, that both his conception and education should be there, that so that name Nazarite, as an inhabitant of that city, might belong to him.

Now follows the second head, which hath two things in it.

1. How his being a Nazarite, or devoted person from his very conception, and education in his younger years, was foresignified in any of these types.

2. How it came to pass that, though he was called a Nazarite by the Jews as in their common language, noting forth only an inhabitant of Nazareth, as Matthew tells us, this should yet withal fall in and serve to fulfil God's intention of his being called a Nazarite, as was by these prophetical types foresignified; and by what a wonderful providence this was brought about, so to fulfil the prophecy.

1. For the first; take the type of Samson, and see how exactly parallel

it falls out to foresignify Christ's being a Nazarite from his conception. Let us but seriously compare the history of both.

Of Samson, Judges xiii. 2, 3, 5, ' And there was a certain man of Zorah, of the family of the Danites, whose name was Manoah; and his wife was barren, and bare not. And the angel of the Lord appeared unto the woman, and said unto her, Behold now, thou art barren, and bearest not : but thou shalt conceive, and bear a son. . . . For, lo, thou shalt conceive, and bear a son; and no razor shall come on his head : for the child shall be a Nazarite unto God from the womb ; and he shall begin to deliver Israel out of the hand of the Philistines.'

Of Christ, Luke i. 26–31, ' And in the sixth month the angel Gabriel was sent from God unto a city of Galilee, named Nazareth, to a virgin espoused to a man, whose name was Joseph, of the house of David ; and the virgin's name was Mary. And the angel came in unto her, and said, Hail, thou that art highly favoured, the Lord is with thee : blessed art thou among women. And the angel said unto her, Fear not, Mary ; for thou hast found favour with God. And, behold, thou shalt conceive in thy womb, and bring forth a son, and shalt call his name Jesus.'

(1.) Observe Samson's wonderful separation from his conception. An angel is sent to foretell it. The prophecy of an angel is recorded : so it is in Christ.

(2.) Both appearances of the angels are afore the conception of either.

(3.) As the angel is sent to a woman utterly barren, to shew Samson's conception should be extraordinary, as to an extraordinary end, so Gabriel is sent to a virgin, who without man's copulation with her had a womb far more barren and incapable to conceive a child than Samson's mother's was. And therefore to strengthen her faith the angel tells her, ver. 36, 37, ' Behold, thy cousin Elisabeth, she hath also conceived a son in her old age : and this is the sixth month with her that was called barren. For with God nothing shall be impossible.'

(4.) The messages sent at and before their conception, to both, concerning these their sons, are parallel.

[1.] That he be a Nazarite of God, that is, holy and consecrated to God from the womb (yea, from his conception, and therefore his mother was warned not to drink wine nor strong drink from this time afore his conception, nor whilst she bore him) unto the very day of his death. Now of Christ, it is at and from his conception, Luke i. 35, ' The Holy Ghost shall come upon thee, and the power of the Highest shall overshadow thee : therefore also that holy thing, which shall be born of thee, shall be called the Son of God.' Now a Nazarite of God, and one holy unto God, were all one ; as hath been said.

[2.] In that the work which each of these were separated unto is declared alike at their conception, as to be saviours of the people. Of Samson it is said, ' He shall begin ' (as being Christ's type) ' to save Israel out of the hands of the Philistines.' And as expressly of Christ it is said by the angel, Mat. i. 21, ' She shall bring forth a son, and thou shalt call his name Jesus ; for he shall save his people from their sins.' Not to insist on this addition which some make, that Herod a Philistine was then king, and the Jews subject to Christ,* when this message was delivered of Christ, as in Samson's time they also were.

[3.] And lastly, how Christ was a Nazarite until the day of his death from the womb, as of Samson it is said, I need not shew. That one text

* Evidently a misprint. I suppose ' him.'—Ed.

speaks it, *obediens usque ad mortem*, obedient until death, all his life long, Philip. ii. 8. Only take this, that at his conception at first, those three fore-mentioned characters or designments of a Nazarite were declared by the angel. 1. Jesus a saviour. 2. The holy one of God. 3. His dignity and pre-eminence over all : ' Luke i. 31, 32, ' Thou shalt conceive in thy womb, and bring forth a son, and shalt call his name Jesus. And he shall be great, and shall be called the Son of the Highest ; and the Lord God shall give unto him the throne of his father David.' To which the types, both of Samson the judge, and Joseph the ruler, do fully answer. Thus also again at his death, those all meet in the inscription on the cross, ' Jesus the saviour, of Nazareth,' or ' Nazarene,' the holy One, ' king of the Jews.'

For the second particular, viz., how it was ordered by God that the Jews should call Jesus a Nazarite ; three things are worthy our notice in it.

1. That God in his all-wise counsel so ordered it, that the name or title Nazarite, which in the Greek is Ναζωραῖος, should be used in the common language of the Jews to express an inhabitant of the city Nazareth, which word also had been singled forth by God to express a Nazarite to himself, one holy and consecrated to himself. It was, as many other words are, *vox æquivoca*, that had two senses equally and vulgarly in use. *Fuit tum nomen gentilitium, tum religiosum*, as *Latinus*, or Λατεῖνος, signified both an inhabitant, or one born in Italy, an Italian, so denoting a man's country ; and was anciently used to signify one that adhered to, and was one of the popish religion, as distinguished from that professed by the Greek churches, or now by the protestant. And this was foretold by Irenæus as the title of antichrist his followers, long before that division was made ; he thus interpreting the mystery of the number 666, Rev. xiii. 18. So now *Romanus*, a Roman, may and doth import one either dwelling or born at Rome, or one of the Romish religion. Or as if a child of an Englishman that had been of the separation at Amsterdam, and educated or born there, should be termed an Amsterdamian, it would import at once both the place whence he came and where he dwelt ; as also (as commonly it doth) that he was of that profession which the English separatists did hold forth there. Multitudes of such instances are producible, and thus it fell out here.

Now that this word Ναζωραῖος was then used to express both, I judge more evident.

(1.) In that we are sure that Ναζωραῖος imported an inhabitant of Nazareth ; for Matthew, who gives him that style, directly pointeth us unto that sense and signification of the word : for he says, ' He came and dwelt in Nazareth : that it might be fulfilled.' He was called a Nazarite, as being vulgarly so styled from that city ; yea and therefore it was that the Jews in scorn so called him, to defame him from that city, which was so vile and mean, as no good was thence expected ; and therefore much less he that was to be the Messiah''should come forth from thence. Also this appears in that in another evangelist, speaking at a time afore that name was given, he is called ὁ ἀπὸ τοῦ Ναζαρὲθ, ' one of the city of Nazareth.'

Then [2.] The scripture or prophets nowhere speaking of Christ's dwelling in the city Nazareth, the fulfilling of the prophecies must be found in this, that this word Ναζαραῖος hath some other mysterious signification, which should be proper and eminent in him that was the true Christ. Now this title ὁ Ναζαραῖος is in the same letters and syllables thereof a Nazarite, or one holy and separate to God. For the Septuagint, translating the Hebrew word for *Nazir* or Nazarite into the Greek, do still use this word with the same syllables and letters. only they sometimes use α, ζα, Ναζαραῖος, sometimes η, or ζη, Ναζηραῖος, whereas Matthew, ω, Ναζωραῖος, and that is all the difference.

And this those of-an opposite opinion object, that because Matthew useth the letter ω, whereas the Septuagint useth α, that therefore it is not the same word which they use to signify a Nazarite by. To which the answer is ready.

For 1. In that the Septuagint themselves do vary it, sometimes writing it with α, sometimes with η, yet in each they alike intended to signify a religious Nazarite. I say, if they alter α into η, in either intending the same word and the same signification, it may bear as well this other alteration of ω, it being but a matter of diverse pronunciation, as Grotius observes, and not a diversity of the word itself, which in differing dialects, when the word is the same, is ordinary in languages, as we see in the Scottish and English tongue (which I mention for vulgar illustration). Yea, the ancient fathers make another alteration, writing it with ι : so Eusebius, Epiphanius, and Nazianzen, terming them Nazireans or Nazirites.

But 2. We all know that nothing is more usual than, in translating a word out of one language into another, to change a letter ; as Miriam in the Hebrew, the Greeks into Maria, Schemuel, Samuel, and the like. And the Syriac, which was the language Christ and the Jews did then speak, did ordinarily in pronouncing the Hebrew, turn α into ω : so as *Nazareth* after the Hebrew pronunciation was *Nazoreth* in the Syriac. Now Matthew in the Greek did incline and conform the termination or sound of the word to the Syriac rather than to the Hebrew, the Syriac being then in use. And so *Nazorean*, or *Nazorite*, is all one with *Nazarite*.

3. I omit to retort, that those of the other opinion that would have Christ here called by Matthew Ναζωραῖος, from *Netzer*, the title in Hebrew which Isaiah gives to Christ, Isa. xi. 1, ' Of the branch,' is far remoter in sound and letters by far. And besides that that is a substantive word, this of Ναζωραῖος is an adjective. But of this afterwards.

It is objected, 2. That Christ is also called Jesus Ναζαρηνὸς, the Nazarene, as well as Ναζαραῖος, the Nazaraian. But *Nazarene* was not used (say they) to signify a Nazarite.

And it is answered again, that if *Nazarene* and *Nazaraian* (that I may in the English variation express it) signified both one, where his city's name is intended, as it is evident they did, then why not both these words also be as promiscuously used for a religious Nazarite, when it is evident that one of them was used to express it, viz., his being a *Nazarite?* There is nothing more usual in all languages than to make such variations, in names of religion as well as other, and yet so as they are still but one word in signification ; as we say sometimes a Grecian, sometimes a Greek, and both signifying either his religion or his country ; a *Roman*, a *Romanist*, a *Calvinian* or *Calvinist;* so if you will, a *Nazarite*, a *Nazarean*, is all one.

And 2. Matthew that holds out to us this mystery, he calls him Nazaraian, or Nazarite, not Nazarene ; so in this place, and so constantly elsewhere. And thus the inscription on the cross (as in John also) and not the other word Nazarene at all. So as Matthew intended to hold forth his being a Nazarite, as well as of the city Nazareth.

The second thing to be noted is, that as Christ was to be a Nazarite from his conception (as in his type of Samson it was foresigned), and also in his younger years of education, as well as when he died, so God in his providence ordered it, that the city Nazareth, from whence he should by the Jews be called a Nazarite, was not only the very place of his education, but also of his very conception; and this is sedulously noted (to complete this mystery) unto us in the story of his conception : Luke i. 26, 27, ' In the sixth month the angel Gabriel was sent from God unto a city of Galilee, named Nazareth, to a virgin espoused to a man whose name was Joseph, of the house of David ; and the virgin's name was Mary.' So then, though Bethlehem was the place of his birth, yet this Nazareth, from whence he had his name of Nazarite, was the place of his conception, to shew he was a Nazarite from his very conception, which hath been the point I have pursued. And as it was the place of his conception, so of his abode and education, until he put himself forth into the world, and appeared as the Messiah. This you have, Mat. ii. 22.

Now, yet further, to add unto Matthew's πληρωθῇ, and to make up his fulfilling of prophecies yet more full, it was foretold by the prophet Jeremiah that his conception should be in one of the cities of the ten tribes,* which the story here in Matthew tells us was Nazareth. The prophet Micah had, before Jeremiah's time, foretold that the city of his birth should be Bethlehem, which the tribes of Judah and Benjamin gloried in, and therefore despised the other ten. The pharisees understood this, as you read in the evangelists, when Herod puts the question to them. But that any of the cities of the twelve † tribes should have any honour of his residence, much less the greatest honour of the laying the foundation of this tabernacle which God, not man, reared, viz., his very conception, they never so much as dreamed of this, especially not of that region or part of the ten tribes, Galilee ; and above all the cities in Galilee, not out of that barren, desert place of all other, viz., ' Shall Christ come out of Galilee ? ' say they, John vii. 41. And again, ver. 42, ' Hath not the scripture said, That Christ cometh of the seed of David, and out of the town of Bethlehem, where David was ? ' And again, ver. 52, ' Search, and look : for out of Galilee ariseth no prophet.' Not so much as a prophet, much less the Messiah, the great prophet. And yet it was apparent, that one of their prophets, Jonah, was a Galilean, 2 Kings xiv. 25. Gath-hepher was a city of the tribe of Zebulon, compared with Josh. xix. 13, which Zebulon was a part of Galilee, Isa. ix. 1.

But as for that city of Nazareth, they are yet more confident that Christ should not come thence: John i. 46, ' Can any good come out of Nazareth ? ' And out of this confidence it was that they styled him so ordinarily ' Jesus of Nazareth ' in scorn, as imagining that alone did carry a confutation and evidence in it that this man of all else could not be the Messiah. So confident are men often of some one unanswerable argument against a great truth, when on the contrary it proves to be the greatest evidence of that truth, as in this case it fell out. But, lo, how Jeremiah had foretold how, though Bethlehem was to be the place of his birth, yet one of the cities of the ten tribes, and that in Galilee, should be the place of his conception (which is the thing in hand), as Isaiah had also that Galilee should be of his preaching. Read Jer. xxxi. 21, 22, ' Set thee up waymarks, make thee high heaps : set thine heart towards the highway, even the way which thou wentest : turn again, O virgin of Israel, turn again to these thy cities. How long wilt thou go about, O thou backsliding daughter ? for the Lord hath created a new thing in the earth, a woman shall compass a man.' Jeremiah, as you know, lived till the Babylonish captivity, and had foretold how the captive Jews should again have liberty, by Cyrus his proclamation, to inhabit their own land, when Cyrus should give them liberty,

* Jer. xxxi. 21, 22.—ED.   † Qu. ' ten '?—ED.

as Isaiah had foretold, and as he promiseth Judah : ver. 23, 24, ' Thus saith the Lord of hosts, the God of Israel, As yet they shall use this speech in the land of Judah, and in the cities thereof, when I shall bring again this captivity, The Lord bless thee, O habitation of justice, and mountains of holiness. And there shall dwell in Judah itself, and in all the cities thereof together, husbandmen, and they that go forth with flocks.' Also God courteth Ephraim, or the ten tribes, who had been long afore dispersed, to return with the tribes of Judah into their cities also, which they should then have free liberty to do. And to invite and allure them to it, they had the prophecies of their Messiah to them both, ' the delight and joy of each,' Mal. iii. 1, and glory of the people of Israel ; and how each should come to have a share in him, the one in his birth, the other in his conception.

1. Of his birth ; that it should be in those parts the two tribes inhabit he prophesies : Jer. xxxi. ver. 15–17, ' Thus saith the Lord, A voice was heard in Ramah, lamentation, and bitter weeping ; Rachel weeping for her children, refused to be comforted for her children, because they were not. Thus saith the Lord, Refrain thy voice from weeping, and thine eyes from tears : for thy work shall be rewarded, saith the Lord; and they shall come again from the land of the enemy. And there is hope in thine end, saith the Lord, that thy children shall come again to their own border.' Now, this properly and exactly relates to the story of his birth, for being born in Bethlehem, which was on the confines of Judea, near Ramah, his birth there was the occasion of the slaughter of many of Rachel's, the mother of Benjamin, her great-grandchildren there in Ramah, and also of Judah in Bethlehem. You all know how Matthew applieth this to his birth : Mat. ii. 16–18, ' Herod sent forth and slew all the children that were in Bethlehem, and in all the coasts thereof, from two years old and under, according to the time which he had diligently inquired of the wise men. Then was fulfilled that which was spoken by Jeremy the prophet, saying, In Ramah was there a voice heard, lamentation, and weeping, and great mourning ; Rachel weeping for her children, and would not be comforted, because they are not.' And to comfort her, he tells her, that together with these lamentations and throes of hers, the Messiah's birth (who was the hope of Israel) should be attended into the world, which would sweeten these sorrows in the end or issue, to the hearts of the rest of the elect, which were to come out of their loins in those times, and then to dwell in those cities. And so this birth of the Messiah, to be in their quarters, was worth this sorrow, and abundantly recompensed it, and was a sufficent invitation for Benjamin and Judah to return to their cities.

2. Then, secondly, he applies himself to Ephraim, or the other ten tribes, as it is expressed, ver. 18–20, and invites them by this argument to turn again with Judah into their cities, that the conception of the Messiah should be in their quarters, and in one of their cities, as his birth was to be in the other : ver. 21, 22, ' Turn again, O virgin of Israel, turn again to these thy cities. How long wilt thou go about, O thou backsliding daughter ? for the Lord hath created a new thing in the earth, a woman shall compass a man.' His meaning is, that this share and interest they and their regions should have in the Messiah, that in one of their cities this strange and unheard-of thing in the earth, and which the first creation knew not, should be ; a woman, and a woman alone, without a man, should encompass a man in her womb, and conceive that *Gebar*, that strong man, that Son of man, the Christ. Now, this he alleging as an

argument to return unto their cities, his scope must be, that in one of their cities this great thing should be done. Now, then, turn we again to Luke i. 26, and the region, province, or shire in which this fell out was Galilee, and the city in that country this of Nazareth : ' In the sixth month the angel Gabriel was sent from God unto a city of Galilee, named Nazareth.' So then, in a manifest contradiction to the Jews, here is some good thing, yea, our chiefest good, comes out of Galilee ; and Nazareth, it was the place of his conception.

Yea, and to view how all things meet yet more fully, as Samson was from his conception proclaimed a Nazarite, and the eminent type of Christ in this of his, so as in allusion thereunto, the word which Jeremiah there useth of Christ's conception hath an eye unto Samson, his type herein. It is not simply that a woman shall conceive a man, but *Gebar*, a strong man, that strong man of whom the strongest man that ever the world had, Samson, was but a shadow, a man filled with strength to overcome all our enemies, and to lift hell gates off their hinges, and to carry them up the mountains, as Samson did. Thus much for the second thing.

CHAPTER VI.

How God wisely ordered it that the Jews should call Christ a Nazarite,
though he was not really born in that city.

The next thing to be noticed is, that God having in these types foretold he should be a Nazarite ; and also in his wise disposement forelaid it, that an inhabitant of Nazareth, and a Nazarite devoted to be more eminently holy and a saviour, should by one and the same word be signified in vulgar use ; yet further stand and admire that wonderful providence of his, whereby he brought it about that the Jews themselves should upon occasion of this city come unawares to give him this name, so to fulfil the prophecies which themselves read and understood not.

Let it be, 1, considered, that our Christ was not to take up the outward legal and ceremonial profession of a Nazarite among the Jews, which his forerunner John Baptist and Samson did. No ; as he professed not himself to be legally a priest, that is, after the order of Aaron, so nor to be a Nazarite, having a vow upon him according to the tenor of their law, but came secretly and unknown to fulfil the substance and reality of both. Now how should this name then come vulgarly to be given him ? No other way but by his having had his known and constant abode from his infancy in that city Nazareth. Then,

2. Consider how contingent a thing that was to fall on't.* The seat of the seed and progeny of David by inheritance, and according to their genealogy, was Bethlehem by Jerusalem, far removed from Nazareth in Galilee. But Herod then reigning, who was jealous of all that might pretend to be heirs of that crown he then wore, these the true heirs, Joseph and Mary, were forced to skulk and retire themselves to these remoter parts of Galilee, as the seat of their dwelling ; and hence it fell out that this his conception fell out to be in Nazareth. Well but,

3. That his conception (so secret a matter) was at Nazareth, the Jews ordinarily would not have known or considered ; nor was it (as it is not) the manner of men to give the name of one's country to the place he was

* Qu. 'out'?—Ed.

conceived. Yea, God ordered that so as, had not Matthew related it, the Jews nor we would never have heeded it ; for as soon as she had conceived, the angel having told her, to the end to confirm her faith, that her cousin Elisabeth, who had been so long barren, had also conceived a son : Luke i. 36, ' And, behold, thy cousin Elisabeth, she hath also conceived a son in her old age : and this is the sixth month with her, who was called barren ;' it is said at ver. 39, 40, ' That Mary arose in those days, and went into the hill-country with haste, into a city of Juda ; and entered into the house of Zacharias, and saluted Elisabeth.' And this they did to rejoice and congratulate each the other. But this performed, Mary returned to Naza-reth, as intending to lie in there, but was just against the time of her delivery hurried to Bethlehem, by reason of a decree that came forth from Augustus the emperor, ' that all the world should be taxed,' Luke ii. 1. And the law of that nation was, as ver. 3, ' All went to be taxed, every one into his own city.' Hence therefore it came to pass, as ver. 4, 5, ' That Joseph also went up from Galilee, out of the city of Nazareth, into Judea, unto the city of David, which is called Bethlehem (because he was of the house and lineage of David), to be taxed with Mary his espoused wife, being great with child.' And this providence was to fulfil the prophecy of the place of his birth at Bethlehem ; which yet not being their constant place of abode, and his coming thither but transient, it still cast a blind amongst the Jews, that though he was so born at Bethlehem, they accounted him as a constant inhabitant of the other place Nazareth. For we read, ver. 39, that ' when they had performed all things according to the law of the Lord, they returned into Galilee, to their own city Nazareth.'

Well but, 4, there is yet a far greater contingency falls out, utterly to prevent his being called a Nazarite from this city, though hitherto the city of his parents' abode. For unless they had abode there, and he with them the greater part of his life, the Jews had never come to have given him this name. Herod being disappointed by the wise men to bring him word of the town where he was born, meant to make the most exact inquiry after this child, that the power and sagacity of so subtle a king could make, to find him out to destroy him. And, lo, no sooner was Joseph returned to his city Nazareth, Mat. ii. 13, but ' an angel appeared to Joseph in a dream, saying, Arise, and take the young child and his mother, and flee into Egypt, and be thou there until I bring thee word : for Herod will seek the young child to destroy him.' Which indeed further strengthens the point in hand, and shews him to have been that true Nazarite, of whom Joseph was the type, in this respect, that when young he was driven into Egypt, as Christ also was. And then again in his return, to fulfil another prophecy spoken of by Hosea, ' Out of Egypt have I called my Son,' Mat. ii. 15. But when in Egypt Joseph's heart was weaned from Nazareth, which was a place of his abode but out of necessity and fear of Herod. And the angel having told him that ' they were dead which sought the child's life,' he came, as is evident by ver. 22, with a purpose to go into Judea ; but hearing that Archelaus, and not his brother Herodias, had obtained the rule thereof, and knowing him to be bloody as his father, it is said, ver. 22, ' But when he heard that Archelaus did reign in Judea in the room of his father Herod, he was afraid to go thither.' And then also being over and above this fourth time ' warned ' (as it follows) ' by God in a dream, he turned aside into the parts of Galilee,' clean beyond his inten-tion and inclination. And upon this occasion, and this alone, it was that, as it follows, ' He came and dwelt in a city called Nazareth,' and so from that time made his constant abode there ; that by this means this 'might be fulfilled' (we have all this while been treating of) 'which was spoken by the prophets, He shall be called a Nazarite.'

For, lastly, upon this occasion, this city being now his continued seat of his education and life till he was thirty years old, the Jews who inquired, and were curious and diligent enough, and did know from whence he came, they out of scorn and malice did give him this title, Jesus, 'Jesus the Nazarite,' or 'of Nazareth.' And this they gave him in contempt, as being in their account a base and unworthy place, so barren, as it was a proverb among them, ' Can any good come out of Nazareth ?' And the devil, he stirred them up to it, himself (say some) first giving him that title, Mark i. 24 ; howsoever he with the first seconds it ; and he did it on purpose to divert the thoughts of the Jews from inquiring;after his birth at Bethlehem, they all cried it up to have been at Nazareth. Then it was generally given out thus by the people, Mark x. 47, Luke xviii. 37 ; and as his fame grew, this name spread also. And that it was out of scorn appears also by this, that as Tertullian saith, unto his time they called the Christians Nazarites, as also Galileans. But lo, what Satan and the Jews designed out of the greatest malice, God made use of the malice of man to attribute to him one of the greatest characters of his being the Messiah, which was to be a Nazarite, and holy unto God by a vow from his conception, which had been wrought also in that city. Thus also he ordered Caiaphas, out of malice, to say, ' One man must die for the people,' to hold forth a just acknowledgment, that Christ by his death should be the saviour of that people, and of all the elect of God in the world. He ordered Pilate to say, and not recall it, that he was ' King of the Jews,' which he did in scorn ; but God thereby proclaimed him his king to all the world in these three general languages, Greek, Latin, and Hebrew.

Some object against this interpretation given, that it is nowhere written he should be called a Nazarite ; nay, nor were Joseph and Samson so called.

The answer is, that these two phrases in Scripture are all one, ' to be,' and ' to be called.' So when it is said, ' He shall be called the Son of the Most High ;' that is, ' He shall be the Son of the Most High.' ' He shall be called the Lord our righteousness.' And so it was true both of Samson and Joseph, that they *were* Nazarites, and are expressly said to be separated ; and it is more true of Christ, that he was such.

Again it is objected, that Matthew says ' by the prophets ;' whereas Moses, that wrote Joseph's story and the law, is distinguished from the prophets ; nor was he that wrote the story of Sampson, in Judges, a prophet : and therefore this allusion cannot be to these.

The answer is easy.

1. That although in stricter sense only they are termed prophets that wrote those books of prophecy, as Isaiah, Jeremiah, and the small prophets, hence you read of Moses, the law, and the prophets, as distinguished ; yet again, in other scriptures, the title of prophet is given to all the sacred writers of the Old Testament. 2 Pet. i. 19, the whole is termed ' a word of prophecy.' And ver. 20, 21, it is styled ' prophecy of the scripture,' as inspired by the Holy Ghost ; so as all scripture, inspired immediately by the Holy Ghost, is termed prophecy : so Heb. i. 1, ' God spake in old time by the prophets,' and then cites the books of Samuel and Chronicles ; ver. 5, ' I will be to him a Father,' &c. ; Acts iii. 24. Samuel, who wrote a story, is termed a prophet ; and all the writers of Scripture from

his time are termed prophets ; and, ver. 21, all are called holy prophets, which have been since the world began.

2. And as to this particular, the thing in hand, it is evident that both Jacob and Moses, whilst they spake this of Joseph the type of Christ, were then a-prophesying as truly as any of the prophets.   Jacob professeth so to do in the beginning of his speech, Gen. xlix. 1, ' That I may tell you what shall befall you in the last days.'   And as evident it is that Moses, in that his repetition of Joseph's being separated from his brethren, Deut. xxxiii. 16, did then also by the spirit of prophecy bless and foretell what should befall him.   And then for that other, of Samson, it is delivered as a-plain prophecy, even before his conception, how he should be a Nazarite, who was therein a type of Christ.   And this, though uttered by an angel, is recorded by a sacred writer, that records it as a prophecy aforehand given.   And thus much of Christ's being vowed and consecrated from his conception.

CHAPTER VII.

That another prophecy of Christ, Isa. xi. 1, *Jer.* xxiii. 5, *and Zech.* iii. 8, *is fulfilled in Christ a Nazarite, or inhabitant of that city.*

I must not conceal, to ingratiate this, another known fair and pregnant interpretation or allusion held forth by many interpreters to another prophecy of him : and I would if there were a thousand of them more, if possible, to fall in into everything about him.   For the more such lines of prophecy about our Jesus meet in any one centre, the more ascertained we are that he is that Messiah that was then to come, and the Scriptures are thereby discovered to be the more mystical, and himself illustrious.   It is evident that Matthew, whilst he says that he was spoken of by *prophets*, not *prophet*, had more in his eye than one, yea, and prophecies perhaps more than of one sort ; and so there will be a πληρωθη, as Brugensis* observes.

Now this other interpretation affirms this name Nazaraian to be an allusion to that mystical and metaphorical name of *Netzer ;* that is, the plant or branch, given him by Isaiah.   Chap. xi. 1, ' And there shall come forth a rod out of the stem of Jesse, and a Branch shall grow out of his roots.'   Seconded by Jeremiah, chap. xxiii. 5, ' Behold, the days come, saith the Lord, that I will raise up David a righteous Branch, and a King shall reign and prosper, and shall execute judgment and justice in the earth.'   And chap. xxxv. 15.   And thirded by Zechariah in two places, chap. iii 8. ' Behold, I will bring forth my servant the BRANCH.'   And especially chap. vi. 12, ' Thus speaketh the Lord of hosts, saying, Behold the man whose name is The BRANCH ; he shall grow up out of his place, and he shall build the temple of the Lord.'   And the name, say they, of the city Nazareth in Hebrew was *Netzer*, or *Natsoreth*, a city of plants (that abounded there, say they), as Jericho was called a city of palms.†   So this of griffs.   And an inhabitant of it, in the Syriac language, then in use, was Noseraio.   So

---

* Lucas Brugens. in locum.

† To name towns from what more eminently groweth and aboundeth therein is usual to this day in those eastern countries, as Herbert in his Descriptions of Persia notes : as Shyras, a town of milk ; Whormoote, a town of dates ; Deagardow, a town of walnuts, &c.   In his first edition. p. 60.

then let us make an apostrophe unto the Jews. You might, O Jews, come to ken and know your Messiah, among other accomplishments of prophecies, by this one, that he whom your prophet calls ' the Plant,' ' the Branch,' it comes to pass to fulfil that prophecy, that he dwelt at Nazareth, which hath its name from plants ; so on purpose afore-designed by God, because it was to be the renowned habitation, and place of education and conception of him whom your prophets had proclaimed the ' top Branch of all your Israel.' And the same providence so disposing it, that whilst you call him Nazarene, and Jesus of Nazareth, you thereby fulfil this prophecy (though not aware of it), owning him, that thereby he should be the branch ; ' The plant God's own right hand had planted.' By which name the prophets had foretold he should be made famous by yourselves, whilst you styled him, ' A man of Nazareth.' Yea, and the prophet Zechariah seems, under that his name, ' The BRANCH,' to point us withal to this place, where this Branch should grow ; ' The man whose name is The BRANCH shall grow out of his place,' meaning this city Nazareth, where he had his conception and growing up ; referring to his education, which was there also until he went forth to preach : and that foretold too in these following words, ' And he shall build the temple of the Lord ' (speaking to Zerubbabel his type, who built the second temple) ; fulfilled in our Christ, who says, ' I will build my church of the new testament.' Which when he went first to lay the foundation of by preaching the gospel, providence disposed so of it that he went out from Nazareth, his place and city, as the 4th of Matthew hath it. So then what Matthew here says, ' He dwelt in Nazareth, that it might be fulfilled, He shall be called a Nazarite,' a dweller in a *Branch* town, answers to what Zechariah says, chap. vi. 12, ' Thus saith the Lord of hosts, Behold the man whose name is The Branch : and he shall grow up out of his place, and he shall build the temple of the Lord.'

But this interpretation hath its lameness, so as, though it may be taken in as an allusion, yet not so literally as the former, much less only or adequately fitted to Matthew's quotation here. For,

1. It cannot undoubtedly be proved that the city Nazareth had its name from *Netzer*, plants. For that town was so obscure, as the name of it is not recorded in the Old Testament, which should decide it. Nor doth Zechariah here use the word *Netzer* for ' Branch,' as Isaiah doth, and that but once, as prophesying of the Messiah. He useth the word *Semah*, as also those other prophets mentioned do. So as if we should entertain that to be Matthew's whole or main scope, we put ourselves upon but one scripture or prophecy, namely, that of Isaiah, who in the letters doth only use that word *Netzer*, all the rest a far differing word. Now when Matthew here says that by being called a Nazarean from the city Nazareth the prophecies were fulfilled ; it is a matter of sameness of names or words that must be intended, to be found in those scriptures which are thus said to be fulfilled. Now the name or word *Netzer* is nowhere else given him but in Isaiah.

Again, that word, as used by the prophet of him, is a noun substantive (as we say), a *Plant or Branch ;* but the title here mentioned by Matthew, to be found in the scripture answering to it, is a noun adjective, signifying an attribute or qualification belonging to him.

But, my brethren, is it not pity that these two interpretations should strive in the womb of this text, the one against the other, if it were possible to reconcile and take in both ? For then you will be sure to have prophets enough wait and attend upon the accomplishment of it.

There have been of those of old, and of late, have endeavoured to take in both and reconcile them, whilst others argue wholly for the one, to exclude the other. So à Lapide, Cartwright, and Jackson, and Hierom of old, as appears by comparing his comment on Mat. ii. 23, and Isa. xi. 1. So as that if we respect the name *Nazoraios*, as Matthew gives it in the letters and syllables thereof, that of Christ being a *Nazarite* doth carry it clear. Yet so as withal there may be an allusion to make it the more full unto Isaiah's *Netzer*, or Christ's being the Branch ; especially considering the name of the city was obscure, and not mentioned in the Old Testament, and so uncertain, whether written by *ts*, or *z*, by *tsade*, or *zayn*, *Notsereth*, or *Nazareth*, primitively in the Hebrew. And if written by *ts*, yet that letter *ts* being often turned in pronunciation and writing into *z*, whereof Drusius and Grotius, and others, give many instances ; and so in that respect well serving, or complying with either interpretation. And it being the Holy Ghost's manner, in things of this nature, to have a vast and comprehensive aim, and by way of allusion in fulfilling prophecies to take more ways than one, I confess I am therefore easily induced to eye and give an ear to both

Only I must withal put in this profession or caution as to my judgment, that if these two cannot be found to stand together (which I see not but they may), that if I must lean to one interpretation rather than the other, I should unto the first, as I have presented it, of Christ his being a Nazarite, the holy one of God, or consecrated unto God. And I do prefer upon all accounts that unto the other for these reasons, besides what hath been afore argued and said.

1. He is called a Nazarite from the city, which is evident by Matthew and other evangelists' testimony. If the question came, whether of the two that city's name was Notseroth or Nazareth, so whether taken from *Netzer*, signifying the *branch* or *griff*, or from *Nazari*, signifying a person vowed to God, it is clear that the latter carries it both in that first of Matthew and the other evangelists, who write the name of that city in the Greek with *z*, not *s*, *Nazareth*, and not *Nasareth*, or *Notseroth*. And secondly, that it is as evident that if, according to the analogy of each of those tongues, you would translate that word from Hebrew into Greek, if in the Hebrew that city's name had been *Netsereth* or *Netseroth* (from griffs and plants), then in Greek it must have been written *Nasoreth* with *s*, or double *ss*, σῖγμα ; for τς in the Hebrew is in the Greek rendered by *s*, not *z*, that is, by σῖγμα, *s* or *ss*, not by ζῆτα, as *Melchitsedec* in Hebrew is rendered *Melchisedec*, by Paul to the Hebrews. *Tsion* is translated in the Greek *Sion ;* so *Tsabbooth* is *Sabboth*, &c., whereas all the evangelists do constantly write the name of that city *Nazareth* with *z*, but not one *Nasareth*. And again, on the other side, when the Hebrew word is with *zain*, then the Greek writes ζῆτα or *z*, as in the words *Zabulon, Zacharias,* and *Beelzebub.*

And again, that this city should have its name from plants or trees growing there, and to be eminently renowned for such, is more improbable, because Zebulon, in which it was seated, was a deserted place in darkness (as the prophecy and evangelists tell us*) ; and on the contrary renowned for such by the Jews, as that usual proverb of theirs shews, ' Can any good come out of Nazareth?' a place so barren and vile above all other places, as that no good, no not of any kind, was growing there, or expected thence. For which cause perhaps this flourishing plant, the Messiah, is said by Isaiah to ' grow out of a dry ground,' Isa. liii. 2, even with an eye to the unfruitfulness of this place and city.

* See Heinsius in Mat. ii. ult.

2. If the importance of these two mysteries pleaded for on each side be weighed, this of his being a Nazarite, in the sense given to have been intended, *dignius est* (as à Lapide says) is of the more worth in the importance of it, that only referring to a metaphorical expression of his being a 'Branch,' and at the highest notes out our engrafting into him as branches into a graff. But this other denotes his personal holiness as God-man, his being dedicated and consecrated to God, separated and sealed by God to the work of redemption, which is the foundation of all; and many other mysteries, as his kingly and priestly offices, all far more glorious than the other, as in the sequel will appear. This will be found most comprehensive, and to take in all the prophets.

3. If we regard the prophecy itself, this name of his, Nazarite, is not in metaphorical words, but in clear and express types, who, as being his types, and for that very end were called Ναζαραῖοι, *Nazarites*, as men in a special manner above the rest holy, separate, dedicated, and consecrated to God, or men crowned with a peculiar excellency above others. And so the Septuagint sometimes translates it ἅγιοι, sometimes ἀφωρισμένοι, separated, ἐστεφανωμένοι, crowned. Now, if they which were his types were called so in all these senses Nazarites, then he in them was much more styled so, and signified thereby to be the reality, the substance, of what they were shadows.

But still I conclude, as I said before, that I wish and hope that both may stand, aud I would there were a thousand more such, of so great a variety and comprehensiveness.

CHAPTER VIII.

That as Christ expressed his will and consent in the dedication of himself to the work, so he shewed his cheerful willingness in all the parts of the performance.

You have had the former part of this great story, his dedication of himself at his conception. The last part follows, to see how he made good his vow from the first to the last act thereof, 'obedient to the death.' I need take no text for it, the New Testament gives everywhere testimony thereof. It were infinite to give you all the passages that argue this his willingness and zeal throughout the whole of his life and at his death. I shall lay afore you but some more eminent and obvious.

It is observable that the very first words you have recorded as uttered by himself, and that when a child, at twelve years old, yea, and that but one speech neither; and this that I am now a-speaking was the sum and eminent import of it: Luke ii. 48, his mother seems to chide him, that without their privity he had stayed behind, and put them to that sorrow and trouble in seeking him, and not knowing what was become of him. What is Christ's answer? Ver. 49, 'Wist ye not that I must be about my Father's business?' As if he had said, It is true you are my parents, and I have been subject to you hitherto in your particular affairs, but do not you know I have another Father higher than you, who hath commanded me, by virtue of my office of mediatorship, other manner of business to be done by me than to attend on you, and wherein I am not to take counsel or direction from you, or ask leave of ycu? For I am not an ordinary son: 'Wist ye not I was about my Father's business?' ἐν τοῖς τοῦ πατρὸς, 'in the things or affairs of my Father,' who is my Father after another manner than you are, and therefore my business is another manner of business than of other children. I am the Christ, the Messiah, and at these years do understand myself well enough to be so; and I have a spiritual work to do, enjoined me by my Father, which all other obligations, though at these years, must give way to. And as elsewhere it is, 'As the Father commands me, so do I,' as John xiv. 31. His will and law is written in my heart from a child; I am engaged to do his will, to perform the office of a mediator, the Messiah, whereof one part is the prophetic office, to teach and to instruct. And to give a specimen or an evidence of it, I have now by his command (this being my first coming up to the temple, my Father's house, where I am to preach hereafter many a sermon) been among the doctors arguing with them, ver. 46. It would seem the first time he came, according to the law, to the feast; the manner being at twelve years to put a difference between a child and a youth, that the males of that age should go up to the temple. Malachi had told he should, as a messenger of the covenant or prophet, suddenly come to his temple: Mal. iii. 1, 'Behold, I will send my messenger, and he shall prepare the way before me: and the Lord whom ye seek, shall suddenly come to his temple, even the messenger of the covenant, whom ye delight in: behold, he shall come, saith the Lord of hosts.' And when he comes first, he will come as a messenger or declarer of the covenant, though but at twelve years of age. As God shewed Moses that he himself was that deliverer to his people (long afore he delivered them) by one act of vengeance upon an Egyptian, so God gave demonstration that this was the angel of the covenant in the temple, almost twenty years afore he came to exercise that function ordinarily. But that which I observe out of it is to the point in hand, that at twelve years old, and long afore, the human nature understood full well his office, and his being the mediator, and did direct his actions to that aim and level. He acted as the Messiah unto his Father, as his Father in another manner than he is the Father of men or angels, and had the law written in his heart at his conception in his eye. To do his will he was careful of, yea, delighted to do that will: I was about my Father's business: yea, I ought to be (says he). This is the original obligation and undertaking my ear was long since bored through to do, viz., this his will. I am not mine own, nor yours, but his servant; I must be in his business. And though now you have a more eminent instance of it at twelve years, you might have perceived it long ago, if you had observed my carriage, and how I have directed my aims; therefore, you see, he blames them: 'Wist you not that I was in my Father's business?' And the word εἶναι ἐν τοῖς, to be in the things of his Father, imports his being wholly in them. And though his Father did not ordinarily, or perhaps had not afore this his appearing at the temple, set him about business extraordinary, or other than such as a child subject to parents useth to be (as, ver. 51, it is after this said of him that he was subject to them), yet he had been in all his course in the things of his Father, and had carried himself as one that walked by a higher principle of obedience to God than other men were bound to. And this they might have observed, else he would not have blamed them for not considering it. And the word εἶναι is to be wholly and continually given up to it, as men in an office ought to be. As Rom. xii. 7, 8, 'Or ministry, let us wait on our ministering; or he that teacheth, on teaching; or he that exhorteth, on exhortation: he that giveth, let him do it with simplicity; he that ruleth, with diligence; he that sheweth mercy, with cheerfulness.' 1 Tim. iv. 15, 'Meditate upon these things; give thyself wholly to them; that thy profiting may appear to all.' That which we translate, and rightly too, 'give thyself wholly to them,' is the like phrase, ἐν τούτοις ἴσθι, 'be in these things.' So then Christ as now, so from his infancy, had been wholly in the things of his Father, and as mediator, directing all obedience as such to him; and not only acting holily, as a child sanctified from the womb, but mediator-like; and he delighted to do it, and shewed so much at his first undertaking. This is the first speech, and it is an early one you have of him, and it imports it. In a word (Christ says), 'He that sent me is with me,' namely, always; 'and I do always those things that please him,' John viii. 29. And he had done so always from his infancy, and directed all to him as a Father that had sent him on that spiritual work. And the Father hath not left me alone, but guided me from the first thus to do (says he); for of his guiding him to do his will he there speaks.

Why should I be large in rehearsing to you all his other speeches which might argue this, how that it was his meat and drink to do the will of God? John iv. 34, 'Jesus saith unto them, My meat is to do the will of him that sent me, and to finish his work.' He was hungry, and yet zeal and desire to do God's will in saving of souls, swallowed up the sense of that hunger and faintness. He delighted to do God's will more than ever hungry man did to eat his meat; and not only at this time, and for this fit, but to do all the rest of the work to the last, to perfect and to complete every part of it. So it follows, 'and to finish or perfect his work.' So then, all his time afore, he had made it his meat and drink, as much as now, and for all years to come, the same zeal was in him, even to the whole, from first to last, as the word *perfecting* implies. And in all this he still directed his obedience as mediator, looking at all he did, not only as obedience due in common as from other men, but as it was the work designed by him that had sent him, and sealed him to this work: see John vi. 38, 'For I came down from heaven, not to do mine own will, but the will of him that sent me.' Still, you see, he fulfils that primitive obligation of his, 'I delight to do thy will, O God.' Yea, it is not only said, as here, that it was more to him than meat to do his will; but further to express his zeal in it, in another place at another time, this his zeal is said to have 'eaten him up,' his strength, and spirits, and all. He was eaten up, and devoured thereby: it swallowed up all his intentions, as the wrath of God is said to have drunk up Job's spirits: John ii. 17, 'The zeal of thy house' (and of thy glory concerned in it) 'hath eaten me up,' says Christ.

CHAPTER IX.

That he did not shrink at the approach of his greatest sufferings, his death, but shewed a cheerful resolution to the very last moment.

Let us instance further, in that which was the hardest piece of his work, and the finishing of all, his sufferings at his death.

1. Afore he came to undergo it a good while, see the frame of his spirit; Luke xii. 50, 'I have a baptism to be baptized with; and how am I straitened till it be accomplished!' He knew the bitterness of that bap-

tism to be such as no creature was able to be baptized with it : Matt. xx. 22, 'But Jesus answered and said, Ye know not what ye ask. Are ye able to drink of the cup that I shall drink of, and to be baptized with the baptism that I am baptized with ? They say unto him, We are able.' Yet, says he, 'How am I straitened till it be accomplished.' How much I cannot express ; and I am straitened that my desire and longings are delayed, and they straiten and contract the heart. Never woman desired more to be delivered, than he to have finished that work ; to have gone over that brook, that sea of wrath, he was to be sunk over head and ears into.

Upon a time when Christ began first to declare the greatness of his sufferings—Mat. xvi. 21, 'From that time forth, began Jesus to shew unto his disciples, how that he must go unto Jerusalem, and suffer many things of the elders and chief priests and scribes, and be killed, and be raised again the third day'—Peter took him (that is aside, as a friend out of love) and began to rebuke him, that he would spare himself, and not provoke the pharisees by zeal ; and 'be it far from thee, Lord' (says he), that never deservedst it, that art the Saviour of men, goest up and down doing good, this shall not be to thee. But how did Jesus take this ? One would have thought he should have taken it lovingly. Absolutely, we never did see Christ so angry, and take a thing so ill. It is said, ver. 23, 'But he turned, and said unto Peter, Get thee behind me, Satan ; thou art an offence unto me : for thou savourest not the things that be of God, but those that be of men.' The word στραφείς, translated 'he turned,' it imports not so much the turning of his body to him, as the turning and change of his countenance unto a paleness or redness, as when a man's blood is up, or when he is moved with anger and indignation. And what said he ? 'Get thee behind, Satan.' There was never such a word came forth of those lips afore or after, given to a saint, as Peter was. All was because he touched him in what his spirit was most eager for ; as anger swells and riseth against what comes in the way and current of men's desires, even as a strong stream against what would stop it. And Christ adds, 'Thou art an offence unto me !' An offence is properly an occasion of stumbling. Now Christ's holy nature was not capable of such an occasion of stumbling, or being drawn to sin, as ours is ; yet Peter's speech had that tendency in it, to divert him from that great work his heart was intent upon. Then at another time Peter would be meddling to rescue him by the sword, John xviii. 11. And though he then received a milder answer from Christ, 'Put up thy sword into its sheath;' yet still you may thereby see how strongly his heart continued set upon the work of redemption that was undertaken by him, and designed to him ; 'The cup which my Father hath given me, shall I not drink ?' Every word speaks the eagerness and strength of his will and resolution therein. Interrogations in that case argue the greatest vehemency. But this belongs to the next particular : namely,

When he came to perform that last part of his obedience, his sufferings to death.

1. As the time drew nearer and nearer for him to take his last journey to Jerusalem, not having many months or days to live, and knew also all that would befall him there, as he had told Peter and his disciples ; the evangelist Luke says of him, chap. ix. 51, 'When the time was come he should be received up' (namely, by means of that cruel death, unto glory), 'he stedfastly set his face to go up to Jerusalem.' I will not dispute whether it was his last journey (which I rather think with Grotius), or that it was half a year afore, as others ; but two journeys to Jerusalem are after-

wards mentioned by Luke (which yet argue not that his disposition, here recorded occasionally, should not be intended of his last journey) ; for Luke tells things not strictly in order of time, but of occasions (as Grotius hath observed). However this all do and must acknowledge, that the scope of this passage was to shew that Christ now toward his end hardened himself, and in all his deportment (which is expressed by face there) set himself to manifest so much, that nothing did or should divert him. Yea, and this was observable in him more than at former times ; for, ver. 53, it was observed by a whole city of the Samaritans, who therefore received him not : ' And they did not receive him, because his face was as though he would go to Jerusalem.'

Hence the exhortation from Christ's example, suffering resolutely for us : 1 Peter iv. 1, is this, ' Forasmuch as Christ hath suffered for us in the flesh, arm yourselves likewise with the same mind ;' a strong resolution, causing a man's mind as boldly and venturously to encounter difficulties, as strong armour doth embolden a man's mind to rush into battle. So then Christ armed himself, steeled his heart, as we use to speak.

And then when he was to eat his last supper, to eat his last (as we use to speak), so it is called, Luke xxii. 16, see what vehemency of desires he utters, ver. 15, ' With desire have I desired to eat this passover with you before I suffer ;' that is, how have I longed with the most passionate desire for the arrival of this last night and meal that I must make, that it would come and hasten, as all men are apt aforehand to do for that which their hearts are set upon. And that to have been his reason is evident by what follows, ver. 16, ' For I say unto you, I will not drink of the fruit of the vine, until the kingdom of God shall come :' the thing signified by the passover, the redemption of the world by my death. This is to be my last drink I shall drink with you ; and now my death comes on, by which you and the world shall be saved and redeemed.

And again, when he knew Judas was to go out to betray him, he said, ' Do what thou dost do, quickly ;' John xiii. 27, 30, as soon as thou wilt, for I am ready and resolved. He dares him, and hastens him to it to shew his own resolvedness. And when he was gone out he claps his hands (as it were) for joy, and utters his joy and triumph in it, ver. 31, ' Therefore when he was gone out, Jesus said, Now is the Son of man glorified, and God is glorified in him.' For he reckoned the stroke now as good as struck, the thing now as good as done, that he should be crucified. For the instrument that was to set all a-work was gone out about it, and he calls his death, his being glorified, because it was the foundation of all that glory himself and his elect were to have. How bitter soever it proved afterwards, his heart at present was filled with joy for the thoughts of the approach of it ; he looks upon it as his wedding day, his coronation day (as in more respects than one it proved) ; as Solomon's heart is said to be filled with joy in the day wherein his mother crowned him. And that so he esteemed it, you have another place to the same purpose, John xii. 23, 24, 28, ' Now the hour is come that the Son of man should be glorified,' which is spoken out of the same passion of spirit as the former ; as if he had said, Now, even now is the time, the longed-for hour, so long longed for, come, wherein I shall be glorified, and do that most glorious work for which I came into the world. ' For this hour I came into the world,' as ver. 27. And this he speaks in relation to his death, so in the 24th verse, as also ver. 27, 28, and 32 evidently shew. It is true, he was struck with terror and trouble at his entrance into it (for here the first thunder-clap that struck him did begin), so ver. 27, 'Now is my soul troubled,' and so troubled, as he adds, 'What shall I say? Father, save me from this hour?' But withal, he renews and recovers that which had been his constant resolution and pursuance. 'But for this cause came I to this hour.' It was a consideration he took in to hearten himself unto it; that he had gone so far, and was now come to it, and should I now recoil? And what was it did glad him, even in the midst of this his trouble? 1. That his Father should be glorified. 'Father, glorify thy name. Then came there a voice from heaven, saying, I have both glorified it, and will glorify it again.' 2. That thereby souls should be saved, which, in ver. 24, he gives this account of, 'Except a corn of wheat' (to which he compares himself, who was to be the root of multitudes to spring out of him), 'die, it abides alone;' as he otherwise must have done in heaven. 'But if it die, it bringeth forth much fruit;' which further, ver. 82, 83, he expresseth, 'I, if I be lifted up from the earth, will draw all men to me. This he said, signifying what death he should die.'

After this he maketh a long sermon to his disciples, when Judas was gone forth to act his fatal design; and Christ, to lose no time, in the mean while enters into a long and large sermon to hearten his disciples, recorded in the ensuing thirteenth and fourteenth chapters of John. And it is greatly observable, how that in the midst of his sermon, in the tenor of his discourse coming to that which most of all did move him to that work, namely, his Father's love, you have the passage, John xiv. 31, 'But that the world may know that I love the Father; and as the Father gave me commandment, even so I do. Arise, let us go hence.' He would needs in all haste be gone, as if he had overslipped his time of Judas his meeting him with his trained bands, and so they would miss of him. He sits upon thorns (as we use to say of one that thinks the time long), for he breaks off in the midst of a discourse, which he assumes again (as if he had forgotten himself), though two chapters afterwards, the fifteenth and sixteenth. Of all works else, preaching, and preaching his last too, his heart was most in; and yet he makes a start in the midst of a sermon to be gone, to be taken and crucified: 'Arise, let us go hence.' He looked on the glass, and saw it was not yet run out, and he sits down again, and preacheth another sermon of the vine and of the branches, occasioned by what he had been administering, the sacrament of his supper, his blood, so signified by the blood of the vine. Well, when that sermon and his latter prayer, chap. xvii., was done, it came to the very point of his bitter execution, he stays not till their pursuivants and Judas with his trained bands should find him out; but as the eighteenth chapter tells us, he offers himself as a sacrifice into their hands (for so all sacrifices were to be brought to the door of the temple by the person that sacrificed), and so to be offered up. And all this he did willingly and knowingly aforehand of what should come to pass, chap. xviii. 4. And these things the eighteenth chapter of John doth punctually and setly relate, from the first verse to the ninth: 'When Jesus had spoken these words, he went forth with his disciples over the brook Cedron, where was a garden, into the which he entered, and his disciples. And Judas also, which betrayed him, knew the place; for Jesus ofttimes resorted thither with his disciples. Judas then, having received a band of men and officers from the chief priests and Pharisees, cometh thither with lanterns and torches and weapons. Jesus therefore, knowing all things that should come upon him, went forth, and said unto them, Whom seek ye? They answered him, Jesus of Nazareth. Jesus saith unto them, I am he. And Judas, which betrayed him, stood with them. As soon then as he had said unto them, I am he, they went backward, and fell to the ground. Then asked he them again, Whom seek ye? And they said, Jesus of Nazareth. Jesus answered, I have told you that I am he; if therefore ye seek me, let these go their way: that the saying might be fulfilled, which he spake, Of them which thou givest me have I lost none.'

We had sinned against knowledge, and he suffers with a full cognisance, and an aforehand deliberation of all that was to befall him. And further (to make us apprehensive of this his will in it), he tells Peter, when he would needs vainly and weakly attempt to rescue him, Mat. xxvi. 53, ' Thinkest thou that I cannot now pray to my Father, and he shall presently give me more than twelve legions of angels?' Alas! he needed not so great a party; his own word, ' I am he,' John xviii. 8, struck them all backward, and might have done dead; and ver. 11, ' The cup which my Father hath given me, shall I not drink it? '

He never shewed any sign of reluctancy, till in the garden he saw what was indeed in that cup his Father did present him with, even his wrath, and being made a curse. And to shew what the nature of a man in itself might in such a case do, namely, shew his abhorrency of so high an endurance, and merely to let us understand so much, to the end we might see his love (for it was meet we should by something understand how much he was put to it), he thereupon cries out, ' Father, if it be possible, let this cup pass.' But as he had, John xii. 27, so here his Father's will quiets all again. And the whole mind of this passage is but to shew,

1. His averseness, as to the thing in itself simply considered, because of the bitterness of it; and,

2. That the whole ground of his submitting notwithstanding thereunto was his Father's will; and,

3. How that, notwithstanding his will stood to it as high as ever, yet only upon that ground, ' Not my will, but thy will be done.'

When they had him in the high priest's hall, scorning and buffeting of him; as he had set his face, as you heard, afore his sufferings to go to Jerusalem; so now the prophet uttering it in his person, tells us how he steeled his heart thereagainst also: ' I gave my back to the smiters, and my cheeks to them that plucked off the hair: I hid not my face from shame and spitting. For the Lord God will help me; therefore shall I not be confounded: therefore have I set my face like a flint, and I know that I shall not be ashamed.'

Lastly, When he hung upon the tree, and had enough to have provoked so great a spirit, so empowered as he was with the sovereignty of heaven and earth to have relieved himself, and to have commanded those nails to have given way, he could have taught them better obedience than to detain their Lord in so great sufferings a moment; and that which did and might have provoked him farther to have shewn his power to rescue himself, was their cruel mockings of him added to all his sufferings, ' Come down' (say they), ' thou that savest others, and we will believe thee.' Well, he still hangs quietly there. ' He endured the cross' (Paul says), ' and despised the shame,' Heb. xii. 1. When in the grave, all the power of death could not keep him there, for he had done his work. But love kept him on the cross, and nailed him there with stronger nails than men or devils could have driven in.

Alas! He could, as Samson, whilst they mocked him, have broke down the pillars of heaven about their ears, and himself have stood erect from out the ruins of it.   In the sixteenth Psalm (made of him) he blesseth God for having given him that counsel to persist in his resolution to die, and keeping the purpose of it fixed in his heart during all those nights in which he had to do with his Father afore his sufferings.   If he, I am sure we much more, have cause to bless God for giving it, and him for following it. Even so, Jesus blessed! Amen.

BOOK V.

Christ's actual performance of our redemption.—In the general, he gave himself for us.—The particular parts of our redemption are, that he was made sin, and a curse; and by his death obtained a victory over Satan, whereby he delivers us from slavery; and hath performed all righteousness which might answer the law for us.—And that Christ, as our great shepherd, takes care to preserve and secure us safe, thus redeemed and freed by him.

*Who gave himself a ransom for all, to be testified in due time.—*1 TIM. II. 6.

CHAPTER I.

That God presently, on man's fall, making the discovery to him of a Redeemer, Adam transmitted the knowledge of him to his posterity, and he was accordingly proposed to the faith of the patriarchs.

THOUGH believers, before the coming of Christ, had in their faith but some obscure glimmerings of Christ the Redeemer, yet they had real apprehensions of such a person to come. And there were certainly some outward glimmerings and rays, in the things appointed to represent Christ shining through that vail. For the difference that the apostle puts, when he handles and compares the point of both and each of those dispensations, ours and theirs, seems to import so much in saying, that 'we behold with open face the glory of the Lord,' 2 Cor. iii. 18; implying that they had some darker, obscure, confused gleams and apprehensions darted into their minds thereof. It is true the person was then veiled indeed, and hid in cloudy and dark expressions and representations, that were but shadows; even as we read of Moses, that his face was covered with a veil, to signify thus much. And Moses being as their mediator then, and *face* being put in Scripture for person, we may say that Christ's person was then obscured; and yet with such a veil as did not utterly darken all perceivance of his glory. It is true, indeed, that they knew not the individual person, who he was to be, as now we do, and is necessary for us to do; as Christ told the Pharisees (who lived under the light of his gospel and miracles), 'unless you believe that I am he, you shall die in your sins.' But that there was one of the sons of men, that was to come, who should be a deliverer, this the saints that were saved generally then knew. Although the vulgar Jew stuck in the letter, as at this day, the veil being on their hearts, as 2 Cor. iii. 15. It is not now on Christ's face, chap. iv. 4, 5, but upon men's hearts.

I shall begin my proof with the first promise in paradise, which apparently was, that a son of Eve, the seed of the woman, was to come, that should have power to break the serpent's head : that is, in plainer language now said, ' who should destroy the works of the devil,' 1 John iii. 8, or as it is in the epistle to the Hebrews, chap. ii. 14, ' Who should destroy him that had the power of death,' and save and deliver from him that had just that very day brought sin and death into the world, and thereupon had the power of death.   And therefore also that person promised was to be more than a mere man, or mere creature.   For how otherwise could he have power to overcome and destroy and break the power of those fallen angels ? yea, and which was more, of God's law, that threatened death ? Now are we to be saved by the knowledge and faith of this person, as Eve (to be sure) first was by the faith on him, and then we.   And the necessity to salvation of that knowledge appears in the case of our first parents. For why else did God thus hastily, in the cool of the evening of that very day wherein they had sinned, discover this, but that the knowledge of it was necessary to their salvation ?   And the same necessity must be supposed to hold for the salvation of others that were to be saved after them. And therefore the knowledge of a redeemer was delivered unto them, to be transmitted down to their posterity.   Adam also living nine hundred and thirty years and upwards into that first world, and a godly seed and race being reckoned from him unto the flood, and those our first parents being godly, and having been the causes of transmitting sin to all their posterity, were the more engaged and obliged, and accordingly zealously moved, to derive down the knowledge of that means, whereby themselves had been recovered, by the which their posterity might be saved also ; and it were strange to think that they should not.   And that, *de facto*, they did so deliver it, besides what the story in Genesis doth relate of the religion propagated in those times, there were some footprints remaining among the heathen of Eve's fall, by name,* of the serpent's venom and infection, for which they made a collision and bruising of serpents, and of a seed, *Jovis Incrementum*, as Virgil calls him, who should be a restorer and confounder of the devil.   Such memorials were left and found among the heathens, though so defaced, as they could not be saved by them, they wanting a spiritual light to accompany that knowledge.   It would be, therefore, I say, unreasonable to think that those who after were to be saved, should be utterly kept by God from the inkling and knowledge of that first promise. For there was no other promise (which we read of extant) whereby those might be saved that were saved.

Now that which I would have observed upon that original promise, is, that there are but two eminent things that promise consists of, First, the deliverance and salvation from the serpent's power, which is the breaking the serpent's head.   And the second is, that a person, one of the sons of men, should effect this, and break his head.   Concerning this my present argument proceedeth.

The all-wise and gracious Lord first saw and conceived the knowledge of such a person necessary for the bringing of the sons of men in to him, as well as of his grace to save them, and therefore contented not himself to make barely a promise of deliverance.   And the necessity lies in this, that the guilty conscience of the sinner, rightly apprehensive of what the heinousness of sinning against God is, and of God's wrath for sin is, even a ' consuming fire,' hath not the boldness to approach to God in its own person, in its own sin, but hides himself, as Adam did.   Nor would man dare to approach to him without a mediator promised to him.   As is evident

* See ' An Unregenerate Man's Guiltiness,' &c., Book ix., chap. 4.

from the people of Israel's desire, that Moses should approach to God for them; and upon which Moses received the promise of a prophet to come after him, like unto him. This also caused Job to wish a day's-man betwixt God and him, Job. ix. 33. And how natural conscience awakened dictates to men the necessity of a mediator, we have an instance in that Highlander, who hearing Mr Robert Bruce inveighing against those sins, of which he knew himself guilty, his conscience being deeply touched, said, ' Ise give him twenty cows to gree God and me.' Poor man! He felt the power of God's word on his soul from that man's ministry; and he thought him to have acquaintance with God, and thought that he might be able to reconcile God to him again. Thus the first grand charter granted to Adam held out the person of Christ as a potent victor over Satan, and mediator for man.

Now this was also succeeded with sacrifices offered to God. Witness Abel, of whom you read, Heb. xi., which way of worship to God sin alone brought in, and which the state of innocency knew not of. And these pointed unto an atonement; and by the saving faith upon the Messiah to come, who had been held forth in the aforesaid promise, was Abel accepted, which Cain wanted, Heb. xi.

CHAPTER II.

That Christ gave himself for us to redeem us.—What is implied in that expression.—We should duly consider the greatness and value of such a gift. —Christ giving himself is a high testimony of his own peculiar love to us.

I have at large shewn the free willingness that was in Christ to perform the work of a redeemer for us, which also these words sufficiently import, ' He gave himself.' He was not passively given up by his Father, but it was a free act of his own; and so gifts are.

We have likewise discoursed the fulness of his abilities and capacities to make satisfaction, and purchase redemption, which no mere creature was capable of, but that his power, being God-man, was as great as his heart was free. Let us now come to the performance, the price, the ransom itself as it is here declared to be, a giving himself. Towards the general opening of this we may observe.

I. How Paul delights in this expression ' he gave,' or ' offered himself up,' both in the frequency of using it, Eph. v. 2, 25, Titus ii. 14, Heb. ix. 14, ' offered himself;' and Heb. i. 3, ' purged away our sins by himself;' Phil. ii. 7, ' emptied himself.' As also in that, when that holy apostle, with application, speaks of Christ's love unto himself, and would set it out to the highest elevation, to affect his heart most deeply, he then useth this expression, ' who loved me, and gave himself for me,' Gal. ii. 20.

II. That what other scriptures do parcel forth in particulars of what Christ gave, this one sums up in this total, as comprehensive of all else. The Scripture elsewhere, yea, the Lord's supper, doth set it forth by piecemeals: his *blood* in the wine, his ' precious blood shed to redeem us,' 1 Pet. i. 19; his *body* in the bread, ' this is my body which is given for you,' Luke xxii. 19; his *flesh* or whole man, ' I give my flesh for the life of the world,' John vi. 51; his *life;* ' I give my life for my sheep,' John x. 15; his *soul*, ' poured out as an offering for sin,' Isa. liii. 10; his giving up all his estates and riches, and becoming poor, 2 Cor. viii. 9; his leaving father and mother, Eph. v. 31, 32, compared. Whatever, I say, other scriptures on the Lord's supper do by parcels inventory forth to us, all and each of these, this one word, ' he gave himself,' doth at once, by the great, summarily comprehend. For to say *himself*, to be sure was his *all*.

III. *He gave*, he gave away ; for what is given as a price or ransom (as this in the text), as also to give himself as a sacrifice, as Eph. v. 2, this is purely a giving away, whereby the giver suffers so much real loss and damage to purchase that redemption. And so the sacrifice was burnt and consumed to ashes, there was perfectly so much loss to him that offered it, as what is given comes to ; and so in giving away his riches, he is said to have become poor thereby, 2 Cor. viii. 9, and to have nothing left to himself, Dan. ix. 26, and that he emptied himself, Phil. ii. 7, 8. There was nothing that was gain to him, but he suffered for the present loss of it, as to his present use and advantage.

IV. *Himself* was that which was given away.' Not *his* only, or what was his, but *himself;* not *sua* but *se* (as Paul said, ' I seek not yours, but you') ; so here Christ gave away not only τὰ ἴδια, what were his own (as proper goods and chattels are said to be a man's own), extrinsecal to him (and thus the whole creation is said to be to Christ, John i. 11), but it is himself, his very person, or what was personally his, whatsoever was most intrinsecally his own, *intimum suum*, and what was, as himself, unto himself most dear and precious, and innate. This is therefore an extensive word, and draws in all of himself (as we shall see anon), the whole of himself, all that could be made of himself, all that he could rap or rend, as we say, that could possibly any way be made away from himself. This in the general. As for particulars, I shall confine myself to such things only as are in Scripture or common speech termed *one's self*, and which, according to the dialect of the Scriptures, about Christ's person, are in a more special manner deemed *himself*. Now what is it that may be, and usually is, called a man's self ?

1. A person's doings, works, operations, and actings, which are the fruits that proceed from and grow upon one's self ; these are reckoned a man's self. Thus when a servant gives up all his actions and service, all his time, and what he can do, that all this should be to his master's use, though suppose that master hath not power over his life, or goods, yet in that case he is said to let himself, to sell himself, to give himself up, to that man's use and service, to be managed all by his master's appointment and command. Or if (suppose) out of love and friendship to another, one employs his whole time and labours, and suffers all his actions to be ordered for the other, though not in way of service, but as a friend ; yet in this case he may be said to give up himself when he is all that while of no use to himself, or to his own private and personal advantages. Whereas otherwise it is the nature of self to work for itself. In this case a man is rightly said to give over himself, when his operations are thus to be disposed of by another. The philosopher says, that ' that day a man is made a servant or slave to another, he loseth half of himself,' half of his reason and thoughts (such was the condition of servants then, especially slaves), they being ordered, disposed of, and subjected to another's will. When Ahab is said to have ' sold himself to work wickedness,' it was by giving up his works, and actions, and ways, to the dominion and power of sin, as a lord and master over him. And on the contrary, the obedience we owe to God in ' keeping his commandments' is called ' the whole of man,' Eccl. xii. 13, because it exacts and takes up the strength and might, and the whole in man

as given up in it, if rightly performed as it ought. Now in this sense, the whole of Christ might be justly said to be given away, and he to have given himself; for all his actions, and whatsoever he did, were wholly at the direction of another, for, and on our behalf, and not his own; and accordingly were wholly directed by him to that end, to serve us according to his appointment: ' I came not,' says he, ' to do mine own will, but the will of him that sent me,' John vi. 38. The Father gave him every jot of his works; and I have finished it, says he. It is his speech at the last of what he had done in this world, from first to last, in John xvii. 4. And so in doing only such works as the Father gave him, he gave away himself to his Father first, and therein to us also. For that work being all, in the earnings of it, wholly for our behoof and advantage, he is withal as truly said to have given himself for us. He was hereby a perfect servant to his Father for us, yea, and ours also. And this also doth Christ in that one single passage, Mat. xx. 28, 'give us the sense and interpretation of, ' The Son of man came not to be ministered unto,' as Lord of all, ' but to minister, and to give his life (as in and by dying, so through the whole course of his life by serving) ' a ransom for many,' that is, for us. He professeth every where that he was not at his own dispose, and so not his own : ' I came not to do my own will;' how often do you meet with it from him. He was not his own, or himself (as we use to speak in that case) in any thing he did here, who yet was himself (by his native right) most free, and had the prerogative to act all for himself, and of glorifying himself another way than this. But this privilege he laid down wholly at his Father's feet, and took up all by a new commission from him, to act all according to his will, and not his own, in order to our salvation. And therefore when he came to die, he says, ' As the Father giveth me commandment, so do I. Arise, let us go hence,' John xiv. 31,

2. A person may be said to give himself, when he gives up the comforts of his life ; and therefore denying a man's self is interpreted by Christ, a forsaking lands, houses, father, mother. And life is put in for the comforts of life, as when it is said, that 'Life lies not in abundance,' the meaning is, the comfort of life doth not. Now all the comforts of this and the other life did Christ part withal first or last, even unto the light of the sun itself, the common privilege of mankind, which was darkened when he was a-crucifying. And then all the joys and comforts of the other world Christ parted with for a time. When it was his due to have been in heaven glorious, he left heaven and all its glories. And then death, which is, as we know, a privation of all worldly things, put a period to all his enjoyments of this life.

3. His manhood of human nature, consisting of soul and body, is called himself, and is meant by giving his flesh for the life of the world, John vi. 51 ; that is, the whole human nature, in distinction from his Godhead, and second person as God, as is noticed in those very words, ' my flesh, which I will give ;' and the giving of the life thereof, as John x., is justly termed the giving himself. And so Heb. ix. 14, the sacrificing thereof (which was a whole burnt-offering) is termed the ' offering up himself.' He ' offered up himself by the eternal Spirit,' that is, by his Godhead, who is that Spirit which quickeneth that human nature. This Spirit was the offerer, and the manhood the sacrificer,* and yet that sacrifice is called himself, even as the body of a man is called the man, so in vulgar speech ; and Mary, John xx. 2, calls the body of Christ, which she thought dead, ' the Lord.' But then the soul is much oftener styled the person ; but take body and soul

* Qu. 'sacrifice' ?—ED.

both, as united into one man, and the offering of both, as so united, that to be sure is the offering of one's self. And in this sense the Scripture, especially that epistle to the Hebrews, opposeth that *himself*, that is, his human nature, to all other sacrifices wherein priests offered up things that were not themselves, but things extrinsecal to their persons, as the blood of bulls and goats. And as when the idolatrous and superstitious Jews offered up their children to Moloch, the fruit of their bodies, the offering up of such things was not in any sense a sacrifice of themselves. But God being made flesh, that is, the second person, the Son, taking a human nature into one person with himself, hence, though he offered but that human nature, yet in opposition to such foreign offerings, he is said to have offered up himself, though the Godhead were not offered up, even as the soul or the person of a man might be said to do, that offers up but his body a sacrifice, and so but his bodily life, though his soul he doth not, and cannot offer ; and in this opposition to things foreign to a person, it is said Heb. ix. 14, compared with verses 11–13, ' But Christ being come an high priest of good things to come, by a greater and more perfect tabernacle, not made with hands, that is to say, not of this building ; neither by the blood of goats and calves, but by his own blood, he entered in once into the holy place, having obtained eternal redemption for us. For if the blood of bulls and of goats, and the ashes of an heifer sprinkling the unclean, sanctifieth to the purifying of the flesh ; how much more shall the blood of Christ, who through the eternal Spirit offered *himself* without spot to God,' &c. Wherein he doth compare Christ, who was God's high priest, with their high priests, saying, that they offered but the blood of bulls and goats, things that could in no sense be called themselves, but he offered up himself; and more clearly, ver. 25, where his offering himself is opposed to the high priests' offering other creatures and not themselves, in these words, ' nor yet that he should offer *himself* often, as the high priest entereth into the holy place every year *with blood of others*,' αἷμα ἀλλότριον, others' blood. So that the blood of bulls and goats, or, by the same reason, the blood of other men (if there had been such sacrifices) as suppose of children, offered up by father and mother (which God required not, though the idolatrous Jews practised it), yet all still had been but the blood of some other thing than himself, αἷμα ἀλλότριον ; but this offering of Christ in opposition was of himself, as that text hath it, αἷμα ἀυτοῦ as also Rev. i. 5.

Now then, if you ask what that was which was the sacrifice, and yet is reckoned himself, 10th chapter to the Hebrews ver. 5 resolves us that it was that body or human nature, both soul and body, prepared to be that sacrifice : ' Wherefore, when he cometh into the world, he saith, Sacrifice and offering thou wouldst not, but a body hast thou prepared me.' So then this is a third sense wherein he offered himself.

Use. Let us set a value upon this gift and ransom, according to the dignity of it. It was the greatness of the price is set forth hereby (that he gave himself, which is the express scope of this text in Timothy, and Mat. xx. 28), to shew the inestimable value of the gift. It was once said of a great bargain, or sale and purchase made by the great, and in the lump, between two great personages, that the one bought and the other sold, they knew not what. And truly, although God knew, and Christ knows, what the price comes to, yet we for whom it was given can never know nor estimate it to all eternity. Oh, never ! nor can we comprehend what this reacheth to, ' Christ gave himself.' It is an unknown gift and ransom this. ' What is his name, or his Son's name,' says Agur, Prov. xxx. 4. ' Canst' thou tell ?' And as little canst thou tell, what this giving himself amounts to; thou mayest as well ' bind the waters in thy garment, and ascend to heaven,' &c., as Agur there speaks, as fathom to the bottom this depth, and sound what an infinite treasure lies sunk therein. It is himself, none but himself that disbursed and parted with it, knows what of himself went from him, when he gave himself. None knows the worth of himself, but himself, Rev. xix. 12. His ' name' is such, as it it said, ' none knows but himself.' None but himself that disburseth it can tell what of himself he parted with, and went from him to make up this payment ; none, I say, but he and his Father, unto whom it was he gave himself, and who set and took the price and made the bargain for our redemption, know the value. We use to set out things of the greatest worth and the vastest sums amongst men, by ' a king's ransom.' It is worth a king's ransom, so you use to say, in saying which you suppose to yourselves some great king taken captive and prisoner by a potent enemy able to retain and keep him ; and how that then his whole kingdom (as the law and manner is) contributes and gives a ransom worthy to restore him to his throne again. And that is estimated also according to what proportion his kingdom may be judged to be in riches, or their prince in glory and dignity. Oh ! what a value then would be set upon a king's becoming a ransom himself, yea, of the great God made one person with our nature, and of his giving *himself* a ransom, who is the King of kings. If God sets a value upon each hair of his children's head (which, to express with esteem, they are said to be numbered by him), then of what esteem with him (think we) must needs every thing of Christ's, every hair of his head be, who is the head, worth all the saints themselves, all the saints together, who are but the body to him ?

There is yet a more special reflection in this speech, ' He gave himself,' as it is in a special manner a setting forth the proper and peculiar love of Jesus Christ himself in this matter; proper, I say, to himself, as distinguished from the Father, and his love in giving him also. Nothing is or could be more expressive of a love, and the greatness of it, than to say, ' He gave himself.' You may therefore observe that they are often joined together ; and where this of giving himself is mentioned, there the other, his love, also is spoken of. Yea, and this is purposely mentioned, as the greatest thing by which his love could be set out. This conjunction we find again and again, Eph. v. 25, ' As Christ loved his church, and gave himself for it.' And a second time by Paul, Gal. ii. 20, ' Who loved me, and gave himself for me.' The highest signification and evidence of love that is found amongst men, is that in a husband towards a wife, that he gives himself to her, and so giving himself, he gives all things with himself, that there needs no more be said or added to signify love. But lo ! here is more, not only Christ giving himself, his whole self *to* his church, as a husband doth, but a giving himself *for* his church, as Eph. v. 23, 25. And that is it the apostle would make impression of upon us, as the greatest demonstration of his love to his church ; that when she was captived to sin and everlasting misery, then he gives himself for her, to save her, as it follows there. We adore and admire his love ; his love in giving himself to us, when by the application of redemption he is made ours by grace. And how great a favour is this to the saints, that live in communion with Christ daily, which they feel in the sweets of a real enjoyment of such a person, so great, so lovely ; which they accordingly take in by the most exquisite spiritual sense, that the presence and gift of such a person requires of them. O, but how great must his love be in giving himself for them so long ago, before they were! although the application of him to them was the end of it. And whereas this transaction of giving himself, they know but by hearsay, and relation of the scriptures, it was what he did for them ' in himself ' (as the phrase is, Col. ii. 15). And so they take it in but by faith. Yet when Christ himself is applied to thy soul, then put but both together, and let the distinct apprehension of each meet in any one's heart, that hath a principle of love to Christ in him ; and what an infinite of love to us will the joint stream of them arise to! Himself given, his whole self, yea, and doubly given ; given to us in application, and that not enough, but given for us first in redemption ; and so given over and over—each of which givings is enough to overcome and confound (with a love's confusion) the stoutest, hardest heart of any, yea, of all believers, when they come to comprehend these things. And it was Paul's prayer for the Ephesians, chap. iii. 17–19, ' That Christ may dwell in your hearts by faith ; that ye, being rooted and grounded in love, may be able to comprehend with all saints what is the breadth, and length, and depth, and height ; and know the love of Christ, which passeth knowledge.' Some interpreters would have it, that the apostle should speak all that of the height and depth, &c., of the love of Christ to us, because that doth follow so immediately. I dispute not that now ; but this I will say, that although the Father's love in other respects exceeds, and is therefore to be extolled for the height, and depth, &c., of it, and is in other scriptures set forth accordingly, in that it was the original of all (for it was he that made choice of the persons that shall be saved, contrived and designed all the grace and glory which each person so chosen shall have ; yea, and his love is also commended to us, in that he gave his only begotten Son, &c., Rom. v. 8, John iii. 16), yet still let me say it, that Christ's love hath this whereby it excels, and which is peculiar to him in this matter, that it was he alone that gave himself. The Father gave not himself. He gave but a Son indeed, yet as a person distinct from himself. And for a father to give a son who is dear to him is love ; but for him that is given to give himself, this in that respect speaks higher. That speaks a strain of more intimacy of love than the Father's is in that respect ; although his Son were never so dear and near to him, and inward with him. But on Christ's part it was himself, and what was proper to himself in distinction from the Father, that that was given by himself. It was he that bare the brunt, that paid the price, out of what was not his only as appurtenances of him, but even out of himself. As therefore, when God would swear, ' because he could swear by no greater, he sware by himself ;' so Christ, when he would give a gift to express and shew his love, because he could give nothing greater, he gives away himself, and that over and over. We are to render to each of those persons that love and honour which is due to them, as the apostle speaks of men in another case, Rom. xiii. 7. And look in what particular thing or respect the love of each of them is proper to each, our affections of love and honour should accordingly uprise and apply themselves to render a suitable return, that is, to give to the Son what is the Son's, and to the Father what is the Father's. Let us therefore bring all of what Christ hath done home to our hearts, under that very respect and consideration that it was he that gave himself, &c. And then withal, let all that can be said to commend the Father's love, let it all come in upon our hearts ; as his giving a Son, an only begotten Son, one in essence and eternal fellowship with himself, as he is God with him ;— ' My Father and I are one ;'—and then let us meditate on God's giving his Son, considered as he is God-man, in that God chose and designed him as

such chiefly and principally, and in the first place for his own peculiar delight, as he says of him, Isa. xlii. 1, ' Mine elect, in whom my soul delights.'
Even that glory which was to be in him, as God-man, was an object in itself more lovely, and dearer unto God for him to please himself with, and to take delight in, than millions of worlds, yea, than all that which he could have made.   And therefore for God the Father to part with such a Son, to give such a Son, and all the glory of his, in which he so much delighted, was infinite love.   But yet still even all this will serve the more to commend the love of Christ the Son to us, that himself was given by himself. I say, in that respect it will be the more heightened on his part also, that he should part with such a Father that so loved him, and his own glory at once.   In and from the Old Testament we find the love of the Father is greatened to us by giving men or nations, when yet they were most wicked, and so most hateful to God of themselves ; to give them for a ransom for his people.   And it is used by God himself as an argument of infinite love, Isa. xliii. 4.   So as still his love is greatened to us by all ; and it is he, and none other, even this Christ (who is God) of whom Isaiah speaks these very things, both in the one place and the other which I have cited.   It is he of whom he says that ' All the nations are but as the drop of a bucket to him.'   Compare for this but ver. 3, 9, 10, 11, of that 40th chapter, with the 12th, 15th, 17th verses, and you will see all these words are spoken of him.   O what a gift was this then !   How much more cause have we to say, than the apostle of the Corinthians' collection for the saints, Oh ! blessed be God for this unspeakable gift.

CHAPTER III.

It is proved in the general, that Christ was made sin and a curse for us, because he, redeeming us who were under the law, must become that which we were in the account and judgment of the law.—That how Christ was made sin for us demonstrated and explained in what respect he was so.—Uses drawn from the doctrines.

It is said, Gal. iv. 4, 5, that ' God sent his Son, made under the law, to redeem them that are under the law.'   Now, whatever Christ redeemed us from, he was himself made for us ; redeeming us from it by being made it.   He that made the law, was made under it for us.   Both he and we were under the law ; but with this difference, we were *born* under it, but he was *made* under it, by a voluntary covenant freely undergoing it.   To be ' under the law' is to be subject to all that the law is able to say or do. So we use to express the condition of a subject, saying he lives under the laws.   And so the apostle expresseth it, Rom. iii. 19, ' What the law says, it says unto them that are under the law.'   So that whosoever is under the law, whatever the law is able to say and exact, to him it says and of him it requires it.   And if Christ will be made under the law for sinners, the law will have full as much to say to him as unto sinners themselves ; that is, as he is their undertaker.

And the law hath more to say to sinners than to any other creatures.

1. It can accuse them, and call them sinners to their faces.   It can arraign them, and lay all their sins to their charge, and will not leave out one tittle in that indictment.   It can say, Thou art a blasphemer, thou an adulterer, thou a drunkard, &c.   It does not, it will not, spare at any time to speak this.

' 2. It can call them cursed for all these sins: Gal. iii, 10. ' Cursed is every one,' &c.

There is the accusing power of the law, and there is the condemning power, as appears by the law in our own consciences: Rom. ii. 15, ' it accuseth,' and, ver. 1, ' it condemneth.' And so you have both a witness to accuse and a judge to condemn in your own breasts, which (as the apostle saith) shews but the effect of the law, which in itself it will do, much more to them that know it in the rigour of it. If therefore he who is our Redeemer will come under the law for sinners, the law will say as much to him as it had to say to us, give him as ill language, exact as hard measure from him as from us. The law is backed with God's justice, and so will not respect or spare the greatness of Christ's person, if he once come under it. As we are creatures, and he our surety, it will as boldly command him to keep the commandments on our behalf, as it would us. Look what it would have said to us as we were sinners, it will as boldly and as freely speak, and speak out against him, only with this differing respect of reverence to him, as by himself voluntarily made under it, whereas we were born slaves under it.

That therefore this clamour of the law might be fully stopped, and we redeemed and freed from whatever the law had to say against us, Christ was made all that we had made ourselves.

As, 1. were we sinners? Christ, that was made under the law, was made sin for us, 2 Cor. v. 21, that sin might ' not be imputed to us,' ver. 19. Again, were we accursed? Christ is made a curse for us, to redeem us from the curse of the law, Gal. iii. 13; that so, by his being made sin, we may say, ' Who shall lay anything to our charge?' Rom. viii. 33; and by his being made a curse, we may as triumphantly say, ' Who shall condemn? Christ hath died,' Rom. viii. 34. So as, though but the one is here mentioned, yet we will handle both. We will both shew how he was made sin for us, and how he was made a curse for us. Indeed, neither of these places do mention both distinctly; but yet either place includes and supposeth both. He had not been made a curse, if he had not first been made sin. He could not be made sin, but he must likewise be made a curse, the consequent of sin. They are two strange words to be spoken of God's Son, and such as it had been blasphemy for us to speak, if God himself had not spake them first. And now that he hath spoken them, we had need take them in a right sense, or else they will be blasphemy in our thoughts still.

1. Christ was made sin for us, 2 Cor. v. 21. By sin some have understood only an offering for sin; and then to be made sin there, and a curse here, comes all to one. I confess it is sometimes so taken, as the offerings in the Levitical law are called sin; but it is not so here, but truly and more plainly for the guilt of sin. And the reasons why it must be so meant here are, *first*, because that which sin is here opposed unto is righteousness: ' He was made sin, that we might be made the righteousness of God in him.' Now, by the righteousness of his made ours, is here meant, not only the benefits which his righteousness deserved and purchased, but his very fulfilling the law; so Rom. viii. 4, ' That the righteousness of the law might be fulfilled in us, who walk not after the flesh, but after the Spirit.' Therefore (as the law of opposition carries it) his being made sin is not only his being made the punishment, the curse that sin had deserved, but even the very guilt and breach of the law itself was made his, even as

his righteousness was made ours. And how this came about, we shall
shew presently.

   Secondly, He was made sin, which he 'knew not,' that is, not experimentally, he was not conscious and guilty of it in his own person : ' he
was made sin, who knew no sin.' Now, if only punishment for sin were
here meant, this were not true, for he experimentally knew what punishment for sin was as fully as we do : Heb. iv. 15, ' We have an high priest
that was touched with the feeling of our infirmities,' and touched to the
quick too. His soul knew full well what it was to suffer for sin ; but he
knew not what sin, the breach of the law, was. He knew not what it was
to act sin ; and yet this which he knew not he was some way or other made,
even made the guilt of sin.

   It is time to explain how, lest any of your thoughts run too far. The
text helps us in it. As we are made his righteousness, so he was made
our sin. Now, we are made his righteousness merely by imputation, that
is, all his obedience to the law is accounted ours, is reckoned ours, even as
if we had fulfilled it, though we knew none of it. It was fulfilled, not *by*
us, but *in* us, Rom. viii. 4. He fulfilled it, not we ; so that there was an
exchange made, and all our breaches of the law were made his ; our debts
put over to him, that is, reckoned to him, put upon his score. That is
all ; let your thoughts therefore go no further. It was ' we that like sheep
went astray,' and not he, and yet ' the Lord laid on him the iniquities of
us all,' Isa. liii. 6. And to be made sin in this sense is but to be charged
and accused as a sinner, and not made really so by committing it. As we
use to say, when we would accuse and prove one to be a thief, we say, I
will make a thief of you ; that is, not make you steal, but prove you to be
such. So this making here is but God's reckoning him as a transgressor.
That phrase is used ver. 12 of Isaiah liii. : ' He was numbered amongst
the transgressors,' reckoned such by God and men. By imputation then
he was counted as one that hath broken the law. And yet (to free your
thoughts from the least mistake) though by imputation, yet not such as
whereby we were made sinners in Adam, which was by imputation, but
originally. Now, Christ was not so made our sin. That which is imputed
may be said to be imputed either by derivation, or else by voluntary assumption, or willing taking it upon one. Now, Adam's sin, though it was but
imputed to us, yet it was by derivation, and by a natural and necessary
covenant. But our sin, though to Christ it was imputed, yet not by derivation, but by a willing, free undertaking or taking them off from us, and
by a voluntary covenant. So that, although he was made sin, yet in that
he was freely made so, therefore that imputation stained not him, nor his
nature ; but he remained holy, undefiled, and separate from sinners ;
whereas the imputation of Adam's sin stained and depraved us his posterity. For though that sin of his was but imputedly made ours, yet so
as we, being one in him, are truly said to have sinned in him ; and therefore his sin is ours, because we committed it, and sinned in him, Rom. v.
12. But of Christ we must abhor to think so. Nay, in this doth the imputation of his righteousness to us differ from the imputation of our sins
to him, that his righteousness is so imputed to us as we, by reason of that
covenant between God and him, may be said to have fulfilled the law in
him, and the law is said to be fulfilled in us, because we were in him ; but
not so are our sins imputed to him. It cannot be said in any sense, he
was made sin *in us,* but *for us* only, or the sin which was committed first
in us, and by us, considered in ourselves, was made his ; for though we

were in him, yet not he in us: for the root bears the branches, and not the branches the root.

Having thus shewn how it was, and in what sense, we will now shew,

I. By Scripture.

II. By Reason.

I. By Scripture. And here take the instance of the scape-goat, over whose head the sins of the people were confessed (Lev. xvi. 21) by Aaron's putting his hand upon it; therein acting the part of God the Father, 'laying the iniquities of us all upon Christ,' and translating them from the people. To which those phrases in Isaiah liii. do refer. And this was in respect of leaving the guilt of their sins, not the punishment of them, upon him. For to express and hold forth Christ as made an offering for sin, that other goat was sacrificed; but the scape-goat was ordained to hold forth Christ's bearing the guilt of our sins, for that goat was carried away into a land of separation, or a place inaccessible. And so Christ, whom John saw as the 'Lamb of God, bearing the sins of the world,' carries away our sins, to an utter abolishing of them from before the face of God, so that, (as it is in Jer. l. 20) 'they shall be sought for, but not found,' they being taken away, as the phrase of the New Testament is. Christ had them put upon him when he was baptized, αἴρων, *suscipiens, portans, auferens*; and principally when he was upon the cross, as 1 Peter ii. 24, 'Who his own self bare our sins on his body' (that is his human nature) on the tree.' So Heb. ix. 28, 'Christ was once offered to bear the sins of many,' and he shall appear the second time 'without sin,' Therefore, now this time he appeared (to John) carrying the sins of the world, but being risen, justified from all those sins, he shall appear without the guilt of them lying upon him. And accordingly, when he was in this life, he demeaned himself as one that had been a sinner, as in appearance such. The flesh he took had 'the likeness of sinful flesh,' Rom. viii. 3. The foreskin of his flesh was circumcised, as if he had been born in sin. So his mother was purified, Luke ii. 23, 24, and offered an offering, as if she had conceived him in sin; and Lev. xii. 2, 6, this was a sin-offering, namely, for that sin which their seed was brought forth in. And as in those rites at his birth, so in his whole life he submitted to the ceremonial law, the intent of which was to be *publica confessio*, and like to penance, whereby they were to profess themselves sinners, and to stand in need of a mediator, and so thrice a year he came unto the temple, &c. All which, if he had not some way been made a sinner, he ought not to have done, for he should thereby have professed that which was not. Yea, in those confessions, those passionate psalms made for him, we find him acknowledging of sin as his own. This will appear by some passages in those psalms which are prophetically made of Christ, and utter the inward addresses of his soul unto his Father. And of all the psalms, or other prophecies of this nature, there is no one except the twenty-second, which can challenge more passages in so small a space, applied expressly unto Christ in the New Testament, than the sixty-ninth psalm. In ver. 4 we have it, 'They hated me without a cause.' This we find applied by Christ himself, as prophesied of himself, John xv. 25. Again, we have it ver. 9 of that psalm, 'The zeal of thine house hath eaten me up.' This you have in like manner, John ii. 19, applied unto Christ. Moreover, the next words of that 9th verse, 'The reproaches of them that reproached thee are fallen upon me.' Lo, you have them applied by Paul as expressly unto Christ, Rom. xv. 3. Again, that passage, ver. 21, 'They gave me gall for my meat, and in my thirst they gave me vinegar to drink;' you know both the story and the application of it by the evangelists, Matthew, Mark, and John. Then that other passage that follows, 'Let their table be made a snare,' you have it applied accordingly unto the Jews that crucified him, for their crucifying of him, Rom. xi. 9.

Now then, so many of these being so applied, why should not those others also be so applied? as when it is said, ver. 4, 5, 'Then I restored that which I took not away; O God, thou knowest my foolishness, and my guiltiness is not hid from thee.' How fitly do these words express the imputation of sin to him. It was a proverbial speech, when a man suffered innocently as to his own person, to say that 'He restored that which he took not,' and so Christ on the cross is brought in here speaking. For as Isaiah tells us, 'He bore our sins;' with *Oh* in the next verse of the psalm he confesseth as his own, having taken them upon him. 'O God, thou knowest my foolishness' (that is my sin, as foolishness it is usually taken), 'and my sins are not hidden from thee.' Which is plainly in other words that which the apostle says of him, 2 Cor. v., 'He that knew no sin was made sin.' The like you have in the fortieth psalm, 'Sacrifice and burnt-offering thou wouldst not; Lo I come,' &c., ver. 6, 7, which how it is applied to Christ you may read in Heb. x, neither can it well be applied to any other. Yet, ver. 12, he says, 'My iniquities take hold of me.' He calls them his, not by perpetration, but by a voluntary assumption, and by imputation, reckoning them as his. So Isaiah liii. 6, 'He laid on him the iniquities of us all.' In the Hebrew it is, 'He caused to meet in him the iniquities of us all.' He was made the great ocean, into which the guilt of all our sins did run.

II Now, second, for the reason of it.

1. He was not only an *inter-nuncius* (as Socinus would have him), or one that came as an extraordinary messenger between God and us, but he was *sponsor*, a surety. So Heb. vii. 22, such as Judah undertook to be for Benjamin, Gen. xliii. 9, 'I will be surety for him and bring him to thee, or let me bear the blame for ever.' Or such as Paul was to Onesimus, Phil. xviii. 19, 'If he hath wronged thee, or owes aught,' says he, 'put it on my account; I will repay it.' Just so doth Christ engage himself unto his Father for us. If they have wronged thee in any thing, put it on my account, reckon it to me, and I will repay and satisfy for it. A surety, whose name is put into a bond, is not only bound to pay the debt, but he makes it his own debt also, even as well as it is the principal's, and he may be sued and charged for the debt as well as he. And so Christ, when he once made himself a surety, he thereby made himself under the law, and so put himself in the room of sinners, that what the law could lay to their charge, it might lay to his.

2. And, secondly, there was a necessity, that if he would take our punishment upon him, and so satisfy justice, he should first take on him the guilt of our sins, 'for the judgment of God is according to truth.' The party whom God punisheth for sin, must be some way found guilty of that sin, or else judgment proceeds not according to right rules. Guilty, not by inherency, yet by imputation and account. For as we can have no interest in any benefit merited by Christ, but we must first be partakers of the righteousness that purchased it, that must first be made ours, and then his benefits; so if Christ will be made a curse for us (which is the demerit of sin), he must first be made sin. And therefore Isaiah, in the 53d chapter of his prophecy, when at the 4th and 5th verses, he had said that Christ our surety was not punished for himself, but 'bore our griefs,' &c., that is,

those that we should have borne, and 'was wounded for our transgressions,' &c., he then goes on to clear it how it was done: ' we,' says he, ' as sheep had gone astray, but God laid upon him the iniquity of us all,' that is, he having first charged upon Christ our sins, which we in our persons committed, when once they were thus laid upon him, God's justice then wounded him for them. Unjust it is not, that a person righteous should suffer for an unrighteous man (Peter affirms it, 1 Peter iii. 18); but then the unrighteousness of that man must be laid upon him and made his.

Thus in general.

But when we say Christ was made sin, what sin was it that he is made, and that was thus imputed to him? Was it sin in the general only, and in the abstract evil of it? Surely more; for how that should be imputed in the universal notion of it, is hard to conceive, though it is true that he apprehended the evil thereof more fully than all mankind ever did, or shall do. The Scripture seems to speak more, and as if he bore particular sins; so all these fore-mentioned places have it. As 1 Peter ii. 24, 'He bare our sins in his own body on the tree, that we being dead to sin,' &c., so over the scape-goat were the particular sins of the congregation confessed. And so in those fore-mentioned psalms he speaks as of multitudes of iniquities, and 'innumerable evils' that compassed him about and came over his head. And as Christ bare sins (in the plural), and innumerable sins, so he bare the sins of all, and every particular man he died for; so, Is. liii. 6, 'God caused to meet in him the iniquities of us all,' he being made as the common drain and sink into which all the sins of every particular man do run, and the centre in whom they all meet; and that meeting implies an assembly of particular sins.

Again, if he bare the particular sin of every man he died for, what were they? Gross sins only, and those which were more eminent for guilt? Why not all and every one, both small and great? For where shall we set the limits? Why may it not be thought, that as there was a bill of all the persons he died for given him (for Christ died not for propositions only, to make them true, but for persons, and therefore is said to ' know his sheep by name,' John x. 3), so also that he had a bill of their particular sins, so as not one sin was left out unreckoned to him. Adam had not a bill of our persons, for his sin is naturally derived to as many as shall come of him; but Christ died out of love to persons, and that out of a voluntary covenant; and so it was necessary that all their names should be enrolled and given him, as himself says, John xvii. 6, ' Thine they were, and thou gavest them me.' And as their persons, so all the sins of all those persons, they were all to meet in him, and to be laid to his charge. And there are these reasons for it :

1. God was to deal in justice with him (as was said), and as a surety he was to satisfy to the uttermost farthing. And if so, it was meet he should have an account, and know the several items of what he paid for.

2. Therein it was that he shewed more love in dying for one than for another; as for Mary more than another, because he bare much for her, and more than for another; which caused her to love him more. And how is it that a great sinner is more beholden to Christ for his dying for him than a small sinner is, but by his bearing more sins for the one than for the other, and so suffering more for him? Which if it had been carried in a confused and general manner, and as it were in a *summa totalis*, without the distinct reckoning of particulars, is hard to conceive how it should be.

3. It was needful, that so a sinner might say with boldness, as Rom.

viii. 33, ' Who shall lay anything to my charge.' *Ne aliquid*, not the least, because that *quicquid*, whatever it was, it was laid to Christ's charge.

And if it now be asked, how this could be, that so many millions of sins should be distinctly considered by him in his sufferings, I answer,

1. He that is פַּלְמוֹנִי (as Daniel calls him, Dan. viii. 13). *Is qui habet omnia in numerato*, he who hath all things before him at his fingers' ends, and as it were in ready coin ready told over, could easily keep a distinct account of all our sins.

2. He who now is in heaven, knows all that is done here below as a man, and hath all the businesses of the world in his head and guides them, and hath all the accounts of the world by heart, so as he is able (as at the latter day he will) as man exactly to give unto every man his accounts, both receipts and expenses, and that to the utmost farthing! For every work shall come into judgment before the man Christ Jesus, be it good or evil. And Peter tells us, he is ' ready to judge both quick and dead,' all that are alive, and all that are dead. He who can do all this, is able to keep a particular account of all the sins which he expiated; and if he did not as man know all things here below (which in themselves are but finite, though to us innumerable), how as man were he experimentally able to compassionate all his saints upon all occasions, and in all their sufferings (as he is said to do, Heb. ii. 18, and iv. 16)? If now in heaven his understanding as man be thus enlarged and vast, why, when he descended into hell (as when our sins were reckoned to him he did), should he not be able as well to take in all and every particular sin of his elect for whom he died? Yea, this stretching of his understanding then, thus to take in all men's sins, did prepare it for that vastness which it now hath in heaven, even as our humiliation makes way for comfort and consolation. Lastly, if Satan could shew him all the glory of the world in the twinkling of an eye, as it were, why might not God shew him all our sins in as full a manner, and set them in order before him?

Use 1. See the immense love of Christ unto his elect, in that he would not only be made a curse, but sin too for them; which he being holiness itself, must needs be most abhorrent of such an imputation. That which we most hate, how do we abhor the imputation and name of! That excellency which we most affect, what an insufferable injury do we count it to be blemished in! For a chaste and undefiled maid to be counted a whore, how nearly would it touch her, how deeply affect her! But for holiness itself to be ' numbered among transgressors,' for God to be called devil, yea, prince of devils, how beyond all expression insupportable must it needs be!

2. Learn we to confess and take upon us our sins in particular. Men's sorrow for sin is usually general and confused. They acknowledge they are sinners, &c., but Jesus Christ's soul could not escape with a general charge (as that he stood in the room of sinners); but the particulars are charged on him. As he says of our persons to his Father, ' Thine they are, and thou gavest them me;' so mayest thou say to him as concerning thy sins, Mine they are, and thou tookst them on thee. And if Christ took them on him to satisfy for them, thou must at least take them on thee to humble thee.

3. If thou canst not confess all thou art guilty of (as thou canst not), yet comfort thyself with this, that Jesus Christ knew all particulars to satisfy for them, and so entreat the Lord to cleanse thee from thy secret

sins, which were not hid from him. What the apostle speaks to terrify hypocrites, that ' God is greater than their hearts,' and knows more by them than they can do by themselves ; that may we consider to our comfort, that Christ is greater than our hearts, and knows more of our sins by us than all we do, yea, and knew them to take them off from us.

4. Make use of Christ's blood and satisfaction, not for thy sins in the lump, but for particular sins, because he satisfied for particulars. Not only spread the plaster over all, but lay particular plasters of his blood to particular sins. And as in crossing a writing which you would not have read, you not only draw lines but also rase and scratch out every word in particular, that it might not be read, so apply Christ's satisfaction, and his being made sin to every tittle and circumstance in sins more heinous, and go over them again and again with cross lines of Christ's blood, especially in two cases.

(1.) When a new sin is a-fresh committed. Christ is a fountain to wash us every day (Zech. xiii. 2) from those daily pollutions that befall us. This was typified out in the old law, when they brought sacrifices upon every particular occasion. Even so should we (not offer up as the papists in the masses) but put God in mind of Christ's sacrifice for particular sins committed. So 1 John ii. 1–3, ' If any man sin, we have an advocate with the Father,' and he was the propitiation for those sins. Or,

(2.) When a sin stares a man in the face much, as David's murder did in his, when he said it was ' ever before him ;' in this case have recourse to this, that Christ did bear it, and apply Christ's bearing of it unto the guilt still as it riseth. And as you lay *aqua fortis* upon letters of ink to eat them out, so still be a-dipping the hands of thy faith in Christ's blood, and through faith applying of that blood to the sin. This do in every prayer and in every sacrament, and thou shalt secretly find the horror of it diminish, and those letters of guilt wherewith it was written in thy conscience, grow paler and dimmer till they vanish.

5. It may serve to strengthen thy faith against particular sins by this, that Christ bore them. Say and plead to Christ when thou beggest pardon, Was not this sin in the number ? And as we make it a great upholding to faith, to consider that God knew afore what we would be, and that we would sin, and yet chose us, and that therefore no sins will put him off, so we may as well make use of this like consideration, that Jesus Christ also, when he died for us, knew what we would be, and what our sins would be, and yet refused not our bill of sins, nor our names given in to him, but bare all those sins of ours in his body on the tree. And if he had meant to have refused thee for thy sins, he would have done it then. When a new sin is committed, we are apt to be amazed, and to call all in question. If indeed thou couldst commit a sin which God and Christ had not known ; if any sin were or could be now new unto Christ, then it might trouble thee ; but there is none that is so, but even this sin that troubles thy conscience so was amongst the rest.

6. See the fulness and completeness of justification, together with the way of dispensing it.

(1.) The way of dispensing it. We think with ourselves, How shall the righteousness of Christ come to be made mine ? Shall I, a sinner, ever become righteous ? O what a wonder were this ! Yet behold, a greater wonder is here ; Christ who is righteousness itself ' was made sin, that so we might be made the righteousness of God in him.'

(2.) See here the completeness of justification. All sins are laid to

Christ, that we might say, *Ne aliquid*, not the least thing shall be exacted of us—Who shall lay any thing? &c., Rom. viii. 33—and that we might with boldness come to a particular reckoning with God, nothing fearing that any exception can be made, or that the least sin was left out of the catalogue which Christ had of them, that should yet remain unpaid for. We may see here the absoluteness of God's pardon, in that, to make sure work, Christ was made sin, and took upon him the guilt of all our transgressions to answer for them; so that God gave us an absolute discharge. Thus, ver. 21, 'Not imputing their trespasses to them;' but looking for payment at Christ's hands, who was made sin for them. In law both the principal and the surety use to stand bound; but God here did from everlasting secretly (as it were) cancel our bond, and keeps Christ's only, and therefore it stands Christ in hand to see our sins answered for. And in that he shall appear without sin, it should comfort us that we shall do so in like manner.

7. It may teach us how to mourn and be troubled; not for punishment only, but for sin as sin also. Christ in satisfying for them not only bare our punishment, but our sins also, which are things distinct from our sorrows. And therefore we in sorrowing for sin should as distinctly mourn for sin as for misery, the effect of it.

8. Those that are the greatest sinners should mourn most for sin, and love Christ most; and this, because he hath borne their sins, and more of their sins than of others. They are to 'love much,' not simply because to them 'much is forgiven,' or that Christ pardons them much, and so passeth a greater act of grace in pardoning them than he does to others, but because Christ paid more for them, he underwent and suffered more that their sins might be forgiven, than for other men. Mary loved much, because much was forgiven her, Luke vii. 47. But Paul goes farther, thereby exalting the grace of Christ, that he came into the world to save sinners, 'whereof I am chief,' says he, 1 Tim. i. 15. As a natural son is more bound to a mother than an adopted son can be, because he, besides his education and inheritance, was moreover born in her womb, and she underwent many painful throes for him (and the harder her labour is with any, the more they should love her) : so we are bound to love Christ, not simply for forgiveness, but also for that he bore us in his soul, and our sins, and had a harder labour of it with some of us, who were greater sinners, than he had with many others.

CHAPTER IV.

How Christ was made a curse for us.—That it was the curse of the moral law, and the whole substance of what it threatened.—Arguments to prove that Christ suffered it.

We have seen how Christ was made sin; let us now see how he was made a curse. The other was but by imputation, but this by infliction. He was made sin, who knew not what it was to sin ; but in being made a curse he knew it to his cost; it entered into his soul and bowels. To explain this a little ;

1. This curse was not merely the curse of the judicial law, or of a malefactor hanging upon a tree ; for the curse which he was to redeem us from was the curse of the moral law, not of the judicial. It was not the curse of such a malefactor's death before men, but before God ; for from that curse

we were to be redeemed, and therefore that curse was he made. And Gal. iii. 10, 13, we have it expressly thus: 'The law says, Cursed is every one,' &c. It is true that this hanging on a tree (on which judicial punishment a curse was pronounced) was made the figure of Christ's being cursed with the curse of the moral law; but that was the curse which Christ was made, and therefore, Deut. xxi. 22, God aforehand typically accursing that death (as aiming at his Son), says of him that hangs on a tree, that he is accursed before him. So that his Son, whom this aimed at, was not only cursed before men, in that he was put to such an accursed death, but was also cursed before God with the curse of the moral law, whereof the apostle brings this as the sign and proof, that that death which in the judicial law only was accursed, was executed upon him.

2. The curse of the moral law, spoken of ver. 10, is opposed to blessing; and as the blessings of God are the matter of his promises, so curses are the matter of his threatenings. Blessings are conveyed by promises, curses by threatenings. The threatenings of the law are the cannons, and the curses in them are the bullets. And as whom God blesseth, he blesseth with all blessings; so whom he curseth, he curseth with all cursings. As there is a fulness of blessings in the gospel (as Rom. xv. 29), so the moral law is full of all curses, which notwithstanding Christ underwent.

3. The curse contains in it the avenging wrath of God, and is more than a bare punishment from God. As God's favour is the life of all blessings, so God's avenging wrath gives weight to all curses. The saints are punished in anger, but not cursed in their chastisements, because they are inflicted on them out of love. But here we must warily distinguish between loving the person punished, and punishing that beloved person out of love. God, though he loved the person of Christ when he punished him, yet he punished him, not out of love, but wrath. When he punisheth the saints, he both punisheth persons beloved, and also out of love, which stirs up anger. But he punisheth Christ out of wrath, and therefore he was made a curse. His person was beloved, but he being made sin, to that end to bear the full punishment due to sin, God therefore out of wrath punisheth sin imputed to him. Not God's wrath, but an anger arising from love, is it that chastiseth us; but it is not so with Christ, the wrath of God was poured forth on him. Which yet differs from his punishing of wicked men, whose persons he hates, and whom he punisheth out of wrath also. But though he loves Christ's person, yet he punisheth sin in him out of pure wrath, and lets justice fly upon him to have its full pennyworths out of him; he lets wrath suck the blood of his soul, till it falls off, as the leech when it is filled, and breaks.

So that, put all these three considerations together, that Christ was made the curse of the law moral, not judicial only; that the curse thereof contains in it all curses; and that those curses are laid and set on with God's wrath; and this will be the doctrine;—

That the whole curse that our persons were subject unto from the law, Christ underwent to redeem us from it. For,

1. That curse which we were redeemed from he was made; but we were redeemed from the whole curse; therefore he was made, or underwent, the whole curse.

2. That curse which contains all curses in it Christ was to be made for us; now such is the curse of the moral law. For as the least breach of the law is copulative, and he that offends in one is guilty of all, so are the curses of the law: he that is cursed with any one is cursed with them all. As there

is a fulness of blessings, so of curses. As therefore a blessed man is called *vir beatitudinum*, a man of blessednesses, Ps. i. 1, as being blessed with all blessings, Eph. i. 3, 'Being heir of all the promises;' so he that is cursed is exposed to all curses ; and so was Christ, and therefore he is called *vir dolorum*, a man of sorrows, as being the centre of them (Isa. liii. 3). And as all our sins met in him, so all our sorrows ; and from his birth all the great ordnance of God's curses were ready charged with wrath, and bent against him, and were all in their order discharged, and let off upon him. And therefore not his suffering, but his sufferings, are mentioned by Peter, 1 Pet. iv. 13. 'Being tempted' (not in one, but) ' in all things wherein we were, sin only excepted,' Heb. iv. 15. *In universali hominum miseria immersus*, says Bernard : τῶν ὁλῶν τὰς πάντας κατάρας διαδίχεται, says Justin Martyr.*
He wholly took upon him all the curses of all ; he was wholly and fully cursed.

Now to give some reasons of it ;

1. The first shall be, because he was become a debtor to the whole law by voluntary suretyship (as was said) for us, and therefore was circumcised, and so made under the law ; and therefore that whole curse and punishment which the law required he was to undergo, ere the law would free him. And for this reason, when he was to suffer anything, as well as to do anything, you shall find him speaking in the language of a debtor, that could not now evade it. So John iii. 14, 'The Son of man must be lifted up :' thus likewise Mark viii. 31, Luke xxiv. 26, and Mat. xxvi. 54, 'These things,' says he, 'the Son of man ought to have suffered.' He was now entered into bond, and it was his duty to pay even the utmost farthing. It is not the custom or manner of the law to abate anything ; and therefore he undergoes the whole curse, or we are not freed.

2. God dealt with him in justice, and justice was that which he was to satisfy ; which could not be till he had borne the whole punishment due to sin. Rom. iii. 25, 26, 'Whom God hath set forth to be a propitiation through faith in his blood, to declare his righteousness for the remission of sins that are past, through the forbearance of God ;' ver. 26, ' to declare, I say, at this time his righteousness ; that he might be just, and the justifier of him which believeth in Jesus.' Compared with Rom. viii. 33, ' Who shall lay anything to the charge of God's elect ? It is God that justifieth.' This justice is shewn in our redemption : for Christ redeemed us not *vi*, *sed justitia*, so in that Rom. iii. 25 ; and not *potestativè*, out of his prerogative and greatness, bearing us out by mere favour, without satisfying justice ; but *rationabiliter*, by a way of equity, *salvis justitiæ regulis;* by paying ἀντίλυτρον, a correspondent ransom, even in proportion, a tooth for a tooth, as the law required, 1 Tim. ii. 6. He was not only to make intercession, but satisfaction. As he is called ' an advocate ;' 1 John ii. 2, so also ' a propitiation :' he has paid for the favour which he now intercedes for. And as he is called an intercessor, so (Rev. v. 6) ' a Lamb slain ;' and by bearing our whole punishment, he made his intercession more prevalent. Yea, I will lay down this for a conclusion, ere I go any further : that Christ was dispensed with in nothing. Justice abated him nothing of that punishment which was due to us. It regarded not the greatness or dignity of his person, to spare him in the least. So that if there had been anything necessarily to have been undergone for satisfaction, which was not compatible with his person, he must not have undertook it. For justice (if God go that way) will have its full due, or nothing. And the reason is

* Justin Martyr contra Tryphonem.

evident; for if Christ had been abated in anything, he might have been abated in one thing as well as in another, and so in all. But he says it was necessary for him to suffer; and the same necessity lay on him to suffer all that was due, as well as anything at all.

But you will say, Did not the dignity of his person avail to some abatement, so as one drop of his blood might have served? The answer is, that indeed the dignity of his person did add an infinite merit to everything he suffered; but not so that any particular should be abated. Again, this his dignity conduced to the acceptation of his sufferings for many persons; that what that one person did should be for many (as Paul says); but it struck off no part of the debt, or of the things to be paid. It caused that that one payment should stand for many; but not that a farthing of that payment should be wanting. But ere we go over any of the particulars, we must answer an objection; which is this, That there were many particular evils of punishments which were ingredients in many of our cups, which yet he never tasted of, as sickness and distempers of body; for his body saw no corruption, neither before death nor after. And many like particular branches of the curse which befall men for sin he met not with. 'Not a bone of him was broken.' How then did he satisfy for the whole curse? Yea, hell itself, and the eternity of its punishments, the worm of conscience, despair, &c., he endured not; how then underwent he the whole curse following upon sin? I answer,

1. (In general) Know that the wrath of God is the whole curse; it is the total sum of all curses, it is the curse in solido, in gross. And as a payment, consisting of many farthings, may be made in one piece of gold, so all particular curses may be undergone in bearing that one great curse, the original of curses, for otherwise the angels now in hell should not undergo the whole curse, seeing many miseries that befall men here they are not capable of. The wrath of God is either expressed mediately, in particular punishments, or immediately upon the soul. Now this immediate wrath eminently contains all mediate crosses in it. The cup of the Lord's wrath, which Christ drank up, is said to be full of mixture; for all evils were strained into it. If therefore it can be proved that Christ underwent the whole wrath of God, it may be said that he underwent all curses, although he had endured none of the miseries of this life. Which (among other interpretations I have elsewhere given) may perhaps be the intendment of those words, Mat. viii. 17, where the evangelist quotes out of Isaiah, that Christ 'bare our sicknesses;' and so by virtue of that his bearing them, he healed them. The meaning whereof is not, that he bare the sicknesses of the body, but that he, sustaining the wrath of God, which was more than the gout, stone, or whatever else, might be said virtually to bear them all, and by virtue of that heal them. And so in that place, Isa. liii. 10, the phrase translated 'bruising him' is by some read, 'He, or his soul, was made sick.'

2. It is in his passive obedience as it is in his active, when it is said he fulfilled every iota of the law; the meaning is not, that he performed every duty; for he performed not the duty of a husband to a wife, or of a magistrate, &c., in this world; but in fulfilling the law of love (which was the sum of the law), he fulfilled all. So in his passive obedience, by undergoing the wrath of God, he underwent the sum of the curse, the curse in solido.

3. It is in temporal curses as in temporal blessings. Many particular good things may be withheld, when yet God 'withholds no good thing

from his children,' in that he vouchsafes them his favour, which is better than all; and so makes up all temporal promises an hundredfold. Thus is it in temporal curses; it was not necessary that Christ should endure each particular, if he endured God's wrath; he fulfilled the whole in undergoing that.

CHAPTER V.

An enumeration of the particulars of the curse which Christ endured.—That assuming our nature, he took also those infirmities which sin hath brought upon us.—That a painful wretched life being the curse of our first father's sins, the life of Christ answerably was filled with miseries and sorrows.

Now for the particulars of this curse, it were endless to go over all those that he endured. We will therefore have recourse to, and instance only in that first curse which was laid on that first Adam, and in his name upon all his posterity, as we find it recorded, Gen. iii. 17–19, ' And unto Adam he said, Because thou hast hearkened unto the voice of thy wife, and hast eaten of the tree, of which I commanded thee, saying, Thou shalt not eat of it: cursed is the ground for thy sake; in sorrow shalt thou eat of it all the days of thy life :' ver. 18, ' Thorns also and thistles shall it bring forth to thee; and thou shalt eat the herb of the field :' ver. 19, ' In the sweat of thy face shalt thou eat bread, till thou return unto the ground; for out of it wast thou taken : for dust thou art, and unto dust thou shalt return.' Compared with chap. ii. 17, ' But of the tree of the knowledge of good and evil, thou shalt not eat of it : for in the day that thou eatest thereof thou shalt surely die.' And to shew how all the particulars of the curse there mentioned were by him undergone will suffice, that curse being indeed the sum and epitome of curses, as the Lord's prayer is of prayers.

It consists of three parts :

1. The frailties man's nature became subject to, tending in themselves to death and dissolution : ' dust thou art, &c.' The curse then seizing on him wasted his body and spirit, and made both subject unto frailties, and to be of a mouldering nature : ' Thou art dust,' says God, ' and to dust thou shalt return.'

2. The miseries and sorrows which man's nature meets with, until he returns unto dust ; which are either,

(1.) The labour and travail he must take to get his living, expressed ' by eating his bread in the sweat of his brow ;' sweat being put (by a synechdoche) for all the labour and travail that man is born unto, ' as the sparks fly upwards,' Job v. 7 ; or,

(2.) The sad and cross events and accidents which befall men from the creature, in the course of occurrences and various passages of God's providence : in that all creatures are at enmity ; the earth brings forth thorns, the forests wild beasts, &c.

3. The third part of this curse is death; both bodily, ' to dust thou shalt return,' and of the soul, ' dying thou shalt die.'

Now to go over all these, and shew how they were undergone by Christ, and how from the cradle to the cross the curse followed him.

It seized on him in the first assumption of the human nature : which was dust as well as our nature is, and subject to the same frailties. The simple assumption of the human nature was no part of the curse, and therefore is nowhere represented to us as such in the Scripture.   It was a condescending indeed to take it, though at first it had been as glorious as now it is in heaven ; but it was no part of the curse.   And therefore when the Scripture speaks of his abasement in assuming our nature, it speaks of it under the investment of frailties ; as in Philip. ii. 7, 8, where it is said ' he humbled himself,' &c., in taking the form of a servant, that is, the nature of man as now made servile and debased, which is therefore expounded in the next words, ' and was found *as a man*,' in the likeness of man.   And so being found, ' he humbled himself,' &c., and therein, in that he was not only a man, but such a man as we, his body of the same metal, mouldry, and weak as ours is : herein became his humiliation.   So likewise, Rom. viii. 3, 4, in that ' God sent his Son in the likeness of sinful flesh,' it is indeed made part of his satisfaction, so ' to condemn sin in the flesh.'   But otherwise simply to assume our nature, though it was the foundation of all his satisfaction, yet it was not reckoned as a part of it ; and though it was that which formerly gave the value to it, yet was it not part of the discharge.   I confess it to have been a minoration or lessening of him in some respects ; for let him take our nature how he will, never so glorious, yet then it will be said of him, ' My Father is greater than I,' which cannot be said of the Holy Ghost ; yet this is not satisfaction ; the assuming our nature simply considered is not part of the curse.   Again, that it was an action merely of the second person ; but satisfactory acts are of Christ God-man, and so he must be supposed to be God-man first.   That the second person would undertake to lower himself so that he might be capable of making satisfaction (which without assumption had not been) is the foundation of the merit of it ; but materially is no part thereof.   But in that this flesh assumed was frail, that makes the assumption of it to be satisfactory ; in that he was found hungry, weary, sleepy, sad and heavy, ignorant of many things, &c., in that he was ' tempted in all,' and after that manner that we are, Heb. iv. 15, these frailties were to be accounted as part of satisfaction.   And though he bare not all our frailties personally, as not sickness—for his body ' saw no corruption,' neither after nor before death, for it would have interrupted and hindered him in the work of our salvation—yet in sympathy and pity he bare them all ; and in that sense fore-mentioned, that place, *he bare our sicknesses*, may be understood, he having a heart soft, and framed to compassion ; therefore, when any of his elect were sick, and brought unto him, he by a feeling pity took their griefs on him, and so freed them.   Diseases also, being rather personal than common infirmities, it was not absolutely necessary that he should bear them. But ' he bare our sorrows,' Isa. liii. 4, even ours in common.

Secondly, For the miseries incident to man's life ; and herein,

1. For his eating his bread in the sweat of his brows (besides that it was in so eminent a manner fulfilled at Christ's death, as it never was in any man ; for in drinking that cup he sweat clodders of blood), how eminently was it fulfilled in doing his Father's will when he lived a public life, travelling over, and preaching in all towns and villages ; his zeal for God's house eating him up, and wasting his spirits, together with his watching whole nights, and many nights together, to pray, &c.; and when he lived a private life, in following a calling of a handicraftsman, and living upon it alone (for his parents were poor, as appears by their offering a poor man's offering, a pair of turtles).   So that by his daily labour he got his food from hand to mouth (as we say), he never working any miracles to supply his own necessities ; but as, when in his public life, he depended upon

what was ministered unto him, so, when in his private life, he lived by his labour. Those who knew his education, and for whom haply he might have wrought, those of his own country, who, ver. 3, are said to have known his brethren and sisters, and himself particularly—those did not only call him the carpenter's son, but more expressly, the carpenter; so Mark vi. 1–3. And it is noted that, at twelve years old, he disputed with the doctors, which was God 'his Father's business;' so that afterwards he 'was obedient to his parents,' Luke ii. 51, that is, doing *their* business, and helping them in their trade of carpentering; this 51st verse, relating to what the evangelist before had said, ver. 49, thereby intimating, that as in that other work of disputing he had been about his heavenly Father's business (which ver. 49 shews), so that now he was answerably employed in his earthly father's work (which the 51st verse declares, saying, 'he was obedient to his parents').

2. For sad occurrences and events befalling him from the dispensation of providence, and the enmity of the creatures, there were more befell him than ever befell any man. He was *vir dolorum*, a 'man of sorrows,' which did all wear and waste him, as griefs use to do us, so that in the judgment of those that saw him, he looked nearer fifty years old than thirty, as that known speech may seem to import. Furthermore, we never read that he once laughed in his lifetime. And,

(1.) For the enmity of the creatures,—besides that in a literal sense the earth might be said to bring forth thorns and briars to him, to such a purpose as scarce ever befell any man, namely, to crown his temples with them ;—at his birth, he is denied a lodging in a common inn ; then, the wilderness denies him bread for forty days, the fig-tree affords him no fruit, and the sun withdraws its light from him. The fathers have many pretty interpretations of that great eclipse, but more witty than solid. The truth is, it was an evidence of God's anger, and of the enmity of all the creatures. Is it in the sunbeams to afford some glimmering comfort to a man in misery? They are denied him. Can darkness add to one's distress, and render it more horrid ? Why, he is enveloped with a Cimmerian darkness, and that in the very meridian and mid-day. Yea (the which was never denied to any but to a man in hell), a drop of water to quench his thirst may by no means be granted him, but instead thereof, sharp vinegar, which their cruelty and scorn do hand unto him.

The sea and winds were once arising up in arms against him, but that he made use of his prerogative and extraordinary power to quell their fierceness. And then at the last he was by all left, and by one of his disciples betrayed, which how it grieved him the psalmist foretold. Then,

(2.) For sad and cross events from the dispensation of God's providence. He met with those which great spirits account the most sad and heavy. He was crossed ere he was crucified, even through his whole life ; as,

[1.] By a mean and poor birth and breeding, which was often cast in his teeth : 'Is not this the carpenter's son ?'

[2.] By a poor outward condition. He was not a beggar indeed, for then he had not fulfilled the judicial law, that there should be no beggar in Israel; but poor he was : 'for our sakes he became poor.' It appears his parents were poor; for at the purification of Mary, they offered only a pair of turtles, which (according to the law) were to be the offering of the poorer sort. Again, he wrought daily ; surely, therefore, it was for his living. And further, he had nothing at his death to leave his mother, and therefore it was that he bequeathed the care of her unto John. Now, how heavy a clog is poverty to a great spirit, and how does it keep him under ;* it puts a contempt upon the greatest virtue, and prejudices the most solid wisdom against esteem. ' No man regarded that poor wise man.'

[3.] By a mean calling. Thirty years lived he in a mechanic trade, and that no better than of a carpenter. Now, for him to be hid under chips, who was born to sit upon the royal throne of Israel; for those hands to make doors and hew logs that were made to wield the sceptre of heaven and earth ; and that he who was the ' mighty counsellor' should give his advice only about squaring of timber ; what an indignity, what a cross is this ! Do but think with yourselves what an affliction it would be to a professor of divinity in an university, to a privy councillor, or (much more) to a prince, for thirty years together to be put to cart and plough.

[4.] By company unsuitable to him, which to a great and noble spirit is as great a burden as anything else whatsoever. For him who from everlasting enjoyed the sweet society of his Father in heaven, and might there have for ever had it ; for him to leave such company, and come down to earth, and here converse with sinners ; how harsh and unpleasing must it needs be to him. And therefore the apostle might well say, ' Christ pleased not himself,' Rom. xv. 3, meaning it of his company. To a man wise and holy, there is nothing more burdensome than the company of men ignorant and sinful ; and the best company he had were his apostles, who, how ignorant were they ! Even so far, that they lay as a burden upon his spirits, inso-much that once he cries out, ' How long shall I suffer you, men of little faith,' or wisdom ? Mat. xvii. 17. They being so incapable of what he said or taught, that most would have been lost, had not his Spirit after-wards brought all unto their remembrance. And, besides their ignorance, they were men clothed with infirmities and sins, and more gross corruptions of foolish ambition and contention. What a burden, therefore, must they needs have been to him who was holiness itself ! Yea (to conclude), every man was a briar and a thorn unto him (as the prophet speaks), and he went through the world against the stream of a perverse and crooked gene-ration, and was a contention to the whole land where he came, which therefore contradicted, opposed, and reviled him, &c. And therefore it is reckoned among his sufferings, that ' he endured the contradictions of sinners,' Heb. xii. 3, which was so heavy unto Jeremiah, that it made him weary of his life : ' Woe is me,' says he, ' my mother hath born me a man of contention to the whole earth,' Jer. xv. 10. So Elias complains that he was ' left alone,' &c., and thus was it with Christ in his times ; yea, all the sins he saw or heard became crosses to him, and went to his heart ; so Rom. xv. 3, where those words are applied to Christ, ' the reproaches of them that reproached thee ' (speaking of God) ' are fallen upon me.' All the blows that blasphemers at any time gave his Father, he takes upon his spirit. And what a life then must he needs live, whose soul was so right-eous ? If Lot's soul were vexed, how must his needs be, whose spirit was so tender of his Father's glory ?

* ' Nil habit infelix paupertas durius in se,
    Quam quod ridiculos homines facit.'—*Juvenal*, Sat. 3, v. 153.

CHAPTER VI.

What were the sufferings of Christ, as bearing the curse of our sins, more immediately foregoing his crucifixion, described in an exposition of the first 21 verses of the 18th chapter of John's gospel.—A garden was the place where he had his first agonies, and was apprehended.—The reasons why such a place was appointed and chosen by him.—The first 9 verses explained, and observations raised from them.

The eighteenth chapter of John's gospel, and that which follows, do continue the story of the sufferings of our Lord and Saviour Christ, as they are recorded by that apostle, who, writing after all the other evangelists were dead, or at least the last of them all, he inserteth divers things which they had omitted, as by comparing the one with the other will easily appear.

Christ, you know, had three offices : he is the prophet, he is the priest, he is the king of his church. His prophetical office he exercised in his doctrine while he was here below, in those sermons and prayers which John and the other evangelists record. Which, when he had finished, he goes forth to his sufferings, to exercise his priestly office also, to offer himself up a sacrifice for his people. And now being ascended into heaven, he there exerciseth his kingly office, in ruling his church, and in ruling the nations in order to his church, and so he will do to the end of the world.

John xviii. ver. 1, '*When Jesus had spoken these words, he went forth with his disciples over the brook Cedron, where was a garden, into the which he entered, and his disciples.*

When Jesus had spoken these words. Which hath a more special relation to that last prayer of his, and that last sermon which he made, recorded by John. When he had fortified his own heart by prayer, and prepared himself to die ; when he had instructed his disciples, and spoken all those truths that he came into the world to speak, and laid a foundation of comfort for them, and had put up prayers for them, and confirmed and strengthened their hearts ; when he had fully done his duty ; when he had spoken these words, he cheerfully goes forth to the place his Father had appointed him to be taken in, and giveth himself up to be sacrificed, and to lay down his life for them.

He went forth. And he went forth with his disciples. What was the reason that Christ went forth, to be taken abroad ? Why would he not be taken in the city, in Jerusalem, in the chamber where he ate the passover, where he might have stayed if he would ?

He went forth, *first*, that he might give his enemies the more free scope to take him, for they feared the people, which was always the great objection against their laying hold on him ; therefore, that that impediment might be removed, he chose to go out of the city, to a place in the fields, in a garden, where they might have full opportunity to apprehend him and to carry him away in the night, without the knowledge of any. And, *secondly*, he did it that his disciples might the better escape ; for had he been in the city, there might have been a hurly-burly, and so his disciples might have been in danger.

And he went forth also *with his disciples.* First, to teach them this lesson, that they are likewise to leave this world and to give themselves up as men that are to suffer with him and for him; that as he himself suffered without the gate (for the beginning of his sufferings, those sufferings that were the sufferings of his soul, his inward sufferings, when he first encountered with his Father's wrath, they were in the garden, which was without the gate, as well as those upon mount Calvary, which were eminently the sufferings of his body), so they also were to go forth with him : Heb. xiii. 12, 13, ' Jesus, that he might sanctify the people with his own blood, suffered without the gate. Let us go forth therefore unto him without the camp, bearing his reproach. For here have we no continuing city,' &c. And likewise he carried his disciples with him, that they might be witnesses of his passion and sufferings more or less, as well as of his resurrection. And he would have his disciples with him too, that he might shew his power the more in preserving them ; for as it follows afterwards, he doth but speak the word, ' Let these go,' saith he, (which was a word of command from Christ, as he was a king), and there was none that so much as offered to lay hands on them. He carried them out with him also that they might see their own weakness and inability to suffer (for they all forsook him and fled), that so they might depend the more upon his strength ; for so oftentimes God doth, he brings us into danger on purpose, as to shew his power in delivering us, so to teach us to depend upon him for ability to suffer. And lastly, he went forth with his disciples, that he might shew them an example that one day they must suffer with him and for him, as they did all afterwards more or less ; only John indeed escaped martyrdom, yet he suffered much, for you know he was banished into the isle Patmos.

Over the brook Cedron. This brook divided Jerusalem and mount Olivet, as Josephus saith. It was on the east part of the city, as mount Calvary was on the west, the two places of sufferings : his taking was in the one, and his crucifying was in the other. He suffered in the east and in the west ; and so indeed the gospel hath reigned, as the sun doth, from east to west. It is called the field of Cedron, 2 Kings xxiii. 4, and the valley of Cedron, because it was an obscure, darksome, shady place, and not because that cedars did grow there, as olives did upon mount Olivet (which is a mistake of some), but it had its name from the darksomeness of the place.

Why did God in his providence order it that Christ should go over this brook Cedron ? It is a circumstance which only John records, for all the other evangelists omit it ; and as interpreters observe, John doth seldom mention any particular circumstance, upon which any emphasis is put, but there is a mystery in it.

We read in 2 Sam. xv. 23, that David and his men went over this brook Cedron, mourning and lamenting, when Ahithophel, his familiar friend, had betrayed him, and Absalom his son sought his life.

Now our Lord and Saviour Christ, whose type David was, this very thing is fulfilled in him ; for Ahithophel typified out Judas : that you have in Ps. xli., ' The man,' saith he, ' that did eat with me, that was mine equal, we took sweet counsel together,' &c. David spake this of Ahithophel in this very journey of his, and it is applied unto Judas in John xiii. 18. Now as David's life was then sought after, so was Christ's now ; and as David went over with his companions, so did Christ with his disciples. As Ahithophel betrayed him, so did Judas betray Christ ; and as David went over with a sad heart, so Christ tells his disciples, that his soul was heavy unto the death.

And that you may see the allusion to be yet more full, in Ps. cx. 7, (which is plainly and clearly a psalm of Christ), it is said, ' He shall drink of the brook in the way, therefore shall his head be lifted up.' He was to sit at God's right hand till his enemies were made his footstool, as you have it ver. 1 ; but before he cometh to be thus exalted, he must drink of the brook in the way, he must go over this Cedron with a sad soul : for the truth is, all the while he was a-going his heart was heavy, and it increased in his going much more. He shall drink of the brook in the way ; not that he drank of the water of this brook Cedron, but it typified out those sufferings which lay in his way to heaven.

Where was a garden. This was the place where he had that sad encounter with his Father's wrath, which made him sweat drops of blood. The soul-sufferings of Christ we eminently read of to have been in this place. Now the fields that adjoined to this Cedron, and that which did border upon this place of the garden (which Matthew calls Gethsemane), was that place which the Jews called *Gehenna*, or *Gehinnom*, or hell, because that Josiah had cursed that place, 2 Kings xxiii. 4, and because that there the great slaughter was done upon the Babylonians, and afterwards upon the Jews. And it was the place which they afterwards called *Tophet*, and it is the only word they had for hell after the Babylonian captivity. It was an execrable place ; and into this place did Christ come; for indeed our Lord and Saviour Christ, he did, in his soul, in respect of the sufferings of it, descend into hell. Now there was a mystery also in this. Adam he was the most eminent type of Christ, so he is called, Rom. v. 13, and in 1 Cor. xv. And the type holds in this, for when we have a ground that such a thing is a type, we may apply it to such particulars as we find suitable. Adam's fall, you know, was in a garden ; Satan there encountered him, and overcame him, led him and all mankind into captivity to sin and death. God now singleth out the place where the great redeemer of the world, the second Adam, should first encounter with his Father's wrath, to be in a garden, and that there he should be bound and led away captive as Adam was. He fighteth with Satan upon his own ground (it became him so to do) ; and here he gives the first great overthrow to his kingdom, and to the kingdom of sin and death. God did suit it so, as indeed he did suit many things in that particular of the first and second Adam. Because (says he, 1 Cor. xv. 21) ' by man came death, by man came also the resurrection.' Because by a temptation let in at the ear man was condemned, therefore by hearing of the word men shall be saved. ' Thou shalt eat thy bread in the sweat of thy brows,' that was part of Adam's curse ; Christ he sweat drops of blood for this, it was the force of that curse that caused it. ' The ground shall bring forth thorns to thee ;' Christ he was crucified with a crown of thorns. Adam his disobedience was acted in a garden, and Christ both his active and passive obedience also, much of it was in a garden ; and at the last, as the first beginning of his humiliation was in a garden, so the last step was too ; he was buried, though not in this, yet in another garden. Thus the type and the thing typified answer one another.

Into the which he entered, and his disciples. Still there is an emphasis put upon this, that his disciples were with him. It is not only said, that he went forth with his disciples, but that he entered into the garden with his disciples, who were to be witnesses of what he suffered, and for the reasons mentioned afore, as also to shew that he had no other guard but them. So much for the first verse.

Verse 2. ' *And Judas also, which betrayed him, knew the place ; for Jesus ofttimes resorted thither with his disciples.*'

Our Lord and Saviour Christ, he knew he should be taken, and taken by Judas, a disciple, and that that was the place appointed by his Father wherein he should be taken; for the 4th verse tells us, ' Jesus knew all things that should befall him.' He knew that Judas would be there that night, and therefore, like a valiant champion, he cometh into the field first, afore his enemy. He goes thither to choose, and singles out this place on purpose.

In this place Christ used to pray most, especially a little before his sufferings; for in Luke xxi. 37 it is said, that ' in the day time he was teaching in the temple; and at night he went out, and abode in the mount that is called the mount of Olives. And all the people came early in the morning to him in the temple, for to hear him.' This was but a matter of seven days before he was crucified; for Christ, when he saw that he must die, and that now his time was come, he wore his body out; he cared not, as it were, what became of him, he wholly spent himself in praying and preaching. He was preaching in the day time, and that early in the morning in the temple, and at night he abode in the mount of Olives; and there sometimes he spent the whole night in prayer privately, and sometimes he took his disciples with him, as now he did.

In this place, which had been a place where Christ received a great deal of heavenly refreshment from his Father in prayer, where he had immediate converse with him, in that place of all others must Christ be first attached, and there must be the beginning of his sufferings. For so indeed God did deal with Christ; he would have all things that were most comfortable to him embittered to him. This was the place of his repose, where he had sweet refreshings from God; and this must be the place where he must encounter with his Father's wrath. He sweat his bloody sweat in this place where he had so often prayed.

And he likewise knowing that this was the place in which he should be taken, made it the place where he prayed most, that every thing might put him in mind, and strengthen him when he came to suffer, to comfort him and to help him, as indeed circumstances of time and place do. If a Christian would choose where he would be taken and hauled to punishment for Christ, it should certainly be in his closet, or in a place where he had prayed most.

Christ had oftentimes afore evaded suffering; he would shift places on purpose; as in John iv. 1, ' When the Lord knew how the Pharisees had heard that Jesus made and baptized more disciples than John, he left Judea, and departed again into Galilee', he flew from them; and so in Luke iv. 29, when they led him unto the brow of the hill whereon the city was built, that they might cast him down headlong, he passed through the midst of them, and escaped away. But now when his last hour is come, and he knew it was the hour appointed him by his Father, now he goes to the very place where he knew Judas, that should betray him, would come.

You shall find this eminent observation in the story as John relates it, differing from all the other evangelists: he endeavours to hold forth in a special manner the willingness of Christ to suffer. Other evangelists hold forth other circumstances of his sufferings; but you shall find all along that John is especially diligent in holding forth the willingness of Christ to offer up himself, which he doth by all sorts of circumstances, as in the sequel will appear. Here it appears by this that (as I said before) he goes first into the field; he goes to the place which he used to go to, and which Judas knew to be the place, and he knew too that Judas would be there.

It was a matter of the greatest moment to hold forth this willingness of Christ to offer up himself, of any other. For there are two necessary things that were to be concurrent in the sufferings of Christ to make it satisfactory for us : the one is the eminency and worth of his person. Had he not been God as well as man, his obedience would never have satisfied God. But the second is a free-willingness to undergo what he did ; for we sinned willingly, therefore Christ, when he comes to suffer, he must suffer as willingly. It is as great and as essential an ingredient to give force and efficacy to his sufferings, as the worth of his person. Therefore, in Heb. x. 7, 8, you will find a great deal of emphasis put upon this : ' Lo, I come to do thy will, O God ;' ' by which will' (saith he) ' we are sanctified.' Both the will of God the Father, and the willingness of Jesus Christ thus to sacrifice himself, was that great circumstance, or more than a circumstance, upon which our salvation depends, and the acceptation of that offering of his. Christ, therefore, to shew his willingness, he goes to the place where he knew Judas would come ; he went thither on purpose ; put himself on this temptation, on purpose that he might put himself into their hands. It was indeed by the commandment of his Father ; for so you shall find, John xiv. 31, ' As the Father gave me commandment, even so I do. Arise,' saith he, ' let us go hence ;' let us go to the place where I must be taken.

That which we find of circumstances in the sufferings of Christ, may oftentimes help us in circumstances of our sinning. Dost thou tempt thyself to sin ? put thyself upon occasions of sinning ? and is that an aggravation of thy sinning ? Thou hast this to help and relieve thee in the sufferings of Christ, that he put himself upon the occasion of being taken, put himself upon that temptation.

And it may move thee to shun and avoid the occasions of sin, for Jesus Christ, that he might suffer for thee, avoided not the occasion of suffering ; he goes to the very place in which he knew he should be taken.

Also those things which had been comforts unto Christ are (through the merit of our sins, which do turn blessings into curse) turned unto Christ into a bitterness. The place where he had prayed, and been refreshed, there is his agony and encounter ; a garden turned into hell. His sweet communion with God there is now turned into wrestling with God's anger falling on him here ; and now through it, on the contrary, we may expect curses turned into blessings ; and the worst of dealings from God to us to be sanctified to our greatest spiritual advantage and comfort.

It is said that ' Judas also knew the place.' Take notice here of the hard-heartedness of the heart of Judas. He had all that time since he received the sop, yea, all the way he went (which was a pretty way from the city), to think upon what he was about to do, that he was going to betray his master, the Saviour of the world, in whom he had for a time believed. Yea, he had that place to strike his conscience ; it being the place where he himself had been often with Christ, and present at many a good prayer, and many an excellent sermon, which he had heard from no less than the Messiah. Whose conscience almost but would have smote him ? Yet so hard, so obdurate is the heart of Judas, that he dares out-face all those prayers and sermons, and to come to that very place to lay hold of his master, and to betray him with a kiss.

An obdurate heart will break through all sort of circumstances and considerations that may keep him from sinning ; so Judas doth here.

And we may learn to aggravate our sins by such circumstances, whereof we shall find many in our lives, if we study our own sinful ways, that God doth suffer to fall out to keep us from sinning, that notwithstanding such circumstances and considerations, yet we should break through all such difficulties and sin against God; this should make our sin out of measure sinful to us. It was a circumstance that much increased the sin of Judas, that he knew the place where Christ used to resort with his disciples (going thither often for freedom's sake of prayer), that yet he would go thither and there betray him.

Verse 3. ' *Judas then, having received a band of men and officers from the chief priests and Pharisees, cometh thither with lanterns and torches and weapons.*'

Judas then, having received a band of men, &c. Judas did not desire this band of men ; he did but offer to betray him. It was the chief priests and Pharisees that desired them ; they went to Pilate (who was the Roman governor), and told him they had a seditious person to take, and implored his help and assistance ; and so he let them have a band of men. And yet it is said that Judas received them ; it is all laid upon him, because in Acts i. 16 he is called their guide ; he was the leader of this cursed band that took our Lord and Saviour Christ ; he was the foreman in it: therefore all is laid on him more than upon them; he is still branded in a peculiar manner, ' Judas the traitor,' ' Judas which betrayed him.' All, I say, is chiefly laid upon him ; for the truth is, Christ took this act of his more heinously at his hands, that had been his disciple and a professor of him, than he did either of the Pharisees or of the Roman soldiers, and his end was accordingly. And therefore Paul, in 2 Cor. xi. 26, when he makes a catalogue of his sufferings, he mentioneth those which he had from false brethren as the worst and chiefest.

The eminent observation that I make out of these words is this, that here is both a band of men and officers from the chief priests and Pharisees. The band of men was the Roman band ; for the Romans having conquered that city, the civil power was in their hands, and Pilate the governor under them kept a band of men about him, which he lends at their request unto the Pharisees and chief priests, to go with their own officers to help to take Christ. All along this story you shall find that there were two sorts of men that God would have, in his providence, to have their hands imbrued in the blood of Christ from first to last. Here is a Roman band, and the officers of the chief priests and Pharisees : here is the civil magistracy, and here is the ecclesiastical state ; for as the civil power was in the Romans, so the ecclesiastical power was in the hands of the chief priests; the Romans, notwithstanding their conquest, leaving them to the rites of their religion still. They would not trust the Roman band alone to do it, for they knew they were not such enemies to Christ ; but they sent their own ministers and servants (and some evangelists tell us that some of the Pharisees themselves were there) to attend them, and see the thing done. The soldiers, poor men ! they went about they knew not what ; they went to take him as a seditious person, and an enemy to Cæsar ; little thought they that the Messiah of the world was there. This, I say, you shall find in the story all along, that two sort of powers were stirred up against Christ. Here was both Jews and Gentiles : ' Why doth the heathen rage, and the people imagine a vain thing ? ' Ps. ii. 1. Both concur here. Here is a band of Romans, and officers of the chief priests; the heathen and the people of the Jews. Christ, as he did die both for Jews and Gentiles, so likewise he would have both Jews and Gentiles to have a hand in his death. And therefore let us not say only that the Jews shall look upon him whom they have pierced, but the Gentiles also shall look upon him whom they have pierced. God would have the Gentiles have a hand in it as well as the Jews. And not only so, but he would have both the civil and ecclesiastical state to join in the sufferings of Christ; for the Pharisees and chief priests they were the ecclesiastical state, they make use of the magistrate, for his assistance, to lay hold of our Lord and Saviour Christ.

They come thither with lanterns, and torches, and with weapons. Although it was full moon then, and therefore the moon did certainly shine, yet, to make sure work, they come not only with torches, that use to give great lights, but with lanterns, that their lights might not be blown out with the wind, and all to seek him, that they might be sure, if he did not hide himself, to find him, or if he did hide himself, to seek him out with their lights. And they came with weapons, too, though they knew he was but a poor man to see to ; but they came with weapons, because they were afraid of the people, and because that Judas had told them how his master had often escaped from them before, as when he was brought to the brow of the hill, &c. ; therefore now to make sure work, both to find him and to carry him away, they come forth with these.

Our Lord and Saviour Christ, he had dealt with them at other weapons; he had often disputed with the scribes and Pharisees ; and the truth is, he had always been too hard for them. But now they come and deal with him at a weapon they thought he should not be too hard for them at; they come upon him with torches and with weapons, and by force they set upon him. And that indeed is the manner of those that oppose the church in all ages. As they dealt with Christ, so they do with his people, and will do to the end of the world.

Verse 4. ' *Jesus therefore, knowing all things that should come upon him, went forth, and said unto them, Whom seek ye ?* '

Still you see the evangelist John holds forth, in an eminent manner, the willingness of Christ to suffer; for that is the thread he spins throughout this whole story, because indeed so much depends upon it. He tells us that Christ knew all things that should come upon him. He did not come to this place unawares ; no, he knew that Judas knew that he usually resorted thither, and he knew that Judas would come thither, as well as he knew that he should betray him, and therefore he comes thither on purpose. And he comes thither first ; and being there, as soon as the band and the officers came, he went forth of his own accord, and said unto them, ' Whom seek ye ? ' He knew all things: he might have hid himself, and evaded his being taken, as he had often done before. No.

There is a case which interpreters here put, whether this example of Christ's be for our imitation, whether we should thus expose ourselves to suffering, choose thus to suffer, or rather decline and avoid suffering in a lawful way, by lawful means ?

The answer is clear. We have divers examples of Christ's avoiding suffering ; as that in John iv. 1, when he did but hear that they knew of him, and knowing their malice, he went and removed to another place. So likewise when he was young, and Herod sought his life, he was carried into Egypt. And then again, when they brought him to the brow of the hill, he escaped. All which examples strongly hold forth, that we may use all lawful means of escaping suffering. But when he knew that his hour was come in which he must be taken aside, and it being by compact between his Father and him, for so it was he covenanted with God to suffer, it became him to shew the fullest and most ready obedience to his Father that could be, to go to the place where he must be attached, to offer himself to them as a prey, to provoke them: ' Whom seek ye ?' Now herein Christ's case and ours in suffering doth certainly differ; we do not know what shall befall us, as Christ did ; for if we did, we ought not to evade our sufferings, as Christ did not ; but because we are ignorant of what shall come upon us, we are to serve the ways of a providence, ways of escaping that are lawful.

Observe from hence, *first*, this. Christ, you see, did not only suffer willingly, but knowingly ; and as his putting himself willingly upon suffering, and into the opportunity of being taken, may help us against our having tempted ourselves (which is a great aggravation of our sinning), so likewise our Saviour Christ's suffering thus with knowledge, deliberately, knowing all circumstances, is a consideration may help us against our sinning knowingly. Hast thou sinned presumptuously against knowledge ? Our Lord and Saviour Christ he suffered as deliberately, he suffered with the greatest knowledge that could be. There was not only the greatest will in his sufferings, but to make up that will more eminent and conspicuous, there was also the greatest knowledge ; he knew all that should befall him, yet he went forth and offered himself.

Secondly, Did Christ know all that he was to suffer ? Certainly then he knows all that we are to suffer. Did he know his own sufferings on earth ? Certainly he knows ours, now he is in heaven. The things we are to suffer, they are called in Col. i. 24, ' the after-sufferings of Christ ;' certainly, then, he knows them. Therefore though thou knowest not what shall befall thee in such or such a course as thou takest in professing his name, yet comfort thyself in this, that Christ knows it. And as he, knowing all things, ventured himself, so do thou, upon the confidence that he knows all things that shall befall thee. Venture thyself too, and trust him and his knowledge for the ordering of all things for thy good, as well as he trusted his Father to do with him what he would. It is our comfort, I say, that Jesus Christ knew all his own sufferings; he certainly, therefore, knows all ours. ' I know thy labour and thy patience,' saith he, Rev. ii. 2. He takes notice of it, therefore fear not the things you shall suffer ; give yourselves up unto his providence, trust his knowledge, for he knows what shall befall you.

It would be miserable for us to know what we shall undergo in this world, for the thoughts of it aforehand would hurt us ; the anxiety of it would trouble us ; it is better for us to be ignorant of it. But Christ he had strength in him, he could know what he should suffer and foresee it, and yet keep his mind quiet and composed ; as you see he did till it came to the very instant. And it was necessary too that he should know all he was to suffer, because he suffered by compact with his Father, which makes a great difference between the sufferings of Christ and ours.

Now he, knowing all that he should suffer, he went forth, and said to them, ' Whom seek ye ?'

Once they would have made him a king, and then he hid himself; but when he comes to be a king crowned with thorns, and knew he should be so to save us, then he hides not himself, but he goes forth to them. Adam, as I said, was his type in his sinning in the garden ; but in this they are unlike, Adam hides himself, and God was fain to seek him out. But here our Lord and Saviour Christ, to shew his willingness to be found, stepped forth, and said unto them, ' Whom seek ye ?' He provokes them rather to lay hands upon him than otherwise. And so much for the fourth verse.

Verse 5. ' *They answered him, Jesus of Nazareth. Jesus saith unto them, I am he. And Judas also, which betrayed him, stood with them.*'

From hence interpreters do observe—and I think rightly—that both these Roman soldiers, and also these officers of the high priest, at their first approach to him, did not know him by sight ; no, nor Judas neither ; for it is said Judas stood with them when he asked them, ' Whom seek ye ?' Afterwards, indeed, he was the first that went to him, and kissed him, and said, ' This is he.' He asked them twice the same question, and they answer both times, ' Jesus of Nazareth,' which clearly argues, that they did not know him to be the man. Therefore some think there was a piece of a miracle in this, that he struck them with blindness, as the Sodomites were that beset Lot's house, or as the servants of the king of Syria were that came to take Elisha. Others think that their eyes were with-led by a miracle, as the eyes of those two disciples that went to Emmaus were, so that though they had often seen him before, and heard him preach, yet now they could not know him. But, however, it is exceedingly likely that these soldiers did not know him, for the Romans regarded not the gospel, nor did they regard the Jewish religion. So far were they from knowing of him, and the officers it is likely they were such as had not heard him. Therefore you may observe this by the way, that the rage of men against the people of God, it is of those that are ignorant of them ; as these here were ignorant of Christ, and these the chief priests and Pharisees set to take him.

They answered, Jesus of Nazareth. They do not say they sought Christ, for they did not own him as such, but they call him by the name of the place of his birth, and by the name of his country. And Christ owns it : ' I am he,' saith he. And he owned that name from heaven when he spake to Paul : Acts ix. 5, ' I am Jesus of Nazareth whom thou persecutest.' Why did he not say, I am Christ ? He speaks to Paul's apprehension,—I am he whom thou knowest and hast heard of by the name of Jesus of Nazareth. He shewed himself to be Christ indeed in his appearing ; but to shew who he was that Paul persecuted, he said, ' I am Jesus of Nazareth ;' for had Paul persecuted him as Christ, he had sinned against the Holy Ghost ; but he persecuted him only as Jesus of Nazareth. So did these poor men, they did not know him to be Christ, only they came to take one Jesus of Nazareth.

Jesus saith unto them, I am he. We should boldly hold forth our profession. When we are asked, Are you a Christian ? Yes. Eusebius reports of one that, being asked divers questions, as what country he was of, and the like, he always answered, ' I am a Christian,' to shew his boldness in his profession ; so Christ here, ' I am he.'

And Judas also, which betrayed him, stood with them. This is noted, first, to shew that Judas was struck backward as well as the rest, for all that company that was together fell to the ground, as you shall see in the next verse. Christ had struck an arrow through his conscience, dashed him, and certainly aimed at him in the confounding of these more than all the rest. Therefore it is added, ' and Judas also stood with them ;' for special confusion shall befall them that profess Christ, and afterwards fall away.

This miserable man (secondly) was wont to stand amongst the disciples, but now he stands where he shall stand at the latter day, amongst those that are reprobates, and the crucifiers of the Lord of life ; that as it is said in Ps. cxxv. 1, ' The righteous shall be like mount Zion, but those that work iniquity, God shall lead them forth with the workers of iniquity.' In the end the Lord doth discover them ; he will bring them into that drove ; they shall fall to that side their hearts are with ; they shall stand amongst them in the issue and end (for God in his providence orders it), with whom they shall stand for ever. And this God doth usually fulfil upon wicked men, though they have a temporary work upon them ; and though for the present they profess the name of Christ never so much, yet at last they stand—and it is a fatal standing—to sever themselves from the people of God, and betake themselves to that side that are persecutors, or otherwise corrupt. So Judas doth here : he stands among Gentiles and officers of the Pharisees and chief priests, an epitome of reprobates, and so he shall stand at the latter day. God will lead forth all men that do work iniquity with the workers of iniquity. To go on.

Verse 6. ' *As soon as he had said unto them, I am he, they went backward, and fell to the ground.*'
Here you see the confusion that did befall them, from the power of Christ, afore such time as they did lay hands upon him. It is prophesied by David in Ps. xxxv. 4, as a curse upon his enemies, and the Septuagint there use the same word that is here : ' Let them,' saith he, ' be turned backward.' It is a phrase that noteth out confusion, and Christ fulfilleth it here upon these Jews in the very letter. ' They went backward, and fell to the ground.'
And he doth not simply say they fell backward, but it is evident he puts it upon the power of Christ, that did cause them to fall backward ; for it is said, ' As soon as he said, I am he,' (or, as others read it, ' He therefore said, I am he,') ' they fell backward.'
My brethren, there was never such a thing done in the world. Tell me in any story that ever any king, Alexander the Great, or the greatest monarch that ever was in the world, with a word of his mouth, did, against men's wills, make them fall backward to the ground. Had they fallen forward, it might have been thought other force behind them had thrown them down ; or it might have been thought they had worshipped him in a counterfeit way, as afterward they did at his arraignment. But to fall backward at the speaking of a word ! In the word of this king, what power was there ! And therefore some of the ancient fathers that are interpreters, they say that of all the miracles that ever Christ did, this was one of the greatest. Some indeed have pitched upon that miracle of his when he whipped the buyers and sellers out of the temple, and said, ' You make my Father's house a den of thieves.' But assuredly this was a greater than that, for there Christ had some kind of weapon, here he had none. He was then, when he did that, surrounded with people that applauded him, for they had newly brought him into the city with triumph, the children crying Hosannah to him ; but here he had none to take his part when these bands came out against him, but eleven poor disciples. There he had to do but with poor men that sold turtles and doves, here with soldiers armed, that came out on purpose to take him ; yet at one word he throws them down. He doth but say, ' I am the man,' wherein he offers himself to them, which makes the miracle the stranger, that that voice which did invite them to take him, that very voice should throw them backward to the ground.

Now, the reasons why our Lord and Saviour Christ deals thus with them before he would be taken are these :

First, Because he would shew them that he was God, gives them this sign of his divinity. And the truth is, if you observe it, he did all along in the course of his life, with his weakness, mingle some specimens of his power and Godhead. Thus when he was a child in the cradle, as an evidence of his Godhead, there came kings, three wise men out of the East, to worship him ; when he was tempted in the wilderness by Satan, he is succoured by angels ; and here, when he comes to be bound, and to be carried away to be crucified, he first strikes them that were to do it backward with a word of his mouth. It is made the property of God alone to consume men with his breath, Job iv. 9 and Dan. x. 17. Now, Christ shews himself to be God by this, he doth but say, ' I am he,' and they are confounded.

Oh, my brethren, if there was this power in the words of Christ in answering but a question when he was in the form of a servant, what power will there be in his words when he shall come to judgment ! What power is there in that word by which the whole world is upheld, as the apostle saith, Heb. i. 2.

He did do it, *secondly*, that they might have some space to repent, that they might have something to strike them, to occasion their repentance. And you see no outward means, no, not miracles, will work upon the hearts of men, if God do not strike them with his Spirit. And you see likewise that men, though their consciences strike them in the very act of sin, and strike them deeply (as this must needs do their consciences here, especially Judas his), yet they will go on. As Balaam, he went on even against the hair as we say, and so did these.

But the *chief* reason why Christ thus confounded them, and struck them backward first before he would be taken, is that which John (as I said afore) eminently and visibly holds forth, namely, to shew that he was willing to suffer ; no man had power to take his life away, they had not power so much as to lay hands on him, they fall down first. All the world might think, and so might they think too, that if with his breath he thus struck them to the ground, with the same breath he might have struck them into the ground, nay, struck them to hell, never have suffered them to rise more ; he needed never to have been taken by them. But when once he had shewed that it was in his power not to be taken, when he had struck their consciences, then he doth willingly give himself up into their hands ; but he would do this first.

And what words are they by which he doth confound them thus ? They were mild words ; no more than this, ' I am he.' Yea, you shall find elsewhere that by these very words he comforted his disciples at other times ; as when he walked upon the sea, ' Be not afraid,' saith he, ' it is I,' or ' I am he.' And after his resurrection, when he comes into the room where his disciples were, he saith, ' I am he ;' and here now he useth the very same words to his enemies, to the greatest terror in the world. The very same words which Christ speaks, and which we his ministers speak, being his words, that are unto some a savour of life, they are unto others a savour of death. He strikes them dead here, as it were, with the very same words that he put life and comfort into his disciples by. At the latter day, when Christ shall appear, the very same look, the very same presence of his, that will be nothing but grace and sweetness to his children, and fill all their hearts with joy, will be horror, and amazement, and confusion to his enemies, and fill all their hearts with terror.

And then another observation I may make from hence is this, that as in this apprehension of Christ, before they prevailed over him, he strikes them with terror, so wicked men do seldom meddle with the people of God, to persecute them, or apprehend them, to condemn them or the like, but Christ strikes terror in their consciences for so doing. As it is in Ps. xiv. 4, ' They eat up my people like bread ; ' they eat them up so heartily, and seem to be so greedy and so mightily hungry after their blood, and after their hurt, that one would think they have no knowledge : ' Have the workers of iniquity no knowledge,' saith he, ' that eat up my people as they eat bread ? ' that they fall so fast to them as they do ? But what saith the next verse ? ' Then were they in great fear, for God is in the genera- tion of the righteous.' And in Philip. i. 28 the apostle bids them, when they suffer, to carry it with a confidence, and to be nothing terrified by their adversaries ; which, saith he, ' is an evident token unto them of per- dition, but to you of salvation, and that of God.' His meaning is, that when men do carry things confidently, being in a right way, usually God's Spirit doth bless that confidence to a double end. *First*, He seals up sal- vation to them that suffer for him ; even while they suffer he breaks in upon their spirits, and fills their hearts with assurance. And, *secondly*, he breaks in also upon the hearts of the persecutors, and strikes them with terror. ' It is a sign,' saith he, that is, a present sign, there is from God, as to you that suffer, inward joy and comfort ; so there is oftentimes terror in the hearts of wicked men that persecute you, which is as it were the first-fruits of hell and of perdition. And so here Christ, to shew that he will one day throw them to hell, he flings them to the ground now. Eccle- siastical stories tell us that the very heathens themselves, though they knew not what they did when they persecuted the Christians, they had oftentimes terrors in themselves while they were executing their cruelty upon the people of God.

And then again, out of this verse, observe this, that the church may pre- vail against the enemies thereof, and make them fall, and yet those enemies may recover and fall upon the church again. Men that shall fall upon the church, and prevail against it, they may for a time fall before it. These very men that God had designed to take Christ, they fall backward first, and they fall backward terrified and amazed ; yet they rise up again, and take him. So is it oftentimes with the body of Christ here on earth, the enemies sometimes are greatly prevailed against, confounded, that one would think they should never rise more ; yet, as Jeremiah saith, ' These wounded men shall rise up every man in his tent, and take the city.' These men, you see, that thus fell backward and were confounded, they were the men that took Christ ; for when Christ had done, and shewed them that he was the Messiah, he gave himself up to them. So it is, and will be, to the end of the world.

Yet you may take it as a certain sign that they shall fall one day ; as this was here, it was a sign that they should fall into ruin and destruction, but they must do their work first. If God come down and help his church, and appear in his power, as here Christ doth, I am sure his enemies will fall backward ; though his enemies, I say, may rise again and take the city. Yet it is a help to our faith that that God that came down as a lion thus, and they were scattered, shall ruin them in the end, that is certain. It is the prophet's expression, when they are all preying like a company of wolves upon the sheep, ' He shall come down like a lion,' and they will all run away presently. Thus, you see, at this day Christ came but down amongst them, and said, 'I am he,' and you know how they all crouched presently.

We see likewise the way that Jesus Christ useth to confound his enemies; it is with his breath, it is with his word. As soon as he had said, 'I am he,' or therefore when he had said, 'I am he,' they fell backward. Still Christ is said to do all his great businesses with a word of his mouth. There is a sword in his mouth that kills them. And in Isa. xi. 4, he strikes them with the rod of his mouth; and antichrist is to be destroyed with the spirit of his mouth, and the brightness of his coming. As it was the word of Christ that confounded his enemies here, so it is that word shall confound them to the end of the world. And if they have any other enemies about their ears besides the word, it is because the word stirs them up. It is the word that works in the hearts of men, and makes them enemies to the enemies of God, and brings them upon them. It is the vengeance of the word which the people of God execute upon wicked men.

You see likewise, when Christ will appear, what a little thing daunts his enemies. It is but a mere word, 'I am he,' and they fall backward to the ground. But to go on.

Verse 7. '*Then asked he them again, Whom seek ye? And they said, Jesus of Nazareth.*'

When they were thus fallen down and risen again, perhaps they went up and down like amazed and confounded men to seek him; therefore he comes to them, and asketh them, 'Whom seek ye?'

This second question carries a mighty conviction, a mighty triumph with it over their consciences; as if he had said, I have told you who I am; and I have told it you to purpose, have I not? Have you not learned by this time who I am, when your hearts are so terrified, that you all fell down before me, a poor man? They had been taught by woful experience who he was, when he blew them over, flung them down with his breath; and it might have turned to a blessed experience had God struck their hearts, as he did their outward man. But still they will not call him 'Christ' for all this, they call him but 'Jesus of Nazareth.'

You see the desperate hardness of the hearts of wicked men, and it is in experience true, no means, no convictions, no miracles, will work upon them. One would have thought that this should have struck the spirits of any men in the world, that a poor man with his breath should cause them to fall down backward, they should be afraid, and not have dared to have laid hold on him. They were afraid indeed afore, that's the truth on't, they had a suspicion that there was more than a man in him; why else had they the Roman soldiers and all their officers armed with weapons? And you see how he falls upon them but with his word, yet still they are hardened. A man would wonder, when there are such evidences of God's taking part with his truth, such providences of God, punishing those that go against his people, yet that men should go on still. Nothing will soften the hearts of those that are resolved in wickedness. There is one instance, and it is to me a mighty one, of the desperate hardness of men's hearts, and that is, of the men that did watch at the grave of Christ. Christ had foretold that he would rise again the third day, and the Pharisees, after he was buried, they come to Pilate, the governor, and say they, This impostor said he would rise again the third day, therefore let us make sure work with him, and let us have a stone rolled upon his grave, and set men to guard it; and so a watch was set. Now while they were sitting to watch him, there comes a great earthquake, and an angel descends from heaven and rolls away the grave-stone, and was so dreadful to these keepers that they fell down, and became as dead men, whereby it is evident that from heaven there was a testimony of his resurrection. They go and tell their masters, the chief priests, all these things that were done; they bid them hold their tongues. ' Say you' (say they to them) ' that his disciples came by night, and stole him away while we slept,' and we will satisfy the governor, and secure you. Though Christ, even by the testimony of their own men, had fulfilled what he himself prophesied, and it was plainly evident to them, yet they hired the soldiers to tell this lie, though the lie contradicted itself (as some have observed); for how could they tell his disciples had stolen him away, when they were asleep? To this desperate hardness do the hearts of men come; therefore never think that truth, or reason, or anything, will prevail upon wicked men; all the means and miracles in the world will not do it, unless God persuade Japhet to dwell in the tents of Shem. In Rev. xvi., when the fourth vial was poured out upon the sun (which is thought to be that execution that is now in the world upon the house of Austria, or whatever it is), it is said, that ' though men were scorched with great heat, yet they blasphemed the name of God, and repented not to give him glory.' And when the fifth vial comes to be poured out (which is the vial upon the city of Rome, the seat of the beast, and it may be some of it is begun to be fulfilled, the little seats of the beast are begun to be removed), it is said, ' The kingdom was full of darkness, yet they gnawed their tongues for pain, and blasphemed God, and repented not of their deeds.' Men that are resolved in their wickedness come to such desperate hardness, that they never repent, let what will fall out. Those that harden themselves against Christ shall be hardened. So much for the seventh verse.

Verse 8. ' *Jesus answered, I have told you that I am he; if therefore ye seek me, let these go their way.*'

Jesus answered, I have told you that I am he. There is a great deal of majesty in this speech, a great deal of exprobration; ' I have told you,' saith he, and I think that I have told you with a witness, ' that I am he.' As was said of the river Jordan, ' What ailest thou that thou fleddest back?' So it might be said of these men, What do you ail that you fall backward at a mean man's only saying, ' I am he'? a mean man in appearance. It is as if Christ had said, you say you seek for Jesus of Nazareth; I have told you that I am he; why did you not then lay hold upon me? Was it a divine power that struck you dead first? Then be warned by it; I am the same man; upon your peril be it if you lay hold upon me. Yea, Christ did intimate thereby that they could not know him, unless he himself had helped them to himself. He said again, ' I am he;' they knew not who was he.

Which still also argues his willingness to suffer, that he should twice put himself upon them, twice say that he was the man. They being as blinded men (for so indeed they were), he might have escaped if he would; but he is so far from that, that he provokes them by a double question to know him. He would not be taken by Judas his sign at first, but by his own voluntary resigning of himself up, for that is the thing (Christ's willingness to suffer) which John doth eminently endeavour to hold forth in this story.

My brethren, these men took pains to seek Jesus Christ to damn themselves; had they bestowed the same diligence to seek him as a saviour, they might have been saved ; had they took the same pains to seek his favour that here they took to seek him to crucify him, he would have manifested himself unto them. There is no man that seeks Christ, but in the end he saith unto him, ' I am he.' And if they have lost their knowledge of him (as many oftentimes do), he saith it the second time, ' I am he,' and provokes their hearts to know him. To all seekers of him he doth so, whether they be those of the left hand, such as these that sought him to crucify him, or those of the right hand, that seek him to be saved by him.

There is one general observation that I shall give you here, upon the occasion both of this miracle and that of healing Malchus his ear ; for he did both these miracles afore they apprehended him, as the context evidently argues ; and although Matthew and Mark relate the story of Peter's cutting off Malchus his ear after his being apprehended, which indeed they do by way of narration, yet it is clear by Luke and John that it was before ; for when his hands were bound it was not a time for him to put forth his hand to heal him. Our Saviour Christ did not put forth any more miracles, or gave any more signs of his divinity now ; but after they had taken him, he is as calm as a lamb. Before, indeed, he doth two things : he terrifies their consciences by casting them backward ; and he healeth him who, like an enemy and a wretch, came to attach him, and it seems was the first that laid hands on him.

Obs. The observation I make from hence is this : You shall find this to be true in experience, that when you are entering into a sin, then will God use that means that he meaneth to apply to keep you from it ; he doth usually do it then ; but after you are entered into it, then your hearts are let go on. So indeed it was here with these men ; Christ useth two means, and notable ones too, two great miracles, before they took him, to strike their consciences, in a way of judgment the one, in a way of mercy the other. But when once they had laid hold of him and got their prey, he leaves them to their own hearts' lusts. So he deals with wicked men, and in experience you will find it true. Therefore, let this be the use of it : observe what God saith to your hearts, what means he useth to your spirits, when you are entering into any great sin. If you neglect cleaving to God then, and making use of those means, you are in danger never to be recovered, but to be left to that sin. And so much for that general observation upon these miracles of Christ.

If therefore ye seek me, let these go their way. Whilst Jesus Christ was ready to be taken, he takes upon him like a king. If you will have me, saith he, here I am ; but I charge you do not meddle with one of these, touch not mine anointed, let them go.

The words are to be considered, first, as they are a command from Christ ; they are not a matter of compact or agreement only with them, or of humble suit, ' Let these go their way ; ' but he speaks as a king, as one that had conquered them before ; he had thrown them backward before, they had felt of his power, ' Let these go their way,' saith he. And that it was a command doth seem to be manifest by this, by the words that follow, ' That the saying might be fulfilled which he spake' (in his prayer), ' Of them that thou hast given me I have lost none.' As he had prayed and had assurance from God of it, so now he gives forth a command about it. For assuredly, otherwise, those which did command those officers to take Christ, did command them to take his disciples also ; their hatred was extreme great against the disciples as well as against the master. And therefore, when all the disciples forsook him and fled, although there was time enough, to shew that Christ's power kept them from taking them, yet when there was a certain young man that rose up, and came out in his shirt in the night, and did but follow him when he was taken and led away, they laid hold upon him, thinking him to be a disciple; and he was fain to leave his linen cloth that was about him, and to fly from them naked. Therefore certainly they had as full a purpose to have taken any that countenanced him, any disciple, as Christ himself, but only here he speaks to them as you see, ' Let these go their way.'

And by virtue of this command it was, that though Peter did provoke them after these words the most that could be, by drawing his sword, and falling upon a servant of the high priest's, and strikes off his ear, which could not but mightily enrage them, yet the command of Christ must stand; he had hold of their hearts, he charged them that they should not meddle with them, and they durst not lay hands on them. Peter endangered himself and all his brethren, that after Christ had said this, he should fall upon them, and strike them with his sword; so that though they had no malice against the disciples before, yet this drawing of swords and striking off an ear, could not but extremely provoke them; yet, I say, Christ's command must stand. And Peter, after this, he comes into the high priest's hall, and there was challenged again and again, yet this word of Christ, ' Let these go,' stood. And John afterward, he comes and stands about the cross, sees him crucified; they had no power to meddle with him, Christ's word stood still, ' Let these go.' It is as if Christ should have said, Well, I will suffer you to take me; but as I have shewn you, by throwing you to the ground, that you cannot take me unless I please, so still, here I am, ' if you seek me, let these go.'

Obs. 1. Observe from hence first, it is a command from heaven, from Christ, that doth deliver his people in all dangers whatsoever. Men could not be in a greater danger than these disciples were in, nor were there ever any men more malicious than these were, yet we see they are preserved by virtue of this word of Christ's, ' Let these go.' In Ps. cv. 14, 15. Though they were strangers, saith he, and though the other were kings, and had power enough to hurt them, yet he suffered no man to do them wrong. God from heaven spake to their hearts, ' Touch not mine anointed, do my prophets no harm;' so doth Christ here speak with the same authority, ' Let these go.'

Obs. 2. Observe from hence, as the power of Christ to deliver us in all dangers, so his willingness to preserve us. He voluntarily resigns himself up to be taken; but as for his disciples, ' Let these go,' saith he. Was he thus willing to put himself in our stead, when he was here on earth? Do you think that now he hath suffered and is gone to heaven, where he is to intercede, to reap the fruit of his sufferings, that he doth not say to his Father upon all occasions, ' Let these poor souls go, I have suffered for them'? If, when he was crucified in weakness, he put forth such a power to deliver his people in so great a danger as these were in, certainly you may trust him upon all occasions to deliver you, now he is glorified much more; unless there be some peculiar reason, some peculiar decree of God's (as there was for Christ himself), that the Father hath appointed us a cup for to drink, and that neither shall not be till the time come. These apostles they were afterwards to suffer; yet Christ, because their time was not yet come, gives this charge to those that took him, ' Let these go.'

This being said concerning the command itself, we will consider the reasons why Christ did preserve his disciples at this time. The reasons are clearly these.

1. To shew that he could have saved himself if he pleased : for he that saved others could have saved himself; he that so with authority did command them to let these go, could have commanded them to have let himself go.

2. He would shew that he alone was to suffer. In this work (saith he) I will have none to be my companions. I stand now in their stead, and their sins are laid upon me, therefore meddle not with these, 'Let these go.' As David said, 'Let thy hand be upon me and my father's house,' so doth Christ say, Let your hands be upon me, let the sword of God awake against the shepherd, but not against the sheep. You know it was the prophecy of Caiaphas, 'It is meet that one man should die for the people;' therefore, if you seek me, saith Christ, I am that one man, let these go.

3. Christ meant to employ them in other services : they were to preach the gospel to all the world, and when they had done they were to suffer. He had other work for them to do, and until that were done, 'Let these go.'

4. They were not yet fit to suffer. Christ he knew the weakness of their spirits ; it is true he could have given them power, but according to an ordinary course, had they been called to suffer now, in that state they were in, they would have all done as Peter did, denied him ; for you see they all fled away from him presently, as soon as he was taken, they would never have held out, the business was too strong for them to undergo at the present. And that this is the reason is clear by the next words, ' That the saying might be fulfilled which he spake, Of them which thou hast given me I have lost none,' implying that if they had been put upon suffering now, they had been lost, their souls would have been undone, they would have denied him. This Christ foresaw, and therefore prevents their sufferings, and so the occasion of their falling so grossly. Therefore, to preserve them every way, both their bodies and their souls, saith he, 'Let these go.'

The observations from hence are these :

Obs. 1. You may see the great care of Christ; when he was to suffer, one would think his thoughts should have been wholly taken up about himself. No ; you see he doth not mind himself, his care was to preserve his disciples : 'Here am I,' saith he, ' let these go.' Was Christ so careful of his disciples when he was to undergo so great an encounter ? How much more doth he take care of his saints now he is in heaven.

Obs. 2. Christ is careful to bring us but then to suffer, when he means to fit us for suffering, and when we shall be able to suffer, and if need be, and so much only as shall need be. That place in 1 Pet. i. 6 contains a promise in it, speaking of sufferings: ' Wherein,' saith he, ' you greatly rejoice, though now for a season, *if need be*, you are in heaviness,' &c. He will not, unless there be need, bring temptations upon you. If Christ had laid sufferings upon them now, they had not been able to have suffered : you see Peter foreswore him upon the assault of a maid, how much more would he have done so, if attached and brought before the high priest. It is Christ's manner not to call us to suffering till we can suffer, nor to lay more upon us than we are able to bear. You know the promise in 1 Cor. x. 13.

Obs. 3. They that are of public use, for whom God hath work to do, till the time appointed in which God will have them suffer, they shall escape abundance of dangers of sufferings. The truth is, had these Jews seized upon Christ and all his disciples at once, they had made sure for* the gospel

    * That is, 'they would have prevented.'—ED.

ever to have been propagated, according to what God had appointed, for he had chosen these men to be witnesses and preachers of it, there had been none left but Paul to preach. They might have crushed the gospel in the very shell, had they taken Christ and all the apostles at once. No ; saith he, ' Let these go.' So long as God hath work for men to do, he will preserve them from being taken and seized upon, and ruined by their enemies. Let no man, therefore, that is in any work and service for God, fear; he shall never be cut off till such time as his work be done, and then to be cut off it is no matter ; he shall not be sent for out of the harvest till he hath reaped that God hath appointed to reap by him. ' Go tell that fox, Herod ' (saith Christ, Luke xiii. 31), ' Behold, I cast out devils, and I do cures to-day and to-morrow ;' and I will do it in spite of him ; he shall not be able, for all he is a crafty, wily fox, with all his cunning, to take me. ' I will work to-day and to-morrow, and the third day I shall be perfected.' Till I have accomplished all my work, till the time come that my Father hath appointed me to suffer in, I will go up and down freely, let him do his worst; and when I have done I will suffer, for I have vowed to do it. So here, ' Let these go,' saith he, I have work for them to do, I must send them abroad into all the world, do not touch a hair of them ; no more they did. So much for the 8th verse. The reason of this is given in the next words.

Verse 9. ' *That the saying might be fulfilled which he spake, Of them which thou gavest me have I lost none.*'
You must not take these words as spoken by Christ, but it is the comment that John, who wrote this gospel, putteth upon Christ's speech immediately foregoing ; and he openeth, through the revelation of the Spirit of God, the true reason why that command of Christ did take place, that the disciples were let go, because, saith he, that Christ had prayed even just before, in the 17th chapter ; for, if you read that chapter, you shall find that Christ, in that solemn prayer which he puts up to his Father, saith, ' Those that thou gavest me I have kept, and none of them is lost, but the son of perdition.' This prayer he had put up just afore, and you see what present need there was of having it answered.
I shall give you two general observations from this.
Obs. 1. We had need to lay up prayers every day before we go abroad and do our business ; for indeed we do not know what dangers may befall us afore we come in again. Christ here, if he had not prayed just afore that all his apostles might be kept, they might have been in danger ; for a great danger they came into, but the efficacy of that prayer kept them.
Obs. 2. How soon are prayers answered ! Christ had put up this prayer but even just before ; and as some think, he did pray as he came along out of the chamber where they did eat the passover, and that he uttered this prayer to his Father walking from thence. For in the last verse of the 14th chapter, saith he, ' Arise, let us go hence ;' therefore they conceive that his sermon mentioned in the 15th and 16th chapters, and his prayer mentioned in the 17th, were all uttered as he went along from the chamber to the brook Cedron. However, certainly it was not long before, perhaps not above half an hour ; and here you see it answered, the thing he prayed for is fulfilled ; ' Let these go,' saith he, and it was done accordingly, they did not touch one of them, ' That the saying might be fulfilled which he spake, Of them which thou gavest me have I lost none.' In Dan. ix. 3, 21, you shall find that Daniel set himself to pray whenas

the evening sacrifice began, and there was a commission presently given to the angel to come and give him an answer. Prayers, my brethren, are presently heard; so was Christ's here, he had an answer presently. So much for the general observations out of these words.

Now the only question for the opening the words lies in this. Those words of Christ's in the 17th chapter—' Those that thou gavest me I have kept, and none of them is lost'—seem to have been put up for the keeping them, in respect of the salvation of their souls, whereas this here (which it is applied unto) is spoken only in respect of the preservation of their bodies, in appearance; ' Let these go,' saith he, let them escape for this time. It is most certain that what our Saviour Christ spake in that place, referreth principally to the salvation of their souls; what is the reason, then, that here it should be applied to this deliverance of their bodies, to a temporal deliverance?

My brethren, all the promises in the Scripture are to be taken in the largest sense that may be. As we say of privileges and favours, they are to be interpreted in the largest sense, so are all the prómises. That promise made to Joshua, ' I will not leave thee, nor forsake thee,' is referred only to the carrying of him on in that war; yet all the elect may apply it to all sorts of distresses, not only that God will never leave them nor forsake them, in respect of bodily deliverances, but in respect of their souls also. So here, on the other side, that which Christ speaks of their souls is extended to their bodies too, and they reap the fruit of it in that respect.

And it argues this too, that that God that saves thy soul, out of the same love saves thy body too; therefore interpret it so, for so John doth here; what was spoken in the 17th chapter of their souls, he applies it here to their bodies. Will God save thy soul? Certainly he will deliver thy body. When we seek spiritual things much, in the height of our spirits, then doth God answer us also in temporal things. And as by the virtue of Christ's resurrection we shall be raised up at the latter day and saved, so by virtue of the same resurrection we shall be preserved here in the world; the same power that shall raise us up then, works for us lesser deliverances now. Paul, in 2 Cor. iv. 10, speaking of the many deliverances he had from temporal dangers, he attributes it all to the resurrection of Christ: ' We are' (saith he) ' troubled on every side, yet not distressed; cast down, but not destroyed, &c., that the life of Jesus might be made manifest in our body.' So here, though Christ did not in his prayer intend so much the preservation of their bodies as their eternal salvation, yet their deliverance from this so great a danger was a fruit of that prayer. The same prayer that saved their souls saved their bodies too; and it was a pawn and pledge to them that their souls should be saved, because the virtue of that prayer wrought a deliverance for their bodies out of so eminent a danger; for who would not have thought but that they should all have been taken, seeing they laid about them so as they did? And it was in answer to Christ's prayer; one would have thought it had been but an ordinary providence, that they were so greedy of Christ that they let the disciples slip away. No; it was an answer to prayer made but a while afore.

Obs. 1. Observe from hence, that of all things else in the world, the greatest care that Jesus Christ hath, it is to preserve all his saints, not to lose one. For he comforts himself in the seventeenth chapter, that of those God had given him, he had lost none, but he that was designed to perdition by God himself; and here it is repeated again, and you see what care he takes for their preservation. My brethren, it would trouble Jesus Christ to eternity (I may say it with boldness) if he should lose one soul that he died for. Are the hairs of your head numbered? Certainly your persons are numbered, and Christ will not lose one of his tale, nor a finger of his body; nay, though thou beest but as a little tip of his finger, or as his little toe, he will have a care to save thee. When he makes up his jewels, he will not lose any, not the least of them. 'Lo, here am I,' saith he, 'and the children thou hast given me,' Heb. ii. 13. 'And this is my Father's will, that of all those he hath given me I should lose none, but raise them up at the latter day,' John vi. 39.

Obs. 2. And observe this too from hence, that Jesus Christ he can keep us in the very midst of his enemies. He gives his disciples here a pass (as I may call it); when there was a band of Roman soldiers, divers of the chief priests, and elders, and officers from them, all about him and his disciples, 'Let these go,' saith he. And all to fulfil this, 'Of those thou hast given me have I lost none.' It is because he rules in the midst of his enemies. Jesus Christ shewed his power before, in confounding these Jews and the rest, by throwing them backward; and now he shews his power as much in preserving his disciples in the midst of them, and so he will do to the end of the world. 'He knoweth how to deliver the godly out of temptation,' 2 Peter ii. 9. He hath the art and skill of it, and the power of it too, for he awed their hearts here when he said, 'Let these go.'

Obs. 3. Lastly, ministers likewise should have the like care, that none of those that are committed to them perish, for so Christ as a good shepherd had. And so much for the ninth verse.

CHAPTER VII.

The tenth and eleventh verses explained, with suitable observations raised from them.—The willingness which Christ expressed to come to die, and be made a sacrifice, and would have nothing to hinder it.

You shall find this (that I may give you a general preface to the opening of the words of this tenth verse, and those that follow) that the evangelists in setting down the story of Christ's sufferings, they do diligently insert the behaviour of his apostles, how they carried themselves. It was an ill time, brethren, for disciples to sin, when their master was to be taken; and yet I know not how many sins of theirs are mentioned. They were fast asleep at that time when he was in his greatest agony. One would think that at that time above all other they should have watched with him, when he was entering into his sufferings for their sins. And now when he was to be taken, you see into what a miscarriage Peter runneth, what a furious rash act he performs. If Christ had pleased, he might have kept them from all these sins, he had power enough to have done it, but he would not. What is the observation from hence?

Obs. 1. That Jesus Christ may be present with a man's spirit, and pray for him too (for he had prayed for these that they should be kept from the evil of the world), and yet that man run into sin. If Christ, when he was here upon earth, did not keep his people from falling into manifold sins and errors, do not think much if sometimes thou art left to sin against him. He made good use of it, he did bring glory out of it; this same rash act of Peter's here, it was an occasion of two things: first, of illustrating the power of Christ the more in keeping of them, according to the command he gave, 'Let these go;' for who would not have thought but that they should all have fallen upon Peter and the rest, and have killed them presently, a company of rude soldiers and officers armed? Yet they meddled not with them. And it was an occasion of Christ's shewing his goodness in healing the man's ear, and of shewing a miracle. And this be assured of, that Christ will work good out of all thy sins, as he did here glory to himself out of this sin of Peter's.

Obs. 2. That God may leave his people to sinning even at that time when he is doing the greatest things for them. But I shall pass that now, because we shall have occasion to speak of it in the following discourse. To speak therefore a little more particularly of this act of Peter's.

Verse 10. ' *Then Simon Peter, having a sword, drew it, and smote the high priest's servant, and cut off his right ear. The servant's name was Malchus.*' You read in Mark xiv. 31, that the disciples, they did all vow that they would live and die with him, as we say; they all promise him that if he were taken that night, they would lose their lives in his defence, that they would; and Peter above the rest he was the forwardest, Whoever leaves thee, saith he, I will not leave thee. Now these disciples, having thus engaged themselves, when they saw that their master would be taken, they asked him, ' Lord, shall we smite with the sword?' So Luke tells us, chapter xxiii. 39. And yet, poor men, they had but two swords amongst them all. And Simon Peter, as he had been the forwardest man in promising to assist Christ, so he is the forwardest in striking, for before Christ gave them an answer whether they should smite or no, he out with his sword and strikes.

Peter, having a sword. There were two swords in the company, as Luke hath it. Christ indeed had said a few hours before, ' He that hath a sword, let him take it;' but he intended it in another sense, and therefore they mistook him. However probable it is that they, knowing Christ was to be betrayed that night, they carried out their swords to fight, having promised to do so before; which may be one occasion of Peter's having a sword; but Josephus and others say (and it is as likely too), that those that came up to the feast (as these did), they travelled through woods and wildernesses, and so were in danger of wild beasts, or thieves, or the like, and therefore they carried swords with them; and besides, it was the manner and custom of the Galileans especially to wear swords, as hath been observed by some. Some interpreters hence observe that it is lawful to wear defensive weapons, which the anabaptists of Germany did use to deny. There is the clearest evidence for it here, for they did not only wear swords, but Christ bids them, if they had no swords, to sell their garments and buy swords; so says Luke chap. xxii. 36. And when Peter had done this mischievous act, in drawing his sword and striking the high priest's servant, Christ did not bid him fling it away, but only to put it up again into his place.

In this action of Peter's there was something good and something bad.

Something good. It is evident first that there was a great deal of zeal and love to his master. He was encouraged to it likewise, because he had seen his master to throw them all upon the ground afore him; thought he, though we be but eleven, and have but two swords, we may venture, for our master will assist us. There was a confidence, a faith, in the power of Christ. And it would seem also that what he did was upon warrant, as he thought; for at the passover Christ had said, ' If any man have a sword let him take it.' He spake it indeed to another purpose (as I said even now), but Peter might take his ground from thence, misunderstanding his master's words.

There was something bad and sinful likewise in this action, viz.,

1. That Peter did rashly fall upon this act; for the disciples having asked Christ whether they should draw, before ever Christ answered, he out with his sword and falls upon the man. Peter had a bold and a rash and sudden spirit, as appeared, as by a world of carriages of his toward Christ, so by this, which was as rash an act as could be ; and it was a folly for him to do it ; for what was he and ten more, that had but two swords amongst them, to encounter with all that band of men that came with weapons to take Christ ?

2. That he went about to hinder our Saviour Christ from dying. That is clear to be a sin by Christ's reproof of him ; for saith he, ' Shall I not drink of the cup that my Father hath commanded me to drink of ? ' Wilt thou hinder me ? Wilt thou go contrary to God's will ? Thou didst tempt me once before, ' Master, spare thyself ;' and now thou wouldst keep me from dying for thee and all thy brethren.

3. That whereas a lawful power had seized upon Christ (a lawful power, I say, though they did it not lawfully), he would lift up his sword against the magistrate, who had sent these men to take him.

4. That he did endanger all the rest of the disciples to have been presently hewn a-pieces, but that the force of those words, ' Let these go,' hindered it.

5. The truth is, there was an injustice in it, Christ having as it were made a bargain with them : ' Here am I,' says he, ' let these go ;' it was injustice in Peter to fall upon them.

Obs. 1. Comfort to those that have bold, and rash, and sudden spirits. Hast thou a rash, a sudden, spirit ? That rashness is sinful, for Christ reproves it in Peter; yet comfort thyself: Peter, that great apostle, was a man subject to the same infirmity. Yet take heed of walking rashly : Lev. xxvi. 40, ' If you walk contrary to me ;' so we translate it ; but I remember Junius translated it, ' If you walk rashly with me, I will walk rashly with you.' If we walk rashly with God, though he love us and will pardon us, yet he may walk rashly with us again, give us a blow afore we are aware, come with some casual kind of cross or other upon us. God is pleased to spare Peter, for he doth not animadvert for every fault ; yet in that place of Leviticus, he expresseth what he will do upon men's rash walking.

Obs. 2. See here the spirit of Peter, how valiant and bold he is, runs into the midst of a band of men, and strikes amongst them ; but, alas ! he did it out of a human courage and valour, because he had said he would die with Christ. This poor man afterwards denies Christ upon the charge of a damsel ; he was afraid of a maid, and yet here he encounters a company of armed men ; he shewed his courage with his sword, when he would not do it with his tongue, as Calvin saith. Let us have never so much greatness of spirit naturally, if we come to any spiritual suffering, and have not grace to assist us, our natural spirit will not help us in it. Certainly this act of Peter's proceeded from his natural spirit and human valour that he had, but when he comes to be put to it to suffer in a spiritual way, Peter shrinks back.

Obs. 3. Good men may carry on a good cause extreme indiscreetly. In appearance this was as good cause to venture one's life in as possibly could be, yet how indiscreetly doth Peter manage it ! He managed it worse than they did that came to take Christ, for you see they did not fall upon the disciples at all, which a thousand to one but they had; whereas Peter, contrary to Christ's agreement with them, falls upon them. As Abimelech said unto Abraham, ' I am more righteous than thou,' in that act: so the truth is, these men were in this respect more righteous than Peter. In managing a good cause, godly people commit such errors as this was, and then all the world takes notice of it. They might have blamed Christ and his disciples, and said, they were a company of rebellious, froward fellows, and the rest of them are like these. This might have been laid to Christ's charge, through Peter's indiscretion.

Obs. 4. Our Saviour Christ would not have Peter venture his life this way. He knew he was better at preaching than at fighting, therefore he would have him reserve himself for that, and therefore he bids him put up his sword. It had been well for this kingdom if some had ventured themselves in a way of counsel rather than fighting. Christ, I say, had other work for Peter. It is good for a man to lay out his life in that which he is best in. Peter, who was designed for an apostle, that had so many precious notions committed to him, for him to venture his life in such a rude manner, it was a great fault.

Obs. 5. Although Christ was an eminent person, the Saviour of the world, yet Christ would not have Peter fight for him against the magistrate, as in this Peter did, because it was against the authority of the magistrate. The sword is committed peculiarly to the magistrate: as Rom. xiii., ' He bears not the sword in vain ;' he bears the sword, not thee;* thou mayest defend thyself in a private quarrel if set upon, but here came out the authority of the magistrate to attach Christ ; and in such a case thou art not to lift up thy sword. ' Put up thy sword again into his place,' saith Christ.

And yet it was the best cause, one would think, that ever was to fight in. If a man might fight merely for religion, I say *merely* for religion, here had been the greatest colour for it in the world. Why ? It was to save the life of Christ, the Lord of the world ; and to fight for the life of Christ is more than to fight for the truth of Christ; yet no, saith Christ, ' Put up thy sword again,' trust me to manage my own cause. Religion may be fought for as it is become a civil right and liberty of a state, for so it becometh when it is enacted by the power of that state; but merely and simply to fight for religion, there is no warrant in the word of God for it. To fight for Christ's life was not warrantable for Peter.

Christ tells him withal (as in other evangelists), ' He that kills with the sword shall be killed with the sword ;' he that will fight in a quarrel that is not warrantable, he himself shall be found out one day. But I rather think the meaning is, thou needest not trouble thyself to avenge my quarrel upon these men, for the sword shall find out this nation for putting me to death ; for so you know it did, the Romans came and took away their city and nation.

Obs. 6. Lastly, When God hath made a promise, and given forth his word, though there may many things fall out to overturn it, yet it shall stand. Christ hath said, ' Let these go.' Peter, you see, had like to have spoiled all ; he goes and runs into a riot which might have endangered them, yet notwithstanding the word of Christ doth stand. When God hath made a promise of deliverance, there shall those things fall out that one would think would hazard the performance, and that through men's own default,

* That is. 'not thou.'—ED.

yet God will bring about the deliverance. So much in the general for this act of Peter's.

And he smote the high priest's servant, and cut off his right ear: the servant's name was Malchus. This servant of the high priest's, it seems, was the first man that stepped forth to lay hold upon Christ, and therefore Peter encounters him first, for as yet they had not taken Christ; for the text saith afterwards, ' Then the captains and the band took Jesus.' It seems, therefore, I say, that this man was the forwardest of the company, which he did either to please his master, or perhaps he was the officer to serve the arrest upon him in a formal way, as we do. Peter now falls upon him first, and cuts off his ear. Some think it was but the tip of his ear, for so the word signifies sometimes, but there is no ground for that, for Luke he calls it the whole ear.

He saith the servant's name was Malchus, which some fetch from the Hebrew root, which signifies one bought. Because as he was a servant, so perhaps his master had bought him with his money, or otherwise obtained him to be his servant. And as Caiaphas, his master, was (as appears by all the story) the greatest enemy of Christ, so this Malchus was the forwardest of all the rest to attach Christ. The obedience of the servant to the master in Scripture, is expressed by lending the ear, and by boring the ear ; and therefore for his doing this out of obedience and zeal to his master, this punishment befalls him. But I pass over that.

Peter cut off his ear. It is certain that Peter aimed at his head, to have cleft that down, but God in his providence directs the blow so, that no more hurt was done but the cutting off the ear. It is strange it should not hit his shoulder, yet you see God guided it so that it did not.

Obs. The observation I have from this is only this, that God in his providence guides and directs blows, and all such casual things as these are. Such passages of providence there are, in guiding the motions of men's hands, and the motions of the creatures, oftentimes for the preservation of us in dangers. And how manifold experiences have we had of them ! Who almost is there but in their lives have been either near being killed, and God hath come in by his providence, guiding and directing such accidents and occurrences, that they have been preserved ! Especially those that are soldiers, they have found strange kind of shots that have been made, and how near they have come to kill them, and yet they have missed. Or else they have been near killing others in a casual way, and God in his providence hath prevented it. I say it is every man's case almost ; we may see many examples of the providence of God in this kind. We see it here towards Peter, and it was a mighty providence ; for had Peter killed this man, had there been a murder committed upon him, there had been such a ground of quarrel that they would have fallen upon all the disciples, and certainly have cut them to pieces ; but Christ had prayed that they should go away free, therefore God in his providence guides Peter's blow, so that he strikes off nothing but the ear, though he aimed at his head ; and Christ heals that ear too, that so his disciples might be all saved and delivered. So much for the tenth verse.

Verse 11 . ' *Then said Jesus unto Peter, Put up thy sword into the sheath: the cup which my Father hath given me, shall I not drink it ?*'

I have observed something before upon Christ's bidding him put up his sword, therefore I shall say little of it now. Jesus said unto Peter. Why unto Peter ? For in Luke he speaks to them all not to draw their swords :

' Suffer you thus far,' saith he. But as he spake to them all, because they
all asked him whether they should draw, so more particularly and personally to Peter, because he had sinned and did actually draw his sword ; for
that is the manner of Christ, to reprove those, and to have those reproved
in a peculiar manner, that sin more peculiarly. He bids him put it up ;
he doth not bid him not to wear it, or not to use it, but to put it up only.
But of that before.

The cup which my Father hath given me, shall I not drink it? In Mat.
xxvi. 51–54, you shall find that Christ useth other arguments to his disciples
to be quiet and to put up their swords. ' How shall the scriptures be fulfilled,' saith he, ' that thus it must be ?' that is one reason. What need I
care for your help, ' cannot I pray to my Father, and he shall presently give
me more than twelve legions of angels ?' and, ' all they that take the sword,
shall perish with the sword.' All these doth Christ give as reasons to them
to be quiet. But the apostle John, writing after all the other evangelists,
inserts what they omitted ; and he mentioneth here another reason, and,
indeed, the highest reason of all the rest, ' Shall I not drink,' &c.

From whence take this general observation, that there may be many
motives and reasons in one action, many considerations that may keep a
man from sinning in one action, though there be one more principal than
all the rest, as this was the principal in Christ.

But why doth he use this argument to Peter more than to all the rest?
Upon a double ground.

1. Because it had been Peter's sin to hinder him from suffering. And you
shall see how his heart still rose against Peter for it. He had once before
said, ' Master, spare thyself.' Christ calls him Satan for it ; and he never
called any of them Satan but Judas : ' Get thee behind me, Satan,' says he
to Peter (Mat. xvi. 23). He saw Satan in it. And now again, when he was
to enter into his sufferings, Peter's zeal was so high that he would have
rescued him out of their hands if he could, and have kept him from suffering ; therefore Christ in a special manner speaks to him.

Obs. To hinder one in any good, to hinder one in suffering when
God calls him to it (though out of a foolish pity), how great an evil is it !
With what a slight eye did Peter look upon this thing of Christ. He
thought it was only a carrying of him to prison, and that the life of a man
should be taken away. He saw not into the bottom of it ; he was ignorant
of the scope of all this, viz., that it was the saving of the world. Peter,
though otherwise a good man, and a believer, he understood it not.

2. Christ speaks this to Peter, not only to lay open his sin in hindering
him, but to lay open his own spirit. ' The cup which my Father hath given
me, shall I not drink ?' He doth not say, A necessity is laid upon me to
drink this cup. He doth not say simply, My Father hath commanded me
to drink it, but ' Shall I not drink it ?' It is a speech that implies that his
spirit knew not how to do otherwise than obey his Father, as if there were
such a natural principle in him, such an instinct that he could not choose
but do it. Even just as Joseph said, Gen. xxxix. 9, ' How shall I do this
great wickedness, and sin against God ?' So Christ here, The cup which
my Father hath given me, how shall I but drink it ? It implies the highest
willingness that can be. For still you shall find this to be John's design,
to hold forth the willingness of Christ to suffer ; that is his project. Therefore he singles out a speech that the other evangelists omit, which most of
all holds it forth. He mentions not the necessity because of the law and
because of his duty, or because the scriptures must be fulfilled. Others

had done that ; but shall my Father give me a cup, and shall I not drink it ? He doth here shew that he doth fulfil the commandment more out of love than any other principle, that he was led by the greatest spirit of ingenuity that could be, for I know not a speech of greater ingenuity than this is, ' The cup that my Father hath given me, shall I not drink it ?'

My brethren, to fulfil the law of God out of a principle of love and ingenuity, it is a higher way of fulfilling it than merely to aim at the letter. Christ indeed had an eye to the command, yet that was not it that principally moved him. It is true, saith he, there is a necessity laid upon me, and the Scriptures cannot else be fulfilled, yet above all this I have a principle in me that moves me. It is my Father, he hath commanded this cup to me, how shall I not but drink of it ? There is a further principle than merely obedience to the law that leads on a godly man, and led on Jesus Christ to obedience. For love, it is the fulfilling of the law; so it was in Christ, and so in his apostles, and in all his saints.

You read in other evangelists, that when Christ was in the garden, but a matter of half an hour before, he had earnestly prayed to his Father that this cup might pass. But when once God had set it on upon his spirit that it was his will that he should drink it, and that it was impossible in respect of his decree that it should pass from him, when God, I say, had intimated this to him in prayer, and he had submitted to it, then he says, ' Not my will, but thy will be done.' Now, you see how firm and strong his resolution was. He that had prayed against it before, when once he knew God's will, and submitted to it, now he longs to drink of it : ' Shall I not drink,' saith he, ' of the cup that my Father hath given me ?' Will you have me go and overthrow the answer I have had of my prayers ? Shall I break that resolution I have taken up and expressed in my prayer ? Shall I not drink of the cup, when I have yielded and submitted to my Father ?

When thou seest God's will determined, or when God hath cast thy heart in prayer one way, and he calls thee to suffer, and hath brought thy heart to yield, Oh! learn then to keep thy heart in that frame, to continue thy resolution, have no more risings against it ! Christ, you see, had not but the highest ingenuity that ever was to it.

Therefore now, you that seek to God at any time by prayer for anything, and you have an answer, you have a resolution drawn forth in prayer, you have a bent, a bias of spirit clapped upon you in seeking God in some particular business, keep to it, hold to it. It is a mighty engagement to have had a man's spirit so and so framed in prayer, when a man can say, I have been afore God in prayer, and my spirit hath submitted, and I have been brought to such a resolution. Oh! take heed of. breaking such resolutions ! You have the highest engagement in the world to continue in them. Therefore, when you pray, mind those engagements that are in your hearts to God in prayer, and keep to them. Christ he came new from prayer now ; he had prayed that the cup might be removed, when God had once set it upon his spirit that it was his will he should drink of it, and he had submitted to it, and resolved upon it, you hear of no more complaints, yea, you hear complaints on the contrary, that he should be hindered in doing it. How often, my brethren, do we come before God, and express ourselves against such and such a sin, we submit ourselves to such and such a way of self-denial, but when we are come from before God, how do our minds alter ! You see Christ's did not in the greatest point that ever was ; when he once had submitted, saith he, I have submitted, and 'shall I not drink it?' He had not the least rising thought against it afterward. We come and engage ourselves against such a sin to God in prayer, and go away with our eyes scarce dry, and are tempted to it again. Oh! how should we think with ourselves, Shall I do that which I have prayed against? which I have engaged myself against? This was Christ's case here: 'shall I not drink it?' saith he. Nay, it is more emphatical, 'The cup that my Father hath given me, shall I not drink it?' He turns the words, the phrase is set in such a posture as hath the most emphasis that can be.

The cup which my Father hath given me. His passion is called a cup; so he himself calleth it, Mat. xx. 22 and Mark x. 38, 'Are ye able to drink of the cup that I shall drink of?' speaking of his passion. And it is called a cup, not only because it was his *demensum,* the portion that was allotted him by his Father; for the manner of the ancients in feasts* was to set every man his cup, or portion of drink that was allotted him, by his trencher, as it were; as we now set bread, so they had every one his cup, every one his *quantum* or portion. And so indeed in Scripture, any portion of affliction or suffering that God doth set out to men, it is called a cup; as in Jer. xxv. 17, 'I took the cup, and I did give it from the Lord into the hands of all the nations, and made them all to drink of it.' So in Ezek. xxi. 31–33, and in Hab. ii. 16. And in many other places you have the cup put for the portion or measure of an affliction. But, I say, he calls it a cup, not only because it was his portion, but I rather think that which is in this place aimed at is, that it was his meat and drink to do the will of his Father. For, you see, Christ is hearty in submitting to his Father: It is the cup, saith he, which my Father hath given me, which speech (as I said afore) expresseth the highest willingness. Now, in John iv. 34, he saith, 'My meat and drink is to do the will of my Father, and to finish his work;' and he looks upon this cup, when once he had prayed over it, as that which his Father had given him to drink; and therefore as it was meat for him to do his will, so it was drink to him, it was pleasant to him (in some respect sweetened by an angel) to take this cup and drink it off.

Obs. 1. First you see the sovereignty of God, to dispose of what cup he is pleased you shall have in your lifetime; which, you see, Jesus Christ here submitteth unto. For a cup it is not only taken for a portion of evil things, but for a portion of good things; and God disposeth unto several men several cups, and of several sizes, as he pleaseth. It is certain that the bitterest cup that ever was was disposed of unto Jesus Christ, therefore no man needs complain.

Obs. 2. Secondly, Christ did not look to what the Jews did, or the Roman band that was with them, that were now round about him, he eyes not them; but still he looks to God, eyes him: 'It is the cup which my Father hath given me.' Peter, you see, he looked only at the Jews as his adversaries. No; Peter (saith he), it is my Father's cup, there is a higher hand in it. So should we do in all our actions; as Job did when he said (Job i. 21), 'It is God that hath given, and God that hath taken away.' 'God hath bid him curse,' saith David of Shimei, 2 Sam. xvi. 10; 'therefore what have I to do with you, ye sons of Zeruiah?' So here Christ carries himself. This is from my Father (says he), I will not have to do with these Jews; it is true I fall into these men's hands, but it is the counsel of my Father; as Acts ii. 23. This Christ looks to; and so, I say, should we do in all our sufferings.

* Stuckius' Antiq. Convival, lib. iii. c. 13.

Obs. 3. Thirdly, It is the cup which *my Father* hath given me. Christ in his sufferings doth not look upon God as a judge. Nor do not you, my brethren, in any of your afflictions. Suppose you see the affliction answering your sin, yet look not upon God as a judge in it, but as a father. It is the cup which my Father hath given me, saith he; and we are to be conformable to him in afflictions. The greatest and bitterest sufferings be sweetened to us, looked upon as coming from a father. It was so with Christ; when he looks upon this as a cup given him by his Father, he looks upon it as his drink, and it is a pleasure to him to drink it off.

Obs. 4. Fourthly, Every man hath a set portion of affliction, every man hath his cup. It is the cup my Father hath given me to drink. Christ himself had his cup, his set quantity; he had a cup that was answerable and proportionable to the sins of those he suffered for; God put in a quantity for every man's sin, and Christ drank it off to the bottom; the sins and the wrath due for them was all wrung into this cup which Christ drunk off, and drunk off heartily. If thou hadst drunk off that cup, there had been eternity in the bottom, and thou couldst never have wrung out the dregs of it; but he drinks it off heartily, and he thinks much of Peter that went about to hinder him of it: ' Shall I not drink of the cup which my Father hath given me ? '

How is his Father said to have given it him ?

By decreeing it aforehand; for he had not yet taken it: he had entered into it indeed, he had tasted of it in the garden, but he was going on to taste more of it; and that cup which his Father by his decree allotted to him, he willingly takes and submits to it.

And let me add this, whatsoever cup it be that God in thy life affords thee, take it, and go drink it off heartily; for whether thou wilt or no, if it be a cup he hath given thee, thou shalt drink it. In Jer. xxv. 15, ' Go, saith God, to all the nations, and say unto them all, Drink ye of this cup; and if any of the nations shall refuse to drink it, tell them, that my people have drunk it, therefore they shall drink it.' Do not therefore only make a necessity of it, and because of a necessity submit, but do it out of that ingenuity that Christ did here; he did not submit merely out of necessity, but with all the willingness in the world, ' The cup which my Father hath given me, shall I not drink it ? '

CHAPTER VIII.

How Christ was taken and bound by those who came to apprehend him, and was thus led away by them, as the victims, or sacrifices, used to be to the altar.—That even this his binding hath an influence on our being loosened from those chains, wherein sin hath fettered us.

Now beginneth the first of Christ his outward sufferings, his sufferings from men; he had suffered from his Father before, in the garden, where now he was, when he sweat drops of blood.

Verse 12. ' *Then the band, and the captain, and officers of the Jews, took Jesus, and bound him.*'

In these words there are two things considerable :

1. The persons taking.

2. The person taken.

The persons taking, are the band, and the captain, and the officers of the Jews.

The person taken, is Christ himself.

And then here is what they did with him, they took him, and they bound him. ' Then the officers, and the captain, and the band took Jesus, and bound him.'

It is said that all of them took him. Certainly all of them at that instant could not lay hold upon him ; but his being taken is ascribed unto them all, because they all rushed upon him at once with a violence. His throwing of them down backward afore had made them afraid, therefore they break forth with violence, and they did all environ him and compass him about, and in that respect it is said they all took him.

You shall find in Ps. xxii. (which psalm we may indeed call a crucifix, it being as clear a story of the crucifying of Christ as Mat. xxvi. is) ; in that psalm, the first thing in the story of his sufferings mentioned there (for the rest are prayers) is, ' Many bulls have compassed me, strong bulls of Bashan have beset me round,' so ver. 12. And again, ver. 16, ' Dogs have compassed me, the assembly of the wicked have enclosed me.' The title of that psalm (as some out of the Hebrew read it) it is ' the hind of the morning ; ' so he calls himself, and they like so many hounds here came round about him in a ring to apprehend him : ' Dogs,' saith he, ' have compassed me,' which hath an allusion to the title of the psalm.

Here is likewise, you see, a particular mention of the persons, here is the band, and the captain, and the officers of the Jews ; both Jews and Gentiles, which I shall give you observations upon anon.

There is one particle, which is a very small one, but there is much in it: *Then*. ' Then the captain, and the band, and the officers of the Jews took Jesus.' Some read it (and rightly too) ' *Therefore* the captain,' &c. Why therefore ? Because that he had afore offered himself willingly to them, they could not else have taken him. There is a great deal of emphasis in that little particle, as there is in every tittle of the Scripture. ' No man,' saith he, John x. 18, ' is able to take my life from me except I lay it down.' These men whom he had thrown down to the ground had never been able to have laid hands on him, had he not expressed himself willing. ' Have I not told you,' saith he, ' that I am the man ? ' And he shewed his willingness too in his expression to Peter, ' Shall I not drink of the cup which my Father hath given me to drink ? ' And ' *therefore* the band, and the captain, and the officers of the Jews took Jesus, and bound him.'

All the other evangelists do not tell us that they bound him when they first took him. Matthew tells us indeed, chap. xxvii. 2, that they sent him bound from Caiaphas, the high priest's hall, to the common hall to Pilate. But that he was bound at the first taking, and that by them that took him, we are beholden to John for this circumstance. Now, the reasons of their binding him (I speak now by way of historical interpretation of the words) are these.

1. Because Judas had bid them (as Matthew tells us) to hold him fast, ' Whomsoever I shall kiss,' saith he, ' that same is he, hold him fast,' Mat. xxvi. 48. For Judas he knew the power of Christ, he was privy to his going through the midst of a whole press of men when they would have thrown him down from off the brow of a hill ; therefore, saith he, when you take him, hold him fast ; and therefore they bind him, and they took him and bound him with that cruelty, that the disciples all ran away.

2. They bound him likewise as one that was worthy of death, and so

thereby to prejudge his sentence. Such the Jews did use to bind, as Jerome says. And it was that which is mentioned, ver. 24, as one great ingredient that had influence into Peter's denial of him, and persisting in it the second time, that he was sent bound from Annas, and continued still bound afore Caiaphas, and so thereby saw there was no hope for him of life, and so the more easily drawn and tempted to deny him.

3. They bound him likewise that they might cast shame upon him, that they might lead him bound, which was proper to malefactors. And, 2 Sam. iii. 33, 34, David's speech of Abner implies it : 'Died Abner as a fool, as a malefactor ? Thy hands were not bound, nor thy feet put into fetters.' Now our dear and blessed Lord and Redeemer, he died like a vile person in outward appearance ; his hands and his feet were bound, at least his hands were bound. And that which might further move them to deal in this manner the more violently with him, was the fetters that he had cast upon them. And therefore in Ps. ii. 1–3 (which Peter quoteth in Acts iv. 25, and applies to the crucifying of Christ), he mentioneth that as the reason : 'Why do the heathen rage, and the people imagine a vain thing ?' They are mightily provoked; why ? 'Come let us break their bands asunder.' Christ and his disciples had extremely bound them and their consciences ; now they are even with him, they clap fetters and bands upon him.

4. They did it likewise in a way of trophy ; and therefore you shall find in Mat. xxvii. 2, when they had bound him, they led him away from the high priest's house, in a kind of triumph, to Pilate the governor.

So you have the historical opening of the words, 'They took Jesus and bound him.' And in all this, and so likewise in whatsoever befell Christ in his sufferings, there was a further mystical meaning, which I term so in respect of those hidden ends in it. Therefore in the next place we will consider what was the mystery of all this. There was nothing befell Christ in his passion, but it was both to fulfil prophecies, and it was for something answering thereunto in us as the cause thereof ; and in the merit of it, and the benefit by it redounding to us, it hath a suitable influence into something about ourselves.

First, All that befell Christ was to fulfil the types and prophecies that went of him. The great and most eminent type of Christ in his sufferings was Isaac, who was the son of the promise, as Christ was the promised seed. And in Heb. xi., the apostle makes him a figure of Christ's resurrection ; and as in his resurrection, so in his offering to death. Now the first thing that Abraham did to Isaac, when he was to offer him up as a sacrifice, was, he took him and bound him ; so saith Gen. xxii. 9. And Christ here, whom Isaac typified, in his death as well as in his delivery from death, was bound.

The sacrifices of the old law, they were first led bound to the priest, and then bound to the horns of the altar, and there slain. So was Christ here.

And so for Christ his taking; for I here put both together. The ark was a type of Christ, and that you know was taken by the Philistines ; so is Christ now.

Adam, he likewise was his type. There was an allusion in the sufferings of Christ in the garden, unto the first temptation in a garden. Adam, you know, sinned in a garden. Christ he suffered in a garden ; there doth the agony meet him, and there he was taken. And what was the first outward act of sin ? How was it put forth ? Gen. iii. 6, 'The woman took of the fruit of the tree' (having first plucked it off with her hands), 'and gave it to her husband, and he took it and did eat thereof.' In answering to this,

Christ, the second Adam, his hands are bound while he was here in the garden. And as his being bound, so also this his being taken by them was foresignified. Thus in Mat. xxvi. 56, when it is said they took him, it is added, 'That the Scriptures of the prophets might be fulfilled.' Now do but look in the margin of your Bibles, what scripture is quoted there ? What is the place of Scripture that the translators of the Bible refer to in that verse ? You shall find it to be Lam. iv. 20, and there it is said, 'The breath of our nostrils, the anointed of the Lord' (the Messiah, the Christ, for so anointed signifies in the Hebrew, the Christ of the Lord), 'he was taken in their pit, of whom we said, under his shadow we shall live among the heathen.' This book of the Lamentation, though it was made upon occasion of the captivity, yet because the foundation of the captivity was laid in the taking away of that good king Josiah—for after his death that people had never a good day, they never thrived—so that book relates to him. And it is clear that the Lamentations were made in relation to Josiah, as well as to the captivity, by that in 2 Chron. xxxv. 25, 'And Jeremiah lamented for Josiah' (and these Lamentations in this book, you know, are the Lamentations of Jeremiah) ; 'and all the singing men and the singing women spake of Josiah in their lamentations to this day, and made them an ordinance in Israel, and behold they are written in the Lamentations ;' that is, in the book of the Lamentations. Now of Josiah it is said, 'He was taken in their pit,' so we translate it ; but others, and the Septuagint agrees with it too, 'He was taken in their sins.' The sins of that people were the cause of his death, which is said to be in the valley of Megiddo, 2 Chron. xxxv. 32.

But whether is Josiah a type of Christ or no, that our translators should refer the taking of Christ to the fulfilling of this prophecy in the Lamentations ?

For that you have Zech. xii. 10, 11. He saith there, that he 'will pour upon the house of David, and the inhabitants of Jerusalem, the spirit of prayer and supplication' (speaking of the time when they should acknowledge Jesus Christ to be the Messiah) and (saith he) 'they shall look upon me whom they have pierced' (meaning the Messiah), 'and they shall mourn for him,' &c. And ver. 11, 'In that day shall there be a great mourning in Jerusalem, as the mourning of Hadadrimmon, in the valley of Megiddon.' Now that mourning there was for Josiah, for there he was taken and arrested with a deadly wound, whereof he died, and was taken and slain in the sins of that nation, and to that do our translators refer us ; and you see he was a type of Christ too, he had kept a passover, as Christ had done, a little afore this. They promised themselves to live safely under his shadow, even as the disciples promised themselves that Christ would presently restore the kingdom unto Israel ; but he was taken in our sins, and our sins were the bands that fettered him.

Secondly, As all this was done to fulfil the types and prophecies of him, so we shall see that our deserts were the cause of it, and that his being bound hath an influence to loose us from something with which we were bound. For there was nothing befell Christ in these sufferings, nothing was done to him, but what answers to something which we had done, and which was to be done toward us.

1. Our sins were the cause of his binding. Therefore in Ps. xl. (which also is a psalm of Christ, for it is, part of it, quoted by the apostle in Heb. x. and applied unto Christ, ' Sacrifices and offerings thou wouldst not have'), saith he at ver. 12, ' Innumerable evils have taken hold upon me; mine

iniquities have compassed me about.' It is plain, my brethren, that Christ speaks this psalm of himself; he reckoned all our sins as his own, and by virtue of our sins encompassing us about, and taking hold of us (which in the garden they did) it is, that these men take hold of Christ, and bind him, he standing now in our stead. For the truth is, Christ he could, like Samson, have broken all these cords asunder. What weakened him? It was because he was fettered with our sins. 'Mine iniquities,' saith he (confessing ours to be his), 'have taken hold upon me;' and therefore these came all about him like bees, like dogs, and seize upon him. We were Satan's captives, therefore was he theirs. In sinning against God we break all bands, as the expression is, Jer. v. 5, therefore is he bound. Our sins took hold of him first, and then the band and the officers had power to take him and bind him.

2. Consider the answerable fruit and benefit of it arising to us. Hereby we were all bondslaves to sin and Satan: 2 Peter ii. 19, ' Of whom a man is overcome, of the same is he brought in bondage.' We were led captive by Satan at his will, so saith the apostle, 2 Tim. ii. 26, Rom. vii. 23. Sin it ensnareth a man: Prov. v. 22, ' His own iniquities shall take the wicked himself, and he shall be holden with the cords of his sins.' And we were not only in the bands of iniquity (as the expression is Acts viii. 23), but we should have been reserved, as the devils and his angels are, in chains of darkness. Such an expression the Scripture hath in the epistle of Jude: ver. 6, he saith, ' The angels which kept not their first estate, he hath reserved in everlasting chains, under darkness, unto the judgment of the great day;' and Peter, Epistle 1, chap. iii. ver. 19, speaks of spirits in prison, which were once disobedient in the days of Noe. Chains of the everlasting wrath of God, and of guilt, should have bound us over to the great day, bound, and bound hand and foot, as you have it in Mat. xxii. 13, ' Take him, and bind him hand and foot, and cast him into everlasting darkness.' This was our condition; and now because we are bound with these chains, to the end that we might be set free and loosed from them, is Christ bound. For it is a certain rule, what should have been done to us, something correspondent was done to Christ; and the virtue and excellency of his person was such, though it was done to his body, it bringeth us freedom from the like due to our souls; and by his being thus bound and led, he himself afterward, when he ascended, led captivity captive. You have a place express to this purpose, and it is a place that plainly speaks of Christ, for it is applied unto him by the apostle in 1 Cor. xv. 55; the place is Hosea xiii. 14, ' I will ransom them from the power of the grave; I will redeem them from death: O death, I will be thy death; O grave, I will be thy destruction.' But what goes before this? See ver. 12, ' The iniquity of Ephraim is bound up.' God had bound up Ephraim and his iniquity together for hell; saith he, I will ransom them. And how doth he ransom them? The truth is, by being bound himself; he standeth bound before God his Father (for he deals with his Father in all this, he doth not deal with the Jews here), and in God's intentions, those fetters that were to be laid upon us were laid upon him, and so he cometh to free us by virtue of himself being bound; and thus as we should have been arraigned before the judgment-seat of God, so was he before Pilate. The analogy holds all along in his sufferings.

Therefore you shall find the scripture follows this metaphor. In Zech. ix. 10, he tells us, by the blood of the covenant we are delivered, being prisoners of hope. And in Isa. lxi. 1, and Luke iv. 18, he is said to be

' anointed to preach liberty to the captives, and the opening of the prison to them that are bound.' And the like you have in Isa. xlii. 7, ' I have given thee for a covenant of the people, &c., to bring out the prisoners from the prison, and them that sit in darkness out of the prison-house.' Hence is it that, when he comes to convert a man to God, he is said to bind the strong man ; Mat. xii. 28. Whence is it that Christ hath this strength in him (I mean meritoriously) ? Because he himself was bound ; it is by virtue of that that the strong man is bound.

3. *Lastly*, Will you consider the heart of Christ all this while ? For under his sufferings it is good to consider that. Certainly Christ's heart was sensible of his sufferings in every particular ; none was ever so sensible as he. Why, you shall find how his heart took it, by that speech of his whilst they were a-binding of him. Matthew tells us, chap. xxvi. 55, that he said to the multitude at that time, ' Are ye come out as against a thief, with swords and staves for to take me ? I sat daily with you teaching in the temple, and you laid no hold on me.' And now they did. And Luke he tells us further, chap. xxii. 52, ' Jesus said unto the chief priests, and captains of the temple, and the elders, which were come to him, Are ye come out, as against a thief, with swords and staves ?' What ? to bind me as a thief ? To deal so dishonestly with me ? This is mentioned as a thing that grieved him, and soaked into his very soul. The dishonour of it did. So to be bound and led was most dishonourable. Thus 2 Sam. iii. 33, 34, David, when he lamented over Abner, expresseth it, ' Died Abner as a fool dies ?' That is, as a bold person, a malefactor, by justice, and law convicted : ' Thy hands were not bound, nor thy feet put into fetters,' as of malefactors it was used to be ; yet this was done to Christ : his hands were bound in, as of a bold person, and so he was led to death. So in Judas his betraying of him, What ? thou ? saith he, my familiar friend, that didst eat bread with me, dost thou lift up thy heel against me ? That was it that did sink into his spirit. And in that Ps. xl. 13, you shall see how this act of theirs pierced his soul, ' Mine iniquities have taken hold upon me ; innumerable evils have compassed me about, so that I am not able to look up.' His iniquities took hold of his very soul, while they were encompassing him about like dogs. And Ps. xxii. 12, ' Be not far from me, for trouble is near.' He saw them coming. All this affected the heart of Christ ; for the psalms lay open his heart, as the evangelists do the outward story. So much now both for the historical opening of the words, and also for that which is the mystery of it. I will now come to an observation or two from all this that was done to our Lord and Saviour Christ, and from the persons that did it.

Obs. 1. First, from the persons that did it, they are, you see, all here enumerated, ' The band, and the captain, and the officers of the Jews.' And Luke saith, there were some of the chief priests there (and by chief priests were meant the heads of the Levites, of which there were twentyfour), and the captains of the temple, as well as the captain of the Roman band, and some of the elders of the people. And it is said of them all, that they took him (though all could not lay hold on him), because they all consented to it, because they all gathered round in a ring about him, that he might not escape. Observe, that God takes notice particularly of every one that has any hand (yea, he doth ascribe the act to them if their consent be but to it) in persecuting his people, as he did here of these that persecuted Christ, for there is the same reason of both ; they are all named, all the sorts of them are enumerated. He takes notice of any one that doth but cry Aha! at any thing that is done against a child of God ; as Edom that cried Aha! and poor Tyrus, in Ezek. xxvi. 2, because she cried Aha! and said she should be replenished, she should have the trade now Israel was destroyed, God takes notice of it, and threatens ruin to her for it.

Obs. 2. But, secondly, God did so order it, that in all the sufferings of Christ, both Jew and Gentile had a hand in them, in every particular action that did befall him. Here was the captain of the Roman band, and the officers of the Jews, and here were the high priests and elders of the people, at the taking of·him ; both the ecclesiastical and civil state. So likewise when he was condemned (for the evangelists carry it along through all the story), there was Pilate the governor, he must have a hand in it; and there was Herod that was the king of Galilee, he was sent to him also ; and there were the Roman soldiers ; and there were the high priest and the rest of that Sanhedrim. Ecclesiastical state, civil state, Jews, Gentiles, all have a hand in every particular of the suffering of Christ.

Obs. 3. Thirdly, From the consideration of Christ's being bound, take this meditation : let no affliction (for all afflictions are called bands by the apostle : ' Remember those that are in bonds, as if ye were bound with them,' Heb. xiii. 3), let no band, I say, be thought too much by you. Be willing to bo bound for Christ, if he call you to suffer ; you see he was willing to be bound for us. And never let the vileness of the persons trouble you, which indeed would even make one's stomach rise, that such should have to do with a man ; consider the Lord of life was apprehended and bound by the basest and vilest sort of men ; for commonly such are those that are employed in such offices. He was taken by the rude soldiers, that certainly handled him rudely and with violence ; for it is said in Zech. xiii. 7, ' I will smite the shepherd, and the sheep shall be scattered.' Now they all ran away when he was bound, therefore they smote him.

Obs. 4. And then again consider, while Christ was bound, all that whole city, the Pharisees and the Jews, they were free. Whilst wicked men do enjoy all liberty and freedom, the church is bound ; so Christ himself was.

Obs. 5. And then further, we should therefore prize all the liberty and freedom that the gospel affords us, because they are all fruits of Christ's being bound ; Christ's being bound was it that purchased all our liberties.

Obs. 6. Lastly, Let the bands of his love draw our hearts, for, as I said afore, he could have broken all these cords, as Samson did those with which he was bound; but the cords of love bound him as well as the cords of our sins. It was these cords fastened him to the cross, more than the nails ; yea, and bound him there more than our sins did,* or else he would never have suffered himself to be bound. As Paul went up bound in the Spirit to Jerusalem, bound up in the bands of love, which made him willing to be bound outwardly, therefore he calls himself the prisoner of Christ, and to have the bands of Christ upon him, to be the bondman, the *vinctus* of Christ ; so doth Christ, he is bound with the cords of love, so they are called : Hosea xi. 4, ' I drew them with the cords of a man, with the bands of love.' Oh let the love of Christ bind us and constrain us (as the phrase is 2 Cor. v. 14), to bring every high thought into subjection, into captivity unto him ; so he was for us. And so much for this first circumstance, or this first beginning of the outward sufferings of our Lord and Saviour Christ, his being bound : ' And they bound him.'

* Qu. ' our sins bound him more than the cords did ' ?—Ed.

Verse 13. ' *And they led him away to Annas first: for he was father-in-law to Caiaphas, which was the high priest that same year.*'

The Scripture doth put much, as upon his being bound, so upon his being led away. And, my brethren, as we go along in opening of these sufferings of Christ, carry in your thoughts still the person to whom all this was done ; it was our Lord and Saviour Jesus Christ. Every thing he did in a way of suffering, how great must it be, think you, when nothing befell him but what was appointed him by his Father, and that in relation to the taking away of our sins !

They led him away. The truth is, his being led up and down is noted in the story as one eminent thing in his suffering, and therefore is not to be passed by. Those that have made the topography of Jerusalem and those places, do account it to be seven miles that he was led up and down from first to last afore he was crucified, which was an exceeding great indignity to him. They hurried him first from the garden to Annas's house ; from thence (as another evangelist tells us) he was led to Caiaphas ; Matthew tells us he was led from thence to Pilate, to the common hall ; from Pilate he was led to Herod ; from Herod he was led back to Pilate again ; from Pilate, when he had sentenced him, he was led to the cross. Thus was our Lord and Saviour Christ tossed up and down, and there is particular mention made of them all, which could not choose but put him to a great deal of pain and trouble.

And, my brethren, do but consider, do but think of any person that is a person of worth, that should be hurried thus up and down from place to place, with his hands manacled, all the people following him, using all manner of indignities to him ; think of one that you praise and value, either for the gospel's sake or otherwise ; I say, do but think of such a one, and then behold our Lord and our Saviour Christ in all his tossings and leadings up and down. I remember there is this expression in one of the psalms,* 'I am as a grasshopper,' saith he, because he was thus hurried and turmoiled from place to place, his heart was sensible of this.

But what is the mystery of this ? For still let us look to the inward part of it, as well as to the history of itself.

First, There was a type in it, for every sacrifice was first led to the high priest, and then offered, Lev. xvii. 5. So Christ, being to be made a sacrifice for sin, he is carried to the high priest. In the way he goes to Annas, indeed, but afterwards from him he was led to Caiaphas, who was high priest that year. And to make up the type more full, which is a thing exceedingly observable, it is said in Is. liii. 7, that after our sins were laid upon him, and that the iniquities of us all did take hold on him, ' he was led as a sheep to the slaughter.' Now you must know that the garden from whence he was led stood at the foot of the mount of Olives, beyond the brook Cedron ; and the gate which was next to that place, through which he was to go into the city, was called the sheep-gate, for it was nigh the temple, which stood on that side of Jerusalem ; and the sheep and oxen (but especially the sheep, for they sacrificed most of them) that were to be sacrificed, were fed in the meadows and fields of Cedron ; and from thence they were led through that gate to the temple to be sacrificed, which therefore was called the sheep-gate. To make up the type therefore more full, and that you may see how the Scripture opens itself in these things, he is led

* It is not easy to ascertain the expression that the author refers to. There is no such expression in our version, nor do we know of any that could be so rendered. —Ed.

as a sheep to the slaughter, to be a sacrifice for sin (for so the prophet saith he was), even through the sheep-gate.

My brethren, 'all we like sheep have gone astray' (so the prophet saith), and because we had taken our wills in sin, and went whither we would, therefore Christ is bound and led away. It was all because of our wanderings. He was led away as a sheep to the slaughter, therefore, in Heb. xiii. 20, it is said he was brought back again, he having been first led away as here to death, as he was brought back again through the resurrection; it is a phrase that hath relation to his being led away.

How are we tossed to and fro, hurried up and down with divers lusts, with every wind of our inordinate affections! Our Lord and Saviour Christ was therefore led from place to place, posted up and down.

And in all these leadings of his, God still would have both the civil and ecclesiastical state to have a hand and some interest in every sort of his sufferings. He was led to Annas, that had been high priest, and then to Caiaphas, that was the present high priest—they were the chief of the church, as it may be called—and then to Pilate, the Roman governor, and then to Herod, the king of Galilee. All the powers that were then in Jerusalem and over Jerusalem, and in those countries, he was brought afore them all, that they might all have a hand and a concurrence in his ruin, that God might make his sufferings every way complete, that all these might cast dishonour and disgrace upon him. For as honour depends upon the honourer—that is truly honour when a person of worth honoureth one—so God would have the disgrace and contempt that was cast upon Christ to depend upon the worth of the persons that dishonoured him. Therefore, whatever was excellent in that state, either of kingly power or ecclesiastical, whatsoever pretended to wisdom or justice, or learning, or religion, God ordered it that all these should have a hand in the condemnation of Christ, and so they had. The eminency of learning and religion was amongst the chief priests, they professed it and pretended to it; of justice, in Pilate; of excellency and kingly power, in Herod. All these concurred. Therefore, if the saints in after ages find that they are condemned by all sorts, let them not wonder at it.

And, lastly, he was led out of the garden, whither he used to go for the enjoyment of communion with his Father (for the evangelists say that to that place he did often resort to pray); and indeed it was his paradise, where he had infinite sweet fellowship and communion with God. Now, as Adam was driven out of the garden, out of paradise, where he had communion with God, as a punishment for his sin, so is our Lord and Saviour Christ led out of this garden, which, I say, was to him a paradise, and carried to die and to offer up himself a sacrifice for sin. And so much now for his leading: 'they led him.'

To Annas first, for he was father-in-law to Caiaphas, which was the high priest that same year.

For the opening of the historical meaning of these words, I shall do two things.

1. Shew who this Annas was, as the text here holds him forth.

2. Open the reasons why he was led first to him.

1. Who he was. Josephus, who writes the story of these times, calls him Annanas. Certainly he was the greatest man amongst the Jews (of a Jew), and of the most illustrious family, which will appear thus. He himself had been high priest formerly: so you have it, Luke iii. 1, 'In the fifteenth year of Tiberius, Annas and Caiaphas being high priests,

the word of the Lord came unto John,' &c. And the high priest was the supremest officer, and in highest place among the Jews, though the Romans had the civil power in their hands. Here, you see, his son-in-law Caiaphas, who married his daughter, or otherwise his son-in-law, was high priest after him, himself still living; and after Caiaphas, Josephus tells us, that Eleazar, a son of his own, was high priest aiso. So that his family was the greatest family among the Jews that lived at Jerusalem, being thus greatened by having the high priesthood successively amongst them, for so they had ; therefore, in Acts iv. 2, you read of Annas and Caiaphas, and John and Alexander, and as many as were of the kindred of the high priest, were gathered together against the apostles at Jerusalem. They followed their old trade still; and as they had their hands imbrued in the blood of Christ, so in the apostles' too. Now, to this man is our Lord and Saviour first brought.

2. Why brought to Annas first? Some say because he being so great a man, and his house lying in the way to Caiaphas (as indeed it did, if we may believe the new description of Jerusalem, and the relation of those that have visited it, for they say we have first shewn you the house of Annas, and then the house of Caiaphas), he was therefore led thither first. But surely that is not all the reason. It is a circumstance not mentioned by any of the evangelists but by John, and therefore here must be some other ground for their leading of him first to the house of Annas. For we read in Mat. xxvi. 57, and in Mark xiv. 53, that all the chief priests, and the elders, and the scribes, were assembled at Caiaphas his house, attending the issue of Judas his plot, and waiting when Christ should be brought thither. For them therefore to interrupt their going directly to Caiaphas his house, where all the council was set, and to carry him first to the house of Annas, it must needs be for some special reason. To me therefore there are these two reasons of it.

The first is that which is expressly mentioned by John himself here in the text, for (saith he) he was father-in-law to Caiaphas ; which implies that Caiaphas, either because he honoured his father-in-law, who was the head of that great family, had given some secret order to the officers to lead him first thither, or rather indeed, because they would gratify that great man, who was the chief of them that had been high priests, and withal because they would gratify Caiaphas too, whom they knew they should please by doing this honour to his father-in-law. They carried him to him as a sight, as a spectacle. Lo, here we have him that is the great enemy to the high priest's office, that would subvert the law, and pull down the temple; this is the prey we have looked long for. And as in a way of gratification Pilate afterward sent him to Herod, so in a way of like gratification he is here carried to Annas first, sent to him as a gift to cheer and glad his heart. As in Rev. xi. 10, in allusion to the death of Christ (for that chapter carries on that allusion), speaking of the witnesses being killed in that place where our Lord was crucified, he saith, ' They shall rejoice over them, and make merry, and shall send gifts one to another, because these two prophets tormented them ;' so here, when they had gotten Christ, that had tormented them so, they were so glad they had got him, that in merriment Caiaphas gives order to have him carried to Annas, as a gift and gratification to him; and so Pilate sent him to Herod. Thus to shew their joy and triumph, they send our Lord and Saviour Christ thus bound from one to another. Lo, here is the man that would destroy the law, and then all our honour must down; we have him now fast enough. For indeed there is nothing that more pleaseth the revenge of people malicious against Christ or against his saints, than to see them in their hands, and to see them under, and to see them down. ' Come,' say they in Ps. ii. 3, ' let us break their bonds, and cast away their cords from us.' And certainly this circumstance is on purpose mentioned by John, as an aggravation of the sufferings of Christ, that they not only carried him to the high priest, but to gratify this wretched man, that was his desperate and most deadly enemy, whom they knew not only hated him, but that of all other men this sight of Christ being taken and bound would be most acceptable to him, they carry him to his house first of all. This, I say, aggravateth the sufferings of Christ the more.

But, secondly, he was carried thither also that there might be an approbation visible before all the people, of Annas his approving of the fact, he being the greatest family of all the rest amongst the Jews. Therefore the 24th verse of this chapter tells us, that Annas sent him bound to Caiaphas the high priest; that was all he did; he did not command them to unloose him, but approved what they had done in taking and binding him, and in a way of approbation sent him bound to the high priest's hall, which was a matter of great prejudice unto Christ, and served a little also to take the envy off from Caiaphas.

My brethren, what a great deal of do is here about a poor man, in view a carpenter's son! And how glad were the great ones of the world when they had got him down! And so it hath been in all ages, the getting down of a poor saint, it hath been the greatest glory to men carnal, as if they had done so great a matter. When they have gotten the witnesses down, as one day they will, they make merry and send gifts one to another. The poor disciples all this while were a-weeping, while they were making merry; so Christ himself said it should be : John xvi. 20, ' The world shall make merry, but you shall weep.'

If therefore at any time we should be made spectacles unto men for Christ's sake, and should be thus served as Christ was, than which there is nothing more grievous to a great spirit, for misery and shame is more than death to a king, and Saul would not fall into the hands of the Philistines, lest they mock me, saith he, 1 Sam. xxxi. 4 ; if, I say, any of us should be so served, made a spectacle to angels and men, as the apostle saith, 1 Cor. iv. 7, do but remember how they led our Lord and Saviour Christ up and down as a trophy, as a sight to cheer and gratify those that were his enemies. So much for this, that he was sent to Annas first, that was father-in-law to Caiaphas. Of Caiaphas it is said,

He was high priest that same year. There are some that would make both Annas and Caiaphas to have been high priests together, because in that place, Luke iii. 2, it is said that John did baptize in the time when ' Annas and Caiaphas were high priests.' But the meaning of that is this, that they were high priests in their order ; in the beginning of John's preaching Annas was high priest, and after him succeeded Caiaphas.

But why is it said he was high priest that same year ?

It is a thing which John observeth, and none else. He useth that phrase by way of emphasis; you have it twice repeated in the 11th chapter: ver. 49, ' Caiaphas being high priest that same year;' and ver. 51, ' He being high priest that year.' And you see it noted here, and noted with an emphasis. Now that it should be twice noted in one chapter, within the compass of two or three verses, and here again, there must be some special reason for it. It is not that the high priest's office did go year by year, as mayors in incorporate towns do with us, a new one chose every year. . It is clear by the story of Josephus, that Caiaphas was seven years (some say more) high priest. It is therefore added, ' He was high priest that same year,' though he was more years besides, yet it fell out that he should be high priest that year, when under his authority, and by his power in a more especial manner, and by his counsel, the Lord of life should be crucified.

And yet withal, 2. It is to note and to hold up this before our eyes, the great corruption that was about the priest's office when Christ was crucified; for in Num. xxxv. 25, and so in Josh. xx. 6, you shall find that according to God's institution the high priests were not to be removed, but he was to continue in that office during his life. And likewise he was to be the eldest son of the family of Aaron. Now to shew that this was out of course; for the truth is, the Jews being oppressed by the Syrian kings, and afterwards by the Romans, they sold the high priesthood as themselves pleased, and put in new ones as often as they would, contrary to the institution of God at first; to shew, I say, the corruption that was then amongst them, this is particularly noted with an emphasis, ' Caiaphas was high priest that same year, though Annas, that had been high priest, was yet alive.'

To give you an observation or two from this. ' He was high priest that same year:' and if you read John xi. 51, ' By reason that he was high priest that year, he prophesied that Jesus should die for that nation.

The *observation* I make from thence is this : that if a man be in a place that is an office instituted by God, though he came into it corruptly, and is not such a one as ought to be in it, yet whilst he is in ¦it, God doth more or less accompany him according to his own institution. This instance here is clear for this ; for it is certain that the high priests then were not lawfully called to that office ; for there were three circumstances which made their calling unlawful (I do not say unlawful in itself for the substance, but unlawful for the act of calling) : 1. They were not of the tribe of Levi, and of the eldest sons of Aaron ; for so the institution was, it should have gone by birth, as in Exod. xl. 15. 2. They had not the place for their lives, but were changed and altered at pleasure. 3. They were chosen by the Roman prætors, and by Pilate the Roman governor, and so it was ordinarily bought and sold for money. Yet notwithstanding Christ, he comes to that worship which this high priest performed, though he came into the place corruptly; and the acts which he performed (he being in the room of the high priest) were valid. I say, the acts he performed as high priest (though unlawfully called), when he went into the Holy of holies every year, they were acts of worship, and they were valid. Why ? Because the office itself was a place of God's institution. For otherwise Christ had not had opportunities to have fulfilled the whole ceremonial law, if that the going in of this high priest into the Holy of holies had not continued and been in use ; but it is clear it continued ; for it is said, Paul went up to the feast, that is, the great feast, when the priest went into the Holy of holies. Christ, you know, he was to fulfil the whole ceremonial law, which he could not have done if he had not come to that feast which was once a year, for there was a curse upon him that did not, his soul should be cut off from the congregation ; and upon that day the high priest went into the Holy of holies, and performed those great acts of worship, that was to be done. If Christ had not been present at this feast, and at these performances, he had not fulfilled the law ; surely, therefore, when the high priest was doing his office, Christ was present, and did communicate in this case with this priest, and with these Jews; and yet this man had not a lawful calling to the high priesthood, for the manner of it; but because for the substance of his calling it was lawful, and he was in that office, the acts he did were valid. Even as it is in the laws of this kingdom; although Richard the Third came into the place of being king unlawfully, yet because when he was in it, it was that lawful place settled by this state, therefore the earls that he made, or the barons, or the acts of parliament that he confirmed, they were all valid; for whilst he was in that place, the place was it (being that which was settled by the law) that gave a validity to all such acts of his. So it is here. And therefore let it never be said, that because ministers are not oftentimes so called to their places as they ought to be, come not in so rightly as they should, by the choice of those whom it depends upon, that therefore they are not lawful ministers;—lawful in this sense, that the acts they do are valid, and are ministerial acts. And indeed it were a hard case if the lawfulness of all men's being baptized, or receiving the sacrament, or the like, should depend upon the lawfulness of the man's being called to his place. It depends upon the office that Jesus Christ hath instituted in his church, and so far forth as there is anything of his institution, he will follow it with his blessing. The ordinances of Christ, the validity of them doth not depend upon the lawful call of the minister; and therefore it is no argument to say, such a man had an unlawful calling to the ministry in that place where I was baptized, therefore my baptism is invalid. For the act and manner of his call may be unlawful, yet he being in that place, he is for those acts a lawful minister of Christ, and his acts are so accounted by God. So it was here. Caiaphas being in the room of the high priest, the acts he did were acts of the high priest, and were valid. And yet further, to shew that God himself respected him as high priest, God put into his mouth that prophecy; therefore it is said in John xi. 51, 'This spake he not of himself, but being high priest that year, he prophesied.' So that God himself was with him as high priest, though for the manner of his calling to this place he was not lawfully and truly the high priest.

Obs. 2. Then, again, another observation that I may make from hence is this. This Annas, it is said, was father-in-law to Caiaphas. You see now by this, how dangerous it is oftentimes to the souls of others to be linked in affinity with men that are carnal and wicked. How many a man's soul is undone by his father-in-law, or perhaps the father-in-law by the son: or the husband by the wife, and the wife by the husband. In all likelihood these two here, Annas the father-in-law, and Caiaphas the son-in-law, are both mentioned as having drawn one another into this great conspiracy against our Lord and Saviour Christ, and joining the more heartily in it, the one engaging the other in this wicked design. And therefore men should very much consider into what families they marry, for if into a wicked family, it may be an occasion of much evil to them. Men are drawn to much wickedness, or strengthened in much wickedness, by their relations, as Annas and Caiaphas were here for the crucifying of Christ, having this relation of father-in-law and son-in-law.

Obs. 3. Lastly, these two, Annas and Caiaphas, they are here noted out in a peculiar manner above all the rest of the Pharisees, as the most eminent enemies, and those that did most malign our Lord and Saviour Christ. Observe that God takes special and particular notice of those that are the most eminent enemies of Christ and his saints. Still you see Annas and

Caiaphas are mentioned : certainly it is according to their hatred ; these two had a deeper malignity against Christ than other of the Pharisees had ; and therefore you read of them again in Acts iv. 6. Annas the high priest, and Caiaphas, and John, and Alexander, they are all reckoned up, they had their hands imbrued in the blood of Christ, and they go on ; and that is the curse of it, that the same men should finish up their iniquity, by laying hold of the apostles too. And in a more special manner you see there is an emphasis put upon Caiaphas, for it is said, ' He was high priest that same year.' It is noted out as the greatest curse that could befall that wretched man, he having so much malignity in his heart against Christ, that it should be his lot to be then high priest, when he had opportunity enough to vent it. So that men of much malice against the people of God, to them doth God give oftentimes most power, and dignity, and ability to do most mischief. Caiaphas he is put into the high priesthood, and the providence of God ordereth it so that this man had a more special enmity against Christ, as the next words imply : ' It was he that gave the counsel that one man should die for the people,' and that man must be Jesus Christ. And so I come to handle that.

Verse 14, ' Now Caiaphas was he that gave counsel to the Jews, that it was expedient that one man should die for the people.'

It implies that Caiaphas was the first man that made the motion to have Christ put to death, and that with the strongest and most taking plausible reason that could be supposed.

In handling this verse, I shall do two things.

1. Open the words.

2. Give the reasons why they are brought in here.

1. And, first, to open the words. ' Now Caiaphas was he that gave counsel to the Jews, that it was expedient for one man to die for the people.' The words, you see, refer to an act formerly done by him. You are therefore to have recourse to John xi. 49, 50, where you shall find the same thing recorded ; only there it comes in as a prophecy, here as a counsel given by himself. ' You know nothing' (saith he there ; he speaks it like a carnal proud high priest, as if he only had knowledge, taking the glory of this counsel to himself), ' nor consider that it is expedient for us that one man should die for the people, and that the whole nation perish not. And this' (saith John) ' spake he not of himself, but being high priest that year, he prophesied that Jesus should die for that nation.' And yet that he did speak this of himself too, is clear by these words in the text; for it is brought in here as his great sin, and a brand is put upon him for it : This is he, saith the text ; even as a brand was put upon Ahaz, 2 Chron. xxviii. 22, ' This is that king Ahaz,' so, this is that wicked Caiaphas; this is he that was the first contriver, the first man that made the motion, that gave the counsel to have Christ put to death.

It is strange that one and the same act should be from the Spirit of God, and called prophecy, and said not to be spoken of himself, and the same act to be of himself, and called counsel, and one of the greatest sins that hath been committed. But the meaning is this, that however he had a most wicked end in this speech, yet notwithstanding, the Holy Ghost (before he was aware) guided his tongue to speak (though he knew it not) that which was a truth, and indeed a prophecy. ' He spake this not of himself,' saith John, that is, not knowing or intending to prophesy, for as it came from him it was spoken out of spleen, and malice, and hatred unto Christ. And yet he took upon him to speak like a high priest; 'You know nothing at all,' saith he; I am now the high priest, and I deliver this to you as an oracle, 'that it is expedient for one man to die for the people;' and the Holy Ghost intended his words should be spoken as'the high priest. 'This he spake not of himself: but, being high priest that year, he prophesied;' not that the high priests used to prophesy, or that he himself used to prophesy, but being high priest *that year*, an emphasis lies in that, wherein Christ was to be crucified, God raised up that ordinance of high priesthood above the ordinary use of it, he being the highest person in that state. And you see he delivers it as a state axiom, and yet with extreme cunning: 'It is fit,' saith he, 'that one man should die for the people.' He doth not say that it is fit that Jesus should die (he doth not express it so at first), or that this man should die, who is a rebel or a blasphemer, 'but it is fit one man (let it be him or any one else) should die for the nation'; and what is one man's life to the nation? And so consequently he implies, that seeing it is this man's lot to disturb the state, and to endanger it by bringing in the Romans amongst us, it is fittest that he should die, rather than the people should perish. And yet if you mark it (to shew the wickedness of his speech yet further), though he puts a public face upon it, and pretends the preservation of the nation, yet the thing he aimed at was the preservation of the clergy only; and that moved him so much. Saith he, 'You consider nothing at all, that it is expedient for us that one man should die.' 'It is expedient *for us*,' that is his expression; for us that are or shall be high priests; our calling will down unless this man be taken out of the way.

So much for the opening of the words.

Now, *secondly*, to give you the reasons why he (having said it before in chap. xi. 50) brings it in again here in this place.

1. It was to set a brand of maliciousness more eminently upon this Caiaphas than upon any man else; 'and to shew also what an accursed man he was in this, that the motive or the reason that should stick with them all, why they should so fixedly resolve to kill Christ (for, you must know, this speech was first spoken at a consultation they had about taking of him), should come first from him. To set, I say, a note and a brand upon Caiaphas in a more eminent manner, is this circumstance here by the Holy Ghost inserted, he being the most desperate and malicious enemy of Christ amongst all the Pharisees; for certainly God chose out the wickedest man among all the Jews to be in the place of the high priest that year, that he and his father-in-law, Annas, should eminently have their hands in his crucifying.

2. It likewise comes in here to shew upon how slight grounds our Lord and Saviour Christ was crucified; it was merely but upon politic considerations (as to them), and that upon but imaginary suppositions neither, that the nation must perish else; for so as it came from Caiaphas it was meant, though God guided it to be a prophecy. And so it clears the innocency of Christ so much the more, that the high priest himself, in his counsel about putting him to death, should only go upon this politic reason, that it was fit one man should die for the nation. They only did it as a state business, and that, I say, but upon a mere imagination that the Romans would else come and take away their place and nation.

3. It is premised unto all the other sufferings of Christ that follow, and it is inserted here in that passage of the story of his leading to Caiaphas, to shew that there was no equity to be expected in all their proceedings

against him   Why ?   Because they had resolved, before ever they took
him, to put him to death, and that upon a state consideration; and therefore they would be sure to keep to their own resolutions, whether he were
innocent or not innocent, whether they could convict him or not convict
him.   And Caiaphas having spoken so peremptorily, 'Ye know nothing at
all, neither consider that it is expedient for one man to die for the nation,'
he being the great oracle in this business, he would certainly prosecute
Christ, according to his own words; therefore there was no favour to be
expected.   And to this end also doth the Holy Ghost record it here.
    4. But to me the chiefest reason is this.   You know it was foretold of
Christ that he should not die for himself; so you have it in Isa. liii. 4,
'Surely he hath borne our griefs, and carried our sorrows: yet we did
esteem him stricken of God and afflicted;' so did the apostles and those that
beheld him.   It was not for himself that he was stricken and afflicted; no,
there was something else in it, it was for others : 'He hath borne our griefs
and carried our sorrows, and he was wounded for our transgressions,' &c.
Now, to the end that you should not only have a word of Scripture for this,
but a testimony also even from the mouths of the Jews, and from the
mouth of the high priest himself for it, hence, therefore, is the Holy
Ghost so diligent to record this passage, 'that it is expedient that one man
should die for the people;' which, though Caiaphas meant one way, God
meant another way; and therefore it is added, 'and not ,for that nation
only, but that he should gather together in one the children of God that
were scattered abroad.'   And therefore, as it was a counsel in Caiaphas, it
was a prophecy in God.   And so you have the reasons why this passage
comes in here.   Now to give you some observations out of it.
    Obs. 1. You see here what mischiefs and sins state policy ofttimes puts
great men upon.   How much state interests prevail to move men against
the saints, and the purity of religion.   State policy here was the cause of
the death of Christ.   And yet this very act of theirs, in crucifying the Lord
of life, brought mischief upon the state.   Here is Caiaphas, he brings the
most authentic state axiom that was ever brought.   It is but a small
matter, saith he, it is but one man's life, and it is better for one man to die
than the state should perish.   He did it, I say, out of the greatest worldly
wisdom that ever man did, and yet you know what followed.   By this we
may come to understand that place in 1 Cor. ii. 8, where, speaking of the
crucifying of Christ, saith he, 'We speak the wisdom of God in a mystery, which none of the princes of this world knew ; for had they known
it, they would not have crucified the Lord of life ;' but, saith he, as for
the wisdom of this world, and of the princes of the world, it comes to
nought, for (as it is, chap. iii. ver. 19), 'The wisdom of this world is foolishness with God, for it is written, he taketh the wise in their own craftiness.'   By the princes of this world it is evident that he means the Jews,
the Pharisees, and the rulers, Pilate and Herod, and the rest that put
Christ to death ; this great Sanhedrim here, Annas and Caiaphas, and their
fellows, and Pilate ; for he went on the same worldly principle too, for
whenas the Jews told him that if he did not put Christ to death he was not
Cæsar's friend, the text saith, 'Therefore when Pilate heard that saying,'
Go crucify him, saith he ; it was state policy did it.   They all thought they
were so wise in putting Christ to death upon this state axiom ; and it was
a fair one.   This wisdom, saith the apostle, came to nought; God made
the wisdom of the world foolishness ; for, alas ! were ever men befooled as
these men were ?   For this very crucifying of Christ was their ruin, that

brought the Romans upon them. Yea, if you read Josephus and others, you shall find that that which strengthened them to rebel against the Romans was their very looking for the Messiah, and the prophecies they had, that about that time the Messiah should come.

Obs. 2. A second observation that I make upon this is this, that a state is not to put a man to death merely and simply for the public good, unless he is an offender. For here this state maxim the Pharisees and Pilate took up, and used as the great plausible argument to the people ; yet it being against a man's life, supposed innocent (whether they knew him to be the Christ or not), it is noted as a high and mighty injury, and as an act of the greatest injustice in them. It is the greatest instance this that can be, that no evil is to be done that good may come by it. An innocent man is not to be put to death, nor innocent men to be injured or wronged (if they be innocent) for a public good. A man's life is not to be taken away merely to save a state. Indeed, if a case of necessity lie, so as that a man offer himself freely up for the saving of a state, as some noble Romans have done, that is another matter ; but to condemn a man to death simply to save a state, ought not to be.

Obs. 3. You may observe, that carnal men, when they would prevail with others to do anything, they will speak to their very lusts. All their hearts here were on fire against Jesus Christ ; Caiaphas now speaks the highest reason to the lusts of the Jews that could be, invents a reason upon which they should put him to death, a most plausible one, colours it over so cunningly as might take with all the people. It is better, saith he, that one man be put to death, than that the whole nation should perish ; he knew this would move them all, and all that is in them. I say he gave counsel to their lusts ; and so you shall have carnal men to do, speak to men's lusts, and vent their own lusts too, vent their own malice ; for so Caiaphas did. ' It is expedient for us,' saith he, for us that are the priests, but puts it upon the people, ' that one man should die for the people.'

Obs. 4. Observe hence likewise, what a dangerous thing it is to be the first mover in any great wickedness. Here you see Caiaphas, because he was the first that gave counsel against Christ, he is noted out in a way of eminency, with this brand upon him, ' This is he that gave counsel that it was expedient for one man to die for the nation.' He did it cunningly and plausibly, but God for all that took notice of it, and lays this great load upon him, ' This is the man.' Therefore, I say, to be the first mover and leader in a wicked business, as Annas and Caiaphas was in the great business of crucifying Christ, is a dangerous thing. And you see one wicked, cunning man will carry the whole. Caiaphas here spake such great reason, that he carried them all ; but such men, of all others, that are the counsellers in evil, and that are the first counsellers in evil, though they glory and pride themselves in it—as certainly as this man did, ' You know nothing at all,' saith he—such men will God brand, as he branded him here, and their damnation shall be great at last. Poor Caiaphas, there was another that gave counsel that Jesus Christ should be put to death afore thou didst, and that was God the Father ; for in Acts iv. 28, 'Both Herod and Pontius Pilate, with the Gentiles and the people of Israel, were gathered together, for to do whatsoever thy hand and thy counsel determined before to be done.' There was not only his wisdom, his counsel, but his hand, his power in it, though it was the greatest sin in the world. Yea, God the Father had given counsel to Christ himself to do it, before ever Caiaphas had spoken : Ps. xvi. 7, ' I will bless the Lord, who hath given me counsel.' And what was the counsel he gave him ?   He bade him die for his people, and he would raise him up; and therefore ' my reins instruct me in the night season,' saith he ; that night when he was in the garden, and when he was before Pilate, God's counsel was to him to do it, beforehand, and he blesseth God, that gave him that counsel.   This psalm is a psalm in relation to Christ, and it is spoken of his death and resurrection.

Obs. 5.   Lastly, observe this, that oftentimes the speeches of great persons (as of fathers concerning their children, &c.), which they do not speak prophetically, as in their intentions, yet they are so in the event.   As Homer brings in the dream of Agamemnon.   So Pharaoh dreamed, and Nebuchadnezzar dreamed.   Yet oftentimes princes and others do utter speeches that have a prophetical meaning in them in the conclusion.   It is dangerous therefore for a man to curse himself, to wish this or that upon himself, for whilst thou dost it in a corrupt passion, out of a corrupt heart, God may turn it to a prophecy ; therefore take heed of such speeches upon all occasions.   And so much for this 14th verse.

CHAPTER IX.

Peter's denial of Christ.—That this was an addition to his sufferings.

There is a great question among interpreters (which I will handle very briefly, because I will not trouble you much with difficulties), whether all this that follows concerning Peter's denial, and the high priest's asking Christ of his disciples and of his doctrine, was done in Annas his house, or in Caiaphas his ?   All yield that there were some things done in Caiaphas his house, and that he was led to Caiaphas, and that from Caiaphas he was led to Pilate, and from Pilate to Herod ; but some would have what is brought in here of Peter, and the examination of Christ concerning his disciples and doctrine, to have been in Annas his house, and by him.   But the case is clear in other evangelists that it was not.   For we read in all the other evangelists, especially in Matthew, that Peter's denial was in Caiaphas his house.   And John here saith expressly that Caiaphas was high priest that same year, and that Peter's denial was when he got into the palace of the high priest, and that the high priest asked Jesus of his disciples and of his doctrine.   Now though Annas was father-in-law to the high priest, yet it was Caiaphas that was the high priest ; therefore all this must needs be done in Caiaphas his house, and not in Annas his.   The plain meaning then is this, that whereas Annas was father-in-law to Caiaphas the high priest, they led him therefore first to his house ; but when Annas had seen him, they (without Annas doing anything to him at all that we read of) led him away to Caiaphas ; and though his leading to Caiaphas be not mentioned here, yet it is mentioned at the 24th verse, where it is said, ' Annas had sent him bound unto Caiaphas the high priest.'   So that, I say, all these things were done in Caiaphas his house, and not in Annas his ; and therefore there is none of the evangelists but John that mention anything of Annas, because, indeed, there was nothing done in his house ; only they brought him unto him because he was Caiaphas his father-in-law, for to see him ; and when he had seen him, he sent him directly to Caiaphas ; the very words, ' to Annas first,' implies this.   And the truth is that Cyril, an ancient Greek father, he brings in even here, afore he comes to the 15th verse, ' Annas he sent him bound to Caiaphas,' and in the copies that he had and had seen, those words were found.　And Beza inclines to that too, and thinks it was an omission in the writer, and that it ought to be here inserted.　So much now for the solving of that question; and so I come to the words of this 15th verse.

Verse 15. ' *And Simon Peter followed Jesus, and so did another disciple. That disciple was known unto the high priest, and spake unto her that kept the door, and brought in Peter.*'

It is the beginning of the story of Peter's denial of Christ, which denial of Peter's is intermingled by all the evangelists with the sufferings of our Lord and Saviour Christ; and I think it is done on purpose, first, to illustrate the sufferings of Christ; for certainly this denial of Peter's did something add to Christ's sufferings; that at that very time when he was asked of his doctrine and of his disciples, one of his greatest and most eminent disciples should be denying of him (for so you see the context runs), which Christ knew, for in the end he looked back upon Peter, and shewed his grief for him, and that he took notice of him, and of what he had done. And, 2, the evangelists do it also for this purpose, to shew the great love of Christ, that though Peter and the other disciples were a-sinning, especially Peter, for he sinned most greviously, Jesus Christ went on in his work, went on to suffer even for those sins that they were then committing. And as Christ knew what Peter was a-doing then, and yet went on to suffer, so he knew what thou wouldst do against him, and yet suffered for thee. But to come to the story.

There are in all the evangelists recorded three several denials of Christ, and that by Peter; and as I go along I must compare the one with the other, and shew that there is no contradiction in what the evangelists record.

In the words here, from the 15th verse to the 19th, you have two eminent things to be considered.

1. The introduction, or the story that delivers how it came to pass that Peter did get into the high priest's hall, which was the occasion of his denial.

2. The denial itself.

1. First, For the story how Peter got in.　John waiting * after the other evangelists, still labours to insert some circumstances which they had omitted.　Now none of the other evangelists tell us how Peter got into the high priest's hall; they tell us indeed that Peter followed his master afar off, but this great circumstance, which was a preparation to his denial, how he got in, and with what difficulty, it is only recorded by John.　And there is a great deal to be observed in it.　But first I shall open it historically, and then give you the observations as I go along.

Simon Peter followed Jesus. The other evangelists tell us that he followed Jesus afar off.　But I shall not speak of that circumstance, intending to keep principally to what John here saith.　It was certainly a mixed action in Peter, that is, an action mixed of love and of fear, of grace and corruption. For that he followed him argues that he had a love in his heart to Christ; yet there was fear mixed with it, for he walketh after him afar off.

The question is here, whether Peter sinned in this, in his going to the high priest's hall ?

Assuredly he did; For, 1. Christ had expressly told him, Mat. xxvi. 2, that he should suffer at that passover; therefore it was unbelief in him to

Qu. ' writing ' ?—ED.

follow him after he was apprehended,' to see the event of it, as Matthew tells us he went for that reason. And,

2. Christ had taken order, when he was first taken, that his disciples should be kept safe, and let free. ' Let these go,' saith he, which was intimation enough that they were unable to suffer; for it follows, ' That the word which he had spoken might be fulfilled, of those thou hast given me have I lost none ;' implying that if they had then been put to suffer, they had been lost, for they were weak and unfit for suffering, and it was not the mind of God to strengthen them to suffering at that time. And therefore in John xiii. 36, saith Christ, ' Whither I go thou canst not follow me now, but thou shalt follow me afterwards.' Thou canst not follow me now, for thou art not able to follow me, neither will my Father strengthen thee to follow me ; but afterwards he followed Christ, even to the cross, for, as ecclesiastical stories tell us, he was crucified as his master was. But yet the meaning of that place is, that as Christ went to heaven in a way of suffering, so he told him that he should follow him thither, but he should not follow him presently in the like way of suffering. And besides,

3. Christ had plainly and fully told him that he would deny him. Now for him, having been thus warned by Christ, and having had experience of his own fearfulness—for having struck off the high priest's servant's ear, he fled away amongst the rest ; and it was not likely that he should be more valiant and courageous in the high priest's hall, amongst soldiers and officers, than he had been in the garden—for him, I say, notwithstanding all this, to be venturing, and to put himself upon that temptation, it was certainly a sin. But still, I say, grace will work with corruption ; his love unto Christ wrought with his fear, and then the words that he had spoken himself, those courageous stout words, ' I will die with thee rather than deny thee,' those rise in his mind, and put him upon going after Christ to see the issue of the business ; and perhaps he hoped that he might happily get in with the crowd, and so not be seen.

Obs. 1. The observation that I make from hence by the way, is this, That we should not put ourselves upon occasions of suffering or danger, till such time as God calls us. It is unwarrantable, and it is sinful so to do. It was so in Peter.

Obs. 2. As it is unwarrantable to put ourselves upon occasions of sufferings, so it is dangerous for us to tempt God by putting ourselves upon occasions of sinning ; to go to the door, as it were, where a man shall be drawn in to sin, as Peter here ; he follows, and he goes to the door, and stands without, hankering to see what shall be the end of it. I say it is a dangerous thing for us to put ourselves upon occasions of sinning, to tempt God, for then you see by this of Peter what the issue is ; when Peter tempteth God, then doth God suffer Peter to be tempted, he leads him indeed into temptation.

But Peter had not got in for all this, had it not been for an unhappy providence to him ; for so I may call it in respect of his sin, though God intended good by it. For the story tells us that another disciple went along with him, and that disciple, being known unto the high priest, went in with Jesus into the palace of the high priest. This is brought in here on purpose to shew how Peter got in, for otherwise there is no reason of mentioning this going in of the other disciple. The providence of God would that here should be two disciples eye-witnesses of Christ's sufferings in the high priest's hall, from whom the rest might have the relation of it. There was Peter and another disciple. He is called a disciple, for that was the name that was given to Christians in Christ's time, and so in the Acts of the Apostles, till they came to Antioch, for then they were first called Christians.

There is a question amongst interpreters who this other disciple was. Some say (and many good interpreters) that it was John, and the reason they give is this, because John in this epistle * when he speaks of himself, he styles himself ' that other disciple,' and never mentions his name, as in John xx. 30. But you shall find that where John speaks of himself, though he concealeth his own name, and saith ' that other disciple,' yet he adds withal, ' whom Jesus loved ;' so you have it in the same 20th of John, ver. 2 But now that addition is not put to this disciple, but it is another disciple which was known to the high priest. And besides, to me there is this great reason that this other disciple was not John, because there is no likelihood (but the contrary seems much more probable) that John should have so much knowledge and familiarity as this disciple apparently had, both with the high priest himself, and so, by virtue of that acquaintance and greatness with him, an interest in his family also ; so that he could command or order to have Peter let in. Now John was a poor fisherman, that lived in Galilee, a country remote from Jerusalem, and came but up with Christ at the feast ; for Christ did not live ordinarily at Jerusalem, but always after the feast went down again into Galilee, the place of his usual residence ; unless he preached sometimes up and down in the country ; and when he went, his disciples went with him ; therefore it is not likely that he should have such interest in the high priest's house. And then again, if it had been John, he would certainly have been questioned as well as Peter, neither would he himself have ventured in, being so well known as it is said this other disciple was. And the Syriac translation favours this opinion, that it was none of John, for it reads it thus, *unus ex aliis*, one of the other disciples, not being one of the twelve. And it was a disciple, though known to the high priest, yet certainly he was not known to be a disciple ; for had he been known to be a disciple, doubtless they had fallen upon him as well as upon Peter, for all his favour with the high priest. And it had been brought in as an argument to Peter, that he was a disciple, because he was helped into the hall by another disciple ; but you see it is not, only they allege that Peter was one of them that was in the garden, &c. But the truth is, when the Holy Ghost hath concealed who this disciple was, why should we go and say, Who is it ?

Obs. From hence I will give you this observation, that Christ he had other disciples besides his apostles ; many hidden ones. You shall find in John xii. 42, that among the chief rulers there were many that believed on him, but because of the Pharisees they did not confess him. And in Acts i. 15, there were a hundred and twenty that met together. So that there were more disciples than the twelve, yet there were many that appeared not, as Nicodemus, that came to Jesus by night ; and they did not appear till after his death. Christ hath many hidden ones that are a long time putting themselves forth in profession. We see it in experience ; it hath been known that men have been long converted, and lived privately in the family, before they made an open profession. And so now, many are favourers of the cause of Christ that do not shew themselves ; but shew themselves they will in the end. This man here, though he would not profess himself openly, yet when he saw a disciple, he would do him a good turn, as he thought he did Peter in having of him into the high priest's house.

* Qu. " Gospel ?"—ED.

The text saith, this other disciple was known to the high priest. The reason why this expression is used, is, to shew that it was a hard thing to get in unless a man had acquaintance, and it was likewise a great favour to come into this Sanhedrim, yea, this very acquaintance of the high priest himself, as it is thought, was not admitted into the inner room where Christ was; for their proceedings against Christ were secret and hidden, they would not have this court kept openly, for the people to see their juggling dealing. Peter, you see, could not get in but by favour of this disciple who was known to the high priest, though unknown to us.

Obs. From thence we may observe, that we should not presently censure a man, that he is not holy or the like, because he holds correspondency, or it may be some intimacy or acquaintance, with men that are carnal; for there may be reason why he doth so, and yet he may be a holy man, as this disciple certainly was, and yet kept his correspondency with the high priest. I will not justify in all things the act itself, but we should not esteem men, or think that therefore they are ungodly, for even that judgment may deceive us.

Now this disciple he went in with Jesus, that is, he went in with the crowd of the officers, and the band of men that went in with Jesus.

He went into the palace of the high priest; into the outward court, so it is in the original. The question is, whether Peter and the soldiers that were about the fire and the like were in one room, and Christ in another? That which breeds the scruple is that in Mat. xxvi. 69, it is said that Peter sat without in the palace; which seems to argue that Christ was in one room and he in another.

The answer is clear, that they were both in one room, that is evident, because the other evangelists tell us that Christ looked back upon Peter. Now it is not to be thought that Christ came out to look upon him when he denied him. Therefore that which is the reconciliation of it is this: whereas it is said he was in the lower part of the hall, the meaning is plainly this, that the high priest and his fellows, they sat in a place more high advanced by steps or so, all within the same walls, and in the lower part of it there was a fire, where Peter and the rest stood; and so Christ being called before them there, he might eminently look over all the room.

Verse 16. ' *But Peter stood at the door without. Then went out that other disciple, which was known unto the high priest, and spake unto her that kept the door, and brought in Peter.*'

That other disciple, perceiving that Peter stood without, and knowing him to be a disciple, and bearing love and goodwill to him, befriends him, goes to her that kept the door, and as some think, betrusts her with this secret that Peter was one of Christ's disciples, which made her so confidently afterward charge him, as you know she did; and so upon this speech he gets in.

Peter stood at the door without. As I said before, it was an unwarrantable action for Peter to follow Christ; he had had warning about his denying of him before, yet you see he would not away, but though he found the door shut upon him, yet there he stands; and as he followed Christ in confidence of his own strength, so here in the same confidence he stands at the door, waiting for an opportunity to get in. My brethren, it is a certain rule and truth, that though another man may suffer for Christ out of a heroic spirit, out of some carnal grounds and ends, yet God will not permit those that are his own children to suffer for him upon such grounds; he will rather give them up to a denying of him, till such time as they are fitted for a true and real suffering; and so he did Peter here.   Above all things, therefore, we should by this example learn to take heed of venturing in ways of suffering out of our own strength, for so Peter did ; he went forth in his own strength, and you see what the issue of it is.

Well; Peter, you see, by the help of his friend, gets in.   The observations that I make upon all this story of letting in Peter are these.

Obs. 1. Observe the workings of God's providence about this sin and denial of Peter's.   The providences of God they were many; I shall mention them here.

(1.) He could not get in : ' Peter stood at the door without.'   Here now God in his providence at first did put an impediment, a bar to Peter's attempt, stopped him in going on to that which should be the occasion of his sin.   Peter he should have taken this for a warning, he should have observed the providence of God in hindering him, but he would not.   In any way or course wherein we find that God in his providence doth put impediments, it should strike our hearts ; and we should look upon it as a call and warning from God to examine our grounds in going on in that way.   If indeed we find our ways such as are warranted by the word, or that our consciences are clear in it that it is a duty, and that we are called to it, then, let there be never so many impediments, we are to go on in it. But otherwise, in a doubtful way, if a man finds impediments, let him observe that providence.   If Peter had done thus when he found the door shut, he had not sinned thus against Christ as he did ; but he still stands at the door, tempting of God, and therefore doth God in the end suffer him to be tempted.

(2.) But yet, though Peter was thus stopped for a while, there comes (after he had tempted Providence) the fairest and clearest providence to bring him in to the high priest's hall that could be.   Peter spake not to this disciple to let him in, but he, spying of him, goes out and brings him in.   So that, on the other side, we are not in businesses to go merely by providences, for you shall find that oftentimes providences do lay fair for occasions of sinning.   Here was as fair and as clear a providence to bring Peter into the high priest's hall, where he should deny Christ, as could be ; nay, the providence was so fair, that one would think that God called Peter into the hall.   We are apt ofttimes to measure our ways by providences much ; but never believe the works of God unless thou hast a word of God first for thy way, for God doth lay snares, especially when men tempt him. When Jonah was to go to Nineveh, and instead of going thither, ran away from God to go to Tarshish, he had the fairest providence that could be, for he found a ship that was fitted and all ready to go to Tarshish; he might now think, here is a providence serves me as fit as can be.   Ay, but he went against the word of God.   And the truth is, so doth Peter here ; and therefore, I say, never be ruled by the providences of God, unless thou hast the word of God, for the providence of God doth as equally and indifferently lay temptations for men as it doth facilitate their way in what he would have them do.   In things which are not God's way, you shall have providences fall exceedingly fair ; and in things that are God's way, you shall have many impediments to the contrary, to try your faith.

When Peter now did thus get in, he thought it certainly a very great favour and courtesy, and a special privilege, that he should, according to his desire, see the issue of things ; for he went for that end, as Matthew saith.   And his friend certainly intended to do him the greatest kindness and favour that could be. There are snares that lie oftentimes in the courtesies and kindnesses of friends. For so there is in this; he did it as a kindness, and the other thought it a favour; but the truth is, it was a great snare, and in the end it proved a fatal business to Peter, as being the occasion of that great and famous denial of his master.

It is strange likewise that Christ, who could tell him he should deny him, would not bid him take heed of the high priest's hall. He could have done the one as well as the other. He, that knew all things that should befall himself, knew what should befall Peter, how it was he should deny him. But yet Jesus Christ, he being God as well as man, he was not obliged to give Peter that *caveat;* but though he knew it, and suffered it for his own glory, yet it is no warrant for us to do so. God may permit sin, he knows how to punish it, and how to get glory out of it, and he himself is not defiled by it; but we are not to permit others to sin. And so much for the 16th verse, and for the introduction into Peter's denial. I come now to the denial itself.

Verse 17. '*Then saith the damsel that kept the door unto Peter, Art not thou also one of this man's disciples? He saith, I am not.*'

That a damsel should be the door-keeper to the high priest, some say (and indeed many of the best interpreters) it was *ex more gentis*, from the custom of the country. Thus, in Acts xii. 13, you read that when Peter knocked at the door, that a damsel went and opened the door; for it was her place so to do. And in 2 Sam. iv. 6, in the Septuagint it is in the feminine gender; it is not in the Hebrew indeed, but the Septuagint, that ancient translation (which shews it was the custom of the country), inserts these words, and the woman that was the doorkeeper was winnowing of corn. I speak it only for this, to shew the reason why a damsel kept the door of the high priest. But others say (and probably too) that the reason why this damsel kept the door, was because that all the servants were now busy, and taken up in attending one way or other; the keeping of the door therefore for the present was committed to this maid. But I take it that the first is the truth, that it was the manner of the country; it being strengthened by those two instances. However it fell out, certainly God ordered it in the greatest providence that could be. For of all men you know how confident Peter was, and how he had said, 'Though all men forsake thee, I will not forsake thee.' He goes forth in his own strength; he had out of his valour cut off the ear of the high priest's servant, falling upon a whole multitude of men, he alone and one other; for there was but two swords amongst them. God therefore ordered it in his providence, that he would confute the pride of Peter this way, that his weakness might be seen to all posterity, and made the more famous: at the speaking of a poor silly maid, he denies his Lord and Saviour Jesus Christ!

Then said the damsel unto Peter, Art not thou also one of this man's disciples? The evangelists they do all reckon up three several sorts of denials that Peter had; yet if you compare the first in Matthew, and the first in Mark, and the first in Luke, with this first in John (which all must be accounted to be but one), the story seems to be exceeding different, if you either consider what the evangelists record her speeches to have been unto Peter, and of Peter, or of what his speeches were unto her. In Matthew, chap. xxvi. 69, the speech she there useth to him is, 'Thou also wert with Jesus of Galilee,' that is, thou as well as others. In Mark it is thus, 'Thou also wast with Jesus of Nazareth;' now Nazareth, you know, was a city in Galilee. And in Luke, chap. xxii. 56, her speech is not to Peter, but to them that stood by, and it was thus, ' This man also was with him.' Now here in John it is a differing speech from all these, ' Art not thou also,' saith she, ' one of this man's disciples ?' And as her speeches recorded by the evangelists do vary, so you shall find that his speeches to her vary as much. For in Matthew, chap. xxvi. ver. 70, it is said, ' He denied afore them all, saying, I know not what thou sayest.' It is the highest kind of negation that can be ; the meaning of it is, I am so far from belonging to him, that the truth is, it is strange to me that you should ask me any such question ; I do not know the least of him ; as if he had never heard of the man before. And so in Mark xiv. 68, ' I know not, neither understand I what thou sayest.' And in Luke xxii. 57, ' Woman, I know him not.' Now here, in John, being asked, whether he was his disciple ? he saith, ' I am not.' How shall we reconcile this ?

The reconciliation is very easy, for they are several speeches of hers, and several speeches of his, whereof some evangelists record some, and others, others. And it seemeth to have been thus (that I may hang and pin them altogether) : this maid she first says to the standers by, ' This man also was with him,' as Luke hath it ; and then she turns to Peter, and says, ' Are not thou one of this man's disciples ?' as John here hath it ; and then she peremptorily affirms it, that she upon her own knowledge had seen him with him, ' Thou also wast with Jesus of Galilee,' as Matthew and Mark have it. Now she, using several forms of speeches, some to the standers by, and some to himself, at the first asking him the question only, afterward peremptorily affirming it, this is it which draws out those several answers from Peter, according to the several occasions ; which all the evangelists severally record, and all these make but this first denial of Peter's.

Others cast it thus (which comes all to one) that she did first ask Peter the question, as John hath it here, ' Are not thou one of this man's disciples ?' as he came in at the door. He answered, ' I am not.' Afterwards going to the fire where Peter sat, and as Luke hath it, seeing him by the light thereof (for so it is in the original), and as the text there saith, viewing of him wistly, with fixed eyes, thought she, I have seen you afore now, and seen you with him. And now she doth not go and ask him, ' Art thou not one of this man's disciples ?' but she plainly saith, ' Thou art one ;' and she tells the standers by so too, ' This man' (saith she to them) ' also was with him ;' and therefore Matthew tells us, that he denied before them all, spake as loud as he could, that they might all take notice of it, ' I know not,' saith he, ' what thou sayest.'

You may likewise see the working of the providence of God even in this too ; as, namely, that such a woman as had seen him some time or other with Christ, should now keep the high priest's door ; for indeed that seems to be plain, that she speaks of her own knowledge : ' Thou also,' saith she, ' wast with him,' that is, thou didst converse with him ; so Matthew and Mark have it. And the truth is, that the coherence here in John evidently carries it so, for here at the 17th verse we translate it, ' Then saith the damsel ;' but in the original it is, ' Therefore saith the damsel,' the coherence whereof is plainly this, that she having observed him to be spoken for to be let in by a disciple, being at the door, minds him not so much at first, but afterwards eying him more wistly by the light of the fire, having formerly seen him, she peremptorily challengeth him : ' She therefore saith unto him,' &c. Now, I say, here was a providence of God, that that woman (it may be none of all the family else had observed him), that she should be at the door and take notice of all these things, that she should come to challenge him, and did challenge him, or else he had not been challenged. Others of them bring other arguments, that his speech bewrayed him, and that they saw him with Jesus in the garden; but the providence of God so ordered it, that of all the family she should be the woman that kept the door, who had seen him and knew him to be with Christ. At first indeed she did not know him so perfectly, therefore she only puts the question to him, ' Art not thou one of this man's disciples ?' But afterward viewing him more strictly, and that by the light of the fire, she comes to know him, and challengeth him in a peremptory manner. So that God's providence did still strongly work in this great business to discover Peter. To get him in, it wrought much, and now it works as strongly even for a discovery. And you shall see other passages of providence afterward in the story, and how strongly they wrought too. And so much now for the historical opening of the words of this verse.

I will give you but an observation or two, and so pass on.

Obs. 1. You see that as God would have it manifested that all sorts of people, Jew and Gentile, civil state and ecclesiastical, all these sorts were against our Lord and Saviour Christ, so all sexes too. There is this damsel here, and another damsel afterward, as Matthew and Mark have it, that fall upon Peter, and challenge him for being his disciple.

Obs. 2. You see likewise the weakness of Peter ; he was but asked by a damsel, and at the first but in a secret way, for I take it this speech here in John, which occasioned his first denial, was when he came in at the door; it was then that she asked him, ' Art not thou one of this man's disciples ?' A damsel, you see, foiled him ; he that was not long before so extreme eager, that he promised he would die with Christ, that he would never leave him, that he would not, promised it three times ; he that in the garden was so valiant as to cut off Malchus his ear, in defence of his master ; this man being left to himself, at a private question that a damsel makes him, falleth into this great lie, which afterwards he seconded with further and greater protestations, as we shall see in the story. If that God doth leave us, what poor creatures are we ! That that Peter who had naturally so bold a spirit, so great a natural courage, one that was a rash and a venturous, a bold and a daring man, as appears by all his actions, especially by that in the garden, when he cut off the high priest's servant's ear ; he that was so bold afterward from the Spirit of God, when the Holy Ghost comes upon him ; this Peter, when he is left to himself, neither natural courage doth assist him, but at the whispering of a maid you see what a lie he tells ; neither doth the Holy Ghost help him, who yet did dwell in his heart. What poor creatures are the most courageous of men, if God leave them ; they will fall short not only of the grace that is in them, and of the power of the Holy Ghost that is in them, but of that natural boldness which they have, for so Peter did.

Obs. 3. When was it that Peter thus foully and grossly denies his master ? It was then when our Lord and Saviour Christ was entered into his sufferings ; when he was arraigned, and arraigned for him, for his sins, before the high priest. Then when our Lord and Saviour Christ was about to do the greatest favour and mercy that ever was done for creatures, and for Peter amongst the rest, then God ordered it that Peter should sin, and sin thus foully and grossly. It was a very great aggravation of his sin, even this, for so the circumstance of time is to any sin. If that, at the same time that a friend is contriving, or taking pains for me, or doing anything for me of the greatest moment, saving my life, begging my pardon, if I should at that time wrong my friend most, how would that heighten my unkindness! This was Peter's case. Yet you see Christ goes on with his work for all that. He knew Peter was a-denying of him, yet that did not make him withdraw his neck from suffering for Peter. Great sins against God, when he is doing us very great mercies, should exceedingly break our hearts, as it did Peter's here; he went out afterwards, and wept bitterly. Whenever we do sin, Jesus Christ is interceding in heaven for us. Our sins do not hinder him from going on to intercede, as Peter's sinning here did not hinder him from going on to suffer for him.

Obs. 4. And then again, Peter being asked whether he was one of his disciples, answers, 'I am not.' He doth not deny Christ to be the Messiah of the world, only he saith, 'I am not one of his disciples.' Yet Christ had said, 'Thou shalt deny me.' He denied, indeed, that he belonged to him. For any man to slink out of the profession of Christ when he is called to it, or out of any truth of his, though he deny not that Christ is the Messiah, and that Christ is come in the flesh, or the great points of salvation, yet it is a denial of Christ. And so much now for the 17th verse.

Verse 18. *'And the servants and officers stood there, who had made a fire of coals (for it was cold), and they warmed themselves; and Peter stood with them and warmed himself.'*
The scope of this relation is only this, to shew the occasion of Peter's second and third denial, which John afterwards tells us of. For though his second denial comes not in till the 25th verse, yet this story here is related as a preparation thereunto: that the weather being cold, the servants and officers were not scattered up and down, but were all gathered together in a ring, and cluster in the midst of the hall about the fire, and Peter he was in the midst of them; and therefore, if there were notice taken of Peter, all must take notice of him, one as well as another; and hence it came to pass that Peter was so mightily afraid, that he went on to deny his master, with oaths and curses, as afterward you read in the story. It was to shew the publicness of his sin, for Matthew saith, 'he denied before them all,' for they were all gathered together in a heap, and Peter in the midst. But to open it a little.

They had a fire of coals; of wood already burned or kindled, to avoid the smoke, because the fire was in the midst of the hall, as Luke hath it.

For it was cold, which might seem strange, because those countries are hot, and it was in the spring time, for it was in March. But this is easily resolved, for you must know that in those countries, as there is an extremity of heat in the day, so there are oftentimes in the spring, as well as in the winter, exceeding cold nights, especially after rain. And it was that night especially a cold night, and that was the reason of the fire.

The observations I make out of these words are only these two.

Obs. 1. It is said that it was a cold night. Now this night, which thus occasionally fell out to be more cold than ordinary, it was that night in which Christ sweat drops of blood in the agony of his spirit when he was in the garden. For that agony of his was not many hours afore this befell him; for after he had supped, he made a long sermon and a long prayer, and then went into the garden, and from thence they fetched him out (all this was within night); and afore the first crowing of the cock this denial of Peter's fell out. It is noted, therefore, by interpreters, as a circumstance

to greaten the agony of Christ, and to set forth the extremity of his sufferings, that in a cold night he should sweat drops of blood, which was contrary to nature, and must proceed, therefore, from that great anxiety and
perplexity his soul was in. It is brought, I say, by divines as an aggravation and evidence of those great soul-sufferings of Christ, more than from
the fear of death, that in a cold night he should thus sweat drops of blood.
It is noted upon that, though it comes in here upon another occasion, viz.,
that it being cold, there was a fire, and Peter stood there to warm himself,
as he might lawfully do, but that he stood in the midst of temptations, and
in the midst of tempters.

Obs. 2. Peter stood in the midst of them; so Luke hath it; for now he
was in, and having once denied him to the damsel, to the end he might not
further be known, he goes and shrinks in amongst the crowd, thinking to
hide himself; and there he stands amongst the enemies of Christ, who
being all full of malice did certainly speak evil of him, and talked their
pleasures of him; but he, standing by, was forced to be silent, said not a
word, suffered all to pass in silence, which was a kind of a denying Christ.
And so, Peter having sinned thus far, God gives him up still to more sin.
It is a dangerous thing, my brethren, without a special call of God, to be in
ill company, especially in evil times. Peter being amongst these enemies
of Christ, it was the occasion of his being challenged, and that was the
occasion of this great sin he fell into. In evil times, if a man be in such
company, either he must be silent, or if he speak, they will be ready to pervert his speech, to put him upon a temptation. We should therefore avoid
all needless societies with carnal people. Take heed of coming into high
priest's halls; you see into what inconvenience it drew Peter to. And so
much for this first denial of Peter's, which I have historically laid open. I
come next to the examination of Christ, in the nineteeth, twentieth, and
twenty-first verses.

CHAPTER X.

*The account of Christ's examination before Caiaphas, in the nineteenth, twentieth,
and one-and-twentieth verses of this eighteenth chapter of John.—We now
come to the other part of Christ's sufferings recorded in this chapter, and
that is a strict examinaton of him.*

' *The high priest then asked Jesus of his disciples, and of his doctrine. Jesus
answered him, I spake openly to the world; I ever taught in the synagogue,
and in the temple, whither the Jews always resort; and in secret have I said
nothing. Why askest thou me? ask them which heard me, what I have
said unto them: behold, they know what I said.'—*JOHN xviii. 19, 20, 21.

Here begins a third part of Christ's sufferings recorded in this text.
You have first his having been taken, and so bound, and then led to Annas
his house in a triumph of glory; now, here is the third, his coming to
Caiaphas his house (for Annas had sent him bound to Caiaphas), who is
called the high priest, because he was that year the high priest, though
others had the name also, for they still retained the title, though they were
out of the office. And being here, they fall to examining of him about his
disciples, and his doctrine. Other evangelists tell us of their examining of
him, and bringing in witnesses against him, concerning some speeches he

spake about the temple, and about his own office, and his being the Messiah; but this examination here, which certainly was the first they began with, and was as the *prodromus* to all the rest, no evangelist hath it but only John.

The time was (some twenty-one years before) when Christ, being but twelve years old, had asked them, and posed the doctors in the temple; and he was then (as he saith) about his Father's business, putting forth then some beams of the Godhead dwelling in him. And now he is before them in a state of ignominy, and he is asked and examined as a delinquent, as a malefactor, as a heretic and seditious person; and he is about his Father's business in this as well as in the former.

And by the way here, afore we come to the particular opening of these verses, let us consider who it was that was thus examined. It was he that was the great prophet prophesied of by Moses, that should come into the world, of whom it was said, that whosoever would not hearken to the words of that prophet which he should speak, he should surely be put to death. Clean contrary now, he being come into the world, he is examined as a false prophet, that they might find cause of putting *him* to death. He that was the truth itself, is examined and charged with false doctrine. He that was the prince of peace, and came and preached peace (as it is, Eph. ii. 17), he is charged with rebellion, and accused to have preached sedition. But, to come to the words.

The high priest then asked Jesus. Then, or *therefore*. Some translate it *therefore*, and so it hath relation to what is said in the 13th and 14th verses, where John speaks of the high priest, and brandeth him to be the man that gave the first counsel that Christ should die for the people. And now they having resolved to put him to death, therefore the high priest asked him of his doctrine and of his disciples, seeking by questions to ensnare him, that so they might have some plausible ground for his condemnation. Others they translate it *then*, and so the meaning is this, that whilst our Lord and Saviour Christ was examining concerning his disciples, then was one of his disciples a-denying of him; whilst he was called in question for them, and it was made an occasion of his suffering, then was Peter committing that foul sin. You see the love of our Lord and Saviour Christ.

The high priest asked him;—as being the mouth of that great assembly, the Sanhedrim, of all the elders and the priests who were met together at his house. For you must know it did belong to the high priest, and to that assembly of elders, to decide all controversies of doctrine that did arise, and to make inquiry into heresies and false doctrines, as appears by that place in Deut. xvii. 11–13, therefore now to deal with Christ about his doctrine, had it been in any thing false or untrue, it had not been unlawful for the high priest to have done it. But see the iniquity of his and their proceedings. They proceed altogether against and without law, for they do not lay any false doctrine to his charge, they bring no witnesses that this and this he had said, but merely, after the manner of the Inquisition, ask him questions to ensnare him; whereas there should have been a complaint made first unto him, and he should have brought forth the evidences, and not go and wire-draw (as I may express it) and examine him upon interrogatories, and so to get something from himself; this was altogether beyond his commission.

He asked him, it is said, *of his doctrine and of his disciples.* The scope of the high priest in this question must be a little considered, for that will give us light into it ; what end it was that the high priest had in it ; and what end likewise it was that God had in it.

The end and scope of the high priest was twofold.

It was *first*, (as I hinted before), to fish out of Christ whether or no he had taught such doctrine as should come within the compass of that law in Deut. xiii. 5 ; for as I said, this great Sanhedrim, the council of the high priest, and the rest of his fellows, had especially to do in the case of a false prophet. Now there, in Deuteronomy, the law is this, ' If a prophet arise that shall revolt from the Lord your God' (as it is in the margin), teach men to apostatize from God, ' who brought you out of the land of Egypt, and set up any other god, that prophet shall be put to death.' Now because that Christ had set himself up to be a prophet, yea, and more than a pro- phet, to be the Son of God, they would have ensnared him by asking him questions of what he had taught, that so according to the law they might put him to death as a false prophet. And because that in that law (as appeareth ver. 6), not only a false prophet was thus to be put to death, but if any one did secretly entice another, saying, ' Let us go and serve other gods'—even as now secretly to persuade any to popery is death by the law of this land,—so it was to turn from the true God, or to turn to any other god ; this the high priest had an eye upon, and would have gathered it out of Christ himself, as appears by Christ's answer, in which he quits himself from any such practice of enticing any secretly, ' In secret,' saith he, have I said nothing.'

And, *secondly*, another end the high priest had was this. They were resolved he should be put to death, and they would therefore fain have gotten something out of him that should be matter or cause of death, and that by the judgment of Pilate. For you must know that all matters of controversy in their own law Pilate would not meddle withal ; but if it touched upon anything that concerned the Roman state, either raising of sedition, or that did touch upon Cæsar, denying of him to be king, &c., of that Pilate was exceeding jealous (and that they knew), and about that he meddled, as being within his cognisance as the Roman governor. You shall read in Luke xiii., that Pilate had mingled the blood of the Galileans with their sacrifices : he killed a great many of them while they were sacri- ficing. What was the reason ? Pilate did not regard sacrifices nor sacri- ficing, and all the schisms that were in that church Pilate took no notice of them, but he let all the sects amongst them enjoy their liberty ; why doth he kill these Galileans ? Look in Acts v. 37, and you shall find that there was one Judas of Galilee, that, in the days of the taxing, went and drew away much people after him, raised sedition, and taught that it was not lawful to pay tribute and taxes to Cæsar. This was it that made Pilate to fall upon a remnant of these Galileans that came up to Jerusalem to wor- ship, and to do it even while they were a-sacrificing. Now, therefore, that which this Caiaphas did fish for was this, to have matter to accuse Christ unto Pilate, for having done as that Judas did, drawn much people after him in a way of sedition. Therefore he tries now if he could get anything that might drop from his own mouth, out of which he might frame an accu- sation ; and therefore the doctrine which he especially aimed in this ques- tion was, Whether he were the Son of God or no ? And hence is it that we find in Luke xxiii. 2, when they came to accuse Christ before Pilate, the thing they urge upon Pilate against him is this, ' He forbiddeth to pay tribute unto Cæsar, saying that he himself is a king ;' and (ver. 5), ' He stirreth up the people, teaching throughout all Jewry, beginning from Galilee to this place.' They would insinuate to Pilate that he had gone up and down teaching this doctrine, and gathering disciples after him, to make a head against the Romans, as being king of the Jews. They put all upon this interpretation, and this was it that Caiaphas, in his questioning Christ, fished for; and thus doth Gerrard interpret the words. And that is the reason that Pilate still saith, he found no cause in the man to put him to death; for Pilate did not meddle with their controversies concerning matters of their religion, not he; but if it were a matter of right or wrong, as Gallio said, a matter of sedition, then he meddled with it. This, I say, was the second thing that Caiaphas aimed at in his asking Christ about his disciples and his doctrine, namely, to find out, if he could, that he had taught a doctrine of rebellion, and did go about to draw disciples in a seditious way after him; which you see is insinuated to be his scope in Christ's answer. You have gone into corners (saith Caiaphas) and into woods, and spread your doctrine in secret, and have taken cunning ways to draw disciples after you. No; saith Christ, whatsoever I have said I have said publicly; ask them that heard me what I have delivered, for I will not accuse myself.

The end that God had in this, why he should be examined about his disciples and his doctrine, it was,

1. To shew that he should suffer for having disciples, that those whom he died for the owning of them should be part of his crime for which they put him to death. Which is a circumstance mightily setting out the love of Christ unto us.

2. To shew what it was that they chiefly maliced him for, it was for having disciples, which was the work of his ministry. And yet they themselves had disciples, for there was nothing more common (as all men know) than for the several sects which were among them (and there were multitudes of them) to have their several disciples, and liberty was given to them so to do; yet his disciples, of all the rest, they maliced; and though they themselves had all the power, yet that vexed them, that he should have any disciples at all.

And they asked him of his doctrine also, as one that had taught new matters, and had not followed the traditions of the elders in all things, but had corrected them in a great many of their false glosses by which they misinterpreted the law.

Neither do they ask him at all of his miracles; not a word of them. Whatsoever made for him, that they meddled not with, but whatsoever might any way make against him, that they might fish anything out of, of that they make inquiry; for his miracles were they that confirmed him to be the Messiah, and confirmed his doctrine. They asked him of his doctrine, as that which was contrary to the law of Moses, and as one that brought in innovations; and they asked him of his disciples, as one that brought in sedition; but that which confirmed the truth of both they speak not a word of. For that is the nature of corrupt men, that which makes for the truth in any cause or business, they let that pass in silence, not a whit of mention of that. 'Believe me,' saith he, 'for my works' sake.' He still confirmed his doctrine by miracles; they would not so much as consider of them, but only barely asked him of his disciples and of his doctrine. 'They asked him of his disciples, and of his doctrine.'

What is the answer now that Christ makes? It is not to the matter of what Caiaphas said or asked him. He declareth neither what his doctrine was nor what disciples he had. Only he deals with them warily, as with a cunning advorsary, one that was skilful to destroy. He would not go and accuse himself, but refers what he had taught to their proof, for it was matter of fact. 'If I have taught anything,' saith he, 'ask them that heard me.' And he answers nothing about his disciples at all, for if whatsoever he had taught had been sound and good doctrine, there had been no guilt in drawing disciples after him. And whereas Caiaphas in his examination did insinuate that he had gone about in a cunning way to draw disciples after him, he clearly wipeth off that challenge: he never went about deceitfully to sow tares whilst others slept; he never enticed any one secretly to any doctrine which he had not publicly taught, but tells them that he did always affect publicness, and he expresseth his affectation of publicness in his doctrine by all sorts of expressions. This in the general.

'*I spake openly to the world, I ever taught in the synagogues, and in the temple, whither the Jews always resort; and in secret have I said nothing.*'

I shall first open the words, and then shew you Christ's scope in this answer of his, as I shewed you their scope in their examination.

First, To open the words. You see our Lord and Saviour Christ answers them fully, and he answers them sharply: 'I spake openly.' The word is παῤῥησία, and it hath a twofold meaning.

1. That for the place where he spake or preached, it was open; so the word is taken, John xi. 54, where it is said, that 'Jesus walked no more openly,' that is, in public view. 'I spake openly;' that is, I did not seek corners to preach in, or to deliver my doctrine.

2. It signifies that he did speak plainly his mind; he spake out; he did not go about the bush, as we say. So the word is used, John x. 24, 'If thou be the Christ, tell us plainly' (it is the same word that is used here); tell us plainly, with a *parresia*, with a freedom and plainness, whether thou be the Christ. And they themselves once gave that testimony of him, that he was regardless of any, and cared not who knew his mind; so Matt. xxii. 16, 'We know thou regardest no man's person, but wilt speak the truth plainly.' So he had ever done. 'I spake openly;' that is, what was in my heart about the truth, I spake it plainly.

And then as he had spoken openly and plainly, so to the world: 'I spake openly to the world,' saith he; that is, to all sorts of men, for so *world* is taken. He did not restrain what he taught to a few disciples only, but he told it to the people also, as the Syriac translation hath it. As when a man publisheth a book, he publisheth it to the world; so saith Christ, 'I spake openly to the world.'

And this, saith he, I have ever done. It hath been my custom from the beginning, as oft as I had any occasion, to speak publicly. It was so at the first; for in Mark i. 21, when he began first to preach, 'He entered into the synagogue and taught.'

'*I ever taught in the synagogue, and in the temple, whither the Jews always resort.*'

There were those two places of public preaching, which he took occasion to preach in, and he instanceth in both. I have taught my doctrine in all the several sorts of public audiences that are amongst the Jews. First, he instanceth in the temple, that is, in Solomon's porch, for that was the great place where they used to speak to the people; and therefore when Christ is said by one evangelist to walk in the temple, another saith, he walked in Solomon's porch, whither all the Jews did resort (for so some read this, whither the Jews always resort), or as others, whither the Jews out of all quarters did resort. Which by the way may be an answer to that which is said, that there were such multitude of believers in Jerusalem, that they could not meet all in one place. Certainly there were mighty audiences amongst the Jews, consisting of many thousands, when they came up to the feast, unto whom Christ preached; therefore at one time in the feast it is said that Christ (to the end they might all hear) 'lifted up his voice and cried, He that is athirst, let him come unto me and drink.' There they all met, and in that respect he had opportunity to preach to many thousands at once, for all the Jews, it is said, came thither; and so that was fulfilled which was spoken of him, Ps. xl. 10, 'I have not concealed thy word from the great congregation.'

The synagogues (which he instanceth in likewise) did differ from the temple thus, that the synagogues they had only moral and natural worship in them, not ceremonial. The temple had ceremonial worship, it was made principally and especially for that, yet so as that prayer and preaching, &c., was exercised in it too; but in the synagogues there was only prayer and preaching, and the moral and natural worship of God, which is to be for ever, and they were for that use only. Now under the gospel, that which God hath made to be the seat of all worship, it is not so much the imitation of the temple or representative worship, but it is the imitation of the synagogues (for so particular congregations and churches are); and therefore in James ii. 2, 'If any man come into your congregations' (the word is, 'into your synagogues') 'with a gold ring,' &c. And in Heb. x. 25, 'Forsake not the assembling of yourselves together;' it is, assembling together in a synagogue. Yet though, for the matter of it, the congregations now be as the synagogues then, which therefore have only moral worship, yet for the privileges and for the promises, they are called temples too, the meetings of the saints in the New Testament are. Every synagogue now, that is, every assembly of the saints, have the promises of the temple made to it. 'You are a temple built up to God,' saith the apostle, 'acceptable to him by Jesus Christ.' 'I ever taught in the synagogue and in the temple.' The doctrine which he had to deliver, he hath chosen all sort of ways to make it public. And he addeth a negation besides.

In secret have I said nothing. These words you have spoken of the great God in Isa. xlv. 19, which he that is God applies here unto himself.

But how is it said that he taught nothing in secret? for in Mark iv. 10, when he was alone, he preached to his disciples. And he made a long sermon here (which John recordeth), at the passover, and he did it when nobody was by but his disciples. And in Mat. xvi. 26, he charged them that they should tell no man that he was the Messiah. And many instances might be given of his often preaching privately; how then doth he say, 'In secret have I said nothing'?

Certainly our Saviour doth not contradict himself or the truth. But this speech of his doth not refer to the act of preaching only, as if it had been unlawful for him to teach in private, but refers to the matter, 'I have said nothing in secret'; that is, I know nothing that ever I have spoken unto any in private, but I have spoken it publicly; I was never shy or chary of my doctrine; I never feared the face of any man; neither cared I if all the world heard me, but I have ever declared the mind of God to the full, and done it with all the freedom of mind that could be. And then likewise the scope of that speech is this, that he had not two sorts of doctrine, which they would have charged him with; that he held forth his best doctrine in public to the world, that so he might gain applause from the people; and another private doctrine which he reserved to himself, and taught it only to his disciples.   No ; Christ was so far from it, that if you read that place in Mark iv., and compare the 10th and 21st verses together, you shall find that though when he was alone he did indeed explain a parable privately to his disciples, and so make a sermon of it, yet what saith he at the 21st verse ?   ' Is a candle brought to be put under a bushel, or under a bed ? There is nothing hid which shall not be made manifest.' And look in Mat. x. 26, you shall see his meaning to be this : though I have opened this parable to you in private, and so preached a sermon privately, yet what I have said in your ear, do you go and preach it on the house-top.   So that Christ professeth the highest plainness and openness that could be, of whatsoever he held, and he had that spirit that scorned to reserve himself, to deliver one thing in private and another in public.   And then he had this third scope also, that he was ready to defend what he had taught, if there were any man that could lay anything to his charge.   I know nothing, said he, that ever I spake in private, but I spake it openly ; therefore if any man can accuse me, I am here ready to defend it.   This is the scope of his speech.

Our Lord and Saviour Christ, you see, he doth not answer a word concerning his disciples.   What was the reason ?

1. Because it was lawful for him, according to the custom that was amongst the Jews, to have disciples.   The Pharisees they had so uncontrolled ; and the Sadducees had so : and you know what great contention there was between those two sects ; so the Essenes, so the Nazarites, so the Herodians, and so others.   And Christ he might as well justify the one as they the other.

2. It needed not : for if he could justify his doctrine, he might justify his having disciples.   If his doctrine were sound and true, there was no guilt in this that he had disciples.

3. He would say nothing concerning them, because he would take all upon himself, he alone would suffer.   Others give this reason : because his disciples had forsaken him, or because he would not betray them, therefore he would not tell who they were.   And they observe this from it, that men should not betray others when they are asked of them, as here Christ did not his disciples.   But I take the second to be the truer reason, namely, that he standing to the justification of his doctrine, his gathering disciples that makes no crime.

There is only this question a little more largely to be insisted upon, whether that all private preaching, that is not in public assemblies, be unlawful ?

1. It is the objection that the papists urged against the churches of Christ in their first Reformation (as Beza hath it in his sermons upon the passion). They say, saith he, that we preach in chimney-corners.   But what saith Calvin ?   It is, saith he, a childish argument to go about to prove by this answer of Christ's to Caiaphas, that in some cases men should not preach the word of God in private ; for Christ's scope in this speech is not to justify the lawfulness or unlawfulness either of the one or the other, but only to shew what course he had held, and to rebuke the impudent malice of his adversaries ; for otherwise Christ had preached not only in the synagogues, but in a ship, and in mountains ; and whenas the Jews went about to suppress him, you shall find that he withdrew himself with his disciples into a desert place, and he did so a long time.   And the disciples themselves did the like for fear of the Jews, as in Acts i. 14 and Acts xii. 12.

2. But, *secondly ;* there is this may be gathered out of it too, as the scope

of Christ, and that justly: that no man should go and spread a doctrine privately, which he will not own and preach publicly, or own before all the world; for so our Saviour Christ did.   It was not but that he taught privately, and so his apostles did too; but as they taught privately, so they did teach also in the temple, and never scrupled to do it.   It is the property of wisdom (as it is Prov. i. 20, 21) to utter her voice in the streets, and to cry in the chief places of concourse, and in the city to utter her words.   It is the devil's practice to sow tares in the night whilst men slept. And the apostle, in 2 Tim. iii. 6, speaks of a sort of men that creep into houses, and pervert silly women.   And it is certainly a sign of falsehood, and argues a lie, to conceal men's minds, or to speak that in private which they will not do in public.   Error and falsehood always shun the light.   Our Saviour Christ, you see, scorned to speak anything in private, which he had not publicly vented, and he was ready to give an account of it; and so did the apostles too; and although they held their meetings, in times of persecution, privately, yet so as what they preached privately, they did not fear to profess publicly.   And it is the genius of the truth, and of them that do profess it, so to do.   The gospel is light, and it seeks no corners, and it ought to seek no corners, but ought to be spoken publicly; Acts v. 20, ' Go, stand and speak in the temple all the words of this life.'   It was Christ's charge to the apostles.

3. Therefore, in the third place, I remember Beza gives this answer: The papists, saith he, need not object to us, that we seek corners to preach in; for, saith he, we desire nothing more than all that ever we preach or hold, to preach it to all the world.   And so much now for answer to that question.

Now, the scope of Christ in this 20th verse (to touch that a little) is this. You see he doth not answer directly to what Caiaphas asketh him; Caiaphas would have had something that he had taught out of him, that so he might ensnare him, which was against the law; for by the law he was not thus to sift him, but to have produced witnesses.   Christ therefore tells them that he had taught what he held in public, and so puts them upon the proof, refers them to what he had delivered, which they were (if they counted it heresy) to bring proof of.   And, secondly, if I have disciples, saith he, I have not gathered them by any secret whisperings or creeping into houses, but it hath been by preaching publicly; and if I have preached anything publicly, and gathered disciples by it, you yourselves may convince me of what I have taught, and here I am to answer it.   So that I say, Christ he doth not go to answer punctually to what the high priest asked him, for he would not give that advantage to so cruel an adversary; but here I am, saith he.   They ought to have produced witnesses in a matter of fact as this was.   And so much for the 20th verse, the opening of it.   I shall open likewise the 21st, and then give you observations out of them altogether.

' Why askest thou me? ask them which heard me, what I have said unto them: behold, they know what I said.'

Our Lord and Saviour Christ, as he had cleared himself in the former words, so here he gives the sharpest reproof, which the high priest to the uttermost deserved, for his unjust proceedings against him; for they were, according to their law, to prove everything by witnesses.   Christ, though he stood at the bar, yet he would shew the greatness of his spirit, he speaks home, you see, and sharply.   It became him so to do; he speaks not railingly or revilingly, but that which shewed both the injustice of Caiaphas, and that he himself, though he stood there before them as a malefactor,

was not a whit dejected. Do you ask me, saith he? I never spake anything privately, but in public, and if there be a fault in gathering disciples,
the fault must lie upon my doctrine; and if there be anything in my doctrine, you have the world to witness against me, for I have taught openly
in the synagogue and in the temple; and do you ask me? And do you
begin now to ask me? Have you not excommunicated my disciples, and
made a law that whosoever confesseth me shall be cast out of the synagogues, and have cast them out because they followed my doctrine? As
you never yet refuted my doctrine, and now you bring no witnesses about
it, do you ask me, that have dealt so injuriously with me and my disciples?
And not only so, but you have bound me, and brought me hither to your
bar, and have nothing to lay to my charge; but what I am accused of, you
would get out of my own words. Do you ask me in a matter of fact what
I have preached, that so you might ensnare me out of my own sayings?
Do you ask me? Will you have me to accuse myself? The law allows
me this liberty, not to accuse myself; no man by the law is to be judged
without witnesses. Produce them. ' Why ask you me? Ask them that
heard me.'

Obs. It is not irreverence to magistrates to defend ourselves in such
cases as these are. Christ doth not stand upon his points as the Messiah,
but as a subject to that state. And men ought to shew great boldness of
spirit in such cases. So the apostles, Acts v., ' Whether it is better to obey
God than man, judge you.' And Paul saith, Phil. i. 28, that such boldness is a token of perdition to the adversaries, and of salvation to the people
of God.

Ask them that heard me. This shews his innocency. I do not desire
you, saith he, to ask my friends only; ask my enemies, the worst I have,
any one that hath heard me, that can testify anything; here I am ready to
defend it; if they will frame up any accusation, I will answer it.

Behold, they know what I have said. That same *behold* hath an emphasis
with it. Some interpreters very probably conjecture, that he did point to
their own officers, who had formerly, when they were sent by their masters
to entrap him, given this testimony of him in John vii. 46, that 'never
man spake like him;' and that therefore he did insinuate this in his speech,
and perhaps did more largely explain it; for the Holy Ghost records but
the sum of things; and so now he gives the greatest justification of himself
that can be: saith he, your own officers (pointing at them) that stand here
at the bar holding of me, many of those can tell what I have delivered; I
have those to justify me, for they said never man spake as I did, therefore
ask them, and never stand asking of me. It is a mighty reproof. I am so
free in myself, and stand so innocent and so resolved in that truth that I
have spoken, that let your own servants and ministers be called, and let
them speak. And so you have the answer of Christ in this 20th and 21st
verses. I shall now give you some observations, and so conclude this story
of Christ's sufferings, which were antecedent to his being scourged, crowned
with thorns, and crucified.

Obs. 1. You may observe that the high priest doth not find fault with
Christ nor with his disciples, for that they had taught without authority.
In another case, when he whipped the buyers and sellers out of the temple,
they asked him, ' By what authority doest thou these things?' But here
they do not lay that to his charge. Certainly they would have silenced him
long afore for his preaching, if it had not been allowable by the custom of
that country. The truth is, that though none but the priests and Levites

that were skilful in the law were to preach, yet divers others did, and were permitted so to do in that state, if they were gifted. The Pharisees did so, and so did Paul, who was a Pharisee, and sat at the feet of Gamaliel; and yet he was not of the tribe of Levi, but of the tribe of Benjamin. And Christ himself did not take upon him to preach simply as he was the Messiah, as holding that forth for his warrant, though that was warrant abundantly for him. And when they come to condemn him, they do not quarrel with him for that, but for the matter of his doctrine, whether yea or no he did teach these and these points, which they would have known from himself, and therefore they asked him of his doctrine.

Obs. 2. You see they object no vice against Christ, only his doctrine to him (for otherwise Christ was innocent), and his having disciples. Observe, then, that his professing Christians should herein imitate their master, that when they come to suffer, they may no way suffer as evil doers; that they may suffer for nothing but the doctrine they have held forth, the disciples they have kept company with, the profession they have made, that it may be barely and merely the truth of their religion they suffer for.

Obs. 3. Still the great charge in all ages that they go about to' lay, as to Christ, so to his people, it is heresy, and it is sedition. This they would have fastened upon Christ, charging him with heresy in his doctrine ; with sedition in gathering disciples to disturb the state, as Theudas and others that you read of in Acts v. ; and therefore they ask him of his doctrine, and of his disciples, and they would have fetched that out from himself, that when he had gathered disciples enow he would presently have rebelled. This they would have made Pilate believe. Both these, heresy and sedition, *in terminis*, were laid to Christ's charge.

Obs. 4. In that Christ answers nothing about his disciples, we may gather this (which indeed I hinted afore), that if the doctrine be good, as to the having disciples that do embrace it, there is no guilt in that. If Christ had done it seditiously indeed, which was it they endeavoured to lay to his charge, therein there had been a guilt. Look of what kind the doctrine is, of that kind the disciples must be. If the doctrine be right, there is no danger that disciples embrace it. Therefore Christ, in Mat. xxviii. 20, bids them make disciples, not to themselves, but to the truth, to their doctrine.

Obs. 5. Observe, that even these men here accused themselves in accusing Christ. There were several of them had several sorts of disciples, but what themselves went on in and agreed in amongst themselves, that they fall upon Christ for; for this is manifest by all the stories of the Scripture, and by their own Rabbins, that in those times it was free to gather disciples. There were three eminent sects among themselves, that still agreed in temple worship; there were the Sadducees, that denied the resurrection, against the Pharisees, and the Pharisees against the Sadducees; there were the Herodians likewise; there were the Esseni; there were the Nazarites. All these were amongst the Jews; and it is evident that after the time of the Maccabees, yea, after the captivity of Babylon, there was a permission of great differences in point of doctrine amongst them. Yet when the true Messiah cometh to teach his doctrine, and to make disciples, they fall upon him for that which they themselves practised. Here were many Pharisees here present that were sectaries (that is the truth on it), but what was a commendation, and tolerable in them one to another, that must not be suffered in Christ; for men will bear anything but the truth. They themselves (saith the apostle in the Galatians) would constrain you to be circumcised and to keep the law, yet they themselves do not keep the law. It is constantly so in experience; they that are opposers of the truth always do so. The papists they suffer a world of differences amongst themselves, they suffer even Jews that are opposite to Christ, and who blaspheme him; but any that do profess but the least of protestant doctrine or worship, how do they oppose them! The Pharisees, you see, did the like, though there was a world of division amongst themselves, and they had a liberty to differ in matters of doctrine, and in matters of a high nature too; yet when it comes to the truth, there they would not permit Christ either to teach any doctrine differing from them, or to have disciples; which yet they themselves allowed, both in themselves and others.

Obs. 6. Those that were the greatest corrupters of doctrine (for these Pharisees and the high priests were those that had corrupted the doctrine of religion by their traditions, as Christ intimateth often in his speeches), they are they that are here most zealous in the matter of doctrine, who themselves, I say, had been the greatest corrupters of it, and had drawn in their several ways several disciples after them, as the manner of those times was.

Obs. 7. This very speech of Christ may teach us this, to take heed of perverting the speeches of men. For this speech of Christ, if you do not take the scope he aimed at, is subject to perversion. He saith that in secret he had taught nothing. Now all the stories of the evangelists shew that he had taught much in private; but (as I have shewed you) his meaning is this, I have not one kind of doctrine that I teach privately and another that I teach publicly. He doth not so much refer to the act as to the matter.

Obs. 8. Though they had authority to examine men's doctrines, yet here lay the evil of their examining Christ, that they should have done it upon complaints first brought before them. It is still as controversies do arise. It was not that the Sanhedrim went and made so many doctrines unto which they would tie men, and they must preach no other; that power even those amongst the Jews had not. It was lawful for men to interpret the Scripture, and that not only by the rule the Sanhedrim set out; but indeed if any controversy did arise upon the spreading of a doctrine, then it belonged to their cognisance, as appeareth by Deut. xvii. If a false prophet arise, and if there were any controversy between blood and blood, case and case, or interpreting Scripture, the thing was to be referred unto them, and it was examinable by that council. But that men should be limited in their doctrine to what all the councils in the world should say, this is not the rule. It was not the rule among the Jews themselves, although that Sanhedrim had that authority which no council ever had since the world began, for it was by divine institution. Therefore, I say, they do not find fault with him because he had not come to know what doctrine he should teach as from them, but that he taught a doctrine contrary to God's law. They indeed acted beyond their authority, to proceed by way of examination; they should have done it by way of charge.

Obs. 9. You see the freeness of truth and innocency; it is able to appeal even unto enemies, unto any, to defend itself. And therefore as we should so preach, so we should so walk, as we may freely and boldly appeal unto any, for so Christ doth here: ' Ask them that heard me,' saith he.

Obs. 10. Oftentimes doctrines and opinions are condemned by prejudice, and upon hearsay only. This Caiaphas and many of those rulers, they had not heard Christ; no, the greatness of their places kept them from that, as oftentimes great places keep men from the means, from that which should save them; but their officers 'heard him, and by the report of malicious and malignant spirits, Caiaphas and the rest were thus informed.

Obs. 11. Lastly, it is the law of God, and indeed the law of nature and equity, that there should not be an oath *ex officio;* that is, that men should not be proceeded against, either in church or otherwise, by a bare examination of themselves, till such time as witnesses have brought an accusation against them. As in Acts xxv. 27, 'It seems to me unreasonable' (it was the speech of a heathen) 'to send a prisoner, and not withal to signify the crimes laid against him.' That rule which is given concerning an elder is true concerning every brother also, though the instance is only in an elder, as one whose credit should be more than another's: 1 Tim. v. 19, 'Against an elder receive not an accusation, but before two or three witnesses.' I do observe this difference, my brethren, and it is very notable: when afterward the high priest doth examine Christ of this truth, whether he was the Messiah, and when he was punctually asked whether he was the Son of God or no, he answers plainly, I am. But when he would examine him about matter of fact, not about the matter so much what he taught, as that he had taught thus and thus, which might be proved by witnesses, then Christ referreth it to witnesses, and would not answer himself. And the reason of the difference to me holds forth this great truth, that no man is to refuse if he be positively asked whether he hold this or that opinion or no. Or if he be asked an account of his faith, or demanded what his judgment is in such or such a thing, he is freely to tell it, especially if they that ask him have authority. It is a thing in which Christ's example is held forth to Timothy by the apostle Paul, that he witnessed a good confession before Pilate and the high priest, 1 Tim. vi. 13. A man is to give an account of his faith to any that will ask him; let him look to it though, whether it be to ensnare him or no. But if any shall come and say, I preached such a thing, which is matter of fact (for as it is preached it is matter of fact), and there are witnesses that can clear whether I did or no, in that case the way is not to proceed by examination of me, but to produce the witnesses, and so to proceed; for no man is bound, in matter of fact, to accuse himself. This I take to be the difference of Christ's answer in this, when the high priest examined him about his doctrine, that is, asked him whether he had not preached thus or thus; saith Christ, If I have preached thus or thus, prove it; there are witnesses enough, I refer myself to them; I will never tell you what I have preached: go to them that heard me, and bring them hither, and then examine me, and I shall give you an answer. But when he came positively to ask him whether he held this or no, whether he was the Messiah, he answered clearly and plainly; for no man is to refuse to give an account of his faith, though it endanger his life, if he be called to it. But for matter of fact, whenas it may be proved by witnesses (and all such things may be proved by witnesses, though it be matter of doctrine), a man is not to accuse himself. It was the proceeding in that great oath that you are now freed from, which, as it was a great oppression, so it is a great mercy to this kingdom that it is taken away.* And whereas they used to allege that Christ accused himself, the case is different; it was not what he had preached in

---

* There were many oaths imposed in those times; but I suppose the reference is to the oath imposed by the Convocation in 1640 (sometimes called the *Et Cetera Oath*), and declared illegal by the Parliament in 1641. See Rapin's History, vol. ii. pp. 321 and 380, or any other history of the period.—ED.

matter of fact, but in matter of opinion and judgment. But as to the matter of fact, 'Askest thou me?' saith he. 'Ask them that heard me.' And this is the law of nature, and this is the law of the Jews; and this was Christ's dealing with a cunning and wary adversary that sought his life; and this, you see, he stands to. I have taught, saith he, where all the Jews come; I have taught in the temple, taught in the synagogues, taught before all the world; and now have you brought me hither, having bound me, and cast me and my disciples out of the synagogues, and ask me what I have preached! Here was the most unjust and unequal proceeding in the world; yet thus they did with Christ, and the disciple is not above his master.

CHAPTER XI.

The last sufferings of Christ coming to his death.—Both the shame and torments are to be considered in them.

We have seen our Lord Christ a man of sorrows and sufferings through the whole course of his life; we have seen him betrayed, apprehended, seized on as a criminal, and brought to examination and judgment; and all these were the fruits of his being made sin and a curse. Now the next part and conclusion of the curse, unto which all the other tend, as so many small rivulets into the ocean, is death; and that,

1. Natural, of the body: 'To dust thou shalt return,' Gen. iii. 19, which phrase notes out the separation of soul and body. So Eccles. xii. 7, it is expounded, 'Dust returns to the earth, and the soul to God that gave it.'

2. Death spiritual, of the soul: 'Thou shalt die the death,' Gen. ii. 17, which words intimate a double death, even another death besides that of the body, and beyond it. Now,

1. I shall shew how Christ was made a curse in his enduring a bodily death; the circumstances whereof do all of them yet add unto the curse thereof. You see that death in itself (whether natural or violent) is by God's first sentence on Adam made a curse for sin. And thus is the death of every man who dies not in the Lord. But yet further, whereas there was but one particular kind of death that was in a more eminent manner, of all deaths else, the most accursed—and that was 'hanging upon a tree'— even that did Christ undergo, so that to be sure he might bear the extremity of the curse herein. And that kind of death was not accursed by God's law and doom only, but was also esteemed to be a curse among the Gentiles. Thus it was among the Romans, who, when they would curse any man unto whom they owed ill will, they expressed it by this, *Abi in malam crucem;* that is, I would thou wert crucified, or Mayest thou die the death of the tree. Equivalent to which is that way of cursing taken up by ill tongues among us, when they say, 'Go and be hanged,' &c.

In that his last suffering the death of the cross (which was the epitome of all), two things are eminently to be considered by us:

(1.) The shame of that death, and the circumstances of it.

(2.) The pains of those sufferings, and the death itself, which is the separation of soul and body, and the conclusion of all. And unto these may the chief of those his sufferings, either preparatory unto, or at his death, be reduced. The apostle, in Heb. xii. 2, draws them to these two heads:

[1.] Enduring the cross, which includes both the pains of his suffering, and death itself.

[2.] The shame that accompanied it, in those words, ' despising the shame.' And Christ himself, particularly summing up all that was to be done to him, and that was foretold of him by the prophets (as he says), Luke xviii. 31, ' Behold we go to Jerusalem, and all things that are written by the prophets concerning the Son of man shall be accomplished.' The main particulars of which, all, he after mentions: ver. 32, 33, he expresseth it in these words, ' The Son of man shall be delivered unto the Gentiles, and shall be mocked, and spitefully entreated, and spitted on; and they shall scourge him, and put him to death;' which particulars, if you will reduce them to heads, do fall into these two :

1. The shame, expressed in three particulars: (1.) Mocked. (2.) Spitefully entreated. (3.) Spitted on.

2. The pains, laid down in two things : (1.) Their scourging him. (2.) Their killing him.

And accordingly we find two especial epithets of excellency mentioned of Christ, when his sufferings are mentioned by the apostles, on purpose to aggravate those sufferings from the worth of the person that underwent them :—the first, that ' they killed the Prince of life :' so says Peter, Acts iii. 15 ; the other, that ' they crucified the Lord of glory:' so Paul, 1 Cor. ii. 18 ; the first serving to illustrate his dying, that they should kill the Prince of life ; the second, the shame of his death, that they should crucify the Lord of glory—the apostle mentioning his glory, together with his crucifying, so to set out the shame of that death above all other, and also as an evil to be considered in his death, as great as death itself, and greater. And accordingly in respect of death he is called ' the Lamb slain,' Rev. xiii. 8, and in respect of shame he is called ' a worm and no man,' Ps. xxii. 6, being trodden on by all men, and his life of so poor a value with them, that they made no more of it to kill him than to tread a worm to death, which to do no man hath the least regret. And accordingly also, Heb. vi. 6, the sin of apostates from Christ is set out by their doing (so far as in them lies) that unto Christ, which the Jews, that put him to death, did to him at his crucifying. It is set out by these two things: 1. That ' they crucify to themselves the Son of God afresh ;' secondly, that ' they put him to an open shame.' And so I reckon this of shame with the curse of his death, because they are thus linked together by the apostles ; and also because indeed, in all death, shame is a part of the curse (and therefore it is said, the body is ' sown in dishonour,' 1 Cor. xv. 43); but especially in Christ's death, for it was more than dying, the kind of death being the shamefullest. And though shame be not mentioned in the words of the curse of our first parents, yet the first fruit, and so the first appearance of the curse (that we read of) even in them, was shame and fear ; it is said, ' they were ashamed,' &c. And so I come,

1. To the shame of this death. It is a great question, whether shame or death be the greater evil. There have been those who have rather chosen death, and have wiped off a dishonour with their blood. So Saul slew himself rather than he would fall into the hands of the Philistines, who would have insulted over him, and mocked him as they did Samson. So that king, Jer. xxxviii. 19, rather chose to lose his country, life, and all, than to be given to the Jews, his subjects, to be mocked of them. And we see that many malefactors that are to be condemned to die, and though, dying as malefactors, any sort of death hath shame in it, yet to avoid a

degree of shame in death, they out of the greatness of their spirits choose
a death that is much more painful, as to be pressed to death, rather than
this same hanging on a tree, which unto this day is, in men's esteem, of all
deaths else, the most ignoble and ignominious.   Yea, confusion of face is
one of the greatest miseries that hell itself is set forth unto us by.   There
is nothing that a noble nature more abhors than shame ; for honour is a
spark of God's image ; and the more of God's image there is in any one,
the more is shame abhorred by him, which is the debasing of it; and so the
greater and more noble any one's spirit, the more he avoids it.   To a base,
low spirit, indeed, shame is nothing ; but to a great spirit (as to David),
than to have his ' glory turned into shame,' as Ps. iv. 2, is nothing more
grievous.   And'the greater glory any one loseth, the greater is his shame.
What must it be then to Christ, who because he was to satisfy God in point
of honour debased by man's sin, therefore of all punishments else he suffered most of shame ; it being also (as was said) one of the greatest punishments in hell.   And Christ, as he assumed other infirmities of our nature,
that made him passible in other things—as to be sensible of hunger, want
of sleep, bodily torments, of unkindnesses, contempt—so likewise of disgrace and shame.   He took that infirmity as well as fear ; and though he
had a strength to bear and despise it (as the author to the Hebrews speaks),
yet none was ever more sensible of it.   As the delicacy of the temper of his'
body made him more sensible of pains than ever any man was, so the greatness of his spirit made him more apprehensive of the evil of shame than ever
any was.   So likewise the infinite love and candour of his spirit towards
mankind made him take in with answerable grief the unkindnesses and
injuries which they heaped upon him.   And if to be abhorrent of shame be
a spark of God's image, so as where more of that image or of glory is in
any one, the more abhorrent he is of shame ; yea, if even those in hell are
confounded with it (they there still retaining so much of God's image in
them), then what must so much shame and contempt be unto Christ, who
was and is ' the brightness of his Father's glory, and the express image of
his person ' ? Heb. i. 3.   Such an image of him as no mere creature is
capable to be ; all which he considered and took in, well knowing what and
who he was, and this before his sufferings.   So John xiii. 3, and also when
he was both at Pilate's and at the high priest's bar.   As therefore the
highest lights have the deepest shadows, so all his ' glory being turned into
shame,' it made his shame the deeper and the greater.

Now if we go over all the particulars of this his shame, never was any
shame like unto it.   There was nothing but shame, and that the utmost
that could be, in all the passages of his sufferings.

This shame I shall set forth to you by these two generals (which will contain several particulars under them) :

1. Their mocking and spiteful entreating of him.

2. Other circumstances, that, through God's providence, were ordered to
accompany his misusage and death, that served to heighten the shameful-
ness of them.

1. For their cruel mocking and shameful usage of him, the very words
that Christ, in Luke xviii. 32, expresseth it in the general by, are very emphatical.   The one ἐμπαιχθήσεται, which we translate, ' He shall be mocked,'
in the derivation of it, signifies ' to make a child of one.'   They made a child
or fool of him by their actions and dealings with him.   Like unto which is
the word that is used of Herod's mocking of him, Luke xxiii. 11, ἐξουδενήσας,
' he made no body,' or ' nothing of him.'   The other word, ὑβρισθήσεται,

principally respecteth contumelious speeches, and injurious despiteful railing at; ὕβρις, noting out the highest kind of injury, and that done out of a despite. It is the same word whereby the sin against the Holy Ghost is expressed, Heb. x. 29, and is there translated 'doing despite.' Now for him whose name is *I am*, to whom all beings are but shadows, for him to be made nothing of, for him who is the 'Everlasting Father' and the 'wisdom of God,' for him, I say, to be made a child of, what an intolerable shame is this! '*Died Abner as a fool dies!*' said David of him. Truly through their usage of him Christ died no otherwise.

But I rather come to those several particular ways wherein they express their extreme contempt and despiteful mockage of him; as,

(1.) Their putting several apparels upon him in derision; one while arraying of him in purple, another while in white, then shifting him into his own clothes again, thus making him ridiculous to all that saw him. Unmeetness and unsuitableness of apparel is matter of shame. Jehoshua the high priest appeared in 'filthy apparel,' Zech. iii. 3, and so Christ our high priest, being clothed with all our sins. For one to be led about in a fool's coat, what a shame is it! Yet thus was he served.

(2.) Their using jeering and mocking gestures. Because he had said he was a king, they therefore make a May-game king of him; and,

[1.] They crown him with a crown of thorns.

[2.] They put a reed in his hand for a sceptre, (though his sceptre was a 'sceptre of righteousness,' Heb. i. 8), to shew how powerless and weak a king he was, who had a kingdom and sceptre as easily broken as a reed. And therefore, to demonstrate his weakness the more in respect of any such kingdom as he assumed a title unto, they strike him with his own sceptre, which is to a king the same disgrace, and much more ignominious, as for an able scholar to have his own argument retorted on him to his own confuting and confusion; as for a valiant man to have his weapon taken from him, and with it to be beaten.

[3.] They hoodwink and blindfold him, and hide his face. Now covering the face is a gesture of shame; Jer. xiv. 3, it is said, 'They were ashamed and covered their heads.' Then they smite him, and when they have done it, they in scorn ask him, Who smote him? because he took on him to be a prophet.

[4.] They smite him both with their hands and with their rods: both are mentioned. And *majus dedecus est manu feriri quam gladio;* no noble spirit can brook a box on the ear, or buffet, but takes it in more disgrace than a wound honourably given. And therefore Micaiah, you know, was smitten on the cheek by the lying prophet, as a token of disdain; for to smite with the hand or fist argues subjection in the party smitten.

[5.] They in mockery kneel to him, and salute him as they did their Cæsar, 'Hail, king of the Jews.' To him whom all the angels (when a child) did worship—'Let all the angels of God worship him,' Heb. i. 6—to whom 'every knee shall bow, both that is in heaven, and in earth, and under the earth;' to him do they in scorn bow the knee, and then as floutingly salute him with an 'All hail, king,' &c. The greater reverence is given in a disgraceful way, the greater the disgrace is; for shame is glory turned into inglory or shame.

[6.] They spit on him; and it was not one or two of them that did this, but many, as it is said. Now this is the greatest indignity that may be. If a father spit in his daughter's face (who yet is an inferior to him), 'shall she not be shut up?' (says God, Num. xii. 14), in that he hath disgraced her. And Isa. l. 6, Christ is brought in, saying, 'I hid not my face from shame and spitting upon ;' they are both linked together. The face is the noblest of the exterior parts of man, as in which God's image doth shine forth, and is therefore called 'the glory of God,' 1 Cor. xi. 7. Now therefore for it to have an excrement, with which men will not defile a clean room they tread on, cast upon it, what a disgrace is it ? And if so, how much more, then, for that face to be spitted upon, in which the ' light of the glory of God' shines far more immediately and more plentifully, 2 Cor. iv. 6. And how disgraces of this nature must needs work upon a spirit so high and so full of glory as his was, we may see (and yet but a glimpse of it neither) by the heart of that king (one of our own), who, being deposed, and by night removed, was in his journey shaved, to the end he might not be known, and set upon a mole-hill instead of a chair of state, and washed with puddle-water, in the midst of which he burst out into this pathetical speech, 'I will yet have clean water to be washed with ;' and forthwith he shed many tears, which in rivulets distilled down his princely cheeks, and cleansed them from that filth wherewith the puddle-water had sullied and besmeared them. What heart would it not affect to read this story of a king ? And how much more did it affect his own heart ? And yet what was he to Christ, who in the midst of all their misusage of him knew well what a kingdom he was born unto! as himself told Pilate.

[7.] They unbare him and make him naked, and then whip him ; and both these to his shame. Nakedness, you know, is shameful ; and, therefore, our first parents,'when they were naked, were ashamed. And then for whipping, it was a punishment inflicted upon none but slaves and villains, never upon a free-born Roman. Therefore how afraid were the whippers of Paul when they heard that he was a Roman. And *mastigia* (or one that is subject to whipping), and a base villain, are all one. Now the reason why they might whip Christ was, that he had taken upon him the form of a servant ; and so they whipped him, as we use to do runaways, which Peter alludes to, speaking to servants, and setting before them Christ's example, 'We like sheep had gone astray, and by his stripes were we healed,' 1 Peter ii. 24, 25.

[8.] They mock him and abuse him by giving him gall before, and vinegar after he was upon the cross, to quench his thirst with. Which therefore Christ is brought in mentioning, as being sensible of the scorn of it, Ps. lxix. 21 (which psalm is a psalm of Christ).

[9.] They wag their heads at him when on the cross, and gape with their mouths ; which is, first, a gesture of despising : so, Isa. xxxvii. 22, it is said of Sennacherib, that Zion had ' despised him and shaken her head at him.' Secondly, it is a gesture of detestation. So, Jer. xviii. 16, it is said of Israel, that ' every one that passeth by her shall be astonished and wag his head at her.' Thirdly, it is a gesture of scorn. So, Lam. ii. 15, it is said, ' they hiss and wag their heads' (at Jerusalem), ' and say, Is this the city that men call the perfection of beauty, and joy of the whole earth ?'

[10.] They mock and jeer him by the most contumelious words that could be—ὑβρισθήσεται, ' He shall be opprobriously reviled,' Luke xviii. 32— yea, they blasphemed him. *First*, In all his offices : as, first, prophetical ; they blindfold him, and smite him, and then bid him prophesy who it was that smote him. Christ will one day tell him that did it who it was. Second, priestly ; he saved others (say they), let him save himself. Why, he was even then a-saving others by bearing their misusage ; he was then, a-doing that for which they mocked him. Third, kingly; ' If,' say they, ' thou be the king of Israel, then come down,' &c. Thus they mock all his offices. So,

Secondly, His person, and his being the Son of God; ' He trusted in God' (say they), ' and said he was the Son of God; let God now save him if he will have him.' And (which is strange) in these and the like speeches they use the very same words that in Psalm xxii. were foretold should be used by them when he should be crucified. \ For these words of theirs you have there recorded, ver. 8; so that, as Paul afterward told them, they fulfilled the prophecies, whilst they ridiculed him. Yea,

Thirdly (Which is an inhumanity unheard of before or since), They mock at his very prayers, which he makes out of the deepest bitterness of spirit that ever creature spake out of, and which were full of the saddest complaints that could be uttered, when he cried out most bitterly, ' Eli, Eli, My God, my God, why hast thou forsaken me ?' They put it off, and turn it into a scoff, as if they understood it not : ' He calls for Elias,' say they in scorn ; as if he had prayed unto a creature, unto Elias, instead of the living God : and ' let us see,' say they, ' if Elias will come and help him.' In Heb. xi., among other persecutions of the martyrs, cruel mockings are mentioned as none of the least, reproaches being to the soul (as the psalmist expresseth it, Ps. lxiv. 4) as the pricking of a sword. Now was there ever such cruel mockings as these heard of ? Christ complains in Ps. lxix. 26 (for it is a psalm of him), ' They persecute him whom thou hast smitten.' When God had smitten him, and he in bitterness cried, ' Eli, Eli, My God, my God,' they turn it to Elias. Take the most hateful malefactor that ever was, one that hath been the most flagitious traitor to his prince and country that ever pestered the earth, and so had rendered himself most abominable and odious to all mankind ; yet, let him come to die for it, and though the rage and fury of men make them not to compassionate his tortures, as being far less than his desert, yet still for his soul, as it stands in relation to God, they wish well to it, and that it may be saved ; their malice rageth not to jeer at the prayers he makes for the salvation thereof. Nay, men are even ready to afford comfort and help unto, and to further such a man's faith, and to join in prayers with, and for him. But these Jews scoff at Christ's very prayers. They speak what they are able to make him despair. If ever the devil was abroad, and the malice of hell in the hearts of men, it was at that day.

In the second place, add unto all these misusages those circumstances that accompanied both his death and mockings, to heighten his shame the more. God contrived all things so to fall out as to make his shame above measure shameful, as our sin had been above measure sinful; he heaped shame upon shame upon him.

The first circumstance here observable is that of time. All this was done to him at the most public time that could be chosen out ; even at the passover, when all the males came up to Jerusalem, and many strangers with them, to celebrate that feast—a concourse like our commencement at our universities, or like the most general assembly you can imagine.

Second is, the circumstance of place. Which,

1. For the publicness of it, was at Jerusalem, the head city of Jewry, a stage the most eminent upon which to be made a spectacle to men and angels. ' Art thou only a stranger in Jerusalem' (said two of his disciples unto himself), ' and hast not known these things ?' Luke xxiv. 18. ' These things were not done in a corner' (as his disciples said). And when God

would shame David, he cast in this circumstance to aggravate it; 'Thou' (says God) 'didst it secretly, but I will punish it before this sun.'

2. (More specially and restrictly) For the infamousness of the place; he was crucified at Golgotha, a place of skulls, as ignominious as our Tyburn. The place had a reproach in it: therefore, Heb. xiii. 13, 'Jesus suffered without the gate,' says the apostle; 'let us therefore go forth to him without the camp, *bearing his reproach*,' namely, of suffering in such a place. It shewed he was an outcast, rejected of men, and as dung cast out.

3. For the persons that mocked him, they were persons of all sorts; kings and rulers, Herod and the elders, the priests and soldiers, together with the multitude of common people that followed him, and that passed by occasionally, yea, the very thieves themselves that were crucified with him. Now the baseness of the persons that contemn one doth add to the contempt. Therefore you shall find Job complaining, Job xxx. 1–10, that those that were younger than he, and whose fathers he would have disdained to set with the dogs of his flock, did mock him: they are (says he, ver. 8, 9) the children of villains, more vile than the earth they tread on, and now I am their song, yea, their by-word,' &c. 'Reproach' (says Christ in one of the psalms made of him) 'hath broken my heart,' Ps. lxix. 20.

4. The death itself was also the most shameful; even 'the death of the cross;' which for his disciples to preach and profess, had in the eyes of all the world a shame in it. Therefore Paul, Gal. v. 11, calls it 'the offence or scandal of the cross.' And if that were a shame, to profess a crucified God, what a shame was it then for God himself to suffer such a death.' The cross was so shameful, that therefore none of all the meanest and basest of the people could be procured so much as to carry it; so that they were fain to compel Simon of Cyrene unto it. And it was the custom ever after to call such as carried a malefactor's cross, *Crucigeri*, as a brand of disgrace. And for himself to carry it (as he did), was such an addition of ignominy unto his death, as for a malefactor to go all the way to the gallows with a rope about his neck.

5. All this was aggravated also by the persons that suffered with him, and their saving one of their lives before his. A comparative contempt is more than a simple one. As,

(1.) That he should be crucified between two thieves, as if he were the prince of them. It is made an heightening circumstance of his shameful death (in Isa. liii. 12), that 'he was numbered amongst the transgressors.' Then,

(2.) (Yet further) That Barabbas, the most infamous thief, seditious person and murderer that was in that nation (and so a proclaimed enemy unto that state), should be voted to live by the common voice of all the people, and this when with the same breath they cry, 'Let Jesus be crucified, let him be crucified.' Pilate put them upon choosing one of these two, and set Jesus in the comparison with Barabbas, on purpose to get Jesus saved, not thinking they would be so shameless as to prefer him to Christ, who was a murderer as well as a thief, and one that had made himself odious unto them all, and whom by their law they were not to pardon or suffer to live. Yet they are content to bring both the blood he had shed (by sparing him), and Christ's also, upon their heads, by crucifying him, rather than to deliver him that was innocent. Thus much for the shame of his death and sufferings.

CHAPTER XII.

The extremity of pain which Christ our Redeemer endured in his body.—His being harassed day and night without a moment's rest.—His being crowned with thorns, torn with rods, and at last crucified.

The second thing to be considered is the pains and dolours thereof, which are all sorts of ways set forth to us in his story.

1. Immediately afore his death, want of sleep, not that whole night only which preceded his crucifying, in which he was kept waking in the high priest's hall, but three or four nights afore, as Brugensis computeth them. He in preparation to his passion, and being now to leave the world, spent those nights in prayer on mount Olivet, and on the days did teach the people in the temple after his coming into Jerusalem : so towards his end, pouring forth his spirit as a sacrifice to God and his people, ere he was offered up as the sacrifice. He knew his tabernacle was now to be dissolved, and he spared not himself, whom God afterwards spared not, days and nights wearing out himself in private prayer or preaching. Luke's words are these : Luke xxi. 37, ' And in the days' (it is in the plural) ' he was teaching in the temple, and in the nights he went out and abode in the mount' (that is, the whole nights, as abiding implies) ' that was called the mount of Olives.' This was his wonted custom for the time after he came into Jerusalem, confirming by his example what in the words afore he had taught his disciples, verse 36, ' Watch ye therefore, and pray always,' &c. And then, ver. 30, it follows, ' And all the people came early to him in the morning' (that is, every morning of those nights, as knowing his manner and wont) ' for to hear him.' These incessant prayers without rest must needs bring a strong body low in spirits, and weary it out. The fourth night, which was Thursday night, he was apprehended after those long sermons made to his disciples, which John hath recorded, and that solemn prayer put up, John xvii.

2. That night and next day they hurried him up and down seven journeys from one place to another (the Messiah had no rest, that those that were weary might have rest in him) according to the compute, of six miles and a half, or seven miles.

3. Whilst he was that last night in the high priest's hall, they smote him with the palms of their hands (which are bones, as our translators render that of Matthew, chap. xxvi. 67), saith Matthew ; and with their fists, saith Mark, and both often ; others add with rods, as the word ῥαπίζειν signifies, derived from ῥαπίς, a rod ; and these on his mouth or face.

4. He had a crown of thorns plaited on his head, where the nerves tenderest of sense do meet. To harrow men with thorns is made a high and grievous torture and punishment, Judges viii. 16. Gideon, when by sense he would teach the men of Succoth, by sense and sore experience to do no more so wickedly, it is said, that ' he took the elders of the city, and thorns of the wilderness, and briars, and with them he taught the men of Succoth.' This crown of thorns was kept upon his head all the time, both in his way to the cross, and whilst on the cross, which pierced those veins and sinews on the temples and forehead, and caused his face, besmeared also with dust in his travel to the cross, to be (as the prophet speaks) more marred than any man's, Isa. lii. 14.

5. Add to this weariness and faintness of spirits, which appeared in the

carrying of his cross. There was that one thing only, wherein they seemed to pity him, in calling to another to help him, Simon of Cyrene. But the truth of the thing was, that he having watched and spent himself so many days and nights together, he failed so much that they feared he would have fainted, and so expired ere he came to the place of execution, and so they should have missed of their designed malice in crucifying of him. We have wearied him with our sins, and this made him weary and ready to faint. Oh, come to him, all ye that are weary and heavy laden.

6. He was whipped and scourged, which was twice, once by Pilate's command, and that to the end to move compassion in the Jews, that so he having suffered so cruel a punishment as was sufficient to assuage their malice, and to satisfy for any crime they could in their own imagination think him guilty of, who in Pilate's had deserved nothing of death, they might relent and cease to desire his being crucified. And when he had scourged him, he brings him forth to public view, and cries, ' Behold the man !' And after that he was again scourged (as John relates it), as of custom the Romans used to do those whom they crucified. And these strokes were laid on, not by the Jews, who by their law were limited not to exceed forty stripes, but by the Roman soldiers, who had no bounds set them, but gave as many and as cruel ones as their barbarous nature pleased, unto an abject man, designed and condemned to the highest tortures.

7. He after all was crucified. The evangelists aggravate not that in the circumstances of it ; only say, ' he was crucified ;' but much is shut up in that one word—the cruelty of that death being known in those days, and by the relation of it in stories, and by those who have made a collection of it, of the manner of it, in these days. The apostle Paul put this emphasis upon his death, ' To death, *even the death of the cross,*' Phil. ii. 8, *cruciatus*, or the pains of the cross, being commonly used by the Romans (among whom this death was frequent) to express the sharpest pains and tortures. The manner of which was,

(1.) The cross, the person to be crucified was being affixed unto, being laid upon the ground, his hands and feet were stretched out as far as they could extend, and then nailed in the hands and in the feet unto the cross ; which the Psalmist, Ps. xxii., expresseth by digging holes (*foderunt*) in his hands and feet, ver. 16, as the vulgar translation reads it. In the hands and feet the nerves again meet and centre, and so they are of the most exquisite sense. Then,

(2.) The rearing up the cross with the man nailed on it (whilst on the ground), and fixing the cross in the hole which was digged for it, with a violent jog to fix it in the earth, as was their manner; this exceeded all the torments of our racks. In the 22d Psalm, ver. 14, 15, himself tells us that it loosened all his bones, or my bones dispart themselves. And it is not only said, as ver. 17, ' I may tell all my bones,' he hanging naked, but further, ver. 14, ' All my bones are out of joint.'

(3.) And thereon they hung till death, their arms and hands bearing the weight of their whole bodies, so as they died of mere pains (and thus Christ hung on the tree, Acts v. 30), exhausting their spirits. For a man to hold his hands but stretched out, what a trouble is it. Moses could not for a day do it, but was fain to be supported.

(4.) And this put them into an exquisite fever, as such pains do, as appeared by his thirst, as Ps. xxii. 15, ' My strength is dried as a potsherd, and my tongue cleaveth to my jaws.'

The last (of bodily sufferings) is death itself, which is the separation of soul and body : unto this the curse reached; and it was not his pains or shame or hanging on a cross that would satisfy, unless he also breathe out his soul.   This was necessary ; ' unless the corn fall into the ground and die' (it is Christ's own similitude, John xii. 24), ' it abideth alone.'   So he, unless he had died, had been (of mankind) in heaven alone.   He was also to be the founder of a will and testament, and that is not of force until the death of the testator ; he must therefore die : Heb. ix. 16, 17, ' For where a testament is, there must also of necessity be the death of the testator. For a testament is of force after men are dead ; otherwise it is of no strength at all whilst the testator liveth.'   And he was to be the death of death, Hosea xiii. 14.   And it is a general rule, what he procured virtue for in man's behalf, he did it by undergoing the same.   Yea, he thereby made death a dead and ineffectual thing, *καταϱγήσαντος τὸν Θάνατον*, destroying death, 2 Tim. i. 10.   This was held forth in the type, Num. xxxv. 28, in that the murderer or manslayer was then set free from his prison, the city of refuge (which was a confinement to them) when the high priest died, but not till then.   Nor should we have been set free unless our High Priest had died.   Now for his soul and body thus to part, and for the Son of God, united to both personally, to continue that union unto that dead carcase of his body laid in the grave, what a debasement was it, besides all considerations else that belong to this head.

CHAPTER XIII.

The greatest of all Christ's sufferings were those of his soul.—What were the causes of those sorrows.—The greatness of those sufferings.—Wherein they did consist.—How it could consist with his being the Son of God, to be forsaken of God, and to bear such extremity of his Father's wrath.

But yet, though we have seen the woe and curse in this life due to us by sin passed over and sustained by Christ ; and secondly, the curse of bodily death undergone too ; yet (as the Revelation to another purpose speaks) there is a third woe, which a guilty conscience fears more than all the other, and which is the curse of curses, ' Thou shalt die the death.'   ' Two woes are passed ; behold, a third woe is yet to come,' which is the great and main curse of the law that is to be undergone (as the text says) before the law be fulfilled.   For as the life promised—' Do this and live'—is more than to live bodily, or as a beast doth, or rationally, as men do ; it being to live in communion with God, as angels do ; so, ' Dying thou shalt die' is more than the bodily death and returning unto dust.   And as that life promised is the favour of God—' Thy favour is better than life,' Ps. xxxvi. 3 ; ' With thee is the fountain of life,' Ps. lxiii. 9, says David—so this death here threatened is from the wrath of God, which therefore is put for hell and death ; as when it is said, ' We are saved from wrath to come,' 1 Thess. i. 10 ; ' This is the second death,' as it is called, Rev. xx. 6.   And it is the original curse, the fountain of curses ; whereas the death of the body, and all miseries of this life, are but the streams.   This is the pure curse, without mixture, as it is called in the Revelation ; the other is the curse in the dregs, mingled and conveyed by creatures.   All other curses light upon the outward man first; and upon the soul but at the rebound, and at the second hand, only by way of sympathy and compassion ; but the immediate and proper subject of this curse is the soul and spirit: ' Indignation and wrath, tribulation and anguish upon every soul that doth evil,' Rom. ii. 9. And this is the sum of all curses, and instead of all the rest. And therefore Paul, when he would express his willingness not only to die bodily, but to endure hell also, for his brethren, as ,Christ had done for him, he expresseth it by this, ' I could wish myself to be accursed from Christ,' (Rom. ix. 3) ; that is, to be separated from all the comfort I shall have by him, and endure that wrath that is due unto me, though undergone by him for me. Which wish of his may help us to understand how far Christ was made a curse for us ; for it was the love of Christ which constrained Paul's heart unto this wish ; and his meaning was to undergo that for his brethren in Christ, which Christ underwent for him, and so far as Christ underwent it, without sin. And so far as Paul wished it without sinning (for he spake it in Christ, and in the Holy Ghost, as ver. 1), so far might and did Christ undergo it without sin also. His meaning therefore was not that he was content to be cut off from being a member of Christ, and so to have no influence of grace from Christ derived to him. No ; that had been a sinful wish, and not from the Holy Ghost. But his meaning is, that he could be content to lose that portion of comfort which was to be had in the enjoying of Christ, and so undergo that displeasure from him which was due unto his sins, by feeling the effects of it in anguish and pain, &c. Thus when it is said, that Christ was made a curse, not only in bodily miseries, but in his soul also, the meaning is not that the hypostatical union was dissolved, or the influence of divine grace restrained, but only, that in regard of comfort he was ' forsaken' of God, and felt the fearful effects of his anger due to our sins, without sin and despair.

In like manner, when it is said, Christ underwent this curse also, ' Dying thou shalt die,' the meaning is not that Christ's soul did die the second death : the Scripture speaks it not, neither are we to speak it ; but thus the Scripture expresseth it, that ' his soul was heavy unto death,' Mat. xxvi. 37, 38. It is spoken of this curse of his soul, which did not work death in it, but a heaviness unto death, not *extensivè* so as to die, but *intensivè*, that if he had died it could not have suffered more. As Jonas is said to be ' angry unto death,' Jonah iv. 10—that is, he thought that misery and cross for which he was angry to be even as great an affliction as death itself, and so he could out of his anger wish for death—so Christ's heaviness was as great as theirs that undergo that death ; yet die he did not; it was but ' unto death,' as Onesiphorus was said to be ' sick unto death,' or as a woman in travail is said to be at the point of death, because if she were a-dying, she could not have more pain. There is such another phrase, Acts ii. 24, where it is said, that Christ ' was raised up, God having loosed the sorrows of death,' ὠδίνας, the throes of death, of which it was impossible he should be held. It is evident that it is spoken of his soul ; for if it were spoken of bodily death, there were no sorrows that remained on his body in the grave, to withhold it from rising again. No ; these sorrows died when he died, and were then ended, and so could not be said to be upon his body, to hinder it from rising. Again, it is not absolutely called death, but ' the sorrows of death ;' that is, the same pains and throes that dying men's souls have, he felt. And it is observed, that the same phrase that is used to express the sorrows of hell, 1 Thess. v. 3, the travail of a woman (so Ps. xviii. 4, 5, the pangs of hell, or birth-throes, as the word signifies), the same phrase [ὠδίνας] is here used, signifying the throes of a woman in travail, and having reference to that phrase in Isaiah liii. 11, ' He shall see of the travail of his soul.' His soul, and not his person, is there properly meant, for it is spoke as of a part of himself, ' He shall see of the travail of his soul.' Those pains were indeed birth-throes to us, they tending to our life, but in him they were the sorrows of death. And so in this he bare the woman's curse in his soul, as well as Adam's curse in his body ; as he did eat in sweat, so he brought forth in pain, and in sorrows unto death ; but yet such as did not kill his soul, it died not, for he was to live to see his seed, and have joy in his soul for them for whom he had had most pain : so it is in Isa. liii. 10. For, thirdly, these sorrows did not ' hold him ;' had they held him, then indeed he had died. And the reason why he died not, was not that he had not the same throes and stabs that use to kill others ; for they are therefore called the sorrows of death, because they were the same which kill all men's souls in hell ; but he was too strong for them, nature was too potent in him, and life too vigorous ; otherwise that which he underwent was enough to have killed out of hand all men and angels ; but him they could not hold, it was impossible. Yet, fourthly, they were loosened, not so as never to have hold of him, or as if he never came in to them (as Bellarmine trifles) ; no, he was in them : (as Ps. cxxiv. 7), ' His soul escaped as a bird out of the snare : the snare was broken, and he was delivered.' The devils they are reserved in chains too strong for them, Jude 5, but he, like another Samson, brake these ropes, these cords. So Ps. xviii. 5, 6, where the sorrows of hell are called cords, for the same word, חֶבְלֵי, signifies both, and so the Chaldee Paraphrast reads it.

And yet, fifthly, because these were truly the pains of death, therefore this delivery of his soul from them is called a resurrection ; and the greatest wonder of his resurrection is ascribed to this ; for the main power of the resurrection was seen in raising his soul, because it conflicted with such sorrows. For his soul had a resurrection as well as his body, which Peter also, to shew he means it here, does distinctly mention, Acts ii. ver. 27. God's promise was, that he would not ' leave Christ's soul in hell ' ; that is, under the pressures of these sorrows ; there is the resurrection of his soul from the sorrows of death expressed ; ' nor suffer the Holy One to see corruption ;' there is the resurrection of his body from the power of the grave, both which make up that greater resurrection of his there spoken of. For to raise a soul from the terrors of God's wrath, does as much deserve the name of a resurrection, and more, as to raise a dead body. Therefore, says Heman (suffering these terrors in his soul), ' I am like the slain that lie in the grave, and wilt thou shew wonders to the dead ? shall the dead arise and praise thee ?' Ps. lxxxviii. 5, 10. And this resurrection Christ's soul had before it went out of his body : for after it went out, it went to paradise, and encountered not with the pains of death ; but before it left his body, it did, and was rescued. And therefore, after that long conflict, for three hours' space, whilst the curtains of the world were close drawn, and all was hushed up in darkness, during which time he had struggled with these sorrows and with God's wrath, which towards the conclusion he manifests by that bitter expression, ' My God, my God, why hast thou forsaken me ?' after that conflict (I say) he cries out, ' It is finished ;' which some divines think not to have reference to the work of redemption, that that work was finished. No ; for that was not as yet finished, his bodily death being a part of it, as also the piercing of his side, and laying of him in the grave ; but the meaning is, that now the great brunt was over, that cup which he so feared was drunk off, his soul was come out of its eclipse, as the sun did then also out of its darkness, which was a shadow or sign of this in his spirit ; unto this it is that those words refer. And that which seems to confirm it is that when first these kind of sorrows fell on him in the garden, the evangelist notes it, saying, that then his soul began to be heavy; and now when they went off him, he shews, that then it was finished.

As therefore we, who are his members, have a double resurrection in our souls whilst they are in our bodies, John v. 25, 'The time now is,' &c., and in our bodies, at the latter day, ver. 29 in the same chapter; so had Christ: one of his soul from the terrors following the guilt of sin, the sorrows of death upon the cross; the other of his body from the grave the third day, which was a manifestation of the first. And answerably those sorrows may be called a kind of death, at least the sorrows of death, in the same sense that bodily dangers and distresses are called dying, as Paul, being in jeopardy every hour, is said to ' die daily,' 1 Cor. xv. 31 ; and so in that sense, and no other, may he be said to have undergone this curse of dying the death. Therefore, Isa. liii. 9, we have his *deaths* in the plural mentioned, not his death only : ' He made his grave with the wicked in his deaths.' So in the original. And in his bearing these sorrows of death was the curse abundantly fulfilled, although he did not die the second death; for that wrath, which is the cause of the second death in others, he underwent; and those sorrows of death, which that cause produceth, he bore; though the same event followed not, his soul died not, as theirs through weakness doth.

Having thus explained and fitted these phrases to our hand, we will now come to the particulars of the sufferings of his soul, which are merely and properly such, and which, as that curse seizeth on wicked men by degrees, so did seize on him by degrees, towards his end. The first mention we have of them is in John xii. 27, four days before his passion, when on the sudden he breaks forth, ' Now is my soul troubled; and what shall I say?' He then saw the storm a-coming, and a black cloud rising, which troubled him ; and in the expectation of it, he saw so much to be troubled at, as he knew not how to express it, but cries out, 'What shall I say?'

The second degree was in the garden, as both Mat. chap. xxvi. from ver. 36 to the end, Mark xiv. from ver. 32 to 51, Luke xxii. 40, and John xviii. 1, 2, do set it down. There it was where the storm overtook him, ere ever he fell into the hands of Judas or the high priest, and he began to feel some drops of it; and indeed the sorrows that there seized on him were such as fetched blood from him ere these his enemies approached him. Whereby was shewn, that he had other and greater miseries to encounter with than from men. And whereas, for all his bodily sorrows, we hear not one groan from him, as neither for his wounding with the crown of thorns, with nails, &c., but ' as a sheep that openeth not his mouth, so was he led to the slaughter,' Isa. liii. 7 ; yet here, in the very entrance into these sorrows, we hear him lamenting : Mat. xxvi. 38, ' My soul is heavy unto death.' He names, and as it were lays his finger on, the part affected, which was not his body, but his soul; it was there where his grief lay. And we have many words and expressions which may help us to see into his grief what it was. Amongst which, the first and lowest expression is λυπεῖσθαι, Mat. xxvi. 37. He had said before, that he was troubled : and we read not so much as of the least trouble of his for outward pains ; but now it is said, he became sorrowful. It was no pain of his body could make his great spirit sorrowful. Sorrow is more than pain, as joy is more than delight. Beasts are never sorrowful properly, and yet they have all sorts of pains of the body, which touch not their souls with a reflection, and so cause sorrow. The cause of Christ's sorrow reached his reasonable soul, which is the proper subject of sorrow, and not the inferior, but the superior part also. Yea, Tully restrains the word *tristis* to sorrow for the punishment of sin and wickedness : *poena sceleris tristis est.* And yet this is but the lowest degree, but the beginning of sorrows, which, notwithstanding, reached as deep as any kind of worldly sorrow could do ; for even David's sorrow or affliction for his son Absalom is expressed by the same word.

Now there were two things which made his soul to be thus sorrowful.

1. The sins of the world imputed to him and charged on him.

2. The curse or wrath of God upon him for those sins.

1. First, the sins of the world came in upon him; and therefore, ver. 38, he is not simply said to be sorrowful, but περίλυπος, which word signifies an encompassing about with sorrows, as David often expresseth it : ' The sorrows of hell encompassed me about,' Ps. xviii. 5. His soul was plunged into them over head and ears, so that he had not so much as a breathing hole. For intention, this sorrow was unto death, and for extension, all the powers and faculties of his soul were begirt, besieged, and imprisoned; and this expression is especially used in respect to our sins taking hold of him. So Ps. xl. 12, ' Innumerable evils encompass me about: mine iniquities take hold of me.' It is spoken by Christ as in his sufferings, for of him is that psalm prophetically made. So that, I take it, this phrase περίλυπος hath a more proper respect to the charging of our particular sins upon him, which began to encompass him, or (as Isaiah's phrase is, Isa. liii) ' to meet in him,' to come about him from every quarter. His soul was so environed and shut up in sorrows (or in prisons, as Isaiah's phrase, Isa. liii. 8, is), that he had not a cranny left for comfort to come in at. Gal. iii. 23, the law is compared to a prison, in which men under the guilt of sin are shut up ; and so was Christ. Now, no temporal mercies do so environ an ordinary man's spirit, but that there is some hole left to take breath at. But sin can do it; and much more all the sins of the world, which now at once did meet at and beset Christ's soul. As Heb. xii. 1, sin is said to be that which ' easily besets us,' and so do both the power and the guilt of it.

2. Secondly, there is yet a further expression used by another evangelist, that respects the terrors of God's wrath, seconding and following upon this his apprehension of our sins, and it is in Mark xiv. 33, ' He began to be sore amazed,' ἐκθαμβεῖσθαι, which is a third expression used concerning his trouble. Our translation rightly renders it ' sore amazed,' for θαμβεῖν signifies to be amazed ; but ἐκ added, signifies the extremity of that amazement, such as when men fall into it, their hair stands on end, and their flesh trembles. It signifies ' to be in horror.' No sooner hath these our sins presented themselves to him, as being our surety, but that withal thunder and lightning from God do presently strike him, and his wrath and curse for them suddenly arrests him; this was it that put him into such an amazement as contains in it both fear and horror. His Father is presented unto him as an angry judge brandishing his sword of justice. And as the delivering of the law made Moses tremble, so the curse of the law made Christ; ' I quake and tremble,' says Moses, or (as David expresseth it) ' My flesh trembleth because of thy judgments,' Ps. cxix. 120.

Now, in the third place, follows the effect of both these two (namely, the imputation of our sins, and the inflicting of God's wrath), which was an ἀδημονία, an exceeding ' heaviness ' upon him. Which word, both Mat., chap. xxvi. 37, useth, saying, ἤρξατο ἀδημονεῖν, which is translated, 'He began to be very heavy;' and the same in Mark, chap. xiv. 33, where it in like manner follows that former expression of his being amazed. Now, this word imports first the deep intention of his mind, so as to be wholly taken and swallowed up with sorrow and amazement, and even to be abstracted from his own thoughts, and to forget all comfort whatsoever, being wholly intent and thinking upon nothing else but God's wrath, with which he was to encounter—so full, so adequate an object is sin and the wrath due unto it, even broad enough for Christ's understanding to be wholly taken up with it. And therefore he hath the thoughts of our salvation, as it were, struck out of his mind for a time; all his powers being so occupied about, and possessed with these doleful sights presented, that they forget their own functions. Some have put a further emphasis upon the word, as noting out, not only an abstraction of the mind, but a distraction also upon the suddenness of the blow, such as might befall him through simple infirmity, deriving it from a privative ἀ and δῆμος, *populus*, because men in distractions are separated from the rest of the people, which, in the sense before given, may be safely attributed to him, namely, that the powers and faculties of nature did for a while forget their functions. Now, all this might be without sin; as the wheels of a clock may be stopped in their ordinary course, and yet not put out of frame or disordered. And this strong intention of his upon wrath was, then, that which God did call for; for Christ's business was to suffer God's wrath for sin; and as taking pleasure in any thing, so suffering too depends upon the intention, insomuch, that some do therefore judge, that even the damned in hell cannot sin, because their thoughts are so intently taken up with wrath, that there is no room for a thought of sin.

Secondly, The word notes out a failing, deficiency, and sinking of spirit; it is *penè exanimari*, as happens to men in sickness and swoundings. So Epaphroditus his sickness, whereby he was brought near unto death, Phil. ii. 26, 27, is called ἀδημονία. So that, we see, Christ's soul was sick and fainted. Thus, Ps. xl. 12, 13 (which psalm is all of Christ, for it is that psalm quoted, Heb. x. 5, 6), where Christ is brought in saying, when he came to offer himself, that 'innumerable evils encompassed him about, and his iniquities took hold of him; therefore his heart failed him.' Iniquities are there promiscuously put for sins and punishments. If sin be meant, Christ our surety now calls our sins his; and being laid to his charge, they take hold of him. If he had stood in his own righteousness he would not have feared, but being invested with, and appearing in our sins, he was afraid, as Adam was, and his heart forsook him; not sinfully, out of distrust, but of simple infirmity of nature, such a failing as a creature, though never so holy, must needs have at the greatness of God's wrath— the creature being unto God's wrath, and before him who is 'everlasting burnings' (as Isaiah speaks, Isa. xxxiii. 14), and a 'consuming fire' (as Moses calls him, Deut. iv. 24), but as the wax is to the fire before which it melts. Which is also Christ's own expression concerning himself, Ps. xxii. 14 (a psalm throughout speaking of his crucifying), 'My heart,' says he, 'was melted like wax;' noting out that natural infirmity and deficiency which was in his human nature as such, now when God approached to him as a consuming fire; so as it was merely a natural failing, not a moral. And this we must know, that in these his sufferings Christ's human nature was left to its infirmities, that he might fully suffer. The Godhead, though sustaining him in union with himself, and in faith towards God as his

Father, yet left him to the natural weakness of a creature, not shewing his power in strengthening him so against his wrath, as that he should not be sensible of it, but in supporting him under it. Therefore, 2 Cor. xiii. 4, it is said, ' He was crucified through weakness,' but ' raised in power.' For in this work of suffering, the Godhead slept (as the fathers express it), and left him to natural infirmities (but not to sinful) ; otherwise he had not been crucified. In respect of which infirmity unto which he was left it is said, Luke xxii. 43, that an angel came to strengthen him. And it argued a great inanition or emptying himself, that the Creator of the ends of the earth, who faints not, and who is the God of comfort, should borrow comfort of an angel.

A third and further degree of this his suffering was that which Luke adds, Luke xxii. 44, that he was ἐν ἀγωνίᾳ, ' at strife,' or engaged in a combat, as the word implies, it coming from ἀγὼν, certamen. And yet there was no man to encounter with ; and the good angel who comforted him did not wrestle with him. Christ had before wrestled with principalities and powers in the wilderness ; but those encounters with Satan fetched no blood from him, as these here do. This agony, this wrestling, was therefore with his Father's wrath, which now had taken hold on him, and under which he now lay struggling. And this I make a further degree of his soul's suffering than the former ; for the former expressions set forth the trouble of his spirit, as but at the first onset and encounter, when first he entered into the lists, and the warning only was given to this bloody combat. Therefore when all the former are mentioned, it is still said in every evangelist, he *began to* be heavy, and *began* to be sore amazed, &c., as noting out those to have been the troubles of his spirit upon the first view, and in the very entrance and beginning of them. But now he is in an agony, in a set battle ; it came now to blows, to wounds, to blood. He sweats drops of blood at this agony, so hot and grievous was it. Neither could fervency of prayer cause this sweat, for it was this agony that was the cause of that fervency in prayer. So in Luke it follows, ' Being in an agony he prayed more earnestly.' What was it then that he encountered with? Even that which Job struggled with ; Job vi. 4, ' The terrors of God,' says he, ' set themselves in array against me.' And for the effect of this encounter and agony, it was answerably greater than the former; it made him sweat drops of blood. All sweat is from weakness, and an overpressing of nature ; and so in him it argues that failing, sinking, and wounding of spirit before mentioned. Dying men do use through faintness to sweat a cold sweat, but never a bloody sweat ; but Christ's soul being now heavy unto death, and scorched with God's wrath, does sweat blood. These dolours fetch not only watery tears from his eyes, but he weeps blood all over, and not by drops only, but clodders, and that in a cold night. Yea, it came through his garments, and that in such abundance as it fell upon the ground, and left the marks of it thereon behind. Adam in innocency should not have sweat nor eaten his meat with labour and pain ; but Christ now tastes of the cup which he desired should pass from him, and it casts him into a sweat of blood.

Well, but yet all this was but the first onset of this great battle ; it was but a skirmish to begin it, in which and after which God gave him a time to breathe, and to go to his disciples, and then come again to the same place. These blows came but at times ; not so thick, but that they suffered him to take breath. He had *lucida intervalla*, some flashes of comfort in this agony, some intermissions, some respite for a time ; but the main and great battle is yet to be fought, even upon mount Calvary, and thither let us follow him ; where, after they had hung his body up upon a tree, and divided his garments before his face, and had a while said and done their pleasures, Christ having made his will, and given heaven to the believing thief, and bequeathed the care of his mother unto John ; after all this, on the sudden are the curtains of the world drawn, and the sun for three hours loseth its light. A bloody battle was now towards, and therefore it was a black day; Christ was to encounter with the utmost power of darkness, and therefore the field he fights it out in is darkness.

Two things were due unto us for our sins :

1. *Pœna damni*, the loss of God's favour, and a separation from God and all good, even to a drop of water.

2. *Pœna sensûs*, the curse and wrath of God. Other things are but either circumstances or consequents of suffering these in those who are sinners. We have them both mentioned ; Job xiii. 24, ' Wherefore hidest thou thy face' (says he to God; there is the punishment of loss and privation), 'and holdest me for an enemy ?' (There is the punishment of sense).

These two are the substance of the pains in hell, and do now both fully meet in Christ.

1. *Pœna damni*, for all comforts fail him. If he desires but a drop of water, it is denied him ; if a beam of light, the sun affords none ; his disciples had all forsaken him ; and whereas heretofore an angel came to him and comforted him, now not an angel dares look out of heaven. His heart had before this melted out of fear, and failed him ; ay, but (says David) ' though my flesh fails, yet God fails me not,'. Ps. lxxiii. 26. But behold, God himself forsakes Christ. So at the end of this conflict he complains, or rather vehemently affirms it (as the Hebrew phrase bears it). He is said to be forsaken, not only in regard of his being kept in the hands of his enemies, as some would have it only meant. For,

(1.) This then would have been uttered by him at the first, when he fell into their hands, and not now at last only. And,

(2.) Though enemies persecute us and have their wills of us, yet we are said not to be forsaken, as 2 Cor. iv. 9, ' Persecuted, but not forsaken ;' that is, though left in the hands of men, yet not forsaken by God ; so that *forsaken* is put in opposition to being left to the persecutions and power of our enemies. But Christ is not only said to be left to the power of enemies, but to be forsaken by God himself, which how it could be, I shall afterwards explain. And this was the extremity of his emptying, emptying to nothing, as Dan. ix. 26, ' Messiah shall have nothing,' that is, nothing left to comfort him ; so his cutting off is expressed.

2. *Pœna sensûs;* he was made a curse, and encountered his Father's wrath, which, *first*, the darkness that was then about him may inform us of. If ever the face of hell were upon the earth, it was at that day. All which while we read not of any word which Christ spake, till at last. So that as darkness covered, so silence hushed all about him, that so he might without interruption or intermission encounter with his Father's wrath. And the place was the air, the very kingdom of the prince of darkness. *Secondly*, the tree he hangs on declares it, which God before had cursed ; and therefore now especially it is that Christ is made a curse, as the apostle intimates, Gal. iii. 13 ; where he speaks as if Christ had never been a curse until now ; and therefore it is that Christ is said to ' bear our sins in his body ' (that is, his human nature) ' on the tree.' And he had no type of his being crucified but the brazen serpent, which of all worms else God had

only cursed. And therefore now it is that the treasures of wrath are broke up, the cataracts of curses set open, and the sluices pulled up, so to let in all our sins upon him, God now ' afflicting him with all his waves.' And when this eclipse by reason of God's wrath went off his spirit, and it received light again, then he cried out, (as was said), ' It is finished ;' which was spoken just before his giving up the ghost, as declaring that the great brunt was over, as was before explained.

There is one thing which yet remains to be done, for the finishing of this point, viz.,

By way of explication, to shew how it might stand with his being the Son of God to be thus forsaken, and made a curse.

1. For the explication (which I put first because it will facilitate and make way for the proofs themselves, both by laying foundations for them, and also by removing prejudices that might hinder the entertainment of them); there are two things which I mentioned as the integral parts of that punishment due to us for sin, but undergone by Christ.

1. His being forsaken by God ;

2. His enduring God's wrath ; both which make up this curse.

I will speak distinctly and apart to the explication of either. And first, how to understand his being forsaken of God, which is not to be understood,—

1. As if the union of the Godhead with the human nature had been dissolved, but so as it might still be compatible, and rightly stand with it. For it was not a forsaking in respect of the essence of the Godhead, but of his presence, and so in a way of sense. The Godhead was not separated, though the operation of comfort from the Godhead were sequestered. The union hypostatical continued still with his soul, now filled with the sorrows of death, as well as it did with his body when he lay in the grave. And so as although his body was united to the fountain of life, yet it might die in respect of a natural life : so his soul, although the hypostatical union continued, might yet want comfort, which is life.

2. Nor yet is it to be understood as if all communion had been cut off in regard of support and the influence of grace ; but only in respect of joy and comfort in and from God's face ; even as the sun hath influence into the generation of metals buried under the earth, whither its light comes not. Though grace naturally followed from that union, yet comfort proceeded voluntarily from it, and therefore might be and was now suspended. *Deus se communicat*, says Scotus, *vel quâ beatus est, vel quâ sanctus:* God communicates himself to the creature, either as he is *blessed*, by comforting it and making it partaker of his happiness, or as he is *holy*, by making it partaker of his purity. Now these two may be severed. God ceased not now to communicate himself to Christ in holiness, but only in comfort and sense of happiness.

3. This his deprivation of comfort was possible ; for he was not yet glorified, as John says. Wherefore as his Deity might and did withhold from his body that glory which was due unto it whilst on earth, and which shone so in his transfiguration ; by the like reason might the Deity withhold all sense of comfort from his soul during that hour. *Subtraxit Deus visionem, non unionem,* as Leo Magnus speaks. Yea,—

4. It was necessary that there should be such a suspension of communion of beatifical comfort, and so a sensible want of it. For had God then communicated himself in that fulness of comfort and joy that was Christ's due by virtue of that union hypostatical, Christ had not felt any sufferings from

man at all, even as many martyrs have not, though a joy unspeakable and glorious. He was therefore to be left to his infirmity, that he might be sensible, and therefore to be forsaken in respect of comfort; and if in respect of some degrees of comfort, then why not in respect of all ? So that,

5. This support was only in respect of upholding his faith ; that as one who walketh in darkness, and hath no light, yet trusts in the name of God, Isa. l. 10, so Christ forsakes him not, but cries, ' My God, my God,' and to the last cleaves fast unto him. And therefore God's forsaking him was not such an one as befell Saul, when he also forsook God. No ; Christ, though he kills him, does still trust in him.

Now in the second place, to explain how he might endure God's wrath, and be made a curse, which is the *pœna sensús*, and the second thing mentioned. There are many difficulties in view, which seem to argue it impossible, and it is therefore the more hardly to be received, both because there is no other instance of one innocent and beloved that was made a curse for another, or that endured God's wrath, as also because no mere creature can be made sin by imputation, but that it must be defiled by it, neither can it bear the wrath of God, but must certainly despair and sink under it. Now all those objections and difficulties which divines bring in against it, I shall take away by these following conclusions, which also explain the point.

1. The soul of a creature, and so of Christ as such, may in itself properly and immediately suffer God's wrath, and not only mediately, by compassion or fellow-feeling from the body. This is evident ; for besides that many have in their spirits suffered the wrath of God in this life, when environed with outward comforts, as David did ; and therefore Solomon calls it the ' wounding of the spirit,' and so differenceth it from other infirmities ;—it is farther evident by this, that in hell the soul suffers immediately, without the body, until the day of judgment. And the reason of this is as plain ; for God is the Father of spirits ; and as the fathers of our bodies can chastise them, so can God the spirit, Heb. xii. 9.

2. That the wrath of God should be thus endured, it is not of absolute necessity that men should be in the place of hell ere they undergo it ; it may be endured here. For the devils, being out of that place and in the air, do still endure it, or at least may ; as the angels when out of heaven, about their ministration here below, are said to ' see God's face,' Mat. xviii. 10. ' Their angels,' says Christ, speaking of little children, ' do always behold the face of my father which is in heaven.' They are said to be *their* angels, in respect of their being sent for them, and their waiting on them ; and whilst they wait on them here below, still their beholding God's face is not interrupted, for they always see God's face. If Paul were rapt up into the third heaven when alive, then why might not Christ in his spirit descend into the nethermost hell, and this whilst in the body, and here upon earth? And if he himself was as in heaven when transfigured, why then not in hell when crucified ? For it is God's wrath that is hell, as it is his favour that is heaven. Many wicked men have a kind of hell here, the earnest of hell hereafter, even as the godly have a taste and earnest of heaven in this life. So had Cain, Judas, &c., but they cannot undergo the full torments of hell here ; and the reason is, because their souls would then die, and their bodies be consumed. The people hearing but the law given by God, thought they should die, of which their weakness was the cause. As ' corruption cannot inherit incorruption,' nor bear alive in this mortal flesh the joys of heaven— ' Who hath seen him and lived ?'—so nor could this corruption fully endure

the pains of hell. But Jesus Christ's soul could subsist in his body, it being backed with the Godhead, even when filled with God's wrath, as well as when filled with glory, as at the transfiguration. The creatures, like an altar of straw, would have been burnt up by that fire if their souls had been to serve for the sacrifice; whereas this altar of Christ's body was covered with brass (as in the Levitical law), to conserve it from being consumed to ashes.

3. It is not a thing impossible or unjust for an innocent soul to have the sins of others imputed to it; no more than it is impossible for a sinful soul to have the righteousness of another made over to it. Now, 2 Cor. v. 21, it is said that Christ 'was made sin, that we might be made righteousness;' and 'not having my own righteousness,' says Paul, Phil. iii. 9. I say, it is not unjust, and therefore not impossible, in case the party innocent be content to become a surety; as Judah was, Gen. xliii. 9, who was content, if Joseph should detain his brother Benjamin, to take that sin and evil upon him: 'Let me then,' says he to his father, 'be always as a sinner unto thee.' And the ground is, because though his own acts make him not a sinner, yet his own covenant and consent do make him a surety; and so oblige him to the other's guiltiness and punishment, and wholly to bear the blame. Thus, Prov. vi. 1–3, it is said of a surety, that 'he may be snared with the words of his mouth;' and so was Christ. It was by his own compact and agreement.

4. A soul having thus taken the guilt of sin upon it, God may justly vent his anger upon such a soul for sin, and express that anger against that soul, as against the sinner, though otherwise God loves him. For it is just with God to inflict his wrath and curse for sin on whomsoever he finds that sin, whether by personal guilt or by imputation. And therefore it is no wonder if he be accursed by God, who hath the guilt of that upon him which God hates, and therefore curseth. If God cursed the earth because of man's sin, which was but his house he dwelt in, then much more must man's surety expect wrath and a curse, who will be so hardy as to take his sin upon him.

5. And further; that soul, though innocent in itself, may be made sensible of the impressions of that anger for sin thus imputed. Those of a contrary judgment think that therefore he could not have been made sensible of God's wrath for sin, because he had not the worm of conscience. But though it be true that Christ had not an evil conscience (which to affirm were blasphemy), that is, not such a conscience as that sin could ever trouble him by way of accusing him (as sinners' consciences do), so as to make him say, What a wretch am I, that I should do thus and thus! (which is one of the greatest torments in hell) though this troubled not Christ, yet his conscience might,—

(1.) Apprehend the evil of sin as fully, nay more, than any of ours; and to see sin as sin is hell, says Luther. And so,

(2.) He might be made conscious of sin, not directly or immediately as sinners are, but by being conscious of his own covenant to take sin upon him as his own. An accusing could not arise from within, but it might from without, as sin was imputed. His conscience might tell him that he by compact did undertake the guilt of these sins which he sees to be thus evil, and so he might come to look upon them as his by covenant; and this with a grief and horror suitable to the evil of them. So Ps. xl. 12, 'Mine iniquities have taken hold on me, so that I am not able to look up; they are more than the hairs of my head: therefore my heart faileth me.'

That psalm is made of Christ. Now, if he confessed sins as his own, he might have grief and dolour for them ; and so though not an accusing conscience from within himself, yet a conscience loaded and charged with them by God from without.

(3.) His conscience, looking at sin as thus evil, and deserving God's wrath, and as made his own by covenant, he might in fear look upon God as a judge. And thus afraid and amazed was Christ in the garden, for then he appeared with our sins on him, and thereupon was afraid, as Adam was ; only Adam out of a guilt that he had done the fact himself, but Christ that, knowing what God's wrath was, he had exposed himself unto it by assuming Adam's sin. And that this may be, appears by this ; for if we have peace of conscience from Christ's righteousness imputed to us, by faith apprehending it to be thus imputed by a covenant, and so rejoice in God as ours, then why (in a contrary way) might not Christ have fears, and terrors, and impressions of wrath from the guilt of sin, which he apprehended as made his only by a covenant between God and him, yet really and justly charged on him ?

6. Neither did the personal union of his soul unto the Godhead put in such a bar or hindrance to all this, or make such an exception, that though the soul of a mere creature might be capable of all this, yet not his, by reason of this union. For he might be forsaken, and the union not dissolved, as was before shewn ; and he might as well be left to endure God's wrath and anguish in his spirit from it, that union continuing, as if he had not been so united. For if the Godhead might and did leave his body to bodily pains for sin (which were fruits of the curse), which yet was thus united to the Godhead as well as his soul, why might not his soul be also left to suffer such torments as the souls of men are capable of ? If it be said, that of all things else the state and relation he stood in towards God by reason of this union would not admit this, that Christ should be accursed of God, and dealt withal in wrath by him, seeing he was his beloved Son ; and that neither could the Father be thus displeased with him, nor could the Son really apprehend God to be so indeed and in truth, seeing he must needs know himself to be God's Son, and so beloved of him all the while ;—the resolution is,

(1.) That God, for his part, might have both these affections towards him at once, although he was his natural Son ; and the reason is evident, for if Christ might bear and sustain two such relations or persons, the one as the Son of God and beloved of him, the other as our surety made sin for us, then might God suitably bear towards him two such contrary affections of love and wrath, and accordingly express them. Or thus, as Christ stands with two respects upon him, as a *Son* and as a *surety*, so did God also in answer to these two sustain two relations towards him, of a *Father* towards him as a *Son*, and of a *judge* towards him as a *surety*. And these two might well stand together ; as in a father that is a just judge, before whom his son is brought as a surety for another's debt, though he entirely loves him as a son, yet he must and ought to condemn him in the suit, and exact the payment of the debt, or inflict some other punishment on him (as the matter he is surety for requires), as he is a judge ; and he is to act both these parts, as the several respects in the things themselves require, justice in this case as well requiring that he should punish him, as well as nature that he should love him. We may see this exemplified in an instance fetched from God himself, and his carriage towards us his adopted sons and children, whom he loves with the same love, though not in the same degree, that he loves his natural Son, John xvii. 23.   God is upon several respects both an enemy and a friend unto us at once ; we are at once both hated and beloved, even whilst we are in the state of nature. God's elect, if considered as invested with sin, and in the state of unregeneracy, upon which God hath pronounced a curse, they are under wrath, and 'children of wrath,' and so pronounced accursed.   And yet at that time their persons, as they are his chosen ones from everlasting, are beloved, and therefore called his people and his sheep.   So were the Jews : Rom. xi. 28, 'As concerning the gospel, they are enemies for your sakes ; but as touching election, they are beloved for their fathers' sake.'   They are at once 'children of wrath as well as others,' Eph. ii. 3, and 'sons of peace,' Luke x. 6 ; and this when uncalled.   Now, thus it may be towards his natural Son, if he over and above takes such a relation on him, of being a surety for sinners ; only with this difference, that God's love to him is natural, because he is his natural Son, and the relation natural ; and his anger but accidental and adventitious, and taken up by him (yet justly), because this relation of Christ his being a surety is, answerably, but assumed and taken up by him.   Yet they are real, both on the one side and on the other.   And therefore, Zech. xiii. 7, where God is said to 'smite the shepherd' (namely, Christ), it is made to be a forced act, as it were, and such as he is fain to stir up himself to do by respects of justice ; and therefore he calls upon his sword : 'Awake, O sword, against the man that is my fellow.'   God considers he is his Son, and natural Son (his fellow), and so he naturally loves him, and cannot find in his heart to strike him ; yet justice must be done, seeing he stands as a surety for sinners, and so he draws his sword ; notwithstanding as being put upon it by arguments, reasons, and considerations moving him to it ; and therefore he is said to awaken it.

In a word, it is one thing to be an enemy, and another to carry one's self as an enemy.   So Job xxxiii. 10 ; says Job to God, ' Why countest thou me thine enemy ?' that is, why dealest thou with me as if I were so, whenas I am thy child ?   Thus did God with Christ.

(2.)   And in the second place.   Christ for his part might have answerable apprehensions and impressions on his soul, notwithstanding he knew himself beloved.   For he might apprehend (according as the truth was) that himself stood at the present under an adventitious relation of a surety, to bear God's wrath for sin, notwithstanding that withal he knew he was God's natural Son, and so beloved.   He might look upon himself as a Son, and a Son performing an obedience to his Father, even in suffering his wrath, and never pleasing him more than now, and in that respect most beloved of him ; and yet withal, as a surety for sinners, and so punished, and in that respect he might apprehend God for the present angry, and full of wrath against him, as being made sin and so a curse for us, yet so as to the end that he might be well pleased with sinners in him.   And both these differing apprehensions of his did Christ accordingly express in that one sentence, ' My God, my God, why hast thou forsaken me ?'   He speaks it as apprehending himself a Son still, and united to God, and beloved of him, and yet forsaken by him, and, as a surety, accursed.   And to this end there were two principles in him, that let in these so differing apprehensions or impressions, faith and present sense.   By faith he knew himself a Son ; therefore Ps. xxii., when on the cross, his trusting upon God is mentioned. And, Heb. xii. 2, it is said, that he 'endured the cross, for the joy that was set before him,' namely, by faith ; and therefore we from his example are there exhorted unto faith (which is the apostle's scope and argument) seeing he thus believed and trusted, who, as it follows there, is 'the author and finisher of our faith.'

7. But there was another principle in him, and that was present sense of the impressions of God's anger : his mind by sight or vision seeing nothing else, and his will by the impressions on it feeling nothing else. Both which principles, as they are in us, so they might be and were in him, we being in faith and sufferings to be conformed to him, and he being in all things tempted like as we are.

8. And therefore, eighthly, all this curse and wrath did not, nor could make him miserable, although uncomfortable, both because he undertook it and underwent it voluntarily (and as the greatest good cannot make a man happy against his will, so nor the greatest evil with one's will can make a man miserable, there being an end obtained to sweeten that estate), and also because he knew he should eluctate out of it, and overcome it in a few hours, as he did when he cried, ' It is finished.'

9. And so, ninthly, this curse was endured by him, without sinning or despair. For the Godhead both helped and preserved him, as his body from corruption in the grave, so his soul from sinning whilst under wrath. And though God left him to the infirmities of a passible nature, to be sensible of all impressions to the full, yet he left him not to any infirmities of sinning, or weakness of unbelief, the ordinary consequents of such sufferings in others. Again, despair ariseth not from the present extremity, but the apprehension of the eternity of those sufferings, and a certain foreknowledge that they shall never have end. Whereas Christ knew he should overcome, and that it was impossible that he should be held of them.

10. Tenthly and lastly. This therefore was for the substance of the suffering itself, the same that we in hell should have undergone ; only such circumstances were wanting and cut off in his undergoing it, as were either not necessary ingredients to the discharge of our debt, or but accidental consequents ; as,

(1.) He descended not, or went not down to the place of the damned, to endure God's wrath there. For seeing that the place of payment is no ingredient into the discharge of the debt, and but a mere circumstance, and that he could endure it on earth as fully as in hell itself, and that, through the supportment of the Godhead, without dying, which no creature could ; therefore though this circumstance were wanting, it detracts not anything from the fulness of the substance of that payment which was due from us, and therefore this may be accounted the same with that.

(2.) He endured it without dying the second death, otherwise than in the sense fore-mentioned. But this hinders it not from being the same in substance that we should have endured, and so it may stand for it. For dying, or quite sinking under this curse, is but the consequence of undergoing the wrath of God in those that are mere creatures, who cannot bear it and live, and so is not any part of the substance of the punishment itself, simply in itself considered. This ariseth only from the creature's weakness, and no more indeed does despair, it being no part of the punishment, but the consequent of it, through the creature's infirmity and sinfulness. As now, suppose two men in a like and equal distemper and heat of a burning fever, the one through the weakness of his brain is light-headed, and raveth, and in the end dieth ; but the other, having more natural strength of body, overcomes the distemper and survives, having through the strength and cool temper of his brain not once lost the right use of his senses all that while ; yet still it may be said, that their distempers were the same, and alike intense for degrees of heat, though the consequents of each were contrary, according to the differing capacities and dispositions of the subjects. Or take two guns charged with like measure of powder and shot: the one breaks and flies in pieces when fire is given to it, when the other holds, as being of more firm and solid metal, or better tempered, or having all its parts more compactly cast according to art, when yet the charge of each is for quantity and force the same. Thus the charging of sin, and of the wrath of God upon men in hell, causeth their souls to despair, and die the second death, through their inability to bear them; whenas the same sins, and the same wrath, though charged home on Christ, yet prevail not to kill his soul, but through his strength and support from the Godhead, his spirit remains whole under them. Despair and dying is but from being overcome, which his soul was not; but as a great fire overcomes a smaller quantity of water cast upon it, so did the worth of his person and sufferings in the end overcome the guilt of our sins, which falls short of the merit of his satisfaction; and therefore this consequent of despair and death followed not upon it. Which therefore being an effect of suffering the pains of hell, is not a part of the substance of them.

(3.) In like manner, for the same reason, though he suffered them not eternally, yet his suffering was the same, and equivalent to what we should have undergone.

For, *first*, eternity is but a circumstance of time, as hell is of place; and not simply eternity, but extremity of sufferings was the punishment due. The lying ever in prison is no part of the debtor's punishment simply considered; for he is to lie there but till he hath paid the utmost farthing (as Christ speaks), which because he can never do, therefore he is never released. But Christ could undergo in a few hours all the wrath due unto sin, and so swallow up death and hell in victory, 1 Cor. xv. 24. That portion or measure of wrath which we by reason of our narrowness could have received in but by drops, and so it would ever have been raining down; that his soul might be and was so enlarged as to receive in at once, even the whole vials and cataracts of it. That cup which is so full of mixture, that we are a-drinking of it down unto eternity, that can he take off unto the bottom, in a few hours. Yea, and by reason of the incapacity of the damned in hell to take in the full measure of God's wrath due to them for their sins, therefore their punishment, though it be eternal, yet never satisfies, because they can never take in all, as Christ could and did,.and so theirs is truly less than what Christ underwent. And therefore Christ's punishment ought not in justice to be eternal, as theirs is, because he could take it all in a small space, and more fully satisfy God's wrath in a few hours, than they could unto all eternity. And this may well be one meaning of those words, Acts ii. 24, that it was 'impossible he should be held by the pains of death,' not only in respect of his power, able to prevail against the power of God's wrath and anger, but impossible in respect of justice, that God should any longer continue angry; seeing that as God's love had such a full vent and sway in Christ, so also had revenging justice its full process against sin in him, and wreaked its utmost, sucking from him so much blood both of his body and soul, as being full it fell off of itself, as fully satisfied.

CHAPTER XIV.

Uses of Christ's being made sin and a curse for us.—We see herein God the Father's love, and his own.—We should not regret to suffer anything for Christ.—Let us obey and worship Christ in soul and spirit.—The troubled in soul should be comforted.—We see the heinousness of sin by the greatness of Christ's sufferings, and the misery of being without an interest in Christ. —We should charge our sins upon ourselves for humiliation.—We should mourn for them, and hate them.

Use 1. See the love of Christ, who laid not his bodily life down only, but his soul. ' The redemption of the soul is precious,' says the psalmist, Ps. xlix. 8 : precious indeed, when it cost not his precious blood only, but his precious soul also. Not with corruptible things, gold and silver, but with the precious blood of Christ were we redeemed. As the body is more worth than raiment or estate, so the soul than the body. Christ gave not his estate only, nor his body only, but his soul.

Use 2. See the love of God, who gave not his Son up only to the hands of men to be executioners of his body, but himself laid on upon his soul ; and that because justice called for the soul, the very soul, ere it would be satisfied. Which no creature being able to reach, rather than we should not be redeemed, he will be the executioner himself ; ties him to the cross, and with his own hand whips him, because no creature could strike strokes hard enough. A tender mother hath not the heart to whip her child for its own fault ; God bruiseth Christ's soul himself for others ; Zech. xiii. 7, ' Awake my sword against the man God's fellow ;' yea, Isa. liii. 10, ' It delighted the Lord to bruise him.' So much was his heart in our salvation, that this (otherwise the most abhorred act that ever was done) was sweetened to him by its end, our salvation, and made a matter of delight, not simply, but in relation to the end.

Use 3. Let us not think much to suffer any thing in our body for Christ ; he hath done more for us, he hath suffered in his soul. All that men can do is but to kill the body, they cannot reach the soul, Mat. x. 28. And therefore all that we can fear from them is but outward, in comparison of what Christ endured, it is but whipping through the clothes ; all that is done to the body, Mat. xx. 22. ' Can ye drink of the cup he drank of, and be baptized with the baptism he was baptized with ?' Rom. viii. 29. He exhorts us to cheerful suffering ; because therein we are conformed to Christ's image, who yet was in suffering the first-born among many brethren, and so had a larger portion in them than ever any had.

Use 4. Did the chief of Christ's sufferings lie in his soul ? Let the chief of our obedience be placed in our souls and in soul-worship. God said to Christ, ' My Son, give me thy soul ;' and Christ says to us, ' My son, give me your hearts.' Obedience in the inward man is the soul of obedience. ' Sanctify the Lord in your hearts,' 1 Pet. iii. 15 : there especially is God ennobled. God seeks for such to worship him as worship him in spirit. ' Bodily exercise profiteth little, but godliness,' &c., 1 Tim. iv. 8. There godliness is opposed to bodily exercise, and therefore godliness is put for the service of the inner man, which is only godliness, in which (Rom. vii.) the apostle says he served the Lord, which he calls serving him (ver. 4 of that chapter) in the newness of the spirit. The papists, whose worship is all bodily, they are all for Christ's bodily sufferings, and deny this is of his soul. But let us place the main of his obedience in the suffering of his soul, and so seeing his love, give up our souls to him chiefly to obey him with.

Use 5. Comfort to those that are distressed in soul.

(1.) You are herein conformed so much the more to Christ.

(2.) He knows the heart of a sinner distressed, and so is moved to pity more feelingly. He became a merciful high priest, in that he was tempted in all things as we, sin only excepted. Pity is more kindly when it is from experience of the like extremity.

(3.) In that he suffered in his soul, he thereby purchased comfort for thy soul. As in other things we make use of Christ's sufferings to relieve us against the particulars we are distressed in, so also let us in this. When we are poor, we may consider Christ was poor that we might be made rich ; when we suffer from men, we may have recourse to this, that by his stripes we are healed : so when in soul, that he was buffeted in spirit to free us ; his soul was heavy unto death that we might be comforted ; God spake to him in wrath that he might speak peace to us. Speaking comfort, in Scripture phrase, is called speaking to the heart.

Use 6. When we think of Christ crucified, let us especially think of the sufferings of his soul, so much forgotten and denied. To this end he ordained the cup in the sacrament ; as the bread to represent to our faith the body of Christ, so the wine the pouring forth of his soul, which is called the blood of the New Testament. That as the blood of the Old was the blood of bulls and goats, in which blood lies the life, as the Scripture speaks, the souls of beasts being but the spirits of the four elements which run in the blood, so that thing which that type signified, was the soul poured out, there being nothing nearer to represent the soul more lively than the blood, with which therefore all was sprinkled.

Use 7. See the heinousness of sin by this, that Christ was made a curse ; as he said, if thou wouldst see what sin is, go to mount Calvary. It is true that the utmost real evil of the thing itself which we call sin consists in this, that it is the transgression of the command of the great God. But the utmost representation to make that evil known to us, is the cross and the curse of the Son of God, blessed for ever. We seldom conceive of the greatness of injuries, as they are in themselves committed ; so we are apt to slight them ; but we do measure them best by the anger and the wrath they beget in the party wronged (if he be not partial in his own cause), and by the furious expressions of his wrath returned back again upon the offence. So whilst we view sin in its direct and proper notion, and that it is an injury against the great God, so we should never have seen the full vileness of it ; for as God is in himself invisible, so is the evil of sin ; and as Christ is the liveliest image of the invisible God, so are his debasement and his sufferings the truest glass to behold the ugliness of sin in, and the utmost representation to make us sensible of it. The throwing down the angels out of heaven, the cursing the earth and all Adam's posterity for Adam's sin, the drowning the old world, and overturning Sodom, and the fire unquenchable which burns to the bottom of hell ; these were such considerations as make us stand amazed and cry out, Oh, what is sin, that thou dost so remember it, or the sinfulness of it, that thou dost punish it in the destruction of the best creatures thy hands have made ! But all these tragedies are but as lighter skirmishes, and but shows of justice and wrath, in comparison of the death and sufferings of his Son. For how greatly incensed must that anger be by sin, which so infinite, so ancient love, to such a Son, could not quench nor yet allay! How deep in guilt must that fault be, for which justice is bold to exact no less satisfaction than the blood of God! For what crimes are kings at any time put to to death? Here God blessed for ever is made a curse, the light and life of the world and fountain of life is killed, the Lord of glory debased, the fulness of the Godhead emptied, emptied to nothing; he who is one with God in essence, in title to glory, is separated and accursed from him and by him, and laid as low as hell; and all this because he was made sin.

Use 8. Think what a miserable and fearful condition it must needs be to be found out of Christ and in your sins. And be assured of this, that either Christ or you must bear the full weight both of your sins, and the curse due to them. That Christ was made a curse may be both an evidence of the certainty of the curse and wrath to come, and of the fearfulness of it. Of the certainty, for if from former examples of God's vengeance upon other sinners like themselves, Peter argueth the assured inevitable destruction of ungodly men, that ' if he spared not the angels nor the old world,' &c., 2 Peter ii. 5, 6; he would therefore certainly not spare them. If further, from the chastisements brought upon his own dear children, God himself bids Jeremiah tell the nations that they should certainly drink— Jer. xxv. 29, ' For, lo, I bring evil upon the city that is called by my name, and should ye be unpunished?'—much more is it argued from this, that he brought all this evil and these curses on his Son. If God spared not the natural branch, nay, the root of branches, which bears all his olive branches, how will he spare those that shall be found wild olives, growing on their own stock, bearing all their wild olives and sins themselves? If he not only upon whom God's name is called, but whose name is in him, did and must drink of the cup, shall not the wicked of the earth drink the dregs of it? And as it may argue the certainty of it, so the fearfulness also. It was an use Christ made of it then when he was a-leading to be crucified, ' If they do this to the green tree, what will they do to the dry?' If he who was a green tree, and was by reason of his sap and fulness of grace no fit fuel for the fire, had no matter in himself for God to be angry with, yet it burns so fiercely on him, standing but in the shade and within the imputation of our sins; if the curse withered him that he looked like a tree growing on the dry ground, Oh, how will it rage upon dry trees, fitted for hell; upon fir trees that are full of, and bring forth, gum and rosin, fit fuel for that fire! And if the whole curse did light on him, and the respect to and dignity of his person abated nothing of it, God spared him not, surely a sinner out of Christ shall be abated nothing neither, but pay the utmost farthing. See in God's dealing with his Son the most vive type and resemblance of the curse to be executed upon all sinful unbelievers out of him. Cursed he is throughout his whole life, as Christ also was made a curse in his. The curse seized on him when he was made flesh, and began to break out upon him in the spots of human infirmities, making him all over like sinful flesh; which curse secretly followed him, and increased upon him in the fruits of it, and left him not till it had brought him to the accursed death, when it appeared to all the world that he was made a curse indeed, when he hanged upon a tree. Why, and cursed wert thou in thy conception, and cursed was the womb that bare thee, and a thread of curses are drawn through the web of thy frail life. And though a sinner may bless himself in honours, riches, pleasures, yet all these have a curse in them unto him; cursed is he when he eats, cursed when he lies down and rests, and cursed when he awakes again; and this curse leaves him not till it brings him to his end, and after that to judgment, when it appears he is cursed indeed, however accounted happy in this life. And learn to see and tremble, and to avoid it, how the curse will then seize on thee by what was done to Christ, if it prove not then that he was made a curse for thee. Then was his day of judgment and ours in him, Isa. liii. 8. And therefore in that day's passages with him, we may raise our hearts up to see what shall be then; what was done to the green tree then, shall be accomplished in a more transcendent manner upon the dry. When they come to lie upon their death-beds, then do their sins and God's wrath come in upon them, as upon him in the garden; they see them written in the curtains, and find their souls environed about with curses, besieged, and see no way out; and then happily their friends stand sleeping or weeping by, but, alas! they cannot help them or save them from that hour, as his disciples could not; miserable comforters thou wilt find them all. And if a minister, yea, an angel from heaven, should come to comfort them, oftimes he cannot. And then comes thy Judas, thy bosom sin, with whom thou hast eaten so many sweet bits, and communed together, and that comes into thy conscience with a troop of curses, and threatenings, and devils after it. And when thy soul sits upon thy lips and is departed, an armed band of hell seizeth upon it, binds thee hand and foot to be cast into utter darkness; leads thee before the throne of God's more private and particular judgment, as Christ was over night before the high priest; where when thou comest thou wilt be examined of all thy ways and works; and as that man in the Gospel that wanted the wedding garment, wilt remain speechless, not able to answer one of a thousand, not have a word to say. Even Christ stood speechless, the guilt of our sins stopping then his mouth. And after sentence then pronounced, that thou art worthy of death, thou wilt be kept in those chambers of death, and reserved in chains of darkness, as Christ was bound in the high priest's hall all night, and there mocked, and whipped, and beaten with many stripes, as the gospel hath it. And in the morning of the resurrection, when the dawning of the day of judgment shall appear, then they shall be more publicly brought forth before the throne of Christ, appointed to judge both the quick and dead, a time when all the world, great and small, shall be assembled to thy arraignment and execution, as all the Jews were then at the feast; when God will shame thee before this sun, and rip up all the hidden things of darkness. As Christ was put to open shame, so shalt thou; and confusion of face shall cover thee, and thou shalt become a loathing and an hissing to all flesh. And though thou hast thy soul filled full of evils, yet God and the saints shall but mock when this thy fear cometh, and laugh at thy destruction, Prov. i., as they did Christ, ' Thou that destroyest the temple,' &c., and ' savest others ;' so will God say, ' I have called, and ye refused ; ye set at nought all my counsel,' Prov. i. 24–26 ; and now let your gods deliver you if they would have you. And this confusion will most befall those who profess themselves the sons of God and were not, that saved others and now are damned themselves; with which they mocked Christ, He said he was the Son of God, and that he trusted in him, and he saved others ; now let him save himself. And then after sentence is pronounced, ' Go, ye cursed,' hurried shall they be, ere Christ riseth off the bench, by angels, Mat. xxv., to hell, the place of execution, where in utter darkness (as Christ also was crucified in a great darkness that was over the land) separated and accursed from God for ever, they shall be punished from his presence, 2 Thess. i. 9, with everlasting destruction; where a drop of water shall be denied them, as it was to

Christ, left naked and destitute of all comforts, stripped as Christ also was, and with the scroll of their rebellions pinned over their heads, for men and angels to read, as Christ's was in all languages.

A second sort of uses are to men humbled for sin, and seeking after faith, to guide and direct poor souls to the right way of obtaining and seeking justification by faith.

Use 9. If Jesus Christ was thus made sin and a curse, the one charged upon him, the other inflicted, then surely all those Christ will save, he will have them also know and apprehend what their sins are, and the curse due to them, though not by way of satisfaction to God, yet by way of humiliation to them. If your sins were charged upon Christ, who knew no sin, there is reason they should be charged upon your consciences. If your sins brought Christ upon his knees (as they did in the garden) before God as an angry judge, they may well bring you upon your knees also. They were yours before they were his, and therefore ere you by faith can come to lay your sins upon Christ and discharge yourselves of them, you must know the burthen of them yourselves. His was but an assumed guilt, yours is proper and inherent. If your sins made Christ's soul heavy unto death, they must make your soul heavy also ere ever Christ will ease you. Christ did so ordain to save you as that you should be conformable to him, and die with him if ever you rise again with him. Now as Christ died and rose again, so must you; and as we are said to rise again with him through faith, Col. ii. 12, so to die with him through humiliation.

Use 10. To this end lay all your sins to your own charge; they were laid to his charge to satisfy God's justice, and thou must lay them to thine own charge, to humble thy soul and to make thee the more thankful. Christ's death keeps many off from troubling themselves with their sins at all: they put off thinking of their sins with this, that God is merciful, and Christ hath died; but that they were laid to his charge hinders not that thou art to charge thyself with them; only thou art to do it to a differing end. Jesus Christ had them laid to his charge to satisfy for them; take heed of taking them so upon thyself, they will break thy back. But take them on thee to humble thee, which thou art therefore to do, because they were all thine ere his; as Christ said to his Father, of his elect, ' Father, thine they were, and thou gavest them me,' John xvii. So on the contrary mayest thou say to Christ of thy sins, Lord, mine they were, and thou didst take them on me.* Thus Isaiah teacheth us to do, Isa. liii. 6, ' We like sheep have gone astray, and God laid on him the iniquities of us all.' And therefore, as David humbled himself,—' Lord, it is I and my father's house ; what have these sheep done ? '—so say, Lord, it is I that have sinned against thee, these sins are all done by me ; what hath this lamb, holy, innocent, without spot, done? And withal, think what an infinite misery it will be to be found in thy sins, if all these sins should be thine own, and not to be taken off by Christ for thee, if it should fall out that thou must die in thy sins (as Christ threatened the Pharisees), that thou shouldst not be eased of the burden of one sin by the death of Jesus Christ. If they made his soul so heavy when they were made his but by imputation, what will they do to thee, whose they are by inherent, by proper and immediate guilt ? If the shadow of them withered him so, what will the true guilt of them in thee ? Thou hast guilt of conscience in thee of them, a conscience of sins which he had not, and yet they made his soul heavy ; what will they do thine ? Thou wilt have despair in hell to make thy torment greater, be-

* Qu. 'thee'?—ED.

cause of that eternity of thy torment, whereas he had faith to uphold him to endure the cross by reason of the joy set before him, which he knew he should receive when the brunt was over. If Christ's soul was so perplexed that he said, ' What shall I say?' John xii. 27, how perplexed will thy soul be, not knowing what to do, but wishing the rocks to fall upon thee to cover thee!

Use 11. If God charged all our particular sins upon Christ, then go and humble thyself for thy particular sins. If God gave Christ a bill of them, do thou make bills and catalogues of them. As Christ knew what he paid for, so he will have thee know what he pardoneth and what was paid for. This will make thee love Christ the more, as Mary did, who loved much because much was forgiven her, and it will make thee see thyself more beholden to Christ for suffering more for thee than another. Thus the thorough knowledge of Paul's sin wrought the more love and thankfulness in him unto Jesus Christ, 1 Tim. i., that though Christ came into the world to save sinners, yet for me, the chief of sinners. And though there are many sins which thou daily discoverest, which thou sawest not at first, yet be not discouraged, for secret sins, though not confessed, may be pardoned; for Jesus Christ bare all sins, and those that are not known to thee to humble thee were yet known to Christ to pardon them to thee. And the confessing particular sins over Christ thus will in the end bring assurance of the pardon of particulars, and be a means to strike off the guilt of particulars; for often when we think such and such sins are pardoned, we yet stick at some one, or such or such, and cannot think them pardoned. Therefore confess particulars, and bring them to God, and say concerning such a sin, Was not this sin, Lord, reckoned amongst the rest unto Christ? This soul-sin that stares me in the face, was not this amongst the rest? Then, Lord, through his bearing of it, take it off from me. And as you are to apply Christ crucified for the crucifying particular lusts, so for the washing off of your consciences the guilt of particular sins. Do therefore as men that would be sure to have a writing crossed and blotted, that the debt-book may not be read, they not only give general cross lines over all the whole leaf at one stroke, but they will (to make all sure) go over every line with their pens, and cross every one in particular out; and so do thou, not apply Christ's death in general, but apply it to every particular sin. And especially against a sacrament, then make catalogues of your sins, for then Christ is crucified afresh afore your eyes. And look, what was done by God to Christ, when he was crucified on the cross for the satisfaction of his justice, that you are to do when you come to view, and by faith to receive, Christ crucified, for the satisfaction of your consciences; for the application of Christ crucified is but the acting over by faith what was done by God. Especially such sins as the guilt whereof doth in a more special manner trouble you, those bring catalogues of at every communion; that although the lines of Christ's blood have been drawn over them with the rest already, yet get more crosses of his blood over them, and use his blood to cross out particulars. And as you do with *aqua fortis*, when you would eat out letters written in a book, if any letters remain more fresh than their fellows, remaining not so perfectly eaten out, you go over them anew; so do with Christ's blood in your consciences, to such sins, the guilt whereof is most conspicuous.

Use 12. Take heed of resting in duties. Christ's active obedience would not have saved you, if he had not also been made a curse, and therefore do you think your dunghill performances, as Paul calls it, will save you? You thereby dishonour Christ as much as the Jews that crucified him ; you bid him come off the cross, he need not hang there for you, you can pray it out, and you can fast sin out yourselves.

Use 13. Rest on Christ alone, especially as crucified. Paul desired to know Christ, and him crucified especially. As they preached so are we to believe.` It is the serpent as lifted up that is the object of faith, so Christ present in the sacrament, not simply the person of Christ, but Christ as crucified and as broken for our sins. Otherwise Christ, considered in the excellency of his person, so he might be an object for the faith of angels, who would have been glad of such a husband; but Christ, as crucified, so he is fitted for sinners, and he becomes not an object of love for the excellency of his person, but of faith and confidence as a means and ordinance for the salvation of sinners ; and though we are to look on him as glorified, yet withal as once crucified. So that faith is to look at once with one eye to heaven, to Christ there as risen, ascended, interceding, so to look down with another eye to that Christ as once crucified and hanging on the cross, as made sin and a curse.

Use 14. Labour for assurance ; so see by faith yourselves one with Christ in all this he did for you, to be able to view yourselves in him when he died, that as by faith you believe you were in Adam when he was in the garden, and ate the forbidden fruit, so that you were in Christ when he fulfilled the law and hung on the cross. Therefore, Rom. viii. 4, the law is said to be fulfilled in us, though not by us, yet in us, because we were in Christ when he fulfilled it, and so it is as if we had done it. Endeavour therefore to apprehend that Christ had not only an eye to thee and thy person, and thy sins when he hung on the cross, but he then stood in thy stead and as thy proxy. This is that which will bring in the comfort. Though casting a man's self upon Christ for salvation through his death is that faith that saves, which is called coming to Christ, yet more is required: Rom. vi., ' Reckon yourselves dead with Christ;' that is, to have died when he died. Faith will help a man to put himself into Christ hanging on the cross, and that is to reckon a man's self as then dying with him; and then you may see all your sins done away, purged away then, Heb. i., and yourselves perfected for ever, Heb. x., that your sins shall arise no more. And to see this, all the world cannot help you, it must be the Spirit, that knew Christ's mind then. Only in the mean time you may go blindfold, as it were, and cast anchor in the dark, and refer the casting of thy state to what Christ did then for thee, that if he bare not thy sins then, thou canst not be saved; desiring God (blindfold) to pardon thee by virtue of what Christ did then. Say, Lord, I refer myself to thy heart from everlasting, and to Christ's heart when he hung upon the cross, and let that cast my condition. And be bold to plead Christ's death blindfold ; by way of questioning with God (though by absolute challenging as yet thou canst not), say, Lord, did not Christ bear these very sins, that affright me so, on the cross ? Did not he condemn them there and cast them in their suit ? Why do they accuse me now ? Say, Lord, didst thou| not give my name to Christ in that bill among the rest ? Was not I written in his heart and thine ? Didst thou not eye my person and sins in his soul as satisfied for them by him ? If so, Lord, pardon them, lift the guilt off from me by virtue of his bearing them. It is lawful to ask such questions : 1 Pet. iii. 21, it is called 'επερώτημα, the interrogating the challenge made of God's favour, by a good conscience justified by Christ's blood and resurrection. So Heb. ii. 4, the church. doth ; and God often whilst a man is pleading and questioning thus, cannot deny it, but affirms it to a man's spirit. Carnal fancy hath a trick to make suppositions, and to put a man by way of supposition into such or such a condition; as suppose I were rich, or were a king, what would I do then? Now let faith make sometimes such suppositions; it is good and warrantable to inure our thoughts to such suppositions till assurance comes. Make the supposition to thy heart, that all this that Christ did, he did for thee; upon such a supposition see how far thy heart would work, and thy affections stir. In suppositions of carnal fancy, you shall find corrupt affections stir, and your heart run out far in them; and in the suppositions of faith you shall find holy affections stir and discover themselves; and as corrupt desires are nourished and increased by the other, so a virtue comes with these to cause a man to love Christ, to hate sin, to mourn for it, that lifts off secretly the guilt of it, easeth the burden, maketh the pinch of it less.

A third sort of use is to them that have got assurance, then to make use of Christ's crucifying and his being made a curse.

Use 15. To cause you to mourn and bleed for sin. His heart was melted through heaviness, and so will yours be to sorrow. His sorrow was to death, yours will be to life. As there is a sorrow to God-ward, 2 Cor. vii., so to Christ-ward; as that God is offended with sin, so that Christ was crucified by thy sin: not to be sorry that it was done, so as to wish it undone, but that thy sin should be against him that did so much for thee unknown to thee. I do not say you are to mourn for the crucifying of Christ as your sin, as some in their rhetoric have endeavoured to persuade men that they were as the Jews; so indeed the Jews, when they are called, shall mourn; but this should make thee mourn, that God should crucify his Son for these sins of thine, and Christ should have such love in him to do it; and so view every sin as dyed with Christ's blood. You cannot say, *I* crucified Christ by my sins, and in that relation mourn, for that was God's act and his own; but you may say he was crucified *for* my sins, and so mourn; both as considering sin as an offence against one that loved you so, and also as considering your very sins as that which was as the weapons, as the instrument wherewith God wounded him. And so you may go over all your sins, and say they fetched those groans from him and those bitter cries; and shall his heart be made sorrowful by them? and shall not mine be for them? Neither is it that you are to mourn for him with a sorrow of compassion, which is all that popish postillers would bring their hearers unto, only such sorrow as a man would have stirred up in him at a pitiful story of an innocent man, or a man of a heroical spirit thus used: this sorrow Christ now regards not, as he did not much then, when he went to be crucified, for said he to them that followed him, 'Weep not for me, but for yourselves;' he regarded not such womanish tears. But to think of thy unkindness to him in sinning, who endured so much, so willingly, to expiate these sins, this is it that is to make the heart to gush. Again, we may mourn for our sins as the crucifiers of Christ, but not as if it were an aggravation of our sins that they crucified Christ, but only of his love, that would be crucified for them and by them. And so, as we say, it is not the executioner kills the man, nor the judge properly that gives the sentence and delivers him up, but the fact laid to his charge, that is it may be said to have been his death; and so may our sins in all this be considered as the cause of all, *peccatum solum homicida est.* So, we may say, the swiftness of our feet to do evil nailed his feet, the works of our hands drave the nails into his, for he was delivered up for our sins. Yea, and of the sorrows of his soul, they were the more immediate instruments and executioners, for they were particularly represented to him, and ran every one with their bodkins and pierced him through; he was beset, as being encompassed about with them, and pierced through and through by every of them; there is not a sin of them but had a stab, and his soul had a stab for it; and in that relation thou mayest mourn over thy sin and his soul and body, and mayest go forth and view every part upon the cross—his hands nailed, his side pierced, his back whipped, and look through his side into his heart, and see it in agonies and horror, and all for these sins of mine,* yea, and caused by these sins, which will make thy heart sweat blood, as his body did, if thou hast any love to him. But above all, thou art to consider his love in all, that is it which above all is to work in this mourning upon thy view of his being crucified. His love was stronger than death; death could not keep him in the grave, but his love kept him on the cross for thee when he was provoked to come down. His pains were great, but his love more; thy sin, and his love in all this, to endure all this for thy sin, this is it must move thee. I will say but this to you: if any of you believers, that have love in your hearts to Christ, had been alive then, and had known from Christ afore that all his sufferings to come had been for your sins, and to save you for them, and your heart had followed him to the cross full of such apprehensions, and you, as John and his mother, had stood by and viewed all that really passed then, and had still had this thought —all this is for me, out of love to me and my sins; I like a sheep have gone astray, and God now lays on him all my sins—and then had gone over in your thoughts all your sins, how would your hearts have been broken and melted! Now, by faith you may view him in this narration, and in the sacraments, as really as if you had been by; so Paul says, Gal. iii. 1, 2. Therefore, get your hearts to melt and break over this crucifix, and put your sins and his love into one cup and drink them off, and see how this potion will work. To bring the murderer to a dead man makes the dead man bleed afresh; but bring thy sins to Christ, and it will make thy heart to bleed afresh.

Use 16. Work your hearts to a hatred of sin upon these considerations also. If a man had killed your friend, or father, or mother, how would you hate him! You would not endure the sight of him, but follow the law upon him (as in the old law they did if they fled not to the city of refuge). Send out the avenger of blood with a hue and cry after thy sin; bring it afore God's judgment-seat, arraign it, accuse it, spit on it, condemn it and thyself for it, have it to the cross, nail it there, if it cry I thirst, give it vinegar, stretch the body of sins upon his cross, stretch every vein of it, make the heart-strings crack; and then when it hangs there, triumph over the dying of it, shew it no pity, laugh at its destruction, say, Thou hast been a bloody sin to me and my husband, hang there and rot. And when thou art tempted to it, and art very thirsty after the pleasure of it, say of that opportunity to enjoy it, as David said of the water of Bethlehem, It is the price of Christ's blood, and pour it upon the ground. Mere ingenuity should move us; say with thyself,

1. If no more but the conformity between Christ and me, shall I live in that to which I died when my head died? thus Paul, Rom. vi.

2. Shall I live upon that which was Christ's death? Shall I please myself in that which was his pain? Shall I be so dishonest, so unkind, as to enjoy the pleasure for which he endured the smart? Shall I spend on

* Qu. 'thine'?—ED.

his score, the score of his love ?   King's children, when others are beaten
for them, it moves them to be as diligent and fearful to offend as if themselves were to be beaten, out of ingenuity; and that Christ was whipped
for us and our sins, should move us as much against them as if ourselves
were every day to be crucified as he was.   I only put this to all your considerations that love the Lord Jesus, if Christ were yet to suffer at the end
of the world, and in suffering to bear all the sins you should commit (as
you heard when he suffered he did), if you had any ingenuity, how wary
would you be how you increased his load, how sorry that you added any
sin, knowing it would be his sorrow ; and shall he fare the worse because
all is done already ?

CHAPTER XV.

*The victory which Christ gained over Satan by his death.—The glory of this
victory displayed by the consideration of the greatness of that power which
the devil had over us.*

*That through death he might destroy him that had the power of death, that is,
the devil.*—HEB. ii. 14.

The victory, yea, destruction which Christ hath upon Satan on our behalf, is the full scope of this text, and follows as the next subject unto that
of redemption of us from sin and the curse, and is indeed the consequent
of that redemption.
There is no text large enough to take in the whole, either of Satan's
power or of Christ's destroying him in respect of that his power, for this
mentions on Satan's part his power over death only as the jailor ; and on
Christ's part, his overcoming him by his death is only spoken of, whereas
Satan hath power, and that chiefly in matter of sin, also, in ruling this
world ; and Christ also destroys or confounds him by his ascension, intercession, and judging both the devils and the world at last.   Yet you well
may upon occasion of these take in all, and it may have this warrant from
this text, that it is said to be a destruction of him (which is a general word
and takes in all), that is, of his person wholly and totally ; and so in all
points of his power besides, as well as in that over death.
And again, Christ's death here meritoriously and virtually reached to all
the power Satan had of any kind ; and so, then, a total rout and destruction of him is in the apostle's scope.
And the story hereof, as gathered from the Scriptures, is our present
subject, and is divided, as the text is, into two parts.
  1. Satan's power.
  2. Christ's victory and destruction of him.
  1. Concerning Satan's power, therein two things are to be considered :
  (1.) What power Satan hath had in the world, and over the elect sons
of men, fallen under sin in common with other men.
  (2.) By what claim or right he came by it.
  2. Concerning the second, Christ's victory, and his destroying him,
therein are to be remarked,
  (1.) The true original ground of the quarrel, how Christ came to be engaged and involved against him.

(2.) The several degrees of Christ's conquests; and they are reduced to two heads:

[1.] The first rout, wherein the foundation was laid of the ensuing victories, and that was got in open battle in the plain field at his death, in and by which virtually the whole was at once won and obtained; and therein I shall shew how justly Satan fell from his power, and lost it: and this I call Christ's meritorious victory.

[2.] Then there is, secondly, the prosecution of this first victory, and the management thereof to his own greatest glory and Satan's confusion. And the parts thereof are,

First; Christ's triumphing over him after the victory obtained in his own person openly, and that in Satan's own dominions, afore God and all the holy angels, and this singly in himself, and in his own person, although as representing us, Col. ii. 15; and this I term his victorious triumph, or the show and demonstration of it.

Secondly; there is his overcoming him in us, then when Satan is still left in actual possession of the whole world, and of the elect among them, whose liberty and redemption it was Christ aimed at. And this hath two degrees:

First; he overcomes him *in us* at our conversion; and,

Secondly; he overcomes him *by us,* and causeth every particular Christian to overcome him in the course of their lives, after conversion. And these two I term Christ's actual prevailing, or getting possession.

Thirdly; a third procedure is Christ his visible setting up a kingdom in this world afore the day of judgment, during which time Satan is shut up, and restrained from tempting the elect, and from deceiving and enraging the world against the elect, as now he yet doth, and heretofore hath done. And this is expressed in the last chapters of the Revelations, chap. xix. ver. 19–21. 'And I saw the beast, and the kings of the earth, and their armies, gathered together to make war against him that sat on the horse, and against his army. And the beast was taken, and with him the false prophet that wrought miracles before him, with which he deceived them that had received the mark of the beast, and them that worshipped his image. These both were cast alive into a lake of fire burning with brimstone.' After which follows chap. xx. 1–3, 'And I saw an angel come down from heaven, having the key of the bottomless pit, and a great chain in his hand. And he laid hold of the dragon, that old serpent, which is the devil, and Satan, and bound him a thousand years, and cast him into the bottomless pit, and shut him up, and set a seal upon him, that he should deceive the nations no more, till the thousand years should be fulfilled: and after that he must be loosed a little season.' And then follows the kingdom of the saints during those thousand years; ver. 4, 5, 'And I saw thrones, and they that sat upon them, and judgment was given unto them: and I saw the souls of them that were beheaded for the witness of Jesus, and for the word of God, and which had not worshipped the beast, neither his image, neither had received his mark upon their foreheads, or in their hands; and they lived and reigned with Christ a thousand years. But the rest of the dead lived not again, until the thousand years were finished. This is the first resurrection.'

Fourthly; lastly, there is Christ his bringing this great malignant unto open trial afore all the world; God, angels, and men; which is at the day of judgment. After which follows the execution of him, in an eternal destruction of him in hell.

There is a glory transcendent that will appear in each one of these particulars, but more in the whole of them all laid together; a stupendously
excelling glory, in comparison unto which victories of Christ, all the great
victories you have seen are but trifles and shadows, that have no glory in
this respect, and therefore ' let not the rich man glory in his riches, nor
the strong man in his conquests, but let him that glorieth, glory in the
Lord;' and in this especially, that he knows himself is one of those poor
captives whom this great conqueror delivered, amongst the rest of the elect
who shall stand up in his lot amongst them.

I. To discourse concerning Satan and his power, and to shew what it is.

In general, it is a kingdom maintained and upheld by him and all his
angels conspiring in one, against Christ and his saints : Mat. xii. 26, ' And
if Satan cast out Satan, he is divided against himself; how then shall his
kingdom stand ?' And whereas every kingdom hath an interest, the interest of this is sin ; Eph. vi. 12, they are said to be rulers of the darkness
of this world, which is spoken in distinction from the good angels, who are
rulers of this world too ; for in that the apostle says, ' this world to come
is not subject to the angels,' Heb. ii. (he speaks of them that are good);
he implies that now they are sent out for the good of the elect, Heb. i. 14 ;
and it argues that this world is subject to them, in order to the good of the
elect. But now herein lies the difference : Satan is the ruler of the darkness of this world, and the riches, glory, and greatness of it being for the
most part obtained and managed by sin and corruption, therefore in ruling
the darkness that is in men's hearts, he also comes to rule and dispose of
these. Even as the pope's power (who is his eldest son) is in pretence
only *ad spiritualia*, yet so as *in ordine ad spiritualia*, he takes on him to
meddle in all things temporal; so his father Satan, having now in commission only spiritual darkness and wickedness, and obtaining this power
over men unregenerate, yet in order thereunto over these children here,
until converted.

These of all other things are committed to him.

1. To entice, as he did Ahab, 1 Kings xxii. 21.

2. To put into the heart, as in Judas.

3. To provoke, 1 Chron. xxi. 1.

4. To bewitch, Gal. iii. 1.

5. To fill the heart, as he did the heart of Ananias, Acts v. 3.

6. To work effectually, and so as to carry all before him, and cause them
to do what he enticeth to, Eph. ii. 2.

7. And, seventhly, to do all this at his will, 2 Tim. ii. 26.

This power of Satan is in respect of sin, or the darkness of this world.
He hath a power over them in respect of death ; so in the text ; but this
power lasts but till the resurrection, and but over men's souls. For when
the day of judgment is ended, it is the good angels that do throw wicked
men to hell, and not the evil angels, Mat. xiii. 41, 42. But in the mean-
time look, as the good angels have the commission for carrying men's souls
to paradise, as they did Lazarus his, Luke xvi. 22, so the evil angels have
until then the commission to carry wicked souls, when by death severed
from their bodies, to hell.

Let us now consider (to set forth Christ's victory the more) the greatness and the extent of this kingdom given to the devil and his angels.

I. As it is in the hands of the great devil placed on his throne, it is a
monarchy over mankind, of all forms, highest for power in all ranks
throughout.

II. For the subject of it, they are (as Christ's subjects also are, Col. i. 16) both things visible and invisible; so that he hath of both kinds, especially the kinds of intelligent natures, subject to him.

1. Angels: 'The devil and his angels.' 2. Us men, wholly captived to him. And further (wherein the upholdance of this great tyrant's cause is), some of these are as natural native subjects that rule with him, and have a common interest of power with him. And they are his angels; but we poor silly men are as slaves captived to them and him. Like as Pharaoh (one of his eldest sons under the Old Testament) had for his natural liege subjects his Egyptians, that ruled over the Israelites with him, and the poor Israelites as captives and slaves unto both. And in this lieth the greatness of the Turkish dominion in part of Europe, Asia, and of the Mogul in East India, to this day. So then he hath all sorts of subjects every way.

3. As unto us men, his power is universal, not a soul of us but is by nature subject to him. We are all born by a statute law his slaves; and Christ hath none but whom he wins over from him, by turning them from Satan unto God, yea, and in the issue he holds and retains a far greater company and number to himself than Christ gets unto himself, Rev. xii. 9. It is one part of Satan's titles, that it is he who deceives the whole world.

4. In us men (the more miserable part of his subjects) he rules inwardly, even as Christ doth in those few he gets from him: he sits and fills and rules our hearts, till we are turned to God.

5. If we consider the length and continuance of this his dominion, as he hath sinned from the beginning, 1 John iii. 8; so he hath entered upon his reign from the very beginning of man's fall, and every man born becomes his subject; neither have these individual devils given place to any, but the same devil that ruled in Cain's time rules now in the children of disobedience, Eph. ii. 2.

6. For success, he hath carried it clear; for he works, and works effectually, in the children of disobedience, and takes them captives at his will, as he lists, 2 Tim. ii. 26.

7. He hath been worshipped as a god, and so hath had more honour and dignity than any prince, 2 Cor. iv. 4. He is there called, 'the god of this world.' Some great conquerors affected to be worshipped as gods, not being content with the highest supreme power; so Alexander and Mahomet; but few obtained it, but the devil hath had both. So it was from the flood, till heathenism was destroyed, and popish idolatry was set up, as it is said, Rev. xiii. 14. Thus therein they worshipped the dragon, who gave his power to the beast, to the end to have worship continued to him in another way under the profession of Christ, even as he had afore. Thus much for the power itself.

II. Secondly, The second part to be discoursed of is, by what claim, right, or title he came to have this power, seeing himself by sinning (afore man had sinned) deserved to be in the nethermost hell.

1. The legal and fundamental claim is God's commission, and that by way of curse upon man. Man turning rebel against God, he justly gave that ungrateful creature, who despised his mild government, over unto the hard and intolerable vassalage of his tyrant. It was a just punishment, that man, who would not have God to rule over him, should be delivered into the devil's power, and it was as great a punishment as could be inflicted. Thus we find, that when David, by way of prophecy, was to curse Judas (who himself was placed in the office of an apostle, or bishop, or overseer,

as Peter interprets it, and applies it to him, Acts i. 16, 20), says he, Ps.
cix. 6,* 'Set in office over him the wicked one, and let the adversary or
Satan stand at his right hand.' The wicked one is the devil; so oft and
usually in the Epistles of John the phrase is used, and in the Lord's prayer,
&c.; and accordingly we read that Satan entered into him, Luke xxii. 3.
And thus in like manner, man sinning at first, God by way of curse and
commission set the wicked one a ruler over him; and this curse was but
suited to his iniquity in a just way, as the law was in Deut. xxviii. 47, 48,
'Because thou servedst not the Lord thy God with joyfulness and with
gladness of heart for the abundance of all things, therefore shalt thou serve
thine enemies, which the Lord shall send against thee, in hunger and
thirst, &c., and he shall put a yoke of iron upon thy neck, until he have
destroyed thee.'
   And besides this curse, there was some appearance of legality in it,
Isa. xlix. 14. The title of Satan's power in Scripture riseth so high, as that
the souls of men are termed his own house. Luke xi. in the 21st verse,
Christ calls them his palace, and all the faculties and powers of their souls
his goods; and, ver. 24, the devil himself terms it his house. And the
grounds of it are,
   1. Of whom a man is overcome, of the same he is brought in bondage
by the law of conquest, 2 Peter ii. 19. He speaks it of sin, but it is true
of Satan, whose interest is the same with that of sins. Man was overcome
by Satan, and caught in his snare; the serpent beguiled our first parents,
and so they were brought into bondage, as unto sin, so to him.
   2. Satan was the father of sin and sinners; and it is his work, 1 John
iii. 8, as holiness is the workmanship of God, Eph. ii. 10. Now the father
of a family was, under the law of nature, the governor and head of it, and
so is the devil, of whom (as I may say) all the wicked family on earth and
hell is named. And God, indeed, cursed the devil himself with this power
for his ruin; and as sin was his work and his invention first, truly he let
him have the monopoly of it; and all sinners came under his patent, and be
workers at the trade under him, as the first inventors of any craft use to have
the privilege to employ others under them.

CHAPTER XVI.

*How it was Christ's great concern and interest to destroy the power of Satan.—
The conquest which he had over him by his death, and his open and glorious
triumph after the victory, expressed in Col. ii. 15.*

   The second part of this discourse is of Christ's part in destroying all the
power of the devil. And therein we are to regard,
   First, the ground of the quarrel betwixt Christ and him; and how Christ
came to be engaged in it. The ground of this quarrel was either, 1. Personal; or, 2. On our behalf.
   1. Personal, as he was God's Son, and natural heir. What was Satan's
sin? It was the setting up a kingdom against God, and Christ his Son.
'He left his habitation' for it, Jude 6. It is mentioned not as his punishment only, but as his sin. He and his angels shook off God's dominion,
and betook themselves to seek their fortunes, and set up for themselves in
                    * See Ainsworth on the place.

this airy and visible world.   Thus in Mat. xii. 26, the bottom reason Christ
gives why one devil opposeth not another, is, for ' how then shall *his kingdom*
stand ?'   You may observe there is a kingdom of his mentioned, consisting
in one common general interest, wherein they all agree.   Now if there were
no other reason but that it is the quarrel of the Godhead, in Father, Son,
and Spirit, Christ is sufficiently in person interested in it on his own, yea,
his Father's, behalf.   For if any rebel against a prince, who is so fit to
suppress and subdue them as the son in his father's behalf (when himself
also is the heir), who so fit as he to fight his father's battles, and to put him
into the throne again ?   But,

2. It is more than whispered, it is talked out by some great and good
divines,* that the spirit and edge of their first sin was pointed against the
Son of God, as he was to be God-man, and so in our nature declared to be
ordained an head to angels and men ; and if so, the quarrel was personal
indeed, for it more particularly touched Christ's propriety and prerogative.
Whether these things were so or no, or that they be sufficiently proved by
these intimations in the Scriptures, I leave every reader to his own judgment ; only if I had not inclined thereto, I had not at all proposed this.
I add,—

3. That it properly and personally concerned Jesus Christ to come and
destroy the devil ; in that Satan's kingdom (which upon his turning head
against God he was in actual possession of) was that which letted or stood
in the way to that of Christ's kingdom, and took up much of the room of
it.   This kingdom Christ as God-man was appointed unto (Heb. i. 2) ;
and it was only as God-man that he was appointed to it, for as mere Son
of God, or second person, he hath it by nature, and not decree.   The appointment also was, that he must win it ere he wears it, as Ps. ii., Ps. cx.,
and 1 Cor. xv. shew.   He must destroy therefore this his opposite, to
make way for the possession of this his own kingdom, and therefore, Mat.
xii. 28, Christ gives this as a manifest undeniable evidence, that the kingdom of God, which the prophets had foretold the Messiah, the Christ,
should (as come from God, and for God) possess and administer, was beginning to be set up upon his coming into the world, and that himself was
the appointed heir therefore, yea, apparent heir, by this probation, that he
did by the Spirit of God cast devils out : ' But if I cast out devils by the
Spirit of God, then the kingdom of God is come unto you.'   The evidence
lies in this, that whilst he did it, he did profess himself to be that very
Messiah to whom that kingdom did belong, and that the rising of his kingdom was the downfall of Satan's.   And so that first promise and prophecy,
Gen. iii., began to be fulfilled, in and by his own very person, viz., ' He
shall break the serpent's head.   Which (saith Christ) you see manifestly
with your eyes ; for with the same breath, at the same instant, he commands the devils forth, and so proclaims himself to be that king to whom
Satan must give way.

But the second ground of the quarrel was on our behalf, and this for
sureness in the text.   The verse afore, the 13th, doth bring in Christ speaking himself as a father of many children, committed to his trust and charge
by God, ' Behold I and the children which God hath given me.'   Christ
is and was an ' everlasting Father,' Isa. ix. 6, and these children were given
to him in and at God's first election, both of Christ himself as mediator,
and them as members, both at the same time, and election of the one was
involved in the election of the other.   Eph. i. 4, They were ' chosen in

* Zanchy, Willet, Suarez, Catharinus.

him before the foundation of the world; thus long afore the fall of man, or Satan's sinning or kingdom, so as Christ was plainly thus long afore entrusted to be their guardian; and such and so great an estate of glory was long afore bequeathed to him.   Therefore these children being by that curse and righteous law (they sinning) become now vassals and slaves of Satan, 'forasmuch then as his children were partakers of flesh and blood, he also himself likewise took part of the same, that through death he might destroy him that had the power of death, that is, the devil.'   It is the very account given in the text, and imports in the coherence of these words with the former immediately foregoing, that these his pupils and children having been long afore given him, and now fallen into the devil's power, that moved therewith, he came to rescue and deliver them (as the next words carry it on, ver. 15).   Thus zealous was Christ for these his children, and to discharge his trust; and thus, Eph. v. 23, Christ being originally and primitively constituted an head to them, this drew him to be a Saviour.   The words there are, 'Even as Christ is the head of the church' (a head first), and 'he is the Saviour of the body.'

These things, as thus relating to Satan, to have been much in Christ's heart, his speeches up and down the Gospel of John and elsewhere shew.   In which you may observe him discoursing, as great princes use to do of their grand opposites, so he of Satan, and the confusion he was sent to put him into; by all which, what his heart was intimately set upon in man's salvation doth eminently appear, as you may read, John xii. 27–32, wherein he mentions this confusion of Satan with somewhat an equal affection he had to that of the salvation of men; and both as those two eminent grand matters in which both God and Christ aimed most to be glorified.   You find him at the 27th verse struck with the thoughts of his approaching sufferings, 'Now is my soul troubled, and what shall I say? Father, save me from this hour;' and yet then checks himself, 'but for this cause came I to this hour;' as if he had said, this was the business I came into the world for, and I must disannul all, if I now withdraw.   But then further he cheers himself up with the great and general end which his death and coming into the world and all served to, verse 28, 'Father, glorify thy name;' unto which God from heaven gave answer, 'I have both glorified it, and will glorify it again.'   Then he specifies two things wherein God was thus to be greatly glorified, by the foresight and prospect of which he further recovers his spirit; namely,—

1. Satan's overthrow, 'Now is the judgment of this world: now shall the prince of this world be cast out,' ver. 31.

2. Man's salvation: ver. 32, 'And I, if I be lifted up from the earth, will draw all men unto me,' and both these at once accomplished by the cross; ver. 33, 'This he said, signifying what death he should die;' which falls in with what the text saith, 'That through death he might destroy him that had the power of death, that is, the devil.'   And with all which also that of John i. 14 doth correspond, 'The Word was made flesh and (ἐσκήνωσε) he pitched a tent amongst us,' as a soldier, for it is a military word; for his end of dwelling in flesh was to destroy the devil in open and plain field, by conquest; and suitably in this Heb. ii. 10, you have him called 'the Captain of our salvation,' then when his destroying of Satan is spoken of.

I pursue next the several proceedings and passages of the victory (whereof the most eminent and fundamental to all the rest is that of his death, as all the places already handled do shew).

I reduced them at first under two general heads, having divers particulars under them.

1. Christ's overcoming Satan *in himself*,* that is, in his own person.
2. His overcoming him *in us* and *by us*. Or thus, there is Christ's overcoming Satan *for us*, and there is Christ's overcoming him *in us* and *by us*. The account of this distinction you will easily perceive by comparing two texts together ; the first, Col. ii. 15, where he is said to have ' spoiled Satan and triumphed over him, ἐν αὐτῷ *(cum aspiratione)* in himself,' and so the margin varies it ; the second is 1 John iv. 4, ' Stronger is he that is in you than he that is in the world.' He that is in the world is the devil, who tempts us with the world; and in overcoming the world we overcome that wicked one (as expressly it is twice said, 1 John ii. 13, 14), and this is Christ's overcoming the devil in us, as these words, ' stronger is he that is in you,' do evidently shew.

What he did in his own person for us are two.

(1.) The great and total rout Christ gave Satan at his death. And,

2. His triumph over him thereupon. Which you have thus distinguished, Col. ii. 15, how, *first*, Christ ' having spoiled principalities and powers,' he *then* ' made a show of them openly' (or made them an open example), ' triumphing over them in himself.' The first was done at his death, or upon the cross. For his cross is that which the apostle had mentioned just afore, as that public open place unto which he had affixed the law as cancelled. And then in coherence with it next follows this, that he did at the same time, to the executioners of the law, the devils, in those words, ' having spoiled,' or disarmed, ' principalities and powers' (namely, on the cross), he overcame the devil : first in the plain and open field, which field was the cross, and the place where it stood, so that the battle was fought there on the cross whereon Christ died. And the text says, ' through death he destroyed him,' which comes to one and† to say on the cross he destroyed him, or wrought his destruction. The word in Col. ii. 15, translated *having spoiled him*, is ἀπεκδυσάμενος, which is properly to disarm‡ (to put on armour, ἐνδύσασθαι, is oppositely used, Rom. xiii. 12), and is a manifest allusion unto what conquerors use when they have gotten the victory ; they strip the conquered of their weapons, and therefore it is here put to express the victory itself by. Though the victory itself is supposed antecedent to this disarming, and the manner of such victors was to erect pillars on which to hang those weapons as trophies, and this sometimes on the very place, either on trees that grew nigh, or upon pillars fixed on the ground. And so he had begun this allusion in the former words in saying, that ' he nailed the law,' as cancelled, ' to the tree of the cross ;' and then pursues it in saying, that through and upon his death he hung up all the devil's armour thereon also ; which, Luke xi. 22, is called Πανοπλία, his whole armour, as it is translated. And this he did as spoils (as our translators here have rendered it). You have this signally expressed, Isa. liii. 12. Piscator reads the words thus, ' Therefore for his part or portion I will give him the great ones, and he shall divide the strong as spoils ;' that is (saith he), he shall have a victory over those evil spirits, principali-

---

* *In himself* is added, says Strigelius, *ad differentiam victoriarum humanarum, in quibus partem sibi vendicat dux, partem milites. Nam filius Dei sine auxilio ullius creaturæ contrivit caput serpentis.—Strigelius in locum.*

† That is, ' as.'—ED.

‡ *Metaphora a bellatoribus victoribus desumpta, qui, hostium spoliatorum armis pro trophæo fixis,* &c.—*Beza, in locum.*

ties and powers, so as to be in his power as a spoil, to carry captive, and use as he pleaseth; and this ' because' (as it follows) ' he poured forth his soul unto death.' And that other reading of our translators comes all to one : ' he shall divide the spoil with the strong,' or ' in the strong.' That noting out the persons that were the object of that his dividing them, and is all one as to say, he shall take their power from them. So then in and by his death meritoriously—because he poured forth his soul unto death— he destroyed him wholly; and Satan and all his power was given up as lawful spoil. Thus our Lord, whilst himself was stripped naked, and they cast lots for his garments, then it was he strips and spoils Satan, and made him wholly naked, without all weapons.

And here comes now to be inquired into the just ground upon which it came to pass, that through or by Christ's death Satan should be bereft of that power which he had (upon the terms formerly mentioned) given unto him. And to be sure he lost it upon Christ's death upon a far more fair and legal right than at first or than ever it was given to him : Isa. xlix. 24, 25 it is thus written, ' Shall the prey be taken from the mighty, or the lawful captive delivered ? But thus saith the Lord, Even the captives of the mighty shall be taken away, and the prey of the terrible shall be delivered : for I will contend with him that contendeth with thee,' &c. Be it literally spoken of Babylon's captivity and redemption, or whatever else, yet this is certain, that that and other were shadows of this of ours by Christ, and therefore applicable in the general thereunto. Now, how far we were lawful captives unto Satan you heard, and God (though the devil be his enemy) will overcome him fairly : *non vi sed justitia*, not by force only, but in justice. ' The lawful captives' (as it is in Isa.) shall be delivered, and that lawfully. It is also a rule fetched from the law of arms, and concertations in games or the like, that ' if a man strive for masteries, he is not crowned' (and so is not reckoned to overcome) ' unless he strive lawfully,' 2 Tim. ii. 5.

The truth is, first, that Satan ran into a *præmunire*, or a forfeiture of all his power, by his assailing of Christ (and if there were no other ground, it were sufficient for the loss of all); he in assailing of Christ, and plotting and contriving his death, went beyond his commission, and God on purpose permitted him to do it, to catch him in his snare. Satan's power over sinful man was not a natural, but an accidental, judicial power, and so perfectly limited by commission, which, if he exceeded, especially if so transcendently (as it fell out in this), he instantly made a forfeiture of it. Know this, then, that Satan's power was over sinful man only; he was not so much as to touch or come near the man Jesus, who was ' holy and harmless, and separate from sinners.' Now, he coming into the world ' in the likeness of sinful flesh,' Rom. viii., this lion, that ' seeks whom he may devour,' boldly ventures on him, and persecutes him to death; for it was Satan that contrived Christ's death : ' This is the hour,' saith Christ, ' and the power of darkness,' Luke xxii. 53. ' Your hour' (speaking to the Pharisees); now you are in the ruff of your power, having me under. But know, says he, you are but the devil's instruments herein, who hath a greater and deeper hand in it than you. ' This is the power of darkness,' which is a further addition, to shew that ' the rulers of the darkness of this world' (as Eph. vi. 12) were also chiefly in it; yea, the utmost of his power concentrated in it, to effect what was in Pilate's, the people's, and the rulers' hearts. The prince of darkness, and the ruler of this world, acted the princes of this world when they crucified the Lord of glory.

But more expressly, John xii. 40, 41, ' You seek to kill me ;' ' you do the deeds of your father therein, who was a murderer from the beginning,' ver. 44. And Christ seems to give a hint of this very reason : John xiv. 80, ' The prince of this world comes, and hath nothing in me,' as matter for him, by virtue of which he should have authority to have anything to do with me. The devil thus foolishly and sillily lost all, and God took the wise in his own craftiness ; and Christ suffered him to go on and to have his whole will upon him, but then took him thereby captive at his will. So God in his righteous judgment ordered that Satan should lose the power that he had, because he exercised that upon Christ which he had not.*

(2.) Consider that it was man's sin which was the sole and only ground of God's giving Satan that power at first ; it was done by way of punishment and curse. Now, if Christ pays by his death (as it was transacted betwixt God and him) a price and ransom for sin, and undergoes all the punishment due to it, then doth Satan's power fall instantly ; for it was wholly judicial, and but part of the curse and punishment upon man.

There was this concatenation or derivation of power : the power of Satan lies in sin, the power that sin hath over us lay in the law (' the strength of sin is the law,' saith the apostle). Now, he, by paying a price or sufficient ransom unto God for sin, the power of the law and devil all fell at once flat, and perished together.

And the chain of these you have in that Colossians ii., where, *first*, in the 13th verse, ' And you, being dead in your sins, and the uncircumcision of your flesh, hath he quickened together with him, having forgiven you all your trespasses.' There is sin gone, both in the power and demerit of it. *Secondly*, verse 14, follows, ' A blotting out the handwriting of ordinances that was against us, which was contrary to us, and took it out of the way, nailing it to his cross.' There is the law cancelled and made void. *Thirdly*, verse 15, and ' Having spoiled principalities and powers, he made a show of them openly, triumphing over them.' The devil falls with these, as his power stood by these.

(3.) Add to these that this Christ, as a common person, stood in the room of us all, and therefore Satan justly lost his power over us all, in that he that represented us all did overcome him.

And here, ere we go any farther, let us stay a while and stand astonished at the glory of God's design herein. There was never any romance ever feigned so strange a story, joined with such a confusion to the person that was conquered, as this represents ; and it is to be taken notice of here, in our transition to that other part, viz., his triumph as a preparation to the glory of it, that Christ a lamb, 'the Lamb of God,' should lie still and *perdu*, having all our persons and sins under that lamb's skin, and form of a servant, ' led as a sheep,' by Satan, ' unto the slaughter,' until Satan should have done his worst, and then as a lion *couchant*, a lion asleep (as Gen. xlix., and Rev. v. 5, 6, a lamb and a lion both), he should rouse up himself from his sleep, and take that very cross that Satan had brought him unto, and hung him upon ; and (as one expresseth it) *baculo crucis*, with the staff, the beam of the cross, break all the devil's bones in pieces, when he had not with all his malice broke one bone of his ; what more glorious ? To overcome then, when himself is overcome !

Thus much for Christ's spoiling, yea, destroying him, virtually and

* *Sic Deo judicante, amisit potestatem quam habuit, quia exercuit quam non habuit*, saith Aquinas out of Austin.—(*Sum.*, part. iii. quæst. 49.)

meritoriously, at his death. His triumph over him next follows. For into those two parts the particulars in this Col. ii. 15 are reduced;[*] even as conquerors first stripped the captives, then led them as examples, tied to the chariot wheels, or else they were driven afore them. In the first, the devil's nakedness appears, in this other his shame and ignominy publicly.

Christ's triumph is thus set forth. 'He made them an example and show of them openly, triumphing over them;' both these expressions falling in to signify the same thing, the allusion is manifestly unto that Roman custom mentioned, after victories obtained, when the chief leader rode in triumph, leading the chieftains of the conquered enemy as an open spectacle. There hath been a question among commentators and other divines, whether or no. Look, as Christ's affixing the law to his cross, and his overcoming and disarming Satan thereon, was an invisible transaction, not seen or observed by any but by God and himself (the reality thereof consisting only in virtue and efficacy), that so, in like manner, this his triumph over the devils should have been but virtual and invisible, and so this his triumph, as those other, all of them wholly transacted on the cross alike. Or whether there was not after that victory mentioned on the cross, a public and open show made, in way of triumph, afore a world of spectators applauding of it. For the decision of this.

1. Therein this difference may be considered between the abolishing sin and the law at his cross, and this other of triumph over the devil; that those first must needs be only spiritually and virtually understood, for sin and the law are not intelligent persons, but only things to be destroyed, and so were capable but of a virtual abolition, as Heb. i. 3.

But the devils themselves, that were the founders of sin, and heads of this rebellion, they were rational and intelligent creatures, and so were capable of being made a real and visible open shame, which was a punishment suited to such. And the manner of the triumphs was to lead the persons and the chieftains, as heads, in open view, to give demonstration of the perfection and completeness of the victory over any prince or nation; now, such were the devils.

2. Although neither this over those damned spirits, as neither that over sin, was visible to the men of this world we live in, yet there is another world, invisible indeed to us, unto whom the shame and ignominy done to these devils might be (as it was) made visible, namely, God and angels, and the spirits of just men, which is the greatest stage.[†] Christ's birth and nativity was known and seen by the angels, when but to one or two in our world; as also his ascension. Now both every word here leads unto this sense, as also the thing considered in itself, and the comparing this with the other.

(1.) The nature of a triumph (to which the allusion manifestly is) was to be a public sight or show, and to have the greater pomp there was a company of spectators to behold it, or it lost what it pretended to be, and was not that which it is said to be. So Tully speaks of the Roman triumphs, that ambassadors were present on horses, the soldiers crying out *Victory*, whilst the conquered were led afore or after the chariots of the conqueror, and this for the glory of the conqueror, and the confusion of the conquered.

---

[*] So Rollock, entering upon that word, 'Made a show of them,' divides them, having spoken *de Victoria in cruce, nunc de triumpho.*—So *Rollock* on that place.

[†] Angeli viderunt traductos diabolos et triumphantem Christum.—*Rollock* on the place. Manifestissima erat et illustrissima coram omnibus coelestibus.—*Musculus.* So also Zanchy.

If there were none there that at present took notice thereof, it were not a triumph, but merely a concealed and stolen victory.

(2.) It is said he made them a public example, and so the word 'Εδειγμάτισεν here, which is all one with παραδειγματίζειν, is used by the Septuagint, Num. xxv. 4, when Moses hung up those kings before the sun; and so by the New Testament, Mat. i. 19 and Heb. vi. 6; it signifies also to make one publicly infamous, yea, to draw and drag him through a company of beholders and spectators.*

All which (if no more were added) argues that some public ignominy was done unto the devils before this solemn assembly.

(3.) The apostle (to fix his meaning) adds 'openly,' ἐν παῤῥησία, which word the Jews have taken into their language to signify a thing done openly, in opposition to what is secretly or hiddenly; and so it is used, John xi. 34, and chap. vii. 4, and chap. vii. 13, and Mark viii. 32. Now, this is that which I urge, that for a thing to be done by way of triumph, on purpose to make infamous, dragging the person made such through a company of spectators, and openly, yet to say it was some invisible transaction, to be viewed by faith only, these things are a contradiction.

3. Thirdly, compare this transaction specified here with other scriptures, and it will resolve, when and how this public ignominy was inflicted on Satan and his angels. And this, added to all the former, satisfieth me most of all.

We read, Eph. iv. 8 (and that epistle is parallel in most things to this of the Colossians, as many have observed), that Christ, when he ascended, led the devils in triumph: 'When he had ascended up on high, he led captivity captive.' This David had prophesied of, Ps. lxviii. 17, 18, and in these scriptures compared, there are two things more particularly expressed.

(1.) That it is an allusion to the triumphs used among the Gentiles, especially among the Romans, with whom they were in their greatest glory; for in their triumphs they led at their chariot wheels their captives; so it is said here in both places, 'he led captivity captive.' And,

(2.) The sixty-eighth psalm speaks of the thousand chariots, who also were those spectators afore-mentioned: ver. 17, 'The chariots of God,' which God commanded to wait upon him at his ascension, ver. 18, 'are twenty thousand;' 'The chariots of God are twenty thousand, even thousands of angels: the Lord is among them, as in Sinai, in the holy place.'

You see, then, how expressly he speaks of the angels who were his chariots, which he rode up in and accompanied him, and he in the midst of them.

When he came down to mount Sinai to give the law, then thousands of angels did accompany him, for it was the law given by the angels. And so those were the spectators of this triumph; and what now is wanting to make it a visible triumph, not to faith only, but the angels?

And further, to carry on the allusion to a triumph, as they had their *missilia* scattered among the people, so of Christ it is said, when he thus triumphed, that 'He gave gifts unto men.'

Thus David, being a prophet, and foreseeing things as they fell out concerning Christ (as Acts ii. 30) spoke afore, as ver. 31, both of the crucifying of Christ, which was a death proper to the Romans, or at least to be brought in among the Jews with the Roman conquerors, and not known

* Significat aliquando per publicum cœtum spectatorum trabere, vel ducere. *Zanchius in locum.; Drusius: Grotius.*

afore unto the Jews; and also of the triumph of his ascension, under the similitude of a complete Roman triumph, as their stories have transmitted the manner of them down to us.

Now, the difference of these two victories, the one at his death on the cross, the other at his ascension, is, that in the first, Christ dealt as a redeemer, with God as a judge; *Cum Deo tanquam cum judice redemptor.* In the other, he dealt, *ut bellator adversus Satanam,* as a warrior against Satan. The first conquest was over Satan's works, weapons, power, doing that for which God gave them up to him as spoils. The other was over his person, as an evidence God had given all his weapons and power into his hands.

Well, but when Christ had given him this terrible *strappado,* hauling him up after his chariot wheels, and then letting him fall again, a fall as bad as the first, Christ goes to heaven, and leaves the devil still in actual possession of power; still, for all he had thus chastised him, and had used him as the vilest varlet that ever was, Christ lets him go like a wretch (though we may not call him so ourselves, yet in relation to Christ, and his usage of him, we may), with possession of all his power, as god of this world, ruling in men's hearts, both elect and others, because he is to have another bout with him; and he suffers him to hold his possession on still in the world, reserving him for a further victory.

CHAPTER XVII.

The victory which Christ obtains over the devil, in us, and by us.—How he not only redeems us, but delivers us from his dominion and power.—That not only Christ in his own person should conquer the devil, and break his power, but that we should bear a part in it with him, is implied in that first promise in Gen. iii., that the seed of the woman should break the serpent's head.—That in all the several parts of that power which Satan hath, and acts in the world, believers, by the virtue and strength of Christ, are conquerors over him.—That in the issue they conquer him as to that power which he hath to tempt them to sin.—The several ages of Christians considered from 1 John ii. 13, 14.—That by Christ believers prevail against Satan as to the accusations of them, which he brings before God.—That Christ, and the saints at last, defeat Satan's designs, and projects, and enterprises, as he is prince of this world.

I come now to the second part or degree of this victory, namely, Christ's destroying and confounding him in us and by us.

1. In us. The devil had still all the elect of God then alive, among all the Gentiles, whom the apostle wrote to and converted, and most of them converted by the apostles in Judea also, fast under lock and key, shut up under sin and wrath, so as Christ must win every soul from him whom he meant to save. Therefore at the conversion of every soul converted (which is expressly a turning a man from Satan to God, a delivering out of the power of darkness, Acts xxvi. 18, and elsewhere), he then comes and begins to bind Satan, and to take his weapons from him, Luke xi. 21. He speaks in relation to throwing Satan out of men's hearts, as well as out of their bodies. For so he applies it, ver. 23, 24; and then it is that Christ begins to execute what virtually he did on the cross, and what at triumphing: he gave a specimen, a public show of that he had power to do. Now,

First, I observe from that place, that the devil, for all the bangs and blows he had at Christ's ascension, that he remains still in possession in men's hearts, and is at peace; and possesseth an elect child of God his heart as his palace, and reckons all his powers and faculties to be his goods and furniture, to use at pleasure.

Well, but Christ having virtually redeemed him on the cross, and spoiled Satan for him and on his behalf then, and triumphed over him in that person's stead, and as representing him, comes now with a writ of execution for all 'his goods detained from him; with a *habeas animas,* to possess himself of all, and actually to take Satan's power. And when Christ comes, he finds him ' armed' (so ver. 21) still, for all he was spoiled on the cross, and as ' strong' in us as ever. For what was then done was but spiritually, and *in merito;* but now he ' binds' him (Mat. xii. 29) to his good behaviour; that is, as in relation to his possessing of, and working in that man, so as Satan is in a chain. Christ claps irons on him, that whereas Satan acted in him afore, as lord in his own house, and he was his jailor; now himself is become Christ's prisoner, bound hand and foot, so as he cannot stir or do anything against us, but with his leave. Then Christ takes possession of all his armoury; so πανοπλία is to be interpreted, ver. 22 (for ver. 21 he is presented armed), so then all Satan's tempting, accusing power, and the things by which he tempts and works, do all fall now into Christ's hands, as his spoils paid for afore; and now Christ becomes actually possessed of them; and as he is King and Lord (to allude to what Christ said from another more general occasion), takes. to himself the power and reigns, Rev. xi. 80. Satan lies bound; his power, rule, his wit, cunning, force, whatever, is at Christ's feet, to order as. he shall give leave, and no otherwise; and he is to have commission from Christ ere he act or tempt.

I conceive thus of it, that as at first conversion, Phil. iii. 12, Christ is said to apprehend, or to take our persons actually, to accomplish in us all that he purchased for us (which made Paul desire to have the whole given him that Christ had apprehended him for, and received then for him of the Father, by a renewed act of donation, the graces, gifts he shall ever bestow and give forth), so doth Christ now by a renewed act take possession of all Satan's power and weapons; so as he cannot use a threatening, he cannot blow up a lust, but by Christ's consent and permission, not in the ordinary providential way only, but by special leave and license; as the attachment of nobles, at least the execution, is by special commission from the prince, but all other persons are left to the ordinary course of the laws, which are to be put in execution by inferior magistrates as they see occasion. And this actual possession of all Satan's power as a spoil is perfect also on Christ's part, as a king, to have it let forth at his dispose; and is perfect in this sense, that Christ takes all, once for all, in our behalf, and to be let out but as shall be for our good; and therefore conversion is called a translating us out of the power of darkness into the kingdom of his Son. We come now under Christ's actual jurisdiction, who hath taken to himself the government of us. The difference the apostle holds forth, 2 Tim. ii. 25, 26, speaking of saving repentance, ' If peradventure God will give them repentance to the acknowledgment of the truth, that they may recover themselves out of the snare of the devil, who are taken captive by him at his will;' whereof the meaning is, that they may not be under Satan's jurisdiction, as afore, ' at his will,' but be so freed as to be able to recover themselves out of his snare.

And because even this first work is a renewed triumph of Christ's over

Satan, therefore Paul says, 2 Cor. ii. 14, that by converting souls, Christ made him triumph; ' Now thanks be to God, which always causeth us to triumph in Christ, and maketh manifest the savour of his knowledge by us in every place ;' even as Christ himself had done upon the cross, in turning out Satan, in judging and casting out the prince of this world out of men's hearts, by convincing men of sin, righteousness, and judgment, John xvi. 11. But now, though Christ hath taken possession of our persons, and hath thrown out of us Satan and his power ; yet so as still Christ lets him loose, and gives line to his tempting power, when, how long, and so far as Christ himself pleaseth, or under such and such laws and rules as are in force in that invisible world between Christ and him ; and on his audit days, when he comes afore God, he gives an account, of which you read, Job ii. 1, ' Again there was a day when the sons of God came to present themselves before the Lord ; and Satan came also among them to present himself before the Lord.' For both good angels, as Zech. i. 10, 11, do at times come and give account of their walking to and fro the earth, as also bad, in that of Job. Christ gives him a commission in such and such cases, and within the compass of such and such rules, to have power to do so and so, and so to tempt us and put us to it ; and he comes to give an account how he hath behaved himself in it. But yet this his binding Satan in conversion of us to God, is an overcoming him in us, and now therein we are altogether passive, even as in the working the habits and principles of regeneration itself, we are said to be delivered, rescued, and the devil cast out for us (we throw him not out) by an eternal hand, by one stronger than he, who comes upon him.

There therefore remains a fourth thing, an overcoming *by* us as well as *in* us, both which is coming on through the whole course of our lives. Christ thinks it not enough to have overcome him in himself, as Col. ii. 15, nor to overcome him in us thus at our first conversion, but he will overcome him by us, he will have our hand actively in it also, and cause us to be more than conquerors in the end.

Now, then, that the glory of this victory on our part, through him that loved us, may be made the more glorious, such are the dispensations of our God, that though Christ hath taken into possession all his power, yet he lets forth a great and large portion of power still unto Satan, to be exercised by commission from himself. Satan is still left to range up and down (and in view as it were loose), to tempt, to afflict, and sorely shoot at these poor souls, thus rescued out of his hands, and all to greaten the victory that yet remains to be accomplished by us. Christ loves to have us joined in it, so 2 Tim. ii. 26, that they may ' recover themselves' out of the snares of the devil ; so 1 John v. 18, ' he that is born of God keeps himself, that the evil one touch him not.' And as we are said to mortify the deeds of the flesh by the Spirit, so to recover ourselves, and keep ourselves from Satan, in a great measure.

That we may the more clearly and distinctly take this into our thoughts, we are to consider that the first promise to mankind fallen was made for a victory over Satan ; Gen. iii. 15, ' I will put enmity between thee and the woman, and between thy seed and her seed ; it shall break thy head, and thou shalt bruise his heel.' Here is a promise consisting of two parts : a former part, ' I will put enmity between her seed and thy seed ;' and a latter part, ' it shall break thy head,' &c. Now there is a controversy who should be intended by ' the seed of the woman,' and who that same *it*, that shall break, should be ? The papists, they take the woman for the virgin

Mary, and limit it to her; and the seed to be Christ only, her Son, and in his own person singly considered, and exclusively of us; and the victory spoken of, ' it shall break,' to be only that of his in himself over the devil by himself alone. Calvin understands by ' the seed of the woman,' the whole spiritual race of believers collectively in all ages, as more directly intended, and Christ only as the eminentest of that seed, and by whom all the rest obtain the victory, and so principally intended. Pareus halves it; understanding by ' the seed,' in the former part of the promise, all believers of mankind; but the *it*, or *he*, in the latter part, prophetically to point out and terminate on Christ alone, the great *he* or *it* that on our behalf encountered Satan (as David alone did Goliah) in a single duel, and ' brake his head.' And it is urged that the Septuagint reads the *it* by αὐτὸς, *he*, and that so it is in all the copies of that translation, and so the Chaldee paraphrast, so Jerome, and others of the ancients. And also that the Greek σπέρμα, *seed*, being of the neuter gender, yet the Septuagint have rendered it *he*, αὐτὸς, and not *it*, so making another difference. I altogether waive that first of the papists, for the absurd glosses they make upon the words in honour of the virgin Mary; and propound that both Christ in his person, and believers in their persons, as considered in and with him, are directly intended in both *seed* and *it*, as making up one and the same; the one as the noun, the other as the pronoun answering thereunto.

1. Christ is intended as the captain or champion in this warfare and victory. (So Heb. ii. ver. 10, Christ is styled, and that in reference to this very victory over the devil, which follows, ver. 14.)

2. All believers, or the children, and his brethren (as in the same place they are called), are also here intended and comprehended, so making one seed—he the captain, they the body of the army, that in their turns overcome Satan also through him that loved them!

And unto this interpretation, all things seem to fall in to make it good, and nothing to hinder it.

1. The Holy Ghost hath (as it were purposely) chosen in the original tongue such a conjunction of words as might admit both senses.

(1.) The word זֶרַע stands indifferent to either, for it is *nomen collectivum*, that signifies a race or generation of many (as is known), and so is applicable to the whole company or family of believers; or it signifies a sole and singular person, as Eve herself (the woman in the text) in the next chapter, Gen. iv. 25, terming that one son of hers, Seth, her *seed*, useth that word זֶרַע, and so that also is applicable to point at Christ, as a singular person, singularly aimed at.

(2.) The pronoun also in the latter part of the promise, הוּא, translated in the impersonal *it*, may as well be translated *he*; the original word will comply with either.* And so as if you take זֶרַע, or *seed*, collectively, then *it* in the impersonal doth fully answer thereunto, as the pronoun to it; on the other hand, if you understand זֶרַע, or *seed*, personally of one singular man, then read *he*; the Hebrew will bear both fruits, so as you may view the words in either of these postures, ' I will put enmity between thy seed and her seed, and it shall break thy head,' &c., that is, Christ collectively taken, or together with the whole body of believers. He and they together shall crush thee, and ' thou shalt bruise his, or its heel ;' or again you may read it thus, ' I will put enmity between thy seed, and the woman's seed,' (taking the woman's seed for that one single person Christ as alone con-

---

* הוּא, ipse vel ipsum.

sidered), ' and he shall break thy head, and thou shalt bruise his heel,' and
so the Septuagint and others alleged have translated it.

2. If we take the materials themselves in these two promises, or two parts
of the promise, and the scope thereof, they will as readily comply with both
these senses ; and then both words and things will be found to conspire in
the testifying hereof.

That Christ personally is directly intended, and his own personal victory,
appears from hence.

1. This was the first promise of the Messiah, who is said to be ' the Lamb
slain from the beginning of the world,' that is, from the fall (as also John
viii. 44, *from the beginning* is taken), and this spoken as in relation to these
words here, prophesying ' thou shalt bruise his heal.' And this is also the
fundamental promise upon which the faith of the whole church lived before
the flood, and after for two thousand years, till it was in Isaac and his
seed renewed to Abraham in other terms, and therefore not to understand
Christ in his own person singly as in himself, and by himself overcoming
Satan, to be directly intended, were to take away that great head of the
church's faith for so many ages. For we read of no other propounded but this,
and so have no warrant to think that there was any other promise extant.

2. And indeed the whole race of the elect of mankind could not, nor cannot be supposed to overcome this so potent an enemy, they being so weak
and impotent in themselves, and now also become in a great respect captive
to him, and under his power. It was necessary therefore to the believing
thereof, that this Messiah or Christ, whom God had designed to be one of
that seed, as the head of them, as Satan was the head of his seed ; and
who should be able (for and on their behalf) first to overcome him singly
and personally himself, and so mortally break his head, as that then the
rest of his brethren might come to set their feet thereon, in the strength
and virtue of him. It was necessary, I say, to the strengthening our
faith, that this our Christ should be presupposed, in the first and chief
place, to be here promised and prophesied of, and directly pointed
at, and not by consequence or implication only, or but as in the crowd
among the whole seed. And can we otherwise think that God, in this
his first proclaiming of this great war and victory to be obtained by mankind, should mention only, and set out in the field so, a company of
the sons of men, utterly disarmed, and having each a deadly wound, and
not propose (as the ground and foundation of the faith thereof) him the
Christ, the conqueror, in whom their whole strength lay ? Yea, could the
devil have feared the breaking of his head by any or all those (put them all
together), so unable even so much as to resist the least tentation of his, unless
God should have aimed and set forth some one extraordinary, one of mankind, that should be infinitely stronger than he ?

3. The seed promised is in a special and singular manner called ' the
seed of the woman' (man not mentioned), as a seed that should be brought
forth not by the ordinary way of generation of both man and woman, and
so doth in the letter of it point more especially at Christ.

2. As Christ singly in himself, so withal the whole seed of believers, as
represented in him, and so representatively in him, are to be understood
in this promise, ' He shall break thy head.' This assertion is made out
by parts.

(1.) That the whole seed of believers are intended in the former part of
the promise, ' I will put enmity between her seed and thy seed.'

(2.) That in the latter part of the promise, ' He shall break thy head,'

Christ is set forth in his own person, so as including too, and representing, the whole seed.

It cannot be denied, but that the curse was intended for all the serpent's seed, as whose head should be broken as well as the devil's ; for they, as well as the devils, partake of the guilt that causeth this curse, namely, they do bruise the heel of Christ himself, or his saints, as well as Satan doth. And the wicked Jews did it personally, and against himself, as Peter chargeth them, ' whom ye slew, and hanged on a tree,' Acts v. 30, as well as the devil himself, that set them on to crucify him. Nor indeed could the devil have done it without them ; and therefore these, and all else, are intended as spoken unto in the curse, as well as Satan. And yet we see that the devil is alone here both blamed and cursed ; the devil alone was present whilst this was pronouncing, and none of them but he ; and so it is carried as if none were cursed but he ; how then can all his seed be included and involved in this curse ? No way but representatively ' in him ;' he alone personally stood by, but yet as the father of them all, and representer and personater of them ; and he alone is made the butt or mark the curse is directed against, but withal it lights upon and is shot against the whole generation of them, and was accordingly considered by God when he sent forth this curse against both him and them. As in like manner when| God, in the 14th verse, cursed the serpent to creep on his belly, &c., he means all the devils, his angels, with him, the whole kind of them, and perhaps as having their heads all in this conspiracy against man, as in their own first fall ; though the great devil (who got the name of ' the old serpent' by it, Rev. xx.) did put it in execution.

Now then answerably on the other side, this our great *he* or αὐτὸς, as John delights to style him again and again, 1 John iii. 2, 3, 5, 6, the devil's great antagonist, our champion, he personally and alone was to encounter him, and fulfil this great promise of breaking his head ; yet considered as the representative of us his seed involved in him. And look how the curse reacheth both serpent and seed ; so the promise, as fulfilled by him, extendeth to Christ and us, to Christ as our great David, that overcame this Goliah for us at a single duel ; then to us as wrapt up in him, and personated by him therein. Seeing that the fates and facts of these two great antagonists, and their several adherents, are within the small compass of this one sentence, ' He shall break thy head, and thou shalt bruise his heel,' so interchangeably set opposite one to the other, in a way (I say) of correspondent opposition ; this rightly supposeth the law of parallel opposition to hold in each, viz., as to this respect, which is the main, that as the devil is cursed with having his head broken, and bruising Christ's heel, and his seed included as accursed therein, also in like manner, in promising Christ that he should break Satan's head, and have his heel withal bruised by him, it is intended that his seed and fellows were represented in and with him. And that seeing the one holds good on Satan's part to this sense mentioned, that the other should on Christ's, as including the seed, especially seeing the Scriptures elsewhere do confirm this truth, that Christ represented his seed in what was done for them.

For the proof of the first. As by the serpent's seed is meant the whole race and generation of wicked men (for other seed the devil hath none) is evident, and of them it is Christ, speaking to the Pharisees, says, ' They are of their father the devil,' John viii. 44 ; and the apostle John the same, 1 John iii. 8 ; therefore by the law of opposition (and here is the highest and most general opposition put : ' I will put enmity between thy seed and her seed ') the whole seed of the godly who were to come of that woman,—'the mother' (upon that occasion called) 'of all living'—that is, that live by faith, must be understood also. And this confirms it, that these that are said to be the serpent's seed were all to be of mankind, and so to be in the literal sense and a carnal respect the seed of the woman, as well as those other, according to natural generation.

The word seed imports a race or generation of men, which is usual, and also it is applied to some one person as well. Thus when Eve had Seth, that one son, she calls him her seed, Gen. iv. 25. And accordingly the word זֶרַע, seed, being a masculine in the Hebrew, the pronoun הוּא, may be translated by the impersonal it, as referring to seed, as it refers to seed, as signifying a whole race ; or he, as personally referring to Christ, who also was in an especial manner the seed of the woman, and not of man, though the other (as Seth) are so called, Gen. iv. 25.

Yet 2. This whole seed is intended, as first represented in that one person Christ, who should by his own strength break the serpent's head for them all, which is clear to be by this parallel reason out of the text. For in that latter promise, ' He shall break thy head,' &c., there is no express mention made of the serpent's seed, or of their being broken, but it is spoken to and of the serpent only in the letter, ' thy head, and thou shalt bruise his heel ;' and yet none will deny but that this part of the curse was intended unto all the serpent's seed of wicked men, as well as to the serpent the devil. Even as it is true that they should bruise Christ's heel (as the wicked Jews did), as well as the devil himself, that set them on to crucify him, therefore they all must be intended as spoken unto in this curse, as well as Satan, though he is alone named ; and how should this be ? But that he, as the father and head of them then, stood by whilst it was pronouncing, and was present, and he alone ; and though in appearance he alone was cursed, and none else, to have his head broken, yet it is evident that all his seed of wicked men were cursed at the same time in this curse directed against him, for they all were to be broken and crushed as well as he, and that for bruising Christ's heel as well as he did. And he, as the father and representer of them, was made the butt of this curse, and therefore was considered by God as the representer of the great devil who lay hid in that serpent. He is understood to have cursed with him all the whole company of angels that fell with him ; and as perhaps having had all their hands in this conspiracy against man, though the great devil only put it in execution. Answerably our great he (as John delights to call him in this, 1 John iii. 2–6), the devil's special antagonist, our champion, is personally designed as the conqueror of him, but we representatively considered in him, whilst himself alone did it, in those words, ' He shall break it ;' and look, as the curse therein reacheth both serpent and seed, but the seed as represented now by him as their head and father of them, so the promise therein extends likewise to both Christ and us : to Christ, as our David overcoming that great Goliah in a single duel ; to us as therein represented by him.

3. So as withal, thirdly, we in our persons are to have a victory over him through his strength, and not representatively only in his.

(1.) Because the victory belongs personally to all those to whom the damage or conflict doth. Now the hurt, the damage we have a personal share in, as well as Christ had. The devil and his seed, by reason of natural enmity put, do bruise our heel, and we find it personally to our cost ; therefore to them also extends that victory, ' It shall break thy head ;'

the same whose heel is bruised are the breakers of his head. And to be sure we receive many wounds and bruisings from him and his, for we feel and groan under them daily, and all the brotherhood in the world with us.

(2.) The enmity that puts the difference, and is the ground of the quarrel, is not betwixt Christ only and the devil's seed, but the whole generation of the just that came of the woman, as experience in all ages hath shewn.

But all this hitherto shews but what was done against Satan in himself, and by himself, and we are therein considered but secondarily and remotely, by way of representation only.

All which have taken up the foregoing part of this discourse hitherto at large ; therefore,

(3.) That this seed shall in their succession and turns bear their parts, and have their share in an actual and personal way in breaking Satan's head, as the intendment also in this prophetic promise, comes next to be evinced.

1. The same of whom it is said, ' Satan shall bruise his heel ; ' the same it is of whom it is there also said, ' He ' or ' It shall break thy head.' So as look who are concerned and have a share in being bruised or wounded in the battle or conflict with Satan, the same here have ascribed to them a proportionable interest in the victory, it being (besides the import that both are so conjoined here) a declared maxim by God, and that as to this very point, that ' if we suffer with Christ, we shall also reign with him,' Rom. viii. 17, 2 Tim. ii. 12. Now all the whole seed or race have their share in their being bruised and wounded by Satan, and therefore also in that other ; the bruised are his breakers. We all find to this day, by virtue of this prophecy, the sad effects of his bruising our heel, as well as Christ did his, and so we too in conformity unto Christ, and therefore we may as well believe ourselves included in the promise itself made to these bruisings.

2. The enmity in the former part, that is the cause of those mutual assailments of each other in the latter part, and the issue whereof is this victory ; I say, that enmity that is the cause both of his bruising our heel, and then of the breaking of his head, is spoken of here as in common to all the seed, as well as unto Christ personally on our behalf, and therefore the combat, and the issue of the war, the victory, are not to be restrained to Christ only, when the enmity, which is the cause of it, is not, but is commensurate and extended unto all.

3. This agrees with the general scope and intent of God's uttering this, made good and proved by the event, and that presently began between Abel and Cain, and hath continued ever since, which is that God here first set up his standard (whereof Christ was to be the standard-bearer under him) four hundred* years before Christ yet came in the flesh, and proclaims the war that was instantly to begin, and to be carried down throughout all ages, and proclaims it in the language of an hereditary war, such as was to be between two houses or families of great and long continuance, to be between two seeds, and so from father unto son downwards, and the *totum genus*, the whole kind and generation of each ; and therefore it is too narrow to restrain it only to Christ the seed, though it is he that is the chieftain, and of whom the whole family in heaven and earth is named, and to whom the glory of all is to be ascribed.

* Qu. ' thousand ' ?—ED.

4. But that which above all convinceth me is, that both in the New Testament we find it affirmed of the saints, that they in their persons are the overcomers of Satan, as Christ hath overcome him in his own person. So 1 John ii. 13, 'You have overcome the evil one,' and 1 John iv. 3, 4, 'You have overcome the world,' and with it the prince of the world ; as the reason which follows evidently argues, 'For he who is in you,' says he, 'is stronger than he that is in the world.' So then not Christ only in himself for us, but he also, and he in us, is to overcome Satan and his together, the world and him that is in it, both serpent and seed.

This victory also is set out in the New Testament in such expressions and phrases as evidently doth allude to this very promise in Genesis, as the accomplishment of it. Rom. xvi. 20, 'And God shall tread down Satan under your feet shortly.' It is God indeed treads him down, and yet it is their feet he is trodden under. Now as the curse of the devil in Genesis, 'It shall bruise thy head,' is an allusion to the serpent's condition, who going on the ground, and being not able to reach the head, yet whilst out of enmity he will be nibbling at the heel, he is liable to have his head crushed by the foot whose heel he thus assaults ; so to 'tread down Satan under our feet' holds as great an affinity with that promise there. Also this being called the enemy, the old serpent, hath an undeniable reference to him that was that serpent, who personated and clothed himself with that serpent, and therein first assaulted Eve, between whom and us the enmity is put.

Yea and Christ himself is pleased to give forth to his apostles, and us in them, our part and share in this victory over Satan, under the same expressions and allusion to this promise, as then bequeathed to us together with himself, Luke x. 19, when speaking of their subduing Satan, ver. 17, and by their ministry throwing him down as lightning, ver. 18, he utters it in those words, ver. 19, 'Behold I give unto you power to tread on serpents and scorpions, and all the power of the enemy.' So then this is Christ's glory, and was the scope of that first promise, that as himself, so also we, should tread on the serpent's, the enemy's head ; and so he came to have a second victory in us, as well as in himself, which as his sufferings in us are termed ὑστερήματα, the after-sufferings of Christ, Col. i. 24, so this overcoming by the saints is the after-victories of Christ. And this second after-victory puts the devil in some respects to more shame and confusion than the first, when he was dressed so by Christ (as we use to speak) of which you heard ; for the weaker the victor is, the more glorious is the conquest ; and the stronger the enemy is and the more equal to deal with, the more glorious is the conquest, and the greater is the shame of his defeat. In Rev. xii. you have the devil described, and set forth with all his royal titles heaped up one upon another, as nowhere else together is the like in Scripture ; ver. 9, 'The great dragon, that old serpent, called the devil and Satan, which deceiveth the whole world ;' such is his power, subtilty, and jurisdiction. And upon what occasion is this great description of him given ? 'Tis after a conquest of him, a downfall : 'he prevailed not,' ver. 8 ; 'he was cast out,' ver. 9, and 'his angels with him,' ver. 9 ; 'cast down,' ver. 10 ; 'overcome,' ver. 11. So then look, as in scorn and as a matter of triumph, a king when conquered shall be proclaimed with all his titles, so is he. And to make all this the more glorious, he sets out a woman, and yet more unequal, a woman in travail, that cannot help herself, much less resist an enemy ; ver. 1, 2, and unto her, that is, the church, is the victory ascribed in the song of triumph that is made upon it ; ver. 12, 'They overcame him by the blood of the Lamb, and they loved not their lives unto death.' This woman and this dragon are set together to shew the inequality of this match. This confounded the devil more, that they, that woman, should be said to overcome, than that Michael and all his angels should be so. It was Abimelech's confusion and pride, Judges ix. 54, ' A woman cast a millstone on Abimelech's head, and all to brake his skull.' ' O slay me,' saith he, ' that men say not of me, a woman slew me.' The woman began the war, Rev. xii., so that she hath the devil under her feet at the end, cast down to the earth, as ver. 9 ; and so he hath the serpent's curse exquisitely accomplished on him, ' Upon thy belly shalt thou go, and dust shalt thou eat all the days of thy life ;' which analogically, as applied to Satan, notes out the most abject condition and extremity of captivation, that as one fully conquered, he should be laid flat on the ground and trodden on, so as to lick the dust of it ; for so captivity, according to the manner of those countries, is expressed by their belly cleaving to the earth, and licking the dust, Ps. xliv. 24, 25, and Ps. lxxii. 9. And therefore though God had cursed Satan to hell afore, immediately upon his fall, 2 Peter ii. 4, ' He saved not the angels that fell, but cast them down to hell;' yet this after curse is a second hell, which therefore is said to torment him ' all his days,' even for ever, that he falls also by the hand and under the foot of man, whom he so much envied and despised. And hereby is not God fully even with him ? Doth he not retaliate his sin upon him to the utmost of the curses? The devil, though in the shape of a serpent, subtilely assaults and sets on the woman, as thinking he could easily deceive and overcome her, as he did, and by her the man. These two, you know, in the type were Christ and his church, Eph. v. 31–33. Well, ' because thou hast done this,' says God. He never goes about to convince him of his sin, (as he did the man and woman), but falls a cursing him, ' The seed of the woman shall break thy head.' The seed, i.e., both Christ the head and Christ the body ; Christ the man and Christ the woman ; Christ personal and Christ mystical, shall do it, as the Scripture calls the church the whole seed, as you have heard.

And whereas he began with the woman, and so prevailed over the man ; on the contrary here, Christ the man deals with him first, spoils and triumphs over him, and then he turns him over to the woman to have a second bout with him. Come (says he to the whole church), thou shalt set thy feet, thy tender feet upon him too, and in my strength shalt crush him. Rupertus * tells it with a great deal of confidence, as having had it, he says, from those that knew it by experience, that if the naked foot of a woman chance to tread or touch a serpent's head, it dies instantly, which a far greater force will not effect. Thus the devil dies not, nor is fully and totally subdued till she hath set her foot upon him also ; and it will be thought that however Christ's so hard tread may break his head, and his power more, yet her tread breaks his heart, and it is no derogation from Christ's, for it is Christ in both. Nay, it is for confusion to that proud spirit, which is as bad as wrath, and therefore after his being judged to hell, he hath the curse of this annexed to it ; yea and for this end (among other) did Christ take up flesh and blood, that is, the weaknesses of man's nature, and not the nature of angels in their strength, that he might, in destroying the devil, therein add confusion to his conquest : it is the reason insinuated, if not expressly given, Heb. ii. 14. And upon the same reason, that the apostle would heighten our conflict with Satan to us (thereby to prepare and awaken us), that we fight not against flesh and blood, but against principalities and

* Lib. 3, de trinit. c. 20.

powers ; by the same is the confusion of Satan rendered the greater, that flesh and blood hath a strength given it to tread upon principalities and powers. But herein as Paul gives the account of it, 'the strength of Christ is perfected in weakness' (it is proper as to conclude the point in hand withal), for the apostle brings it in upon occasion of Satan's being sent to buffet him ; 'A messenger of Satan,' as some, or the 'angel Satan,' as others, was sent to buffet him, 2 Cor. xii. 7, 8.

If we would further know the particulars and the glories of these Christ's victories over him, achieved by the saints, we must estimate them by that threefold power and advantage which Satan hath still left him over the saints.

1. In ruling the world, to bring afflictions on them.

2. In accusing them to God.

3. In tempting them to sin. And the saints have an answerable victory over all ; and these victories also obtained in a fair and rational way, by and according to equitable rules, and not by extraordinary force. So that in handling these three ensuing particulars, I must carry along three things through each particular.

1. Satan's power.

2. How the saints, or Christ by the saints, do defeat him.

3. How each of these defeats is done by rule, in a rational legal way. Which latter renders these victories on our parts more slow and tedious, but more glorious. You have a maxim, 2 Tim. ii. 5, that no man is crowned that doth not strive lawfully ; Christ himself did not overcome him by mere force, but in an equitable way, as was shewn ; so nor do we.

1. Satan hath over us a tempting power unto the greatest sin ; you know he is called the tempter. I will begin with that ; Peter, that had been worried by him, cries out to all his fellows, 1 Peter v. 8, 'There is a roaring lion' (look to yourselves), 'who always goes up and down seeking whom,' of us believers, 'he may devour ;' and his outcry is τῇ ἀδελφότητι, to the whole brotherhood of saints in the world, 'Be sober, be vigilant ; because your adversary the devil, as a roaring lion, walketh about, seeking whom he may devour.' It is as if one should have given warning to a company of children (suppose those in Elisha's story) a bear, a lion is broke loose, hungry and roaring, seeking whom he may devour ; and who knows whom he may light on ? as elsewhere, Paul, Gal. vi. 1, 'Lest thou or thou be tempted.' For Paul knew that after he is cast out at conversion, as in the fore-mentioned Luke xi., he attempts to make re-entries. He not knowing who are true believers, who are not, maketh the same assaults and stormings upon men savingly converted that he doth on temporaries ; which made Paul so jealous of all his converts, lest by some means the tempter should have tempted them, 1 Thess. iii. 5. In this work of temptation Satan is permitted to exercise abundance of power, more than in any of the former, unto astonishment of themselves and angels ; and they are so put to it, that indeed it may be asked, where is the blessedness you spake of ? What is become of those great good tidings of perfect victory over him on the cross and ascension ? And the actual possession of all his power by Jesus Christ, and taken from him at our conversion ? The apostle hath a very high expression, Eph. vi. 12, shewing how much the saints are put to it in this particular, 'And having done all to stand.' He had said afore, 'We wrestle not with flesh and blood, but with principalities and powers.' It is true, indeed, God will not suffer us to be tempted above what we are able to bear, yet suffers to the utmost what we are able to bear ; that is, he leaves us but to just so much grace as shall be suffi-

cient, 2 Cor. xii. 9. Many a righteous man is scarcely saved in this respect, his temptations are so strong, his jailors so many; yet still I may say what was said of Joseph, Christ's type and ours, I may say the same of every Christian, ' The archers have sorely grieved him, and shot at him, and hated him,' Gen. xlix. 23. These arrow-masters (as Ainsworth reads it), his brethren, his mistress, his master, they all put him unto great trials and temptations, and so do these arrow-masters, these forgers of those fiery darts and arrows (as in the same Eph. vi. 16 they are called), every Christian. But Christ hath promised, as there he did of Joseph, ver. 25, ' But his bow abode in strength, and the arms of his hands are made strong by the hands of the mighty God of Jacob.' There is no victory but there is a battle, no battle but there must be a permission to use wiles and utmost force. We read of both in Satan, who is called the lion and the serpent. No man is crowned, unless he strive lawfully, 2 Tim. ii. 3, therefore Christ will do so, the devil shall have fair play, yea, and sometimes do his worst; and this makes the victory the more glorious, James i. 12, ' Blessed is the man that endureth temptation : for when he is tried, he shall receive the crown of life, which the Lord hath promised to them that love him ; ' that is, one who hath gone through them and overcome them, though with infinite batterings and bruisings of spirit. Nor are temptations there to be limited to outward afflictions, but to extend it unto trials for sin. For it follows, ver. 13, 14, ' But let no man say when he is tempted, I am tempted of God : for God cannot be tempted with evil, neither tempteth he any man : but every man is tempted when he is drawn away of his own lust, and enticed.' Now that the saints, after some years' experience in Christianity, have usually some experience of their having overcome that evil one, and that so as to be a pledge unto them of their full and final overcoming at last (of which that in the Rev. ii. 7, 13, ' To him that overcometh I will give the crown of life,' is to be understood), is a certain truth ; and I shall open but one scripture that makes good this previous overcoming in hand : 1 John ii. 13, 14, ' I write unto you, fathers, because ye have known him that is from the beginning. I write unto you, young men, because ye have overcome the wicked one. I write unto you, little children, because ye have known the Father.' Ver. 14, ' I have written unto you, fathers, because ye have known him that is from the beginning. I have written unto you, young men, because ye are strong, and the word of God abideth in you, and ye have overcome the wicked one.' It is attributed here (you see) to the middle sort or age of Christians to have overcome that wicked one ; by which is meant the devil up and down this epistle ; and that the overcoming him is spoken in respect of lusts, or temptations unto sin, is evident, because it is made the ground of an exhortation that follows, not to love the world, nor the things of the world : ver. 15, 16, ' Love not the world, nor the things of the world. If any man love the world, the love of the Father is not in him. For all that is in the world, the lust of the flesh, the lust of the eyes, and the pride of life, is not of the Father, but is of the world.' And his argument unto these young men (of whom he says, ' they have overcome') lies thus : you have had already some experience of victory, having been in some battles and conflicts with the enemy, fighting against sin, Heb. xii. 14. It hath cost you hot work, and will you now give back, and lose all you have fought for, and grow faint when the battle declines, and experience gives you so clear a hope of an assured victory? No ; but on the contrary therefore, be encouraged still to fight it out. Again, you may observe that this is twice said of them with repetition, and therefore is a matter of eminency to be noticed. This for the coherence of the words of that text of Scripture; now, to explain them, let us remark that he reduceth the state of all Christians to three sorts of degrees: babes, young men, and fathers ; making the ground of his allusion the proportion that grace, or the new creature, hath with what is found in nature in the sons of men, wherein those three ages are eminently distinguishable. And look, as if a naturalist were to set out the genius, dispositions, and attainments of childhood, man's estate, and old age, he would take that which is most proper to each of these ages, so doth the apostle here in characterising these three ages in Christianity.

1. Babes in Christianity know the Father, are taught to run to God as to a father, and to abound in expressing filial and childlike dispositions and instincts towards God as a father, and are trained up as children, and are allured with toys, and held by the arms and taught to go, and are carried in the arm rather than walk.

2. Old men in Christianity know him that is from the beginning. The property of old age in nature is to talk of things ancient and long ago done; these they are taken up withal. Now, the heathen* could say, ' Who is the most ancient? ' God, whom Daniel calls ' the ancient of days.' So Christ is too, 1 John i. 1, ' That which was from the beginning,' who, ver. 2, is ' that eternal life who was with the Father.' And for all those great mysteries of the gospel in election, and the transaction of the Father with the Son, a story ancienter than the world, these things grown Christians delight to speak of, and are taken withal, the knowledge of which is that Paul boasts most of, Eph. iii. 2.

3. Of young men, the proper excellencey is their strength, Prov. xx. 29, and they boast of wrestlings and victories; and if they be military men, they have had experience of overcoming the enemy in the field, and are thereby fleshed and animated to any encounters.

Now as all true Christians are born for soldiery, and conflicts with sin and Satan, so the apostle points out that time between their being babes, and whilst they are growing up to a virility and strength, and to a spiritual manhood. And during that age is the proper season and most eminent field of a Christian's life,† in which the bloodiest battles with lusts and temptations of that kind are fought, and in which time (where there is truth of grace) there have fallen out some comfortable experiments of victories, though still the assaults may be renewed and continued; for John (you see) distinguishes them from babes by this very thing. The truth is, that in the first age humiliation for sin hath stounded lusts ; the Spirit, by John Baptist's voice and ministry, hath blown upon all flesh ; hell and the curse, and fear of damnation, &c., have withered all excellencies, or things desirable, and these are succeeded with sweetness and supports, which add to the deadening of their spirits unto temptation to sin ; and that present frame of spirit reduceth them often to think they shall never commit a gross sin, as Peter, that he should not deny his Master ; and so they are censorious of others, and then God spares them. Babes are fed with milk, and not led unto the field unto great or notable encounters, or else the exercise of their spirits lies in point of justification, and seeking Christ's righteousness; yea, and then all the affections upon either the account of self-love, or gracious love, are stirred and run in one.

* Plutarch in Sympos.

† *Romana Juventus* was the poet's style of the soldiers; so among the Jews too ' Let the young men play afore us,' 2 Sam. ii. 14.

channel in pursuit after salvation of a man's self. But when once the soul is settled, these first stounds of humiliation and frights are over, and lusts have come to themselves again. And then when the soul is in some measure quieted by faith, and yet not assured of eternal salvation (so as wonted fears are kept under, but yet the soul attains not joys unspeakable and glorious, which should as much heighten the affections that way as fears had stirred them that other) ; when also those mercenary assistances and auxiliaries which self-love afforded are recalled and withdrawn, and if any sweetnesses were they are abated and gone, and so what is purely grace (which now is of itself grown up to some degree of strength) is left to shift for itself, and to fight its own battles alone ; then usually come the bloody conflicts, then is the trial whether lusts and devil, or soul and Christ, should overcome, and whether Christ hath begotten truth of grace, and owns it upon some assaults or other, and in some trial and experience of victories, that it may be said, ' Ye have overcome that evil one.' For one of these two cases have fallen out, either Peter's case or Paul's, either such Christians have been kept and not foiled (we read not that Paul ever was), or if they have been foiled and overcome for some acts of sinning, yet that hath in a recovery occasioned (as it were) a new conversion, which was Peter's case, who went out and wept bitterly, and brought in a new strength and recruit. And either of these are and must be reckoned an overcoming that wicked one. It is no matter (that is, as to this point) that thou hast been overcome ; for if God recovers thee still, and renews thee by repentance, thou hast overcome. A town that hath been often besieged, and yet never won or taken (as that virgin, maiden city of Venice) ; and another into which the enemy hath made great entries, and yet hath been beaten out again by them that are within it, these are both of them victorious. In these cases God accounts of it as a great matter that grace remains and is not excussed ; and therefore John adds here, ' Because ye are strong, and the word of God abides in you.' The word of God abides in you both as the cause of these victories and as the signs of them, that it should still so abide after all, when the battle hath been so great and sore, and it was doubtful by the passages that fell out in the castle who had the worse or who the better. Yet this is reckoned a signal of the conqueror, that he keeps the field, and is found standing to his ground, and is where still he was, and retains and holds his standard. That the seed of God still remains, and the word of God abides, this is an evidence of victory : and Christ so expresseth it, ' I have prayed that thy faith fail not.' For after sore, great, and many such temptations, a temporary work is worn out, and abides not ; yea, when a man is strengthened to continue to maintain the battle, and not fling his weapons down, so long sin hath not the dominion, but Christ will bring forth judgment to victory.

Now, the reiterated experiments of having thus in part, and at times, overcome or continued the fight, is to men of that age a pawn and pledge that they shall finally overcome. It is so in the thing itself, and is often made such to their faith : ' Experience breeds hope, and hope maketh not ashamed,' as Rom. v. 4, 5. Soldiers that have been in many cruel battles, and are yet alive, and have their limbs whole (though with many fears), and have fought it out, and got the victory, though perhaps often rallying and giving ground, they come to have stout or strong and resolute spirits ; and whereas others' hopes (namely, of babes) of perseverance, is built only upon God's faithfulness, these further have the experience of the issue of many a combat to cause them the more fondly to hope ; and in this sense some have understood these words, namely, 'You have overcome the wicked one;' that is, 'you shall overcome,' expressing that which is future in the time past, to shew the certainty of it for the future. But that cannot be the immediate and direct meaning, because the future overcoming is as common to believers * as to young men, that is, that they shall overcome, whereas the apostle's scope is by way of eminency and distinction to the other, to set out what is more proper and peculiar to young men; only this sense comes in in a collateral way, that that experience which that age attains to is an evidence unto them that they shall finally and in the end prevail. Even as Joshua, when they had as yet made some progress of victory over their enemies, he bade the eldest † of Israel come and set their feet on the necks of their enemies, Josh. x. 24; and in the assured confidence of the promise of God at first made, whereof they hitherto had had such experience, he speaks thus unto them, ver. 25, ' Fear not, neither be dismayed; be strong and of good courage : for thus shall the Lord do to all your enemies against whom ye fight.' And so it is here.

The second thing that belongs to this, is the glory of these victories of Christ by us, as thus they are carried on to the end of our days; which, that it may appear, the terms or laws set between God and us are to be considered. In the entrance of this discourse I proposed that our overcoming Satan was not transacted by a sole mere outward violent force or restraint, a pure arbitrary prerogative put forth by Christ on our behalf; for so he could keep him off from tempting us at all, but that Christ leaves him at times to encounter with us, and to do his worst; yet upon certain laws and terms set between us by Christ, upon which it is he puts forth that force, and so according to those laws it is we overcome. That maxim holdeth here, 2 Tim. ii. 5, ' And if a man strive for masteries, yet is he not crowned except he strive lawfully.' So then laws are set between these combatants, else there were no dealing with the devil; and such as wherein his utmost skill and cunning to deceive, entice, persuade, provoke are displayed.

The first law is, that though he should prevail to blow up and inflame a man's lusts and affections with those corrupt instruments of his, he sets upon the will, yea, and the will itself be much won over and inclined, even ready to yield, yet if the major part thereof (which is the executive power in a man) keeps fixed and comes not off, so long a man is said to overcome; so as Satan must not boast that he carried it so or so far, but in that case the victory is decided to be on our part, and not on his. Every man's will is his castle, as the law speaks of a man's house, and if a man retains but ' power over his own will' (as the apostle in another case expresseth it, 1 Cor. vii. 37), which is seen by a man's either not morose indulgency or actings over a sin in fancy again, or not perpetrating it outwardly; in this case God pronounces on our sides that we have overcome, though in the assault we have had our hearts much wounded and pierced through with fiery and inflaming darts, that at the instant did transport our affections : Eph. vi. 13, στῆναι καὶ ἀντισθῆναι, if we be able but to ' withstand and stand.' You may observe how that all the weapons there reckoned up are but defensive, as helmet, shield, &c.

We only stand and deny; ‡ and accordingly says Peter, 'whom resist, stedfast in the faith,' 1 Pet. v. 9, that is, by faith we are to retain the power of the will; so likewise 1 Cor. vii. 37, ' stedfast in heart, having power over one's own will.' I observe also that in Rev. xii. our overcom-

* Qu. ' babes ' ?—Ed.   † Qu. ' captains ' ?—Ed.   ‡ Qu. ' by faith ' ?—Ed.

ing Satan is expressed by his not prevailing (ver. 8, 9, and 11 compared), namely, in the issue. I inquire not how many times he prevails, that is not the measure God goeth by. This may be set out by comparison of what befell Eve and Adam (whom Austin still styles *fortissimus ille*, that Samson and most strong one in comparison to us) in innocency; or rather, in the full strength of the image of God, consisting in holiness and right-eousness, and that complete in them.

(1.) We have the same vertibility of will which they had (take it merely as it is a will), the strongest purpose whereof is, as I use to say, as easily diverted and turned aside as the strongest push of a rapier by a straw.

(2.) Take Adam's will, and it had perfect command over his affections, so that not a desire, not a velleity, could stir to move it, until it gave way, yea, gave forth a command unto it. As in a well-framed watch or clock, an under wheel doth not stir until the upper first themselves hath moved it. It must be so in them that the understanding and will were to begin to be seduced ere an affection waved this way or that. ' The serpent deceived Eve,' the text says. It is a slander upon God's image and workmanship as it first came out of his hands, and that absolute perfect government God set up in Adam's soul, to say, that lusts and affections (the popular part of man) had power to move themselves, which yet the Jesuits and Arminians have cast upon it. No; the will itself was as the Almighty, that had the winds in its fists. Adam then had nothing inward to tempt him or draw him aside ; but we have a body of sin and death, full of life and activity as to sin, a weight that presseth us down, sin that besetteth us round, lusts that fight against the soul, and not only lusts to entice the will, but the will divided against itself, that we cannot do what we would. It was as easy for Adam to will good as it is for us to wish anything, to think or move a toe, the whole bias of the bowl led him that way ;* but now at best you have flesh lusting against the spirit, that you cannot do or will what you would. But then nothing without or within should check or foreflow any good motion in him, and yet the devil overcame them.

(3.) Yea, and the devil had not power to come within him, to represent unto and fire his fancy, to inflame his affections, or suggest by inward motion and incitations (as he doth us) for why else did he take an external shape to tempt him in ?

(4.) The devil overcame them the first onset he made, yea, and upon a lighter skirmish, yea, and both of them at once, and it was not long a-doing; they easily, presently, and soon yielded up all. How great then is the glory of that grace in us (who are every way so disadvantaged), that our wills should be able to withstand and to stand. The apostle in his own example hath celebrated it, 2 Cor. xii. 7, a thorn in the flesh, an angel of Satan, was sent, ver. 7, to shew that God's grace was sufficient, and that his strength is perfected in weakness, and that he hath ordained strength in babes and sucklings to still the enemy and avenger, Ps. viii. 2.

2. A second law which is set by Christ between him and us, that if we do thus hold out to resist the devil, we so overcome him as he must flee from us ; and that is a victory indeed, when the enemy is forced to fly for it. You have it expressly, James iv. 7, ' Resist the devil, and he will' or ' shall flee from you,' for it is not put upon his will there, but what is the event and issue of such resistances. Souls that are assaulted still more

---

* Tanta facilitas in Adamo vellendi et agendi benè, quanta nunc cogitandi aut movendi pedem, quanta sola velleitatis. Nam nihil interius aut exterius fuit quod retardaret motum.—*Jansenius* out of *St Austin*.

fiercely every day than other, are ready to say, Where is the promise of his
fleeing, for I find his temptations doubled ?   Well, but God hath said it;
and understand it as he hath meant it, and you shall find it true.   The
sense that I give of it is,

(1.) That for all fierce and set temptations there is a time limited to
Satan, though we know not the measure or limits of it; sometimes, and to
some, shorter; sometimes, and to some, longer.   It is termed the 'hour
of temptation,' Rev. iii. 10 ; and so Christ says too, Luke xxii. 53, 'This
is your hour, and the power of darkness.'   Now during that time, and whilst
it is appointed to last, Satan may, yea, doth after many renewed resistances of thine, come upon thee yet more fiercely; but there is a period,
until which if thou dost hold out, he must flee from thee.   Why should
there not be a set time for his temptation, as well as his persecution ?   His
commission therein is, ' for certain days ;' as Rev. ii. 10, ' Satan shall cast
some of you into prison, and ye shall have tribulation ten days,' but then
the keys are remanded and taken from him ; and so it is here in this case
too.   Now then,

(2.) The law of that concertation is, that if the soul be found resisting
him at or until such a time, though perhaps with many intervening foils,
that then he must be packing and gone ; let him look to himself.   It seems
not only to express a promise to us, but a law that concerns him, he will
and shall flee : even as that in Gen. ix. 6 contains both a promise and a
law, ' He that sheds man's blood, by man shall his blood be shed.'

(3.) It is expressed in the way of a military engagement, and an issue
such as is in war.   The words afore are, ' submit' or ' subject yourselves
to God,' and then follows, ' Resist the devil, and he will flee from you.'
And he had spoken afore of their ' lusts warring in their members,' ver. 1, 2,
of which lusts (as all know) the devil is the leader.   He had spoken of God
as the sovereign Lord, and giver of more grace, of grace opposite unto our
lusts, ver. 5, 6.   Now then, says James, if you would in this war prevail
against your lusts, my counsel in the first and chief place is to submit or
subject yourselves to God, become subject to him, as the word is, Rom. xiii.
1, 5, ' unto the highest powers ;' that is, as weaker states use to do when
they are engaged in war against an enemy too potent for them, their wisdom is to give themselves up as subjects to some other opposite prince, that
may defend and protect them, and supply them with aid.   So here these
to God are advised to subject themselves, that he may seasonably come in
with help in time of need.   Now when the soul hath first thus committed itself,
and put itself under God's protection, then, and upon that occasion (if you
observe it), it is that he utters this, ' Resist the devil, and he shall fly
from you.'   It is as if such a king or prince, that is engaged for such a
town or city under his protection, that is besieged and beleaguered long,
should send word unto them, hold but you stoutly out your resistance, and
I will come with forces myself that shall raise the siege, and cause the enemy
to depart.   And in such engagements there use to be the most punctual
observances and trusts.   Thus doth the apostle, as in the name of God, utter
this here ; subject yourselves to God, and resist the devil manfully, and he
shall flee from you, God will enforce him to do it.

(4.) Give me leave to give in my apprehension of this promise, he shall
flee from you, φεύξεται ἀφ' ὑμῶν ; I know the word is used simply to express
a sudden and swift removal, for which that Mat. x. 23 is cited by Beza.
' When they persecute you in one city, flee into another ;' yet usually it is
a flight out of apprehension of danger (at least) and even there the word

imports danger in the cities where they are persecuted; and here it is coming after an exhortation to a warlike resistance, it seems such a flight as is out of such an apprehension. Some say it is out of pride that he goes away, as being ashamed and as scorning to be resisted so much or so often. But the devil is not wrought upon by an affection of shame; he would by his good will continue the assaulting us even to the end, to weary us and tire us. It riseth then so high, as it is some way out of a fear of some real hurt that he knows is coming upon him if he desist not; yet, alas! what can he fear of damage from us, who are but flesh and blood? But from God (who, as was said, is engaged in it to take our parts) he may. God will come in as an assistant, with a force and power to raise his siege, if he continues his assaults longer than such a time; so as when he thus sees a stronger than he coming, he is forced to take his heels and run away. It is certain that at times God rebukes and chastiseth Satan; what else is the meaning of that prayer of the angel Christ, Zech. iii. 1, 2, and the angel Michael, Jude 9, ' The Lord rebuke thee.' The devils were in fear of a torment when cast out; or else why say they, ' Why comest thou to torment us before the time ?' Mat. viii. 29. Perhaps when the commission as at first granted is expired, when he is cast out at conversion, he is for a while confined to dry places, where he hath little trading for doing mischief, which makes him walk melancholy, and is a vexation to him; as also where he hath tempted men to great sins, he is confined to the place where the facts were committed, Mat. xii. 22. And why may it not further be thought in this case, that as when wicked men, who are the devil's instruments, do assault the saints, and draw them before their tribunals, that if they demean themselves so as in nothing to be terrified by their adversaries, Phil. i. 28, that then as there God strikes the hearts of their adversaries with terror, as he did Pilate in the case of Christ (for it follows, ' which is in them an evident token of perdition, as to you of salvation, and that of God,' that is, as God fills your hearts with seals and tokens of his love, so others at some* time with horror). Why may not the like be thought to befall the devil, when we manfully resist him, and that of God? Sure I am, the promise is (Rom. xvi. 20,) that when he should have done his do (as we say) in causing divisions in the church of the Romans, and that God had quieted those divisions, Satan is not only said to be overcome, but to be trodden under feet. He is a serpent, and fears his head to be bruised, to have a broken pate after he hath bruised our heels, and therefore flees; but this is in case we be standing out to resist him.

But in case we be overcome by him, as sometimes in such conflicts with him we are, by reason of our own lusts, and he prevail so as to lead us captive, yet two things do make a glorious victory even in this case.

1. In that this man that is overcome recovers himself again out of the snare of the devil, through the supply of the Spirit of Christ that is in him, and stronger than Satan who is without him; and this is glorious in another respect, *bis vincit qui victus vincit.* He is twice a conqueror, who is so after having been vanquished. It is made a glory for the people of God to take them captives, who had made them captives, Isa. xiv. 2. Even Christ himself, in his sphere and capacity (though not overcome by him in sin, yet in sufferings, &c.), suffered himself to be overcome, and to be nailed to the cross, so as the devil thought he had him fast and sure, and then he removed but his foot, and crushed him all in pieces. Now then when Satan

* Qu. ' same ' ?—ED.

hath even devoured and swallowed up a poor saint, 1 Peter v. 8, so as he
hath not only a foot in his snare, but his whole man in his belly, as to all
outward appearance, as he had done Peter as well as Judas, for he was
going (like Jonah) into the belly of this Leviathan, and had the weeds
about his neck; then to have Christ with one look, with one cast of his
eye, to break that man's heart, and to cause him to repent, so that the devil
must give him up again, to have his prey thus taken out of his teeth, it
doth mightily confound the devil.   Yea, and further, occasionally to make
use of that his sinning to provoke him (through zeal and repentance) to do
the devil more mischief,—so as Peter's denial, upon his repentance, made
him more stout and resolute than ever (as in the Acts you read) as being
converted he was strengthened so, as he turned three thousand souls at
once; and David's murder provoked him to teach sinners, and it hindered
not but that God converted many thereby, as Ps. li.—and personally working in the party sorrowing with godly sorrow, more zeal, and revenge, and
desire, &c., 2 Cor. vii. 11.   This is perfecting God's strength in our weakness, as 2 Cor. xii. 7, 8.   And by the way it is strange that Satan sent to
tempt should be termed a gift, as ver. 7 of that chapter, 'A thorn in the
flesh was given me, a messenger of Satan,' or the angel Satan, 'to buffet
me;' was it ever heard the devil was a gift?   Yes; in respect of the issue
of his temptations, as well as to suffer (and his temptations are termed
affliction and suffering, 1 Peter v. 20, 21), the bruising of our heel was a promise, as well as the breaking of his head.
    2. A second thing which in this case renders it glorious is, that often
when a soul is overcome in respect of its lusts, yet at the same time it is
enabled by faith to say, I shall yet overcome and be a conqueror, and in
the confidence thereof to give thanks unto God aforehand.   Such a courage
as this daunts an enemy exceedingly (especially when he knows he must in
the end be worsted), that when he hath a man down and under him, that
man yet spits in his face, and says to his teeth, I shall yet rise and tread
thee down.   Thus Paul in the name of believers, when he was driven to
the war, and taken captain,* sighs forth, 'O miserable man that I am!
Who shall deliver me?'   And in the foresight of the victory, cries, 'I thank
my God, through Jesus Christ,' Rom. vii. 25.   Well, Satan (says the soul),
thou hast me now under, but I shall up again, and say, as the church in
the prophet, 'Rejoice not against me, O mine enemy, though I fall; I shall
rise again, but thou shalt be trodden down as mire in the street.'   God
shall tread down Satan under your feet shortly.
    Christ's dealing with Peter is a strange instance, wherein you may per-
ceive Christ's care to support his faith, though he knew he should be foully
overcome. 'I have prayed,' says he, 'that thy faith fail not,' Luke xxii. 32.
Christ knew the effect of this promise would not be to keep him, and preserve him from falling; and he gives him an assurance he should recover;
and to that end to strengthen his faith before the sin committed, even with
the same breath he foretold he should so heinously transgress, he assures
him he should recover from it.   There is a talk by carnal spirits that deal
with God upon the terms of self-love only, and the covenant of works, that
assurance of persevering hurts a man's spirit, and exposeth him the more
to sins.   If this were true, then is Christ to be blamed in this; he ventures
it with Peter's spirit, and the efficacy of his intercession, he lays in provision
for faith beforehand to feed upon, against he should be overcome by sin,
and sets a cordial by him afore the disease; so much doth he delight in

* Qu. 'captive?'—Ed.

the triumph of faith in falls. You know Paul's triumph, Rom. viii. 37, 'We are more than conquerors through him that loved us.' And why? Because of the persuasion begotten, ' for I am persuaded neither death, nor life, nor angels, nor principalities, nor powers,' &c. He puts in to strengthen faith what needed not, what are not real, but only supposed enemies, as the good angels; nor heights, nor depths, that is, Satan (as Rev. ii. 24), that is, the strangest temptation that Satan can invent, or throw us into, cannot overwhelm us. He had first said neither death nor life; and I confess I have been most pleased and comforted with the putting in of life, that that shall not separate. I have feared life and the snares of it more than death, or angels, or devils. As for death, it despatcheth a man's sins and dangers in respect of them at once; it, like Samson, pulls down an old house, that kills all the Philistines together with himself; but it is life which a Christian is most apt to fear, knowing his own weakness, and the strength of lusts, and varieties of temptations; but here is a man's life insured (as is the merchants' language), and an assurance put in for life, and so against all hazards of sinnings, and therefore we are more than conquerors, because in and during the conflicts (which in view and to sense are dubious, and hazardous which should overcome), faith persuades us we shall overcome. Yea, *Vicimus! Vicimus!* (as with or after prayer he cried out ere he knew the event). Ye have overcome the wicked one, 1 John ii. 12. It is as good as done; yea, *in ipso bellandi ingressu sumus victores.* All that is born of God overcomes the world, 1 John v. 4. In all battles else men fight *dubio marte*: sometimes the one side carries it, sometimes another; so as they are doubtful of the event, only relieve themselves with this disjunction; *Aut mors certa, aut victoria læta,* either certain death, or a happy victory. Fight the good fight of faith, with assurance of success, says the apostle. It is a good fight indeed wherein there is ground for an assurance of victory, and a man can afore view sins and temptations, as that general did a goodly army of the enemies, and go aside and laugh out to God in confidence of the victory. Thus Christ, when he was presently to enter into the field of cross and wrath, and devil: ' Now is the Son of man glorified,' John xiii. 31; he says it beforehand.

When Satan hath any way prevailed by tempting us, he hath an accusing power before God, Rev. xii. 10. There is great joy in heaven when the accuser of the brethren is cast down, who accused them before our God day and night. I take the meaning to be this, that God professing himself, though a father to his children, yet to judge without respect of persons here in this life, in temporary judgments, his own children as well as others, and to go by the same rule therein; which you have in so may words emphatically, 1 Pet. i. 17, ' And if you call on the Father, who without respect of persons judgeth according to every man's work.' Hence therefore, when they sin, God hath given power to Satan freely to come and urge his own temporal threatenings, and his worst; professing withal, that unless they be wrought about to overcome his accusations by their repentance evangelical, he must and will proceed against them. And herein Satan pleads not before God as a mere slanderer; God would never be moved with that; but as an accuser that urgeth what the word of God saith against such and such sins, and inordinate walkings. And Satan hath upon such occasions leave to come to heaven (or elsewhere, I dispute not) and to appear with the sons of God, the good angels, as you see, Job i. 6. Christ's ears are pierced with his complaints day and night, so that text speaks. Yea, and if Satan had not power with God to do a great deal of mischief this way, there had not been such a rejoicing when Satan was overcome, as you read of, Rev. xii. And herein God deals by rule between us and Satan. God will have Satan fairly laid on his back. He useth not mere prerogative. The good angels are grieved at your sins (as they rejoice when they see a soul turned), but shake their heads and say nothing; we read not of their accusation. Yea, 2 Peter ii. 11, 'Whereas angels, which are greater in power and might, bring not railing accusations against them before the Lord' (he had spoken of the levellers of that age, who found fault with their magistrates, and their mis-governments and callings, promising liberty, ver. 19, by rebelling against him), says Peter, you do in this that which the good angels do not do : they, when they see magistrates miscarry, they, though greater in power (both than those magistrates and than you poor earth-worms, their subjects), yet bring not an accusation, blaspheming them, βλασφημοῦντες, which is, Jude 9, interpreted by this, that when Michael strove with Satan, it is said he did not bring a railing accusation. The meaning is, he brought none, for he said no more, but this, 'The Lord rebuke thee.' He went not to God with the story of his crime, but left it to him silently ; and as for them they quietly behold the face of God, to have commission from him to punish them if he think meet. So that this of Peter is spoken by way of distinction of good and evil angels. Evil angels go presently and bring accusations against men before the Lord, but the good do not complain, no, not of the devils themselves, when they oppose them.

Now Christ invalidates all these accusations of the devil by his own interceding and pleas in the force and virtue of his own blood, and therefore he is termed a righteous advocate : 1 John ii. 1, ' We have an advocate with the Father, Jesus Christ the righteous.' An advocate is the perfect opposite to the devil his being an accuser. It is one that takes off accusations by contrary pleas before some court, and his are righteous pleas all. Of this transaction you have a representation in that vision, Zech. iii. 1 : when Joshua was to be brought anew into the execution of the high priest's office, the devil stood at his right hand to resist him ; and what it was he spread before God against him you may understand by Christ's speech : ver. 4, ' Take away the filthy garments from him ; behold I have caused thine iniquities to pass from thee.' They were all his sins. Is this man (said Satan to God) a fit man to be a priest over the house of God, that hath sinned so and so ? instancing in particulars ; and so he pleads against any of you, when to be ordained or called to the ministry, or any place of eminency. Now Christ, the angel of the Lord, ver. 2, he on the other hand stands up for Joshua, ' The Lord said unto Satan, The Lord rebuke thee, O Satan.' And observe his pleas ;—

1. He pleads God's election. The Lord that hath chosen Jerusalem as his people, and place of his worship, whereof Joshua was by inheritance the leader and instrument, for whose sake he was to be placed in that office.

2. Is not this a brand plucked out of the fire ? ver. 2. Hath he not suffered sufficiently for those his sins already ? And wouldst thou have him confounded ? Such things as these Christ pleads, and take away his sins, says he, &c. Many such transactions as these pass for and against us in heaven, when we little think of it. But Christ's glory is not only to overcome him as accusing us in and by himself, but further causeth us to overcome him. I had once thought that Christ only deals with Satan in his accusing of us, and alone confounds him ; but that Scripture, Rev. xii. 10, 11 verses compared, ' The accuser of our brethren is cast down,' say

the angels, ' which accused them before our God day and night ; and they overcame him by the blood of the Lamb, and by the word of their testimony,' &c. This Scripture (I say) plainly shews, that not Christ only, but they, overcame him, and that as an accuser. He urged their failings, and how ? As in Job's case, that if tried and put to it they would deny Christ, and blaspheme him to his face ; now they overcome him.

First, As to their sins, by the blood of the Lamb. They pleaded that, and confessed their iniquities. If we confess our sins, and plead Christ's blood, God is just to forgive us, and the blood of Christ cleanseth us from all sin, 1 John i. 7, 9.

Secondly, They overcame and silenced him many of them in the other accusation by continuing constant in the testimony of the truth, and by not loving their lives unto death, which in the end silenced Satan, and moved God to assuage the persecutions of the Christians, and turn them into a glorious liberty.

Thus when a believer hath fallen into sin and the snare of the devil for it, as again and again Paul to Timothy expresseth it, 1 Tim. iii. 7, and 1 Tim. v. 14, that the devil hath occasion to reproach him unto God and unto men (although as for his reproaches of them to men it often falls out that his commission is to use his own trade of lying, and he is restrained from what are indeed their sins), however Christ upon this sends down his Spirit (unknown to them) into their souls, Rom. viii. 25, 26, and he intercedes as fast in their hearts, urgeth such and such promises and pleas as Christ in heaven doth on their behalf. He breaks their hearts, causeth them to confess their sins, 1 Cor. vii. 1, to mourn after a godly sort, gives them repentance, carefulness for time to come, revenge and hatred against them, and fear for falling again, and intermingled with apologies drawn from their own frailty, Christ's blood, intercession, &c. And thus (as there) they approve themselves clear in that matter (namely, wherein they had sinned, and for which they repented), clear, that is, before God, and according unto God's rules ; and so (as was said), though God judgeth without respect of persons, yet they having thus judged themselves, they stand *recti in curia*, according to the equity of God's rules, not by extraordinary power, but by law ; which you find, 1 Cor. xi. 31, ' If we would judge ourselves, we should not be judged.' And thus the devil is baffled, and the man restored.

Thirdly, Satan hath the power of ruling and governing the carnal party of men, which the Scriptures term the world. He is therefore termed ' The prince of this world,' John xii. 31 ; and he that deceives the world, Rev. xii. 9. And the chiefest trade and design he drives, and advantage he makes of this his government over the world, is so to mould and make up the fashions of this world, as by them to persecute the saints, Rev. xii. 17. For persecute them immediately he cannot by himself alone, although those other powers, as to accuse them to God, and to suggest and urge temptation, he hath of himself singly and separately assigned to him ; yet to bring persecution on them herein he must shroud himself under the power of the world, and make use thereof, and work mediately thereby ; yet so as such proceedings against the saints are more attributed unto him than unto the world. Insomuch as that whole Roman empire, being acted by him to persecute the saints (ignorant of what themselves did therein), is termed the dragon and the old serpent, Rev. xii. ; as he that deceived the world, and was *anima mundi*, the soul and form of that world that then was, and so unto this day.

Now as the saints then by their prayers and tears, and holding forth the testimony of Jesus, overcame that world that then was, and thereby are said to have overcome the devil as prince of that world, so they have done it in several ages again and again since ; in overcoming and working all those new and great alterations in the world in relation to religion that have been made, and the devil hath still been overcome and laid on his back by them. And therefore, John xii. 31, when Christ says, ' Now is the judgment of this world,' he adds, ' Now shall the prince of this world be cast out.' The judgment or reformation of the world (as, John xvi. 8, the word is used) is still the casting forth of the devil, who rules and informs it, as the soul doth the body. And so far as they overcome and make changes in the world, as it is opposite to Christ and unto them, so far do they overcome the devil also.

Take but a view of the course and proceedings of matters since Christ's time downward to this age, and you that know how the world hath gone must also acknowledge that there have been a many new worlds, and faces of things, and as the apostle terms them, 1 Cor. vii., ' fashions of this world, which pass away.' The world hath been put into a great many new dresses and shapes; and under all powers the devil still hath sought to shroud himself, and carry on his mentioned interest, which hath always been to form up the multitude of men and their spirits so, and to mould the customs and laws, and power, that he may have wherewith to persecute the saints more or less, which is his trade.

And he hath wisely applied himself still to the times and spirits of men to effect this, and sharked to do it (as I may so speak), as the saints have driven him out of his worldly works, and hath made the best of it in his losses. For the saints have unroosted him out of his former works often, and put him upon new seekings of his fortune, and altering his play many a time.

For the making forth of which you may observe how Christ and his apostles, speaking of the world which they did live in, with this indigitation or designation, ' This world.' So Christ in that John xii. 31. And so the apostles, and that not in opposition to the world to come (as, Heb. ii. 5, the apostle speaks), but as in specification of that present world which was then in Christ's and the apostles' times, which, Gal. i. 4, Paul calls ' the present evil world.' Even as Peter styles the truths that were passing then, ' the present truth,' 2 Peter i. 12. Paul speaking at once both of the state of the world that then was, and also of the devil's rule in it (as it then stood), expresseth himself thus, ' That the spirit that now works,' says he, ' in the children of disobedience,' Eph. ii. 2. There was a present world in Christ's and the apostles' time, the power, the swing, customs and laws of which then carried it against the saints, and Satan was in it. There were the received laws and customs of the Jewish religion, which had a toleration throughout the Roman empire, when the Christian had not ; and also the rites of the old heathenish religion, I need not tell you how prevalent, which the apostle called ' the rudiments of the world,' Col. ii. 8, and ' the traditions of men,' that is of that world that then was. Now the saints they overcame that world that then was, both Jewish and heathenish, not only in their single persons swimming against the stream, and in not being entangled with the weeds at the bottom of that stream, that is the good or evil things thereof : 1 John v. 4, ' For whatsoever is born of God overcometh the world.' But they plainly overcame the whole. You all know the alteration made in Constantine's time, three hundred years after Christ. You read of a great shock and battle, Rev. xii. 3, made by the great red dragon with seven heads and ten horns (which, as I may so speak, was the arms of the Roman heathenish empire, as set out by the Holy Ghost), which cast or body of government the devil inspired, and so is called the dragon, the devil, as fortified herein; hence therefore it is plainly said, that they, the saints overcame him, ver. 11, ' And they overcame him, as there was no place found for him and his angels in heaven any more,' ver. 8. There was not one man left in some years that were seen to worship one of their heathenish gods. And in doing this (which is the glory of it), God came not down from heaven with thunderbolts and miracles to over-come, but kept to his ordinary laws of providence in ruling the hearts and spirits of men. He turns the emperor Constantine unto the Christian faith, and he turns about the world upside down, as they spake in the Acts; and now all the power was for the saints, which before was against them. Well, the devil was unroosted, and his palace or castle (as Christ calls it), his fortifications or works, as then formed to annoy the saints out thereof, were slighted, dismantled, and himself clean turned out, and turned naked to shift to the wide world as we say. It is said immediately thereupon, Rev. xiii. 1, ' And he stood upon the sand of the sea.' You know it is read so by some, who make those words the close of the former chapter, and applied to the devil, who (as Mede* says) being deprived of the Roman empire, and put out of course and play, was put to his trumps; and because he could not rule and sway things thereby any more, he stands melancholy and naked on the sand of the sea, waiting to see what new form or face of a new world would arise next out of the sea. Now the sea was the multi-tudes of nations and people, then altered, both to a new form of government, as also turned Christian; and thus chap. xvii. 1, 15, the many waters, or the sea the next beast rose out of and sat upon, is interpreted. Well, the devil upon that interim observeth which way the waves tumbled, unto which he is as the wind or breath, he soon spied out a new advantage; only seeing the world was turned Christian, he applied his government of the world unto the spirits of men, and he would be a Christian too, that is, carry on his designs and affairs under the profession of Christianity. And so that corrupt, ignorant world that then was, being brooded upon by this spirit that breathed upon these waters, did in the end bring forth a new form of government, and religion of popery; the power and laws whereof, through Satan's efficacy, the whole world that then was, went again after, and made war against the saints, and overcame them, as ver. 3, 7. And this our forefathers have told us.

Well, but the saints are born to overcome this devil, and a thousand of his worlds, if you could suppose them. Let him put himself into, and shroud himself under what worldly power soever; let him draw his lines of fortification anew, and build them as high as heaven, or as firm as the great mountains, yet they shall conquer him. And how they have overcome him in that power also, the 14th, 15th, 16th, 17th, 18th chapters, and the stories of that Reformation of religion in all these protestant countries, tell you, and they are the saints that have done, and by their prayers shall do it: Rev. xvii. 14, ' The Lamb shall overcome them, for as he is Lord of lords, so they that are with him are called, and chosen, and faithful.' And in doing this, he did not come down from heaven with flashes of lightning or Egyptian plagues, but kept to his ordinary rules of proceeding by which he hath governed the world in all ages, making changes in them, sometimes making use of men's lusts, as of Henry the Eighth; otherwhere turning

* See *Mede's* Clav. Apoc.

the hearts of princes to embrace the gospel, as in Germany and Sweden; elsewhere inflaming the people unto popular tumults, and a hatred of idolatry, as in Scotland; sometimes in giving up princes to oppress them in their civil liberties as well as in their consciences, and so to move them to cast off the yoke, as in Holland; sometimes entwisting in one interest civil rights, and the interest of religion, as in France : all which, however done, and done but by the laws of. providence ruling men's spirits, have been done at the prayers of the people of God.

Well, but when protestantism was set up, and the reformed religion, so as there was again a new dress or fashion of the world (as the apostle speaks of it, 1 Cor. vii. 31), yet still he made a shift so to form even the truth of that religion up into a mixture of such common laws and constitutions, that had the supreme power and people so to back them, as he could still and hath still used that present world to oppress multitudes of the saints; and how the power thereof hath been broken, and the devil again put out of trade, and made a reformado, as to the persecuting part of this our age; and it hath been the prayers of the saints have brought it about. He is half an atheist that will not acknowledge it, and say, ' Verily there is a God that judgeth in the earth.'

And in this interim the devil is, upon those great alterations we have seen, in his dumps and musings hovering over this island, and waiting how to form up a worldly party, and unite them in a common interest, such as may serve to persecute again, more than with the lash of the tongue; and this present world is as fit for it as ever any. And as it was then, so it is now; those that are after the flesh will persecute them that are after the spirit, Gal. iv. 29. And the devil waits but how to draw his line anew, and to raise up a fortification to effect it, which, whatever it will prove to be in God's just permission, yet in the mean time, know that you have overcome the devil more than men, or than that present constitution of the world forepast, and have routed the devil in subduing the power of men. In overcoming the present world, you overcame the devil much more, and this Paul knew and informs us, that we fight more against principalities and powers than against flesh and blood. And I say unto you, rejoice not that armies or nations have been subjected to your prayers, but that the spirits, the devils themselves, have been so; though above all, rejoice that your names are written in heaven.

CHAPTER XVIII.

The last and complete victory which Christ and his saints have over the devil, both before and at the day of judgment.

The third sort of Christ's proceedings against this common enemy are more open and judicial. For when he hath let him try his skill and power every way (as hath been shewed) to annoy us, and that in all sorts of attempts, as against us made, Christ hath for thousands of years still baffled and confounded him by us; which, because it is but invisibly done, he is not ashamed at it, but would persist to eternity in this way (if the world should last so long), therefore Christ hath resolved to deal with him more openly and visibly. And so it became him, that when he had enabled us to overcome him in a regular way, then to fall upon him in a hostile and judiciary way. And this hath two degrees.

1. When the world, the time and seat of his rule, shall grow towards a conclusion, then a strict restraint shall be clapped on him.

2. There will be a bringing him to open judgment.

1. A strict restraint shall be clapped on him towards the end. It is time; he had chains clapped on him from his very fall, 2 Peter ii. 4, and yet he hath been hitherto as a prisoner at large, that hath had liberty to walk up and down with his chains, to take the air, as he is 'the prince of the power of the air,' says the apostle, Eph. ii. 2. Well, but when the world draws to an end, he shall be bound up in chains, so as (at least) his ruling power over this world (which hath been the fairest flower in his crown) shall be taken from him, whilst he yet sees (to vex him) the world of men on earth continue to go on in its succession before his face. How far his tempting power will be taken away I will not argue, but that he will towards the end be universally restrained of his ruling the nations (as he had wont) to persecute the saints, I think there is ground for it; Rev. xx. 1, 2, 3, 'And I saw an angel come down from heaven, having the key of the bottomless pit and a great chain in his hand. And he laid hold on the dragon, that old serpent, which is the devil, and Satan, and bound him a thousand years, and cast him into the bottomless pit, and shut him up, and set a seal upon him, that he should deceive the nations no more, till the thousand years should be fulfilled.' You might, without much hesitation to your thoughts, think when this is to be done. If we had no more, it is enough signified in Rev. xx., that the time is the last hour or two before the dawning of the great day, and shutting up of the darkness of this world. And what is this revelation but a prophecy of the fates of the church and world? Rev. i. 1 and chap. iv. 1. The world, therefore, now that is a-drawing on its last scene, is not yet so to end but there shall be a little time for the devil to play his pranks a little while, ver. 3. But more particularly, whereas it hath been shewn how in his ruling power the devil, the old serpent, was beaten out of his holes; and we have seen how this mountebank, who deceives the whole world, in his several stages he hath set up in the world, hath still been beaten down, and been forced to build new. First he had Judaism, then heathenism, in the room of which he hath set up popery, Rev. xii. 13.* We have seen how, when all the world turned Christian, an antichristian beast rose up, and all the world went wandering after him, for ver. 4, the dragon gave him his power, and his seal, and great authority, and they worshipped the dragon that gave power to the beast; and you read of this new beast's rule until the 19th chapter, ver. 19, 20, 'And I saw the beast, and the kings of the earth, and their armies, gathered together to make war against him that sat on the horse, and against his army. And the beast was taken, and with him the false prophets that wrought miracles before him, with which he deceived them that had received the mark of the beast, and them that worshipped his image. These both were cast alive into the lake of fire burning with brimstone.' Now, when Christ and his army (which are the saints) have clean defeated and made an end of this last beast and his power, so as that they have had a fair and open victory in the view of men over the devil, and all this world, and this the last trial of skill assigned him, for Christ resolves to lay all the powers of the world—oppos-

---

* The 15th and 16th chapters are the degrees of his coming. The 17th the explication who and what he should be. The 18th the funeral song of the great city that is borne up by him. And chapter 19, the fatal overthrow. [See the author's exposition of the Revelation, in vol. III. of this series of his works.—ED.]

ing his kingdom—fairly, and in a human way of conquest, on their backs (according unto that chap. xiii., 'He that killeth with the sword shall be killed with the sword), so as the devil that had acted all these is now left a naked devil, beaten out of all his fortresses; what then immediately follows? Rev. xx. 1, 2, 3, 'And I saw an angel come down from heaven, having the key of the bottomless pit,' &c. Now, says Christ, yourself, the great actor in all these tragedies, your time is come, your turn is next at last, that 'he who led into captivity should be led into captivity,' that yourself must be bound otherwise than you have been; and bound from what? Why, from deceiving the nations: ver. 3, 'That he should deceive the nations no more,' either by tempting or ruling them any more. And he never deceived the nations more than in the time of popery, therefore this his binding must be after all; and then, to make sure of him, casts him into the bottomless pit, shuts him up with a seal upon him; here is the devil fast, and so it is as a restraint before his last fatal trial and judgment.

I will not prosecute this further; you know where else to find it argued. To convince you that there is to be a kingdom of Christ and of the saints for a thousand years, read the following verses; during which time it is meet, yea necessary, the devil be in hold, as you see he is.

2. The last scene, or final proceedings of Christ against him, is his bringing him and his angels into personal and open judgment before God, angels, and men. And herein, to make this victory and destruction full and complete, you that are the saints thus opposed by him shall be his judges. And there cannot be supposed a fuller victory than this, that after you have overcome him, all sorts of ways related, and God hath trodden him under your feet, that then at last you should sit and be his lawful judges, of all his wickednesses, enmities, and temptations acted against yourselves. Now, look, as Christ triumphed over him openly, visibly, Col. ii. 15, before angels, and the spirits of just men made perfect, so shall you then with Christ more visibly and openly, even before the world. This you have, 1 Cor. vi. 2, 3, 'Do you not know that the saints shall judge the world? Know you not that we shall judge angels?' This judging of Satan I shall explain and prove by these steps.

(1.) That the devil as well as men shall be brought to open judgment; this is plain both by Jude 6 and 2 Peter ii. 4, 'The angels that kept not their first estate, he cast them down to hell,' so Peter, 'and reserved them in everlasting chains under darkness to the judgment of the great day;' so Jude; 'or delivered them into chains of darkness to be reserved into judgment,' so Peter. I understand the transaction of it to have been thus.

[1.] That upon the angels' first sinning, there was a present throwing of them into hell, namely that place and state they shall for ever be in after the great day, as a taste of what in a greater fulness they after judgment should be condemned unto; yet so as,

[2.] They were presently let out again into the air, by reason of which they have liberty and freedom of spirit, and they rule this world, which if in full torments they could not do, Luke viii. 31. They, as dreading that place of hell, besought him he would not command them into the deep, that is, their former hell.

[3.] Yet in the mean time, whilst they are at liberty, they are as prisoners in chains, suffered to walk up and down, and thereby marked out as reserved to an assize or judgment of the great day. And under this allusion, their condition seems to me to be different from that of men, wicked men, with whom God is yet in treaty, for they go under bail of Christ's death, that hath purchased this forbearance for them, as space to repent. These, I say, were never yet actually cast into hell (as the devils upon their first sin were), so as these are not actually prisoners, as those are that are entered into prison, and belong to it, although they have permission to go abroad. And to shew they are so, they carry chains of that prison about them (which what they are I stand not now to determine), which chains are badges that they are reserved unto a more open visible judgment of the great day. The conclusion of all is this; look, as hell itself is said to have been prepared for the devil and his angels, originally for them, so they sinning first go into hell fire, prepared, &c., and so the judgment of the great day was appointed for them first. They in both are the *mensura* and pattern of wicked men, and therefore both Jude and Peter mention their judgment first in the head and van; and then of wicked men, the old world, and Sodom, &c.

(2.) We are, secondly, to take notice that during this vacation or time of liberty to them, the account and score of their sinning runs on, and is daily added unto, so as they heap up thereby matter of judgment, which shall be brought forth, and charged upon them at that great day. Herein is one difference between the case and condition of the spirits of wicked men deceased, and of these devils. The spirits of such men are said to be in a strict sense *in prison*, 1 Peter iii. 19; and so the spirits of those in Sodom are said by Jude to have been made an example, ' suffering the vengeance of hell fire'; so as men's souls shall answer but for the sins they have done in the body, 2 Cor v. 10. Cain shall answer for no more sins than what his soul did in his body; his score of sinning runs not on since he was in hell; he is not only truly and actually a prisoner, but detained in prison, and suffers a fulness of wrath, as there a man's soul is sure to do, and that takes away the demerit of sinning; but with the devils that go abroad as prisoners in chains, and as belonging only to that prison, it is otherwise. What sins they commit personally, or in tempting us, shall then be accounted for, which is proved.

[1.] Because the devil is cursed for having tempted both Eve and Adam, thus it is pronounced, ' Cursed shalt thou be above all the herd or cattle of the field,' Gen. iii. 24. So that not his own first sin in falling from heaven shall be reckoned to him only, but also all his tempting of us.

[2.] And again he in after times should bruise the heel of Christ (which was four thousand years after), and of the whole seed of Christ; therefore his head is to be broken, namely, in vengeance for his bruising Christ's heel there is a total breaking of his head. Now if he be cursed for those, and his head to be broken for those, then he is to be judged and cast into hell for those as reckoned sins done by him, which are matter of judgment. For in that he says, ' Cursed shalt thou be above all cattle,' &c., he designs his punishment in hell, and his meaning is, thy punishment shall be greater than of all wicked men, the cattle of the field. And our saviour's words of them are, ' Go ye cursed into hell fire, prepared for the devils.' He is cursed, therefore, with hell fire for his sin, and that as the pattern of sinners, and all other that are cursed and punished in like manner.

[3.] It is expressly said, 1 John iii. 18, that he sinneth from the beginning, as continuing so to do, and what he doth being reckoned and imputed to him, it is not only that he sinned at the beginning, but he sinned continually from the beginning; and this suits his scope, which was to shew that that man that continued in a course of sinning was of the devil; that a worker of iniquity was of the devil as his father; for lo! says he, in like manner the devil thus sins in a perpetual constancy.

(3.) You the saints are to be his judges, so 1 Cor. vi. 2, 3. Christ had first declared this to be the privilege of the twelve apostles, to sit, and to judge the twelve tribes of Israel; this Paul enlargeth to all the saints, ver. 2, 4. 'Know you not the saints shall judge the world,' all the world, yea the angels? And he speaks of judging in a time * and proper sense, then when the whole world is to be judged at the judgment-seat of Christ; as when causes are heard and judged in courts, and persons are condemned or acquitted, according to the nature of the fact. For he brings it as an argument why they should not carry or transfer the civil controversies amongst them about matters of this life to earthly judicatures, but rather to end and decide them among themselves. Ver. 1, 'Dare any of you, having a matter against another, go to law before the unjust, and not before the saints?' And in the chapter afore he had shewn how God had given power to them as a church to judge them that are within, and so to cast out that wicked person. His argument to this had not been proper, if he had not intended the like time* and proper way of judicature at that great judgment to be committed to them; where though Christ shall be the great judge, yet they shall sit judging, as Christ says, as co-assessors, discerning the guilt, and carrying in the sentence, Luke xxii. 30, Mat. xix. 28. And ἐν ὑμῖν is by you, ver. 2; the world shall be judged by you, ver. 4. His inference is from hence set them, καθίζετε, put them to the chair, that are least esteemed in the church, for at the latter day they shall sit and judge. And that he speaks it of all saints is plain; for, he saith, 'We shall judge the angels, and know you not that the saints shall judge the world;' and not the greater saints only, but small and great; for he infers from it, 'set them to judge who are least esteemed in the church,' having before founded it on this, 'that if the world shall be judged by you, are you not worthy to judge the smallest matters?' And to heighten their dignity herein, he first says, 'they shall judge the word,' namely, of men; and then I tell you more, yea, the angels. As Christ's glory is, that God made two worlds for him, visible and invisible, Heb. i., Col. i., so our glory is, that we are constituted commissioners to judge two worlds, visible and invisible, such two large circuits we have. Thus much for the explanation and proof of it.

Now, then, my brethren, let us lift up our hearts, and raise up our thoughts, in the expectation of this 'great day,' as still the New Testament styleth it. It is termed great in respect of those great things which shall be done in it. A great and glorious day it will be, not only in respect of the splendour of the concourse of all of mankind unto one assembly, all that have been from Adam, all angels and saints will be there, 1 Thess. iii. 13, but also it is great in respect of the things and matters to be judged. All the human affairs of this world, which the apostle calls things of this life, ver. 4, which the great ones of the world are the judges of, he reckons among the smallest matters; so he terms them, ver. 2, in comparison of the things that then should be transacted in a way of judicature, which will be the exact scanning and trial of all actions as they pertain to eternity, that is, the spiritual good or evil that is in them, and as they tended to the honour or dishonour of the great God. These are the proper subjects that belong to the cognisance of that day. And now to have all the affairs of the whole world, of men, of all their thoughts, plots, counsels, actions, and that under the consideration, as good or evil, to have them all under

* Qu. 'true?'—ED.

this cognisance, laid open and committed to the censure of the saints with authority, what an infinite dignity must this be to them! Yet so he heightens it, 'If the world shall be judged by you, are you unworthy to judge the smallest matters?' ver. 2, by which he means all those things that are brought before human courts, of what kinds soever; and then thereupon he rises higher, ver. 3, 'Know you not that we shall judge angels?' as those whose story and transactions afford higher and greater matters by far than the story of this whole world will do?

Now, then, how and in what manner the world of mankind shall be judged, in the same kind and manner shall the angels also be, for he casts the same line over both. Now, how shall the world of men be judged? Why, every work, whether it be good or evil, shall have an exact trial: Eccles. xii. 14, 'For God shall bring every work into judgment, with every secret thing, whether it be good or evil;' and, 1 Cor. iv. 5, 'Judge nothing before the time; the Lord will come, who both will bring to light the hidden things of darkness, and will make manifest the counsels of the hearts;' importing that at that time all will so be discovered by the Lord, who is ready to judge the quick and the dead, as every saint shall be able to judge too.

Now, then, think with yourselves, if you knew but all the affairs of this present age, all the secrets of states, state ends, maxims, rules, principles, lusts of all the monarchs, of all the nobles in the world, to have (as he told the Assyrian king) all that is said in the king's chamber revealed, yea, that are in his thoughts, which are unsearchable, by which they rule and reign, and you had all the story of this age, past and present, nakedly spread before you, what infinite delight would this afford you! To have a prince's cabinet, a few letters or transactions published, how greedy are men of them! Now, you know (says the apostle) you shall have a greater story one day, and of infinitely higher worth and elevation; you shall judge the angels, 2 Pet. ii. 10, 11. The apostle, comparing earthly magistrates and dignities (and in his time they were the greatest that ever were, namely, those in the Roman empire), he says of the angels, that they are greater in power and might; and as the good, so the bad; for they contend each with other upon all occasions, as appears by the story of Daniel, chap. x. and chap. xi., and by that passage between the devil and Michael in Jude. The devil's monarchy is the greatest that ever was. The apostles and Christ, that had a prospect into that invisible world, termed him the prince of the world, greater than Cæsar, than the great Turk or Mogul, &c.; they are but as petty constables, as one comparing the power and state of our European princes with those eastern monarchs speaks. The angels they are the rulers of the world: Eph. vi. 12, 'So as we fight not against flesh and blood' (in comparison of them our contentions against the world are not considered), 'but against principalities and powers.' Men are but as the puppets above the stage, when these act all. And again, the transactions between God and Satan are many, as the story of Ahab and Job shews; and also those between the good and bad angels are great and various. Now, then, as these grandees of this invisible world excel in power and wisdom all the petty rulers of this world, so the passages and transactions amongst them and by them, their policies, enmities, animosities, &c., must needs excel all other. Satan is renowned for his stratagems, his wiles. He outwitted Eve, and soon deceived her; yea, and the whole world too, Rev. xii. 9. We are not ignorant of his devices, says Paul, 2 Cor. ii. 11. And further, his wickednesses are spiritual, sublimated wickednesses.

The worst of earthly tyrants and monarchs are but carnal wickednesses unto them; and all these shall be laid open, and sentenced to a suitable punishment. All the secret counsels of his heart, his over-reaching and going beyond poor souls, the utmost and extremity of that malice and envy he acted all with, shall be detected, and thou a poor believer shalt be a judge of all these. Then shalt thou see Beelzebub the great devil, and all hell with him (that is, his angels), brought forth in chains, and Christ opening all their sins, even here in this world, where they did all the mischief. What a glorious and triumphant sight (think you) will it be to the primitive Christians to see Nero or Julian stand forth, led and haled before the judgment-seat of Christ! How much more to see this dragon and his angels, that inspired all these in all their rage and malice, and to have all the stories of their actings ripped up for six thousand years' continuance. In Isa. xiv. 10–18, when the king of Babel was brought down to the grave, it is said all hell went forth, all kings and nations he had tyrannised over went out to meet him, so great a spectacle it was: 'How art thou fallen, O Lucifer, son of the morning!' And even that is an allusion (as the ancients have conceived) of Satan's fall and ruin.

Particularly for thy comfort, O thou tossed, and bruised, and weather-beaten soul, how will it rejoice thee if it were but to hear Christ as on thy behalf openly to rebuke Satan, and to say thus to him, Didst thou, Satan, spite, malign, vex, and provoke unto sin this poor saint; those thoughts didst thou dart in, this train didst thou lay for him, as the fowler doth for a silly bird; and no sooner hadst thou drawn him into thy net to commit the sin, but thou didst run to God and accuse him of that which thou seducedst him to do, whilst he, poor soul, went weeping bitterly, as Peter when he had done evil? And now will Christ say, I will save him, and damn thee; and that for all the sins which he committed through thy instigation, of all which thou art the father more than he. And then how comfortable will it be to hear Christ excuse thee also, that the spirit was willing but the flesh was weak; and then to lay the load on him, and adjudge him to so much the greater torment because of what he did to thee; this will be much and great joy. But further will Christ say, Come thou, even thou, weak soul, up hither, sit down here by me, thou shalt be his judge, thou shalt sit on my throne with me; yea, more, as I triumph over him, so do thou now, and not as over one vanquished only to thy hand, but as over one instantly to be condemned and adjudged to hell; and thou shalt see it enrolled before thy face ere thou stirrest off this bench, and when thy sentence hath concurred with mine, I have in readiness here about me, to revenge all their disobedience, the good angels, armed with another manner of power than ever before, who shall throw them down to hell, and take and burn them with fire and brimstone. What can be supposed a perfect victory, and triumph of Christ and his saints over the devils, if this is not?

CHAPTER XIX.

Christ's fulness for our justification.—His fulfilling the law for us.—That justification doth not consist only in pardon of sin, and therefore it is not Christ's passive obedience alone which is imputed to us.—That the whole righteousness which is in Christ is imputed to us for righteousness.

Having largely proved and explained how Christ performed that part of our redemption, which consists in freeing us from the guilt, and curse, and punishment of sin, which he did by himself being made sin and a curse for us, what remains is to prove that he fulfilled the law, and performed all righteousness for our justification; and that he is ' the Lord our righteousness,' as well as our sacrifice and ransom. I first lay down this general proposition.

Prop. That the whole righteousness which is in Christ is imputed to us for righteousness.

The terms or words of the proposition should he explained by some distinctions, to avoid all ambiguities, and to prevent mistakes; but instead of multiplying distinctions, which often confounds instead of clearing the truth, I shall premise two or three things, to shew in what limited sense the proposition is meant, and to be understood.

1. When I say, *the whole righteousness which is in Christ,* I do not understand that essential holiness of the divine nature which is in Christ, who is God; for I perfectly reject and abhor the dream of Osiander. I mean then that acquired righteousness of Christ God-man; for though Jehovah is called our righteousness, Jer. xxiii. 6, yet that righteousness which is of God is not ours.

2. We must also cautiously discern between the righteousness of the mediatorial office (from which Christ is deservedly called the alone mediator) and the merits of the righteousness of Christ the mediator. For as God will not give his glory to another, nor indeed can give it (and therefore I deny the essential righteousness, by which he is God, to be communicated), so neither will Christ give away the glory of his mediation. That righteousness of the office, by which he is mediator, cannot be imputed. But as in logic we say that the whole nature of the *genus* is communicated to the *species,* but not generical natures by which it is a *genus,* for then the *species* would be a *genus* too; in like manner I assert the whole righteousness of Christ the mediator to be communicated, but not the mediatorial righteousness.

3. We must also make some distinction concerning this righteousness of Christ, which I assert to be imputed to us. For I do not include in it the righteousness of Christ the mediator, as now glorified in heaven, which righteousness yet is continued; but the alone righteousness of Christ performed by him in his estate of humiliation on earth is to be understood. For though he is said to be raised for our justification, Rom. iv. 25, viz., that his righteousness and the merit of it might be applied to us, yet he cried out on the cross, ' It is finished,' John xix. 30, and after his death he ceased to merit anything, as he will also cease to make application of his merits to us after the day of judgment, when God shall be all in all. And when he is said to be a priest for ever, Heb. vii. 17, it is to be understood that he is so in his intercession, not in meriting for us. As also when his righteousness is called ' everlasting righteousness,' Dan. xi. 24, it is meant of the duration of its value and virtue, not of the continuance of its external acts.

4. Nor do we take in all which he did while he lived here on earth. All his extraordinary works, as miracles and the like, are not to be included. They rather transcend the predicaments of the ten commandments than are parts of the righteousness of the law. They were proofs of his divinity, and the signs and badges, rather than the duties, of his office. He indeed by them shewed himself to be the only mediator, but he did not act the mediator in them. And he did them that men might believe in his righteousness; but they were no ingredients of that righteousness on which they were to believe.

Now to give the right state of the controversy: protestant divines asserted against the papists, that all our righteousness, by which we are justified, is the imputed righteousness of Christ; but what is in question among divines of the reformed religion is, whether the whole righteousness of Christ be imputed.

There is a twofold obedience visible in Christ in his humbled state: one, which consists in the conformity of his life to the law; the other, in undergoing death, and the curse of the law: of which the first is called in the schools active, and the other passive, obedience. To which may and ought to be added, the holiness of his nature, which is the principle of both the former obediences.

There are some who not only exclude that sanctity of his nature, but all the active righteousness of his life, from that righteousness which is imputed to us. They say indeed that both the holiness of Christ's nature, and the obedience of his life, are of great advantage to us, and that they concur to the obtaining of our justification, as conditions qualifying the mediator for that work, and as requisite to be in the person who is our high priest: Heb. vii. 26, ' For such an high priest became us, who is holy, harmless, undefiled, separate from sinners, and made higher than the heavens.' But yet they deny all this to be, together with his passive obedience, imputed to us in the room of our righteousness; for they affirm that it all was acted by Christ for his own sake, and on his own personal account; for Christ was bound to it as a creature and son of Adam, born under the moral law, and as a son of Abraham under the ceremonial law. And one debt (say they) can never be discharged by another. But they believe his passive obedience to be only imputed, both because Christ did undertake and perform it, not for himself, but purely for our sakes, and also because they esteem it an adequate and sufficient matter of our justification.

But we lay down this contrary assertion, that both the holiness of Christ's nature, and all that work of humiliation (which the apostle includes in the name of ' obedience unto death'), was both undertaken and accomplished for our sakes, and that it gives its joint mark with his passive obedience to our justification; in a word, that all this righteousness of Christ whatever, is imputed to us, as proportionate conformity to that righteousness which the law requires from us.

Which assertion I shall both explain and demonstrate by a few conclusions (of which the proposition which I have laid down is the sum) mutually linked together, and which, being rightly applied, will preclude the chiefest objections of the contrary side.

There are two principles in which both parties agree, and which therefore remain not now to be proved.

The first of which is, that that righteousness by which a sinner may appear righteous, ought to consist in a perfect satisfaction of the law. For though it cannot be called the righteousness of the law, that is (as the apostle hath interpreted it, Phil. iii. 8), the proper performance of the sinner, who, as being under the law, owes all obedience to it; yet as this righteousness is in the person who is our surety, and made under the law for us, it stands good in law as fully satisfactory; for God gives a declaration of his justice in the justification of the sinner, Rom. iii. 24, but justice is not satisfied unless the law be so too. Whence the apostle concludes in the last verse of that chapter, ' We establish the law.' And indeed since the ' righteousness of the law' is said to be ' fulfilled in us,' Rom.

viii. 4, though performed only by our sponsor, it shews that by the gospel there is not made any exchange of the righteousness, but only of the persons.

The second principle that is mutually agreed on is this, that this satisfaction of the law is the proper righteousness of Christ, and that it is ours only as imputed, since he is our sponsor and surety, Heb. vii. 22, and made under the law for us, Gal. iv. 4.

These two principles, as granted by both, being thus laid down, I shall build upon them some conclusions subordinate to one another. The first of which will inquire and resolve, what and how much is that righteousness, in the abstract notion of it, which the law requires from the sinner, and how many parts there are of our justification? Whereby also will be evinced wherein a full conformity unto the law doth consist. The second conclusion will search out what and how much righteousness and conformity to the law may and ought to be found in Christ our sponsor, and to be imputed to us; where it will be demonstrated that this must be no other than the whole righteousness of the law. And both propositions compared together will demonstrate the cause why it must be so.

Conclusion 1. In the covenant of works, or the law, there are two things on our part that occur distinctly to be considered. 1. The fulfilling of the precept; which precept is twofold: *affirmative*, Thou shalt do this, to which alone the promise of life is by God graciously annexed. The other is *negative*, Thou shalt not do so and so, lest thou transgress. 2. There is the payment of the penalty if the man transgressed; Thou shalt surely die.

There is a great and observable, and to our purpose a material, difference between the precepts with the annexed promise and the denounced punishment. And the difference is this, that those precepts are absolute parts of the law, which by the right of creation simply and externally oblige. But the imposition of the punishment is only added as a conditional appendix, nor are we subject to it any otherwise than on certain conditions. To which this other thing may be added for the farther confirmation of it, that the mind of the lawgiver, which is indeed the law, primarily, absolutely, and *per se*, requires obedience by the precepts, but it threatens and exacts punishment as it were secondarily, and *per accidens*.

Conclusion 2. From this follows the second conclusion, That though in the primitive state of innocence we were only obliged to an obedience purely of the preceptive part of the law, yet being fallen into sin, we now are subjected absolutely to the precept and punishment together, and unable to discharge them.

The reason of it is drawn from the former conclusion which I laid down; because, since the penal payment is only conditional, and not so much required in the law, as in the appendix of it, it will not, though satisfied, invalidate that absolute and eternal obligation of the law itself. We are held bound by a double debt and by a double right. As creatures we are obliged by the law of creation to obedience, and that not only for the time past, but the future: and withal, as offenders, we are obliged by the right of the judge to undergo the punishment. Hence it is also evident, that the mere suffering of the punishment is not sufficient to the satisfaction of the law, because it doth not adequately answer that primary and absolute design of the legislator, who would rather have obedience than the death of the sinner. As thrusting the debtor into prison doth not vacate the debt, so neither doth the throwing of a sinner into hell satisfy what he owes; for one debt can never be discharged by the payment of another. Nor was there ever any law, even among men, either promising or declaring a reward due to the criminal, because he had undergone the punishment of his crimes. Now then the obligation of thy surety, O sinner, who undertook for all these thy debts, will not be less than thine. His passive obedience will not suffice unless joined with his active, nor his active do the work, if not followed with his death, whether that obedience future is to be performed, or was now at present owing. The active obedience alone would suffice if thou hadst not sinned, but then thou wouldst not have needed this surety; but now the righteousness required by the law is to be considered as lost by thee for the time past, and now therefore it will not be enough to render the principal debt, when thou hast contracted a new obligation to punishment, for thou wast unable to pay at thy appointed time. But be it so, that the death of thy sponsor, O sinner, shall be able to discharge all the past debt, and to cancel thy bond; yet since the law is an eternal covenant, and thou art an immortal soul, it will for the future require a new obedience from thee, and that to all eternity. But that penal payment of thy sponsor for thee, avails to no more than to restore thee to the same state in which Adam stood at the first moment of his creation; and though he had delivered thee eternally from all thy fore-acted sins, and past omissions, which are in number finite, yet he doth not supply to thee to be imputed that active righteousness which the law exacts from thee for the future. Hence the angel, in Dan. ix. 24, foretold concerning the Messiah, that 'when he had made an end of sins, and had expiated iniquities,' he should also 'bring in everlasting righteousness;' which being put upon thee, and thou being clothed with the Sun of righteousness, thou mayest in heaven be accounted righteous before God. For the grace of which thou art partaker, and which inhereth in glorified souls, though it be most perfect, can never attain to the righteousness and justification of the law, since to that, that old covenant must be antiquated and rendered invalid.

But as the death of thy surety will not restore thee to a state of righteousness, so neither would it ever bring thee to life. For the promise of life is made only to the doers, 'Do this, and thou shalt live.' And therefore justification of life, as the apostle calls it, Rom. v. 18, is attributed to the abounding of the gift of righteousness. And hence another corollary flows, which shall be the third conclusion.

Conclusion 3. All *that* is required to the justification of a sinner, which heretofore was requisite to the justification of Adam, and of the blessed angels. Nay, something more is required to our justification, because we are held bound by a double debt. For as it is certain that more is required to the sanctification of a sinner, since it is described not only by a mere simple creation out of nothing, but by the mortification of the old man, and the abolition of the body of sin, to which it is necessary the new creature be added, so the like account is to be stated in the justification of a sinner (of which sanctification is an image); the whole of it is not accomplished in the taking away of sins, as the angel speaks, unless, besides this, an active conformity to the law be added. Also to reconciliation (which is the effect of justification, and bears the likeness of its cause) all that is required which is requisite to procure a new and simple friendship, and something more, since it is the receiving of an old enemy into favour. Peace and pardon is first to be acquired; nor this alone, but also the old favour is to be obtained. This is apparent from the example of Absalom, who was not satisfied with peace and pardon obtained, 2 Sam. xiii., unless he saw the face of his father, and experienced his former favour. The same is also evident by the joint testimony of the angels, enumerating peace on earth, and good will towards men, as distinct parts of reconciliation, Luke ii. 14. To whom also the apostle doth accord, Col. i. 19, 20, 'It pleased the Father that in him should all fulness dwell,' viz., of righteousness and holiness ; but to what end ? ' That peace being made by his blood' (for the merit of his blood extends no farther than peace), 'God, by him might reconcile all things to himself,' ver. 20, which declares something farther than mere making of peace, and that to be obtained also by that fulness, which God to this end would have to dwell in him.

That all which was requisite in Adam should be an ingredient into our righteousness, is also evidently true, unless they will assert that we are constituted less righteous in the second Adam than in the first, when the apostle on the contrary affirms, that the gift of righteousness doth more super-abound in Christ, Rom. v. 15, 17. And indeed it is necessary that it should more super-abound, since more is required to our justification than to Adam's.

Hence at length ariseth the fourth conclusion, and which shall be the last in this order.

Conclusion 4. As many things as are required from the sinner by the law, it is necessary that so many concur that he may be restored into a state of justification, as parts of his justification, of which there are two the chiefest.

(1.) An absolution both from the punishment, and from all crimes and guilt of the fact, which answers contradistinctly to the negative part of the precept, ' Thou shalt not do this,' and to the annexed appendix of it, the denunciation of death. And by this absolution the guilty person is so acquitted, that he is freed from the obligation to punishment, and also is reputed never to have committed such sins.

(2.) There is a pronunciation of the person to be righteous, by which he is reputed to have done all those things which the law commands, and is adjudged worthy of eternal life, which is conformable to the affirmative part of the precept, and to the annexed promise.

And we may find so many parts of justification distinctly assigned in the Scriptures. The first of them is asserted by the apostle, Rom. iv. 7, 8, ' Saying, Blessed are they whose iniquities are forgiven, and whose sins are covered.' Ver. 8, ' Blessed is the man to whom the Lord will not impute sin.' The remission of sin in ver. 7 respects obligation to punishment. The not-imputation of sin, ver. 8, respects the act of sin itself, of which the person is so acquitted, so as not to be reputed guilty of the fact. For whereas in human courts of judicature there are two things take place : the accusation of the fact, which is the work of a witness, and the condemnation, or adjudging to punishment, which is the work of the judge ; the contrary seems to have place in God's court, when the business is there transacted concerning the justification of a sinner. He is judged so free from all punishment, as it is said, ' Who shall condemn him ?' Rom. viii. 34. And he also is absolved from the fact, as it is said, ' Who shall lay any thing to his charge ? ' ver. 33. He so imputes not sins, that neither the memory nor mention of them remain, and so that none are found, Jer. l. 20.

And this may be called the state of a believer's innocence, as the condition of the first father Adam when new created, and when he had not acquired any righteousness to himself by doing the law, is rather called a state of innocence than of righteousness; which though to suppose to be a certain middle state (by descending from a state of righteousness to a state of sin), would be a vain and foolish fancy; and such an one, imagined by the papists, wherein they say man was in his pure naturals, we deride as an absurd figment. Yet in the justification of a sinner, which is by ascending from a state of sin to a state of righteousness, such a middle state may at least be supposed. For there is a great disparity of reason which may be assigned between this case and the other.

1. For, first, whereas righteousness was what by nature ought to be in man, and necessary to him in his primitive state, he must therefore of necessity, when deprived of this original righteousness, fall into a state of sin. But that gift of justifying righteousness, all of it freely flows from God, and therefore both in pardoning our sins and in giving us Christ's righteousness, his grace illustriously shines out, and is to be acknowledged; and therefore such a middle state is supposable: that we may the better make a distinction between those two gifts, and to give the greater illustration of them, God, who bestows one benefit, not being bound to confer the other, Mat. xx. 15.

2. The justification of a man in his primitive state did flow from his own proper righteousness, though there was a justifying act of God concurring with it. And in man thus considered, a mere want of righteousness, though he had committed no sin, yet could not be called innocence, because that righteousness was what ought to be in him. But the justification of a sinner, as it supposeth nothing in the man, so neither doth it expect or wait for something to be in him, but it is a pure act of God, and imports a respect to the mind of God justifying, who, as he calls those things which are not as though they were, so he can look on those things as not due which are due, and by pardoning remit them. Therefore a pardoned sinner may be said yet to want that righteousness which ought to be in him; yet since justification expects nothing in the subject, God of his mere grace may pronounce him to be innocent; and by his remission he may account that privative want of what should be in man for a mere negative.

In a word, though pardon and the consequent imputation of righteousness are never to be separated (so that the state of innocence, in which I have but made a supposition a pardoned sinner to be, is never really existent), yet they are not to be confounded; and therefore, that we might have distinct thoughts both of the one and the other, I made the foregoing supposition.

The same is to be said concerning acquitment from death, and acceptance to life, between which a middle state may be supposed to be, though the subject not existing, viz., a state of annihilation, which if God should vouchsafe to the sinner, it would be a favour, since Christ says of Judas, that ' it would have been better for him if he had not been born,' or if he should be annihilated.

Therefore over and above the man's absolution, there is some other thing to be added, viz., the imputation of righteousness; to which is annexed, acceptance to life, of which the apostle speaks distinctly, Rom. v. 19, when he affirms the obedience of one man to constitute many righteous; which in the preceding verse he had called justification of life, or to eternal life; which contains in itself two parts of righteousness, as the law also requires, viz., a habitual holiness of nature, and active righteousness of life. For since we are to be constituted no less righteous in the second Adam than the first Adam was to be, as we said before; and since Adam in law appeared righteous, both by habitual holiness in his created nature—which certainly God approved as conformable to the law, since he approved of all his works as good—and then at length active righteousness, viz., a perfect fulfilling of the law was to be added to justification of life; since these, I say, were requisite in him, it also is necessary that we should be constituted righteous before God by both these righteousnesses imputed.

And thus we have finished the first part of this discourse; and you have heard an entire conformity to the law, both active and passive, to be required to the justification of a sinner. We now hasten to the second part, which is to treat concerning the righteousness which is in Christ; and here in like manner I will frame four conclusions.

Conclusion 5. That so many parts of righteousness, as completing the whole righteousness of Christ, are in like manner to be seen in him, as you heard them to be required in the law, and to be parts of our justification, and which seem to be a sufficient payment, and proportionated answerably to our debts, as also exactly to agree to the assigned parts of our justification, as matter adequate, accommodated, and squared to it. There is no need of a long and large enumeration of particulars. Would you have freedom from the curse of the law? Christ is made a curse, that he might redeem us from the curse of the law, Gal. iii. 13. And he bore our sorrows, Isa. liii. 4. Would you be so acquitted that your sins may not be imputed? He who knew no sin was made sin for us, 1 Cor. v. 21. Neither in his death alone was he numbered among transgressors, Isa. liii. 11; ' who was separate from sinners,' Heb vii ; but also in his life, in his most exact subjection to the ceremonial law, by which he professed himself to be the greatest sinner, since those rites were a public confession of sins. And Christ was circumcised (as Austin rightly observes) as if he had been born in sins; and the like may be said of his other observances; and so both imputatively and reputatively he was made sin, that it might not be imputed unto us. Now I place his obedience to the ceremonial law to the account of his passive obedience. For what is more grievous than for him who knew not sin but as the greatest of all evils, to act the part of a sinner in the likeness of sinful flesh, not only in suffering, but in observing those ceremonies of the law which were required of men as sinners to observe; what thing I say, more sharp and grievous than this, could so much as be imagined?

Do you desire a righteousness of nature to be superadded to all this? That holy thing is called the Son of God, Luke i. 35, that by that sanctification of our nature in him, he might condemn sin in the flesh, Rom. viii. 3.

Do you further desire a righteousness of life? As he came not to dissolve the law, but to fulfil it, so he did perfectly accomplish it, John viii. 29. And to what end did he this? The apostle gives an answer, Rom. x. 3, 4, ' For they, being ignorant of God's righteousness, and going about to establish their own righteousness, have not submitted themselves unto the righteousness of God.' Ver. 4, ' For Christ is the end of the law for righteousness to every one that believeth.' Christ is the end of the law, not destructive of it, but to perfect it (as Austin says); but in what? In justification, of which the apostle there speaks, when he says this in opposition to a man's own righteousness, which the Jews endeavoured to establish. It was, indeed, the part of the law to justify in man's primitive state, and to that it was ordained; but Christ only attained the accomplishment of this design. And for whom? Not for himself, to justify himself only, but ' he is the end of the law for righteousness *to every one who believeth.*' Whenas the end of the law was the righteousness of man, Christ, being now made ' the Lord our righteousness,' is called the end of the law. But by what obedience to the law is he so ? What ! By his passive only ? No; for that same righteousness must Christ bring, which if it were not brought, the law would be frustrated of its end, or he could not be said to be the end of the law. But that righteousness is active ; and to put it out of all dispute that this righteousness is meant, the apostle adds, that ' the law says, that by doing a man shall live,' ver. 5.

Conclusion 6. The sixth conclusion follows, that all this complete righteousness in Christ, and which answers the law, since it is not wholly due from him, but hath the nature of merit in it, therefore it may be imputed to the sinner. Let it be granted, that if some part of his righteousness was due for himself, that could not be imputed ; yet this also must be insinuated, that if the obedience of Adam, as well as his sin, by virtue of the covenant made with us as in him, should have been imputed not only to him, but to us, though all of it was due from him for himself, why is there not the same reason in some respect that the righteousness of the second Adam should be so too ? Let Bernard be heard speaking in this cause. What ! Is it to be feared (says he) lest thy righteousness, O Lord, should not be sufficient both for thee and me, when of God thou art made righteousness unto me ? (And he speaks of that which is active.) It is a short cloak indeed which cannot cover two ; it will, O Lord, both cover me and thee.

But what though we grant it, that supposing this righteousness of Christ be due from him for himself, that it would not suffice at least for other sinners ; yet the contrary is proved by instances of its being meritorious, which then it is when it is not wholly due from Christ on his own account.

As to Christ's passive obedience, there is no doubt of its meriting ; and the same will appear to be true of all the rest. I will begin from Christ's birth.

The sanctification of his human nature is a natural due to him, it is true ; but since the divine person assuming it was before that assumption free whether he would assume it or no ; and in assuming man's nature, though most holy, he abased himself, and in this yielded obedience to his Father, Phil. ii. 7, 8; and he so assumed it, that after the assumption that holy thing born is called the Son of God, Luke i. 35 ; hence it will obtain the account of merit, since it was not in all respects due from the divine person. This holy thing indeed is called the Son of God, as the blood of Christ is called the blood of God ; but yet this Son of God did not want that holiness of the human nature, being himself full of the essential holiness of God, and therefore it was not in all respects due from him. It was for us Christ was holy: John xvii. 19, ' For them,' saith he, ' I sanctify myself.'

But this will be more clearly evident concerning Christ's obedience to the moral law. For,

1. The greatest part of it was not at all due for himself as man, at least not due in that manner as he performed it. For he might have been man, and yet have lived always in heaven, and then he would have been free (as now glorified he is) from many duties to be performed, both to God and man in this life, which yet he, whilst he lived amongst men, performed for us.

2. Whenas that holy one is called the Son of God, shall he not have

the prerogative of a son, and not of a servant only? And when he is called the Lord of the Sabbath, why not also of the rest of the law?

3. What though we grant him to have been subject as a creature, yet the obedience is of the whole person, and he is called 'the Lord our righteousness.' What therefore as a work would be entirely due from the human nature, shall be called the merit of the mediator God-man.

4. What though he now, made under the law, and become a servant, is held bound to the servitude of the law, as other men are kept, under the punishment of death? Yet, since the person assuming was before at his own dispose, and it was only to make satisfaction for us that he took upon him that condition of a servant, this service, though due, will be meritorious. For all motions have their specification and denomination from the begining and end of them. And as the danger is the greater in that condition, wherein now, having made himself a servant, he is bound to perform this service for himself, so much greater will be the merit, that for our sakes he exposed himself to that danger.

And this is yet more evident as to Christ's obedience unto the ceremonial law; for though he was indeed by nation a Jew, and a son of Abraham, yet unless he had been a sinner, he was not bound to it, as only the sinners of the Jews were subject to it. And though those rites of the law at that time were the manner of divine worship, yet they were not to be observed but by sinners. Since, therefore, this whole obedience was performed for our sakes, and he was born for us, and made under the law for us, the whole of it may be imputed to us.

I will also add this: that since there was no need that these things should be done on the sole account of being qualifying conditions of our high priest, or as conferring merit on his passive obedience, since the alone dignity of his person brought enough of both these, Heb. ix. 14; therefore all this obedience is performed on our account, and ought to be imputed to us, since otherwise it would be to no purpose. But this will be more clearly demonstrated in the following conclusion, which is this:

Conclusion 7. All these single parts of the righteousness of Christ, though they are of an infinite merit intensively, yet extensively they are not so, but in their imputation unto us for righteousness they are to be limited to that kind of righteousness only to which they belong.

To explain the meaning of the conclusion, and to illustrate it by a parity of reason. Let us consider, that as all the merits of the whole righteousness of Christ performed in man's nature are not extended to the angels, Heb. ii. 6, 7—though as to mankind they would suffice to save and justify innumerable millions, and therefore they are said to be, though not intensively, yet extensively, infinite—so there is the same reason in all the several parts of the same righteousness compared one with another; so that though the merit of the passive obedience avails to cancel all our debts of suffering or punishment which are within its sphere, nay, and is sufficient to expiate the guilt of the sins of the whole world, yet it cannot stand in the room of the active righteousness required by the law, because it is out of its sphere and kind. And so in like manner neither can the active righteousness of Christ avail to discharge the due parts of the passive; and therefore though each of them is intensively infinite, yet not extensively.

So then, whereas there is a double debt of punishment and obedience required in the law from us sinners, the passive righteousness, though in itself of infinite merit, will not suffice for both of them; and therefore, since an entire satisfaction of the law is exacted from us, the whole righteousness of Christ, active and passive, ought to be imputed. And God will require obedience as a satisfaction to the law, not only redundant in a singular kind of merit, but as accomplished in its own particular way and kind. And for this he would have all fulness which denotes perfection of degrees, and all fulness as denoting a perfection of parts, to dwell in Christ, in order to our reconciliation, Col. i. 19, 20, that we might be complete in him, Col. ii. 10. As it is thus in other parts of our salvation, so in justification also, since Christ is all in all, and is made all things to us, ' wisdom, righteousness, sanctification, and redemption,' 1 Cor. i. 30; where, since by ' wisdom ' may accommodately be understood inherent righteousness, in which sense it is often taken by a *synecdoche*, and by its redundancy there it ought so to be understood, Christ is made all the other things to us by the imputation of his righteousness, *sanctification* by the merit of the sancti- fication of his nature, *righteousness* by the merit of his active obedience, and *redemption* by his passive. And in the same order, though inverted, he doth in the like manner enumerate the parts of justification in his epistle to the Romans, as remission of sins by Christ's death, chap. iv.* And in the beginning of chap. v.,* he says that Christ is made redemption; and then in the end of that chapter he says, that he constitutes us righteous by his active righteousness, which to be meant there is certain, both in that he calls it obedience, and not only so, but righteousness, and also that he calls the effect proportionate to in† justification of life. And it is more clearly manifest from ver. 17, where, comparing it with the alone disobe- dience of Adam, he says, ' If by one offence death reigned by one, much more shall life reign by one, in them who receive that abundance of grace, and of the gift of righteousness.' The comparison is so made, that the gift of righteousness is said to be abundant, not in merit only, but in quantity and number, for the multitude of the acts of righteousness seem to be opposed to the one disobedience of Adam ; therefore the alone passive right- eousness is not understood ; therefore his active is also imputed to us, and in respect of that too he is made righteousness to us. But when at last, in chap. vii., he had complained of the inherent remainders of sin, which he calls the law of the members of the flesh and of death, he comforts him- self at the first and second verses of chap. viii, in the justification obtained for him by the sanctification of Christ's human nature, which, therefore, in opposition to the other law of death, he calls a law of the spirit and of life; that is, a spiritual and inward law and principle of life, which he also affirms to be inherent in Christ ; and this (saith he) hath freed me from the law of sin and death ; and ver. 3, he affirms Christ sent in the likeness of flesh obnoxious to sin, and yet free from it, to have condemned in his flesh sin which was in ours. Which parts of justification, when the apostle had perfectly enumerated, he adds this as a conclusion in ver. 4, ' That the righteousness of the law might be fulfilled in us;' that is, that that absolute, complete, and universal conformity and satisfaction to the law, in suffer- ing the punishment and death, or obedience of life, and holiness of nature, required of sinners, being found in Christ, and communicated unto us by imputation, is said to be fulfilled in us, as if we had accomplished it. The whole righteousness therefore of Christ, as it ought to be imputed, so *de facto* it is imputed unto us.

* These references do not seem to be correct. The former would appear to be to Rom. iii. 25; but the statement that ' Christ is made redemption' occurs nowhere but in 1 Cor. i. 30 quoted above.—Ed.

† Qu. ' it ' ?—Ed.

Let me, to conclude all, add an eighth and last proposition, with which I would not farther lengthen out the discourse, if it were not necessary to clear up the truth asserted.

Conclusion 8. Though these parts may be considered divisively, as composing the merit of our imputed righteousness, yet in the imputation itself they coalesce into one entire and undivided righteousness; nor is one part to be considered separate from the other. The conclusion is thus to be understood, that though, in the execution or performance of this righteousness, the parts of Christ's obedience were accomplished, one distinct from another, and successively, and at length completed by various acts, his passive obedience after the active, and the active after the sanctification of his nature; and though, secondly, an afflicted conscience meditating on its whole misery, and considering by piecemeal the several parts both of the sin and of the punishment, can therefore in that very righteousness of Christ, apprehended by faith, and therefore imputed, run over all the several parts of it as a proportionate remedy, and applicable to every one of his distempers; yet such a division is not to be thought of in the imputation, as though that was successive, or that one part of Christ's righteeousness was applied to us after another. And the reason is this: the law, since it is a handwriting, is not to be cancelled, till it be satisfied to the last farthing. Therefore no part of the debt can be said to be paid, unless it be all considered as paid, and the bond cancelled. Therefore the active righteousness of Christ cannot be said to be imputed, unless also at the same time his passive righteousness be supposed to be imputed; and on the contrary, not his passive without the active. For though the merit of one part (suppose it the passive righteousness) doth not depend on the other, viz., the active, yet the imputation of the merit of each part depends upon the other. Hence the apostle, 2 Cor. v. 21, says Christ is 'made sin,' and hath taken away the guilt and punishment of it, ' that we might be made the righteousness of God in him.' Not as if that passive righteousness was that by which we appear just before God; but this active righteousness would not be imputed, but upon supposition of the other. Hence therefore it comes to pass that, the whole work of justification is attributed to one part of this righteousness, and of right may be so, as it is often attributed to the death of Christ; which is often inculcated by the assertors of justification by Christ's passive righteousness alone. Thus we are said to be reconciled by Christ's death, and the like; and thus also the sanctification of Christ's nature is said to condemn sin in the flesh: which expressions are not to be taken in such a sense, as if the whole merit of imputed righteousness might be found in Christ's death (and so likewise as to the other), but because the imputation of his other righteousness depends upon this, as this also on the other. But it is attributed most often, and chiefly, to Christ's death, for several reasons, the principal of which is this: because it was the last part paid which cancelled the law's whole handwriting, and was as it were the completing of all the rest.

But yet of this we are to be advised, that though the whole force of the imputation flows from each part, and in the imputation a one, entire, and undivided righteousness is to be considered as resulting from all the parts together, yet this doth not hinder but that one part of your justification may be more attributed to one part of the righteousness than to another (as remission of sins to the death of Christ, and justification of life to his active obedience). For the like is found in sanctification; though the whole sanctifying virtue and energy flow together from his death and resurrection, yet mortification is rather ascribed to the virtue and power of Christ's death, as quickening or vivification to his resurrection; because mortification hath a greater similitude with his death, as the effect useth to have with its cause. So likewise remission of sins is rather attributed to Christ's death; justification of life to his active obedience, because of the greater congruity and correspondent proportion. As a whole, Christ is made mediator; and that he might be a fit one, it was requisite that he should partake of the natures of the persons between whom he was constituted mediator, and yet both of them should coalesce into one person, but without confounding them together; so that the whole mediatorial work should proceed from both natures, should reside in both, and should be ascribed to both, both of them concurring to every work of the mediator; and the whole Christ is mediator. In like manner it is as to the work of this mediation; and so the matter is, that both the active and passive obedience in our one entire justification bears some resemblance to the two natures of Christ in one person. For since we owed both of them to the law, he performed them both; and yet in the performance they were not divided one from the other (that I may allude to that of David concerning Saul and Jonathan), but were joined with a most strait and indissoluble bond. For Christ in his life had suffering actions, and he sustained in his death active passions, as Bernard speaks. But in the imputation and application of them to us, they coalesce with almost a hypostatical union into one entire righteousness; so that our whole righteousness proceeds from both, and resides in both, and it may be attributed to both, that the whole righteousness is imputed to us.

CHAPTER XX.*

That the perfect holiness of Christ's nature is imputed to a believer, to justify him against the condemnation of original sin.

The right context of Scripture is half the interpretation; and therefore I will shew the coherence of this with the foregoing chapter.

Now. These words refer to the former chapter, and it is as if he had thus spoken, 'It therefore follows from what I have said.' What had he said? He had made in his own person the lamentable complaint of a poor regenerate soul in his constant conflict; often foiled, and somewhat prevailed upon, as in ver. 23, 'The law in my members brings me into captivity to the law of sin.' But it is but the captivity of a prince, one of a prince-like spirit, though put upon drudgery to do what he hates: 'What I hate, that do I.' And for holy duties: 'I would do good,' says he, 'but find no strength for it.'

He describes here a regenerate man at his worst. It is evident he speaks of a godly man, one in Christ: 'O wretched man that I am, who shall deliver me? I thank God, through Jesus Christ our Lord,' says this man. Therefore he is a man in Christ. It is the greatest misery in the world to such a one to be thus beset with sin. There is no cross like it, and therefore, says he, ver. 24, 25, 'O wretched man that I am, who shall deliver me from the body of this death?' Ver. 25, 'I thank God, through Jesus Christ our Lord. So then, with the mind I myself serve the law of God; but with the flesh the law of sin.' He gives thanks for that deliverance he had in his eye; that he should be delivered from the power of sin at last,

* This chapter should evidently have had prefixed to it the text, Rom. viii. 1–4.—Ed.

and that he was freed from the guilt of it at present. And in the 25th verse he makes it clear he intends such a one (viz., a godly man) : ' So then,' says he, ' I myself with the mind do serve the law of God.'

Mark then the scope : ' There is therefore now,' &c. As if he should say, If it be the case of a man in Christ, to be as I have said ; if he that yet serves the law of sin in a great measure, is yet a man in Christ, because in his mind he serves the law of God ; then plainly there is no condemnation to such a one ; for here is the worst case you can suppose him in. I will premise two or three things.

1. That what is said between ver. 1 and ver. 5 is meant of justification.

2. That there is yet a conflict between grace and corrupt nature ; and yet no condemnation. It is meant of non-condemnation for the corruption of our nature. It might have been said, So far as a regenerate man is sinful, so far he is liable to condemnation. No, saith he, ' There is no condemnation to such a man ;' for he is ' in Christ,' and shall be preserved in him.

There is no condemnation to them who walk, &c. 1. They are in Christ Jesus. 2. They walk not after the flesh, but after the Spirit. These two restrain non-condemnation to such. Their being in Christ is the true original ground why there is no condemnation to them. Though their conflict be great, and corruptions strong ; yet being in Christ, and flying to him for help, there is no condemnation to them ' who walk not after the flesh, but after the Spirit.' This is a description who these are.

But does he mean it of such as are led captive by sin ? Is there no condemnation of them ? He must intend it of such, or he had said nothing. He is led captive ; but there is a spirit of regeneration in him that works against his lusts, even in the midst of his captivity. A poor soul hath some weak resistances against sin, even whiles he commits it. There is a thread of the renewed nature still runs through him ; he hath a pulse still, though it be but weak, and Jesus Christ knows it. There is a stream of spirit runs out against sin, and that is his walk. For otherwise, when a man has but weak resistances against sin, and is overcome, he would be out of Christ, and be in a state of condemnation.

Obs. 1. That our being in Christ, and united to him, is the fundamental constitution of a Christian. The state of a Christian is expressed so : Rom. xvi. 7, ' He was in Christ afore me ;' that is, he was converted afore me.

Obs. 2. That union with Christ is the first fundamental thing of justification, and sanctification, and all. Christ first takes us, and then sends his Spirit. He apprehends us first. It is not my being regenerate that puts me into a right of all those privileges, but it is Christ takes me, and then gives me his Spirit, faith, holiness, &c. It is through our union with Christ, and the perfect holiness of his nature, to whom we are united, that we partake of the privileges of the covenant of grace.

For the law of the Spirit of life in Christ Jesus. What is the law of the spirit of life ? It is known by its opposite, sin and death, that is, inherent corruption. So then the law of the Spirit of life in Christ Jesus is the holiness of his nature. It is called, ' the Spirit of life,' because it is the same that is in Christ. It is born of him, and this quickens us.

Why called a *law ?* For two reasons. 1. The inherent holiness of Christ's nature is called a law in Ps. xl. 8 (which is of Christ), ' Thy law is within my heart.' His delight to do God's will flowed from the writing of the law in his heart. 2. Because being in him, it had a right and authority to free us. A law has power to justify or condemn ; and this law, being in Christ, has power and authority to free us, by virtue of our union with him. And if you would know what is the reason that there is no condemnation to those in Christ, notwithstanding all the remaining corruptions that are in them, it is because there is such a perfect holiness in Christ, which being mine by my union with him, frees me from the law and power of sin and death.

Hath made me free, &c. As if he should say, It is the case of all the saints ; what belongs to me as a Christian, belongs to every one that is such, though ever so weak and small.

For what the law could not do. There was no remedy else. Had God made us new creatures, yet so far as corruption goes, so far had we been liable to condemnation. The law was too weak for that work, to free us from the condemnation of indwelling sin. I have a corrupt nature, and I am but flesh, and therefore can do no good upon it. A man is dead, and you will give him physic ; but though it be the strongest in the world, it works not. The man is dead ; that renders the strongest physic perfectly weak. And thus all the helps that are, if given to corrupt nature, could do nothing as to the freeing you from the power of sin ; but Christ is the only universal remedy, Acts xiii. 39.

What did God therefore do ? He ' sent his own Son in the likeness of sinful flesh, and for sin condemned sin in the flesh.' The holiness that is in Christ's nature takes away the condemning power of original corruption in us. *In the likeness of sinful flesh*, that is, with all the frailties that for sin were brought upon the flesh of man. Nay, he came into the world as one that was born in sin. He took upon him the personage of one born in sin. He was circumcised ; which signified the cutting off of original corruption. And his mother must be purified, as being defiled by the bearing of a sinful child. He bore our likeness every way. And the end of this was, to condemn sin in our nature. He was but the likeness of sinful flesh, yet had power to condemn that sin which is in us.

Condemned sin in the flesh. That is, he put it out of commission. If sin had its full power and authority, as by Moses' law it would have, it would condemn us ; but being put out of office, it is to be executed. It is condemned by the holiness of Christ's nature ; and being condemned itself, it cannot condemn you. This is in respect of corruption yet remaining, than which nothing can be more comfortable to a poor soul.

What is the ground of this assertion ? There are two reasons for it. One is, that whatever Jesus Christ did or suffered in this world for us, it hath an efficacy to free us ; it is as good law as ever was. The law says, ' Cursed is every one that continueth not in all things written in the law to do them.' And it speaks it to all that are under the law, Gal. iii. 10. How is this curse removed ? By as good law as that it came in by ; ver. 13, ' Christ hath redeemed us from the curse of the law, being made a curse for us.' He took sin upon himself, and so freed us. Everything that Jesus Christ did, it was for us. He was circumcised, and this by a just law procures for us the circumcision of our corrupt nature : Col. ii. 11, ' In whom also you are circumcised.' You were circumcised with him, because you you were in him, and so this his circumcision is yours, and made good upon you. This condemned sin in your flesh. There is never a sore we have, but Christ has a plaster for it.

The other reason of it is, the ordination of the Father. God sent his own Son, and he sent him for that very purpose, for sin. What came Christ into the world for ? For sin ; not to sin himself. He had not come into the world but for sin, namely, to take it away. He took away actual sin by his suffering; and original sin, by his taking on him the likeness of sinful flesh, which in him was perfectly sanctified.

And he was the Son of God. Had God created a man holy, and only put him into the world in the likeness of sinful flesh, that would not have taken away our sins. But for the Son of God to take on him our nature, that only could do it, 1 John i. 7, ' The blood of Jesus Christ his Son, cleanseth us from all sin.' The blood of angels could not have done it, but from the Son of God in our nature comes this virtue.

That the righteousness of the law might be fulfilled in us. The law had a righteousness against us; and ' whatever the law saith, it saith to them that are under the law;' and what the law saith, it saith it to sinners. Well, let the law say what it will, Christ answers it. It says, You are a sinner. Well, but Jesus Christ was made sin for me. You are under the curse. True, but Jesus Christ was made a curse for me, that I might be made the righteousness of God in him. The law is answered here again. There be three parts of justification. *First*, The taking away of actual sin; this is handled in chap. iii. ver 24, ' All have sinned,' &c. His passive obedience takes away the guilt of actual sin. But, *secondly*, we ought to have an actual righteousness reckoned to us. This is handled in Rom. v. 18, ' As by the offence of one, judgment came upon all men to condemnation; even so by the righteousness of one, the free gift came upon all unto justification of life.' The active obedience of Jesus Christ made many righteous. Justification lies not only in pardon of sin, but in the righteousness of Christ imputed to us, and imputed to us as Adam's sin was.

But the law is not fulfilled yet; for we have corruption of nature in us. The apostle therefore in this Rom. viii. 4, he brings in the *third* part of justification, viz., That Christ came into the world in our nature, and fulfilled the righteousness of the law, in having that nature perfectly holy. And now the righteousness of the law is fulfilled in all parts of it; here is a perfect justification, and we desire no more.

CHAPTER XXI.

That not only our legal, but our evangelical, righteousness is excluded from bearing any part in our justification.—Phil. iii. 9, explained and proved, that the apostle there renounceth not only his legal and pharisaical, but his evangelical, righteousness.

*And be found in him, not having mine own righteousness, which is of the law, but that which is through the faith of Christ, the righteousness which is of God through faith.—*PHIL. III. 9.

There are two things to be considered and proved.

I. That by his own righteousness, the righteousness which is of the law, is meant his inherent righteousness of sanctification, wrought in him after his conversion.

II. That by the righteousness which is by the faith of Christ, and the righteousness which is of God upon faith, is to be understood the righteousness of Christ, which was out of himself (and not his own) imputed by God, and received by him, through faith.

These are two righteousnesses so inconsistent one with the other, that if a man will *have* (as the word is) the one, he cannot be partaker of the

other. And accordingly we find in his own case and example, that he perfectly resigns up, yea, renounceth the one ; 'That I may be found, not
having mine own righteousness, which is of the law,' and wholly betakes
himself unto the other ; ' but that which is through the faith of Christ, the
righteousness of God which is upon faith.' And both the renunciation of
his own, and his eager contention after this other, do respect his righteousness of justification, or serve to set out the true righteousness thereof,
both negatively and affirmatively ; wherein he would be found afore God, so
as to be sure to be justified. This is a matter of infinite moment for every
Christian rightly to understand, and to exercise his faith about, in like manner as our apostle here doth, and that daily, both by way of renouncing
what is a man's own righteousness, and by way of dearest acceptation and
embracement of the other, which is done by faith.

The terms of opposition stand thus.

1. Not 'mine own' righteousness, but the 'righteousness which is of
God.'

2. Not the righteousness which is ' of the law,' but, the righteousness
which is ' by the faith of Christ ;' *law* and *faith* standing in terms of utter
incompatibility, as in respect to this righteousness.

Let the reader take this along with him, that whatever this his own
righteousness, &c., renounced, will prove to be, as also the opposite righteousness which he betakes himself to, and which he calls ' the righteousness of God through faith, and the faith of Christ' (whatever that also
in the arguing may prove to be), that he yet speaks of both as in respect
to justification, or his being accounted righteous before God at the latter
day.

There are none of any opinion, that I know of, that deny a righteousness for justification here to be meant ; only the quarrel is, about what it
is should be meant by that righteousness he calls ' the righteousness of the
faith of Christ,' and ' the righteousness of God,' as which he would have
for his justification ; and oppositely, what his ' own righteousness,' and
' which is of the law,' should be that he renounceth. But all agree, that
both are spoken in relation to his justification, both what righteousness he
would at no hand have to be justified by ; and also what he would be justified by.

And if you view the controversy about justification, in Paul's other epistles,
you will find it stated under the same terms that here it is. See Rom. iii.
ver. 20, ' Therefore by the deeds of the law shall no flesh be justified in his
sight : for by the law is the knowledge of sin.' Ver. 21, ' But now the
righteousness of God without the law is manifested, being witnessed by the
law and the prophets ;' ver. 22, ' Even the righteousness of God, which is
by faith of Jesus Christ, unto all and upon all them that believe ;' which
place exactly corresponds with this ; and in both, that righteousness, which
is in opposition to that of the law, is made our righteousness, whereby we
are justified. So as I need not trouble myself any further, that this in the
9th verse is spoken in respect to justification.

1. But the question is concerning his negative, what he should mean by
the righteousness of the law, which he would not have to be the matter of
his justification ; whether he means that old pharisaical righteousness which
he had aforehand mentioned, ver. 6, ' Touching the righteousness which
is in the law, blameless ;' or whether the inherent righteousness he had
acquired since his conversion, namely, that of true holiness, and his acts of
faith in Christ, and repentance for sin, should be that righteousness which

he here renounceth as to his justification, though otherwise never so excellent and desirable, and useful to other glorious ends and purposes.

2. Then again the question will be as touching the affirmative ; what that righteousness of God, and of faith, should be meant, whereby he would be justified. The question is, whether the righteousness of the new creature in us, as it contains all the actings and principles of faith, repentance, and new obedience, thence flowing, as complex together, and wrought by the grace of Christ in us, be not the righteousness here intended ; or whether it be not the righteousness of Christ alone, which was *extra* or out of Paul himself, but as imputed by God, and received only by faith, and imputed to him upon faith, was the matter of his justification in the affirmative part, when he says, ' But that' (righteousness, namely) ' which is through the faith of Christ, the righteousness which is of God upon faith.'

In speaking to these two, I shall not travel into the whole doctrine of justification, but keep strictly unto what the text leads me to in this 9th verse.

1. I begin with the exposition of the negative clause : ' Not having mine own righteousness, which is of the law.' Herein are two things.

(1.) Some evidences that his own righteousness in himself, after his conversion, and not only or chiefly that old righteousness under pharisaism, is meant in this his renunciation.

(2.) That this interpretation comporteth well with the phrases here used, to style that after conversion ; both,

[1.] His own righteousness ; and

[2.] Which is of the law.

And the necessity of speaking to these things lies in that appearance which is on the adverse side ; that sanctification and obedience after conversion are not our own, because wrought by Christ (say they) and the grace of God. Nor is it to be styled (say they) a righteousness of the law, because it is new evangelical gospel obedience, and wrought by the faith of Christ, and is termed God's righteousness, because he is the author of it anew.

I shall first give some general arguments that his old pharisaical righteousness afore conversion is not meant ; but,

1. For a first evidence, I observe how he had despatched his renunciation of his old pharisaical righteousness over and over before ; and that expressly, and particularly, and apart ; enumerated ver. 5, 6, and he utters that part in the time past, as that which he had done when converted, at his first acquaintance with Christ ; and how he did it ' for Christ,' that is, for his first obtaining of him ; and for his sake, then, which he expresseth, ver. 7, ' What things were gain to me' (that is, in his opinion to obtain life by), ' those I accounted loss for Christ ;' he speaks in the time past. But this here I say, he speaks in the present time now, long after his said conversion, and so in a separate manner from that foregone. And now he speaks after this manner, ' And doubtless I count all things but loss.' And in this speech are included not only (if at all) those things past, but all things whatever he had, that were his own of any kind, but especially what was his own righteousness inherent in him after his conversion, which yet was his own in a true sense ; all which, as to the point of justification, he professeth to undervalue in comparison of Christ, and that righteousness which he had by the faith of Christ ; as even he had despised his old righteousness before conversion. For the evidence of this let us consider, that so it was, that at that present time wherein he spake

this, there had been a new stock of inherent righteousness gained and acquired by him, which Christ had wrought in him upon and after his conversion ; and therefore it was in a true and proper sense his own righteousness (as I shall anon shew) in distinction from that without himself, which is through the faith of Christ. All which new-wrought righteousness succeeded in the room of that old righteousness of pharisaism, and which was now to him the best thing which he had, or could be supposed to have, which might properly be called his own, and wherein (if in anything) he might have cause to glory anew. So then there is in this 8th verse a second or superadded renunciation, of new things acquired after conversion, and increased in him unto that present time he wrote this, and it is expressed in this 8th verse with a new comprehensive addition of all things he had to that *now*, or present time he wrote this in, wrapped together with those things that in time past were or had been gain, ver. 7. And that he involves all, both old and new, is plain both from the forepart of that, ver. 8, ' Yea, doubtless, and I count all things but loss.' Of the old he had spoken, ver. 7. This ' all things,' therefore, here extends itself further than to those things which he had renounced in the verse before, even to all things else whatever beside those. And then he again redoubleth his speech, out of the vehemency of his spirit in this point, ' I have suffered the loss of all things ; ' as if he had said, I then broke (as we use to say) once for all, and for altogether. I suffered a shipwreck of all past, present, and to come, either which then I had in lading of old stock ; yea, and for time to come, of all future expectations from what righteousness should be again laden in me. Remember that he speaks it especially in relation to justification, so that he reckoned all the stock of righteousness which he had to trade with as not in the least valuable, to come in payment of that strict and complete righteousness required by the law. The light of which did then come upon him (as in Rom. vii. 9, 10, in his own person, and of his own conversion he speaks), and discovered to him that a universal perfect righteousness was it which was ordained for life, Gal. iii. 10. I thereupon (says he) suffered the loss of all, past or to come, as to the obtaining of eternal life by any righteousness of my own for ever. His timing it, ' I have counted all things loss, and I do at present count them but loss,' hath this plain meaning, that those all things he had then, and these all things he hath now as well as then, he doth alike, as to his justification, count dung. He had once for all at his conversion renounced his old righteousness, to the end to win Christ then, whom he thereupon did actually win. He came not then to him with any righteousness of his own to be justified thereby. And thus in the same way and manner he came to him still, and still he repeats the same language, ' I do count them all dung that I may win Christ,' in the same way of treaty as at the first ; and still he speaks of justification. As thus therefore he at conversion had long before cashiered his old pharisaical blamelessness as for justification, so he did at present in the like manner also undervalue and count dung all that was of his own righteousness, since to the end he might win Christ, and together with him that righteousness which was Christ's properly, instead of any of his own of what kind soever, or had ever been wrought, whether by grace after or without grace before. He came not to Christ with a new righteousness to be justified thereby now after his conversion, which he had not at first. And it is one and the same Christ also whom he would win, perfectly, entirely, and wholly the same in both, and for ever. There is not a new justification by Christ after, that was not from the first, but from first to last he is one and the same Christ; as he is said to be yesterday, and to-day, and for ever.

If any therefore should query, whether under these his present new things (as I may call them) he should involve his own righteousness acquired at, and by, and since his conversion unto Christ? I would reply, That his 'all things,' what was before, and is at present (as thus set in opposition unto Christ, and what was Christ's, as here they are), must surely be included in * this particular of his own new righteousness; for it is plain he means all things besides Christ, and what is purely Christ's, whom he would win, for which he thus accounteth all loss; and otherwise he would have excepted it. But he is so far from excepting it, that in the 9th verse he begins to specify that of all other as intended·; and so descends from that general of all things to make special and particular instances of that new righteousness of his own; and therein to shew, that as he had accounted all things in general but loss to win Christ, and to have an interest in his person, as in ver. 8, so that he accounts particularly all his own righteousness but dung that he might have Christ's righteousness, the righteousness which is through the faith of Christ, the righteousness of God by faith; than which coherence of 7th, 8th, and 9th verses, nothing can be alleged more consonant of one thing with and to another.

And I would demand of the opposites hereto, in what respect it can be understood that he should account all (even what was his new acquired righteousness) to be but dung, but in respect unto Christ's righteousness, which was out of himself? For in all other respects, as, namely, that it was the image of Christ, purchased by Christ, and wrought by Christ, so he set a high value upon it; and therefore it could be for no other respect he would trample on it as dung, but as in comparison to that righteousness which was Christ's, and derived by faith. Neither needed he to have thrown that away (as he doth) to win Christ's person; for the having it was not only consistent with Christ, but flowed from being 'found in him.'

2. Let us attentively mark the posture, or his placing of those following words about this his 'own righteousness,' and his 'being found in Christ.' He says not first in order that, not having mine own righteousness, I may be found in Christ, and so thereby have that righteousness which is by the the faith of Christ; which in all reason should have been the ranging of the words if he had intended in this place that old righteousness which he had had out of Christ; for look, as in the former verse he had first said, 'I have suffered the loss of all things, that I may win Christ,' so here, if his old righteousness had been meant, he would have first said, 'That not having mine own righteousness, I may be found in Christ.' For it is absolutely necessary unto our having Christ at first conversion to renounce and throw away in the first place whatever is our own, that we may obtain him; this, in the order and course of things, is absolutely necessary to be done, as a man's hand that is full of dirt must first empty itself, by throwing that away, ere it can receive and take into itself a new handful that is offered to it; and therefore in that order it would have been here expressed, whereas he placeth it in a different posture; and in the first place saith, 'That I may be found in Christ,' and then, 'not having mine own righteousness, but that which is of the faith of Christ,' &c. What doth this broadly insinuate other than this, that upon his being found in Christ (which above all he in the first place here desires), that that righteousness of his own which he hath had, or desires to have, wrought and

* Qu. 'in his "all things" . . . must surely be included this'?—ED.

continued upon his being found in 'him, might not be that righteousness which he would be justified by (for a righteousness to be justified by is his scope), neither that what thereof he hath hitherto had, or shall ever have from him, upon his being found in him, as being a righteousness of his own. The having which righteousness is not opposite to his being found in Christ; for he first supposeth his being in Christ, and supposeth it to have been wrought through his being in Christ, and to accompany and go along with his so being (whereas his old pharisaical was perfectly opposite to his being in Christ, and had been first absolutely renounced by him); but this new righteousness, flowing from Christ in him, though it were not opposite to his being in Christ, yet it being (as to the point of justification) opposite to that other righteousness, which is Christ's own righteousness, wherein justification doth alone consist, he therefore renounceth this of his own, after he is found in Christ, as to such a purpose; and had good reason so to do, because God had provided a much better, infinitely better, righteousness of his own as the donor, and of Christ himself as the worker, to be imputed to him and received by faith.

And this considered, the plain scope of the apostle in this verse is, That whereas there was a twofold righteousness, and both flowing from union with Christ, and a man's being one with him, or being found in him;—

1. One being a righteousness of sanctification, which is from Christ as the author of it, which yet he calls his own, because wrought in himself as the subject of it, though by Christ as the author.

2. Another, which is the righteousness of justification, which is the righteousness even of Christ himself, and God's righteousness, as he calls it, imputed to him upon believing, and received by faith.

And he is to have one of these for his justification, to plead afore the judgment-seat of God. In this choice I would not have that of *mine own*, I have had from him efficiently, says he, since I was found in him; but I would be found in him to have that righteousness of *his own*, which is conveyed by a faith, going out of myself unto him for it. For if I betake myself to mine own new righteousness, though I have it from him, yet because it is mine, it comes under the power and jurisdiction of the law, and will be judged of by the tenor of it; and so I must abide by a sentence according to the law, in case I seek to be justified by it, and thereby, if I plead it, I shall be cast.

Add unto this (not to make a new argument of it) that he having first said, 'And be found in Christ,' it had been utterly preposterous to have added after it, not having mine old pharisaical righteousness. For his not having, or renouncing, that old righteousness, must necessarily be supposed first done, ere he could be found in Christ. This were as absurd as for a wife new married to a second husband, her former husband being dead, for her to say, I would be found married to my second husband, and not found married to my former husband, whenas he is supposed first dead, and so that marriage and obligation utterly dissolved, ere she could be married to the new. To what purpose should she say, she would be found married to her new husband, and not to her old, whenas he is dead, or she could not seek to be found in the other? This is the apostle's own comparison, Rom vii., speaking of the very case afore us, namely, how the law being first dead, and we unto it, then it is we became married to Christ. I will for more plain evidence sake set down the words, from ver. 1 to ver. 5, ' Know ye not, brethren (for I speak to them that know the law), how that the law hath dominion over a man as long as he liveth? For the woman that hath an husband is bound by the law to her husband so long as he liveth : but if the husband be dead, she is loosed from the law of her husband. So then if, while her husband liveth, she is married to another man, she shall be called an adulteress ; but if her husband be dead, she is free from that law ; so that she is no adulteress, though she be married to another man. Wherefore, my brethren, ye also are become dead to the law by the body of Christ, that ye should be married to another, even to him who is raised from the dead, that we should bring forth fruit unto God.'

3. A third evidence is from the mind, meaning, and drift of his spirit, or the pulse thereof, as it beats in uttering those words, ' Not having mine own righteousness.' We must consider that he is not here upon a set delivering doctrinal assentions (though they are to be inferred thence), but upon a declaration of what was now, and had been since his conversion, the continual exercise of his spirit towards Christ, as to the point of his living on him for justification through faith, in this verse; as in respect unto living on him for sanctification, and other things, in the other following verses. This to be his general scope is apparent by the particulars he pursues, and the manner of his declaring it, namely, in his own example, which he presseth on them after, ver. 15 and 17, ' Let us therefore, as many as be perfect, be thus minded : and if in anything ye be otherwise minded, God shall reveal even this unto you. Brethren, be followers together of me, and mark them that walk so as ye have us for an example.' Now this being a daily exercise of his faith, in living upon Christ for a righteousness to be justified by, he doth express his vehement solicitude, and most earnest heedfulness and wariness, that his spirit should be carried right, and be sure that he pitch upon what was the true righteousness that God had appointed to justify men by, as being a matter of infinite moment ; as his discourses in his epistles to the Romans and Galatians do shew, it being said therein, that it is the glory of the gospel to reveal that righteousness, &c. His inserting so careful a renunciation negative, *not having*, as entering a caution about it over and above, shews this. And indeed to be guided unto the right truth in this point is a matter of wonderful difficulty and spiritual nicety, if I may in that word express it ; for the thing in itself is truly such, souls being apt to stumble at this stumbling-stone, as Rom. x. 3. And hence it is we find him here, in the practice of his soul concerning this thing, to have been most wary, as to the management of his soul about it. He had been deceived once in this point, and thought that righteousness to have been unto life and justification, which proved to be to condemnation and death, as Rom. vii., and he would not now be deceived a second time. Whilst therefore he says, negatively, ' Not having mine own righteousness,' he utters at once a great and real danger, if he should pitch upon what is not his true righteousness for justification, and withal, a most perfect jealousy and fear he had of this righteousness, lest he should be left unto it after all as his only righteousness. But especially, lest his own spirit should in the daily exercises of it be tempted unto that righteousness he intends, so as to mind and regard it as that which looked like unto that righteousness which he desires, now he is found in Christ, to be justified by, he speaks as a man that avoided a serpent. Now let us but consider, whether such an exercise, and frame, and apprehension of spirit as this, doth or might at all suit with the supposition of his old pharisaical right-eousness, to be the object of this exercise of thoughts and jealousies, &c. ; or at least, whether of the two, this other of his new acquired righteousness of

holiness, since he was found in Christ, doth not find more compliance and agreeableness to this exercise of his specified, and so to be intended far rather as the subject thereof.

(1.) For us to imagine that he meant to express any apprehension he had lest he might be found in his own pharisaical righteousness at the latter day, and so in respect of the danger of the thing itself to befall him, this were irrational. For from whence should that arise? Not from any suspicion he should ere he died return unto it again, either to trust in it for his righteousness, or that he should act according to the principles thereof again; this were to suppose he thought he might one day be tempted from Christ, whom his soul so dearly pursued after, and betake himself to his old course, and turn pharisee again, according unto those principles he had then walked in. Nor was it that he, falling from Christ, and from what righteousness he now had, should have no other left for him at the latter day, but that old righteousness, to stand upon afore God at that day; for he was sufficiently convinced that that was no righteousness. It cannot then be the apprehension of that fate to befall him that made him so solicitous. This is as to what may be supposed in reality.

(2.) Nor was it a fear and jealousy he had lest his own heart should betray him unto a recourse unto it for his justification, as once when he was without Christ he had, and lived on it. But the righteousness he here speaks of was a righteousness concerning which he expresseth a jealousy of, lest by having it in his eye in his daily exercise of faith for justification, he might derogate from that other righteousness he had in his aim.

The words import an avoidance of being found to have it, so much as in our thoughts, to any such purpose; not so much as to cast an eye, or look at any time upon it, as any way a righteousness to be regarded as for his justification. He would not be found having it in his eye, nor the least glance towards it, for any such purpose; much more, not having any such reliance in the least degree upon it, not for the whole world. And he speaks it not only for the present, but for the future all along, during the whole course of his following life, and not in relation only to his being found in it at the day of judgment. For the whole current of his speech, whereby he utters both this and what follows, shews what was the exercise of his spirit, the vehement contention of his soul, which he daily acted touching his justification, he therein speaking of himself as a practical example unto others, as was said ver. 10. Also he utters his care, that if possible God might never take him tardy in this manner in his own righteousness, not for a moment in his life.

Now, if his *not having mine own righteousness* hath this respect in it, then for us to think and imagine that this care and solicitude and daily practice of his should be ever used, and taken up about his old pharisaical righteousness, fearing lest his heart should ever be entangled with that any more, this would be yet far more absurd. What! that Paul, who had been so long and so highly acquainted with Christ, should be afraid of his own spirit, lest it should in the exercise of it be found looking any more unto that old, cast, unrighteous (wholly unrighteous) righteousness, or to have the least regard thereto, much less to have a thought of any expectancy of a righteousness of it, or from it, who can imagine it? Nay, I may say, it were a high folly to conceive that this old righteousness could have the face, or front, or appearance to tempt his heart in the least thereunto. Certainly not; for he had been so thoroughly and unrecoverably convinced of the utter wickedness (instead of its being a righteousness) of all those who are in that condition, as he had taken a final and eternal farewell of that, whatever should become of him, or whatever other righteousness he might betake himself unto ; and that so fully and finally, as that never any such thought should so much as look into his heart again, much less be entertained any more.

There is no ordinary convert that hath been thoroughly convinced of the unrighteousness of his estate in nature, that ever returns unto a good opinion thereof any more. ' The law came, and I died,' says our Paul of himself, Rom. vii.; and all his thoughts of life by the law did perish therewith ; as when a man dies, it is said, that ' his thoughts perish.'

But oppositely, if we take into consideration that other inherent newwrought righteousness of sanctification within him and us, though wrought by Christ and by grace, there is a real and continual likelihood lest that should be ever and anon offering itself to our thoughts, to be looked at for our justifying righteousness ; and so that interpretation thereof will well bear all this jealousy and exercise of spirit about it, as to this matter. The root of the old corruption of self-confidence doth still remain, when the old righteousness that formerly was the matter of that confidence is wholly cut off, withered, and dead ; and ever and anon that old root will be sprouting forth of new branches of confidence from that new righteousness; and daily temptations and puttings forth there are thereto. That spick and span new creature, the image of Adam's holiness in his creation, and of Christ the second Adam, is alluring the eyes of the soul unto itself, to trust in it; and because it is a true righteousness before God, and accepted by him,—as Acts x. 35, ' But in every nation, he that feareth God and worketh righteousness is accepted of him,'—though not for justification; yet we are apt hereupon to be diverted from Christ and his righteousness for justification by glances at, yea, porings upon it, as our righteousness for justification also. He that discerns not such workings of spirit in him knows not his own heart; yea, and there is a prevailing of this in some men's hearts who are godly, that hath occasioned the pleading for this new righteousness, and arguing for justification by it.

There is nothing so natural to us in all estates as this, both before we have grace and after. Before we have grace, we trust to moral righteousness : see Rom. x. 3, ' For they being ignorant of God's righteousness, and going about to establish their own righteousness,' have not submitted themselves unto the righteousness of God.' Men do *sibi fidere* (as the Stoics' maxim was), trust to themselves ; and after grace, upon the same principle, we are apt to trust to our own holiness, even because it is our own, upon which ground he here renounceth it. Men are wonderfully prone to value, or at least regard it too much as a righteousness of their own. It is a saying which the papists quarrel at Luther for, yet spoken by him for this respect now mentioned and insisted on, and now fetched out of deep experience of the haunts of his own heart, in having recourse unto what was in himself : *Cavendum est a peccatis, sed multo magis ab operibus bonis ;* a man must take heed of his sins, but much more of his good works. And the danger of the heart's so trusting to them (which our apostle was infinitely sensible of) is, that in so doing, a man doth derogate from what God and Christ are (as was said) most tender of, and most jealous in. At so great a height do they hold up the value and the esteem of their own justifying righteousness above all other things, wherein their glory is concerned.

There was then a just reason for the apostle's entering his protestation so vehemently against this righteousness, and uttering his fear and jealousy of his own heart about it, and lopping off continually those sproutings of it as they did arise. And whenever he came to exercise faith about justification, he had reason to speak resolutely, what righteousness he would have, and what not.

Only let me put in this caution ere I conclude this. Far be it from us to understand his vote and desire here, not to have a righteousness of his own, of sanctification simply, or not at all; his desire is sufficiently shewn to be after that, even to a perfection of it, in ver. 12; such a perfection as, if it had been possible, he would have attained that which those shall have that are risen from the dead, yea, and to have had his whole portion and allotment of holiness, which was in Christ's hands to bestow, presently bestowed upon him, ver. 11–13. And yet, whilst he would thus have it to glorify God and Christ, he would not have it as his righteousness to stand by for his justification afore God, nor would he have his heart regard it to any such purpose. But as so considered, he divests himself of it, and undervalues it, for that super-excelling righteousness of Christ.

4. My fourth and last argument is, that this his old pharisaical righteousness was not a righteousness, *nedum justitia*, as Chamier and others have urged. I add this to what they urge this way, that after his being so enlightened and possessed against his old righteousness, and seeking to be found in Christ, he would not, at any hand, have styled that as a righteousness, nor give it the honour to name it such, but the perfect contrary, even utter wickedness and sinfulness. Would he call (think we) his persecuting the church, though out of zeal to the law, whereof at ver. 6 he had spoken, and which in his pharisaism he esteemed as a part, yea, the eminent top and crown of his legal righteousness, when he did it out of zeal for the law,—would he now call this a righteousness of the law upon any account whatsoever?* The issue and upshot of which zeal was to leave upon him the style of his having been the chiefest of sinners, 1 Tim. i. 15. And would he honour this with the denomination of a righteousness? It is true indeed, that of that other part (the best part) of his deportment in conformity to the outward letter of the commands ('the oldness of the letter,' as elsewhere he slights it), he thus speaks in the same ver. 6, that 'touching the righteousness which is in the law, he was blameless;' yet he minceth it you see. He durst not say, he was *righteous* according unto it, in the least degree, but only *blameless;* that is, he had an outward conversation as might obtain the name of blameless as afore men, that were not able to charge him with the breach of it in an outward gross act. But this was far from that righteousness which the law commands, by the righteousness of which he aimed to be righteous, but himself confesseth he was but blameless afore men at best. But now, the righteousness he had of sanctification, since he was converted, had a true, real, inward conformity to the spirit of the law in the inward man, and so a righteousness (though imperfect) answering to the spiritual part of the law (the newness of the spirit, as Rom. vii. 6), as well as the outward; he was now 'a Jew inwardly,' and not in the letter, 'whose praise is not of men, but of God,' Rom. ii. 29, and so had now, and never till now, a true righteousness of the law inherent to renounce for Christ. But now he had. For in this respect, 'he that doth righteousness is righteous,' 1 John iii. 7. In that former state he was in a true sense 'without the law,' Rom. vii. 9; that is, without the true spiritual light of the law, and therefore much more was he then without any true righteous-

* Thus Bishop Downham urgeth it.

ness of the law in the least degree. It was then neither a righteousness, nor of the law ; and therefore, if we consider the thing itself, that which he calls his own righteousness must be that since his conversion.

But you will say, he speaks thus of it, according to the opinion himself had of it whilst a pharisee. Then he did within himself verily think it to be a true righteousness, and it was esteemed such by others ; and therefore he speaks of it at that rate here, as often in Scripture we find things spoken of according to the opinion men have of a thing ; and so, that on this account it should be, that he styles the righteousness of the carnal Jews their own righteousness, Rom. x. 3.

The reply is (and it strengthens the argument), that you must consider the time and season wherein he spake it, and so spake it according to his own opinion of himself at that season. It is at the present time now, many years after his conversion, he says it, as in ver. 8 he had indigitated : *I do*, and *I do at present*; and the season was when 'the darkness was now past,' 1 John ii. 8, and the true light had now shined. And therefore he now speaks of things as they were in reality ; 'the commandment came,' and so I, having the true light of it, 'I died', saith he, Rom. vii. 9, to all that which I esteemed to be righteousness, and for life afore. And I am in so deep a conviction of it, as never after will I call it righteousness any more. And therefore, looking now upon it with the same eyes, now when he uttered this, that he did then at his conversion, he would not deign it the name of righteousness, not now at least, who at best had entitled it but blamelessness, even just now afore, but would rather affirm no righteousness to be at all in it.

And though speaking according to the opinion that others had or might have of themselves, he terms theirs their own righteousness, when yet they never had any ; yet here, speaking of himself, in his own present case, and of his righteousness, at a season when indeed he had both a new righteousness of his own, truly such, and having had it long, and also new eyes to behold things with, and was able to judge righteous judgment of things as they were ; should he now be thought to speak at such a rate, and call that a righteousness, which he afore never truly had, but in a false opinion of it ? What should he thus express his old opinion of it, and mean that, rather than that which is in itself a true righteousness, and which, to be sure, he had now in truth : this, namely, of sanctification, conformable unto the law, as it is a rule of holiness ? Who can think thus of the apostle ?

When those that were saints, already converted, speak of themselves, and of their righteousness, renouncing it as to their justification, as the apostle doth here, Isa. lxiv. 6, they speak there of it in this manner, 'But we are all as an unclean thing, and all our righteousnesses are as filthy rags;' and Dan. ix. 18, ' We do not present our supplications afore thee for our righteousnesses, but for thy great mercies.' Can we think that these meant other than the righteousness of true sanctification they had, though defiled with sin ? Yes ; certainly of their new nature, as the best thing they had since their regeneration; and so is this speech of our apostle here to be paralleled and understood.

The next inquisition is, whether the new inherent righteousness of a believer may be termed a man's own righteousness ?

The ground of the objection made by those that would have the old pharisaical righteoussness only to be so understood is this, that they do distinguish and say, that that only is properly a man's own righteousness, and of the law, which is done by the strength of those principles a man had in nature, and the force of that light and motives or provocations of the law, either that of nature or the moral law ; and so may truly and properly be termed our own. But that which is after conversion, that is not to be called ours, because wrought by the help of grace, and is called God's righteousness in that respect. And this objection may be edged with this, that when the legal righteousness of unregenerate men is spoken of, there indeed it is called a man's own righteousness ; as of the Jews, Rom. x. 3, 'For they being ignorant of God's righteousness, and going about to establish their own righteousness, have not submitted themselves unto the righteousness of God.'

The answer or reply is, that inherent righteousness after conversion is styled frequently in Scripture ours, or our own, and the very principles and habits of graces, though infused by God, yet because we are the subjects in whom they are wrought, and into whom they are infused, they are therefore truly styled ours. Nay, nothing is more ours, says Zanchy on the place,* insomuch as it is said, not only that they are wrought in us, but that we ourselves are the workmanship that is new created when these inherent graces are wrought, Eph. ii. 10. When Adam was created of God, and all his graces with him, I hope it may be said his virtues were his own. And thus, the principles or habits wherein we are passive, are yet styled ours. Then the actions, works, and operations which flow from thence are much more ours ; for therein we actively concur with God, and they are our actions and works, flowing from the vital principles of habitual graces and man's will, &c., which are in ourselves, and indeed ourselves. God gives indeed, that we may will, and gives us to will, but still it is we that will. There is nothing more the gift of God than faith, Eph. ii. 8, yet that faith given us is reckoned (I trow) our faith. Christ terms it their faith, Matt. ix. 2, and thy faith, ver. 22 ; and your faith is spoken of in all the world, Rom. i. 8.

Thus all other graces, and the workings of them, are called ours.† 'From me is thy fruit found,' Hosea xiv. 8 ; from God as the efficient, and yet thine as the subject. The prayers we make, although one exercise we perform, is more the work of the Holy Ghost in us, Rom. viii. 26, 27 ; yet it is said they are our prayers, and not the Holy Ghost's prayers, or that they are his prayers.

3. We may consider that it is so called in opposition to that righteousness that is another's, which is ours no otherwise than as imputed to us ; it is not inherent in us.

Now, if you will further see the ground the Scripture gives why the righteousness that is thus ours, though by grace, is excluded from justifying of us, it is even because it is ours, *subjectivè*, or subjectively, although wrought by the grace of God efficiently. And by the way, it is strange that those men that make good works to depend more (or as much at

---

* *Nihil magis nostrum quàm quod est infusum a Deo.*—Zanch. in verba.

† 'The sincerity of *your* love,' says the apostle, 2 Cor. viii. 8, which is called *theirs ;* because, though wrought by God, chap. ix. 15, which he thanks God for, as an unspeakable gift, yet was wrought and subjected in their wills, as ver. 10 of the 8th chapter, ' You have begun not only to do, but to be willing ; ' and yet was from God, who works in us to will and to do of his own good pleasure, Phil. ii. 13. Why should I instance more ? ' Both your faith in Christ and love to all saints,' Eph. i. 15 The like, Phil. i. 5. So, good works, ours : ' *Thy* good works,' Rev. ii. 2, and ' *thy* patience,' chap. iii. 10. ' In *your* patience possess your souls,' Luke xxi. 19. Ps. xviii. 20, 26, 35, ' According to *my* righteousness God recompensed me.'

least) on the will of man than on the grace of God, in God's co-working
with man, and whilst they are discoursing upon that head, do derogate
from that grace so much—that yet they should, when they treat of the
point of justification, then magnify these works by this, that they are the
effects of the grace of God, and not our own, so to prefer them to the
dignity of justifying of us, detracting from the grace of God in both; whilst
we that ascribe so much to the grace of God in the working of grace in us,
further than they, even to his working the will and the deed, should yet
contend that these works of grace are excluded notwithstanding from all,
or any ingrediency into our justification, because they yet may be truly
termed our works, and our righteousness, comparatively unto a more divine
glorious righteousness, which is another's, which is styled here, ' the righteousness of God,' as wholly his, abstracted from any thing that is of his
work that is in us, and in full opposition to this other of ours. Rom. iv. 2,
' For if Abraham was justified by works, he hath whereof to glory, but not
before God.' And the instance from his example is such as is invincible;
for he speaks not of Abraham's works afore his conversion, when in Chaldea,
and an idolater, and so to exclude boasting therein, but when *in medio pie-
tatis cursu*, when he was in the midst, and in a high course and progress of
holiness, many years after his conversion; and to that time that speech of
his being justified (which follows) doth evidently refer, ver. 3, ' But what
saith the scripture? Abraham believed God, and it was counted to him
for righteousness.' For if any one in reasoning will fetch a maxim or rule
out of an instance, that instance or example must extend and be proportioned to that rule; and that rule or maxim also must suit and agree with
what the instance alleged most properly concerns and is extended unto.
Now, the apostle's maxim afore had been, Rom. iii., that God is so, or in
such a manner, a justifier, ver. 26, as to exclude boasting by works; ver.
27, 28, ' Where is boasting then? It is excluded. By what law? of
works? Nay; but by the law of faith. Therefore we conclude, that a
man is justified by faith, without the deeds of the law.' And for the proof
of what works that maxim reacheth or is extended unto, he brings Abraham his being justified by faith without works, even then when he had
done and wrought so many holy works after conversion. Thus in this
succeeding chap. iv. at the beginning. Therefore necessarily must this
maxim extend to those and such works of Abraham as were after conversion in a special manner; and from that instance of Abraham, it must be
intended as a general rule to all believers, and to exclude all men's works,
though never so holy, as well as his. Yea, if we examine it, that is the
very ground and reason why those works are also excluded, as well as those
afore; and it will prove to be even this in my text, that they are our own,
though wrought by the grace of God. Than which nothing is more point-
blank against their assertion and evasion. The ground or reason whereupon his and all the saints' works after conversion are excluded from any
influence into justifying us, is, that *boasting* be excluded.

And if it be further demanded, wherein should the danger of boasting
lie, if we were justified by such good and holy works after conversion?
This is reduced to no other but the very same in my text, that a man might
say, they were his *subjective*, and that they are acts of his will, and a righteousness of a man's own, although efficiently wrought by God.

The other instance for this is Eph. ii. 8–10, ' For by grace ye are saved
through faith; and that not of yourselves: it is the gift of God: not of
works, lest any man should boast. For we are his workmanship, created

in Christ Jesus unto good works, which God hath before ordained that we should walk in them.'   Where observe,

1. That therefore works are excluded, and faith only admitted, upon this account, to exclude boasting ; consonant unto Rom. iii. 27 and 28, ' Where is boasting then ? It is excluded. By what law ? of works ? Nay ; but by the law of faith.   Therefore we conclude, that a man is justified by faith, without the works of the law.'

2. That yet, these that are excluded are such good works, and holy principles of grace, together with their works, as are wrought in Christ, and by the grace of God (which is full to the point now in hand), for, ver. 10, he says, ' For we are his workmanship, created in Christ Jesus unto good works, which God hath before ordained that we should walk in them.' Here, both the principles are said to be of God : ' we are a new workmanship, created in Christ to good works ;' and also the works themselves are said to be from God, in those words, ' which God hath prepared that we should walk in them.'   He hath prepared them, and prepared us, in that he formed and fashioned us anew, and hath ordained those works also, but still not to give us the right of salvation by them.   But for that he hath ordained faith (that wholly ascribes all to his grace and to Christ) to do that ; so as it is all one with him to say (as here he doth), ye are saved by grace, and saved by faith ; but holiness and works, and the new creature, he hath ordained only to be the way to the possession of that salvation, which grace through faith doth interest us into.   So there it is said, ' that we should walk in them.'   And these good works and holy principles are also but a part of that salvation given us.

3. And chiefly, observe how he gives this as the very reason why their works are excluded ; because, although wrought every way by this grace, yet because (as is manifested) we are the subject of them,' we are his workmanship,' and 'that we should walk in them.'   This we spoils all as to justification and salvation ; for there would arise such a boasting as God could not bear, if we were saved by them, that is, so as to obtain right of salvation thereby.

Yea (which I most of all observe, this is the contrary unto what our bold asserters do argue), whereas they say, that because they are of grace, therefore they may justify without prejudice to grace ;—

4. The apostle carries that very thing as the reason to the contrary, and to exclude all inherent holiness after conversion, ver 10, as well as afore, even for this reason, because they are the effects of a new creation, and so given upon a supernatural account of mere grace, and anew bestowed by grace, after the great forfeiture of the first creation-holiness, and due to man's nature then, if God meant to have created man at all.   Which holiness so bestowed, and upon that account, did then justify man, and was so appointed to do, as the phrase Rom. iv. 4, spoken of the covenant of works, is ; which yet I would rather translate dueness than debt.   But that privilege works had by the law of creation was utterly forfeited by sin, and God laid his hand upon the forfeiture and took it, and took justification into his own hands, as that it should never be so more.   But if he justified a second time, it should be every way by grace, so and in such a manner as not at all by works of what kind soever.   Which account is given in the instance of Abraham, in that Rom. iv., and more fully Rom xi. 5, and is therefore called God's righteousness ; super-creation, supernatural righteousness, so that this maxim ariseth invincibly out of this place, Eph. ii., that the borrowed and restored grace of holiness, since the fall,

shall never justify ; but these works upon conversion are such ; read ver. 10, ' For we are his workmanship, created in Christ Jesus unto good works, which God hath before ordained that we should walk in them.'

God was infinitely tender of his glory, in point of justification, above all other of the parts and pieces of the application of salvation unto us, and so to preserve the glory of it to himself, and as that it should be his righteousness alone, and his Son Christ's ; for in other respects, and to other ends, he admits works to have some share, notwithstanding they be ours. Thus when we shall come to possess heaven, and that degree and measure of glory allotted us, it will be said, that God rewards us *secundum opera*, according to works, though not *propter*, or for works. So far good works are admitted ; and yet the saints are therein kept from boasting, because the fundamental original right, and great charter unto salvation, is past afore, and given upon another account ; and in point of justification, and our right to heaven, God is so tender and jealous, as he utterly and altogether excludes works, for giving a right thereunto in the least. It is the apostle's words, Rom. iii. 27. He will have nothing to do with them when it comes to that action of his ; he hath not, nor will ever have, any regard to them therein, nor should he ; and therefore the apostle had no eye to them here. But it is God's righteousness, wholly God's, and no way, or in no respect ours, but merely receiving it ; which is here set as the opposite to Paul's ' my righteousness,' in the text.

CHAPTER XXII.

That God appointed Christ to be the great shepherd, to take care of the elect souls given to him.—The mighty care and diligence which Christ exercises in discharge of this office.

Now the God of peace, that brought again from the dead our Lord Jesus, that great shepherd of the sheep, through the blood of the everlasting covenant, make you perfect in every good work to do his will, working in *you that which is well pleasing in his sight, through Jesus Christ; to whom be glory for ever and ever. Amen.—*HEB. XIII. 20, 21.

The reason of the pertinent coherence of one thing with another in a parcel of Scripture is often at first view not obvious; as here, why Christ as ' shepherd,' and then his ' resurrection,' are expressed under these phrases of being ' brought again from the dead,' and that ' by the blood of the everlasting covenant ;' how these should suit at first view is strange. And yet there is a great harmony in the jointing every one of these one with another. Therefore, for the opening the words, I shall do three* things.

1. Shew their aspect or reference to what went afore.
2. Shew why he brings in this title of *shepherd* in this epistle.
3. Shew their correspondency among themselves, and pertinency of each to each ; together with each particular.
4. Shew their reference to the prophecies of the Old Testament.
1. As to their reference to what went afore, we may consider them,
(1.) In their immediate reference to what went just afore.
(2.) Remotely, to some principal matters in this epistle.

* Qu. ' these ?'—ED.

(1.) As they refer to ver. 17, 18.

[1.] Where he had made mention of himself a pastor over pastors and churches, an apostle, and other their ordinary pastors, and from thence suitably upon this next occasion of mentioning Christ, he speaks of him as 'the great shepherd,' over apostles and all, and as one that could do that for them which no apostle could do, viz., to 'perfect them in every good work.' None of them were sufficient for one good thought of themselves, 2 Cor. iv., much less for any good work, or for every good work, especially to perfect others whom they were set over in the Lord, which Christ their shepherd could through their ministry; and therefore addresseth his prayer for this to God through him.

[2.] Himself (who was a great instrument through Christ of good unto their souls) was now absent and far off from them. The last foregoing words were that they would pray he might be restored to them the sooner; and here he chooseth forth such expressions about Christ, &c., as might prompt them with fit matter, or the most effectual arguments for that request, and a help unto their faith in that particular: though this is done obliquely, the matter here more directly serving unto that other petition that follows. But this argument lies in this, that that God who had brought back the great shepherd by his blood, &c., that the same God (who only could) would restore him to them out of all dangers, &c., through the same blood.

Obs. 1. Jesus Christ bears and bore the same offices whereinafter he places his officers under him in the church, thereby sanctifying of all offices and officers, which is a great comfort to church officers, and to the people of God and churches. He hath the title of Διάκονος, minister and deacon of the circumcision, Rom. xv. 8, and Mat. 20, 28, and Mark x. 45, Luke xxii. 27; bishop or elder, 1 Pet. ii. 25; a shepherd or pastor, 1 Pet. v. 1, 4, 5; an apostle, Heb. iii. 1; only with this difference, he the *great* shepherd, he the *chief* bishop, &c.

Obs. 2. The blood and resurrection of Christ, as of the great shepherd, do in their virtue bring ministers, that have a good conscience, and their people, together again. God restores them when driven away and scattered; fetcheth them out of prison, from silence, &c., yea, out of deaths and dangers, and brings them and their people together through the efficacy of these, 2 Cor. iv. 11, 14. There is not a church-meeting we have, but it is in the virtue of Christ's blood and resurrection.

(2.) The words are a prayer in the conclusion of this epistle, and the materials of it do refer to some principal matters treated of in this epistle, whereof the sum is gathered up into a prayer as the conclusion.

[1.] In this epistle the apostle affects to set forth Christ under several titles which the Old Testament had given him, and which had been taken for granted to be intended of the Messiah by the Jews themselves he wrote to. As,

1. A captain of salvation, chap. ii. As the angel that appeared to Joshua styles himself, Josh. v. 14, 15.

2. The apostle, chap. iii., or him whom God would send as the prophet like to Moses, chap. iii. 1, 2, and so on.

3. The great high priest, chap. iv., and so throughout this epistle.

4 And accordingly here at last in this prayer he attributes to him another title of shepherd, as famous in the prophecies as any, which includes all of his offices, as I shall shew.

5. Under whom these Jews were become as sheep, one shepherd and

one sheepfold; and all, both Jews and Gentiles, who are under him, called unto peace and unity by the God of peace.

6. He had treated also of that new covenant, chap. vii. 8, 9, &c., whereof Christ was the founder.

7. Of that blood of his, which had confirmed that covenant, chap. ix. throughout.

8. Of the virtue of that one offering, potent and effectual to perfect for ever them that his blood sanctifies, Heb. x., even to a non-remembrance of sins for ever, and procuring God to be at peace for ever, ' I will remember them no more.'

9. Of God's raising him up ' to sit down at God's right hand, having ' purged away our sins;' so chap. i. and chap. viii.

10. He had treated of the everlastingness of this salvation and covenant and redemption.

11. And as all along, and especially towards the conclusion of the epistle, having exhorted to many good works and duties, thereupon he shuts up all with this prayer, the sum of all these, containing a motive and persuasive in them with God, a most efficacious one to move him to grant power to enable them to do all those things which he had exhorted unto, and such as had themselves withal in them the most operative virtue perfectly to work the same in us, namely, his blood and resurrection. And ' that God' (prays he) ' through these make you perfect in every good work, to do his will, working in you that which is well-pleasing in his sight, through Jesus Christ; to whom be glory for ever and ever; Amen.'

Observe a great ground for ministers to gather up in their after-prayers the strength of what hath been said in the sermon, which the ancients styled a *collect*, as in the Common Prayer appears to this day in making a brief collect of what had been just afore read out of the Scriptures, and forming them up into a short prayer.

Why is it the apostle should insert this title of ' shepherd' and ' great shepherd' in this epistle?

Ans. The pertinency of his doing so in writing to the Hebrews doth many ways appear. The Jews expected the Messiah to be as a shepherd to them, as David their king and Moses had been, who were types of him. Moses and Aaron, Ps. lxxvii. 20, ' led the people as sheep.' David, Ps. lxxviii. 22. And under the name of David as a shepherd God had promised the Messiah to them, Ezek. xxxiv. 23, ' And I will set up one shepherd over them, and he shall feed them; even my servant David, he shall feed them, and he shall be their shepherd.' And Christ himself, when he came, had represented himself to them under that notion, John x., throughout that chapter.

Now those prophecies giving him that title, it was meet the apostle should somewhere in this epistle refer unto this, being as great, and the prophecy thereof as eminent, as of any other he in this epistle citeth; and it is his apparent design throughout the epistle to refer unto and quote out of the Old Testament what was most eminent in Christ, either about his titles or offices; only he chose to do this of his being a shepherd here last in a breviary by way of prayer.

That he hath such an eye and scope in this is evident by comparing the passages here, and those prophecies together.

I shall but single forth that one place, Ezek. xxxiv., and compare it with what is spoken here.

1. There, God promiseth to make a covenant of peace with his people

by Christ as a shepherd, so ver. 25 ; and here you have, 1. God in relation to this performance styled ' The God of peace ;' 2. The covenant also mentioned.

2. There, he promiseth to ' set up over them' this shepherd, ver. 28. Here the God of peace ' brings back' this shepherd, or, as Capellus reads it, ' brings up,' ἀναγαγὼν, from ἀνάγω, *rursum revocare;* for it may be ἀνὰ and ἄνω both, and so *to bring back, up,* or *to set up,* as the word in Ezekiel is.

3. There, he styles him that ' one shepherd,' ver. 23, which is in the import of it all one, as to say, ' the great shepherd ;' τὸν μέγαν, says the apostle here, as pointing to that one only shepherd ; in the prophet, *unicus,* or the only ; as of the church, Cant. vi. 9, ' My dove, my undefiled, is but one ; she is the only one of her mother, she is the choice one of her that bore her.' As Christ also says of himself, ' I am that good shepherd,' and I alone. For he adds, all shepherds else are but hirelings, John x.

4. There, in Ezekiel, he is called ' a prince ;' here, ' the Lord.' But the Jews little imagined what manner a shepherd he should be, and in what strange manner set up to be so. They indeed dreamed chiefly, and most of them, him only to have been so entitled in relation unto such deliverances outward as Moses had given them, and a prosperous state, such as David had set up, and Solomon, taking the covenant of peace for that of outward prosperity. They little thought this shepherd must be con-secrated, and made such, by his own blood. Hence therefore,

5. The apostle points them here unto those other prophecies of him, which punctually had described him to be such a shepherd as he here speaks of him, and how that that covenant of peace prophesied of by Ezekiel of him was to be made by his blood, and that it was a peace for their souls, and he a shepherd thereof, and for the doing away of their sins, and ruling and strengthening them to every good work, wherein principally this his office of shepherd was seen.

The first of the prophecies which under this relation he refers unto, is that in Isa. liii. 6, ' All we, like sheep, have gone astray ; we have turned every one to his own way ; and the Lord hath laid on him the iniquity of us all.' And therefore, withal, he there prophesies that he that was to be theirs, and our shepherd, was himself to ' be brought,' first, ' as a lamb to the slaughter,' &c., ver. 7. And here, his being ' brought again back' imports his having been first led away to death ; hence from that of Isaiah it appears that he who was their shepherd was first to be as a lamb offered up, and to give his life for his sheep : as John, x. 11, himself says, ' I am the good shepherd : the good shepherd giveth his life for his sheep ;' even ' that Lamb of God' John pointed to, and Peter, 1 Epistle chap. i. 19, ' But ye are redeemed with the precious blood of Christ, as of a lamb without blemish and without spot,' and the Lamb's blood in the Revelations often ; of whom, and of which sacrifice, all their sacrifices were types. It is highly observable, that the gate through which he was led to be crucified was termed the sheep-gate, for the sheep that were to be sacrificed were kept in meadows without that gate, and so were led, as he was, to be sacrificed, but they in the temple ; all which sheep and sacrifices and temple were types of him and his sacrifice, as in the same Isa. liii. 10. The apostle had even now said, Christ ' suffered without the gate,' in mount Golgotha, unto which he was led, as the other sheep were through that gate to the slaughter, as it is also expounded and applied by Philip, Acts viii. 82, ' He was led as a sheep to the slaughter ; and like a lamb dumb before the shearer, so opened he not his mouth.' It is also as evidently by Peter applied to him ; for having in his 1st chap. ver. 22 termed him the ' Lamb without spot,' by whose blood we are redeemed, in the 2d chap. ver. 24, 25, he cites some of those passages out of Isaiah of him, ' by whose stripes we are healed,' and what we were, referring us unto the rest, ' We, like sheep, had gone astray ; and God laid on him the iniquities of us all ;' which he interprets in ver. 24, ' Who his own self bare our sins in his own body on the tree, that we, being dead to sin, should live unto righteousness : by whose stripes ye were healed.' And that this he did for us as our shepherd, that was to lay down his life, as so as a sheep be led unto the slaughter, for us his sheep who had gone astray ; thus ver. 25 of that 2d chapter explains to us, ' For ye were as sheep going astray ; but are now returned unto the shepherd and bishop of your souls.' And again look as Isaiah says, that ' as a sheep afore the shearer, he opened not his mouth,' Isa. liii. 7 : so Peter hath it, ver. 22, 23, ' Who did no sin, neither was guile found in his mouth : who, when he was reviled, reviled not again ; when he suffered, he threatened not, but committed himself to him that judgeth righteously ;' thus manifestly expounding and applying that 53d of Isaiah unto him, both as a lamb in his death, as he was a shepherd in his resurrection.

And considered either as lamb or shepherd, we find that God being angry with him whilst thus he bore our sins, insomuch as he is said in his wrath to have smitten this shepherd with his sword, and smitten him unto death, Zech. xiii. 7, ' Awake, O sword, against my Shepherd, and against the man that is my fellow, saith the Lord of hosts : smite the Shepherd, and the sheep shall be scattered.' And that is another prophecy the apostle here looks in, and refers unto. And thus God was first a God of wrath against him for our sakes, God having laid upon him the iniquities of us all, and remained such against him until justice had satisfied itself thereby : ' The chastisement of our peace lay upon him,' or chastisement for our peace, Isa. liii. 5 ; and die he did for these sheep.

3. Because he was led thus as a sheep unto death, by which his dying is expressed by the prophet, therefore most pertinently of all other expressions he singles forth this, that he was ' brought back again from the dead' here, so setting forth his resurrection, and his being set up a shepherd over us. He was slain without the gate, and his dead body was laid without the gate, buried in a tomb there without the gate ; but God ' brought him back again' from the dead, and he came into Jerusalem among his disciples, and elsewhere, and then was also carried ἄνω, up to heaven, as the word also signifies.

And that this phrase here of being ' brought back from the dead,' thereby expressing his resurrection, should yet couch under it, and impliedly point unto that manner of his dying, of being ' led unto slaughter,' may elegantly be exemplified by the like parallel in the like opposite way, and *ordine inverso*, in that of our conversion to Christ (in which we are conformed to his death and resurrection). Now this our conversion to Christ, Peter termeth a ' returning to the shepherd of our souls.' From whom was it that Peter fetched this expression ? Even out of that contrary phrase, which, I say, had used to express our state afore conversion, and much as ' we, like sheep, had gone astray, and turned every one to his own way :' this is Isaiah's expression only ; but the apostle on the contrary, and in allusion to this, as fitly sets out our repentance, ' But are now returned to the shepherd of our souls,' ver. 25, which had imported our having turned away from him; and so conversion is a returning to him. And,

4. Because by his death he made our peace—Isa. liii. 5, 'The chastisement of our peace was upon him'—and by his blood made that peace for us, as Col. i. 20; hence God, that was wroth with him then, when he was led to death, and himself smote him (which phrase is used in Isa. liii. 4, as well as by Zechariah, and interpreted to be God's bruising him himself, ver. 10), is now upon a new style (when he brings him back) enstyled, 'The God of peace,' and that both towards him and us: Eph. ii. 14, 'He is our peace,' by dying, 'that he might reconcile both unto God in one body by the cross, having slain the enmity thereby,' ver. 16. God's justice being satisfied, his anger assuaged, and now he raiseth up Christ, as a God of peace, and thereupon both justified us and him; and in token he was at peace, he let our surety thus out of prison. It is in the same 53d of Isaiah, ver. 8, 'He was taken from prison and from judgment;' the suit was ended. I quote still such places wherein his dying as a lamb, &c., are mentioned, and for us as sheep. And,

5. Because this was done by a covenant betwixt God and him; therefore here that covenant is also mentioned, as it is also in the prophecy wherein first his being set up as a shepherd is spoken of, Ezek. xxxiv. 23–25; it is said to be by and with a 'covenant of peace,' ver. 25.

6. Yea, and in Ezek. xxxvii., having at ver. 24 promised to give them this one shepherd, he adds, ver. 26, 'I will make a covenant of peace, and it shall be an everlasting covenant;' even as in express words here it is styled 'the everlasting covenant,' when he speaks of him as of our shepherd, and this these other prophecies alluded unto also.

7. Here it is said, 'the blood of the everlasting covenant,' even as that by which Christ himself was raised up, &c. For by his blood, and the merit of it, it was that himself was raised up, after that our peace had been fully made up by him: John x. 16, 17, 'Other sheep I have, which are not of this fold: them also I must bring, and they shall hear my voice; and there shall be one fold, and one shepherd.' Ver. 17, 'Therefore doth my Father love me, because I lay down my life, that I might take it again.' Yea, his mediatory glory he did purchase over all anew, and so his resurrection, by his death, though not his personal: Rom. xiv. 9, 'To this end Christ both died, and rose, and revived, that he might be Lord both of the dead and living.' Phil. ii. 8, 9, 'And being found in fashion as a man, he humbled himself, and became obedient unto death, the death of the cross.' Ver. 9, 'Wherefore God also hath highly exalted him, and given him a name which is above every name.' All which was by covenant between God and him; as in that 53d of Isaiah, 'because he made his soul an offering for sin,' God promiseth to raise him up, and 'he should see the travail of his soul,' &c. And,

8. In using this phrase, 'By the blood,' &c., the apostle refers us to another passage in the prophecy of the same Zechariah, chap. ix. 11. And God makes Christ this promise, 'By the blood of thy covenant' (he speaks to Christ), 'I have sent forth thy prisoners out of the pit.' Zechariah speaks much of this shepherd, and those false shepherds that should then be when he should come amongst them, in several places of the same prophet; and in this 9th chapter he speaks of 'the flock of his people,' ver. 16; and the meaning of that speech, that by and for the merit of his blood it is that he gives forth all deliverances to his people from all evils, as from the grave and hell, and by merit of the blood of the same covenant which

they were delivered by, it was that Christ himself was, and whereby God brought Christ back again from the grave and hell; and because it was not done simply by mere contract and covenant, but also by merit, therefore it is not said only here that by his covenant he was brought back, but 'by the blood of his covenant' he was brought back.

And still you see (and it is to be observed) that all these prophecies of him were uttered when either he is prophesied of: as, 1. A lamb slain; or, 2. As a shepherd for his sheep; or, 3. As a shepherd set over his sheep; all which doth the apostle contract and gather together into one sum in these few words.

9. Because God as the God of peace sanctifies us throughout—1 Thess. v. 23, 'And the very God of peace sanctify you wholly,' &c.—and sanctifies us by covenant through Christ his blood, and the virtue thereof, as also through his being raised from the dead; hence in the force and influence of all these he here prays, ver. 21, 'Make you perfect in every good work to do his will, working in you that which is well pleasing in his sight, through Jesus Christ,' &c.; because Christ had by his blood, and once offering of himself, 'perfected for ever them that are sanctified,' as Heb. x. it is said.

10. And lastly, that Christ was proposed to be such a shepherd as should perfect his sheep in holiness and good works, and that God's covenant was with him, is as express in that Ezek. xxxvii. 24, 'And David my servant shall be king over them; and they all shall have one shepherd: they shall also walk in my judgments,' &c.

Thus you have seen that the words are a contract or sum both of this epistle and the prophecies; and having been thus opened in their correspondencies one with another, as also with the prophecies, I single out but one observation.

Obs. Christ is a shepherd, a great shepherd, that great shepherd mentioned by the prophets. All those patriarchs that were shepherds were types of him. Abel (whose blood in crying is made a type of his, chap. xii. 24) was a shepherd, and a type of him. And as in Abel blood and shepherd met, so in Christ here, a great shepherd and his blood are joined. Moses, a shepherd and a type of Christ; 'A prophet like to him' who, with Aaron, 'led the people as sheep,' Ps. lxxvii. 20. David, a shepherd, who, as a king, 'guided the people by the skilfulness of his hands,' Ps. lxxviii. 72, and therefore their shepherd is named by his name, Ezek. xxxiv. 23. A testimony we have recorded of the devils themselves (as in the Scripture, that he was 'the Son of God,' 'The Holy One of God,' so in heathen story), that he was that great shepherd. Plutarch, endeavouring to give a reason why their oracles ceased, says, 'That one Thamus a shipmaster, who, sailing, was warned by a voice that when he came right over against Palodes (in his voyage to Italy), he should cry aloud, *Magnus Pan mortuus est*,* which having done, there was heard by all the mariners a lamentable groaning and yelling of spirits. And indeed it was so that the cross of Christ (who was crucified in the days of Tiberius) was the cause of the oracles' silence and defect, which from that time never gave answer to any.

I. This title of shepherd implies both his natures.

1. His Godhead. A shepherd is of a superior kind to the sheep, they being beasts, and the shepherd man; Ezekiel, in chap xxxiv. 31, interpreting that his parable of the shepherd and sheep, 'And ye, my flock of my pasture, are men, and I am your God, saith the Lord.'

---

* The great shepherd is dead, Pan, the god of shepherds.

2. His manhood. Zech. xiii. 7, ' My shepherd, and the man that is my fellow ;' says God in Ezek. xxxiv. 24, he their shepherd is said to be ' one among them,' or *in medio eorum*, that is, (as that phrase elsewhere), he is of their nature. As he is man, he is called the lamb ; and this lamb is shepherd also, as those words import, Rev. vii. 17, ' The Lamb shall feed them.'

II. This title implies all Christ's offices.

1. Of king. Kings were called shepherds, ποιμένες λαῶν, &c. : thus Ezek. xxxiv. 24, where, as Christ is called their shepherd, so their prince, as he who guides and leads his sheep, Ps. xxiii. 2, John x. 27, as David and Moses did the people, and ' judgeth between sheep and sheep,' Ezek. xxxiv. 20, 21 ; he will judge those that push them ; and at the latter day it is said, The Son of man, the king, sitting on his throne of glory, shall as a shepherd separate the sheep from the goats, Mat. xxv. 31, 32, and in that respect in the next verses is styled the king, verses 34, 40.

2. Of priest. John x. 11, ' I am that good shepherd, that give my life for the sheep.'

3. Of prophet. *Pastor à pascendo*, he feeds them ; John x., Ps. xxiii. 2, 5, and in Ezek. xxxiv. 23, it is ingeminated, ' He shall feed them, he shall feed them,' that is, eminently and immediately, as doubling the speech doth indigitate (as Ezek. xxi. 27, it doth). Thus much what this title of shepherd in the general doth import.

III. Christ is called, that great shepherd.

1. In respect of other under shepherds ; so 1 Peter v. 4, ' And when the chief shepherd shall appear, ye shall receive a crown,' &c. And here the apostle having made mention of other inferior shepherds, verses 2, 3, in this verse he calls him the chief shepherd ; yea, kings are styled shepherds, but Christ is the shepherd even of those shepherds, as being the ' King of kings.'

2. He is a shepherd of souls. The souls of men are his flock, 1 Peter ii. 25. One soul is more worth than all the world, which is the rate this shepherd himself, that went to the price of them, valued them at.

3. In respect of the extent of his flock ; he is shepherd over all, both Jews and Gentiles. John x. 16, ' There shall be one fold, and one shepherd.' Christ having in the former part of that verse spoken of other sheep which were not of that Jewish fold—he had had another great flock among the Gentiles—he therefore adds, ' And them also I must bring, and there shall be one fold,' &c. Paul was the apostle, but of the uncircumcision, and Peter of the circumcision, Gal. ii. 7, and both the one and the other but for their age ; but Christ is the shepherd of all, yea, and both in the Old Testament and the New. In the Old, Eccles. xii. 11, he was then called that one shepherd, from whom the masters of assemblies, the ministers, rulers, and elders of the synagogues, had all their words given them, and their assistance to speak them. Of the New I need not instance.

4. In respect of propriety ; the sheep that Christ feeds are his own, John x. 14. It is not so with other shepherds, that are ministers under him ; they are but as hirelings in respect of any propriety of feeding sheep, says Christ to Peter. They are *my* sheep, says he, not *yours*; and they are his because he bought them : ' The flock of God, which he purchased with his own blood,' Acts xx. 28. He bought us, and is therefore called there in the text both shepherd and Lord, having bought them by laying down his life for them, John x. 11.

5. In respect of his abilities.

(1.) In a particular knowledge of all the persons who are his sheep ; though they be of that vast extent and variety, yet ' he knows every sheep by name,' John x.

(2.) In skill ; to heal and apply him to all their sicknesses, weaknesses, wants : Ezek. xxxiv. 16, ' I will seek that which was lost, and bring again that which was driven away, and will bind up that which was broken, and will strengthen that which was sick : I will feed them with judgment.' *With judgment;* that is, with convenient food and physic for every one, as their condition of sickness or strength requires.

(3.) In respect of power.

[1.] To make them his sheep, by a new creation. He first bought them, then makes them his sheep : ' We are his sheep, and he made us,' Ps. c. 3 ; that is, he made us to be his sheep, and ' not we ourselves,' as some do read the words.

[2.] To strengthen them, with strength in the inward man ; which no other shepherd can do for his sheep. He is able to make them perfect in every good work, as in the text.

[3.] He protects them all against all them that push them, and would drive them out of their pasture, or otherwise any way injure them, and ' judgeth likewise between cattle and cattle.' Ezek. xxxiv. 20, 21, 22, ' Thus saith the Lord God unto them, Behold, I, even I, will judge between the fat cattle and between the lean cattle. Because ye have thrust with side and with shoulder, and pushed all the diseased with your horns, till ye have scattered them abroad ; therefore will I save my flock, and they shall no more be a prey ; and I will judge between cattle and cattle.'

[4.] He hath all power effectually to keep them, and to bring them invincibly to salvation. John x. 27, 28, ' My sheep hear my voice, and I know them, and they follow me : and I give unto them eternal life ; and they shall never perish, neither shall any man pluck them out of my hand.'

The USE is of comfort to all that are Christ's sheep : in the application of which there will still more of the greatness of our shepherd be further set out, though in a consolatory way ; which I rather chose to do than in a mere doctrinal.

1. In general ; if Christ be our shepherd, and such a shepherd, ' what can we then lack ?' It is the comfort that David draws from it, Ps. xxiii. 1 ; ' I send you as sheep among wolves,' saith Christ, Mat. x. 15 : it was spoken when he sent them out to the cities of Judah, and when they returned he asks them, ' Did you lack anything ?' Luke xxii. 35. And how came this to pass, but because he was the great shepherd, who went with them all the while ? And though you now, in this age, are as sheep in the midst of wolves, yet you see he spreads your tables, gives your * ordinances in the midst of your enemies ; and what do you lack ?

But, more particularly, consider his promises as a shepherd.

1. To give you pasture. John x. 9, ' They shall find pasture ;' says he, I will see to that ; yea, Ps. xxiii. 2, ' Green pastures, the paths of righteousness.'

2. Fresh springs also, as well as green pastures. So it follows there, that is, fresh comforts, springing from the fountain of comforts. Thy heart is dry and barren to day ; the next prayer thou makest, or sermon thou hearest, thou findest a new spring ; as they in their travel to Sion, Ps. lxxxiv., ' that dig up fountains still,' ever and anon when they are athirst. And this spring is by Christ himself interpreted to be his ' Spirit, which he

* Qu. ' you ' ?—Ed.

gives to them that believe,' John iv. 14; 'even rivers springing up to eternal life,' and so never ceasing until you come to heaven.

3. Particularly; those green pastures are ordinances. As,

(1.) A good fold, as Ezek. xxxiv. 15, that is, a good church, which is the seat of ordinances, a good church and holy saints to be in and with. Thus Cant. i. 7, 8, 'Tell me, O thou whom my soul loveth, where thou feedest, where thou makest thy flock to rest at noon: for why should I be as one that turneth aside by the flocks of thy companions?' And again, 'I will bring them into the fold,' as Christ's speech evidently implies, John x. 16; and it is he that gives thee a heart to join with such where thou mayest be most edified: as in that Cant. i. 8 you see how, in answer to her desire, he directs and guides them whither to go: ver. 8, 'If thou know not, O thou fairest among women, go thy way forth by the footsteps of the flock, and feed thy kids beside the shepherds' tents.'

(2.) Over that he sets and finds out pastors and elders for thee, both according to his own heart, yea, and according to thine; that is, who do and shall suit the state and condition of thy soul the best of any other in the world: Jer. iii. 14, 15, 'I will take you one of a city, and two of a family, and I will bring you to Zion: and I will give you pastors according to my heart, which shall feed you with knowledge and understanding.' It is a promise made to gospel times, agreeing with Matt. xviii., as the phrase of taking two or three of a city and tribe shews. He will either bring thee to the best means, or make those means thou hast the best to thee.

(3.) He provides and prepares all the good sermons thou hearest, and puts those words and prayers too into his ministers' hearts and mouths. These are all 'from him, as from that one sphepherd:' Eccles xii. 11, 'The words of the wise are as goads, and as nails fastened by the masters of assemblies, which are given from one shepherd.' Yea, in their providing of them, Christ as the great shepherd, that knows the state of every one of his flock, brings to their mind this goad to prick forward such an one's heart, that nail to fasten on such an one's spirit (as there), according as any one hath need. It is he that 'feeds them with judgment,' Ezek. xxxiv. And when he hath given fit words for them to speak (the pertinency of which to every one's heart they are not aware of), he then gives assistance in the delivery, and drives in that promise or command home to the nail's head; makes that goad of rebuke or exhortation to pierce a thick and brawny heart, and makes it tender.

(4.) He farther feeds them with the strangest, yea, strongest, sweetest, and most soul-heartening food that ever was, even with his own flesh and blood: 'My flesh is meat indeed, and my blood is drink indeed;' and so some have understood the coherence of these words here in the text, that he is a shepherd ἐν πῷ αἵματι in his blood, as feeding them therewith, and giving it to save them; and so refer those words, not to his being brought back again, but to his being a shepherd in his blood. This for the first ground of comfort: his promises as he is a shepherd, and we the sheep of his pasture, as we are called.

A second ground, that Christ is a shepherd who is careful, as the opposition of Christ and hirelings shews, John x. 13. That office exacts care: the sheep take none, the shepherd all; and that which obligeth Christ to this care is his propriety in his sheep. Other shepherds are only hirelings and servants; and though faithful, yet only but as servants; but Christ cares for them as being their owner. They are 'his own sheep;' as therefore the apostle reasoneth, Heb. iii. 5, 6, 'Moses was faithful in his house as a servant, but Christ as a Son over his own house; which house we are.'

This his care appears,

1. In seeking them out, both at first conversion, 'and after when gone astray, as many ways they do, and are apt to do. Thus, Ezek. xxxiv. 11, 'I, even I, will both search my sheep, and seek them out.' The word implies a search even through the whole wilderness, every hedge, every bush, every corner. Christ leaves the ninety-nine (as in the parable) to seek the poor one that is astray, and seeks all the wilderness over, Luke xv., and in the mountains, Matt. xviii. 12, 13, yea, and looks at it as his duty so to do. John x. 16, 'Them also I must bring in,' says Christ there. It is my Father's command; as Laban required his tale of Jacob, so will God of Christ.

2. When he hath found them he makes sure work with them to keep them, Luke xv. 5. They are not only in his hands, but he lays them on his shoulders, and holds the fore feet with one hand, and the hinder feet with the other, and yet they will be struggling, but that he hath long hands that still reacheth them, and holds them, and pulls them in again.

3. His care is seen in his inspection into the flock, and visiting his sheep, abiding *in medio earum*, in the midst of them, or among them: Ezek. xxxiv. 11, 'I, even I, will both search my sheep and seek them out.' The one of the two words there used implies the searching of them out, and the other inspection. The Septuagint translates it ἐπισκέψομαι, to *visit* or *oversee*. Hence the apostle, 1 Pet. ii. 25, doth join both, calling Christ 'the shepherd and bishop,' or overseer of our souls,' ἐπίσκοπον. He knows all their wants, and looks to all their wanderings; and as Jacob watched whole nights with the sheep, so Christ does neither sleep nor slumber, but keepeth Israel.

The third ground is, that Christ is a shepherd who is pitiful: Matt. ix. 36, 'When he saw the multitudes, he was moved with compassion on them, because they fainted and were scattered abroad, as sheep having no shepherd.'

1. To young converts: Isa. xl. 11, 'He gathers the lambs with his arm, and carries them in his bosom.'

2. To those that are with young, he gently leads them (as in the place last quoted); that is, the grown Christians, or any that are in pains of travail, not to overdrive them, as Jacob did not his flock, Gen. xxxiii. 13; and in Ezek. xxxiv., there are more instances of his pity: as,

3. To those that stray after their having been brought to the fold, he seeks them out again: ver. 12, 'I will deliver them out of the places where they shall be scattered in the cloudy and dark day.' Temptation is as a cloudy day; it is a walking in darkness, as Isa. l. 10. No beast so apt to wander as sheep are; Christ seeks them again.

4. The weak he strengthens, who have feeble knees and faint hands, so ver. 16; and also,

5. The sick and broken he heals. Sheep are apt to break their legs, and fall into ditches (heavy temptations), and of all creatures are most subject to diseases; but Christ binds up their wounds and heals all, it being the greatest work of a shepherd to look to such things.

6. He shews his pity and care in providing rest and lying down for them, Ps. xxiii. 2; and, in Cant. i. 7, 'Thou makest thy flocks to rest at noon,' in the heat of the day, whether in case of distresses, pressures, hard drivings, or persecution, by giving them comfortable intermission, and some-

times for a long while quietly and safely to enjoy his ordinances : as Ezek. xxxiv. 25, ' And I will make with them a covenant of peace, and will cause the evil beasts to cease out of the land ; and they shall dwell safely in the wilderness, and sleep in the woods.'

Use 2. The second use is of exhortation to men to turn to him. We are all as sheep going astray. Oh now return unto the shepherd and bishop of your souls, 1 Pet. ii. 25; else God will say, as Zech. xi. 9, ' I will not feed you; that that dieth, let it die,' &c., which is as much as to say, Let thy soul die in a ditch, and there lie; I will not regard it.

BOOK VI.

Of Christ our high priest, as entered into the holy of holies in the heavens.—
How we are to treat and converse with God and Christ Jesus, under the
notion of his being our high priest, and being entered into the holy of holies.
—And of our having liberty to enter thither to him, and to converse with
him there, through faith, in prayer.

Seeing then that we have a great high priest, that is passed into the heavens,
Jesus the Son of God, let us hold fast our profession. For we have not an
high priest which cannot be touched with the feeling of our infirmities; but
was in all points tempted like as we are, yet without sin. Let us therefore
come boldly unto the throne of grace, that we may obtain mercy, and find
*grace to help in time of need.—*HEB. IV. 14–16.

CHAPTER I.

The words of the text explained, That Christ is our great high priest.—Wherein
the greatness and excellency of his priesthood consists.

THE apostle had set forth Christ as a judge, to whom we must give an
account, ver. 12, 13, and here he sets him forth as a most gracious and
merciful high priest. The former he did, to persuade the Hebrews to get
true faith, and to beware of a temporary faith. The latter he does, to encourage them to continue in the true faith. And it comes very seasonably
in after the former. For whereas he had told them, that Christ knew and
observed every thought, and that his word was *κριτικός*, critical in observing
and finding out the least by-end, not a thought could escape Christ's all-
piercing eye, they that were sincere-hearted, being conscious of so many
imperfections and infirmities in all they do, might think with themselves,
If he with whom we have to do be so severe as ver. 12, 13, describe him
to be, how shall we have anything at all to do with him? how shall we
hold in with him? Wherefore the apostle in an instant quite alters and
changes the scene, and presents Christ in a new habit, and puts on him his
high priest's robes. As before he had presented him sitting in his judgment seat, with his sword (the ensign of his justice) in his hand, able to
' divide between the marrow and the joints,' so now he tenders him to them
with the heart of a high priest, most tenderly affected towards them in all
their infirmities, and as sitting upon a throne of grace and mercy-seat, to
which with boldness they might draw near.

From which coherence observe that—

Obs. Jesus Christ can and will shew himself the most exact and severe
judge ; and likewise the most tender and merciful high priest. He is called
(you know) both a lion and a lamb. Yea, you have both in one and the

same chapter, and the one in the next verse, immediately following the other (even as here also the like), Rev. v. 5, 6. A lion is of all creatures the most fierce and furious, yet generous in his wrath; and a lamb is of all the meekest. And he is set forth under both; not in respect of those two several estates of his when on earth, and now in heaven, as if a lamb in respect of his carriage here, and sufferings here below, but a lion now, possessed of his power and glory in heaven. No; but a lamb as now risen again, and as taking the book out of God's hand, and so to be God's commissioner to govern and judge the world. For that is the scope of that chapter. He therefore, as he is now in heaven, shews himself a lamb as well as a lion. And a lion and a lamb are creatures of all others the most contrary. Yet Christ hath the heart of a lion, and the heart of a lamb too, because he is and was appointed to be the perfect image of God, Heb. i. 3, and the executioner of all God's decrees, both of justice and mercy, on the elect and reprobate. Through his human nature, the Godhead is to express his extremest severity, and likewise the tenderest bowels of mercy; and therefore Christ's heart was fitted and tempered unto both, according to the exactest mixture and proportion that might be. God himself said of the angel who went with the Israelites (which was Christ, and in an allusion unto which type this representation of him here, ver. 12, 13, doth come in), 'My name is in him,' that is, my attributes; as of mercy, so he went with them to lead them into Canaan; so of justice, therefore provoke him not, for he will not spare you; and yet of mercy also, for else he would not have gone with them.

Use 1. This shews us the excellencies of Jesus Christ, who hath all perfections in him to the height, and mixtures of contraries in their full perfections. Such a man we love as hath a spirit of all compositions: when highest meekness, and greatest courage and stoutness are met in one, how amiable doth it make one! Even such an one is Christ: read his description in Ps. xlv.

Use 2. We should therefore look at them both in Christ, and carry the representation of them both at once in our eyes. Men either look upon him as all mercy, and so presume; or as all severity, and so tremble to come at him. The devil then makes a false Christ of him in either. The lamb can be angry: you read of 'the wrath of the Lamb.' And so the lion can be lamb-like and gracious. Poor souls in desertion look at Christ only as armed with his sword, and so tremble to come at him; as that child in Homer did, when his father in complete armour took him up in his arms. When Christ looks sternly on thee, yet he may have a father's heart to thee, under that vizor of terror.

Use 3. We should have a mixture of affections, namely, of fear and love, answerable to this mixture in Christ; so Ps. ii. 11, 12, 'Serve the Lord with fear, and rejoice with trembling. Kiss the Son, lest he be angry.' And yet again, 'though his wrath be a little kindled,' yet rejoice, and come boldly to him as a Saviour. And let us serve him without fear also, for he is a merciful high priest. So in the 45th Psalm he is set forth as a loving husband, greatly delighting in the beauty of his queen, who sits at his right hand, and is familiar with him. And yet she is taught to know her distance: 'He is thy God, worship thou him.'

Use 4. It should be an encouragement to poor souls, who are sinners, and tremble at every threatening, and are afraid when they hear or see Christ angry, when he rends and tears wicked sinners in pieces, when they see judgments on the earth. You do well indeed to tremble, as children when they see the servants beaten. But consider withal that he is a gracious God to you, when his anger is never so much against others. Like a loving husband that is general of an army, though he hath been in the field killing and slaughtering men that are his enemies, yet when he comes into his tent, he is as loving to his spouse as ever, and with the same arms embraceth her, with which he ruined them in fury. Such is Christ; he can be and.is as loving and familiar with his own, and will use them as kindly as if he were not angry at all. And yet men can hardly so command their passions, but that they will run out one way; and when they are angry with others, they are morose, not placid even to their wife or friend. But it is not so with Christ; he can act both parts to the height, and loves to do it. He can turn his fierce look on others, to the most gracious smiles on thee, and that in the twinkling of an eye. Think but how that, at the latter day, his anger will be at the highest, and yet how loving will he be to his own! It will be the strangest sight that ever was, when in the same countenance the greatest fury and the most sweet smiles of grace shall lodge and appear together, as then they will. Therefore in Isa. xxvii. 4, when God was in his armour, and in battle array, against his enemies (as it is in that verse), yet then to his vineyard, to his own, he says, 'Fury is not in me.' No; I am not angry with you (says God), though indeed against briars and thorns I am, and will burn them together. When he is most angry, fear not to go forth to meet him, but rather go rejoicingly out to him; for he will use thee lovingly, if thou humblest thyself before him, Isa. lxiv. 5. Thus much I have said as an introduction to the words of the text, and from the coherence of them.

The words divide themselves into these three parts:

1. Two eminent duties exhorted unto.

2. Three especial discouragements from those duties.

3. A ground of encouragement unto those duties (notwithstanding these discouragements) fetched from Christ's high priesthood in heaven.

1. The duties exhorted unto are two.

(1.) To hold fast our profession. Whereby is meant, that cleaving to Christ by faith and obedience, whereby we do profess him to be our Saviour, and do put our confidence in him. Heb. iii. 1, he is styled 'the high priest of our profession;' that is, whom we profess to be our high priest, by cleaving to the doctrine and religion which he is the high priest over. All professions have some eminent founder or chief of them, of whom the professors have their denomination. The Jews' religion had Moses and Aaron, to whom therefore they are said to cleave; and the Romish religion and profession hath the pope for its chief. He is the high priest of it, *pontifex maximus;* and therefore they of that profession are called *pontificii* and papists from him. In like manner the true Christian profession hath Christ for the high priest of it, and therefore we are called Christians. Now, then, to cleave constantly to Christ, by faith and obedience, in all things, whereby he is magnified and confessed to be our high priest, both in heart and life; this is to hold fast our profession. And because this is chiefly done by true faith, which as a hand takes hold of Christ and holds forth in life the profession of him; therefore he bids them hold the profession: κρατῶμεν, *let us hold,* &c. And because that faith hath great oppositions and discouragements, that might pull them from it or it from them, therefore he bids them hold fast or strongly; for so the word signifies.

(2.) The second duty exhorted to is to come, viz., by faith; for by it we are said to come to God and to Christ, 1 Pet. ii. 4 ; to draw near, Heb. x. 22. I take it therefore especially to mean coming to God in prayer. As in Ps. lxv. 2, ' O thou that hearest prayer, unto thee shall all flesh come.' And that is meant here ; for the word translated *boldly* is μετα παρρησίας, liberty of speech and spirit. Come boldly and speak out your needs and complaints. And therefore also the help that is given is called βοήθεια, that is, help upon crying ; and this is correspondent to the ground of encouragement given from Christ's high priesthood, which is an office of prayer and intercession. And therefore the apostle encourageth against all our exigencies, both miseries from without and guilts of sins within ; including both these in that one word ' infirmities,' as things wherein Christ our high priest will pity us. For these are all either expressed or evidently implied in the words. The two first are expressed under that one word ' infirmities,' ver. 15, whereby both persecutions and afflictions from without, and sins, are meant. That under infirmities, miseries, and persecutions, and all outward evils are meant, appears from 2 Cor. xii. 5, and chap. xi. 30. His outward distresses the apostle calls his infirmities. And these he means here ; for he comforts them against these by this, that Christ in all these was tempted. Therefore, notwithstanding them, ' hold fast your profession ;' you have a high priest to pity you in them.

Yet more especially by ' infirmities' he means sins, which indeed are the greatest pressures, and which we therefore need most comfort against, and that the pity of Christ be shewn therein. And they are the greatest discouragers of us in our coming with boldness to the throne of grace for help against those outward evils ; and therefore they must be intended here. And accordingly we find the word on purpose used but three verses off in this very discourse, continued, about this high priesthood in the type of Christ. In chap. v. 2, the apostle shews the qualifications of a high priest then under the law, and he recites them to shew that the same virtues, as towards us, are found in our high priest, but without sin. He was the high priest under the law (says he), one that ' could have compassion on the ignorant, and them that are out of the way,' *i. e.*, upon sinners (for by ignorances and strayings from God, sins are meant), in that himself (says he, speaking of the high priest) was clothed with infirmities, that is, with sins ; which might move him out of a sense of the like sins in himself to offer the sacrifices of every sinner which should come to him. And again, you have the same expression used again of the high priest, chap. vii. 28, ' For the Lord maketh men high priests which have infirmities,' that is, sins, such as the people had ; which is spoken in direct opposition unto Christ his being holy, undefiled, and separate from sinners, ver. 26. But though as concerning Christ his having any infirmities on his part, the apostle had exempted him, and put in an exception before the words of my text, saying, that he was ' tempted in all things, yet without sin ;' yet as to the pitying part, viz., to have compassion on us, under such infirmities, his scope is to the full to shew that he is, and must be, a high priest that can have compassion, more abundantly than those narrow-hearted priests could have, though they were compassionate upon other grounds than he. They, for that themselves were clothed and surrounded with the same infirmities of sin that the people were, therefore pitied them. But he, though without sin, yet hath that innate compassion, and a heart so made up of mercy, that he is much more able to compassionate such even in their sins, which are their greatest infirmities. So then under the word *infirmities* sins are intended, and in his alleging the parallel of the high priest in respect of compassion towards sinners which are out of the way, his scope and intention must necessarily be to shew that Christ is thus also. His allegation had been to no purpose at all, if not unto this; and so it refers to and explains what is said in my text, that he is 'touched with the feeling of our sinful infirmities;' and they therefore are here mainly intended. And further, to that end he shews, that though he kept himself from being tempted with evil and sin, yet he came as near as might be, being tempted by Satan unto sin, and vexed (as the word in some copies signifies) with all sorts of sins, yet still without sin. He came, I say, as near therein as might be, that he might be able to pity us experimentally. Even herein again, because the apostle means infirmities of sins, as well as of miseries and outward temptations, therefore the comfort and remedy which they are directed to seek, and encouraged to find at the throne of grace, is in relation unto sins. He mentions both grace and mercy: 'that you may obtain,' says he, 'grace and mercy;' grace to help against the power of sin, mercy to take away the guilt of sin. And our own pressures of all other are those of sin and corruptions; and above all things our hearts (who are true Christians) are carried forth to obtain grace, and mercy for and about them. So as however that grace to help against all other infirmities is meant, and we may find in Christ both grace to supply wants, and mercy to give deliverance; yet there being two things in sin—corruption and guilt—therefore to be sure we need grace and mercy to serve against these two, more eminently than against all evils else. And these are the evils which the saints' hearts do most implore grace and mercy against, and therefore these are above all intended by the apostle here.

Obs. 1. Jesus Christ is a great high priest; concerning which in general, whatever title Christ hath, this of greatness is added to it. 'A prophet he is of a truth;' and '*that* prophet', said they, John vii. 40; yea, that '*great* prophet,' say they, Luke vii. 16. John was a prophet, 'yea, more than a prophet,' says Christ of him, Mat. xi. 9. But then, 'I am not worthy to untie the latchet of his shoe,' says John of Christ. A shepherd he is, but with this addition, 'that great shepherd,' Heb. xiii. 20. A king he is, but, Ps. xlvii. 2, 'the great King;' it is a psalm of Christ's ascension: ver. 8, 'The King of kings, Lord of lords.' A priest he is here, a high priest; yet that is not title high enough, but he is a 'great high priest.'

As King of kings, so Priest of priests, that in all things he might have pre-eminence, Col. i. 18. When the person is great, all his titles are such. Princes who are eminently excellent, have by their subjects the title of *Great* affixed, as Charle*magne*, Alexander *the Great*, Henry *le Grand*, &c.; and shall not Christ be exalted, yea greatly exalted? Ps. xlvii. 9.

Use 1. Men who have great friends, how do they bear themselves upon them, and have great hopes, great thoughts, and great looks! So, Rabshakeh bore himself upon Sennacherib; and what big words doth he speak! 2 Kings xxviii. 19, 'Thus saith the great king;'—and shall not we, who are Christ's servants, bear ourselves as much upon our great Lord and master? as Paul often calls him.

Use 2. Let us serve him as becomes his greatness; not with the halt or lame. Shouldst thou send such to thy prince, would he accept such services? 'I am a great King,' says God, Mal. i. 14.

Use 3. Let us become little, that Christ may be great, and appear such. As his alone is goodness, so his alone is greatness, 1 Chron. xxix. 11. Let us become cyphers to set his greatness out. Let us be content to decrease, that he may increase, as John did; and, like the moon, the nearer we come to this sun, the more we should, yea we shall, wane; it is our glory so to do. This in general.

Now to shew more particularly how Christ is a great high priest. This is spoken of him,

1. Comparatively to Aaron, who was a high priest; but Christ is a great high priest, whose priesthood the apostle compares with his throughout this epistle. I will not now shew all the particulars wherein Christ doth exceed; only in this I instance, that Aaron's priesthood was but a shadow, not so much as a picture, compared with his. So he concludes that discourse, chap. x. 1. As a king-at-arms, who goes before a true king, such was Aaron to him; and therefore but a low, and a mean, a little high priest to this great high priest.

(1.) In the Levitical law there was a plurality of priests, which argued imperfection; but 'they truly were many,' says the apostle, Heb. vii. 23, and all could not perfect the work; which plurality of theirs is implied, ver. 11 of the 10th chapter, 'every high priest;' but Christ was but one, ver. 12. They were but as so many candles, that successively were burnt out, and gave but a dim light; but he as the sun, which is the meaning of that, Col. ii. 17, where the apostle, speaking of all the fore-running types, which were 'the shadows of things to come,' says, 'but the body is Christ'; who (as his scope there was to shew) hath disannulled all those shadows by his coming unto the world; and therefore can be no other body but of the sun itself in that comparison intended. For otherwise the shadows do begin to exist but when the body comes; but where the sun casts its beams, shadows fly away. Now as the sun is called the 'great light,' Gen. i. 16, because it alone doth that which all the stars and candles cannot, so Christ alone discharging this office is called the great high priest.

(2.) They 'daily ministered,' and 'offered oftentimes,' and the 'same sacrifices;' but Christ he did it but 'once,' and that 'for ever,' so Heb. x. 11, 12.

(3.) These many priests, with their many sacrifices often offered, 'could not take sins away;' but Christ by one offering took away all sins, and 'perfected us so for ever,' that our 'sins are remembered no more,' ver. 14, 17. But I will no longer insist on this comparison, for it is not worthy of it, it being a thing very uncomely to compare the body and the shadow together. Therefore I come,

2. To shew how he is a great high priest in himself, absolutely considered.

(1.) In his person, 'higher than the heavens,' Heb. vii. 26, that is, than the angels, and so all creatures; for not of place, but of personal dignity, is the highness there meant. And as hell is put for devils—'the gates of hell shall not prevail,' &c.—so there, heaven for angels, and 'such an high priest became us,' as it is there. And in this sense he is said to be ascended to heaven, when he was not yet ascended in place, but only by the union hypostatical, John iii. 13. This his personal worth and greatness is mentioned in the text, as that which is the foundation of the greatness of his office, 'Jesus the Son of God.' Other offices make the person great, and his dignity the more; but here the person dignifies the office, and makes it great. For from hence proceeds all the worth of the sacrifice he offered, and of the intercession of this priest: the worth of his sacrifice being attributed to his being God—'the blood of God'—and the prevalency of his intercession to his being the Son. Other officers (if great) must have a great deal of outward state and pomp, as kings have, and ceremonies of reverence are invented to make them seem great; and as themselves are human ordinances and creations, so they have human inventions for state and pomp, because they want personal greatness to bear up respect. And such a priest was Aaron and his fellows, which (I take it) is the meaning of that Heb. vii. 16, ' He was made a priest, not after the law of a carnal commandment,' which is spoken in opposition to the priests of the old law, who were indeed made thus, and it was all their making. The priests of old were of themselves no more fit to be priests than others of the Jews ; it was merely a law which made them such, no peculiar personal worth in the men: as the law makes a child as true and as great a king as a man grown. And, accordingly, they had carnal rites, which the law also prescribed, in the observance of which their priestly power and dignity did lie, and thereby was supported ; and so were priests ' after the law of a carnal commandment ' (so the law ceremonial is called, and thereby distinguished from the law moral, which is called spiritual, Rom. vii. 12, 13, 14). For the persons being weak, as other men, they had rites, such as were glorious garments, a glorious temple, &c., to make their office great ; which yet were but fleshly, that is, weak (as Eph. vi. 12, flesh is taken, ' not with flesh, but with powers,' &c.), and which wrought in the fleshly part of men an estimation of greatness. But this priest ' is made after the power of an endless life.' By power, he does not simply mean that authority given Christ by his Father's institution ; for so these Levites also were ordained : Heb. v. 4, ' No man takes this honour to himself, but he that is called of God, as was Aaron;' but he understands thereby, that personal power, and those eminent abilities which were in his person inherent, and which moved God to pitch on him, whereby he was not a king or priest dressed up, or set out with ceremonies, and carnal rites of reverence, but endued with power inherent, whereby he was able to shew himself a priest indeed. And as he was ' declared to be the Son of God with power,' Rom. i. 4, so also to be a priest with power. He had the power of a priest in his person ; which consisted chiefly in this, that he had the power of an indissoluble life (as the word is), that whereas it was requisite that he should die, to undergo God's wrath, which would have sunk the souls of men and angels, he could outlive it, and all the powers of death could not hold him ; as Acts ii. 24. ' I lay down my life, and I take it up again,' says Christ ; and so can survive to perform the rest that belongs to that office. And hence the word of the oath pitched on him, as one of himself consecrated and carved out for it, and none else ; so ver. 28, ' The law maketh men high priests which have infirmities, but the word of the oath, since the law, maketh the Son, who is perfected,' as the word is, ' for evermore.'

2. Secondly, It appears how great a priest he was, by the great trust which was reposed in him. We judge and esteem of the greatness of offices, by the great trust that is reposed in them. This made Joseph's office great, and himself the greatest man in Egypt. So with us, the high treasurer's place is great, because of the trust; and so the lord keeper's, &c. Now of Christ it is said, Heb. vii. 22, ' He became a surety of a better covenant.' It was an infinite trust which God committed to him. All those ' great and precious promises ' must be made ' yea and amen ' in him. All God's oaths and covenants must otherwise have been disannulled and cancelled ; yea, heaven must have been dissolved, and all the souls saved under the Old Testament sent down again, if Christ had not been a faithful high priest. All the glory of God's justice, all our souls which God so loved, all our sins which he desired so to be pardoned, all God's plots hung upon him, all his affairs were committed to him (I mention all these, because

they all concerned God's glory as well as our salvation, and therefore are called 'things appertaining to God,' though 'for men,' that is, for man's good; and he was faithful in them all, Heb. ii. 17). He trusted Christ, as Pharaoh did Joseph; and was not this a great high priest then? All the good things that Christ meant to bestow, the purchase of them was committed to this high priest. All God's holy things he was minister of, Heb. viii. 2 and ix. 11. All which argues the excellency of his ministry: Heb. viii. 6, 'He hath obtained a more excellent ministry, by how much he is the mediator of a better covenant, which was established upon better promises,' and of greater trust, which he was to make good.

3. Thirdly, The great solemnity that was at his instalment argues his greatness. It was by an oath, Heb. vii. 20, 21. Not so the Levitical offices. Those offices which were small, and of no great account or trust, but put in and out at pleasure, were wont to be bestowed without an oath, but great ones with an oath. And this very reason is indeed given why Christ was made with an oath, ver. 22, 'Insomuch as he was a surety of a better testament;' that is, betrusted with the rich promises of a greater covenant. Yea, further (which may be matter of wonderment unto us, as differing from all other investitures), not he himself so much doth take the oath, as his Father that made him, which was a transcendent and unheard of honour.

At the first erection of this office, and placing this great officer, God himself took an oath; whereas the usual way is, that the party that enters upon the office takes the oath; but here, God himself swears. Heb. vii. 21, 'This priest was made with an oath,' says the apostle; and by whom was this oath taken? Not by him who was made the priest, but by God himself (that made him) when he made him: 'He was made with an oath, by him who said to him' (mark it, by whom it was taken), 'The Lord sware, and will not repent, Thou art a priest for ever, after the order of Melchisedec.' This oath indeed was first taken from everlasting, when God first called him to his office, but was then solemnly renewed, and again rehearsed over, when Christ first entered upon this priesthood in heaven, being now set at God's right hand, as appears by comparing Heb. v., 5th and 6th verses, and Ps. ii., 6th, 7th, and 8th verses, with Ps. cx., ver. 1, 4, where, when God had set Christ down at his right hand, as Ps. ii. 6 and Ps. cx. 1, then he rehearses this oath, as ver. 4 of that psalm; yea, renews it, as Heb. v. (quoting both these psalms to this one and the same purpose) doth shew. All this was to assure us how much God's heart was engaged in this business of his priesthood, which it should be exercised about, namely, the pardoning of sinners. Christ's office in heaven is the pardon-office. He is a priest over it, to sue a pardon out for sinners. And the reason why God thus sware, rather than Christ, was because the business to be effected by this office being the pardon of our sins, which was dependent upon God's will, and to be procured at his hands through Christ's mediation and intercession; now therefore, to assure both us and Christ himself likewise, when he took on him this office, that his intercession should never be in vain at any time, for any souls that come to God by him, or that he sues for, God the Father takes this oath. Because Christ's office in interceding being to sue for pardon, and it being the Father's part to grant it: in this case, the oath is rather taken by the Father, to assure both us and Christ for ever of his covenant to hear Christ, and grant what by virtue of his office he requires; and that is, the pardon of our sins, which is the work of the office, that is, the thing that the oath intends, and not simply the confirmation of his office to him, but the effect of his office, that it should procure pardon, as is evident by chap. viii. throughout. An oath to a covenant or promise argues the greatest seriousness that may be. Even he who doth betrust him, is so satisfied in him, as he takes an oath for him; he exacts it not of him; he would not shew so much diffidence in a person so great and faithful, and able for the place; but he swears for him, that he should be a priest, and he would not repent; yea, he foresaw that in Christ, that he could never have cause to repent that he saved men by him. God swears, as glad to engage him in it.

4. Fourthly, He is a great high priest in respect of the continuance of his office; for what was it God sware to? 'Thou art a priest *for ever*,' says the apostle, glossing upon this oath: Heb. vii. 23, 'They truly were many priests' (that is, in succession one after another, though there was but one priest at once), 'because they were not suffered to continue by reason of death.' They were but as so many candles (as was said) that burned out, and others were set up in their rooms; yea, and some were deposed afore death; they were not suffered to continue, though they continued to live; so Abiathar. 'But this man' (says he, ver. 24), 'because he continueth ever, hath an unchangeable high priesthood;' for that cannot pass to any other, but is for ever in himself; and he can never lay it down, as he cannot lay down his person, or his being the Son of God. For that is the reason given, that seeing he himself continueth ever, his priesthood likewise shall continue ever. Now, offices that are of great trust, and withal are perpetual and for one's life, and cannot be taken away, are ever accounted great. It is this that makes the office of a king so great, because he is not subject to a deposition. Therefore he must needs be a great high priest, who hath a priesthood that cannot pass from him; yea, if he should lay it down, there is none in heaven or earth worthy to take it up. Princes consider well whom they put into places, out of which they cannot again remove them, and that hold not upon a *quam diu se bene gesserint*. Now such is this office wherewith Christ is invested. But God knew him so well aforehand, that himself durst swear for him, and that he would never repent of his placing him in it.

5. Fifthly, Christ is great in his love to us to become a priest for us: John xv. 13, 'Greater love than this hath no man, that a man lay down his life,' &c. By undertaking of which he became a priest; and so it may be said, as in the Acts, 'With a great sum purchased he this office.' Great was his love thus to become a priest for us, that he was equal to God his Father, and as great as he, that he should descend from his greatness and become lesser, to be a priest for us; and the lesser his person became, the greater his priesthood. For now his Father (as Christ is a priest) is greater than he, John xiv. 28. Yea, Christ became 'lower than the angels,' Heb. ii. 7, and yet lower, even than men; 'a worm, no man,' &c. And by how much lower his person became, by so much is his priesthood made higher. And so at once the greatness of his person made him alone fit to be this high priest (as was said); and yet withal, the lowering of all this greatness, even to nothing, made his priesthood to be so high and great. So that it hath both a height and a depth in it to make it great; and so his love is said to have (Eph. iii. 18, 19,) such 'a height and a depth in it, as it passeth knowledge.'

6. Sixthly, He is a great high priest in the sacrifice which he offered; which, Heb. ix. 23, is called a better sacrifice than those of the law, so much as heavenly things are better than the shadows of them; as it is

there, and chap. x. 1. 'For he offered up himself,' Heb. ix. 14, 26. And what a sacrifice was that! God himself hath not such another Son to offer, he has no more such sacrifices. Had he sacrificed millions of worlds of innocent men, and holy angels, even hecatombs, they had been but as mites to the riches of heaven and earth, in comparison to Jesus Christ: 1 Cor vi. 20, we are said to be bought with a price ; *magno pretio*, so some read it ; for what a sacrifice must that needs be, wherein all the riches, glory, and excellencies of God-man were emptied, and (as sacrifices of old were to be) consumed and burnt to ashes, to nothing ! And all he offered was his own, by such a title of personal propriety (as second person), as it was not God the Father's (though his also as God's creature) : so as he borrowed nothing, but was himself priest, sacrifice, altar, temple, and all.

7. Seventhly, He was a great high priest in respect of the temple and tabernacle that was made for him to officiate in. You guess at Aaron's and his successors' greatness by the glory of the tabernacle first, and then of the temple, and therein of the holy of holies, the wonder of the world. But the heavens were made for this man to be a priest in; and it is the highest end, next God's glory, that they were made for. He is a heavenly man, yea, 'the Lord from heaven,' as he is called, 1 Cor. xv. 48 ; a priest higher than the heavens ; and therefore he must have a place suitable to perform the great part of his office in. And, therefore, as it is said, that ' it became us,' or, it was necessary for us, being sinners (if saved), ' to have a priest,' who for the excellency of his person should be ' higher than the heavens,' so likewise it became the excellency of his person and high priesthood, that he should have a place to administer in, ' above the heavens.' And that is also noted in the text as a circumstance that makes him a great high priest, that he is ' entered into the heavens,' and officiates at the ' throne of grace' (ver. 16), the highest place in heaven, as the mercy-seat was in the holy of holies. Yea, he purchased this place by his blood, and laid down a price for it ; and therefore is said to ' enter into the heavens by his blood,' Heb. ix. 12, 24. Yea, he had a temple and a tabernacle yet more excellent than the heavens, a building made of better stuff. You will wonder what that should be ; his own body and human nature, which was the true temple, as he says, John ii. 19, ' Destroy this temple.' It was ' God's tabernacle,' Rev. xiii. 6, the ' holy of holies,' Dan. ix. 24, in which the ' fulness of the Godhead dwells bodily ;' which in the local place of the heavens it doth not, nor is personally united to them ; and that is it which makes this his manhood more high than the heavens, and to be called ' a greater and more perfect tabernacle, not made with hands ; that is to say, not of this building.' The apostle speaks it of Christ's own body ; for of the heavens he speaks besides in the next verse, ' By his own blood he entered into the holy of holies' (ver. 12) ; namely, the heavens, than which this of his body is the greater and more excellent tabernacle, ver. 11.

Use. Let us hold fast our profession against oppositions of men. The apostle speaks to them in suffering times, and we may say it in difficult times. And it is to be held fast : there is danger of being pulled from it by the adversaries. Men who have great masters bear themselves upon them, and are bold to wear their livery. The three children saw God in his greatness, and contemned Nebuchadnezzar ; and so did Moses as to Pharaoh, whose wrath he regarded not. Let us still view how great a high priest we have, and give back in nothing. Paul loves to have this.

often in his mouth ; 'Jesus Christ my Lord,' so Phil. iii. and elsewhere : as courtiers use to cry, 'The king my master.' Now why should not we be as bold as they ? For he is able, and will bear us out against all that do oppose us. 'We are not careful,' said the three children, 'to answer thee, O king, in this matter.' They saw God to be great, and able to bear them out. So we, seeing our high priest to be so great, let us hold fast to him, and he will hold us fast, 'and none shall pluck us out of his hands,' John x. 28. He is a great high priest entered into the heavens, who will also, if we hold fast to him, bring us thither. Men cleave to great persons in great distresses, when they can give them any great hopes. 'Can the son of Jesse give you vineyards and olive-yards ?' said Saul, when he feared the people's departing from him. But have any of your great masters places in heaven to bestow ? Have they mansions and offices there to dispose of ? (may our high priest say). But Christ hath ; 'He is passed into the heavens.'

CHAPTER II.

The words of the text explained.—What is meant by the holiest.—How we enter in thither.

Having therefore, brethren, boldness to enter into the holiest by the blood of Jesus, by a new and living way, which he hath consecrated for us, through the veil, that is to say, his flesh ; and having a high priest over the house of God ; let us draw near with a true heart, in full assurance of faith, having our hearts sprinkled from an evil conscience, and our bodies washed with pure water.—HEB. X. 19–22.

My subject from out of these words is, How in prayer, especially secret prayer, to converse with Christ our great high priest, entered into the heavens, and we to follow him thither by faith, and treat him there when we pray as being entered into the holiest with him.

The art and skill of this high converse with him in the heavens, is the apostle Paul's : who of all the apostles (if not alone) hath most insisted on this particular. And in this epistle he unfolds the mystery of Christ's high priesthood, as it was veiled under the type and shadow of the Levitical high priesthood of Aaron, and his successors. And writing to the Hebrews, now turned Christians, he speaks both the doctrines and duties of the gospel in the Old Testament characters, and conciphers them. But in a special manner he had explained the mystical signification of that eminentest part of Aaron's priesthood, in his officiating on that most solemn 'day of atonements,' when he went into the holy of holies (which was the sum and complement of the high priest's service), to be Christ 'entering into the heavens' as an high priest for us (of which you may read largely, though intermingled with other things, from chap. iv. ver. 16, and chapters v., vi., vii., viii., ix., and so on in this 10th chapter, unto these words). And in these words (my text) he comes to the duties, or practical part that belongeth to us thereupon as inferred from thence : which likewise he utters in the language of the types of that day's rites and solemnities.

And of all those gospel duties, he begins first with this very thing which I have singled forth for my subject, viz., How to converse with God, and Christ, now he is in heaven, in allusions unto the type thereof, and there to transact our concernments with him ; which being the first of all the other exhortations made, shews it was a principal one, and most genuinely inferred from the foresaid type. And to that end he *first* informs us, in ver. 19, of our right and privilege, that are saints under the New Testament, viz., to enter into the holiest, and to go to him our high priest thither; and the foundation of that privilege to be his blood, ver. 19. And withal, *secondly*, pointing us the way which our high priest hath paved and consecrated for us to come thither to him, ver. 20, himself having first entered as an high priest for us, ver. 21. And then, *thirdly*, in ver. 22, he sets forth the duty and qualifications of those that will so come, and which they that enter must seek for, or bring with them; and these drawn and inferred either from the type of the people's part, performed on that day, or by the high priest acted for them, or on their behalf.

There are three or four things or phrases in the text which I account it requisite to explain, to make way for the founding of this my subject on the words, ere I proceed upon it.

First, That by ' the holiest' here is meant the highest heavens, into which Christ is entered, and where Christ is resident, and whither we are bidden to come and enter, and whereof the holiest in the temple was the type. This is so much known to the most of intelligent readers as it needed not to be insisted on, but for the more unknowing their sake. And they may understand from our apostle that the tabernacle of Moses, and afterwards the temple of Solomon, consisted of two courts or rooms (see 1 Kings xvi. 17, 19), one before the other; which the apostle exactly describes, to the end that all might understand this very thing I am upon. Chap. ix. ver. 2, 3, ' For there was a tabernacle made; the first, wherein was the candlestick, and the table, and the shewbread; which is called the sanctuary or the holy. And after the second veil, the tabernacle, which is called the holiest of all.' ' And the priests,' he says, namely, ' the holy, went into the first* every day to sacrifice,' ver. 6. ' But into the second' (which was the holiest) ' went the high priest once a year,' &c., ver. 7, which second he again calls, ' the holiest of all,' in ver. 8. And at ver. 9 he tells us, that this ' first tabernacle' (so he calls the whole, consisting of these two apartments) ' was a figure for that time then present.' The figure of what? The apostle plainly unriddles and explains it; ver. 24, ' Christ is not entered into the holy places made with hands' (that is, into those earthly tabernacles which the priests entered into every day, and the high priest once a year entered into), ' which are the figures of the true; but into heaven itself, now to appear in the presence of God for us.' So then we are sure that the heavens are the holy places; and the heaven Christ is now in is the holiest, and figured out by that holiest of all. I will not at all detain you with the question, whether there be not in the heavens a first court, which Christ passed through, of which the court of priests was the figure, into that heaven of heavens, of which the holiest of all, which then the high priest entered into, was the figure. The apostle, in that last place cited, doth in the plural mention both, in saying, ' the holy places,' and that they were ' figures of the true,' and it is certain the true here are the heavens. And yet again when he interprets what those places did signify, he says, ' heaven itself,' in the singular. It is enough to my present purpose, that the highest heavens is here meant by the holiest; those which Christ entered into, and where now he is, and into which we are here invited to come in; and into which our hope is said to be (in like allusion) to enter as an anchor, into ' that within the veil; whither the forerunner is

---

* Qu. ' into the first, namely, the *holy* ' ?—ED.

for us entered,' chap. vi. ver. 19, 20.   And 'that within the veil' is plainly
an allusion to the '.holy of holies.'   So the apostle would have us to mind
and observe, from his foresaid description, chap. ix. ver. 2.   After the
second veil was the tabernacle, which is called the holiest of all.

The *second* thing to be explained is, what is meant by entering.   Our
éntering (for it is spóken of us, and our entering) into the holiest; that is,
into heaven.

1. We all know that our going to enjoy and possess heaven, after this
life and world are ended, is termed àn entering into it : Matt. xxv. 23,
' Enter into thy master's joy ; ' and Acts xiv. 22.   And Christ's entering
into his glory, and into the heavens (as in this epistle), is said to be when
he ascended.

But here this our entering must be understood of what is to be, and what
we are to do, in this life.   We being invited upon the' declaration of our
right to enter in, ver. 19, to come to, as the word is, ver. 22, or draw near.
And it is as an act to be done by us in this life ; an entry and coming with
liberty of speech, as the word translated liberty and boldness, in ver. 19,
also signifies.   And withal to ' come to,' and ' draw near,' doth import an
act of ours ; and that to be with such and such dispositions as at that present are to accompany that act of drawing near, and to be exercised therein,
all which dispositions are concomitants of this life.   Moreover, it is as an
entry whilst we are *in via*, in the way ; *viatores*, wayfaring men (as the
prophet 'Isaiah, chap. xxxv., terms us) ; so ver. 20, we are to enter ' by a
new and living way,' consecrated for us, and that is in this life.   In the
other world we are at our journey's end.

Yet 2. There is an entering into the kingdom of heaven in this life,
which is when we are first called and converted, and born again, which
indeed is done but once for all, whereof baptism is the seal; of which those
places are to be understood : John iii. 5, ' Except a man be born of water,
and of the Spirit, he cannot enter into the kingdom of God ;' which phrase
is also used, Matt. xix. 23, 24, and Mark x. 23, 25, that ' a rich man shall
hardly enter into the kingdom of God ;' that is, is hardly converted ; and
is spoken upon occasion of the rich young man's refusal to come unto
Christ.   But this initial entrance is not meant here; for he supposeth them
he speaks to, to have been as to this respect entered already ; and therefore calls them brethren, ver. 19, and supposeth them to have a right
already to enter : ' Seeing therefore we have boldness,' or ' right to enter '
(as many interpret it), so upon that right invites them to draw near; whereas
the new birth is that which gives that right first, as John i. 12, 13, and
therefore is not meant here.   And again, that entrance into the kingdom of
heaven by effectual calling at first, is as an entrance into a state, or such as
into a city, to be at first admitted a free denizen of it (the state of grace,
as Rom. v. 1) ; but is an admission into a condition or privilege, namely,
that the kingdom of heaven should belong to us.   It is to be *cœlo donatus*,
made a citizen of heaven, Phil. iii.   But this here is an entrance as into a
house, ver. 21, where some one dwells whom we would speak withal ; and
liberty of speech is that which this entrance serves unto.   And this is into
the holiest, you see, as into a place, in allusion to the high priest's going
into the tabernacle, as a holy place; and such was Christ's entrance into
heaven, as into the holy place, as was said, chap. ix. ver. 24 ; and this of
ours is into heaven, as his was.

3. It rests then this be an entrance into heaven in this life, by our performing such acts of drawing near, and coming to God, and our high priest

there, as are to be continued and increased after our first conversion, and performed between it and our entering into the actual fruition of the glory of heaven. And that there are such actings of soul, in the exercise of which we do truly and really enter into heaven, and are so called, the Scriptures are not wanting as to the using this phrase in that sense. The apostle, 2 Peter i. 11, having exhorted unto an exact diligence in all good works after calling, and unto adding all sorts of graces, as occasions call for the exercise of them, and to abound therein ; from ver. 5 to 10, he then proposeth four or five spiritual advantages that will accrue thereby, proceeding by a gradation in them, ver. 10. And the last and highest of them is in ver. 11, ' For so an entrance shall be ministered unto you abundantly, into the everlasting kingdom of our Lord and Saviour Jesus Christ.' This is narrowed by most interpreters* unto an abundant free entrance into heaven, and reception of our spirits by Christ at our death ; according as we have abounded in good works, to be filled at our death with joy and comfort answerable ; as also at the latter day, when Christ shall say, ' Come, ye blessed ; for ye saw me hungry,' &c. And it is certain that the word *enter* is used of our taking that full possession of enjoyment after death of the kingdom of heaven, as Acts xiv. 22, and frequently elsewhere ; yet I find Calvin to take in unto this, the promise of all those rich supplies and assistances, which God vouchsafes all along during this life, whereby to bring us to heaven. And some protestant interpreters since,† take it to include assurance in this life, and a promise that eternal life, and the happiness thereof, shall open itself to you more and more, or be set open wider unto your spirits, so as to enjoy the larger sense thereof in your souls, that you may more amply and freely pierce into the inwards of heaven, and enjoy the sense of that life in a larger measure. I have in the margent cited these, that I may not appear alone in giving this sense ; though I take the words to extend to both, viz., unto our entrance by way of full fruition in the other world ; the comfort whereof at death God often gives to those that have abounded in holiness, that their souls are in heaven whilst in their bodies, and in the suburbs of heaven. And they crowd not in, but have the great broad gates set wide open to them. Yet withal, also, that in the mean time holy walking procureth, ministereth, or affordeth in the very doing, the privilege of a more abundant entrance into heaven every day more and more, all along this life ; by Christ's manifesting himself to them ; as John xiv., upon ' keeping his commandments.' And in the coherence of the words in Peter with the foregoing, the promise hereof comes in last, as an increase or surplusage of the former privileges (all which are in this life). One mentioned, ver. 10, was, that we should thereby ' make our calling and election sure.' And this of ' abundant entrance' is not the same with that ; not a repetition of the same matter, of assurance namely, but an addition of a distinct and further benefit ; a further, and indeed the highest, degree attainable in this life, the top of his climax, or highest ascension of such attainments. As if he had said, you shall not only ' make your calling and election sure,' but you shall enter more and more into heaven, and live in heaven aforehand whilst you live, and take an ample possession of it in the first fruits thereof, which yet is called but an entering (though often still renewed), because it is at

* Dutch Annotators.

† Amplior introitus, *i. e.*, felicitas et vita æterna amplius pandet, et explicabit se vobis, ut copiosius, et liberius penetrare possetis in regni hujus partes interiores ; et frui vitæ illius sensu, in ampliori mensura.—*Dixon in verba.*

highest in this life but an imperfect attainment; and in comparison of the latter full entrance, which is upon death, but as an entrance, a first entrance, and first fruits and earnest, and yet said to be an entrance. And thus, Heb. iv., 'we who have believed do enter into rest;' and therefore going on 'from faith to faith,' as Rom. i., we enter further into rest, as faith increaseth, every renewed act being a renewed entrance; and thus we are entering all our life long. And this Jacob, that so extraordinary saint and patriarch, had enjoyed long afore death. He says, 'This is the house of God, and this is no other than the gates of heaven,' which in that vision (wherein he saw Christ and the angels) he had been taken up into, Gen. xxviii. 17. Yea, and every soul that walks very holily, and abounds in it, though he enter not into the joys of heaven, such as are 'unspeakable and full of glory,' yet he may truly be said to go further up into heaven, in his so walking, and to obtain larger room and place there than other men, though holy. He enters further up into the country every day, into the heart of it, as we use to say,—though it be true that every true Christian is passed from death to eternal life, from hell into heaven;—and when possession or fruition shall come, such a man will find a more rich and ample provision to have been made for him there against he comes.

4. But if, in the last place, more strict inquiry be made, what actings, exercises of faith and holiness, the apostle doth here in this my Hebrews' text, more especially intend, and calleth an entering into heaven, and a coming to, and drawing near? I answer:

(1.) In general. All gospel worship and ordinances, which therefore by way of inference from this here in ver. 19, he in the 23d exhorteth not to forsake. And we must consider that his exhortation, begun in the 19th verse, is an inference from his discourse afore of the Jewish worship, and particularly of that on that solemn day of atonement, when the high priest went into the holiest, which was the highest worship that the Jews had prescribed them; and was a day of pure worship. They were to do no work thereon. Yea, and was styled a Sabbath of Sabbatism, the queen of sabbaths, and above all other sabbaths whatsoever. And you may observe how in the beginning of this chapter, wherein he goes on to interpret and unfold the mysteries of this day's solemnity, he styles them that come to it, 'the worshippers,' 'the comers thereunto,' verses 1, 2, and from which (namely, that his discourse, doctrinally treated by him in three chapters afore) it is he deduceth his exhortation here. So then gospel worship and ordinances may in general be understood to be an entrance into heaven, and the dispositions required in ver. 22, to be the inward qualifications requisite unto all such worship.

But (2.) in a more special and eminent manner, I conceive, he understands prayer, and especially private prayer. And I am so far from being alone in it, that I find myself compassed about with a cloud of interpreters, who, almost generally, carry it unto prayer. I could fill a leaf with their names and sayings to this purpose upon some or other of these. And that parallel-like exhortation (which many of them do allege for this), Heb. iv. 14, 'Seeing we have a great high priest, that is passed into the heavens, Jesus the Son of God;' and ver. 16, 'Let us come boldly to the throne of grace.' The exhortation there, 'Let us come,' is a coming by faith in prayer, imploring for help in time of need and distress; so the psalmist useth the word to 'come to God:' Ps. lxv. 2, 'To thee shall all flesh come.' How? 'For thou art a God hearing prayer.' It is a coming then by prayer. And the word here in my text, 'let us draw near,' προσερχώμεθα, is in the original the very same that is there in chap. iv. 16. And in the next chapter to this where my text is (the 11th), ' He that cometh to God' is one that ' diligently seeks him;' and that is by prayer. But if it were as it is translated ' draw near,' it likewise importeth prayer : James iv., ' Draw near to God, and he will draw near to you ; be afflicted, and mourn,' &c. Again, in that parallel, chap. iv. 16, it is a coming to God ' to obtain mercy, and find grace to help.' And all that speaks prayer. For these are the aim of a soul that invocates God by prayer, to obtain his mercy for pardon ; and grace for supplies of all their spiritual wants, and other needs. And also the word βοήθεια there used, is a crying out for help in case of extremity. Likewise the word there translated ' boldly,' μετὰ παῤῥησίας, *with boldness,* is properly ' liberty of speech.' And what is that but to come and speak freely to God our needs, and boldly to use all sorts of pleas with him, which grace and mercy in him do afford, to obtain relief, and succours, to pour out our hearts afore him ? And is not the very word also that the apostle chooseth here in my text, to form his exhortation in, the very same ? ' We having boldness, let us come,' or draw near ; that is, having liberty to speak, and speak out our minds, our whole hearts, let us come and do it. Every word in that Heb. iv. speaks prayer ; and with that exhortation there doth this here correspond and agree. The allusion also here of entering refers unto the Jews, their coming to worship, which is styled an ' entering into God's courts,' Ps. c. ; and their coming with praise and thanksgiving (which is a part of prayer, 2 Tim. i. 1*) in the 4th verse of that psalm, ' Enter into his gates with thanksgiving, and into his courts with praise : be thankful unto him, and bless his name.' But further, the special allusion of this whole paragraph, my text, being specially made to the worship and practices of that day wherein the high priest entered into the holiest (which phrase of entering into it is so often repeated in this epistle), this brings it yet nearer home unto prayer as meant, and shews that it is a coming to God and Christ by prayer. For both on the high priest's part that day, as he went in by blood into the holiest, so by incense to make a cloud, and by these two alone he went into the holiest : Lev. xvi. 12, 13, ' And he shall take a censer full of burning coals of fire from off the altar before the Lord, and his hands full of sweet incense beaten small, and bring it within the vail : and he shall put the incense upon the fire before the Lord, that the cloud of the incense may cover the mercy-seat that is upon the testimony, that he die not.' This all of us that come into the holiest are to imitate. Now, not only incense betokens prayer (as in the psalms), which was required on the high priest's part, but on the people's part also. It was required of them, that whilst incense was offering, they should pray without : Luke i. 9, 10, ' According to the custom of the priest's office, his lot was to burn incense when he went into the temple of the Lord. And the whole multitude of the people were praying without at the time of incense.' And if on the times of the ordinary days of worship, much more on this day, the day of atonements, which was appointed also for the people for prayer ; for they were to fast and afflict their souls for sin, Lev. xvi. 27, 28, which they then confessed, even of their whole lives ; and was therefore joined with prayer, as that duty did require, for atonement.

So as everything falls in, that prayer bears the main of the apostle's intendment and exhortation. And those qualifications, ver. 22, of ' a true heart,' &c., do come in but as concomitants, to make the prayer acceptable.

* Qu. ' Phil. iv. 6 '?—ED.

CHAPTER III.

That it is the privilege of believers under the New Testameat to enter into the highest heavens by faith, and with the apprehension of faith.—An invitation to them so to do.—The dispositions which are required to make them meet for such a heavenly converse.

These things premised, I reduce the words to these four heads :

I. That all that are believers already, under the New Testament, their privilege is, that when they worship, especially in prayer, that they should by faith, and with the apprehension of faith, enter boldly into the very highest heavens ; and placing themselves there, to seek communion and converse with God, through Christ ; and with Christ himself as our high priest, themselves considered as they are in heaven ; and we by faith present there, together with God and Christ ; in brief, when we pray, we should in an immediate manner set ourselves to enjoy communion with God and Christ, as they are in heaven.

II. A free and open invitation here made, with an exhortation thereunto ; which invitement you have amply pressed, and enforced with the highest encouragements to persuade confidence in so doing ; namely, thus to approach God and Christ in the highest heavens. These two heads you have in the 19th, 20th, 21st verses, ' Having therefore, brethren, boldness to enter into the holiest, by the blood of Jesus, by a new and living way which he hath consecrated for us, by the veil of his flesh ; and having a high priest over the house of God ; let us draw near,' &c.

III. The inward dispositions or qualifications that are required to make them meet for such a heavenly converse, and. which are to make their prayers prevalent to have power with God ; to obtain what we pray for :

1. With which therefore we should enter and approach ; or,

2. Which we should put forth, and exercise in the time of performance of that duty of praying ; and, as much as in us lies, to endeavour not to come off without them. Or,

3. At least, which we do in our prayers, should chiefly seek for at God's hands, and implore his grace and mercy to help our infirmities therein ; these, above all things else that we pray for ; without doing which, we shall much fall short in our obtaining those other things prayed for by us ; and these you have in ver. 22, ' Let us draw nigh with a true heart, in full assurance of faith, having our hearts sprinkled from an evil conscience, and our bodies washed with pure water.'

I have proposed this third head under these three several branches, that it may take in and comprehend all sorts of believers ; all of them either having or performing either the one or the other of these three. For if we should understand and limit the scope of these qualifications, to be all and every of them absolutely necessary conditions ; that is, such as without each of which, unless every believer brings with him before he prays, he is not, nor shall be accepted, nor his prayer regarded ; we must exclude many of the righteous. For it is certain that many do want ' full assurance of faith ; ' which speaks a higher degree of faith, and especially an assurance that their persons are accepted. Many also fall short of having their consciences* so fully sprinkled from an evil conscience ; as to their own sense (as that phrase would import, even to the sense of their consciences, of which hereafter), that their own hearts should not condemn them ; in the guiltiness of many sins that God is pleased to let lie bound, even upon them

* Qu. 'hearts?'—ED.

that are saints, for as long as his pleasure is, thereby to humble them. And to confirm this, if we take the scope of the apostle, I look upon the words to be an invitation, with an exhortation; and the scope of that exhortation to be, what dispositions those that would pray as in heaven, when they pray, and that would pray after such a heavenly rate, should labour to attain, and either bring such with them when they come, or at least are to seek after, to obtain them in praying, and by prayer. And so these things to be proposed here, as principal matters to be prayed for. And so they serve as rules of direction to praying, as well as for qualifications requisite thereunto. I find but two interpreters that have touched upon any such scope; and they are in Flaccius Illyricus upon the words, of which afterwards. The other is worthy Mr Dixon, who hath well observed on that word—' in full assurance of faith '—that God's meaning is, that he likes it better to come with a full assurance of faith, though he despiseth not the weakest, nor quencheth faith in the smoke, not yet risen into victory in the flame. To which I add, it being an exhortation, exhortations are usually made in the strain of highest attainments, not the lowest and weakest. The apostles did exhort to many things weak Christians might be long in attaining. For the copy or samples you set afore learners use to be with the perfectest, when yet they write or work very much short of them. And so here the meaning is, that God indeed would have you come in full assurance ; and this he proposeth as that which you may obtain, and exhorteth unto it as what he most desires, and would have in you. Also, consider that yet the weakest believer hath a faith, so far as to cause him to perform the main thing exhorted to ; and that is, to come to God and Christ, and also with a true heart in prayer. Again, it is certain that those, whoever they be, that have these dispositions, he or they obtained them by prayer. And therefore they cannot be all absolute conditions aforehand in all cases ere we come to pray. For themselves are obtained (I say) by prayer first, and much seeking of God too. And how many poor souls do bitterly complain of the want of these !

IV. And each and the whole of these, both duty, invitation, privileges, &c., are inferred from, and represented under, the analogy and similitude of that special solemn worship, and the rites thereof observed and performed by the high priest and the people upon the great and memorable day of atonement; once again celebrated with extraordinary sacrifices on purpose appointed for that day, besides the ordinary for every day, the high priest carrying the blood for those extraordinary ones, to make atonement, into the holy of holies, which he entered into but once a-year. All which was accompanied with confession of sins and prayer, the people also universally coming up to that assembly, and' were present at that solemn worship, keeping that day with afflicting their souls for the sins of their whole lives past, which therefore must needs be joined with prayer on their part for the pardon of them ; as Lev. xvi. 12, 17, where it is said the high priest carried incense within the veil, with which, if you compare the practice of the people, what it used to be whilst incense was offered ; as in Luke i. 9, 10, ' according to the custom of the priest's office, his' (namely Zacharias) 'lot was to burn incense when he went into the temple of the Lord: and the whole multitude of people were praying without at the time of incense ; ' it appears that the people prayed that day, incense on that day being offered in the holy of holies, by the high priest, for an atonement in the same, Lev. xvi. 29, 30, which day was called the day of atonements ; and in like respect styled the fast, Act xxvii. 9.

From the types of which the apostle deducts his exhortation here, in these four verses, and speaks to the Hebrews in the language thereof; carrying us up from that holiest to heaven, unto God, and Jesus our high priest there. And he presseth the substantials of our inward worshippings, in ver. 22, from the performances of that day, especially in prayer. For, as this day's solemnities were the top of the Jewish worship, and spent in fasting, prayers, and confessions of sin by the people, so is prayer—these duties and qualifications of our person in prayer—the height of our Christian religion.

For the first. That it is our privilege, and the gospel dispensation calls for it, that when we pray we should set ourselves to enter in, by faith, immediately into heaven, and converse with them as they be in heaven, and we together with them.

Instead of more literal proofs, this text being evidence sufficient, requiring us thus to do, I shall give reasons and demonstrations of it.

1. A reason in general. The gospel (the doctrines of it being totally heavenly, and the blessings of it heavenly, Eph. i. 4) hath exalted, raised up, and enhanced all things thereof to an heavenly state, in their several proportions and kinds. Like the elixir, it hath turned all the legal alchemy, or carnal earthly ordinances (as Heb. ix. 1 they are there called), into celestial; as in the same Heb. ix. 22 they are styled, even all the things represented by those types. The gospel itself was styled, with difference from the old covenant, 'the kingdom of heaven,' and that by Christ himself, when he began to preach it. The very preaching of it is termed an exaltation of those that heard it unto heaven, Mat. xi. 22 ; and a speaking from heaven, Heb. xii. 25. And that is spoken in comparison to Moses giving the law, whom he there oppositely terms, 'him that spake on earth.' Yea, and this speaking from heaven is attributed to the sermons of the apostles, and ordinary ministers, unto the Hebrews and other Christians, to the end of the world. And if their sermons, which are ordinances by the ministry of another speaking to us, are a speaking of Christ's from heaven ; what then are our prayers, especially private prayers ? For they are purely mediate* effluxes of the soul to God himself, without the intervention of any outward *medium*, but what is in and from a man's own soul, elevated and assisted by the Holy Ghost, as Rom. viii. This may certainly be entitled, praying in heaven.

Our conversation (if such as becomes the gospel) is to be in heaven, Phil. iii. 20. But prayer is here made, comparatively unto that ordinary conversation, an entering into heaven in so eminent a manner, as if that we walked out of heaven when in our callings, &c., and entered anew sometimes, but now and then, and that when we pray and come to worship. Likewise where Christians' state is to sit together in heavenlies with Christ—Eph. ii. 5, 6, 'Even when we were dead in sins, hath quickened us together with Christ; and hath raised us up together, and made us sit together in heavenly places in Christ Jesus '—if you be quickened, and have the least of spiritual life begun in you, then hath Christ placed thee in heaven ; and our actings in prayer should be in its degree (and this exercise doth excel all other) answerable to our state, and therefore should be a praying as persons in heaven. Certainly if any part of worship, this in the nature of it, above all other, calls for it.

This reason is but a general, from the heavenliness of the gospel.

* Qu. 'immediate'?—ED.

CHAPTER IV.

The privilege of believers under the New Testament illustrated, and proved
by the difference between them, and believers under the Old Testament, who
had not this freedom of entering into the holiest.

There is a further special account to be given of this privilege, from a
difference between the manner of the dispensation under the law, and now
under the gospel, as in respect unto this particular of prayer ; together with
an explication wherein this difference lies of us from the old Jew, who yet
directed their prayers unto God that was in heaven, and implored him to
hear in heaven when they prayed, as in 1 Kings viii. you often have it, and
elsewhere abundantly.

That there was and is (notwithstanding this now said of them) a difference of privilege between them and us in this respect, it is plain that this
exhortation in the text, to come boldly into the holiest, is spoken oppositely
to what was theirs, specially when compared with other passages of this
epistle concerning them ; the text also styling this our manner of coming
into the heavens to be a ' new way initiated,' or ' new begun,' (as the word
' consecrated ' in ver. 20 doth also signify), by the flesh of Jesus rent, as
ver 20, and by his blood, ver. 19, newly shed, as the words in the original
do import, of which further after.

Concerning which difference,

1. I will not hold you in the briers of a dispute about the meaning of
that difficult place of our apostle, chap. ix. 8, affirming that to the people
of the Old Testament, ' The way ' (that is, for us) ' into the holiest of all was
not yet made manifest ; while as the first tabernacle was yet standing ;' that
is, whilst the Jewish worship was yet in force, which was until Christ the
true high priest was ascended up unto his holiest, the heavens. The
plainest meaning to me is, that the mystery of this was kept hid, in a great
measure, that Christ might have the greater honour in the discovery of it,
upon and after his ascension ; and also to shew, that by virtue of his blood
it is that any do now, or ever did, enter therein. But still so as, whatever
de facto was then, that the godly entered into heaven at death, yet the way
to be through Christ's entering, this was not then manifest (I take hold of,
and keep to, the proper import of the word). He says not that none had
in reality, or indeed, not entered, for Enoch and Elias had, but that it was
not manifest ; nor yet was it that it were altogether unknown to them
that they should one day come thither, for the patriarchs knew it, and
expected it, Heb. xi. 10, 14, 16. All which still was but with a glimmering, obscure light ; as a dark shadow. I take, therefore, the apostle's
meaning in the same sense that the same apostle speaks it, of the whole
mystery of the gospel itself. Eph. iii. 5, ' Which in other ages was not
made known to the sons of men, as it is now revealed unto his holy apostles
and prophets by the Spirit.' Even so this particular of it was not manifest,
that is, in that clear manner that it is now, upon Christ's ascension. The
very apostles (in the name of whom Philip seems to speak it), John xiv. 5,
say, ' Lord, we know not whither thou goest, and how can we know
the way ? '

My inference from this is, that if the way of entrance at last into that
holy of holies was not then so manifest to them, then much less was this
way of worshipping and praying, by an immediate entrance of themselves

(through Christ) into heaven itself, whenever they prayed; and as present with their high priest himself, to present themselves by faith unto God through him, and so offer up their prayers to him; but stood as aloof, as men on earth, whilst they prayed unto God as dwelling in heaven. But this the apostle in my text hath taught us; and this way, I may safely say of it, was not manifest then as it is now. But,

2. Besides the obscurity of the knowledge of this way of praying, they were preoccupated from such an address immediate, into heaven itself (such as we have), in that God appointed another place of his residence, viz., his temple on earth, and therein specially the holy of holies, ¶calling upon them to look unto, and make their addresses to him, as dwelling also there; whereas now he hath appointed heaven itself immediately for us in prayer to come into, when we come unto him, where also our high priest is present. Their case stood thus: they knew, indeed, that God's dwelling-place was heaven, and that when they prayed, God heard in heaven his dwelling-place; and therefore when they prayed, they spread forth their hands towards heaven, as Solomon in his prayer did. But yet withal, they were first called upon to do homage to God, as sitting on his throne on earth; as sitting between the cherubims on the mercy-seat, which covered the ark in the holy of holies. So Hezekiah directs his prayer, 2 Kings xix. 15, 'O God, that sittest between the cherubims;' and others in the psalms the like. And thereupon also, when they prayed (though in private prayer), they were bidden to look 'towards the holy place and temple;' as Ps. xxviii. 2, 'Hear the voice of my supplications when I cry unto thee; when I lift up my hands to thy holy oracle.' This oracle was the most holy place, where the ark, the mercy-seat, and the cherubims were; as you find 1 Kings viii. 6, and chap. vi. 5. And in this manner Solomon, in the dedication of his temple, directs his own prayer made by himself, and unto this course directed the people also: in that 1 Kings chap. viii. he prays unto God, that dwelt in heaven, to hear in heaven; and yet draws down their eyes towards that house on earth, as dwelling there; ver. 27–30, 'But will God indeed dwell on the earth? Behold, the heaven, and the heaven of heavens, cannot contain thee; how much less this house that I have builded! Yet have thou respect unto the prayer of thy servant, and to his supplication, O Lord my God, to hearken unto the cry and to the prayer which thy servant prayeth before thee to-day; that thine eyes may be open toward this house night and day, even toward the place of which thou hast said, My name shall be there; that thou mayest hearken unto the prayer which thy servant shall make toward this place. And hearken thou to the supplication of thy servant, and of thy people Israel, when they shall pray toward this place: and hear thou in heaven thy dwelling-place; and when thou hearest, forgive.' So as they took God up, as dwelling in both places; but first looked to his dwelling-house, or himself as dwelling on earth. And from thence their faith was to climb up to him, as dwelling in that other, the most holy house in heaven, whereof this on earth was the type; and thereby was to their weakness a help unto their faith in prayer, to have God so near them (as the phrase is), as on earth; that God should come down to earth, and there had a visible dwelling-house amongst them; as Exod. xxv. 8, 'And let them make me a sanctuary, that I may dwell among them;' which he had not again on all the earth.

And hence ariseth a manifest difference betwixt their condition and ours, that though they prayed unto God that was in heaven, and to hear in heaven, yet,

(1.) Themselves looked upon themselves as standing afar off, at a distance from heaven, whilst they were a-praying; and entered not themselves by faith into heaven, as we are here called upon to do. I may therefore again say, this way of prayer in the holiest was not then manifest, as it is now. And,

(2.) Though they desired God would hear in heaven, yet the cry of their prayer and the eye of their faith were directed first unto and towards his holy of holies on earth;* from whence, as by a rebound (as I may so speak), it should as by an echo ascend up into the ears of the Lord of hosts in heaven. Even as a man directing his speech, going immediately to such or such a hollow place, or cavern, the sound thereof comes back at second hand by reflection, to one that is further off: and their intercourse with God in heaven was like as if one should send a letter, or a petition to a great person, who had two dwelling-houses, one in a city, the other in some village very far off from that city; and the man is appointed to send his petition or letter directly to the country-house, but directed to him withal in his standing house in his city. So as indeed the holiest saint of them looked unto God in both, and did homage to him as dwelling in both, and were not to neglect either. Whereas we take a direct course to heaven when we pray, and divert not the least cast of an eye to anything on earth wherein God should be. We look not to the right hand, nor the left; not to one place more than another: ' Let prayers be made everywhere,' 1 Tim. ii. 8., spoken in opposition to the Jews looking to their temple.

And one reason of this was, that God dealing then with them as children under age, Gal. iv. 1, and instructing them by figures of the time (as Heb. ix. 24, where he speaks of and applies that maxim to this very thing we are upon), he therefore would have a figurative house to dwell in; not such as in common he is said to dwell in all the earth, but separated from the rest of the earth; which house was consecrated by himself, and wherein his glory and shadowy presence did often shine and appear from forth the oracle, the holy of holies, and filled that temple: and thither their faith and prayers were to approach him first, and take up by the way, as we say, in their addresses to heaven. God condescended herein to the weakness of them whom he trained up as children. And it was a way of worship fit for children, and suited to their capacity; and yet sanctified unto them, because thus appointed by God.

You may perhaps in part understand an Old Testament Jewish heart, and that of one that was truly penitent, by the spirit of that poor publican, whose character and frame of spirit Christ hath lively set forth to us, Luke xviii. And therein view the distance which they keep. He was a sinner truly humbled, and an expectant of mercy. It is said, ' He went up to pray in the temple,' ver. 10; so then it therein falls pat with the subject afore me. Now, observe what confirms the foregone differences (as on their part) I have given. 1. ' He stood afar off;' so ver. 13. There is the distance I spake of. 2. ' He would not so much as lift up his eyes to heaven;' but, 3. applied himself, and his prayer unto God, as sitting on his mercy-seat in the holiest: in those words, ' But smote upon his breast, and said, God be merciful unto me a sinner.' It is that word—God

* The word which Calvin useth of David's praying, in the 3d Psalm, when he fled from Absalom was—*David recta se ad tabernaculum convertit, unde promiserat Deus se propitium fore servis suis.* On the words of the 5th verse—*Mediam viam tenuit, ne vel signum visibile contemneret, quod Deus pro temporis ruditate instituerat: vel super-stitiosè loco affixum quicquam de gloria Dei carnale conciperet.—Ibidem.*

be merciful to me—I take hold of for this. In the original, the word ἱλάσθητι, that is there used, is a verb answering to the noun ἱλαστήριον, the mercy-seat; and unto ἱλασμός, a propitiation for sin, as 1 John ii. 2. And so it is as if he had said, According to that mercy, thou, O God, that sittest between the cherubims, over and upon thy mercy-seat (which is called ἱλαστήριον by the Septuagint, and owned by the apostle, Heb. ix. 5), declaring thereby that thou art and wilt be propitious and merciful to poor sinners, according unto that mercy thereby set forth, be merciful to me a poor sinner, that am at this distance from that thy holy place thou dwellest in. Yet I do look unto that thy mercy-seat, and to thee who sittest thereon; and have my eye and hopes fixed wholly thereupon for pardon. And though I dare not look up to heaven itself, where thou dwellest, yet my soul looks toward this mercy-seat, whereon thou sittest on earth. You may, I say, understand hereby the level of a Jewish faith. And that word ἱλάσθητι, as spoken by him, shews that they understood, though darkly, what that mercy-seat did signify. That God, that sat thereupon, was merciful, and favourable to expiate and make atonement for sins, and then to cover, and pardon them, as the Hebrew word importeth (of which more afterwards); unto which the word ἱλάσκεθαι, and ἱλάσκειν answereth; signifying both to make atonement or reconciliation by Christ (so Heb. ii. 17), and also to be merciful and forgive, upon such a reconciliation made: as by Dan. chap ix. 14, and Deut. xxi. 8, ' Be merciful, O Lord,' &c. Now of this man, Christ says, he went away justified. He being humbled, and having this faith. I but observe here how yet he stood afar off, two courts off from the holy of holies, where this mercy-seat was: yea, in the remotest place, out of that outermost court, did this man stand; for it is comparatively spoken unto that nearer approach which the Pharisee forsooth made, he going up unto the highest part of that outward court; thither he crowds up himself with confidence, even next to the door of the priest's court: but into that priest's court none was to enter but a Levite. Well, but here, in this Heb. x., we see the faith we are exhorted unto: ' Christ being come, an high priest of good things to come ;' not as then, but in a shadow revealed, we are bidden to ' enter with boldness :' yea, to draw near, when we are entered, with full assurance of faith, and confidence, even into the holy of holies; the heaven where Christ is sitting at the throne of the majesty on high. Under the law, the holiest saint of that people was not to enter into the first earthly mundane tabernacle, into which the priests came. Yea, some have said, they were not so much as to see into it (but that I am not fully resolved of; for they brought their sacrifice to the door of that first tabernacle, and one would think should see it sacrificed too for them) ; but enter they did not, that is certain. And to that end there was a veil, called the first veil, placed at the entrance of the first tabernacle of the priests, to shut out the people ; as well as there was a second veil placed afore the holy of holies, as the apostle plainly insinuates, Heb. ix. 2. I will not dispute whether it was to hinder the people's sight of what was done in the priests' court, as well as the second veil hindered the priests' sight of what was in the holy of holies ; but, to be sure, it forbade entrance to the people, if not wholly debarred their sight.

This practical instance I have, as by the way, and in the middle of my discourse, inserted, to shew the difference mentioned of a Jewish faith and prayer, and as giving light to the rest of my discourse on this argument.

I proceed to confirm the former notion further.

II. As in this manner they directed their prayers unto God in his temple, on their parts, so answerably on God's part he both promises,

1. That his eyes shall be open, and his ears attent unto the prayer that was made in that place. 'For now' (saith he), 'I have chosen and sanctified my house, that my name may be there for ever: and mine eyes and my heart shall be there perpetually.' And in 1 Kings ix. 3, it is added by God, 'My heart shall be there perpetually.'

2. It is *de facto* said and spoken of God, that his hearing of their prayers was out of his holy temple, as well as out of heaven; and to send forth help, and blessings, and deliverances of his people upon their prayers; yea, and to work all his works of wonder, which he executes over the whole earth from out of his temple, his dwelling-place on earth.

But especially in the deliverances of his people: Ps. iii. 4, 'I cried unto the Lord with my voice, and he heard me out of his holy hill.' It was uttered by David when he fled from Absalom, as the title to the psalm is (he having before placed the tabernacle and ark on Zion,* the city of David, 2 Sam. vi. 12, 17, which he calls in that Ps. iii., 'The holy mount'); and that speech of his here hath an aspect and reference unto those passages in the story of his flight, 2 Sam. xv. The high priest did offer to carry the ark with him into the field, ver. 24. No, says David, let it stand in its proper place, in the tabernacle appointed for it, ver. 25; and, thought he, my prayer shall be towards it, as it is placed in that ordained seat which God hath appointed. And his prayers having been heard, though at that distance from the ark itself, he glorifies God that had heard him at that distance 'out of his holy hill' (thus Calvin glosseth on the words); David's faith glorying and triumphing in this, that whilst Absalom, who came and possessed the city of Jerusalem, and so had the outward presence of the temple and ark with him (and let him take that to himself); but David, in the mean while, though removed from it, bent his prayers thither, and those prayers prevailed, and were heard therein (says he), whilst his wretched son was rejected, who had the local being of the ark close by him and with him, for he was possessed of Jerusalem (let these things be compared with the story). In like manner, Ps. xx., he brings in the people praying for their king; their petition, ver. 2, is, 'Send thee help from the sanctuary, and strengthen thee out of Zion.'† And lo, as he hears the prayer in his sanctuary, so the performance of it is likewise said to come from God, as dwelling in the sanctuary; from thence it was he gave forth his commands for the execution; and yet so as heaven thereby was signified too. And therefore, upon this experiment, David (who was the king they had prayed for) strengthens his faith for the future: ver. 6, 'Now know I that the Lord saveth his anointed; he will hear him from his holy heaven with the saving strength of his right hand.'

Many other like passages you may find scattered up and down in the Psalms and elsewhere; that what God doth at the prayer of his people, he is said to do it in his temple; that is, that from out of his temple the sentence to come forth, to render recompence to his enemies, is said to be a voice out of his temple. Isa. lxvi. 6, 'A voice from the temple, a voice of the Lord that rendereth recompence to his enemies.' For God sat as a

---

* Fateor quidem cœlum alibi sæpe vocari sanctum Dei palatium; sed hic non dubito quin respexit ad Arcam: quæ jam in monte Zion locata erat.—*Calvin in verba.*

† Hoc est, auxilietur tibi e monte Sion: ubi Arcam fœderis locari jubens, domicilium sibi illic delegit.—*Calvinus in verba.*

judge in his holy temple, and ruled thence the whole earth, Hab. ii. 20.
And Ps. xcix. 2, ' The Lord is great in Zion; and he is high above all
people; '—' and terrible out of his holy places,' Ps. lxviii. 35. The great
deliverances of his people when threatened to be besieged by Sennacherib
and his host in Hezekiah's times; Ps. lxxvi. 2, 3,* ' In Salem also is his
tabernacle, and his dwelling-place in Zion. There brake he the arrows of
the bow, the shield, and the sword, and the battle. Selah.' Observe how
it is said, ' There he brake,' namely, in his temple, his habitation there.
For unto that his temple doth the coherence in the verse afore carry it, for
that was last in mention, and with the greatest emphasis above the former;
either Jerusalem or the land of Judah, ver. 1. And ' there he brake the
spear,' &c., that is, frustrated and made void all their weapons prepared for
the battle, though not one stroke were struck; so he is said to ' break the
arm of the king of Egypt,' Ezek. xxx., that is, to weaken his power. But
that which puts the greatest notoriety upon this, as to our purpose in hand,
is that in the story we read how that Sennacherib's overthrow was from
Hezekiah's prayer in the temple; for upon Sennacherib's letter, and Hezekiah's hearsay of the blasphemy, he took himself thither, went instantly
into the temple, and began his prayer thus: ' O thou God of Israel, that
dwellest between the cherubims.' He invocates him under that style of
his dwelling in the holies,† and so hearing prayers there. Thus you have
it recorded both in Isaiah and in 2 Kings xxix. 15. And how suitably, in
answer hereunto, it is said here in the psalm, that God gave forth sentence
presently out of his tabernacle; yea, and that so suddenly too, as that the
very execution is said to be done there, that is, from thence. And yet
again, in the 8th verse of the psalm, it is said to be a sentence from heaven
too; ' Thou didst cause judgment ' (so called because it was the sentence
of God as a judge) ' to be heard from heaven.' Thus Hezekiah prayed, and
thus God heard; and both as in the temple.

---

* Unto Sennacherib's invasion doth Calvin refer it, for which he gives his reason.
And Piscator, in the very title, doth the same. And Ainsworth, on the last verse,
aptly applies it to the chieftains of Sennacherib's army, which is a most apt accom-
modation of the conclusion of the story, with a concluding admonition given to kings
and princes; ver. 12, ' He shall cut off the spirit of princes; he is terrible to the
kings of the earth.' The word translated *princes*, is *antecessors, leaders* (see Junius's
translation), next to kings (which follows), God doth cut off their spirits; gather or
take away their spirits, their lives, in a moment, at once, and with as much ease and
liberty at pleasure as a gardener prunes the leaves and branches of vines, or as he
would gather the bunches of the grapes when fully ripe, and makes no matter on it
to do it. How fitly this doth correspond with the event in that story, you may see
but by reading these few words, which are the conclusion of that story too, in
2 Chron. xxxii. 21, ' And the Lord sent an angel, which cut off all the mighty men
of valour, and the " leaders " and captains in the camp of the king of Assyria.' And
for those other words in the Psalm, ' He is terrible to the kings of the earth,' take
those other words in the same verse in the story, ' So he returned with shame of face
to his own land.' What a dread and confusion must it needs strike the heart of that
haughty prince with. But that was not all; read but the verse, ' And when he was
come into the house of his god, they that came out of his own bowels slew him there
with the sword.'
† Qu. ' holiest' ?—ED.

CHAPTER V.

That there is a fair and open invitation to enter into heaven when we pray.—
And in such a manner to pray, as those that are thither entered.

It being the condition of many New Testament saints (so much of Moses'
veil remaineth on their hearts), that they dare not approach so near as to
believe themselves in heaven, or to be ' called up to heaven '* when they
are to pray: they hope indeed in the end to enter in thither when they
die (and it is true they shall), but stand at present afar off;—our apostle,
therefore, vehemently exhorteth them in these words, to draw near, ver. 22 ;
and to enforce this his exhortation, tells them they have a liberty, yea, a
right to enter. And then he follows, to back that, with other most potent
arguments to persuade them hereunto.

Concerning this his scope, in the general, observe,

1. That this invitation, with that exhortation, ver. 22, is of such persons
as are actually believers already ; for it is of such that at present have a
right to enter, and cause of boldness. 2. That they are supposed to have
a true heart, and a saving faith wrought in them ; and thereupon are exhorted to draw near, yet nearer, with a full assurance of faith, which is a
further degree of faith, in believing their right and interest, and of the
acceptance of their persons and prayers when they come. And such a
faith of *assurance* always presupposes a first act of faith of *recumbency* to be
already begun ; it is that begins their interest ; which faith of recumbency,
the apostle Paul saith, was the foundation faith of himself, and Peter, and
the other apostles and Christian Jews : Gal. ii. 16, ' We believed on Jesus
Christ, that we might be 'justified.' Likewise 3. Those he thus invites
and exhorts, he termeth ' brethren.' ' Seeing therefore, *brethren*, we have a
liberty, &c., let us draw near,' or ' come to.'

There is another invitation to come to Christ, which is on purpose
directed to such as are but as yet under a work of preparation unto their
coming to Christ ; namely, of those ' that are weary and heavy laden : '
Mat. xi. 28, 29, ' Come unto me, all ye that labour and are heavy laden,
and I will give you rest. Take my yoke upon you, and learn of me, for I
am meek and lowly in heart, and ye shall find rest unto your souls.' And
that indeed is that coming to Christ by souls that are now a-converting.
And so the exhortation there is for them to put forth that first act of faith,
which they never had done before, that they may be saved. But this here
is an invitation with an exhortation to those that have come to Christ for
salvation already, that they would enter into heaven in prayer. And it is
certainly a mistake in those interpreters that do extend the direct scope of
this here unto men who as yet have not believed, to come in at first to believe. I say this is not the direct scope of our apostle ; though I acknowledge (to the honour of this portion of Scripture) that many of the grounds,
persuasives, and instructions here given believers to come into heaven, by
prayer to Christ, may powerfully be made use of as pertinent invitements,
persuasives, and directions to those whom we preach to ; and by themselves
to persuade them, being humbled and heavy laden, for their first coming to
Christ. As, namely, 1, That they are immediately and directly to come to
Christ, as the way to God the Father : as my text also teacheth, and as
Christ is here represented. And 2, To come unto him as a high priest,
to sprinkle their consciences with his blood, as ver. 20, 22. Likewise, 3,

* As, Rev. xi. 12, it is spoken of the Witnesses.

To come to him as a high priest that is ' over the house of God ; ' and so as to him that hath the power and commission of admission of souls into that house at first, the household of God his Father, to own and receive them. And this is most proper unto the first act of faith. And 4, To come to God the Father with Christ's blood ; to be 'justified by him freely by his grace, through the redemption that is in Jesus Christ, whom God hath set forth to be a propitiation through faith in his blood ; ' and thus to be ' sprinkled from an evil conscience,' that is, from the guilt of all their sins : which, chap. ix., he terms a purging by his blood their consciences from dead works (which word *dead works* is proper unto the sins and state of a person that hath been unregenerate ;* their works are wholly dead works). And 5, To come both to God the Father and the Son, to give them true and sincere hearts unto God and his interest. Also 6, To have their bodies (put synechdochically for the whole man) washed, that is, sanctified by pure water ; and their outward conversation made holy and pure by the power of the Holy Ghost, working as clear water.

And as all these are undeniably the main substantials of saving conversion, and which humbled sinners invited to come to Christ do seek for at Christ's hands and God the Father's, so they are all found in the text. And it is also as certain, that after we have believed and been converted, that these are the great things which in prayer we drive at, and treat with God and Christ for, even ever after, till we come to heaven. And so the words of the text may serve for both.† And the most of these you will find in David's renewed faith and repentance, in Ps. li. And indeed it falls out that all the same essentials that are wrought in, or that are to be sought by, converts at the first for their salvation, the very same the most growing Christians are to continue to exercise in their renewals of faith and repentance in prayer ; as David there did. And like as that invitation, Mat. xi., ' Come to me, all ye that are heavy laden,' &c. (directed to beginners), yet serves many a poor soul's turn, that hath been long and truly turned to Christ ; when in temptations, that doubt sins afresh come in upon them ; and the Spirit of God makes use thereof for their relief ; so on the contrary, this invitation, &c., in my text, though setly intended for believers already as encouragements to prayer, may with an easy alteration be used and turned into persuasives unto those that have not yet believed, to persuade them to come in.

2. It is a universal invitation of all such. He exhorts them, therefore, under the title of *brethren*, and speaks it as including himself and all other Christians : ' Seeing we have, brethren, all of us the like liberty, let us draw near, even whoever is a brother with us.' As if he had said, in this matter, both of privilege and of duty, we are all alike ; the case is all one with me who am an apostle, and all my fellow-apostles, with all Christians. The weakest in faith and hope may crowd into heaven, together with the strongest ; you may all come into the holiest, and get up into it, as high as you can get.

Yea, 3. This exhortation and invitation is specially directed unto the

* See Calvin on those words.

† There is this seeming appearance for the other interpretation, that in ver. 19 it is called an entrance, which in usual speech notes a first beginning to enter. But for answer. 1. Every new prayer is a new entrance into the holiest, in comparison to thy ordinary walking in thy calling. Every time we pray we are to enter into heaven. 2. That act of drawing near, or approaching, ver. 22, supposeth one first, as ver. 19, entered into the holiest ; and notes a going on further, to approach to God there.

weaker sort of Christians (if to any more than others), that stand farthest off; that is, that are under the greatest discouragements in their own spirits to come, and are most backward and stand aloof in and through the sense of their own unworthiness, or weakness of faith and holiness. Unto you it is I more especially speak, of all others. As if he had more familiarly said, Come you and draw nearer, you that stand afar off, the outmost of all the company. Come to, why keep you at such a distance? Your right to draw near is as much as ours that are nearest. Like to that proclamation of peace, Isa. lvii. 19, 'To them that are afar off, and them that are near.'

These generals being forelaid, to clear the apostle's scope—all which I might have reserved to applications at last, but perhaps do stand as advantageously at this entrance; not only to shew this drift (necessary at the first), but chiefly that all sorts may know how to make use of, and apply the encouragements that are now to follow unto themselves. For that which I purpose to insist on are the persuasives with which this invitation is strengthened. And as the thing invited to is the greatest, namely, a communion with God in the heavens, by faith in praying, through Christ, as if we were with him there—the summary of this Scripture—so the invitements, or things inviting, or proposed to us to persuade us to the exercise of this, are the most alluring and forcible; and all framed after the image, and similitude, or allusion unto the coming to God in his own house, by the Jewish worshippers, or comers unto (as they are styled ver. 1 and 2 of this chapter). And when they came to pray in the temple, especially on that day of atonements, who are thereby said to appear before God, to approach and draw near (although with that local distance from the holiest); as also after the similitude of the high priest his entering into the holiest, both as high priest and in behalf of the people. For remember to carry along with you how I have proposed these as my pattern, to draw the particulars of what in this subject I shall handle, and shall keep it all along.

CHAPTER VI.

An enumeration of the particular invitements unto communion with God and Christ, by thus, in praying, entering into heaven through faith.

1. The invitement is to come to God's house; which you have *in terminis* proposed, ver. 21, even to his standing house of his continuing and everlasting abode. The usual and common style that invitations run in, is, Will you come to my house, and see me there? And if you read but what the holy men of old (that were kept at that distance) speak of, what entertainment they found when they came to God's house, (as Moses' tabernacle and temple were called), the type of our heaven, and what they express of it in the Old Testament language, you must needs expect far higher from God, when you shall in prayer come to heaven to him. They speak of the fatness of God's house: Ps. xxxvi. 8, 'They shall be abundantly satisfied with the fatness of thy house; and thou shalt make them drink of the river of thy pleasures,' noting a fulness of all that is good. Of goodness: Ps. lxv. 4. Come to a great man's house, and what a plenty do you find it furnished with; when you come but as a stranger, at times, and not as an indweller. Yet their holy of holies was but the shadow of good; of goods, in the plural; so in the original, Heb. x. 1; that is, both of what is substantially and truly good, and only good; as also plenty of all sort of good things. And notice, that he precisely speaks this, in Heb. x., of their holy of holies, as

the shadow into which their high priest there, he says, went. Thou comest to pray; that is thy business; and lo! when thou settest thy foot but in, thou mayest behold a new world of heavenly good things, which this earth affordeth not. All that thy soul needs for itself, to be sure, are to be had there, and from thence, by faith and prayer, in this life. Thy soul hath a choice set afore it; and my text tells thee, thou mayest be bold to pray for whatever is truly good, the commodities of that place which God hath given thee but a heart to will and desire and to pray for. And what good is there, or can be, which God's house will not afford?

But 2. Who is it in that house we are invited to come to, and speak withal there? God, who is the master and owner of the house, the supreme Lord of it. The house of God, saith he, which Christ is over, ver. 21, and set over by God his Father to be the governor of it, whereof the Father is the original owner, which Christ therefore calls his Father's house, John xiv. and which, although it be Christ's own house also, yet but as the Son's, Heb. iii., so as God is thereby set forth to us, as he to whom we are invited to come, and by whom we are invited to come.

The good welcome to any house, and the entertainment, depends on him that is the supreme in it; and therefore it is God (and that as here propounded) whom we are ultimately to come to. It is God we ultimately come to, and in prayer do and must apply ourselves unto. For this house is called the holiest, ver. 19; so called, because the holiness of God dwells there, in the high and holy place, created by him on purpose to display his glory in; which that and other scriptures term his throne, as Christ also enstyleth heaven. And there his face is to be seen, his presence. Even Christ here is said but 'the way,' ver. 20; but God is our journey's end. Where there is a way, there must be a journey's end. Though we are come to Christ first by faith, yet it is that he may 'bring us to God,' 1 Peter iii. 18, and that we may have access through Christ's own going to heaven, who was to appear in the presence of God, Heb. ix.

Now what entertainment you may have coming to God in his house, take in Old Testament language also; 'They shall be abundantly satisfied with the fatness of thy house; and thou shalt cause them to drink of the rivers of thy pleasures;' out of the same himself drinks of, even of the pleasures God himself hath. His own blessedness is thy utmost happiness. There can be no higher entertainment, than to be at the king's table, and to eat of what himself eats, and to drink of what himself drinks; 'of thy pleasures,' saith he. As also Christ, 'Enter into thy master's joy.' And sipping hereof thou mayest have* in this life (if thou seekest it in prayer as for thy soul), find the first fruits. For David spake this of what himself, and many Old Testament saints, had in their prayers to God, and other worshippings of him at their temple, or towards it, in this life found; Ps. lxv. 2, compared with ver. 4, 'O thou that hearest prayer, unto thee shall all flesh come. Blessed is the man whom thou choosest, and causest to approach unto thee, that he may dwell in thy courts. We shall be satisfied with the goodness of thy house, even of thy holy temple.'

But 3. The liberty (as our translators in the margent) and freedom that is proclaimed to us to come, being added to these, makes the invitement fair, and far more encouraging. The former are the real inducements, but this addition makes the encouragement as to us; and that is the third branch. For if the plenty the house affords were never so much, the entertainment never so great, yet if all this be not accompanied with a freedom for us

* Qu. 'here'?—ED.

declared, that we may come and be welcome, we should be afraid, and still keep at a distance.

Now for the clearing and demonstration of this, I must a while insist upon the interpretation of the word, ἔχοντες παῤῥησίαν, which is translated *boldness;* 'having boldness.' As that which is purposely set to declare this liberty to us.

The original word hath a large comprehension in it, of such senses and imports* as do abundantly fall in to make good this third branch I am now a-speaking to, and doth render this invitation yet more fair.

I shall here give a premonition concerning the translation of the word παῤῥησία, here rendered boldness.

I acknowledge that in that parallel place to this, Heb. iv. 16, 'Let us come with boldness,' (where it is the same word παῤῥησία) it doth signify a bold confidence in us to come, &c. But there it is a simple exhortation, and the whole of the exhortation. But here it is made the ground of the exhortation that follows. 'Let us therefore come,' &c., that is the exhortation. And 'seeing we have the boldness,' &c., that is, the ground premised or forelaid, to draw on the thing exhorted to. Again, there it is joined with μετὰ, *with* boldness, as an act of confidence within ourselves, which we are bidden to come with. But here it is, ἔχοντες παῤῥησίαν, which is translated, 'We having this boldness,' as having an act of boldness and confidence already begotten in ourselves, which, as it stands in this place, seems not so proper unto that following exhortation, verse 22. And my reason is, because in that exhortation boldness or confidence (as it is a grace in us wrought) is one main thing exhorted to in that clause, namely, 'with full assurance of faith,' that is, with full confidence and persuasion, which is that which causeth boldness as the effect of it. And thus it would be as if he had said ; 'seeing therefore we have the boldness, &c., let us come to, or draw near, with full assurance of faith ;' which in sense and substance are all one and the same thing. Yea, and it were to make this boldness (supposed), which is the effect of assurance of faith (as was said), to be the ground or persuasive, and so the cause of this assurance of faith, and of our coming with this assurance.

But yet unto this objection it may be answered, that some good beginning of boldness and confidence being wrought already in us, encourageth us to enter ; and that then Christ gives more assurance and confidence. For as faith begun goes to Christ for more increase of itself—'Lord, increase our faith'—so doth confidence, for more confidence. Like unto that exhortation, Ps. xxvii. 14, 'Be strong,' or of 'good courage' (which are all one), 'and he shall strengthen thy heart.'

It is far more congruous to interpret it thus : seeing we have such cause of confidence, or such ground of boldness, which by a metonymy is so called boldness, let us draw near with full assurance. And indeed our best interpreters do understand, and carry all the particulars that follow after, or that come between in this 19th, 20th, and 21st verses, yea, and this word itself unto this : to beget assurance of faith, which we may draw near with. They turn all those lesser streams into that one channel, that they might all fall into this issue of creating assurance and boldness in us, which each doth naturally tend unto.

* Junius, who first cast these verses into the form of an invitation, expresseth it thus. 1. *Domus est aperta*, the house stands open, it is but our coming. 2. *Jus ingrediendi datum*, a right for us to enter, given us, ver. 19. 3. *Via comparata*, the way cast up, made plain, consecrated for us, ver. 20.

That therefore which comes to be my present work, is to explain the particulars that follow, in this their tendency, viz., as they are grounds of encouragement unto us, to come and enter into heaven, when we pray ; as that which all and each particular tends unto, as the true centre of them. As for example ; take that one, that Christ, being our high priest, is entered into heaven for us, and there resident to entertain us, &c.: this affords us just ground of confidence and boldness, to enter thither to him with full assurance of faith, that we shall be received, and accepted, and our prayers.

And in order to this issue, unto which all those other particulars in their several tendencies drive, I begin with this very first word itself, ' Seeing we have the liberty,' &c. ; and I will give you the unfolding the word παῤῥησία, translated *boldness,* as it serves to manifest this third branch, the freedom and liberty we have to enter into heaven, &c.

Our translators have in the margent varied it, *liberty.* This I choose rather to follow, and insist upon.

The Greek word is an extensive word, and comprehends many things in the significations of it ; whereof what shall serve to the present purpose, I shall particularise. It comprehends all sorts of what you use to term freedom and liberty.

1. A freedom from fear, or shame in coming, that may arise from the sense of unworthiness. Many that are invited to a great man's house may be bashful to come, and incident to shame. But we sinners, who have been made sensible of our vileness, as all believers have been—' I am ashamed, and blush to lift up my face to thee, O God,' &c., Ezra ix. 6— and likewise fear, which ariseth from guilt, which guilt, condemning us in ourselves, works fears. Now the word here used imports the removal, first, of shame : 1 John ii. 28, ' Abide in him ; that, when he shall appear, we may have confidence, and not be ashamed before him at his coming.' The word translated *confidence* there, is the same as that here. Also of fear, which ariseth from guiltiness condemning: 1 John iii. 21, ' If our heart condemn us not, then have we confidence towards God.' The same word: it imports a being freed from fear. Malefactors found guilty had their faces covered, for the shame of their guilt, and so hurried to execution ; as Haman's face was covered, no more to appear before the king. In the gospel, when Christ asked him, ' How camest hither without a wedding garment ?' he was speechless. Whereas παῤῥησία is an appearing without shame, or cause of shame, ' with open face to behold the glory of the Lord ;' their sins being forgiven, there will never be any cause for it. And so as if he had said, we have good ground to appear before God, and look him in the face with free and open countenances, not as guilty persons ; for, if we believe, our sins are forgiven us. Likewise upon the same ground we may appear, and enter without fear.

The word also doth import a freedom from any cause of danger, that might be supposed upon a man's doing this or that. And therefore in the negative, one is said not to have παῤῥησία, to walk openly, and abroad, when his person may be supposed to be in danger if he does, John xi. The Jews consulting to destroy Christ, ver. 53, at the 54th verse it is said, οὐκ ἔτι παῤῥησίᾳ, that Jesus walked no more ' with freedom.' It is translated ' openly,' but it is the negative, the same word that is used here. He forbore to appear in public, withdrew himself as apprehending danger. And the very acceptation of the word fearlessness from danger, is exceeding useful to be taken in, here in this place ; for it plainly serves to express a difference between us under the New Testament, and the Jew under the Old. And the apostle carries it much in his eye and scope, and offers to set out those differences thereby, to exalt and magnify the gospel.

Now it is evident that God carried things so, under his Old Testament dispensations, as to keep them under a fear of being cut off from their people, and so of death, if in their approaches to the public worship they omitted or neglected such and such observations prescribed them.

(1.) Take for instance the case of the high priest, in his goings into the holy of holies (for it is pertinent to the purpose in hand ; for the allusion here is made thereunto). How solemnly was he forewarned to take heed how to perform the outward rites prescribed, in his officiating on that day, with this threatening, ' that ye die not.' You have it twice inserted and rehearsed in Lev. xvi., (the ritual for that day). It is at the beginning of the prescripts, ver. 2, and in the middle, ver. 13. It was matter of danger for him to enter in thither ; and must needs cause fear to him that entered, lest he should through omission have miscarried, or through casual uncleanness. But we are here invited to enter into the holiest, upon the assurance of the contrary : that we have a παῤῥησίαν, no cause of fear written over the door of our entrance. Therefore let us draw near, but with a true heart, and full assurance of faith, and there is no danger at all. Likewise,

(2.) The inferior priests and Levites, in their officiatings and transactions about the utensils of this the holiest, about the ark, namely, and the rest in Num. iv., when the tabernacle was to be taken in pieces, and removed by the Levites ; when Aaron and his sons (who are only appointed to do it) had taken down the veil afore the holy of holies, and had covered the ark therewith, ver. 5 and ver. 8 ; and in like manner all the sanctuary, and the vessels in it, had been covered by them with other coverings appointed for them ; what says ver. 15 ? ' And when Aaron and his sons have have made an end of covering the sanctuary, and all the vessels of the sanctuary, as the camp is to set forward ; after that, the sons of Kohath shall come to bear it : but they shall not touch any holy thing, lest they die. These things are the burden of the sons of Kohath in the tabernacle of the congregation.' And also ver. 20. The Kohathites that were to be employed about those holy things, ver. 18, yet at verses 19, 20, it is said, ' But thus do unto them, that they may live, and not die, when they approach unto the most holy things : Aaron and his sons shall go in, and appoint them every one to his service and to his burden. But they shall not go in to see when the holy things are covered, lest they die.' They were neither to see those holy things with their eyes, nor touch them with their hands. Oh but, brethren, the case is altered with us under the New Testament. Read 1 John i. 1, where the apostle, proposing Christ unto us believers of the New Testament, whom he deciphers to be him ' that was from the beginning,' and ' the Word of life,' him, says he, ' whom our eyes have seen, and whom our hands have handled ; that which was from the beginning, which we have heard, which we have seen with our eyes, which we have looked upon, and our hands have handled, of the Word of life.' Such familiar converse had the apostles with him, when he was come, whom the vessels of the sanctuary, the ark, &c., shadowed ; and whom the apostle doth in these words there expose unto all the spiritual senses of all believers (for the acts of New Testament faith on Christ are said to have the exercising of these three senses there mentioned ; hearing, seeing, handling ; and of the other two also in the Scriptures).

And this very comparing, as to this very respect of fear and danger, between the 'state of the Old Testament and the New, our apostle doth institute and at large spreads forth in chapter xii., towards the close of this
Epistle, from verse 18 to verse 25, and instanceth on the one part how it
was with the Jews' spirits at the giving of the law, when God brought the
shadow of heaven down so upon the mount, Exod. xxiv. 10.   They, Moses,
Aaron, and the seventy went up the mountain, and they saw the God of
Israel, and under his feet the body of heaven, &c.; and utters it in the
same word wherein the exhortation in my text speaks in : Let us ' come to ;'
and there it is ye are 'not *come unto* mount Sinai' (as they were), ' which
might not be touched, insomuch as if a beast' (that was not capable of the
command) ' touched the mountain, he was to die ; and so terrible was the
sight, that Moses' (their mediator, to approach to God for them) ' said, I
exceedingly fear and quake.'   Thus it was on the Jews' part, in their coming
to.   But oppositely he sets out our coming to, with all that is amiable,
delectable, and alluring ; ver. 22, ' But ye are come unto mount Sion, the
heavenly Jerusalem,' &c. ; whither to come there is no danger, but all that
may make blessed.   The danger is only in refusing, as ver. 25.   In that
other their coming, there was presented on all hands a danger ; yea, of
those who by warrant from God were called up into the mount, and saw the
God of Israel.   As in the same Exod. xxiv. 11 is repeated, and that they
did eat and drink before him, it is in that verse recorded as a wonderful
thing, that ' God laid not his hand upon them ;' he did them no hurt.   It
is noted as a strange, extraordinary thing, that they should come down
again, without being destroyed.   They were in danger ; yea, but we are
invited: let us come to ; seeing we have a security, a freedom from fear
and danger, a $\pi\alpha\rho\rho\eta\sigma\iota\alpha$, to enter.   So the text; there was never no man
got any hurt by entering into heaven to pray.   These are the first step
and the lowest of the import of this word.   And I begin with this the
lowest, because I mean to make a climax, or an ascent of the significations
of it.

2. It is a liberty to enter; and that importeth all free leave to come,
licentiam intrandi, licence to enter, if you have but a will.   According as
we use to say, You may come if you will.   There is no extrinsecal bar or
hindrance from without ; no unwillingness or want of freeness in the hearts
of God and Christ, the inviters; but all heartiness and readiness to entertain
those that will.   And they may take as freely when come, as they may come
freely without needing any new invitation: ' Whosoever will (come), let him
take of the waters of life freely.'

And so you may take in the freeness that is in the heart of him that in-
viteth you, though not upon the signification of the word here, yet upon the
merit of the thing itself.   I confess that the word $\pi\alpha\rho\rho\eta\sigma\iota\alpha$, in my text, imports not directly this freeness as in the heart of the inviter, but yet sup-
poseth it; for whence is it that you have the freedom to come, but because
he that biddeth you come hath that freeness in his heart ?   And this much
the word that is annexed in that passage of the Revelation doth fully make
up: ' freely,' $\delta\omega\rho\epsilon\grave{\alpha}\nu$, is the word, which notes an offer of the inviter, out of
pure liberality and munificence, to proceed from a largeness of heart; a free
heart in the donor; and in God out of pure grace.   And thus these two
are yoked together, both grace and freeness : Rom. iii. 24, ' Freely by his
grace ;' and Rom. v. 15.   You may therefore come and take (and by seeking you do take) freely, on God's part ; that is, without his the least thinking much, or grudging at it by God, or ever upbraidure afterwards for it

(as James hath it): 'God gives richly,' yea, with his whole heart, 'and upbraids not.' Therefore so far as your will is within itself really, and in earnest raised up to desire, seek, and ask, and continues in that posture, so far you have freedom, without any check, to take. And the waters of life are those streams of blessedness in grace and glory, all that heaven affords. So you have it declared in the beginning of the same chapter: Rev. xxii. 1, 'And he shewed me a pure river of water of life, clear as crystal, proceeding out of the throne of God and of the Lamb;' that throne is in the holiest.

But who is this that says this? Our Lord Christ himself, and that from heaven: ver. 16, 'I, Jesus,' &c. It is I that speak those things that you have now heard, and that follow in ver. 17. And take notice that they are my last words that ever I will speak to men on earth. And being to speak but this one, I choose and leave it as my last farewell unto the sons of men. Yea, they are the last words I ever intend to have written by any apostle, or other penman, as Scripture given from me, or by my inspiration; so ver. 18, 'If any man shall add unto these things,' &c. So much must we suppose his heart to be deeply engaged in this saying above all other. And that he might be believed in it, he again sets his seal to this and the other sayings in this book, as the close of all: 'He that testifieth these things, saith surely, I come quickly,' ver. 20. They are Christ's words also, as those, ver. 16 and 18, and the seal of all; not the angel only I send, but I myself testify these things. And yet I alone testify them not; the word is συμμαρτυροῦμαι, I witness with another witness; not the angel he sent (for as he, the faithful witness, 'needed not the testimony of man,' as in John, so nor of the most glorious angels from heaven); but I witness, and the Spirit with me, ver. 17, yea, and my Father, who himself from heaven witnessed this of me: 'This is my Son, hear him,' and believe him. And whatsoever I speak' (says he elsewhere), 'even as the Father said unto me, so I speak,' John xii. 50. And therefore if ever you believe, or will believe, any word of his, believe this. And to be sure it is of the most concernment to you, of any word that ever he spake, and you shall never have any such word from him anew until himself comes. And lo, it is to invite you (till himself shall come to you) that you would come in the mean while unto him, for whatever you have a will to have which himself hath; and if this speech of Christ's extends to those (as sure it doth) who do not yet believe on him, to invite even such to come for life at first, as Matt. xi. 28 it is intended, then much more it intends those that have come already, that they would continue to do it until he comes; for such have a right and boldness, says the text: Let us therefore come, &c. But,

3. It may be said, and is by many, though I have free leave to come, and ask freely, and need not be either ashamed or afraid, but I cannot speak what I desire. There is for this a further signification of the word παρρησία, a relief which will prompt you in this. It signifies, in a most proper meaning of it, a *freedom of speech*, which imports two things: 1. Free leave and liberty to the thing itself, to what you will speak, according to God's mind warranted in his word, 1 John v. And 2. Not as it is a leave to speak only, but a new endowment of spirit in you, emboldening you to utter your minds; an enlargement of heart to express your desires one way or other acceptably to God. And this must needs still hearten you; for the business you are specially exhorted unto is to pray, and to ask, as I proposed it at first.

And that it is a most proper signification of the word cannot be denied, and is generally agreed among critics. And the New Testament so useth it frequently, and it is often put for plainness of speech, when one speaks what is in his heart; as it is there, John x. 24, 'If thou be the Christ, tell us plainly' (it is the same word). The etymology of the word παῤῥησία is from πᾶν, omne, and ῥῆσις, dictio, a telling all.*

By nature all men's mouths through guilt are stopped before God: Rom. iii. 19, 'That every mouth may be stopped, and all the world may become guilty before God.' And so when they come afore God to pray, being condemned in themselves, guilt stops their mouths, and they are speechless, as he, Matt. xxii. 12.

But when a man is, by faith and regeneration, become actually a member of Christ, Christ gives him a new mouth as well as a new heart, ' a spirit of prayer and supplication.' There is a ceremony, that after the pope hath made a new cardinal, and put him into that dignity with Esto cardinalis, he hath a further solemnity (which they term the opening a cardinal's mouth), which is to give him leave to speak and vote with the rest of them. This he doth in a vain show, having no power to give more ability of speech than he had before, but permission only; but, to be sure, Christ hath power, and doth exercise it to them whom he makes fellows with him and members of him: ' Open thou my lips,' &c., Ps. li. And it is a wonderful work to see how Christ gives to poor weak souls, ignorant and dead-hearted afore conversion, how he gives, I say, a glorious liberty and freedom this way to ask what concerns their own salvation. When Paul's three days of lying in of the new birth were not yet out : ' Behold he prays,' saith Christ from heaven of him, Acts ix. 11. And whereas they know not what to ask, Christ sends his Spirit into such souls to help their infirmities, Rom. viii. And what we are not able to clothe with words answerable to our desires, or to express what we desire, he draws out inward groans and sighs unutterable. And God knows the meaning of the Spirit, that is, of the new creature which he hath wrought within us, as if they had expressed them in words. He knows what it would have when it yet cannot utter ; so that very soul hath a vent one way or other, either by inward words (and the groans, desires, and thoughts, and affections of the mind and·inward man are in Scripture often termed words), or else by outward ability of speech, whence there is nothing in our hearts but are one way or another made known to God by us. The word παῤῥησία is, as I said, πᾶν ῥῆσις, to tell all. It warrants thee to go and tell God all. A soul hath liberty to pour forth his whole heart: Ps. lxii. 8, ' Pour out your hearts before him.' To pour out implies, 1. A fulness of matter, which the heart, conceiving within itself, pours forth on the sudden, and easeth and disburdeneth itself of it, and empties the soul of all that is in it. Yea, God enlargeth the heart, and

---

* Acts ii. 29, ' Let me speak freely to you,' says Peter (the same word). And there it is both a taking free leave to do it, and also to utter what was in his mind freely about it. ' Great is my freeness of speech to you,' says Paul, 2 Cor. vii. 4. His heart was so enlarged by love to them, as in the verse afore, ' You are in our hearts to die and live with you,' that he tells them he can say anything unto them, ver. 4, and pour out his very soul. And Pectus dissertum facit. Here it imports a power of affection to utter one's heart ; and in Acts iv. 27, the apostles and the whole church prayed, that the apostles might ' speak the word with all freeness,' not boldness only (as it is translated), but with all ability to utter the truths of it ; for it is all sorts of freedom, as there. They were filled with the Holy Ghost, as there, who is said to give utterance to them, chap. ii. ver. 24. Such as were of free spirits to express themselves are called παῤῥήσει ἀστήροι.—Arist. Rhet., lib. ii.—[Qu. ' παῤ-ῥησίαστικοι ' ?—Ed.

causeth good materials for prayer to boil up within a man's spirit, and by these fore-preparings of the heart provoketh the soul to prayer, and to pour them all forth ; and so is fulfilled that of the psalmist, ' God prepareth the heart, and hears the prayer.' And thou mayest, in telling God all, use plainness of speech (as was observed the meaning of the word to be), even as plainly as ever thou art able to utter them ; as thou wouldst do to any, thy dearest friend, all thy griefs, fears, wants—Ps. xxxviii. 9, ' All my desires are afore thee ;'—yea, all thy sins, and then mayest make ' apologies for thyself' (as the word ' clearing of yourselves' is, 2 Cor. vii. 11). I mean not excuses, but all sorts of pleas which may move God to pardon thee, which thou findest in the word belonging to thy case. Thou mayest take all the words to thyself, Hos. xiv. 2, that free grace hath written and prompted in this book, and use them as pleas for thyself.

And what a mighty encouragement then is this third branch, being added to the former?

4. The word παῤῥησία hath a promise from God, that follows it, annexed to it, and entailed upon it; and that is, that God will grant whatever of heavenly and spiritual things you ask. This you have, 1 John iii. 21, ' Beloved, if our heart condemn us not, then have we confidence towards God.' And it follows, ver. 22, ' Whatsoever we ask, we receive of him, because we keep his commandment, and do those things that are pleasing in his sight.' The word in the 21st verse, ' confidence,' is our word here in the text. And he mentions it there for this end and purpose, to encourage : that if with confidence and boldness we use and exercise the fore-mentioned freedom of speech in praying (for the word imports boldness, and freedom of speech both), then whatever we ask we shall receive of him, sooner or later. If you take it an universal promise (as it is whatsoever), then understand it whatever blessings, spiritual, heavenly, as Eph. i. 3, they are styled. We are to make our prayers as placed in heaven (as was said); and our prayers shall be answerable thereto ; and the liberty that our desires take in asking should run after things heavenly, as our affections are called upon to be: Col. iii. 1, 2, ' If ye then be risen with Christ, seek those things which are above, where Christ sitteth on the right hand of God. Set your affections on things above, not on things on the earth.' Look what commodities that country affords ; there you may be free, and as free in asking them, as you have hearts raised up to desire them. Yea, and you have in effect the things you ask given you; if your hearts so ask them, and from your souls ask them. Those are the commodities of that place, and of its own growth ; only take in what follows in the same ver. 22, ' Because we keep his commandments, and do those things that are pleasing in his sight.'

CHAPTER VII.

The exercise of faith in prayer, which aptly present themselves under the notion of coming to God, and Christ as our high priest, so far as the type of the high priest, when he went into the holy of holies, doth represent.

I limit myself unto that converse with Christ, and God through him, by faith exercised in prayer. And therein I intend but only such exercises in prayer as aptly present themselves under the notion of coming to God, and Christ as our high priest ; so far as the type of the high priest in the times of the Old Testament, when he went into the holy of holies, doth represent. And yet therein I shall instance in some more principal ones that are obvious in that day's rites, leaving your own thoughts to search and find out more of the like (that are to be found therein, not insisted on by me), for your own help and advantage.

1. Acknowledge thine infinite unworthiness to enter and to draw near; as being so high a privilege. You read, Lev. xvi. 17, that the very priests in the old law that entered daily into the first tabernacle, Heb. ix. 6, ' accomplishing the service of God,' that yet when the high priest went unto the holy of holies, they were all turned out : ' And there shall be no man in the tabernacle of the congregation, when he goeth in to make an atonement in the holy place, until he come out, and have made an atonement for himself and for his household, and for all the congregation of Israel ;' as to shew, that as it is Christ alone that makes our atonement, so withal our utter unworthiness to come thither to him.

2. Acknowledge that it is purely by the blood of Christ thou hast the right and boldness to draw near ; so my text, ver. 19, ' By the blood of Jesus.' Shall I tell you, Christ himself having been made sin for you, and undertaken for sin, should not himself have entered into the holy of holies, but by and through his own blood, first shed ; and therefore it is express in the 12th verse of the 9th chapter, that ' by his own blood he entered into that holy place.' He had not come thither else. And the reason is, that although in his original, personal right, it was his inheritance, and ordained for him, yet having appeared with sin for us in this world, that is, with the guilt of our sins taken on him, a demurrer stood to hinder him the possession of it. And compare for this Heb. ix. 26 and 28. In ver. 26 it is said, ' He once, in the end of the world, appeared, to put away sin by the sacrifice of himself.' And observe how this is plainly called an appearing with sin, and was his first appearance in this world ; for in ver. 28 he says, ' Christ was once offered to bear the sins of many ; and unto them that look for him shall he appear the second time without sin, unto salvation.' This second appearance without sin, shews his first to have been with sin, which is also expressly said, ver. 26, ' bearing' (as the word is in that verse) ' the sins of many ;' which his bearing of them, and then his offering of himself for them, was that which did put them away from himself, as well as from us ; and was the reason why that, after he had done this, that he is said to appear the second time without sin.

Yet let no man here apprehend, as if I meant that Christ offered one sacrifice for himself, and then for the people, as his type the high priest is observed to have done, with difference from Christ our high priest is by our apostle, chap. vii. 27, ' Who needeth not daily, as those high priests, to offer up sacrifice, first for his own sins, and then for the people's.' And the reason is, because the high priest was a sinner himself, by inherency; and therefore they are there called his own sins ; and so he needed to atone for himself apart by one sort of sacrifice ; as in Lev. xvi., you read how on that day he did ; and so he might be capacitated to offer another for the people's, each of which he did at two successive turns and vices, as you find by comparing the 6th and 11th verses with ver. 15. But it was infinitely otherwise with our high priest; as it follows in that Heb. vii. 27, ' This he did once, when he offered up himself.' He made but one work of it, in one entire sacrifice of himself ; and the reason of that was, because they were really and indeed our sins alone which he was to suffer for ; but made his only by imputation, he barely taking on the guilt of them. And it was himself was the sole sacrifice (as there). And thereby it came to pass, that in offering up himself for our sins, he, by that one act of but one sacrifice, discharged himself of the imputation of them ; even as a surety that is bound for another, by paying the full sum of the debt for that other at one single payment, acquits himself of the debt, and the principal debtors too ; until which be done (in case he whom he is bound for be utterly insolvent and unable) he stands bound for himself, as well as the debtor.

But still so as until he had performed this, and brought his blood shed for our sins, and himself came in the virtue of his having been offered up for them, there had been no appearing for him in heaven (as not for the high priest into the holiest without blood). There was no room for Christ himself there, not according to God's ordination and compact with him, until that were performed. God would have shut heaven gates against him without his offering made ; and Christ himself, in the 16th of John, insinuates as much : ' The Spirit shall convince the world ' (the Gentile world that was to be converted) ' of (my) righteousness,' by the apostles' ministry of righteousness ; that is, that his righteousness was the true righteousness, ordained to justify men, when they had first convinced them of sin, as in the verse afore he directs them. And he gives them this invincible evidence that it was, as he had formerly taught, the true righteousness, ' Because I go to my Father, and you shall see me no more.' Was that such a sign and wonder, may some say, that he who was the Lord from heaven, and whose right and due therefore it was to go thither at any time he would, without more ado, could there be the least supposition made, that they might see him sent down again ? You must know that he speaks of himself as having undertaken, with his Father, to perform a righteousness for sinners here on earth, to take sins away, ere he should come to him in person ; without the exact fulfilling of all which righteousness first, there had been no coming for him thither, so as to keep his standing there ; but they should have seen him again. My Father would not have admitted me ; I must have come back again to have completed what had been wanting, if anything had been. Take it therefore, says he, as an invincible evidence, that all will be finished according to agreement with my Father, that ' I go to my Father, and you shall see me no more.' And therefore it is called, ' the blood of the covenant, by which he ' (Christ himself) is said to be ' sanctified,' Heb. x. 29, where, setting out the sin and punishment of a deserter of Christ, he says, ' Of how much sorer punishment shall he be thought worthy, who hath trodden under foot the Son of God ; and hath counted the blood of the covenant, wherewith he was sanctified, an unholy thing ?' the word he, &c., not so fully referring to the apostate, as if he had been ever truly sanctified by that blood, as it doth unto Christ's having sanctified himself thereby, in offering up himself a sacrifice unto God. And that clause is added to aggravate the sin of apostates, in counting that blood to be but as ' a common thing,' whenas Christ himself, whose blood it is, was consecrated thereby, to be the mediator of the New Testament. In the same sense that chap. xiii of this Epistle, ver. 20, Christ himself is said to be ' brought again from the dead, by the blood of the everlasting covenant ;' his very resurrection was from the merit of his own blood.

Yea, heaven itself was to be purified with his blood ; for though we sinners never had been there to defile it, yet because sinners were to come thither, it was to be purified. And so in the type, Rev. xvi. 16, when the high priest was entered into the holy of holies, he was to ' make an atonement for that holy place, because of the uncleanness of the children of

Israel.' And it was not for their ceremonial uncleanness only, but because of 'their transgressions in all their sins.' Brethren, this is strange, that the place called 'the most holy,' whereinto the people never entered, no, not by one room off (for they went not into that first tabernacle that was afore it), that their ordinary sins should reach and defile that holy place, so as that an atonement, or expiation for sin, must be made for the place. How was it then defiled? Persons only, not places or things, are capable of having sins imputed to them, whether they be their own sins or another's. For persons only are capable of the guilt of sin. Yet 1, By a relation that places may or do bear unto persons, they are defiled, Titus i. 15. And it was ceremonially seen in the defilement of the leper's house and walls. And so, although the people, during that dispensation, were not to come thither, yet the high priest came in their stead, into the most holy place, on purpose to make an atonement for all their sins, as being the place appointed and ordained by God to have an atonement made therein for their sins. And in relation unto the making that atonement for them as sinners, the very place wherein it was to be done was itself first to be sanctified and atoned, which the high priest was to do, with the blood he brought thither with him, distinctly and apart for the place, and then to make the atonement for them. Their sins were of so great a guilt, as the very holiness of the place forbade any atonement to be made in it for the sinners, until itself were purified with the same blood.

Now this type was to be fulfilled, and it is certain that the holy of holies that was then was the type, or (as the 24th verse of Heb. ix. styles it) the *demonstration*, or *scheme*, or *pattern* of the highest heavens, unto which place in the end (though it was not manifest as then to the old Jew), yet they and we, even all the saints of both testaments, were ordained unto, are at last to come. Thence and therefore it came to be necessary, that the holy place of the heavens was to be purified by Christ's blood, as Aaron's most holy place was instituted to be purged by the blood of those his sacrifices; so as it was not only, or so much to fulfil the type; which yet, they being given out afore as types, was necessary; for though they be but shadows, yet they are prophetic, and must have an answerable performance in the truth and substance signified thereby. But the original reason, and for which the type itself was appointed, was, that the holy of holies in the heavens was itself fore-ordained to be the place for us sinners to come unto, and did bear in God's fore-decrees the relation of being their eternal house they are to dwell in for ever. And God's holiness and purity is such (having made that place the seat of his presence-glory, and placed his throne there), as to shew how deeply he resenteth sin; he would have the place of his children's residence (having once been sinners), it being so near to him, and afore his face, first purified, as well as the sinners themselves. Not that it was defiled in itself, for the presence of God makes it most holy; but even that was it made it to be too holy for sinners. And therefore, in relation to its becoming their actual abode there, it was now to be atoned for their sakes. And upon both these reasons, especially the latter, it was, that this, which was the truth and substance of the type, was not so much to be conformed to the type, as the type was framed and formed by this fore-ordination of God's, which was the original prototype of all. And upon this it is that the apostle pronounceth in the 23d verse of the said Heb. ix., 'It was necessary that the patterns of things in the heavens should be purified with these; but the heavenly things themselves with better sacrifices than these.'

But besides these general grounds of analogy of the type and antitype, the words of the next verse do expressly determine, that the heavens, considered as the place, were purified by Christ's person and blood. For it follows, ver. 24, ' For Christ is not entered into the holy places made with hands, which are the figures of the true ; but into heaven itself, now to appear in the presence of God for us.' They are those places in the heavens (heavenly places as they are elsewhere rendered) answerable to those on earth, that were to be purified. And he here speaks of them as of the place or places, as the word ' entering into' imports. Even as when in Eph. ii. we are said to ' sit in heavenlies,' it is aptly and necessarily to be understood, ' to sit in heavenly places ; ' for so the word sitting doth require. Thus likewise here, the word ' entering into heavenlies ' argues those heavenlies spoken of to be the places of heavens ; whereof the tabernacle, or tabernacles of Moses, which were also called the tabernacle, in the singular ; of these, as the place or places, the apostle says, ver. 21, ' Moreover, he sprinkled with blood both the tabernacles, and all the vessels of the ministry.' So that not only the vessels, the furniture, the *suppellex*, the utensils in the tabernacles (and accordingly the saints that are to be brought in thither, that is, into heaven), but the place itself that contained them, was purified also by Christ's blood, that it might receive sinners, and be their *domicilium*, their habitation for ever. And of all these, both tabernacle and vessels, he says that they were figures and patterns of the true in the heavens, in their several kinds of analogy. The tabernacle itself, the utensils of the things in that place, and all to be purified with better blood than these ; and especially the place of holy of holies in the heavens ; for in ver. 24 it is peculiarly specified and said of it, ' For Christ is not entered into the holy places made with hands, which are the figures of the true ; but into heaven itself, now to appear in the presence of God for us.' And in that place, the mercy-seat, we read, was sprinkled with blood ; and the pavements of the place that were afore the mercy-seat were sprinkled seven times. Lev. xvi. 14, ' And he shall take of the blood of the bullock, and sprinkle it with his finger upon the mercy-seat eastward : and before the mercy-seat shall he sprinkle of the blood with his finger seven times.'

I cast this in further, to shew the necessity of Christ's blood for our entering into the holy of holies in heaven ; either now by faith, or hereafter by possession and enjoyment, that even the mercy-seat itself, the throne of grace, that is, of God himself, whereon 'God, merciful, gracious, long-suffering, pardoning iniquity, transgression, and sin,' sitteth, that that also was sprinkled with blood, Lev. xvi. 14.

But you will say, Did God's mercy-seat need sprinkling with blood, or a being purified ?

No, surely, not in itself. The mercies of God are pure and holy mercies, Acts xiii. 34 ; τὰ ὅσια, ' the holy things,' they are called (see the marginal note). But yet if sinners shall come to have mercies from God, his mercies must be mingled with Christ's blood to purchase them, that God may be just in having received the atonement, and ' the justifier of him that believeth in Jesus.' So as still in respect of us that are sinners, the mercy-seat must have blood, that we may be justified, even as the heavens were to be purified with blood, because sinners were to enter there.

The conclusion of this is, that if the heavens were to be purified with Christ's blood because of us sinners who were to come thither, yea, if Christ himself having undertaken for sins could not have entered thereunto unless he had brought the virtue, efficacy, spirits of his own blood with him, and that in and by the merit thereof it was that he entered thereinto, and that his very human nature was through the imputation of our sins to him, when he 'tabernacled among us,' John i., was to have an atonement made for it by his blood, and by the rending it in two, in the separation of soul from his body, that so he (as representing us) and we as one mystical person with him, might enter into heaven, and else not; then whenever thou comest to pray more solemnly (whereby thou enterest and approachest unto that holies in the heavens), acknowledge how it is by and through his blood that thou, a wretched sinner, not by mere imputation such only, but in reality of guilt; and that thou shouldst be in hell, whilst thou art admitted into heaven itself, whilst thou prayest, Oh! this blood, this precious blood! let it be precious to you, and let him be precious that shed it. And because he was so precious in his person, though debased, therefore it was that his blood is so precious, as you may collect by comparing 1 Pet. i. 19 with ver. 6 of chap. ii. His person made the blood precious; for it was the blood of him that was 'made higher than the heavens,' Heb. vii. 25; yea, 'of God,' Acts xx.

CHAPTER VIII.

Another exercise of faith in praying is to confess all our sins unto God over Jesus Christ, as typified by the live-goat, the scape-goat.

Confess all thy sins unto God, over Jesus Christ, as the live-goat, the scape-goat. What the signification of this is I hope I shall make you understand. There was that day, and on that day only, when the high priest was to go into the holy of holies; before he went in, in order to his going in, there were two goat-kids presented afore the Lord. Look into Lev. xvi. 3, 'Thus shall Aaron come into the holy place;' and at ver. 5, 'He shall take of the congregation of the children of Israel two kids of the goats for a sin-offering;' and then at ver. 7, 'The high priest shall take the two goats, and present them before the Lord at the door of the tabernacle of the congregation;' and then at ver. 8, 'He cast lots upon the two goats;' and the one lot is said to be 'for the Lord,' because that goat that lot for the Lord fell upon was to die, and to be sacrificed to the Lord for sin. And again, ver. 9, it is said of that goat that it was the goat the Lord's lot fell upon; for it was set apart, and appropriated to him as a sacrifice, and so the Lord's in a special manner, in comparison to that other, namely, by way of sacrifice; as it follows in that ver. 9, 'Aaron shall offer him for a sin-offering.' And afterwards he was 'burned without the camp,' ver. 27. And the other lot is said to be for the scape-goat, that is, for its escaping being sacrificed as the other was. And it follows, ver. 10, 'But the goat, on which the lot fell to be the scape-goat, shall be presented alive before the Lord, to make an atonement with him, and to let him go for a scape-goat into the wilderness.' And they both are called a 'sin-offering,' ver. 5; that is, both were ordained to take sins away. And this latter goat, that stayed and lived, is said, ver. 10, to 'make an atonement with God' as well as the dying goat did, but each in their several ways: the one by bearing our sins and the punishment of them by death, the other by escaping, and by his life carrying them away. You read not that he was carried away into the wilderness to be there destroyed, nor was he in that which belonged to its part made at all a sacrifice. But look, as the dying goat was made an atonement for sin in his way, by sacrifice in dying, so the other let go alive made an atonement in its way, namely, by carrying away the sins confessed over him into the wilderness, by means of his life. And that was transacted by confessing their sins over the head of that live-goat, after that the other goat had been offered as a sacrifice for them, that their sins being so confessed and sacrificed for, he might carry them away : ver. 9, 20, 'And after he; hath made an end of reconciling' (namely, the sacrifice), 'he shall bring the live goat;' ver. 21, 22, 'And Aaron shall lay both his hands upon the head of the live goat, and confess over him all the iniquities of the children of Israel, and all their transgressions in all their sins, putting them upon the head of the goat, and shall send him away by the hand of a fit man into the wilderness : and the goat shall bear upon him all their iniquities unto a land not inhabited, and he shall let go the goat in the wilderness.' Brethren, will you have the mystery of this ?   Our dear Lord and Saviour Jesus Christ, he is both these goats in the types, but as considered under two different notions, viz., Christ dying for sin in the first, and Christ risen, and alive, and carrying sins away into the wilderness. But you will ask, Why two such utterly differing types ? Might not one have served ? Brethren, the case stood thus, no one type could represent these two grand mysteries of Christ at once ; and therefore God's institution was, to represent one piece of him by one type and another piece of him by another. Now, the same individual goat that was killed was not to be raised again, being a brute creature (that is proper only unto men).. Hence he takes one goat that should die, to represent Christ in dying, and as such bearing our sins and punishments ; and he takes another goat that lives, to represent him alive again. You find the like parallel to this in the case of cleansing the leper, Lev. xiv.   There were two birds, ver. 4, one to be killed, ver. 5, and another, called the living bird, that flew away : ver. 4–7, 'Then shall the priest command to take for him that is to be cleansed two birds alive and clean, and cedar wood, and scarlet, and hyssop. And the priest shall command that one of the birds shall be killed in an earthen vessel over running water. As for the living bird, he shall take it, and the cedar wood, and the scarlet, and the hyssop, and shall dip them and the living bird in the blood of the bird that was killed over the running water: and he shall sprinkle upon him that is to be cleansed from the leprosy seven times, and shall pronounce him clean, and shall let the living bird loose into the open field.'   You read in Rev. i. 18 how our Lord speaks of himself, saying, 'I am he that liveth, and was dead ; and, behold, I am alive for evermore.'   You read in Rom. v. 10 what singular differing purposes these two especially serve for : that as we are 'reconciled to God by the death of his Son,' as a sacrifice, so we are 'saved by his life.'   There is his death, to pay the price or ransom for our reconciliation, and there is the actual application or communication of eternal salvation unto us ; and that is said to be by his life. You have the like both again, in Rom. iv. 25, 'He was delivered for our offences:' there is the dying goat; 'and he rose again' (and liveth) 'for our justification:' there you have the living goat.

Sin is done away two ways by Jesus Christ; either meritoriously, by the sacrifice of himself, in dying, as the price paid, which the Scripture everywhere speaketh of: Heb. ix. 26, 'Once in the end of the world he appeared, to put sin away, by offering himself, and bearing their sins,' as ver. 28. Secondly, there is a taking away of sin by the actual application to us of what his death merited for us ; and so Christ takes sins away when we believe and come to him for pardon. The word John Baptist hath in John i., comprehends both ; ' Behold the Lamb of God, that takes away the sins of the world : the word is αἴρειν ; it signifieth both, 1. To bear the guilt of them, and then John saw him bearing, and loaded with all our sins upon him, which did bring him to the tree, and caused him to die ; ' He was made sin for us, who knew no sin.' And, 2. It signifieth to take away sins by a removal of them from off our persons ; to which the Latin word *tollo* answers, but the Greek word αἴρεω intendeth both. First, take the dying goat, and that is Christ, ' bearing the sins of many,' as 1 Pet. ii. 24, when he was crucified ; ' who his own self bare our sins in his own body upon the tree.' And thus to lay our sins upon him to this end, that was God's act, and his own, in taking our sins upon him, not ours. We were not then, neither did the saints that were then alive, understand or think of it ; but that was God's, and transacted between God and Christ. ' God was, in Christ, reconciling the world to himself ;' who ' made him sin for us, and a curse, that knew no sin.' And God, says the prophet, ' laid on him the iniquity of us all, when his soul was made an offering for sin ;' and therefore also the dying goat is called ' the Lord's lot.' The priest did but barely cast the lot, but it was God that disposed it to that goat ; he would have him die. Nor do you read that the priest that was a-doing did confess our sins over the goat that was to die ; it was a single sole act of God's. And so he bore them in his being sacrificed and offered up.

But come we, secondly, to the living goat, Jesus Christ. And he, after he hath made an atonement by his death, is yet to take our sins away by an actual justification of us. And in respect both to his sacrifice and offering up, as also for the application of it to us by faith to justify us, at and upon our believing, he is called a ' propitiation for us.' 1. In respect to that made at his death, in 1 John ii. 2, ' Who is the propitiation for the sins of the world.' This must be understood of him in dying ; for there were many in the world, and yet to come into the world, he was made a propitiation for, who as yet believed not. But, 2.—Rom. iii. 25, ' Whom God hath set forth to be a propitiation, through faith in his blood.' Observe here how he is said to be fore-ordained to be a propitiation, through faith on that his blood, which was afore made a propitiation on the cross. For then it is his atonement comes to be actually a propitiation to us, when we through faith come in to God and plead it, and not till then, and that in a true and real sense. This his being a propitiation in that place, must therefore be understood in the application of him to us. And we may distinguish of them thus : the one is Christ, a propitiation *for* us ; the other, the same Christ, a propitiation *to* us, even in the same differing senses and respects, that the live goat and the dying goat are, in the foresaid Lev. xvi. 5, both called a sin-offering and for atonement. And now when this atonement is to be applied unto us at our conversion, and ever after, then it is indeed that the actings on our part come to be done towards the pardon of our sins : as to believe on and plead his death and blood, and also what the type instructs, viz., to come to him as he is now alive, and lives for evermore ; for him to take our sins to himself and take them away from us ; to lay hold on him with both hands, as it is in Lev. xvi. 21, and confess our sins over him ; and until then we remain in our sins, for all that he was offered as a dying goat for us. And this is the thing that I have aimed at and made way for, in telling you this long story out of the Old, and the mystery out of the New Testament. The priest, we see, did confess over this live goat; and therein the high priest performed the people's part, for it was done in a way of confession, and that act in no sense must be ascribed to God, in his laying our iniquities upon Christ. He confessed not them for us. So then we, when we would be saved and forgiven, must perform that part, and come and confess our sins over Christ, the live goat. God the Father hath done his part in sacrificing his Son, and Christ, the dying goat, hath done his part in purchasing our pardon; but he as the living goat must do another, and that is, both to cause us to come to himself, and lay both our hands upon him, and confess it was God's part to lay our sins upon him; but it remains to be our part to lay our sins upon him, by confessing them over him and afore him to his Father, now he is alive for the pardon of them. Look into the type, in Lev. xvi. 21, 22, it is most express: Aaron, at the 20th verse (mark well), when he had made an end of reconciliation (that is, when he had done his work, belonging to that of the goat to die, killed him, and then sprinked the blood); 'Aaron shall lay both his hands upon the head of the live goat, and confess over him all the iniquities of the children of Israel, and all their transgressions in all their sins, and send them away into the wilderness. And he shall bear them away into a land not inhabited, and he shall let them go alive into the wilderness.' The mystery of this I take to be, that after the reconciliation made for us·by Christ in his death, which was done without our knowledge, he then rose again, and is alive to justify us. But then we must come to him, acknowledge, as the priests did, and confess them in their names, all the sins of all the people of Israel, of what kind soever. And then this live goat carries them away into the wilderness.

If you demand·the mystery there of the answer,* it is a like expression to that in Micah vii..10, that ' he will cast our iniquities into the depth of the sea.' What is thrown thither never rises more; as that roll into Euphrates, to signify Babylon, should never rise again. Heaven is not indeed a wilderness, to which place our live goat is ascended; but it is in the utter taking away of sins, and hiding them for ever, so as never to be found or remembered, which is here aimed at. And so Christ takes sins away, and carries them into that oblivion and forgetfulness, as none can find them, ' never to be remembered more,' as the Scripture speaks.

The issue which I drive at is, as to exhort you hereupon, when you come more solemnly to converse with Jesus Christ in the holy of holies, or with God through him, not only at your first conversion and faith on him, but when you come setly to pray, especially on great occasions, to lay hold on Jesus Christ with both hands (as it is in this type), that is, with all your might; and then to confess all your sins particularly over him, as the high priest did over the head of the live goat, who by his resurrection and ascension into heaven, is escaped from death and wrath for sins; and in confessing them, transfer them from off yourselves, and implore him to take them upon himself; discharge yourselves of them, by desiring him to take them, who knows what to do with them, not now to suffer for them; he hath done that once perfectly for ever; but to carry them away to an utter forgetfulness, and to be thy advocate to God to remember them no more; seeking of God not to impute thy sins to thee, but to him that was made sin, that thou mayest be made the righteousness of God in him. And so to

* Qu. ' The mystery thereof, I answer?'—ED.

make an exchange with Christ; he to take thy sins, and to bestow his righteousness upon thee instead thereof.

And secondly, To make use of this notion to help them over one difficulty, which those, whose judgments are that Christ died not for all men intentionally, may, or perhaps do sometimes meet with, in their coming to Christ. They must not, nor ought to, come to him now to die for them; that is past and over, and were vain and blasphemous. Nor yet can they assuredly say and believe that Christ died for them, and bore their sins in particular. And although that declaration Paul makes, brought home to the heart, that 'Christ came into the world to save sinners,' he speaks indefinitely: sinners, and all sorts of sinners, even the greatest, for he saved me, says he there; though this be a sufficient ground to draw a sinner that sees himself lost utterly, and sees Christ with a spiritual eye, as John v., to come to him; yet if this course in the way of believing that I have now urged be well weighed and made use of, it may conduce to ease the heart much more, as to any such stick and demur in his coming to Christ. For though I cannot plead that whilst he was a-dying, he had my sins for my particular laid upon him by God, yet now he is alive again, I may, as now I have been instructed, come in my own person to him, and lay my hands upon him to be the live goat for me, and confess all these my particular sins to him and over him, and also unto God and before God, having his Christ by him present in the view of my faith. And that I may lay all my sins upon him with this end and aim, joined with the most vehement implorement of him, that he will freely take the guilt of them off from me, and carry them into a land of non-remembrance, as into a land not inhabited, and therefore never to be found, and to mediate with his Father, to pass an act of oblivion upon them, and remember them no more. And I may be sure and certain, that I am warranted thus to confess and lay my sins upon him, to the end that he should carry them away; and that this is an act, as now to be performed by me and him. And I may now come to him to do it for me in my particular. And my faith needs not proceed here upon an indefinite ground, that should any way admit of a scruple, whether I am the person that he intends or no; for I am, and every humbled sinner is, now absolutely and definitely required to do all this for his own salvation, and for his own particular. And this admits no doubtfulness at all, nor requireth a certain resolution first to be had by us, that God laid upon Christ at his death his iniquities. And it is a great relief and help to the exercise of our faith, and an infinitely gracious dispensation of God, to ordain such a type, as after was left for us to perform this part, in a way of our coming to Christ, after this manner; to become a propitiation and atonement for us in particular, through faith in his blood. That God, I say, hath left us so certain a way and course for us to put in practice; and in the practice and exercise of it, confessing our sins with mourning and brokenness of heart, that therein we shall certainly find Christ, and God through Christ, take away our sins thereupon. And this, this performance upon the day of atonement, teacheth us to do.

Exercise faith for the forgiveness of all thy sins. This that day's practice doth for our comfort in a special manner instruct us unto; for it was that which those days' sacrifices were ordained for; that whereas they had particular sacrifices appointed for particular sins, as occasionally they were committed, for which they were to bring a trespass-offering to the priest, and he by offering his sacrifice for him, made an atonement; and the promise was, it should be forgiven him; of all which you read in Leviticus, the 4th, 5th, and 6th chapters : yet, notwithstanding these, as also that there were daily sacrifices, twice a-day (of the intendment of which afterwards), the expiation on this day was singularly appointed for a general pardon of all sins at once, passed unto the end of that year ; for that outward, typical, legal atonement signified no further, there being, as the apostle says, a new remembrance of sins every year, so as they were forgiven by the year, as we say, and yet universally. All which I shall demonstrate in the close of this head.

But I find it necessary for me to speak first of the intent and scope of those particular atonements for special sins, because that will give some light towards the clearing that universal atonement of this day.   And also the knowledge thereof will conduce to the comfort of believers, and to the direction of the faith of believers, in case of occasional sinnings.

CHAPTER IX.

Of occasional sacrifices for particular sins.—Their intendment then, unto us now.

Now, as touching those particular sacrifices for occasional sins, we find how that there were some special sins that were excepted, and left out from having atonement made for them by those kind of sacrifices ; as, namely, murder, adultery, and blasphemy.   And this hath occasioned a great stumbling to some men, lest their being types of gospel proceedings in pardoning, the sacrifice of Christ's blood should not extend to such sins as these, but the same exception should now continue.   Now, to solve this, and to clear up the matter of our universal pardon, which is now the thing I drive at, the first inquiry must be into the ground of difference then made ; what that should be, that there should be no occasional sacrifice for those sins, was appointed.   Some have founded the difference to lie in this, that murder and adultery, &c., being sins apparently against conscience and special light, and therewith committed with consent of will, deliberately, and upon that ground no atonement ; and that those other sins, for which expiation was made by sacrifice, were only sins of ignorance ; and that that was the reason why those of murder, &c., were excluded from atonement.

Thus some have deemed, because that at the entrance of those commands and prescriptions for such particular sacrifices, in Leviticus, chap. iv. God seems to limit them, for which such atonements were to be made, unto sins of ignorance, as the general rule about them is in ver. 2, ' Speak unto the children of Israel, saying, If a soul shall sin through ignorance against any of the commandments of the Lord concerning things which ought not to be done, and shall do against any of them.'   But yet that that was not the ground of that difference, it is manifest ; in that in chap. vi., there is the same provision of expiation made for sins against conscience, and deliberately and willingly committed.   As in case of a man's having had goods of another man's, or some other matter committed to his trust ; or of a man that had violently stole, or taken anything from another ; and the person entrusted having so defrauded his neighbour, did besides utterly deny any such thing to have been committed to him, and so added a lie to his theft, which alone was against knowledge ; yea, and yet more wickedly had superadded oaths to those lies and denials, forswearing himself ;—here were sins sufficiently against manifest light of conscience, and a whole cluster of such, and as high against (simple) knowledge as high could be, and as deliberate as deliberate can be.

Yet notwithstanding, upon restitution, ver. 5, he shall bring his trespass-offering unto the Lord, and unto the priest; and the priest shall make an atonement for him before the Lord, and it shall be forgiven him; for any thing of all that he hath done in trespassing therein;' verses 6, 7. Nor is it limited to circumstances of times, as if he had but once or twice done thus.

It is an error of the highest cruelty unto souls, as well as of derogation to God's grace and Christ's satisfaction, which the Socinians have taken up; that for gross heinous sins against light, committed after believing, there is no forgiveness to be expected from the covenant of grace; but if any, it must be by an extraordinary way of mercy, and not by virtue of the ordinary covenant of grace. But what it should be which hath induced them unto so desperate a condemnation of many poor souls that were penitents after such sins committed, this I have much wondered at. Whether it were to make their profession of religion highlier admired; or perhaps rather, that they in their other doctrines, levelling Christ's most extensive meritorious sacrifice with the sacrifices of the old law, in their affirming that Christ's sacrifice doth take sins away but in the same way and manner that the sacrifices in the old did (though they acknowledge Christ's sacrifice to be the more excellent); that therefore they should measure the extent of Christ his taking our sins, by the scant standard of the particular occasional sacrifices instanced in the law, in their taking away of sins; and from thence to judge, that as the sacrifices of the Old Testament served not to signify the taking such great sins away, that therefore Christ's also should testify and declare (for no higher end do they make of it) no more of God's favour towards sinners, than to pardon such sins as those particular sacrifices did extend unto the pardon of. For they would make Christ's sacrifice, though they would seem to cry it up for excelling above those of the law, yet to be but metaphorical and figurative, even as those were; that is, merely serving to signify and shew that God was pacified, and in favour and grace with us; but not at all by way of merit and satisfaction from the merits of Christ's sacrifice, no more than through those of old.

But you see that even according to this their own measure taken from them (which is most wicked), that particular sins against conscience, and those of a heinous nature, were forgiven upon the atonement made by those particular sacrifices; neither was there any exception against their atonement, though reiterated, or again and again committed.

But, blessed be God, we have not so learned either his grace or our Christ; nor do we esteem that infinite satisfaction of his, once offered up for all the sins of the whole world, at so low a rate; as if it had no further efficacy than what is figurative (as those of the Old Testament were of), or of no larger extent of dominion over sins, for the expiation of them, than what those several particular occasional sacrifices did reach unto; which were so limited unto those sins, because, although the expiation of such sins against knowledge fore-mentioned, made atoneable by such occasional sacrifices, did signify to them that were believers, that such sins as they were, committed against the moral law, were made pardonable through Christ's satisfaction to come, as well as sins committed of mere ignorance. For Christ's sacrifice was fore-signified in all the sacrifices, and so in these; and so may confirm our faith, that for such sins in a special manner Christ's sacrifice was ordained, so to relieve the hearts and souls of such as have

become guilty of such sins; that if any man so sin grossly, Christ is a propitiation, a high priest, a ready advocate at hand upon such an urgent
occasion, to plead his sacrifice for their pardon; as in 1 John ii. 1 2, 3,
and 1 Cor. v. 1, 2, 3, and the latter end of the 5th verse. Yet there was
a further larger intention of God's appointing these occasional sacrifices to
the people of that nation, and as they were members of that: a nation and
typical church;—that as every sin deserved corporeal death, as well as
eternal; and these especially God was pleased to remit, and pardon them
unto them upon sacrifice; after which externally performed, they still stood
and remained members of that nation, and not to be cut off from that land
for them, yea, and might still have the privilege of that outward communion in their holy things, temple-worship, &c.: for we must know that
God was to be considered a sovereign judge unto that people in a double
respect. 1. As he is the judge of all men (as his style is, Heb. xii.), or
'judge of all the world' (as Gen. xviii.). Or 2. As he took upon him to
be the king of that nation in particular, and sovereign governor of that
country, in such a manner as he owned no other people in the world. And
thereupon set up their judges, and chose David, and his seed after him,
immediately as his lieutenants; and thereupon gave them judicial laws for
the government of that nation. And in this latter respect he appointed an
atonement by occasional sacrifices for such sins as deserved eternal death
from him, as he is judge of all the world, which yet, as judge of that
nation, he was pleased to appoint and receive an atonement for. And so
these sacrifices in that respect, and absolutions thereupon, are to be referred unto his judicial law; from which privilege he yet exempted the sins
fore-specified, adultery, &c., which he, as the supreme law-giver of that
kingdom, had peremptorily designed for a being cut off from that people.
And this was the ground of difference of such sacrifices, acceptable for other
sins, when not for those.

Yet, notwithstanding this political end and use of such sacrifices for such
sins, that they might continue free denizens of that church and kingdom,
this did not hinder or prevent and exclude the faithful amongst them from
having an eye unto that other use and end mentioned, a spiritual forgiveness of those particular sins, as an atonement for their souls, whenever they
had occasion to offer such sacrifices upon their sinnings. Yea, they were
therein called thereunto; for sacrifices were not mere civil acts, as presents
made unto a civil prince, but religious, as unto God that was offended.
Yea, they were called sin-offerings, in common with all other that were
sacrifices for their souls; and the blood of them was sprinkled seven times
afore the Lord, before the veil of the sanctuary, and on the altar of incense,
with all such rites performed about the blood that were used in the daily
sacrifices; as you read Lev. iv. from ver. 4 to the end. And of all sacrifices with blood (whatever they were), God indifferently and alike says, Lev.
xvii. 11, that the life was in the blood: 'For the life of the flesh is in the
blood, and I have given it to you upon the altar, to make an atonement for
your souls; for it is the blood that maketh an atonement for the soul.'
And therefore the one as well as the other served for the expiation of their
souls, if any of them did so sin. Moreover, the circumstances of those particular sins were forgiven as well as the outward fact. And therefore these
sacrifices were expiations, if they had true faith, for their souls. Accordingly, you find in the forecited Lev. vi. 7, in the case of foreswearing a
man's self, &c., the atonement, his sacrifice runs in these terms, 'It shall be
forgiven him, for any thing he hath done, in trespassing therein.' Wherein

God, supposing that many aggravating circumstances might accompany such sins, beside the outward fact, let them have been what they may prove to be, they shall be, even *anything* therein, forgiven him.   This a burdened conscience amongst them would take heed of; for circumstances lie heavier on the soul than the act.

And surely if David could spy out a soul-forgiveness for such sins as were exempted from particular expiation by sacrifice, namely, his murder and adultery, for which there was no particular sacrifice allowed to atone him from bodily death; and therefore says to God, 'Thou desirest not sacrifice' (namely, for these sins), 'else would I give it,' Ps. li. 16; yet, notwithstanding, he cried out for a soul-forgiveness of them : ver. 7, 'Purge me with hyssop, and I shall be clean ; wash me, and I shall be whiter than snow.'   And again, ver. 16, 'Deliver me from blood-guiltiness, O God, thou God of my salvation; and my tongue shall sing aloud of thy righteousness.' He expresseth how he had in his eye a further righteousness—even that which the apostle calls 'The righteousness of God through faith'—then surely from hence I argue, that if David had committed any of those other particular sins, for which a particular sacrifice was appointed, his faith in offering that his sacrifice would have looked for soul-forgiveness of that sin.   And in like manner, other believing Jews, in their particular offerings for those sins, had or might have had an eye unto the like forgiveness also.

And the use and comfort from the instances of these particular atonements under the Old, may be very great to us under the New Testament, to relieve our faith in the case of relapsing into presumptuous sins against conscience, and those the most heinous, reiterated, and deliberately committed ; and that notwithstanding such, we are not excluded, but may have access to God through our high priest for the forgiveness of them, in the faith and invitation of his sacrifice ; which certainly being the truth and substance of all sacrifices whatsoever, must be supposed to have been the ultimate end and scope of all, and aim in them all, and to have an infinitely greater efficacy to do away any, or all particular sins, in the moral guilt of them, than those mere shadows had, to expiate either individual guilts of corporeal death, or to be so much as significant also of the forgiveness of their souls, as in the shadow.

Yea, and I further suppose, that this was one special aim and intent why God did appoint such occasional sacrifices for occurring * special sins ; to teach and instruct us (as did the saints in those times) to turn unto our only priest and mediator Christ Jesus, and unto God through him, in a more set and solemn manner, for a special atonement of such occasional sins—which the apostle terms, being 'overtaken in a fault,' Gal. v. 1—as they do or may fall out, over and besides our daily begging forgiveness for sins of ordinary infirmity and incursion.

And I have made the larger excursion about these particular sacrifices for particular sins, because I take it—the apostle John doth—under the language of allusion unto the atonements made by the sacrifices of old, direct us unto the like practice, to have an alike recourse unto Christ our high priest and propitiation for occasional sins.   In his First Epistle, chap. ii. ver. 1, 2, 'My little children, these things write I unto you, that ye sin not.   And if any man sin, we have an advocate with the Father, Jesus Christ the righteous : and he is the propitiation for our sins, and not for ours only, but also for the sins of the whole world.'   For the obtaining the

That is, 'meeting.'—ED.

special and more direct aim and meaning of which words, we may look back and consider how he had in the foregoing chapter first spoken of the forgiveness of such daily unavoidable sinnings, as accompany believers in their strictest walkings : chap. i. ver. 7, ' But if we walk in the light, as he is in the light, we have fellowship one with another ; and the blood of Jesus Christ his Son cleanseth us from all sin.' And how that for these there is a pardon of course (as we use to speak), though yet upon our confessions thereof. And we may by comparing them together observe, how in this chap. ii. he proceeds to a special case of believers' sinnings ; and that is the case of sinning more grossly : ' My little children, these things I write unto you, that ye sin not ' (that is, willingly and deliberately, against that light, which he had said, chap. i. 7, that the saints ' walking in, have fellowship with God, who is light ') ; ' and if any man sin,' that is, who so sins against his own light, and contrary to the light of that fellowship with God he is called to enjoy and walk in, this is the case. Now in the words afore, chap. i. 8, he had apostolically declared against a state of perfection, the saints having no sin at all ; the experience of himself, *if we*, and all other believers, utterly confutes that dotage. ' If we say that we have no sin, we deceive ourselves, and the truth is not in us ;' and thereupon exhorts us, ver. 9, ' If we confess our sins, he is faithful and just to forgive us our sins, and to cleanse us from all unrighteousness ;' meaning ordinary infirmities, that fall out in those that walk most exactly. It had been utterly incongruous that after this he should come in with an *if*, ' If any man sin,' &c., unless he had intended such kind of sinnings as were not included in those ordinary sinnings that accompany all sorts of believers. It is therefore a special exception of sins committed against light, and with deliberate indulgency of our wills ; and also that first of those passages, ' These things I write, that you sin not ;' after those his foregone so positive assertions against the perfectionists of that age, is not that you never have no sin in you, for that had been in vain, and contradictory to what God had declared to be a truth, during this life ; but in that coherence it hath its scope, that you never sin against your light ; and that is attainable in this life, which his fellow-apostle Peter thus utters it, ' That you never fall ;' that is, willingly, against the knowledge and dictates of your spirits. And that apostle in that place shews it to be attainable.

Thus much concerning peculiar sacrifices for special sins, and the use our faith is to make of them, which was the first branch.

CHAPTER X.

Of the general atonement made for all sins once a year, when the high priest went into the holy of holies.

I come to the second branch, which was the main thing proposed and intended under this head at the beginning of it, viz., that there was a general atonement, when the high priest went into the holiest, for all sins, once a year ; which we are to make improvement of, to seek the pardon of all, and any sin whatever throughout our whole lives, from and through our high priest, who is now resident and officiating in the holiest.

The Jews then had indeed, besides those occasional expiations, and this general atonement once a year, ' continual sacrifices,' as the Old terms them ; offered up ' daily,' as the New ; twice a day, morning and evening sacrifices, in the first tabernacle, which were offered up also by the high priest, Heb. vii. 27, as well as the ordinary priests, Heb. x. 11. And these also were types of Christ, and of his one alone sufficient sacrifice (for he and his one sacrifice were the substance of them all, Heb. viii. 3, 4, 5; Heb. x. 1 ; Heb. ix. 11) ; and they were offered up for their own sins, and the sins of the people: Heb. vii. 27, ' Who needeth not daily, as those high priests, to offer up sacrifice, first for his own sins, then for the people's ; for this he did once, when he offered up himself.' And not occasionally only.

But over and besides both these sorts of atonements, God did institute this solemn expiation once a year, upon a solemn day, which is therefore by way of singularity called the day of atonement, and appointed not for this or that particular sin only, as the occasional were, but for all sins whatsoever. And likewise that day's atonement excelled those other daily sacrifices. 1. In the style it bore, in that the day was ὀνομαστικῶς, called ' the day of atonement' throughout Moses. It carried the day from all other days in that respect. Moreover, the killing and offering of that goat that day was in like manner singularly styled, ' the sin-offering of atonements,' Num. xxix. 11, whilst yet the ordinary daily sacrifices that were atonements also are made mention of; so that as the day, so the sacrifice proper to the day, is above all other the sacrifice of atonement ; as if none had been such, but only it, which shews the eminency of this atonement. And,

2. All the particular solemnities, rites, and sacrifices performed that day, declare as much ; for they had all those ordinary sacrifices that were offered up every day, offered up twice on that day also, as duly as on any other day, Num. xxix. 7–11, Lev. xvi. 24. And there were, moreover, two extraordinary special sacrifices, of a bullock and a goat, that were proper to that day, killed in the outward sanctuary. And then their blood was carried into the holy of holies ; and no other blood of sacrifices, not any of them was so employed, or made use of to that purpose ; no, not the blood of those daily sacrifices, although offered up on that day, as was said, whereon the high priest did go into the holy of holies, was not carried in by him. But of those only, namely, of the bullock and the goat peculiar to that day. Moreover, it was the bodies of those two which were burnt without the camp on that day, and not the other beasts sacrificed on that day ; as in Heb. xiii. 11, the apostle expressly limits them : ' The bodies of the beasts,' says he, ' whose blood is brought into the sanctuary by the high priest for sin, are burnt without the camp.' All which remarks do denote the super-excellency of that day's performances ; the lines and shadows thereof being drawn nearer to the life, in setting forth

I. Christ's crucifixion, as a sacrifice in the first tabernacle ; which eminent note the apostle puts upon it, ver. 12, ' Wherefore Jesus also, that he might sanctify the people with his own blood, suffered without the gate.' As also of Christ's making atonement in heaven, whither he has gone to appear in the presence of God for us ; and pleading that his blood, and from thence applying it to our souls, by sprinkling of it upon our hearts and consciences, so as all the substantial parts of his mediation were most conspicuously held forth in that one day's ministry.

II. All this was to signify, as the issue and tendency of all, the extent of that atonement to be universal as to all sins, and the signification thereof to have been the special design of that day, with difference from both occasional and daily sacrifices, and is indeed so expressly notified and inculcated, as makes it seem an appropriate end of it ; for I find not to my observation, that of any other of these daily sacrifices it is in express words said, with a note of universality, ' for all sins,' as of this day's sacrifice it is. This honour had this day's work alone, to be the open and public testification of this privilege which we have by Christ's sacrifice, that it is for all sin, it being utterly impossible that the blood of bulls and goats should take away sins, as Heb. x. Here was, I say, a condemning remembrance of all sins past, which came up before God, and in their consciences, every year, and therefore God applied a *catholicon* or universal outward plaster every year; and yet that did but outwardly skin over the sore every year in a carnal Jew's heart, but not healed perfectly and thoroughly, but so that it would break forth again. Yea, the very renewing of these sacrifices every year was a real testification that even these yearly sacrifices took not sins away; for why else should they be renewed again and again if the guilt of them did not remain? Which are the apostle's arguings, Heb. x. 1–4, yet the intention was to publish an universal pardon for sins past at every year's end, when the atonement was made; such as that law could give, but withal in the shadow and type of it, minding them of a perfectly extensive atonement which was to come, which should take away all sins at once. By one thing* God would take away all sins of the comers to worship. Now by the same reason that sacrifices every year served to take away sins past for that year, and therefore are called the sacrifice once a year, by the same reason the sins of the nation, in a like manner coming up in remembrance before God every day, the daily sacrifices served but to signify the atonement of them for that day, and reached no farther; and because a remembrance of them was renewed every day, therefore it was that the sacrifices were renewed every day. But in this day's sacrifice there was a remembrance every year, yet not of that year's sinning only, but of all sins past whatever, to the time of the years then ending; so as there was atonement then made for all sins past whatever.

And if it be said that murder and blasphemy were excepted, I further answer, No. They were not left out from the intent of the significancy of that day's atonement, which was to point them unto Christ's atonement, which should be made by him once for all, for all manner of sins; the intent of his sacrifice not being at all to exempt men from bodily death, which by the judicial laws of supreme governors is due to any crimes. It was not the design of this day's atonement neither to expiate any crime under that consideration, but it was significant of an atonement for the sins of their souls, by a more perfect sacrifice of Christ's to come. There was left this remark of imperfection on it, that it was reiterated every year, thereby to drive them to eye and expect the most perfect sacrifice signified by these, which should perfect for ever them that are sanctified (as in that 10th chapter of the Hebrews he concludes that his discourse of this type), and he but once for all offered up. If therefore any sins were under the type excepted for any respect, yet that one sacrifice to come was beforehand ordained to take away all at once; as Acts xiii. 38, 39, Paul told his countrymen, ' Be it known unto you therefore, men and brethren, that through this man is preached unto you the forgiveness of sins: and by him all that believe are justified from all things, from which you could not be justified by the law of Moses;' neither moral, nor ceremonial, nor judicial. And he spoke it to signify this, as far as that present dispensation would bear, that there was an universal atonement for all sins put into the great charter of that day's pardon. It is not anywhere in express words said, or

* Qu. ' offering'?—ED.

uttered of any of them, that they were for the forgiveness of all sins; but this honour had this day's work, and issue, alone to be the open and public testification of this privilege, which is the point I drive at for your comfort and direction.

I am loath to make a dispute of it, whether the daily sacrifices were *re ipsa* instituted to hold out an universal forgiveness of all sins. I rather rest in this as a rule, that the legal ordinances and sacrifices, as they were imperfect shadows in themselves, so wherein their imperfection in their signification should lie is much to be judged of by what we find said, or declared of them, when they are spoken of as to their proper intent and extent; and therefore I think it safest to say, that the difference between the sacrifices of this day, and those daily, may be, that the daily sacrifices eminently pointed at a continual forgiveness of sins as they were every day committed; they were for the errors of that day, as the name imports. But these sacrifices, and the expiation by them once a year, was ordained for all sins past of their whole lives, especially that had been committed that year. They were forgiven by wholesale, by the great and lump, on that day, though even in these sacrifices this mark of imperfection was left upon them, that there was a legal condemning remembrance of sins past.

Now that this universality of pardon of all sins was the great design of this one day's atonements, is in most express words, and not in figures, avowedly declared, and so often repeated, as all men must acknowledge that to have been the eminent scope thereof. For, 1. It is commanded that all the people should ' afflict their souls' for all their sins, Lev. xvi. 29. I say ' for all their sins,' for so the very next words warrant me, which are the reason annexed to that commandment, ver. 30, ' For on that day shall the priest make an atonement for you, to cleanse you, that ye may be clean from all your sins before the Lord.' And, 2. When the two extraordinary sacrifices were killed, and their blood taken to be carried into the holy of holies, this is the declared intent of both : Lev. xvi. 15, 16, ' Then shall he kill the goat of the sin-offering that is for the people, and bring his blood within the veil, and do with that blood as he did with the blood of the bullock, and sprinkle it upon the mercy-seat, and before the mercy-seat. And he shall make an atonement for the holy place, because of the uncleanness of the children of Israel, and because of their transgressions in all their sins : and so shall he do for the tabernacle of the congregation that remaineth among them in the midst of their uncleanness.' Again, 3. When that extraordinary atonement, by those sacrifices, was perfected, and that the high priest came forth from out of the holy of holies, then Aaron took the live goat; ver. 20–22, ' And when he had made an end of reconciling the holy place, and the tabernacle of the congregation, and the altar, he shall bring the live goat : and Aaron shall lay both his hands upon the head of the live goat, and confess over him all the iniquities of the children of Israel, and all their transgressions in all their sins, putting them upon the head of the goat, and shall send him away by the hand of a fit man into the wilderness. And the goat shall bear upon him all their iniquities unto a land not inhabited ; and he shall let go the goat into the wilderness.' Here are still, you see, both all and all sorts of sins in three several words expressed ; to the end that all sins whatever might be sure to be comprehended. Again, you have that *all* inculcated in the last verse, as the special design of that day, ver. 34, ' And this shall be an everlasting statute unto you, to make an atonement for the children of

Israel, for all their sins, once a year. And he did as the Lord commanded Moses.'

The occasional sacrifices served but for the expiation of particular emergent sinnings, and each served but for one turn, for that one sin, and no more. And if they fell into the like again, a new sacrifice was to be offered for that second, and so a third. And yet in them the believing Jew might spy out another manner of sacrifice, shadowed out for their souls. Again, in the daily sacrifices they might discern the same sacrifice typified, for daily sins committed every day, whilst yet the ritual sacrifice itself reached but to that day's sins. And still there was a remembrance of all these sins every year: Heb. x. 1, ' For the law could never with those sacrifices which they offered year by year continually make the comers thereunto perfect;' and ver. 2, 3, 'For then would not they have ceased to be offered? because that the worshippers once purged should have had no more conscience of sins. But in those sacrifices there is a remembrance again made of sins every year.' And this shewed the imperfection of that ritual sacrifice; yet still so as in the type and shadow it adumbrated a universal pardon, through a perfect sacrifice once offered to come : ver. 12, ' But this man, after he had offered one sacrifice for sins, for ever sat down on the right hand of God;' in which there would be ' no more remembrance of sins,' ver. 17.

And although neither this day's atonement, nor no other of these forementioned legal sacrifices, served not to acquit them from those sins excepted, as murder, adultery, or blasphemy, so far as God, as king of that nation, in his judicial law (as was observed) required bodily death for them, that day's expiation freed them not from that extreme punishment, whether they had been committed afore that solemn day or whether they had been discovered after that day's expiation had passed upon them. They could not have pleaded that day's atonement to free them from death; no, they died without mercy, as the apostle tells us.

But still all these did, in their several significancies, set forth that one perfect and all-sufficient sacrifice, which was the substance and centre of them all. And as these on that great day performed excelled all the other in the significancies of it—they being offered on purpose on that day the high priest went into the holy of holies, thereby, firstly, notifying this our high priest's alone sacrifice immediately afore his entrance into heaven—so especially, and most eminently, they were designed to shadow forth the extent of that of Christ his sacrifice, as reaching to the pardon of all sins, holding out a universal pardon of all sorts of sins, of what kind soever (but only that against the Holy Ghost, which in the 10th chapter the apostle alone excepteth). This was the proper intendment of that day's atonement. And if in those occasional sacrifices for grosser particular sins, the believers then might understand thereby, that there was a sacrifice for the forgiveness of their souls represented thereby, as well as a present freedom from the punishment of God's either immediately cutting them off from their people, or by the hand of the magistrate, according to any judicial law, threatening bodily death; then for the like reason the sacrifices and atonements of that day being so expressly and loudly proclaimed to be for all their sins whatever, they must be understood to have intended a like universal atonement of sins unto all that come unto this great high priest, confessing their sins, afflicting their souls for them, and seeking to be sprinkled with his blood, and their bodies washed with water, as it hath been explained.

And therefore let it be observed, that the high priest alone performed the whole of that day's service, which was to be done in either tabernacles, whether of extraordinary or ordinary sacrifice, to shew that there was one, and but one, great high priest that was to come, who should ' by one offering perfect for ever those that were sanctified,' Heb. x. 14 ; in whose sacrifice all the sacrifices concurred and met, as lines in a centre ; whether it were those of the high priest once a year, which he had instanced in this Heb. x. from ver. 1 to ver. 11, or of every priest daily ministering, in ver. 11. These are all swallowed up as shadows into this great body and substance of them.

But especially this day's atonement, instituted to signify this general atonement, is for this cause so largely insisted on, and above all others explained, and exposed to our notice by our apostle in the 9th and 10th chapters ; as also chap. xiii. ver. 11, 12. And those atonements made by the ordinary priests, but in one passage of chap x., ver. 11, although their daily services also imported the daily taking away of all sins for every day.

Seek then to Christ, to cause his face to shine upon thee, and his Father's through him. This I mention upon two grounds, proper to our high priest's being in the holy of holies, from the type in Lev. xvi. You read how the high priest took incense, with coals of fire, from off the altar of gold, and then going into the holy of holies, with the censer of gold, with those coals, and casting the incense thereon, he caused a cloud of smoke to ascend : and thereupon God manifested himself in a glory shining on the cloud. For this compare ver. 2d with the 12th and 13th, ' I will appear in the cloud' (so God promiseth, ver. 2); which how it was fulfilled, the 12th and 13th verses tell us, ' He shall take a censer full of burning coals of fire from off the altar before the Lord, and his hands full of sweet incense beaten small, and bring it within the veil : And he shall put the incense upon the fire before the Lord, that the cloud of incense may cover the mercy-seat that is upon the testimony, that he die not.' The cloud of incense, or the smoke thereof, typified prayer, as in the Psalms. And answerably, and in allusion unto this, the penner of the 80th Psalm doth in the name of, and for the people, frame his prayer thus, ver. 1 : ' Give ear, thou that dwellest between the cherubims' (in which was the holy of holies) ; ' shine forth ;' so, ver. 1. Then, in ver. 3, ' Cause thy face to shine, and we shall be saved,' which he repeats twice after in that psalm. His faith then penned that psalm for them, had in his eye that promise of God's appearing in the cloud : as in Lev. xvi. Witness the compellation he gives of God, ' Thou that dwellest between the cherubims.' He understood full well, that although himself, nor the people, on whose behalf he made this prayer, did follow God into the holy of holies personally themselves, but the high priest only ; and that yet that appearance of God's in the cloud from the mercy-seat unto the high priest, when he went into the holiest, did signify that unto those that looked by faith unto that mercy-seat, and invocated God with fervent prayer for grace to help them in their occasional or constant need ; that God would shine forth, and appear unto them, in answer unto their prayer graciously, some way or other, especially when it is the face of God himself which they seek, and that their hearts are carried out in prayer to seek the shine thereof.

We must know that the phrase of seeking God's face is more largely used ; for seeking his face, that is his favour in any particular request we would obtain at his hands. And it is a wonted speech in Scripture used to that purpose. But it is taken more strictly for seeking the shine of his favour itself to be manifested to a man's soul. It is the character of saints in the Psalms, 'That seek thy face.' And when their hearts are pitched upon that request above all things else, Oh then, he that dwelleth between the cherubims will shine forth according to their desire and his promise; as he often did unto particular persons, amongst them that came to the temple to worship. God shone forth upon their souls whilst they were praying there, which caused David to utter his request in this manner, in Ps. lxiii. 2, 3, ' To see thy power and thy glory, so as I have seen thee in the sanctuary ; because thy lovingkindness is better than life, my lips shall praise thee.' Observe how he says, ' so as I have seen thee in thy sanc-tuary ;' calling to remembrance God's gracious treatings with him in former times, when he used to come there to worship.

There are two things contained in that petition, ' shine forth,' which do thou, when thou conversest with God and Christ in this sanctuary, seek for at their hands.

1. That he would cause the light of his countenance, in his electing love, to shine upon thy soul ; that is, to give thee the assurance with a taste of his lovingkindness or special love borne towards thee, in which he at that present doth graciously accept thee in his beloved, and from everlasting had pitched and fixed to manifest towards thee in his Son. This is David's meaning there ; for one sight which he desires to behold him with in his temple, is that of his lovingkindness, which he therefore specifies in the following verse : ' Thy lovingkindness is better than life,' ver. 3. And this is one and a chief part of what my text intendeth, by ' drawing near with a full assurance of faith ;' that is, with assurance of our being accepted of him ; the shine of which David desired to have from out of his temple, whilst his faith looked to the holy of holies, unto which my text invites us to come in heaven.

The 2nd is to manifest himself to a man's soul : to ' see his glory and his power, as he had seen it in his sanctuary,' ver. 2 ; that is, to have a view of his personal excellencies and glories. And thus I interpret it ; for the wonders of power and glory which God shewed by outward works done for his people were works in the execution of them acted out of doors, as we say. They were transacted abroad, and in the world. The sights therefore which in the temple he sought to see were those of his personal greatness, power, and glory within himself, which were the cause and workers of those wondrous effects from out of his holy temple, as those abroad in the world are said to be.

And if you apply this to the seeking the face of Christ, the direction then is, that thou wouldest seek a view of him, not simply in his high priesthood glory (which is his office), and so what therein thou needest to have from him, to make use of him for, as thou art a sinner, but a view of the glory of his person abstractly from his office ; when therefore, Ps. lxxx. 1, he says, ' Thou that dwellest between the cherubims, shine forth,' and ver. 3, ' cause thy face to shine,' the highest and furthest intendment of those petitions is, that he would shine in his personal excellencies. For indeed the face of God and Christ are put for the person of each : 1. Of God ; ' Thou shalt have no other gods before my face ;' ' to behold the glory of God in the face of Jesus Christ,' that is, myself*. 2. Of Christ ; 2 Cor. iv. 4. And his face imports, as the lifting up the light of his coun-

* Qu. ' " before my face," that is, myself. 2. Of Christ, 2 Cor. iv. 6, " to behold," &c. ?—ED.

tenance in his love and favour, so the excellency and glory of his person : as in 2 Cor. iv. 4, the glory of God shines in the face of Jesus Christ. The word προσώπῳ is, *in the person of Christ.* And that which follows shews it is his personal excellency mainly intended, 'who is the image,' says he, ' of God;' which both in Col. i. and Heb. i. are primarily spoken of him in respect to his personal glory. Now, in that 80th Psalm, where it was we founded this head, 'O thou that dwellest,' &c., 'shine forth,' as ver. 1, so he begins ; but then in the 3d verse it follows, 'Cause thy face to shine,' which face of his is elsewhere styled his beauty, which denotes the excellency and glory of his person ; and is also still spoken of him as shining in and from his temple, and as therein and from thence he was to be viewed, Ps. xxvii. 4, 'To behold the beauty of the Lord, and inquire in his holy temple.' And that beauty is eminently termed his holiness, Ps. cx. 3. And as his favour, grace, and love is the light of his countenance shining towards us, so his holiness is the personal glory in himself; as that vision in Isaiah, chap. vi. 1, given of Christ when on his throne. That throne is that seat in the holy of holies, whereon (now he is ascended into heaven) he sits at the right hand of God, with his angels about him, worshipping of him as there. And the place or scene of that throne is in the vision made the holy of holies in the temple ; for it is said that his glory (that is, the train and gleam that came from it) 'filled the temple,' that is, the rest of the temple from the throne. Now, that glory is that of his person ; for Christ himself refers this of Isaiah unto himself, John xii. 41. Now, that glory there in Isaiah is said specially to be his holiness, as appears by the angels celebrating him and that his glory with crying out, 'Holy, holy, holy,' therein adorning* him for that, as wherein his glory specially consisted ; which, when Isaiah saw, you read how he was affected with it.

Also heaven is the holy of holies, and it is the personal glory there of him doth there appear (who is the most holy, and the Messiah, and the anointed one, Dan. ix.), which our Saviour desireth we might behold, John xvii. 24. And therefore a forehand sight and glimpse by faith of this his personal glory (and so far as faith is capable of it) is of all sorts of actings, or receptions rather, by faith the most desirable and delighting, and fills the soul with glory ; whom 'having not seen' (that is, as we shall do), yet so far seeing as faith will capacitate us, and may carry us, this works 'joy unspeakable and full of glory.' And such sights the primitive Christians were much inured to, 1 Pet. i. 8.

It falls out sometimes that when thou thyself comest to him, and afore him, that himself doth cause some rays of that more mean and little beauty that is in thy soul also (which is •the reflection of his shining on thee) to break forth afore him, whilst thou art in his presence. And he, to please himself in thee, draws out thy love to him, and causeth thee to tell him— he thereupon enlarging thy soul that way whilst thou art a-doing it—how well thou lovest him ; and to relate to him how holy thou wouldest be, which will in us to be so is our greatest holiness in this life ; and herewith do both God and Christ wonderfully delight themselves, as in Ps. xlv. it is said both of the Father (for his speech it is) and of Christ the Son, 'He is thy Lord, and worship thou him; so shall the King,' that is, Christ, 'greatly delight in thy beauty.' And, Eph. v., Christ doth 'present the church to himself.' How, and why, to himself? You have heard how he presents us to God; but here it is said he doth it to himself, as his spouse, for of

* Qu. 'adoring'?—Ed.

that he had spoken afore.　He takes a view of a soul that comes to him, and is taken with her himself first, and pleaseth himself first in her; and then covereth her all over with his righteousness, and then gives or takes a kiss of her himself, and so presents her to his Father.　Now, therefore, when thou comest afore him, obtain (if possible) ere thou comest off or out from him, a view of his person and of his holiness and beauty; and beg hard, be instant for it.　And to that end I counsel thee, let thine eye be fastened on him in what he is in himself.　See what thou canst spy out to be in him, or from him, over and besides thy redemption by his priesthood, that should make thy heart more to cleave to him, and more to love him, and delight in him.　And when but the first glimpses, and thereupon motion of such affections, do rise and enkindle, follow them, and blow up those sparks to a flame; let thy heart dwell upon such interviews.　Likewise every holy strain or disposition of spirit, which he draws forth out of thy heart, out of pure love to him, whilst thou art in his presence, they are so many gleams and lines of beauty in thee, with which his heart is delighted, whether they be brokenness of heart, and relenting pangs of sorrow for sin, or submission to his will with all cheerfulness, because it is his will, putting thy mouth in the dust, in thy deepest trials and temptations.　Or that thou canst, with all that is within thee, fall a-blessing him for what he is in his own blessedness and glory, though thou should not be partaker of it in him, and with him, rejoicing that Christ he is with the Father at his right hand in glory, whatever becomes of thee; which Christ told his disciples, that if they loved him they would have done; because I go to the Father.　These are each so many casts of a gracious beauty in thy soul, with which in thy converses with him he is ravished.　These interviews and intercourses of love of the soul to Christ, and of Christ to the soul, you may read of Cant. 7th chapter throughout: both on Christ's part, from ver. 1 to 10; and on the church's part, from ver. 10 to the end.

But to wind up this head, and to bring it back again to the language and signification of the type itself, which we began in, and made the rise of this head.

There were two things in that holy of holies, principally ordained to represent our Lord Jesus Christ: 1. The ark, whose residence was continually therein; 2. The person of the high priest, who came in but once a-year, and then whilst he was in it, did but personate our Lord to come to heaven. The ark itself alone I take (and submit it) typed forth his very person, simply considered.　A chest it was, made of plain boards of Shittim wood, covered both within and without with pure gold.　The wood signified his humanity, the gold his divine nature, as joined both in one; the fulness of the Godhead dwelling in him bodily, and enclosing or encompassing his human nature, with the fulness of itself, Exod. xxv. 11.　And this ark is termed the glory and beauty of God, Ps. lxviii. 71; as also of all Israel, 1 Sam. iv. 21.　And it was under that style declared of his person, by old men, when but eight days old, Luke ii. 32, 'the glory of thy people Israel.' Crowned also it was with a crown of gold, denoting all excellency and right of the dominion; having the testimony or covenant of the law in it, as Christ had the law in his heart, Ps. xl.

The second representative was the high priest, who came in but to perform the works of a priest, who was the type of Christ's office of priesthood, which is but additional to the glory of his person.　By these two we are taught to view, and that distinctly: 1. His person, and the glories thereof simply considered, and that of his office in performing the work thereof, as a mediator for us, and as an atoner for our sins. And as the ark was the most eminent, and first bespoke to be made, Exod. xxv. 10, so is and was the person of Christ first ordained, and is to be esteemed accordingly, in and for his person, the most precious above all other, being 'the most holy,' Dan. ix. And certainly his person is far more excellent than any, or all his offices for us, and accordingly to be sought for by us; and the privilege hereof Christ hath promised to some special favourites of his: John xiv. 21, 'He that hath my commandments, and keepeth them, he it is that loveth me; and he that loveth me shall be loved of my Father, and I will love him, and will manifest myself to him.' Mark how he says, 'I will manifest myself,' having said, I will manifest my love, in those words, 'I will love him,' as distinct from and short of this. Now, to love us, as in his own heart his love is seated in common to all believers, whereas this is uttered as a special favour to them that keep his commands, in a special and intense manner; and therefore is meant of the manifestation of that his love. And then the next words, 'I will manifest myself to him,' is a further additional, beyond that discovery of his love or his Father's; and so of his person, which is usually called himself. And it was a privilege not vouchsafed the apostles until himself was ascended, and poured out his Spirit on them. And then their union with his person, as his with his Father's, was manifested to them, as in the verse afore, ver. 20, 'At that day ye shall know that I am in my Father, and you in me, and I in you,' which is expounded by this speech of his in ver. 21. Sure I am (that so I may still express it by the type which hath led me unto this) that the perfection of that glorious state which the saints on earth shall attain unto, is typified forth under the shadow of the holy of holies, in a comparative unto the foregoing states of the church less perfect, described by the model of the outward court; and then the court of the priests, whereof Rev. xi. 1, 2, and the last verse gives us the scheme. But after these two courts are passed in ver. 1, 2, it is said, ver. 19, that 'the temple of God was opened in heaven, and there was seen in his temple' (the seat of which was that part of the temple called the holy of holies) 'the ark of the testament.' Oh how will men then more continually rejoice in the contemplation of his person, and above all, love him, value him for what he is in himself, and for himself; whereas now it is a rare privilege vouchsafed to some, and yet attainable, but will not in the height of it be communicated, until these more imperfect and dead-hearted churches, the court of priests which foregoes it, be purged and more refined; and that by the laying dead the two witnesses, which are both the churches themselves, the golden candlesticks, and the persons of the most eminent professors, both of ministers and people. After which, though we with the rest of the New Testament saints are said all to enter into the holiest, when we worship, as in the text; yet God hath provided last for them of those times, after their resurrection and ascension into heaven, that is, a more conspicuous glory of intercourse with Christ; such as is an enjoyment of his person, as the ark in the holy of holies, in comparison unto what is now but as in the court of priests. And yet let every one now seek it, by growing up unto perfect holiness, and keeping his commandments; for unto such that promise is in all times made, and is to be attained by some that seek it, as a fore-running glimpse and pledge of the like, as then more common glory of the saints in those times.

www.ingramcontent.com/pod-product-compliance
Lightning Source LLC
Chambersburg PA
CBHW060446100426
42812CB00025B/2714